The Complete Guide to Flower & Foliage Arrangement

The Complete Guide to Flower & Foliage Arrangement

Edited by Iris Webb

DOUBLEDAY & COMPANY, INC.
GARDEN CITY, NEW YORK

Dedication
To all who love flowers and foliage, but especially my NAFAS friends

A  Book

Edited, designed and produced by
Webb & Bower Limited, Exeter, England

First Edition in the United States of America

Library of Congress Cataloging in Publication Data

Webb, Iris.
The complete guide to flower and foliage arrangement

Bibliography: p.
Includes index.
1. Flower arrangement. I. Title.
SB449.W37 745.9'2 78-20711
ISBN 0-385-15119-5

Text set in 9/10 Century Schoolbook

Printed in Great Britain by
Cripplegate Printing Company Limited

Bound by Webb, Son & Company
London and Wales

Contents

Foreword

In this lovely book Iris Webb has given us a new perspective on the many varied aspects of arranging with flower and foliage materials. As a judge and teacher of flower arranging as well as a practising gardener she brings a wealth of knowledge and personal experience to both the creative and practical sides of flower arranging.

The art of flower arranging has been practised for many centuries in both Western and Eastern cultures, giving today's arranger an eclectic heritage to draw upon. This comprehensive book covers the styles of arranging from the beginning up through the avant-garde trends of today. It is only through an understanding of the basic techniques involved and the evolution of plant design that one has the knowledge to support one's own creative endeavors. A book such as this one which combines a foundation in the techniques as well as an historical perspective of the art is an invaluable aid to flower arrangers, whether they are just beginning or are experienced practitioners.

The art of flower arranging is a purposeful objective of the National Council of State Garden Clubs. We are affiliated with the National Association of Flower Arrangement Societies of Great Britain and share with them many interests and activities. Garden Club members use flower arranging both to express their individual creativity and to encourage the cultivation of many new varieties of plants for use in our homes and for shows. Like anyone who enjoys creative activities, Garden Club members are always searching for new ideas. This informative publication will be a welcome addition to any flower arranger's library.

March 1979 VIRGINIA W. WEAVER
Flower Show Schools Chairman
National Council of
State Garden Clubs, Inc.

An antique mirror reflects some of the flowers arranged by Mary Pope in a Worcester porcelain shell. Included are *Beloperone guttata* (shrimp plant), *Hoya carnosa, Sidalcea malviflora, Diplacus glutinosis*, pelargonium and *Asarina procumbens* (antirrhinum)

Introduction

In the year A.D. 1560 when Levinus Lemnius, a Dutchman, visited England, he commented: 'Altho' we do trimme up our parlours with green boughes, fresh herbes or vine leaves, no nation does it more decently, more primmely, nor more sightly than they do in England.' A sixteenth-century Eastern poet named his school of flower design, it is said, from a phrase in the Buddhist text which means 'Plucking a flower and smiling slightly' – based on the belief that Buddha held a flower and gazed at it, and that his companion smiled his understanding. These two examples serve to illustrate that centuries ago in two widely separated parts of the globe, men – and no doubt women too – were sensitive to the importance and the inspiration of nature, and that they were conscious of the fragile and ephemeral life of flowers and foliage.

This book is devoted entirely to the artistic and practical study of foliage and flower arrangement. It covers the historical background, tracing it through pagan and religious uses to period, traditional styles and on to the modern, free form and abstract designs of the present day. Clear and detailed information is given for the beginner, the intermediate and the advanced flower arranger, including that concerning the development of the Western styles which depend on the use of a profusion of plant materials, and of the Eastern styles which use line and bring space within the pattern as a design element. The reader is made aware how one art form has naturally influenced the other, and vice versa.

The subject of flower decoration has enthralled men and women of all cultures and civilizations since antiquity. There is a permanency in the pattern of this specialized interest which has lasted through the centuries. Understandably the cultures, social conditions and geographical backgrounds have influenced the many styles and their uses. This aspect, by itself, makes a fascinating and compelling story. One curious fact of flower arrangement is that those who are drawn to it seem to find in the impermanence of their work an added attraction rather than a deterrent. Artists, poets and writers have always derived inspiration from nature for their practical work, and their painting, sculpture and writing provide constant and lasting pleasure. This is not the case for those who work with plant material, who in a sense can be compared to musicians who are happy to give momentary life to the work of a composer, or to dancers who interpret the work of the choreographer in a dynamic but purely transient way. For their part, flower and foliage arrangers must be content to create decorations that can bring only short-lived happiness and pleasure as if writing on sand, aware that the incoming tide will sweep it all away.

Perhaps it is the constant challenge, the necessity for a perpetual awareness of the beauty of nature, the changing seasons and colours that provide the lure. The ability to perceive the infinite variety of shapes, forms, colours and textures available in creative designs develops what is known to flower arrangers as 'the seeing eye'. The great attraction of this art form is that it provides an outlet for the latent creative talent that everyone possesses to some degree and, what is more, it can be practised alone in your own home or with a group of people with similar interests. It is a perfect therapy and also a practical one within the reach of everybody. In a world of confusion and noise it can provide inner quiet and happiness and relax tensions.

The aim of this book is to enable all those who are involved or interested in flower arrangement, whether as a beginner or at an advanced level, to widen their knowledge and increase their understanding in all spheres of the art and craft. The reader should be able to choose containers, plant materials and designs that are in harmony with a stately home or a simple cottage, as well as for a church or a modern airport lounge. Clear diagrams, simple text and fine illustrations are provided, and together they should inspire confidence and pleasure in the novice as well as the more proficient arranger.

The National Association of Flower Arrangement Societies of Great Britain (NAFAS) was formed in London in 1959. Mrs Mary Pope of Dorchester was the Founder President. The aim of the Association is to encourage the love of flowers and to demonstrate their true decorative value in the home. The membership is open to both men and women of any age irrespective of race, colour or creed. The National Association is the official organization of the flower arrangement movement throughout Great Britain. It guides and exercises control of the movement and co-ordinates the functions of the twenty Area Associations throughout the country. Judges, demonstrators and lecturers are instructed and trained and enabled to qualify at National or Area level. There is also an Education Committee for Teachers and the Association publishes its own quarterly magazine, *The Flower Arranger*. In addition, there is a Publications Committee responsible for publishing excellent instruction leaflets and booklets. In its comparatively brief existence NAFAS has attracted 100,000 members, and there are clubs in virtually every town and city in the United Kingdom. Approximately one million pounds has been raised for charities, and it has become a great driving force with affiliates from all over the world. Among these are the State Garden Clubs of America and Ikebana International.

'Hollyhocks' by Jan van Huysum (1682–1749)

Acknowledgements

My appreciation and sincere thanks go to: Mary Pope for her Foreword; the NAFAS National Officers, Council Members, Education, Photographic and Publications Committees; and the countless friends and students who have given me continued help and encouragement during the long preparation of this book. In particular, my thanks to the major contributors – all valued personal friends with whom I worked so happily. Doris Hunt undertook the compilation of the Index and Glossary and gave other much-valued help. Jean Taylor's helpful advice was greatly appreciated.

I am deeply grateful to Mrs Howard S. Kittel and Mrs J. Elmer Weaver of the National Council of State Garden Clubs Inc. for their wonderful and ready help in reading the manuscript and making valuable comments on it. In addition, my thanks go to Virginia Weaver for kindly consenting to write the Foreword to the American edition.

Finally my thanks to my husband and son, both Richard Webbs, whose kindness and patience I can never repay.

Iris Webb

Editor's Note

The flower arranger cannot work without the flowers, leaves and seedheads of the growing plant. There are millions of different trees, shrubs and plants, of infinite variations in colour, shape and form. Climate plays a vital role in what will be available for the arranger. Some plants described as 'wild' or 'weeds' in one environment, can be rare and treasured in another. Travellers, seamen and emigrants have found and noted plant varieties new to them and carried them back to their native lands. Emigrants have taken to their new homes plants they loved or required for food purposes. The rhododendrons and azaleas – among countless other varieties – that are commonplace in many modern gardens, were first collected by the great British professional plant hunters in the nineteenth century. Inevitably anyone writing about plants known to be specially useful to a flower arranger, will do so from personal knowledge and experience gained in his or her own garden.

George Foss, who has spent a lifetime working with cut flowers and foliage with Constance Spry, writes of his gardening experiences in southern England. His references to 'mild' or 'sheltered' or other climatic conditions, can be applied to local conditions wherever the reader lives. The plants, shrubs and trees he grows originated in many different parts of the world, and comparatively few are native to Britain. This is not because he has specialized in any particular varieties. He is a very good and keen gardener and the plants he grows are available virtually anywhere, depending of course on local conditions. Some plants that are confined to the house in one country may be hedge plants in a warmer climate. Nevertheless, the name of the variety remains the same in reference books and nurserymen's lists, together with cultural instructions suitable for the country where the reader lives.

Nomenclature of plants

The Swedish naturalist Carolus Linnaeus (Carl von Linné, 1707–78) was responsible for classifying many thousands of plants by devising a system of Latin nomenclature. Included among these were 6,000 ferns and 250,000 species of flowering plants. His system, the basis of modern botanical nomenclature, is used internationally, so that regardless of the many different vernacular names, wherever you live – be it Australia, America or Europe – you can quickly identify a plant in your reference book or nurseryman's list. Let us take as an example the word *Acer*. This is the botanical Latin name for the maple tree. (The word acer also means 'sharp', referring to the hardness of the wood which the Romans used for spear-shafts.) There are delicate shaped Chinese and Japanese maples, sturdy Canadian red maple trees, common sycamores in Britain, mountain maples in North America and maples in Asia Minor, Persia, Caucasia and elsewhere. All can be identified by the use of the prefix *Acer,* followed by the name of the variety.

A serene water scene with primulas and waterside plants contrasting with the splendid foliage of *Gunnera manicata*

List of Arrangers

The publishers and the editor have made every effort to identify the arrangers whose designs have been used. Where this has not been possible the source of the photograph has been given.

In all cases where arrangements by the author(s) of the chapter are included these come first; other arrangers are then listed in alphabetical order.

1. What is Flower Arranging All About?
Iris Webb, 15 top.

2. Practical Knowledge - Tools and Care
Iris Webb, 24, 25, 26.

3. Basic Principles
Iris Webb, 39; Violet Stevenson, 38.

4. Traditional Design
Iris Webb, 47 bottom, 48 top, 50, 52 bottom left, 56, 57 top left, centre and right, bottom left; Dora Buckingham, 51, 53, 55; Joan Chambers, 49; B. Channon, 48; Mabel Drew, 61; Joan Ewing, 57 bottom right; Richard Jeffery, 45; *Source:* Scott Lauder, 60; *Source:* NAFAS Education Committee, 58 left; *Source:* NAFAS Photographic Committee, 46; F. Stewart, 59; Eve Taylor, 47 top, 58 right; Jean Taylor, 52 top and bottom right.

5. Categories of Design
Iris Webb, 66 top, 67 left; Erik Bering, 62-3; Isabel Crichton, 70 bottom; Molly Duerr, 64 top; Monique Gautier, 75 bottom left; J. E. Hamilton, 68 top right; Irene Hawkins, 68 bottom; Headingley Flower Club, 68 top left; Elsie Holden, 74 bottom centre; Mrs P. Howard, Auckland, 74 bottom right, 75 top right; Edna Johnson, 66 bottom; Glenda Kroll, 75 centre left; Moira MacFarlane, 72 top right; S. Madan-Mayers, 70 top left; Contessa Camilla Cagli Malvasia, 74 centre left, 75 bottom right; Margeren Morrow, 74 bottom left; *Source:* NAFAS Photographic Committee, 71 top left, 72 top left; Judy Pownall, 71 bottom left; Mrs E. Rhodes, 69 top left; Winifred Simpson, 67 right, 70 top right, 73 bottom right; George Smith, 65; Eve Taylor, 64 bottom; Jean Taylor, 73 top right; Dorothy Tuffin, 71 top right, bottom right; Virginia Weaver, 74 centre right, 75 top left; Theo Wiggin, Victoria, BC, 74 top right; Win Wilsher, 69 top right, bottom left.

6. Drying and Preserving, Foliage and Florist Flowers
Avril Cresswell, 86 centre left, 87 bottom left; Kit Gasser, 78 bottom, 86 centre left, 87 bottom right; Freda Hart, 86 bottom left, 87 top left; Mrs Lansdowne, 79 top left; *Source:* Scott Lauder, 80 left, 81 right, 82 right; Peggy Lovell, 86 top left, bottom right, 87 top right, 88 right; Sara Marquadt, 85 top right; Renee Mottershead, 89 left; *Source:* NAFAS Photographic Committee, 77, 83, 84; *Source:* NAFAS Teachers' Association, 82 left; Joy Spence, 85 top left, bottom; Elizabeth Tomkinson, 80 right, 89 right; Daphne Vagg, 81 left; Alan Wheeler, 88 left; Nan Whiston, 79 right.

7. Favourite Flowers and Designs in the Home
Iris Webb, 93 top right, 94 top right, bottom right, 96, 97 top right, 98; Peggy Crooks, 93 bottom, 99; Edna Johnson, 95 top left; Elsie Lamb, 97 bottom left; Betty Mustoe, 91; Eve Taylor, 95 top right; Jean Taylor, 94 bottom left; Nan Whiston, 95 bottom right; Win Wilsher, 93 top left.

8. Special Occasions
Arrangements on pp. 102-111 by Eve Taylor; arrangements on pp. 112-115 Richard Jefferys; Irene Wright, 116.

9. Designs Requiring Special Techniques
Iris Webb, 127 right; Margaret Farrell, 123 top; F. Gill, 131; Sylvia Lewis, 124 right; *Source:* NAFAS Photographic Committee, 122 bottom, 123 bottom, 127 left, 129 top left; Judy Pownall, 124 left; Marjorie Sanders, 125, 126; Pamela South, 122 top; Alan Wheeler, 129 bottom and top right; Win Wilsher, 130.

10. Plants for the Flower Arranger's Garden
George Foss, 138 top, bottom, 140, 145, 147 bottom right, 149 left, 150 top, bottom.

11. Historical Background
Iris Webb, 158; Joan Forrest, 157 right; Margaret Hallows, 165; Doris Hunt, 166 top left, top right; Mary Hunt, 159 bottom right, 160; Lilian Martin, 161 top right, bottom right, 162 top; Kay Rusden, 159 top left; Marjorie Sanders, 158 left; Eve Taylor, 159 top right; Jean Taylor, 162 bottom; Elizabeth Tomkinson, 156 left.

12. Church Flowers and Church Festivals
Peg Aldridge, 178 bottom; Frederick Burdock, 168-9; Jean Cook, 176 top right; Louise Cook, 177 top; Isabel Crichton, 174 bottom right; Joan Dunne, 170 top; Doreen Gillard, 172 bottom right; Janet Harwood, 181 top; Joan Herridge, 171 bottom right; Doris Hunt, 171 top left; Mary Hunt, 172 top right, 175 left; Flower Rota Helpers, Ideford Parish Church, 177 bottom; Edna Johnson, 173 left, 174 top left; NAFAS/St Paul's Cathedral, 173 right; Brenda Peppiatt and Daphne Spring, 180; Mary Pope, 172 top left, 178 top; Jean Roope, 181 bottom; K. Sagar, 176 bottom right; Daphne Spring, 179 top, 180 and Brenda Peppiatt; Jean Taylor, 174 bottom left, 175 right; Joan Weatherlake, 174 top right, 176 centre right; Jo Whaley, 170 bottom; Nan Whiston, 179 bottom; Beatrice Wilde, 171 top right.

13. Colour
Jean Taylor, 184, 187, 189, 190 left, right, 193, 194, 195; Marion Aaronson, 187 right; J. Abbott, 191 left; Bill Lomas, 185.

14. Additional Design Elements
Joan Weatherlake, 197.

15. Modern and Abstract Design
All arrangements by Marion Aaronson.

16. Exhibition and Show Work
Winifred Simpson, 217.

17. Ikebana - the Japanese Art of Flower Arrangement
All arrangements by Stella Coe.

18. East and West, Differences and Influences
All arrangements by Pamela South.

I. What is Flower Arranging All About?

And one might therefore say that in this book I have only made up a bunch of other people's flowers, and that of my own I have only provided the string that ties them together.

MICHEL DE MONTAIGNE 1533–1592

'Portrait of a Little Girl'. From a painting by Cornelis de Vos at Chatsworth House

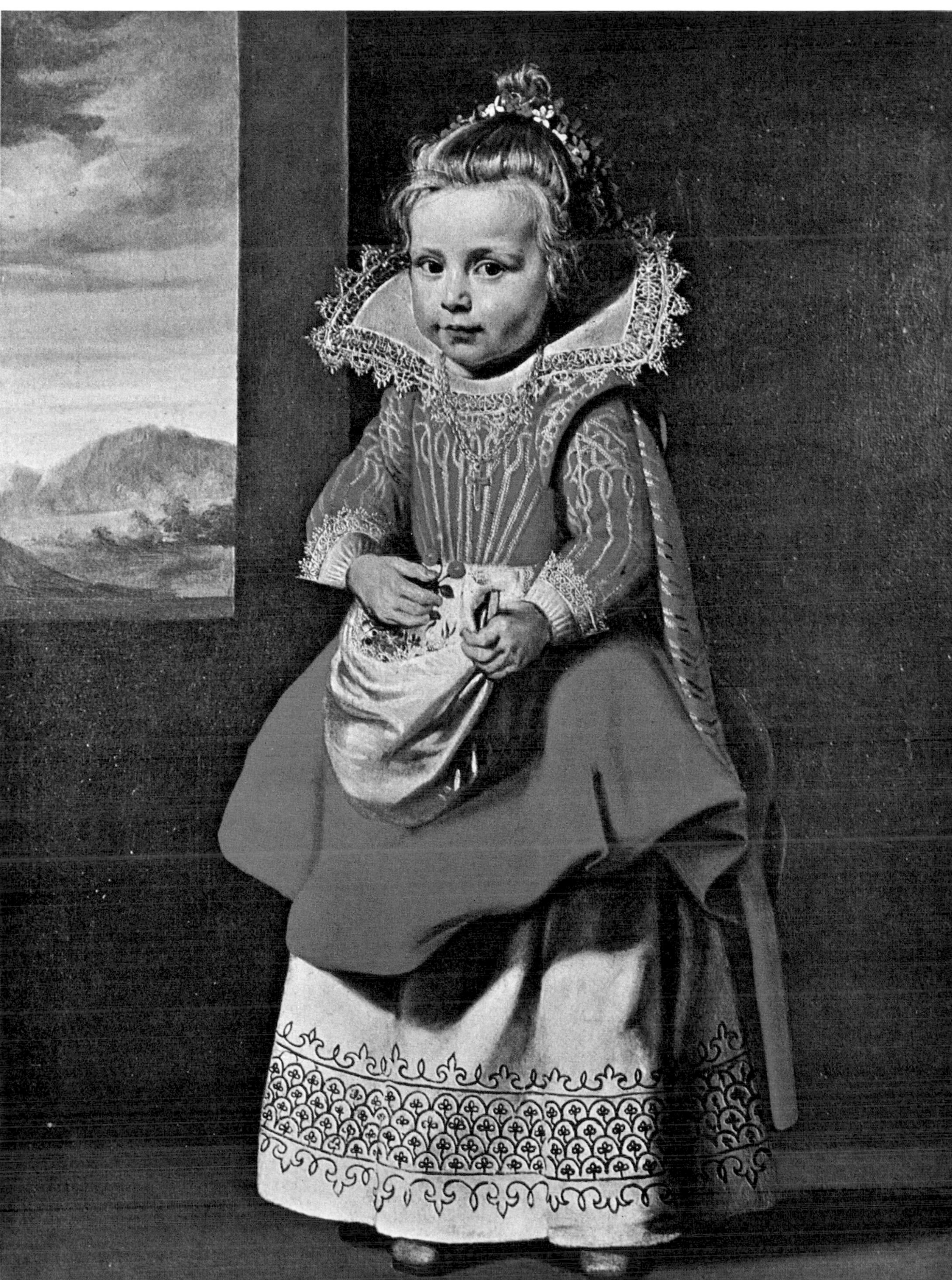

Beginnings

Most people start their flower arranging experience as children picking wild flowers during a walk, or daisies on their garden lawn. It is instinctive, a natural and happy reaction to the colour and beauty of the flowers, and not usually prompted by adults. Children's posies have the artless grace and charm that belong to 'folk' work of all kinds. They have an authentic feeling that cannot be imitated. The small bunch clutched in the fist, or put in a small basket, is brought back to the house for those at home to see the treasure and to share the pleasure it has aroused. The child learns at once that, if the flowers are to last, they must be put in water. So the first step is taken. An understanding begins that these colourful things are 'living' and must be given different care and thought than is accorded the other inanimate treasures that the child collects, such as sea shells or small pebbles. The choice of what container the water and flowers are to be put in is, as a rule, decided by what is at hand, and the length of the stems of the flowers. Usually jam jars, meat paste pots or other small and valueless containers that can be found in kitchen cupboards are chosen.

But as children grow they become more perceptive about their surroundings and of the variety of flowers to be seen. They observe that the choice has widened. Soon they may gather garden flowers as well as wild ones, and they are aware that unusual blooms can be bought at the florist. For most of these cultivated flowers the jam jar or meat paste jar no longer looks quite right, nor is their capacity adequate for the quantity or varieties available. So the next and logical step is a bowl or a vase of some kind. This is where the once wholly enjoyable and simple task becomes complex and frustrating. The small, narrow neck of the pot or jam jar that supported the stems so well has gone. The flowers and leaves fall about and look a mess. It becomes clear that some knowledge of how to make them stand in an orderly fashion is necessary. Not only that, but the discovery is made that bowls and vases have varying textures and colours, and this creates uncertainty of another kind. The attraction and love of flowers remain the same, and by now there is an awareness that a room or house without flowers tends to look, and feel, institutional and dead. This then is what flower arranging is all about. It is the realization that, although leaves and flowers will if fresh always look lovely, in the right hands their loveliness can be enhanced. In the wrong hands, however, they can look muddled, overcrowded and misplaced.

Detail from 'A Day at the Sea' by Charles Hunt

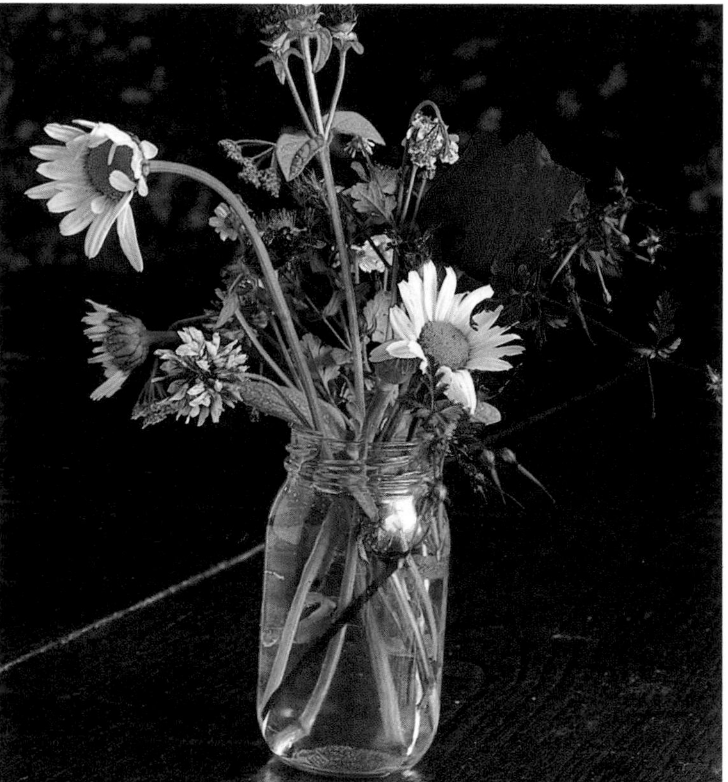

The first step

Basic skills

Basically there are no hands that are right or wrong. It is just a question of whether an individual is willing to acquire the simple skills and then apply them to the handling of plant material and the choice of containers. There is a tendency to create something of a mystique about the art of flower arrangement and to treat those who excel at it as though they possess great gifts. Of course there are a limited few who are quite exceptional arrangers, possessing a sense of design, colour and artistry which is outstanding. In every creative skill this will be true of certain people, and they are usually described as 'naturals'. This does not mean that the majority of those with good average artistic sense and intelligence, with knowledge of the requirements and a willingness to apply them, will not achieve consistently high standards. They must also possess patience for trial and error, for there will be much of this. It is after all generally accepted that time, patience and some study are required if you are to become a proficient cook or dressmaker. No less is needed for the handling and arranging of flowers and foliage.

The flower arranger uses living material, whose beauty and interest can be lost altogether if it wilts or flags. This means that she must develop her knowledge of how to make leaves and blossoms survive, as well as how to pick, purchase or grow – how to treat the severed plant material and also how to select it. The durability and lasting quality vary dramatically. A knowledge of which flowers and leaves will combine interest and beauty and also remain fresh five days or a week (in the right conditions) is a necessity for the flower arranger. It can be compared to the need for a chef to recognize, in his raw materials, what is necessary for the dish he prepares, and its suitability for the occasion at which it will be eaten. This kind of know-how is acquired by growing, handling, conditioning and arranging flowers and foliage, and of course learning from the experience gained by others and made available to the beginner.

Environmental influences

Bringing flowers into the house, whether from the garden, hedgerow, or from the florist, immediately creates yet another problem. Houses, flats or buildings are usually architecturally different, but in some respects they are standardized. The exterior of one dwelling may be identical with another, but past the threshold the décor will vary with the individual taste of the inhabitant, or the functional use of the building. Colours, furnishings and lighting all are going to play a part in how the flowers will either be suitable and please, or sadly fail in their purpose to become an extra feature of an overall scheme. Scale or size relationship is all important too. The small pot of honeysuckle that looks just right on the windowsill of a country cottage would be lost in the salon of a stately home or large public room in a hotel. Equally, a large and flowing pedestal of generous foliage and flowers would be an encumbrance in the country cottage or two-roomed flat. So, thought has to be given to the décor and the scale of the background into which the finished flower arrangement is to be fitted.

As will be shown in Chapter 11, there is nothing new in the practice of placing flowers in the house. While the first flower decorations were placed in temples and churches, relatively soon afterwards the custom was introduced into dwelling-places where civilization had made people sensitive to their surroundings. It should be noted that flowers and foliage are used for other than aesthetic purposes among primitive peoples. When life is confined to a struggle for sheer survival, there is an essentially different response to the wonder of flowers. Primitive people tend to endow certain trees and plants with supernatural or mystical qualities. Examples of these are the banyan tree in the East, and the mandrake root, the elderberry tree, the oak and the mistletoe in the West. Through all history there is evidence and confirmation that the response of men of all races, civilized or primitive, to the plants and flowers and trees of nature, is one of instinctive joy and happiness, coupled with a wish to be involved with them. It is clear that primitive man felt that in the struggle for existence plant life was endowed with certain mystical qualities. First he would see the seed falling on the ground. Later, he would notice these same seeds grow, blossom and turn to fruit, then either die back into the ground or continue the same

Above: the simplest of arrangements; spring flowers, whose beauty is almost self-sufficient, enhanced with a blue silk ribbon. The arrangement includes freesia, lily of the valley, *Narcissus jonquilla* (wild jonquil), *Stephanotis floribunda* and a single tulip

Left: the strange contortions of the banyan tree's aerial roots create a feeling of uneasiness because of their deviation from the usual tree form. From a painting by Sir Charles D'Oyly

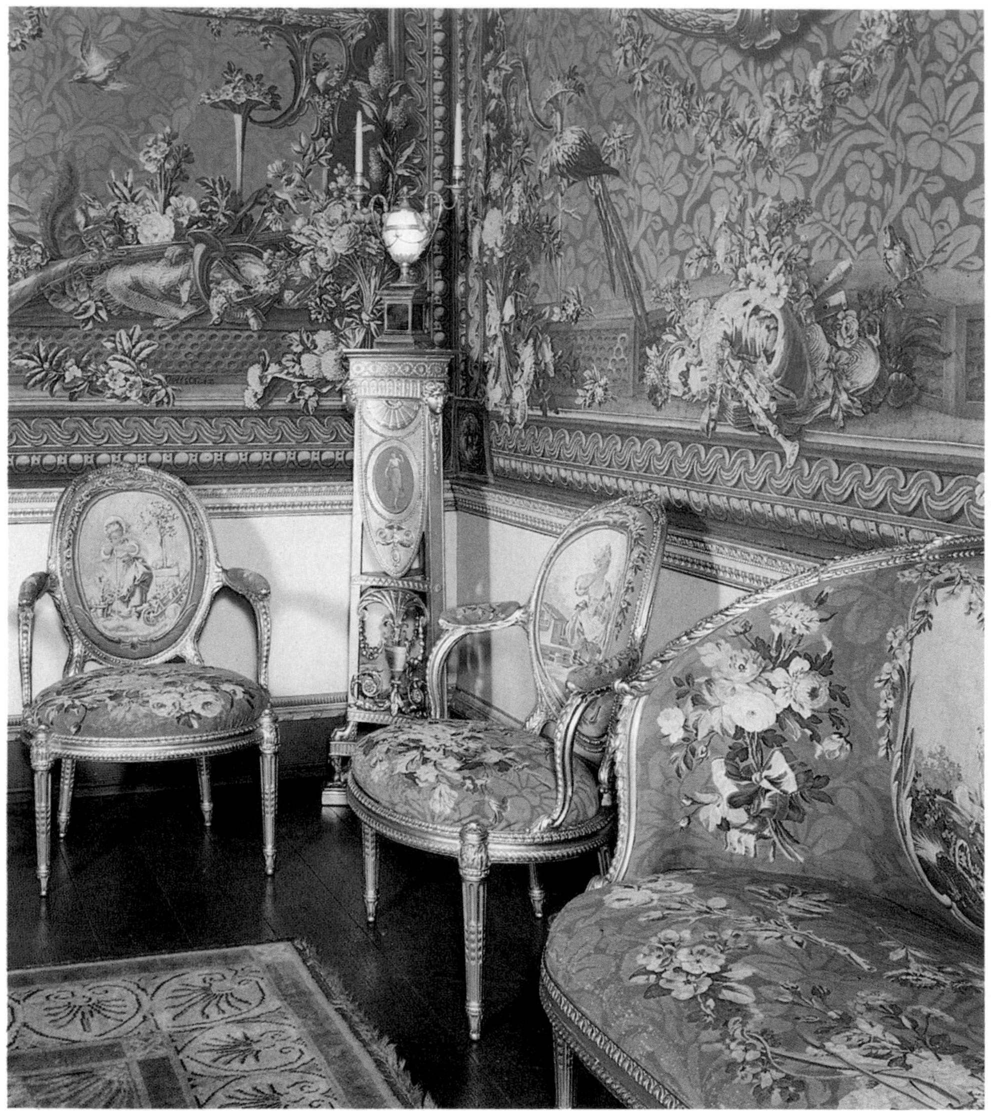

cycle. This cycle of life being beyond his reasoning, to him it could only come from some mystical and supernatural source. So flowers and plants became sacred. Offerings were placed under or in trees, later in temples and then in houses and churches. The centuries passed; the life and surroundings of man became more diverse, more sophisticated, but something remained constant, shared by men of every race and environment. Nature in all its aspects, and certainly in plant material, has always been respected – loved – by man, such that he has singled it out and chosen it to be his special associate, whether in his cultivated land or his temple or church. His decorative art – in metal, porcelain, glass, paintings, sculpture and fabrics – bears witness to his devotion to the classic or simple shapes of all kinds of flowers and leaves. Century after century certain styles evolved, to be replaced in turn, but still the same theme of flowers, leaves and branches was used by men to express their wish to perpetuate beauty. There is no other form or shape that has been so universally accepted and carried along through the ages as a symbol of beauty. Sometimes colour has been added in paintings, but more often it has been the vine and its tendrils alone, the chalice shape of a blossom, or the rounded form of a seed, that have been captured in metal or wood for all times. There is here an aspect that the flower decorator should note. It is that shape and form are the most important aspects for the human eye. Colour plays a part by affording added aesthetic pleasure. Countless artists of all kinds have shown their joy in the outlines of leaves and all other natural plant forms. They have not depended on the evocative quality of colour, for the materials in which they worked were perhaps muted in tone, but relied more on texture, such as wood, stone or metals.

Above: bouquets of flowers are used in the wall hangings and the silk brocade of the upholstery in a background of *vieux rose*. They add charm to the elegance of this French interior
Far left: a contrast to the profusion and bright colour of the style above. This example of Jacobean fabric design shows the use of stylized plant forms, disposed with space around them. Thus the strong shapes and fluid movement of the branches and leaves play a vital part without stressing colour
Left: another example of how plant forms have given inspiration. A lovely glass jug (from the Victoria and Albert Museum, London) which the designer has embellished with water lilies and their leaves. The translucence of the glass is enhanced by the choice of a flower which grows in water

Above: plant forms carved in wood are used by Grinling Gibbons here as a surround to a portrait of Henry VIII after Holbein

Design characteristics

Grinling Gibbons is an example of a master hand in wood carving who revelled in the forms of nature portrayed in wood. These shapes of rounded fruits, flowers, grasses and twining vines owed nothing to the colours endowed to them by nature. That this beauty of form alone has long been recognized is convincing evidence that in all design the basic **shape** and **form** are the most important characteristics, and that while **colour** can add an arresting further dimension it is not the major design feature. Flower arrangers arrive at this discovery a while after being caught up by the exciting, often dream-like qualities of colour. Observe the arranger of experience and her love of green flowers, and of the muted colour of driftwood or dried and preserved materials. Her eye has travelled beyond the immediate magic of colour and is ready for the more lasting features of shape and form. This does not mean that she no longer uses and enjoys colour, but that she draws upon it with more discernment, observing how one colour can enhance and complement another, or provide exciting contrast. The forms and shapes of plant material carved in alabaster or wood, or shaped in metal, provide complete satisfaction and bring aesthetic pleasure to the eye. Should these same satisfying forms and shapes have paints or enamel added to them, then the pure pleasure of observing the curves, lines and swelling forms would probably be spoilt rather than enhanced.

The rapid growth and interest in the art of flower arrangement, and the consequent rise in the standard of decorative flower work, mean that the designs of the more expert and experienced arrangers are seen and admired by many hundreds of thousands of people. The use of simple but classic shapes and forms, rather than dependence upon the visual impact of solid colour, has no doubt awakened in many viewers, too, an understanding of the design potential offered by nature. How apposite are the words of the Italian painter Lippo Lippi: 'If you get simple beauty and naught else, you get about the best thing God invents.' It is significant that the superb Corinthian stone columns are crowned with acanthus leaves carved in stone as their embellishment. How often do we see stone pineapples used as finials. The delicately decorative carved chains on Robert Adam mantelpieces are reputed to be based on the lovely *Garrya elliptica* catkins. Grinling Gibbons loved to include in his carvings an open garden pea-pod with the row of spherical peas enclosed by the parallel lines of the two sides of the pea-pod.

It would be wrong and foolish to give the impression that colour in flower design is a purely secondary consideration. On the contrary, it can bring the necessary drama and 'punch' required at times, and some combinations can be almost breath-taking to look at. The stimulation of contrast, however, without

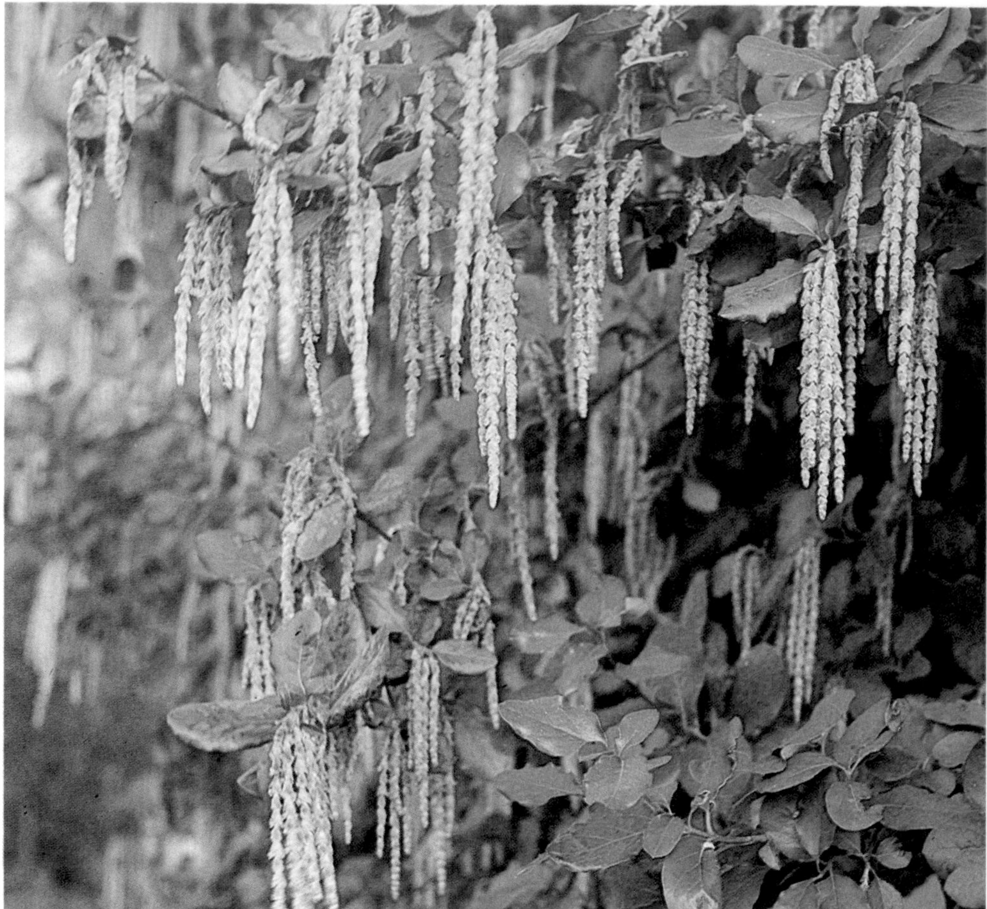

Garrya elliptica, a shrub which flourishes on a north wall. A closer look at the form of the silken catkins reveals a series of graduated bell shapes. Their stylized forms can be discerned in the design above the Robert Adams fireplace and on its side panels (below)

Fine stone columns with their ascending vertical lines fittingly crowned with the sculptured shapes of the acanthus leaf

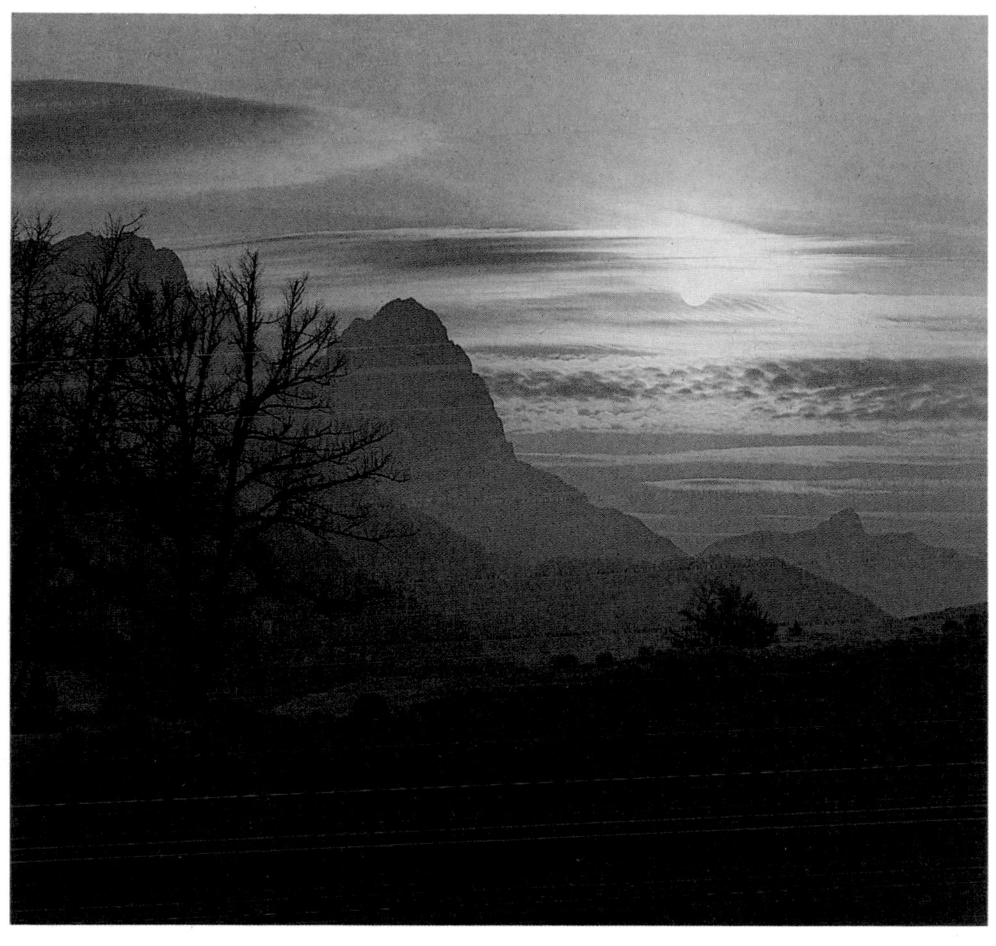

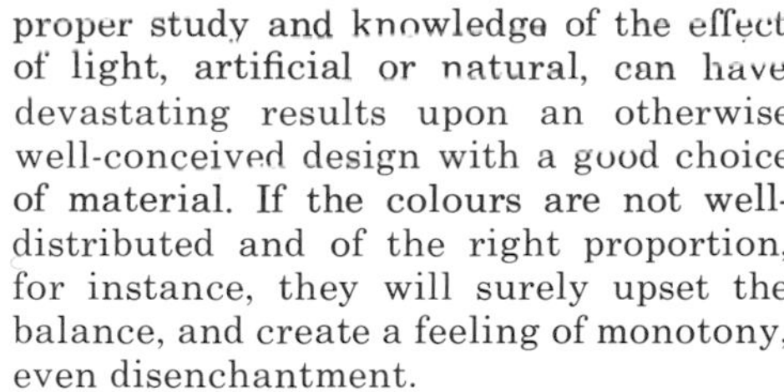

proper study and knowledge of the effect of light, artificial or natural, can have devastating results upon an otherwise well-conceived design with a good choice of material. If the colours are not well-distributed and of the right proportion, for instance, they will surely upset the balance, and create a feeling of monotony, even disenchantment.

Another aspect of nature, the sky, presents at all times a fine panoramic background of changing forms and shapes. Here, it is not usually colour that is the dominant factor, but simply the cloud formations and movements. The eye never tires of watching this natural and ever-changing spectacle. Sometimes a sun-

set or sunrise will suffuse the horizons with exquisite colours ranging from deep red, purple and golds to the faintest shell-pink. The sight can bring exclamations of admiration. However, it is questionable whether it would be quite so pleasurable if these were the colours of the heavens for all and every day. Nature has provided a roof and ceiling to the world that does not challenge the eye but has movement and changing forms which are ever-pleasing. In the same way nature offers an immense variety of restful colours – greens of all tones and shades, the quiet brown sand colours of rocks, stones and wood, soft blues and slate greys – in the materials that make up the universe. Against these muted and restful tones nature paints in a medley of rich colours, sometimes with dramatic impact: for instance, a curtain of purple bougainvillaea against deep jungle green, or a haze of soft hyacinth bluebells below a canopy of the palest of green beech leaves, or a splash of scarlet berries among almost black-green holly. Another variation is the cool beauty of a water-lily against the background of its own leaves and of water. There seems to be an element of surprise, and restraint in most cases, in the way nature, left to its own devices, distributes colour. It is as if it seeks to draw the eye and thoughts of man to the importance of an unobtrusive background. Here surely is a clear message for the flower arranger if she will heed it, applying it in her own use of colour in design.

People of discernment are aware of this need to understand the qualities of colour and, in particular, that this whole exciting extra dimension in design can either provide the master touch or simply offend the senses by over-use, whether it be décor or dress. It can be best developed through constant observance of nature, in all its varieties of shape, form and tone. On occasion, sometimes in gardens but more often in public parks and places, man brings together strong, vibrant and opposing flower colours and groups them in serried lines and patterns. The result is rarely pleasing to the senses and seems to inflict on the eye a sense of shock, far removed from the pleasurable feeling conveyed by the more gentle 'surprise' of a simple spilling of colour with indefinite boundaries. That is the way of nature. This then is what the flower arranger must hope to achieve when she uses the materials provided by nature. Yet it is not easy to bring together leaves and flowers from different plants and shrubs so that their grouping seems like natural growths intermixed. However, by observation of plant growth, and by avoiding clutter and too much contrivance, it can be done with increasing confidence.

The message of flowers

All moments of special significance in life are linked universally with the arrangement of flowers. At a christening, the font is rimmed with the small and simple flowers emblematic of childhood. Earlier, the mother of the child will have had flowers of congratulations sent to her bedside. At weddings, a profusion of flowers is exhibited in countless ways: the church and the reception area are decorated, the bride and bridesmaids carry flowers and often wear them in their hair. The groom and ushers, as well as families and friends, wear them too. The bride will almost certainly have received them from the groom when he was courting her and wished to show his love. When grief, sadness and illness come into people's lives, then flowers again are present to console, to express love as a last gesture, and to lift the hearts of those who mourn. On great occasions, stately functions, or at a barbecue or dinner party, flowers are in evidence. They are inextricably woven into the pattern of modern life as they have been since the beginning of time. The world over, men have seen in them a unique and precious quality that sets them apart. At certain moments that really matter, man uses flowers to express feelings for which words seem inadequate – joy, love, sympathy. Life fortunately is not purely one broken succession of major emotional events, and therefore flowers have not been kept exclusively for such occasions. Indeed, everyday life can be rather mundane and routine; and, just as

Three examples of the work of nature. The muted, misty perfection of the bluebell woods contrasts with the cool clarity of the lily petals against their background of water, and the vivid drama of purple bougainvillaea

Above right: the work of man shows how over-regimentation in line and the use of strident contrasting colour fails to evoke the same aesthetic response

Below: 'Summer Flowers', a late nineteenth century painting by Maud Goodman (detail)

the presence of flowers helps to elevate the spirit and the quality of living on special days, so can it in more routine situations. Flowers on the dining-table or in the living-room, or sent when a friend is ill, still play an indispensable part. For they speak of happier things, of gardens to those who live in the city, and bring gaiety to the shared meal, or help soothe the misery of pain and illness.

So if our lives, and the events that take place in them, are linked with flowers, then it follows that we should know how to grow, cut and buy them, and how to care for them too. Having acquired the flowers and leaves, it is also necessary to know how to arrange them so that their beauty can be enjoyed to its full advantage. Then one must find out what is best to put the water and flowers in, for display and in order to keep them as fresh as possible. In addition, one must learn how best to select and place flowers for a particular need or occasion. Flowers console and bring happiness. Learning to arrange them and their foliage not only helps develop one's artistic gifts, but induces tranquillity of mind, a falling away of inner tensions. The tools required are few; and soon the mind and hands of the arranger come to be guided by the flowers and leaves themselves, so complete and happy is her absorption in them.

2. Practical Knowledge -Tools and Care

Knowledge is of two kinds. We know a subject ourselves, or we know where we can find information upon it.

SAMUEL JOHNSON 1709–1784

A basket, which has an inner lining to hold water, contains early spring flowers

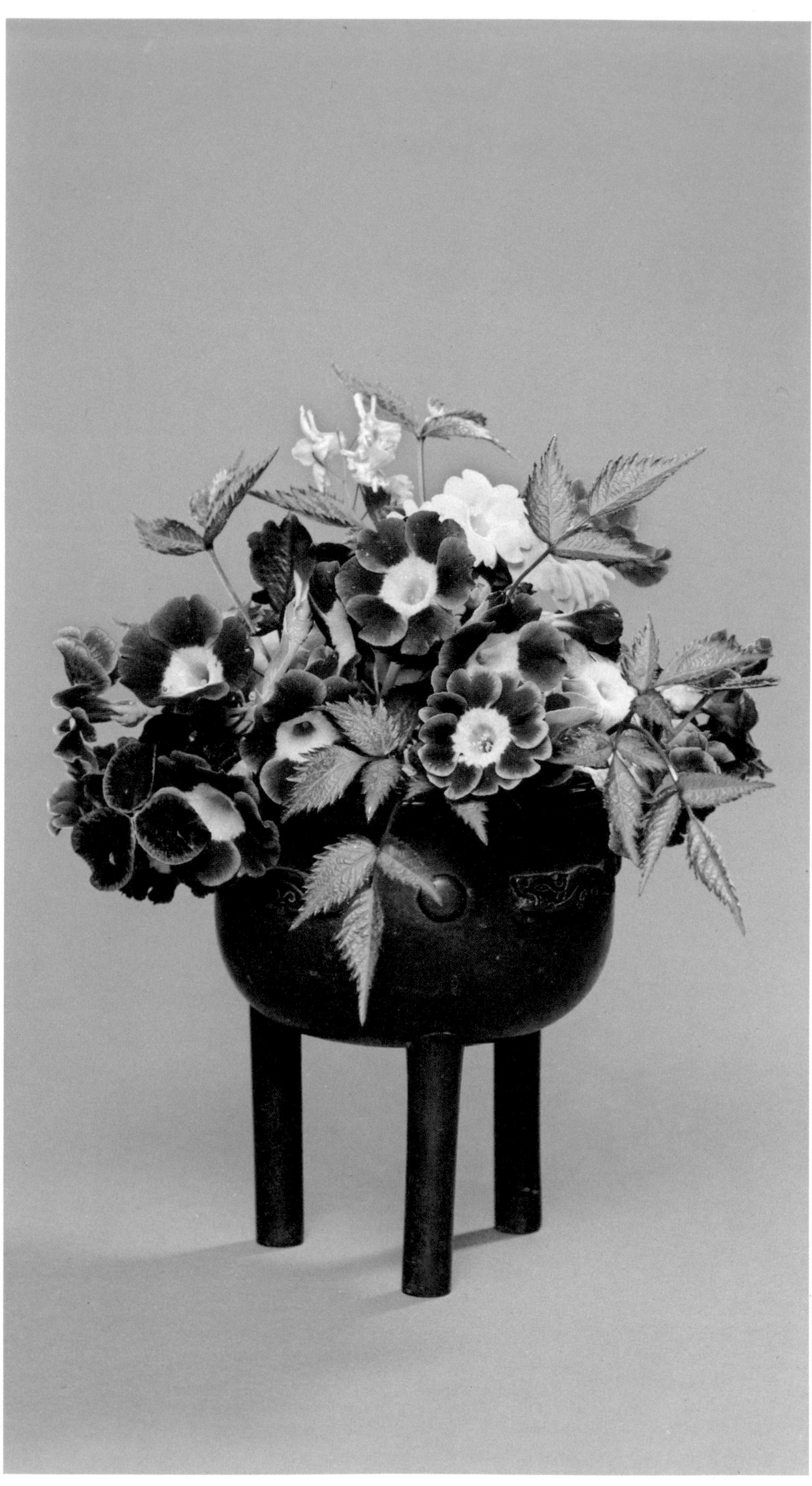

The white paste eye and velvet petals of auriculas have appealed to flower artists through the centuries. Here they are displayed in a simple bronze container

When the practical 'putting together' or construction of a design is attempted, it is necessary to train and use your fingers, combined with certain tools and equipment. Flower arrangement is an art, skill and craft. All crafts require certain basic tools. In flower arrangement this equipment is known as *mechanics*. The dictionary defines art as 'a human skill'. 'Skill' is described as 'cleverness at doing something – either from practice or from a natural gift'. A craftsman is 'one skilled at making something'. So, 'cleverness at doing something' – skill – comes either 'from practice, or from a natural gift'. Nature has been the inspiration of artists, poets, and writers from the beginning of time. It is likely that anyone drawn to flower arranging will be endowed with 'the natural gift' referred to. My experience is that it is just not true that certain individuals have a monopoly of brilliance and intuitive creativeness. Of course there are some people who have talent greater than others, but the average flower arranger possesses all the latent skills, which will develop 'with practice'. This fact should be borne well in mind by the novice.

Two maxims I learnt from the Education Authorities when doing my teacher's training diploma were: 'Students learn best by *doing*' and 'Students learn best from each other'. The truth of these two sayings has been proved to me throughout the years during which I have taught hundreds of flower-arranging students. So 'skill' comes 'from practice', which in other words is 'doing'.

If you do flower arranging you will be drawn inevitably to other people with the same interest, and this is where you will learn from each other. Reflect that you are following an interest that ordinary men and women have practised for generations. Inevitably, some will have been more gifted, more persevering, than others. Consider too that concentration on the basic essentials, knowing what they are, and then practising them, will lead to your own success in your chosen interest and craft. The knowledge that 'practice makes perfect' should not only encourage you to persevere but also create in you the feeling of confidence that all sensitive, artistic people need to acquire, in the early stages – but not too much, otherwise another essential quality, modesty, in the face of the challenge will be lost.

One of the best and most sensible ways of gaining confidence will be to acquire a limited set of well-designed, good quality tools and equipment. Few are required, and with care they should last a lifetime.

This chapter on *basic* requirements is for the beginner. Therefore, on the subject of containers, I will describe only what is needed to start with. Containers can be very costly, and, until you know and develop your own style, you could spend a lot of money unnecessarily. Later in this book I shall describe in detail and illustrate specific period, traditional, modern and abstract containers. Try to limit your collection when you first begin.

Containers

This is the word used by flower arrangers for the receptacle into which the plant material is placed. Obviously it must hold water, or water-retaining material, such as plastic foam. 'Container' could be called an 'umbrella' word, for it covers any shape, size, colour, etc., and any substance from plastic to pottery, china, metal and so forth. The words vase or bowl are inadequate for the vast choice of articles now used. Avoid patterned or highly coloured containers, since they can clash with the pattern and colour of your flower design. 'Earthy' colours such as muted dull green and brown-green will serve you best for practically all the designs you wish to make. These are the colours nature itself provided as the starting-point.

Remember you can paint over a pattern or change the colour of a container. Should you do so, use matt rather than gloss paint, for a shining surface draws the eye from the flowers and foliage. Avoid small containers to begin with. They are restricting and more difficult to use, and in them your mistakes are more apparent, sapping your confidence. Matt black is useful on a container but tends to bring in a 'sophisticated' feeling. White tends to be cold and is rather dominant too, unless

Above: these containers harmonize in colour and texture with the simple arrangements of spring flowers and foliage displayed in them
Left: among this collection of containers there are some valuable antiques, but the readily-available ones of simple material and design will probably prove to be more generally useful

Primroses and their own leaves in a suitable lidded basket

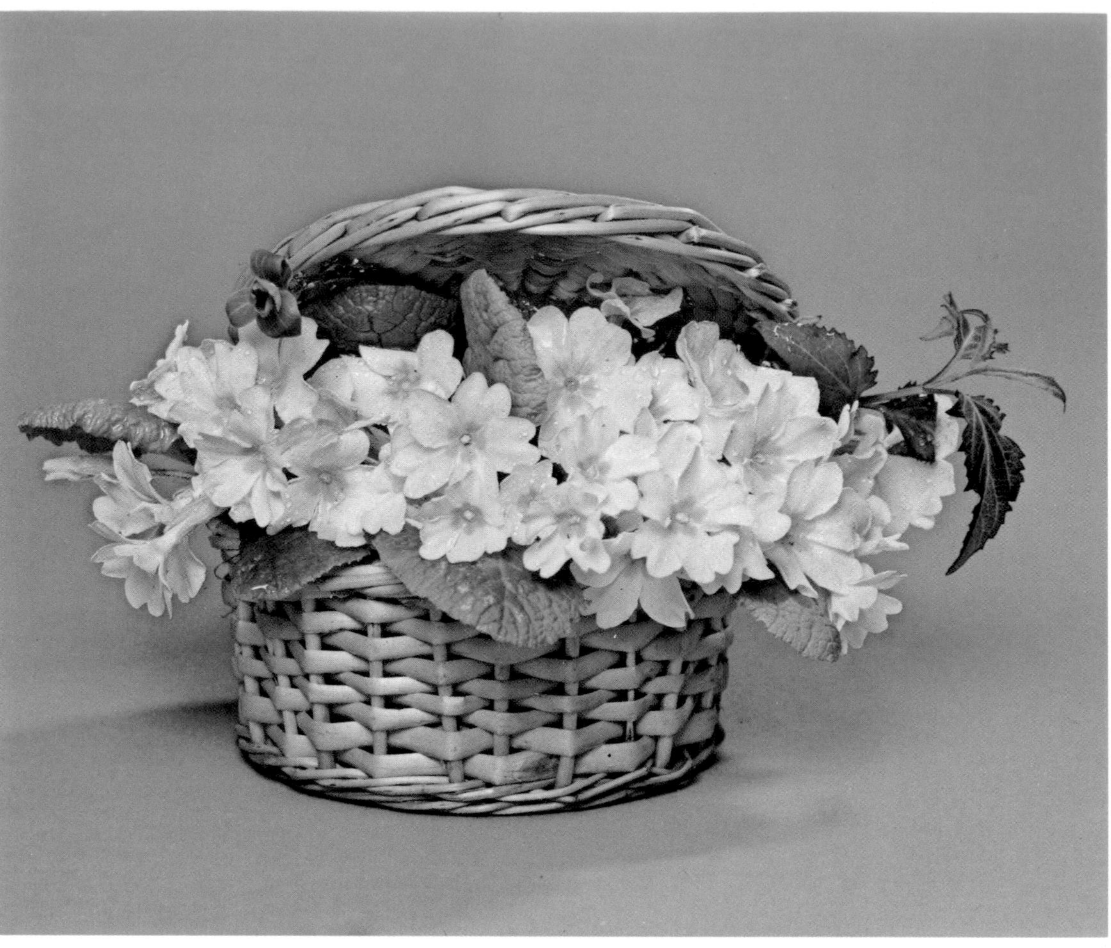

you want a cool look. It is wiser therefore to keep to the earthy colours. All plant material looks good in baskets and basketry – probably because here again is another natural material. Hand-thrown pottery is always sympathetic and usually has a simplicity lacking in more ornate porcelain. Even home-made containers blend better, providing they are well finished.

Copper, pewter, brass and silver look excellent with most plant material. Furthermore, there seems to be some kind of chemical reaction in the water when plant material is put in metal containers, and this helps to keep the material fresh. A 'loaf' baking tin painted on the outside, or a 25-cm (10-in.) baking tin, provide good water depth and space for flowers, and set them off well. Many casseroles and similar dishes lend themselves handsomely, often made as they are in muted earthy colours. Plain bowls, whether round, oblong or any other shape, are all very useful. Containers raised on stems – known as *footed containers* – such as goblets, cake stands and candlesticks, are known to add grace and elegance to the design. On the other hand, low oblong pottery dishes look very well with designs, water playing a decorative part when the plant design is at one end of the dish. If such a dish is very shallow, then use a well pinholder (described later in this chapter) so that the plant material has sufficient water.

Excellent upright containers can be made by cutting the top off a plastic holder such as those made to hold washing-up liquid. Fabric or a nylon stocking can be glued on to them, and they can then be painted or have substances such as the kind used to fill holes and cracks in walls spread on them. Sand or shells added to the paint while it is still wet afford added textural interest. Interesting paint colours can be combined to get metallic effects. Plastic containers tend to lack stability because of their light weight. In tall containers this snag can be overcome by putting sand or stones in the bottom. This can also be a means of raising the pin-holder so that stems do not have to reach down to the bottom.

Strip-lead can be bent into low dish shapes, the dull grey looking particularly pleasing. Pieces of bark, tree roots, and other articles such as shells also make unusual containers.

Equipped with the simple containers described, you have enough as a beginner to go ahead and make yourself proficient with first designs. During this period you

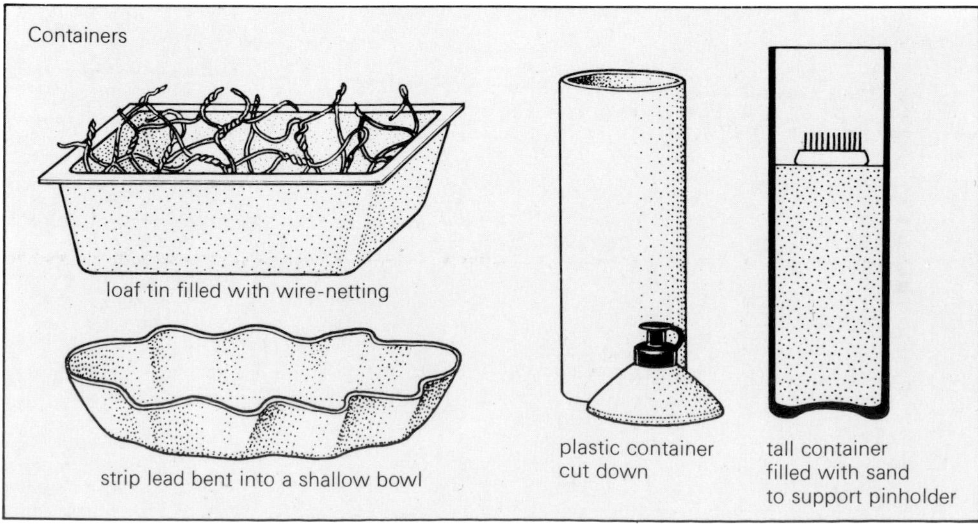

will soon learn and decide which type will be of most use to you. When you have reached that point, you can start to buy containers that are more costly. You will find anyway that, however many containers you may buy, make, or have given to you, you will in the end still find the basic ones described continuously useful, and will come to look on them as old and trusted friends which will never fail you.

Bases

A base is not an essential (except to protect furniture), but it can do a great deal set under a container, providing it is in harmony and in good scale with the overall design. 'In harmony' means, for instance, choosing a velvet-covered base for use only with an elegant design. A simple design would, in contrast, accord better with coarse linen or hessian fabric. A base of wood, or a piece of slate or stone, combine happily with simple designs. More sophisticated work may look better on a polished marble base.

Providing the material, colour and texture of the base chosen are suitable for the plant material used, and in scale with the design, then any shape or substance is permissible. Rush and bamboo mats and 'rafts' are excellent standbys, as the natural material they are made of blends well. Oriental stands, both high and low, have been imported in quantity and most antique shops stock them. They are suited to arrangements using a branch of blossom and a few flowers.

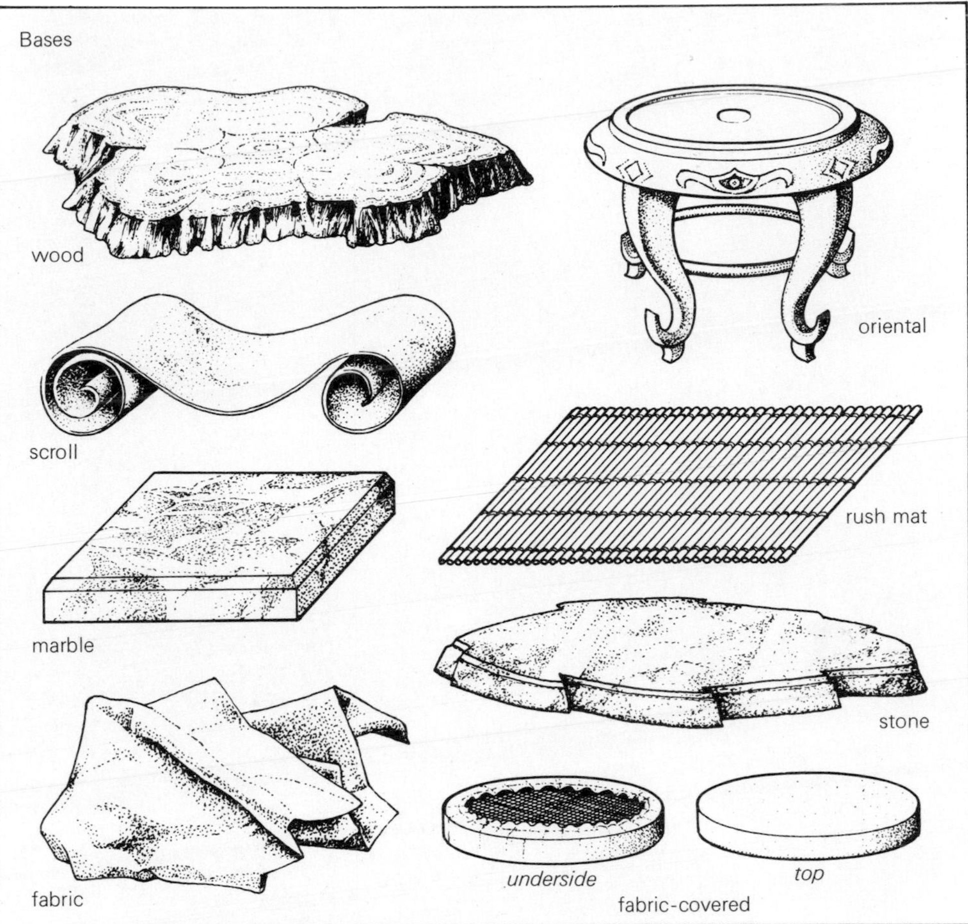

Bases can be used alone, in place of a container, if a well pinholder or small container is placed on the base. The mechanics must be concealed, but this is easily done by foliage or a piece of bark, or pebbles. Bases add not only variety, interest and sometimes contrast, but they also provide considerable visual weight at the bottom of a design, which can be useful in certain circumstances. However, they should not be used unless they play a part and enhance the overall design. Unless this is the case, they can make a design look overdone and too contrived.

Cake bases, such as are used for wedding-cakes, can be covered by sticking fabric on them, or making several covers of different fabric and colours with an elastic edge wide enough to go over and under the base. Wood or hardboard can be cut in all shapes and covered with fabric or painted, polished, etc. Should you use a piece of fabric not mounted on a base, then great care should be taken to see that it is not too voluminous and that it is carefully arranged. As mentioned, a practical advantage of using a base is to protect furniture on which an arrangement is placed, but if it is not part of the design, a near-invisible circle of plastic will do as well.

Pinholders

When buying your pinholder, there are certain things of which you must be aware. One is that you should avoid buying one made of plastic. The reasons are that the light weight gives no stability, and that the pins bend under the weight and pressure of a wooden stem and it is virtually impossible to impale the stem end on them. If you buy a metal pinholder take care that the pins are not set too close together, or too far apart. Close pins are meant for very fine stems such as sweet peas, while wide ones are for use with heavy wooden branches. The most useful size for general purposes is the round-shaped metal pinholder 6.5–7.5 cm ($2\frac{1}{2}$–3 in.) in diameter. A pinholder has a round lead base in which sharp-pointed pins are embedded close together. Make sure the pins are long and sharp or your stems will tend to topple over. The base should be solid and heavy. Because of the metal pinholders are fairly expensive. However, if you take care of them they last many years and are almost indestructible. They should be kept very clean and all bits of stem, leaves and so forth should be washed out after use. If the pins are bent after pressure, straighten them. Never place plastic foam on the pins without first placing a piece of nylon stocking under the foam. After use, you can just strip the nylon off, avoiding choking up the pins of the holder with foam.

Ideally an arranger should own three sizes of pinholders: a really small one about 3.5 cm ($1\frac{1}{2}$ in.) in diameter for very tiny containers and second placements in a design; a general purpose one of 6.5–7.5 cm; and a really large, tough heavy pinholder with a wide heavy base and pins set well apart. The latter is for pedestal work, or really large designs using heavy boughs and stems. A beginner rarely needs the first and third sizes until she is more experienced.

The well-type pinholder, sometimes called a **kenzan**, is invaluable if used on a base instead of a container, or in a shallow container. It is a pinholder welded into a metal base cup. They can be expensive, so if you buy one make sure it holds sufficient water to maintain the plant material you place in it. Many of them are made very shallow and with straight sides. If possible buy one with the sides sloping outwards. Small size and straight sides tend to restrict the plant material. However, you can make a very good substitute for the manufactured well pinholder by dropping an ordinary pinholder into a tin of just the size to hold it and deep enough for sufficient water. Many empty food tins are excellent for the purpose and only need a coat of matt black or green paint to disguise them.

When you put a pinholder in a container place three or four small balls of plasticine (or other adhesive clay) around the perimeter of the base. Place the pinholder where you wish to make your design and then give the base of the holder a firm slow

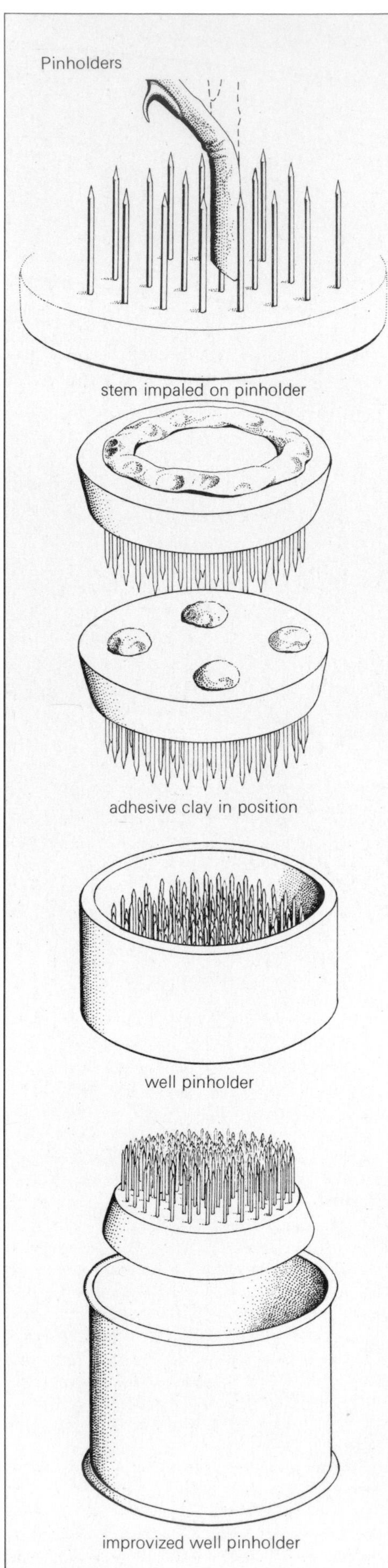

turn until the plasticine balls are flattened and adhere to the container or base. Pinholder, container and clay must be *bone dry* or they will not stick together. The container and pinholder will then be as one unit and there will be no risk of the holder skidding when you fix your stems. A firm base will help eliminate much of the frustration and nerve strain felt by the beginner and put confidence in its place.

Clamps

These are similar to the clamps used by carpenters, but in this case specially made for holding driftwood. They are sometimes mounted on the base of small pinholders which have their pins pointing downwards. These pins are then placed on the pins of the general purpose pinholder. Driftwood is often extremely tough and cannot be impaled on ordinary pinholder pins. There are several other methods of fixing driftwood, and these are described in Chapter 9. It is helpful to know that should a stem be very thin and refuse to be supported by the pinholder, the difficulty can be overcome by fastening a few centimetres of a thicker stem to the base of the thin one. Alternatively you can place the thin stem into a short length of another hollow stem. When using heavy stems with top weight, which causes leverage, small pinholders put upside-down on the holder that is being used make excellent ballast and provide good anchorage.

Wire netting supports

Wire-netting can be bought by the metre or yard from ironmongers, hardware and garden shops. You will need about 1–2 m ($3\frac{1}{4}$–$6\frac{1}{2}$ ft), which will be sufficient for containers of all sizes. It is essential that you insist on 5 cm (2 in.) mesh. Smaller size mesh will mean that when the wire is crumpled up for use it becomes so solid it is difficult to get the stems through, which is frustrating. The wire has a selvage running down each side made of twisted double wire. This is to give a firm edge if the wire is used for, say, chicken-runs. It is of no use to you and should be cut off. Then cut a piece of 5 cm mesh as wide as the container and about three times its depth, if you are using a deep container. Make it into a U shape. The cut ends or 'snags' should be a little above the rim of the container, with the wire in a slightly dome shape in the centre. The snags are invaluable for holding stems in position and are bent around the stems as

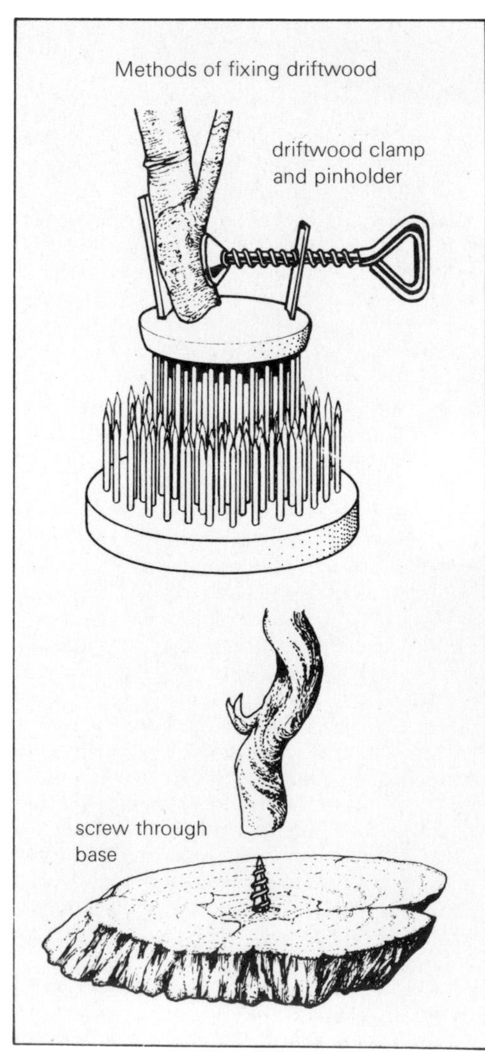

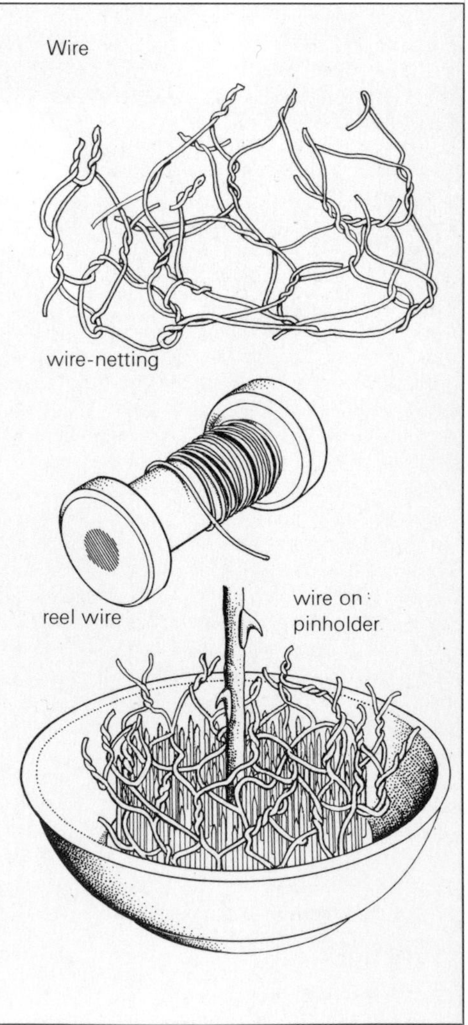

they emerge from the container. Push the wire down into the cavity of the container, seeing that it is spread evenly and not too low, about rim level. The pinholder will have been previously fixed to the bottom of the container. If the container has a rim edge folded, or handles, these can be used to help hold the wire in place. If necessary a piece of thin wire, or string, or two rubber bands can be threaded through the wire, or placed, as you tie up a parcel. After arranging your flowers these can be snipped away, should they show. The great advantage of using wire netting as a support is that it allows the plant material to take up the maximum of water. Being galvanized it does not rust and is virtually everlasting compared to plastic foam. It allows a looser construction, which has a less tailored look than the arrangement made in foam.

Plastic foam, moss, water-retaining materials

Plastic foam (there are several varieties available) is excellent and has brought a new dimension to arranging. It can be wrapped in plastic and then be used in containers that would be porous with water (alabaster, wood, etc.); it cannot scratch valuable silver or glass; and it can be cut with a knife to fit containers with small or difficult apertures, such as shells. Even so, beginners are advised to persevere with wire-netting and pinholder until they are really proficient at placing stems correctly, and can achieve good visual balance and design. The most important aspect is that they will be training their fingers to handle and manipulate stems. A stem placed in foam stays exactly and firmly just where it is placed. A stem put in wire requires more skill and patience to stay put, and this proficiency must be acquired. The arranger must study the 'flow' of stems to achieve good results, whereas in foam stems can be placed at the angles required. After gaining this knowledge and skill arrangers will find foam invaluable.

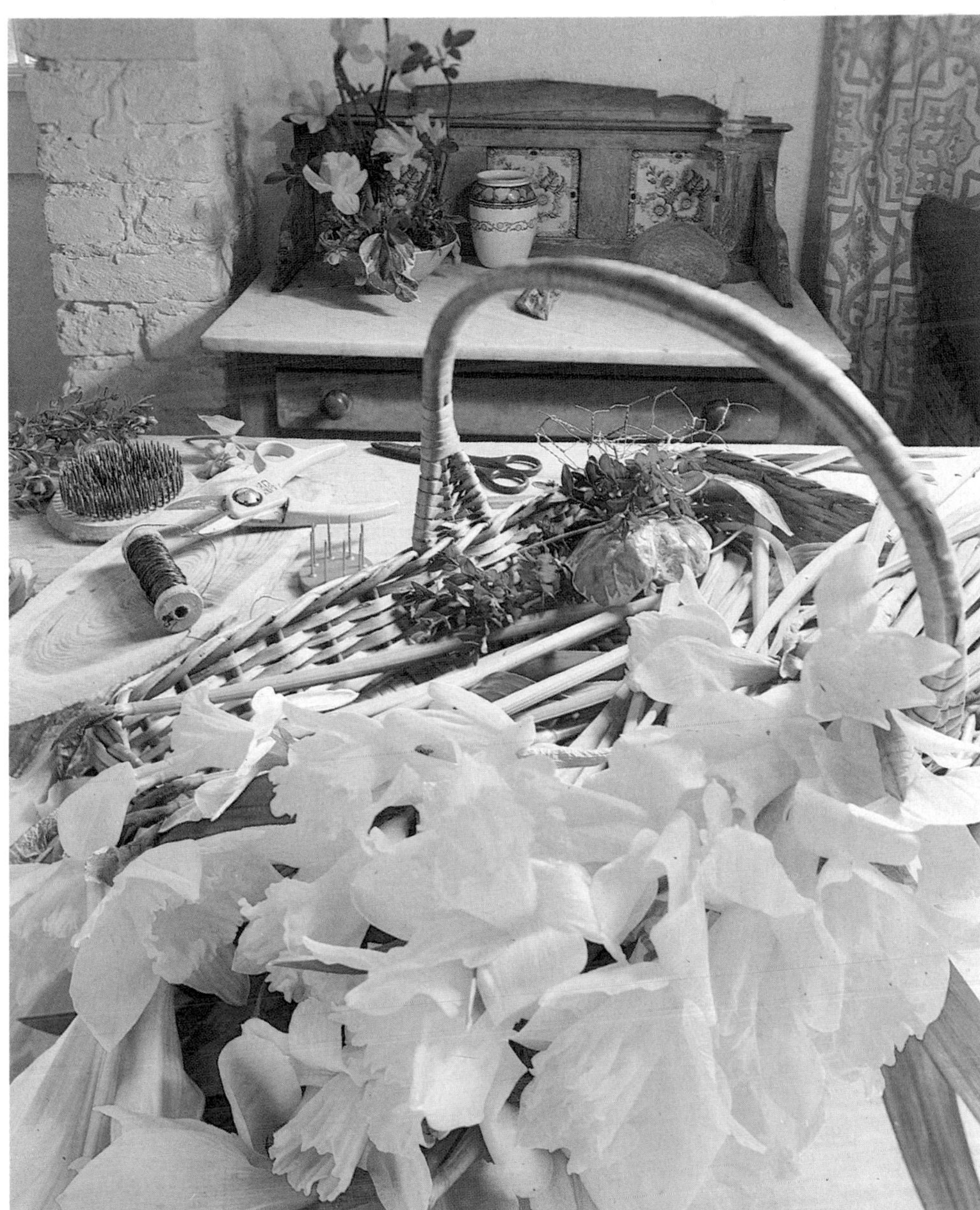

A basket filled with the first flowers of spring inspires everyone to start arranging in the home. The necessary tools are evident in the picture

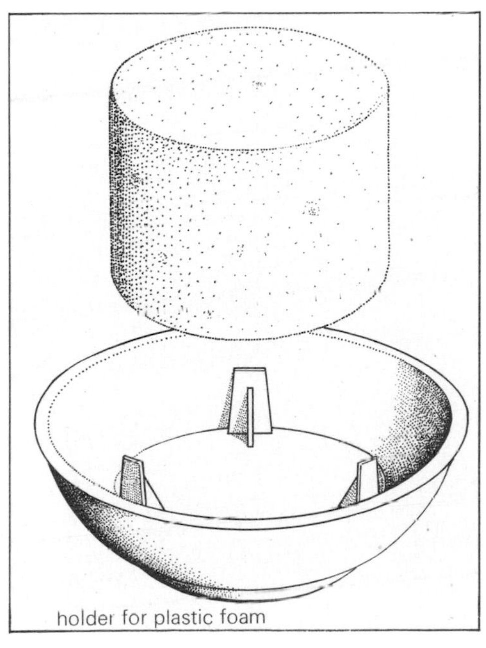

holder for plastic foam

If a thin girdle of wire-netting, or 2.5 cm (1 in.) mesh wire-netting, or fabric netting such as oranges are packaged in, is used, it will help to keep the foam intact. After some use the foam tends to break up and disintegrate as tough stems open it up. Aim to get as much use out of the foam as possible, as it is not particularly cheap. Leave a small space between the container edge and the foam so that you can add water when necessary – usually daily – as the foam dries out. Before using, place the foam in cold water deeper than the block. When it is ready for use it will sink to the level of the surface of the water. A large block will require about twenty minutes and will absorb about 3 pts (1.7 l) of water. Small rounds take about ten minutes to absorb the water. Once foam has dried out it will not take up water again, so it must be placed while wet into a sealed plastic bag when not in use. Special holders are made – a pinholder with a few long pins to hold the foam, or plastic dishes with spikes to impale it. Plastic foam is no use for really soft sap-filled stems, and indeed some flowers of this kind will wilt in it and not survive, particularly the early spring bulb flowers. Sphagnum moss is excellent water-retaining material, particularly useful when making swags and garlands (described in Chapter 9).

Tools and Equipment

Flower cutters and scissors Buy the very best you can afford. Make sure they are well balanced, have good cutting edges and are not heavy and clumsy in design. They will be constantly in your hand, and these aspects really matter. Do not try to make do with kitchen or ordinary scissors, for they will not stand up to the work involved and they will be ruined for their intended use. It is essential to have clean-cut ends to your stems and the tools made for the task will not cause rough, torn edges. Small floral secateurs are the most useful purchase, for they deal with woody stems rather better than the flower scissors. The scissors specially made for the arranger are excellent, but cutters have the extra bite for woody stems. Some use a penknife, which gives a clean cut without crushing the stem, as the nip of cutter or scissor may do, but knives are not quite so easy to use.

Knives An old knife is useful for stripping bark off stem ends, and for removing thorns from roses, although special tongs are made for the latter task.

Nail scissors These are helpful when defoliating stems.

Flower buckets Tall florists' buckets of green plastic and with a lifting handle each side are best. They provide a good depth of water, and have an advantage over ordinary buckets which have a central handle that damages the flower material.

Watering cans Use a small one with a long thin spout for topping up your designs without disturbing your work.

Water sprays These are quite valuable for spraying a fine water-mist over an arrangement, prolonging the lifespan dramatically. Avoid spraying soft petals such as lilies, as they will discolour.

Tubs A small plastic dustbin, kept out of doors in the cool, is excellent for immersing foliage for a conditioning period.

Reel wire Keep some about the same thickness as fuse-wire, and another slightly coarser variety. It has many úses.

Stub wires These short stiff wires are sold in bundles for splinting or holding stems. Medium gauge is the most useful.

Florists' tape For twisting round dried stems.

Funnels and small tubes For raising stems in large designs or for broken stems that are too short. The longest funnels are about 30 cm (1 ft) and they range down to a few centimetres in size.

Cocktail sticks Useful for impaling fruit used in a design.

Plastic sheet Keep one for working on to safeguard your furniture from plant litter. In addition, keep a supply of plastic bags to carry material and a small hand-towel for mopping up.

It is natural that people should wish to enjoy flowers and foliage in their homes as well as in gardens. The fact that in order to provide this source of enjoyment the flowers and leaves have to be cut from the parent shrub or plant will mean that they will be deprived of sustenance. With this in mind, anyone who cuts flowers and leaves should always be conscious that, whereas other designers and artists use natural or man-made substances as raw material for their work, the flower decorator is working with material that has life. This is not to encourage an over-sentimental attitude: the same person who would hold up his hands in horror at the thought of a flower or stem being cut to be enjoyed indoors would probably, without a

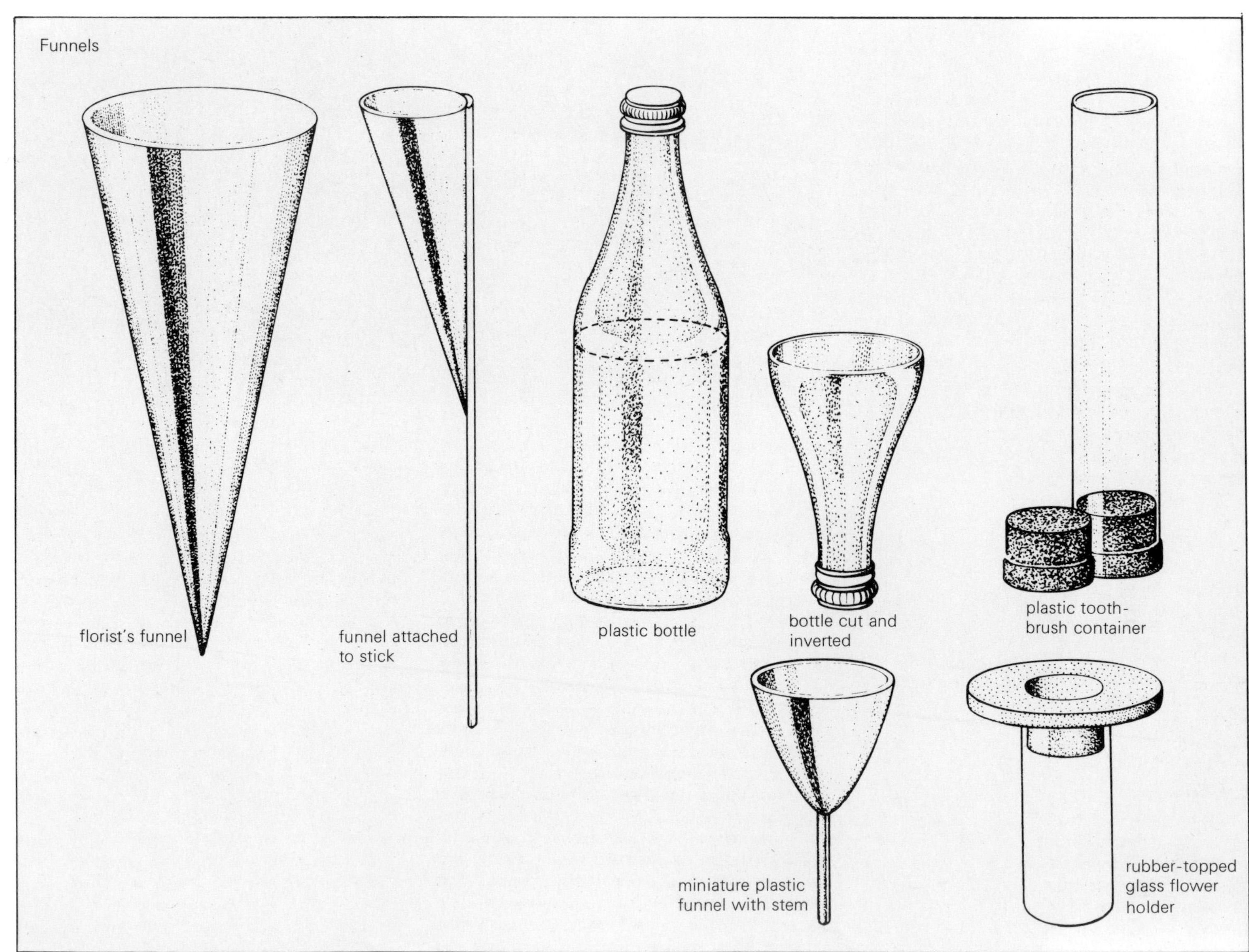

qualm, cut the head off a growing lettuce and cheerfully set about tearing the leaves up for the salad bowl. Roses and many other shrubs benefit from pruning, and judicious picking will often control excessive leafiness, shape a tree, or encourage new growth. The flower arranger who provides aesthetic pleasure and the vegetable grower who satisfies physical needs seem to be a good combination in living. Thousands of flowers and plants that were not commercially viable have been saved from extinction by flower arrangers growing and caring for them in their gardens. It is significant of the association's rôle that NAFAS had its origins in the Royal Horticultural Society, has close ties with that organization and provides a feature at the annual R.H.S. Chelsea Show. The National Council of State Garden Clubs Inc. in America are as renowned for their conservation projects and planting of roadside verges as they are for their flower arranging.

Cutting

Like gardeners, who are well aware that their plants will die without care and sustenance, no-one who cares sufficiently about flowers and leaves to want to enjoy their loveliness in their homes would willingly allow them to wilt and die. To prevent this, the cut ends of stems should be put in water at the first possible moment after cutting. If you are cutting in the garden, try to do so in the early morning or the evening. Place the flowers and leaves in a bucket with some water in it. When you make the cut, do so at a slant so that the greatest possible area of stem core is exposed to take up water. If the stems are tough, slit them for about 2.5 cm (1 in.). If there is a thick bark, scrape it off for about 5 cm (2 in.) and remove any thorns that make the stems difficult to handle or arrange. Strip off any leaves that grow down the stem to its base and which will be placed under water when arranged. Under water these leaves will only decay and exude bacteria in the container.

The sap or watery fluid in a stem can be compared to blood in the human body. When a flower or plant stem is cut the plant stem forms a scab or callous which seals over the wound just as human blood eventually coagulates when flesh is cut. Air locks can form behind this scab and the water cannot be taken up the stem. It is therefore, always necessary to re-cut the stem end (particularly florists' flowers or others that have travelled) for about 2.5 cm (1 in.). This should be done under water to prevent a further air lock forming.

Conditioning

The processes of conditioning flowers and leaves make a difference of literally days' more life to cut plant material. It is true that some varieties of flowers and leaves 'stand up' better than others. Experience quickly teaches you which these are, but *all* varieties will respond with a fresh crisp appearance and longer life to correct conditioning. These are the procedures:

Boiling Using an old pan kept especially for the purpose (for some stems exude poisonous fluid), hold the stems together and stand them in about 2.5 cm (1 in.) of boiling water for about a minute. Take care to protect the flower heads by wrapping a cloth below them so that the steam cannot scald or damage them. This treatment will remove some of the air in the stem and break through any seal, so that the stem can take up the water freely. The boiling water sterilizes the stems and kills any bacteria that could shorten the life of the flower.

Singeing This process is particularly necessary for stems that exude a milky fluid and 'bleed' freely, such as poppies or spurges. Without the burning the fluid would eventually coagulate and prevent water intake. The method is very simple. Hold the stem end in a flame (candle, gas or match) until it is blackened. Should you find that you need to re-cut the stem to a different length when you are arranging the flowers, then re-singe them.

Water-filling Many flowers, (e.g. lupins and delphiniums) have hollow stems. These should be up-turned and filled with water direct from the spout of a water can or with a small funnel placed in the stem end. When the stem is full, plug it with cotton wool or a small piece of plastic foam, either of which materials will draw the water up the stem after it is replaced in water.

Foliage conditioning Mature foliage (other than grey leaves which will become sodden and lose their greyness) should be immersed in water overnight or for some hours. Foliage absorbs water through its surface tissue. Young foliage needs to be submerged for about two hours only, as it can become waterlogged. Evergreens – especially if grown in urban areas – may be dust-laden and dirty. A quick swish around in warm water and a little washing-up liquid will make them fresh and bright. Rinse in clear water.

Stems Whichever process of conditioning you use, immediately afterwards stand the stems in deep warm water. Two hours is the absolute minimum for this, but overnight or about eight hours is best, in a cool, draught-free and fairly dark place. Stems then become what is known as turgid – or full of water – and will last well. Nothing takes the place of this initial deep drink.

After care No plant material will continue fresh and crisp unless its water needs are carefully maintained. If it does not actually die it will certainly wilt and look miserable if the container or foam is not topped up daily.

Draughts Avoid draughts at all costs for they dehydrate plant material.

Dry atmosphere Central heating is the worst offender and much can be done to prolong freshness and life by the use of an atomizing spray of fresh water. Remember leaves and some petals absorb moisture through their surfaces. Avoid spraying fleshy petals such as lilies that will turn brown.

Heat Electric lamps emit a surprising amount of heat and it is obvious that positions in full sun, near fires or any sort of heat will kill flowers. Choose the place in which they will stand with care.

Wilting To revive flowers or leaves, re-cut the stem under water, put the stem end into boiling water for a minute, protecting the flower head from the steam; float the flower in water; or refresh it head down under water – or do all three things.

Cleanliness Wash equipment (containers, wire-netting, pinholders, etc.) after use, in water containing a little mild disinfectant. Dry everything before putting away. Keep cutters clean and sharp. The bacteria that grows in neglected equipment shortens the life of flowers and leaves. If it can be said that 'bad workmen blame their tools' it is quite certainly true that tired and wilting flowers are due to poor or skimpy conditioning.

Florists' Flowers

Many people living in cities or towns have no gardens and are forced to depend on the florist for their material. House plants for foliage and preserved and glycerined leaves are great standbys. Much can be done to augment bought flowers by using these auxiliaries and also by picking bits from window boxes and tubs on verandahs and patios if you have them. Imported roses, lilies, gladioli, carnations and chrysanthemums can be obtained from florists most of the year now that air freight has extended the seasons. Most of the flowers mentioned are remarkably long-lasting if conditioned as described. Spring, summer and autumn bring many other seasonal flowers into the shops so those without gardens will have a wide choice. One might even suggest that in some ways they are more fortunate: the flowers offered them are usually in peak condition, while the gardener has to buy his plants and bulbs and stand the hazards of weather before achieving success.

A good guide to the freshness of flowers is to look at the stamens and see that they are not too developed towards the seed stage. Shop around in the first instance to find a good source and then make your florist your friend. Remember that, like you, he or she has chosen to work with flowers and will appreciate your shared interest in the subject.

3. Basic Principles

Choosing each stone and pressing every weight,
Trying the measures of the breadth and height;
Here pulling down and there erecting new,
Founding a fair estate by proportions true.
ANDREW MARVELL 1621–1678

The proportions of the Human figure, after Vitruvius, a pen and ink drawing by Leonardo da Vinci c. 1492. (Academy, Venice)

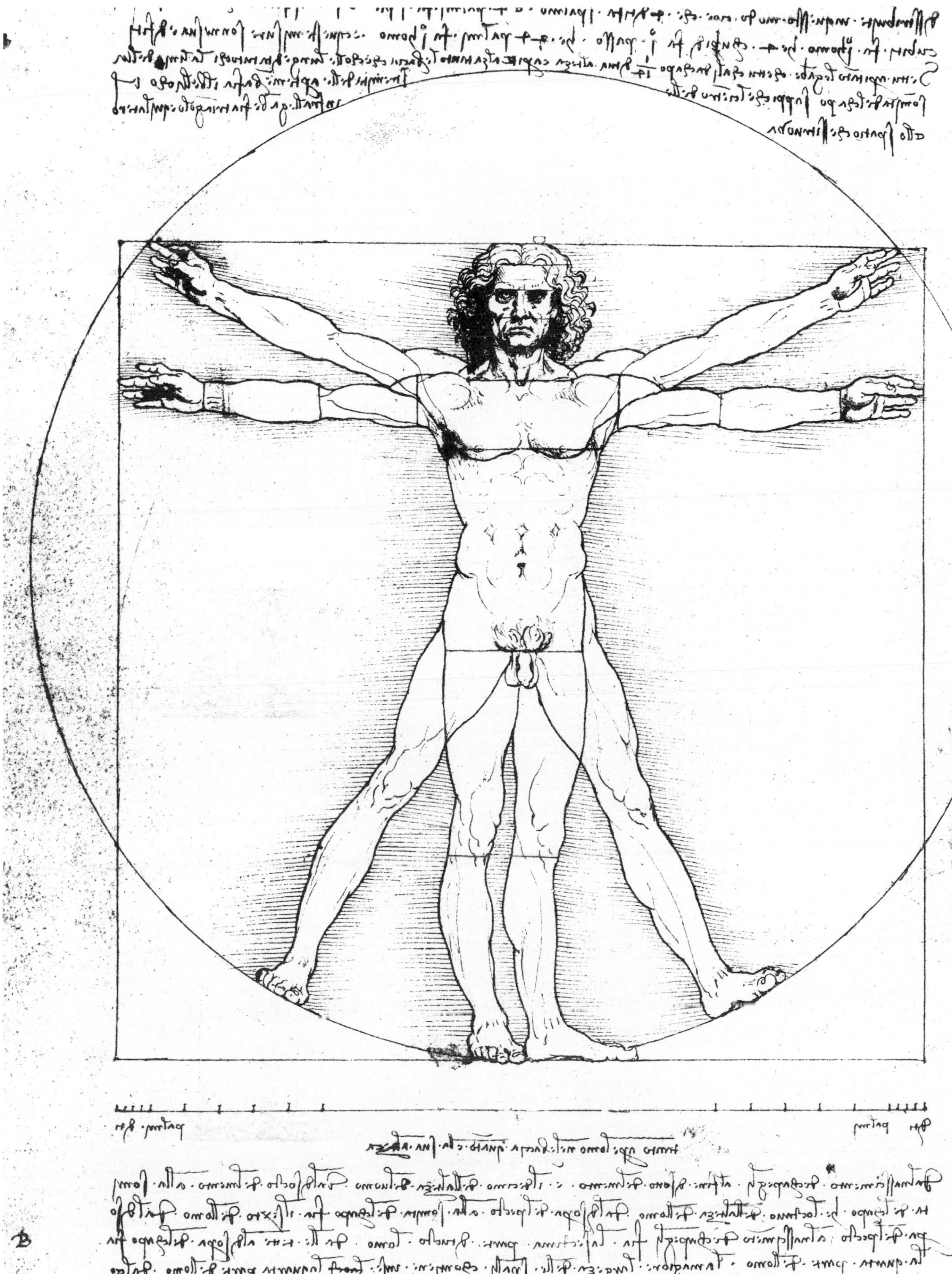

Design

It was once said that all great journeys must begin with someone taking the first step. Everyone has enjoyed putting flowers or branches in a pot, in just the way it pleases them. Then a moment comes when they feel they could do it all so much better with a little more knowledge and understanding of how to create a more satisfying design. We have used the word **design** because this is the most important clue to where the previous arrangements will have gone wrong.

Providing the plant material is fresh, and in good condition, the flowers and leaves are likely to be satisfactory and lovely. The key to the end result – as to whether or not a pleasing and satisfying overall design is achieved – will rest in *how* the arranger has gone about her work. Let us suppose someone is given a length of lovely fabric, from which she is expected to create a well-cut and finished dress. If she is familiar with dressmaking skills, she will almost certainly succeed. Someone without this same knowledge would undoubtedly end up with an ill-fitting and useless shape. Worse still, she will have ruined the fabric for ever. The whole exercise will have been a waste of time and effort, as well as of good material. Equally flowers and stems, like a dressmaker's fabric, need cutting, shaping and handling with practised skill. An understanding of the basic principles of design is therefore essential when taking the first steps towards acquiring the skills of flower arranging.

They are not difficult; in fact, by the time people are adult, many have a fairly sound understanding of good and bad design. However, unless their job has required them to apply the basic design principles to specific tasks, they probably work by instinct rather than through knowledge.

To create a design it is necessary to formulate an idea in the head and then, in almost all cases, to translate that idea into a form or shape by means of lines or curves on paper. Houses, furniture, clothes, cars and aeroplanes all start out this way. This leads to a moment when the lines and curves drawn on paper come to be translated, a crucial stage handled by the craftsman or manufacturers who produce the finished article.

Flower designs do not usually start out with lines drawn on paper, or with the careful and exact measurements required by architects or a clothes manufacturer. Certain crafts and skills have been mentioned, and in their case an error in measurement could well result in doors that will not open, ill-fitting collars, and similar faults. In flower arrangement, the 'idea' of the form and shape of the finalized work is held in the mind alone, and will be translated into the required design by the response of the eye of the arranger and the use of her hands. Crafts require measurement, but in this art it does not apply. It will be a question of response by the creator of the flower arrangement as to how her work is shaping, and whether it is looking good. But this personal response is not enough by itself. Certain principles of design must be mastered too, if the result is to be of pleasing proportions. However, you may rest assured that however advanced your work becomes, the same simple basic principles will always apply. This is as true of an everyday arrangement in a bowl on a coffee-table as it is of the most way-out modern or abstract design.

What are these basic principles and how did they come about? There is nothing new about them, nor were they decreed by one person. They have evolved over the centuries from prehistory through the days of Ancient Greece, when much thought was given to the subject of attaining perfect proportions in all things. The splendour of their buildings, though now in ruins, shows how well the Greeks succeeded. The remains of these buildings are the admiration of the world and thousands of travellers are drawn to visit them. The whole subject of good design, and how it is achieved, is a fascinating one and worthy of study in depth. The essence of the matter is that the lines and proportion found to be most pleasing and harmonious to the human eye can best be seen in the uneven distribution of visual weight, such as in the proportions of the human body. Lines of equal length, being without variety, tend to become monotonous and boring to look at. Envelopes and books, for instance, are usually oblong in shape. Yet they would be just as functional if they were square. One good reason why they are normally rectangular is because uneven proportions have more visual appeal. The same principle of unevenness applies to flower arrangement design,

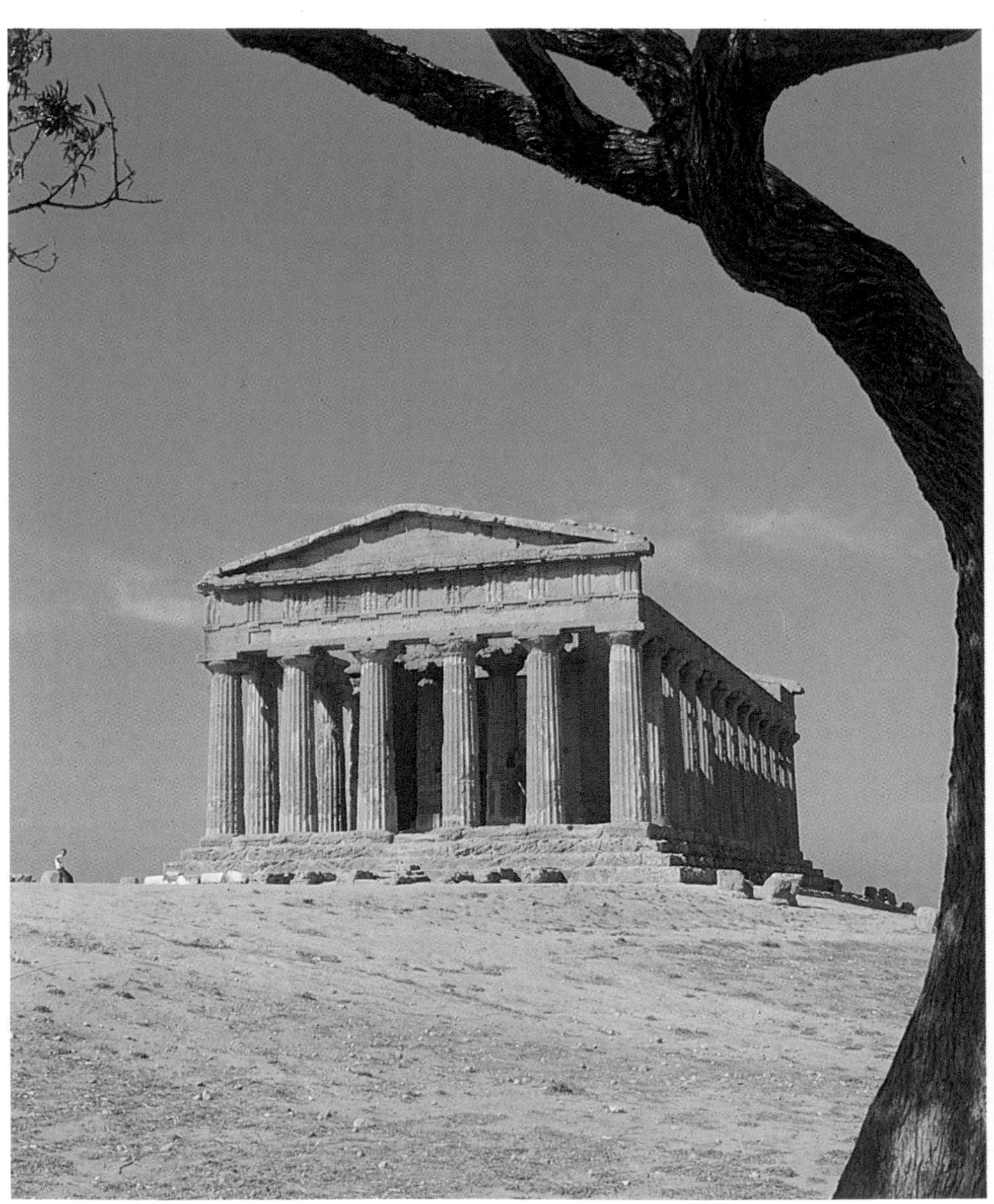

The Temple of Concord at Agrigento, Sicily

which you go about in the following way.

First you must use a suitable container, in which flowers can be placed in water. This can be an upright vase, thin and tall, or a low round bowl. There are, of course, dozens of variations of these two shapes. The same principles are used to achieve the correct proportion for the completed arrangement, no matter what shape of container is used. The main height lines or width lines (according to whether the finished design will be vertical or horizontal in feeling) should be *at least* one and a half times the height or width of your container, whichever is the greater measurement. Obviously the vase will be taller than the bowl, and the bowl will be wider than the vase, but in either case anything less than the proportion indicated as between flowers and container would look squat. There is grace in long lines. Think how tall and slim the top fashion models are. Observe how a tapering spire enhances a church building. Go to the limit in length that your eye and artistic sense tells you is satisfying. You will be surprised how easy it is to decide, and you will know instinctively as soon as you reach the maximum. The effect will look good until the tip of the line goes beyond a certain point, whereupon it will suddenly appear overdone.

What is the main line to decide upon when you arrange plant material? What does it consist of? How is it chosen? Whatever design you envisage (vertical, horizontal, etc.), to get the proportions of the overall design correct, you must take hold of the piece of plant material that you have selected to form an important *main line*. You hold it at the base of the stem (for this is where you will make the cut), and place the tip of the stem either up the container or across it (whichever is the greater measurement). Then add a half of this measurement *at least* again to the stem length, testing it by holding it in your container and seeing if the added portion is right. Then, and only then, you cut the main line stem and place it in position.

It cannot be emphasized too strongly that this final cut must be made only when you have come to a firm decision about the length of the main line because, once severed, the stem end can never be replaced. Therefore, to achieve success you must choose your main line with infinite care, for whatever else goes into your design afterwards, it will be this that plays a vital role. Standing more or less alone, while other lines become more obscured and less dominant, it leads the viewer's eye to the whole design.

In **vertical design** the *width* lines are reduced and stylized to accord with the *height* line length. It will depend on the plant material being used, and the kind of design, but your eye will respond when you find the correct width length. Whereas you will have sought out an almost straight stem for your main height line, you should look for a slight curve in the width lines, so that you have a gentle 'flow' and not an angular hard line at the sides of your design. In a **horizontal design** the width lines become the main line, and the height line is compressed down until the eye (or the requirement of the occasion) is satisfied. For instance, the horizontal design is most used on dining-tables, and here it is important to keep the height line reasonably low. However, sometimes a horizontal will be needed on a side-table, and then the height line in the centre would look better taller.

Horizontal width and vertical height

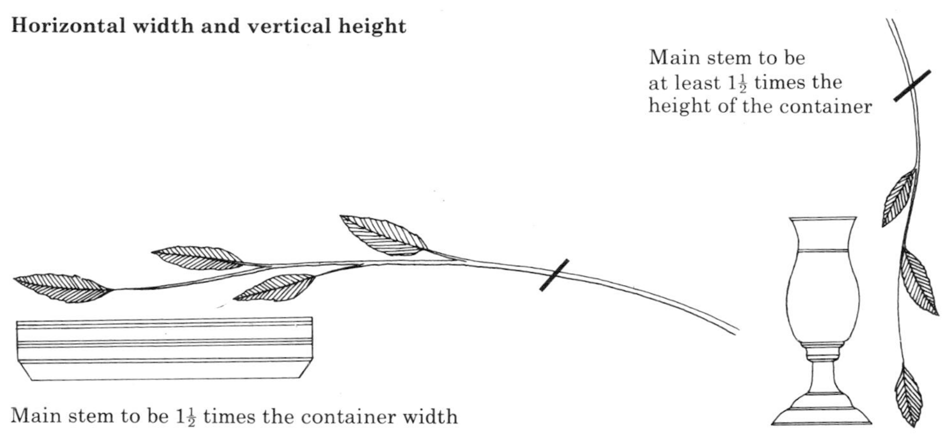

Main stem to be 1½ times the container width

Vertical arrangements

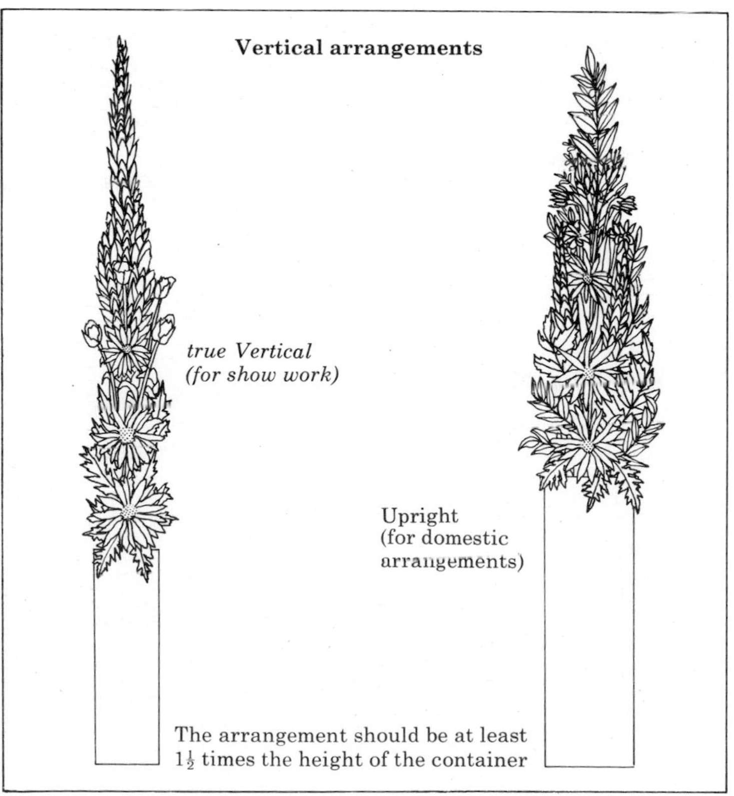

The arrangement should be at least 1½ times the height of the container

Horizontal design

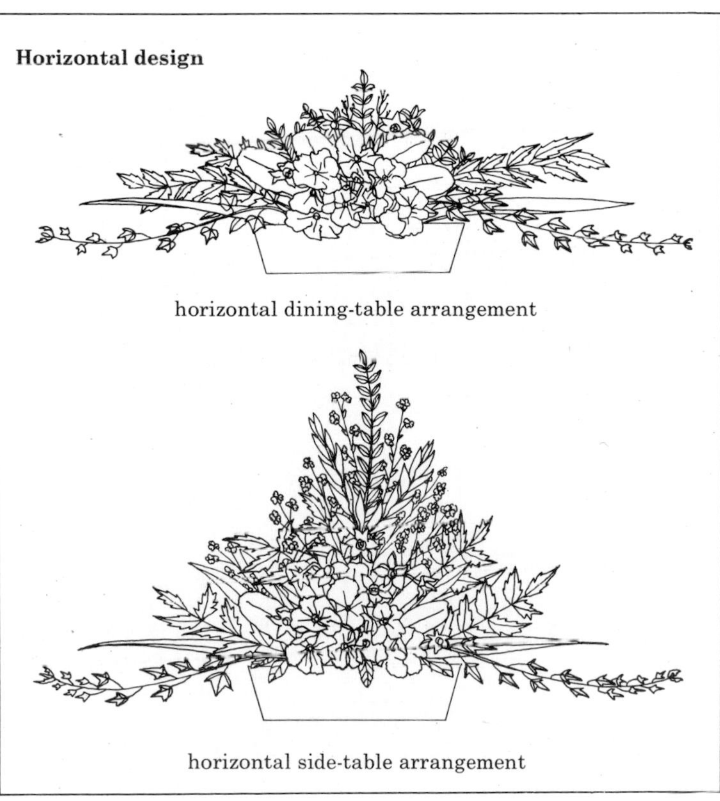

horizontal dining-table arrangement

horizontal side-table arrangement

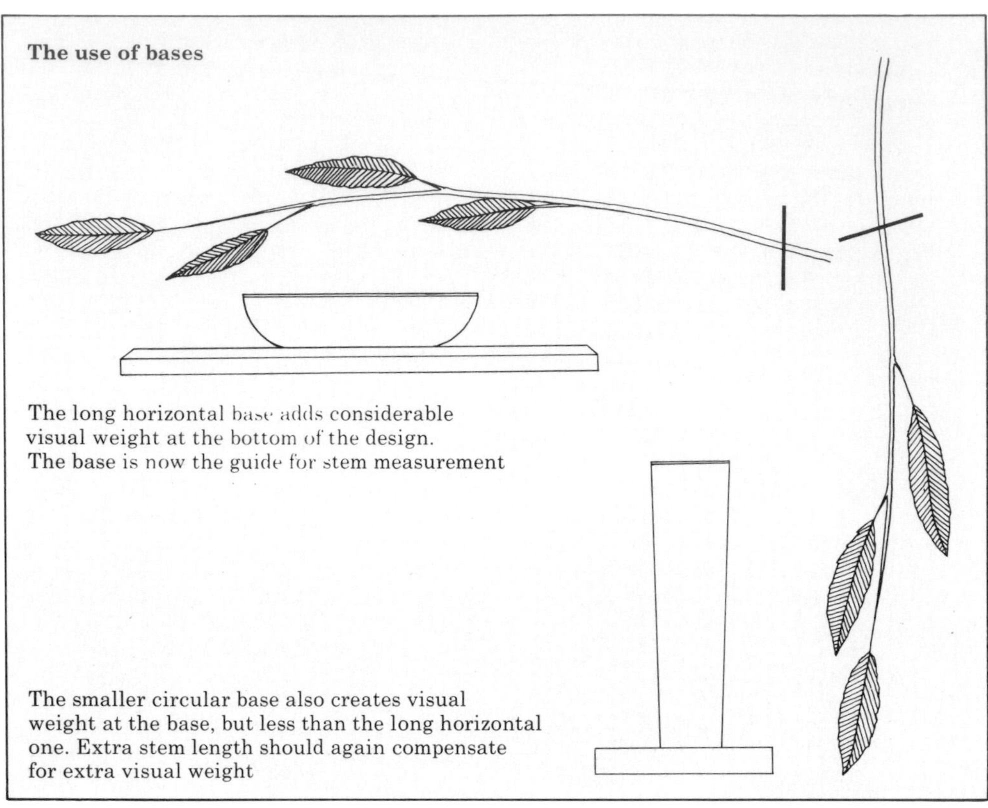

The use of bases

The long horizontal base adds considerable visual weight at the bottom of the design. The base is now the guide for stem measurement

The smaller circular base also creates visual weight at the base, but less than the long horizontal one. Extra stem length should again compensate for extra visual weight

main line placement

2nd placement

3rd placement

The 2nd and 3rd placements should flow with their natural curves to the right and left

If a *base* – made sometimes of wood or other material – is placed under an arrangement, it immediately becomes a part of the overall design, and its length, if greater than that of the container and its contents, must be the deciding factor for the main plant line length. Each individual arrangement will vary of course, but your eye will at once discern where lies the greater measurement of the container and how much this must be elongated by the same measurement of stem, plus half again *at least*, according to the kind of design, the plant material used, and where the finished arrangement will stand. In time, and with constant practice, your eye alone will tell you the correct scale, but it is essential, until then, to carry out this measuring procedure.

You now know what is meant by the phrase 'main line'. Except in modern and abstract design the plant materials selected for this main line should be fine and elegant and without any blemish from insect or weather damage. Broad heavy lines or leaves prevent the eye moving down to the materials placed lower in the design and appear to 'press down' on them. It should be about the only nearly straight stem, all the others used having more grace if they possess a slight curve, particularly the width stem lines and those used at the edge of the design. Fortunately most stems grow with natural curves, dictated by the habit of the plant, or through being drawn to the light, or because other branches restrict their growing space. If each piece of plant material is examined with care this natural curve can be seen. Stems should then be placed so that the 'flow' follows the natural curve of the stem, to the left or right side of the main line placement. Failure to look for, and observe, this aid to achieving a 'natural growth' appearance in the finished design is the major reason for the muddled appearance in most inexperienced arrangers' work.

The objective should be to make your design appear as close as possible to a natural growing group of plant material such as we see in a garden or in the wild. It is bound to be a stylized interpretation because in most cases flowers and leaves that grow on totally different plants will be used together. This is why the student must observe and follow nature if the design is to be successful. Live plants need rain and soil and the minerals they contain for their food and nourishment, and therefore, all their stems and branches depend on the main stem of the plant or tree for their survival. Similarly, the arranger plans her whole design around the important main stem, so that the whole design flows from it. This point at the base of the main stem is called the *source of springing*.

Observe a tree on the skyline in winter, when its leaves have fallen. The perfect symmetry and filigree of the branches all

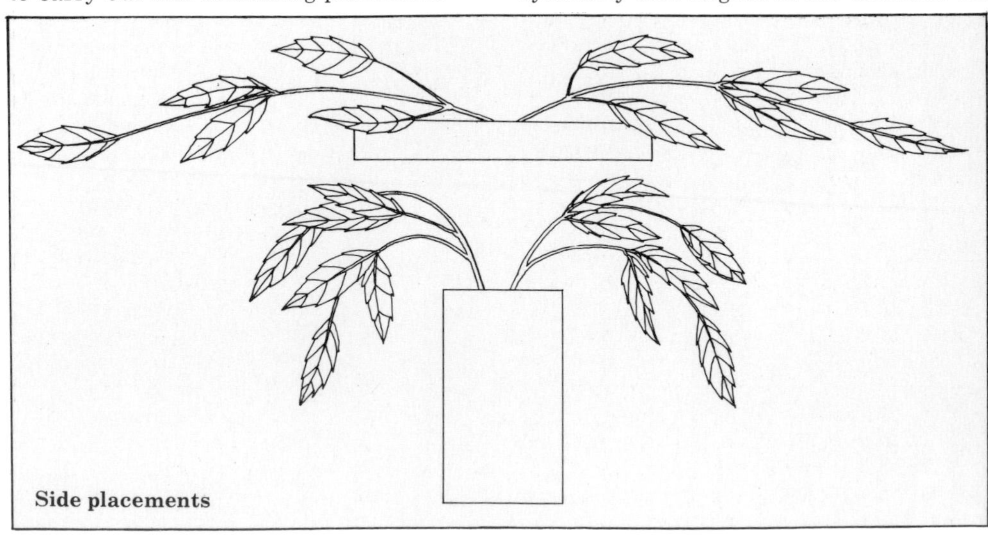

Side placements

converge to the main stem. Look at a daffodil bulb and see how all the leaves, the flower and its stem rise from the small narrow opening at the neck of the bulb. Everyone has seen these structures of nature. If your design is to convey a pattern reminiscent of a formation in nature, then you must understand and follow the structure used by it.

Another important pattern of nature to follow is the bud, half-opened bud and blossom, in that order; and in using leaves, fine, medium, dense and heavy ones. This is the natural order of development of growth, and the placements should follow it in that sequence. Fine at the top and edge of the design, then medium, and then at the base the dense and heavy. Not only does such placement look more natural, but it serves another important purpose. The eye of the viewer starts at the top of the design and is then 'led through' the graduating forms, without a sudden check of a heavy shape just as her eye had been interested and was enjoying the shape, colour and texture of the main line tips.

This placement of graduated forms and shapes also has a descriptive term in flower arrangement design, namely *transition.* It is important to entice the eye of the viewer through the arrangement as you have conceived it. In that way you will hold his interest and pleasure, which is what such design it all about, and why you created it. A solid chunk of leaves and flowers will look static and dull, and after a glance at such an assemblage the viewer will lose interest. The importance of encouraging the eye to 'move' through the design has been stressed, which brings us to the *focal point.* This should consist of the largest and darkest coloured flowers; or a change in shapes or of form or colour, as can be provided by berries or fruits; or a change in texture achieved by means of shining and reflecting leaves, or the matt appearance of succulents. Any one of these design elements will do, but not all of them. Whatever it may be, make your selection with great care, paying particular attention to contrast. This design feature also has a name: more commonly known as the focal point, it is also called the *area of repose.* The 'repose' referred to is that of the eye of the viewer. A good successful design will bring various pleasures, through the blending or contrast of colours and textures, the gradations in shapes and forms, leading to the 'feature', upon which the eye will ultimately fasten. A most important basic principle to memorize is that the focal point should always be found at the base of the main stem – with the exception of **free form modern** or **abstract design**, which follows different principles.

This, then, is how you set about making a composition – a bringing together of all the different elements to create a harmonious and unified picture. In doing so you

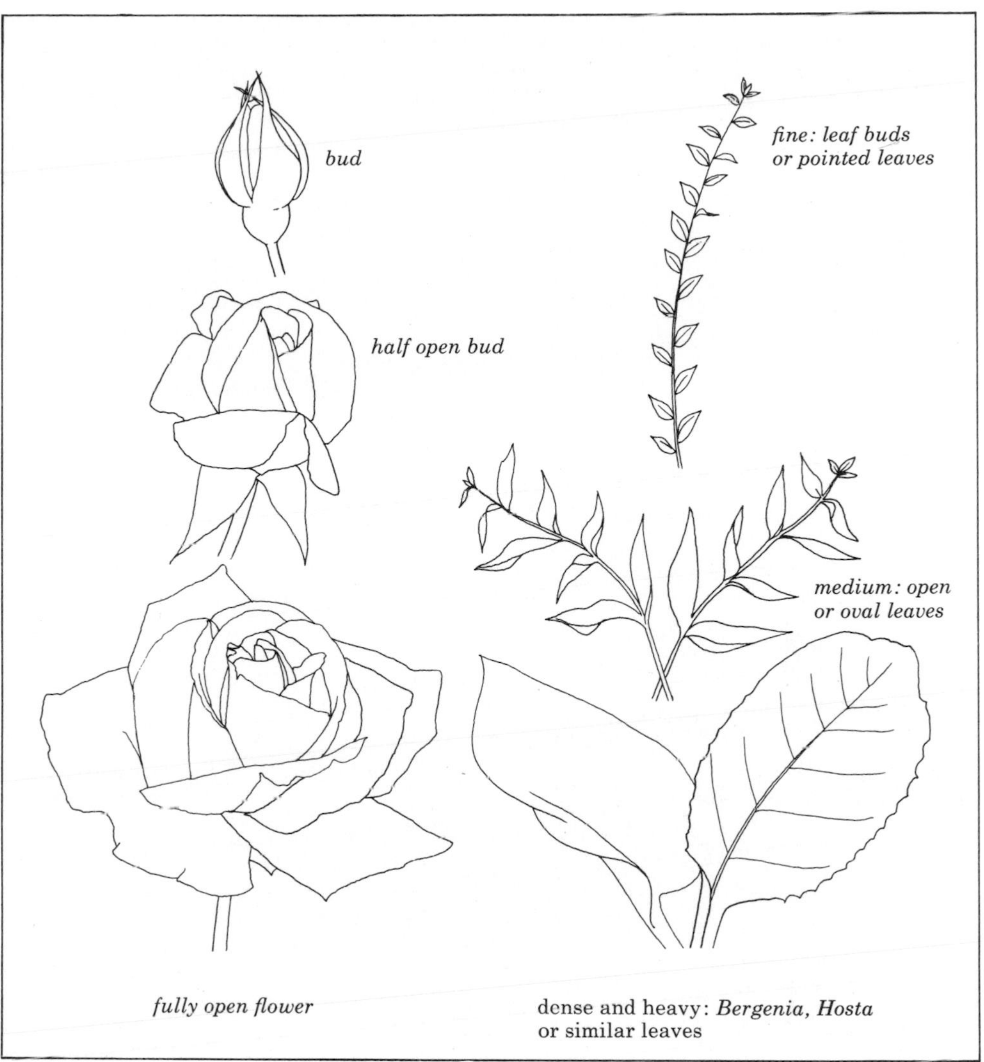

Completed design: sequence of foliage

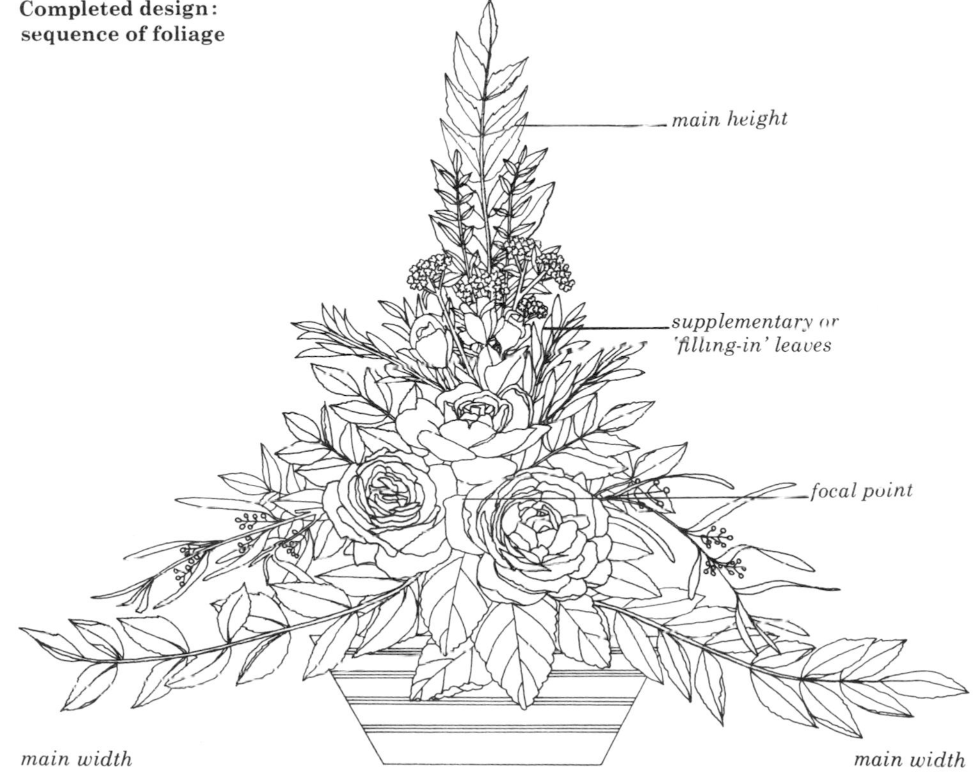

will have exercised an understanding of one of the four basic principles of flower arrangements, namely design (form and shape). You will know how to apply it to the overall design, depending on whether the outline is to be *triangular, horizontal, vertical, crescent* or *all-round*, among countless other shapes. You will also have observed the forms and shapes of the plant materials and how they differ, and within the overall design you will have brought them together so that they create not only a good design *outline shape,* but so that they converge to the base of the main stem and the *source of springing.* In that way the plant materials used will follow the growing structure of nature. Finally, there will be the container and/or base which will bring to the completed design its own form, shape, colour and texture.

Almost all of this 'design plan' will take place in the mind of the arranger before she actually handles any of the components. The thought process will probably follow a pattern of the following kind: 'I want to put an arrangement of flowers and foliage on my dining-table for a dinner party. I must use a container that is low and will not take up too much space, as the party, and the table, are not large. I will use this (or that) container.' This is the starting-point. The container chosen for the occasion and the place it will be seen in (for this varies widely) will be selected in the way that clothes are chosen and influenced by the occasion and the time of day, and where they will be worn. This particular dinner party is to be a small one, rather formal, therefore the arranger gives thought to the variety of flowers that are available in the garden or from the florist. Their colour, shape and whether they will show to advantage in artificial or candle-light must all be taken into consideration. Foliage too must be considered. Once she has thought out a proper plan, the arranger can start putting it into effect.

Harmony

Harmony is the next of the four basic principles. It is a happy word that has all the characteristics ascribed to it in the dictionary. How can it be applied to the arranging of flowers? Unless through weather or growing conditions or insect pests, blooms and leaves are damaged, the raw material at the arranger's disposal will allow for complete 'harmony'. It is only when these same growths are cut and placed beside others, by human hands and not by nature, that disharmony can creep in. Take, for instance, nasturtiums, with their vivid colours, their gay, flat, umbrella leaves, the ribbed textures and the round forms of their seeds, their curving stems – all in harmony with each other. They would be in harmony if put in a bright, shiny brass bowl, a brown basket, or a pottery bowl of the right size, and then placed on a cottage window-sill.

But let us now take another simple flower, the lily of the valley. This flower has a delicate and fragile beauty. The small bells have the appearance of pearls held by threads to the fine stem. The chartreuse green of the leaves with their sheath-like blades complement perfectly the blooms

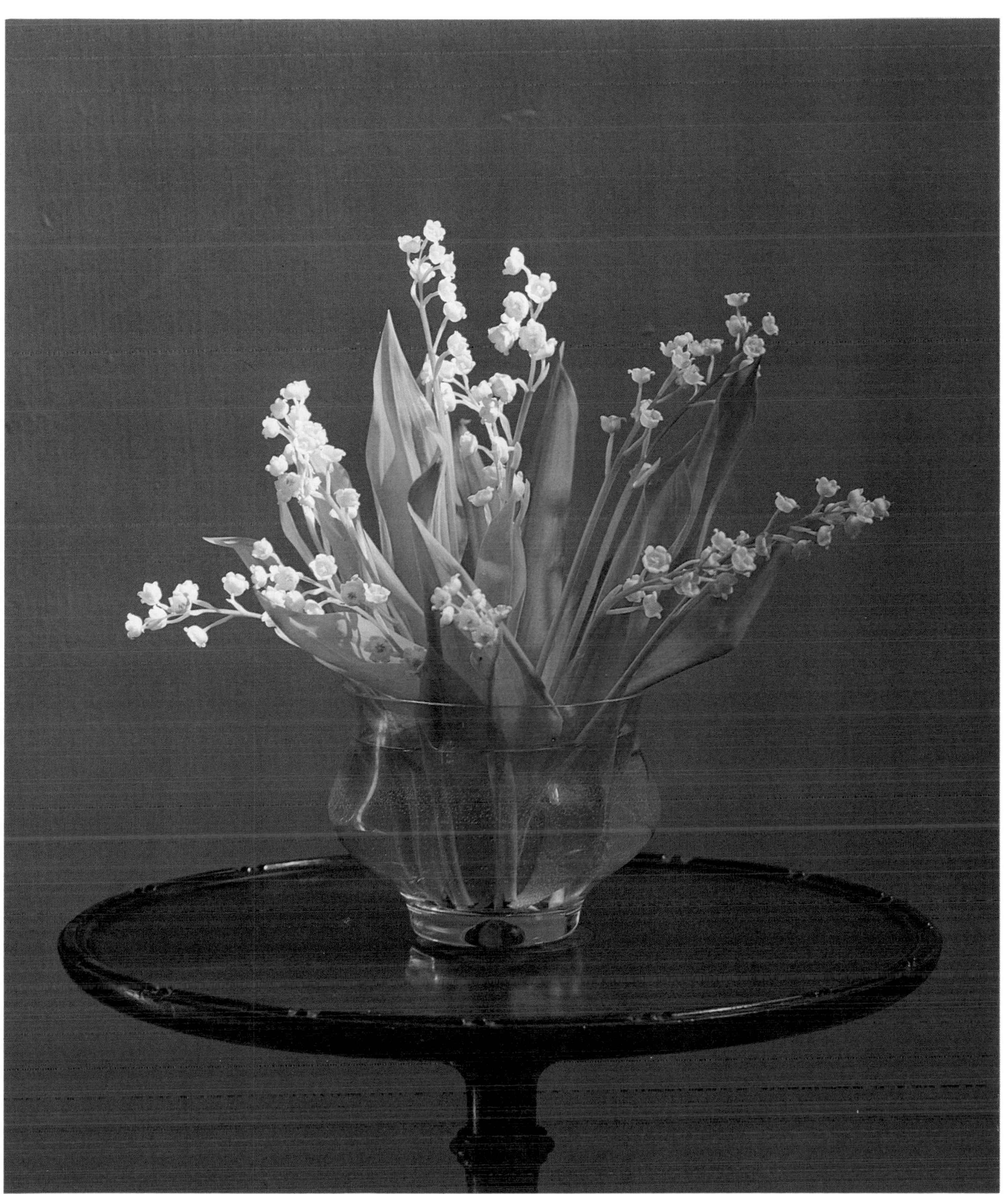

Left : the warm, vibrant colours of nasturtiums are accentuated by the highlights of the copper container

Above: the challenge presented by the fragile beauty of lilies of the valley is met by placing them in a glass container on a polished wood surface

themselves, with their sweet fragrance. These flowers should be placed where their delicacy and scent can be enjoyed at close quarters. Brass with its warm colour, or the coarse texture of basketry or pottery, would be too challenging for them, too much in contrast. For lilies of the valley one thinks of cool silver, glass or fine porcelain, and of setting a small bowl of them, flowers and leaves, on polished wood. The strong light from a cottage window-sill would not allow the special qualities of the small white bells to be appreciated, whereas the sun striking the robust, colourful nasturtiums and the brass bowl would bring a touch of warmth and gaiety to a room.

Different flowers and different settings are to be enjoyed in their own particular way. Bringing such flowers as nasturtiums and lilies of the valley together in any one of the described containers, or placing them in unsuitable settings, would at once introduce disharmony. People give careful consideration to their choice and use of clothes and food. Equally, they can give a little thought to flowers, their containers and their setting, and to the purpose and occasion for which they are wanted.

The two kinds of flowers mentioned above undoubtedly look their best with their own foliage only, but sadly they are among the few exceptions. Roses provide another example. The majority of flowers are generally enhanced by the leaves, seedheads and blossoms of other plants rather than by their own. This is another way the designer of a finished arrangement must exercise her skills and sensitivity to shape and form, to create a harmonious combination. There are occasions when soft grey foliage will do more for pale pastel colours than the more usual green leaves. The use of delicate leaf forms or vine tendrils can bring a special quality to flowers that are rather heavy looking. Perhaps the addition of smooth matt leaves, or serrated edges, will bring a more interesting texture and shape. All such details of design will be components in the final picture presented to the viewer.

The three basic shapes of container

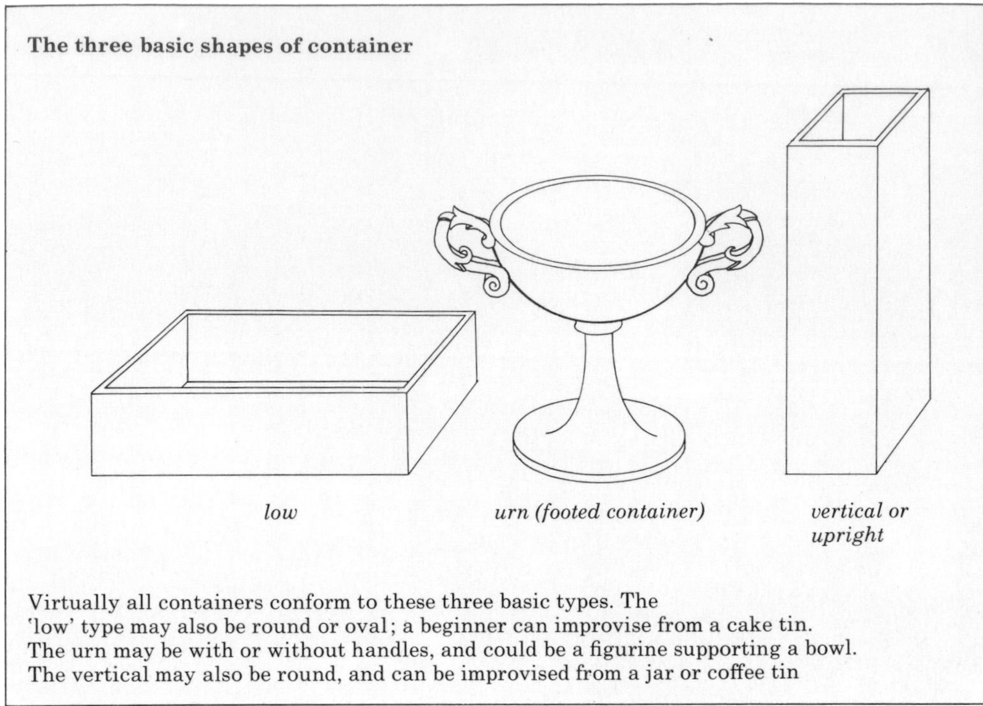

Virtually all containers conform to these three basic types. The 'low' type may also be round or oval; a beginner can improvise from a cake tin. The urn may be with or without handles, and could be a figurine supporting a bowl. The vertical may also be round, and can be improvised from a jar or coffee tin

Scale

The third basic principle is **scale** or 'size relationship'. It is not necessary to labour the differences in size to be found among flowers. They vary from the tiny head of, say, a forget-me-not, to the dinner-plate size of a giant sunflower. Leaves, too, can be fine as a blade of grass right up to the mammoth cardoon or grey artichoke leaf. In between these extremes there are flowers and leaves of every conceivable shape and form. And of course they come in a profusion of colours. It will be apparent that exquisite little flowers require a sea shell, thimble or snuff-box to enhance and not obliterate them. Also that the leaves and flowers of large, noble and classic proportions for their part require large classical urns in stone or metal, or heavy, impressive-looking bowls to be in character and scale with them. Large containers also provide the necessary space for water as well as weight at the base, both visual and physical, to allow for good size relationship. Stability is essential for the heavy stems and their leverage.

In between the miniature and the very large scales there is an immense range of flowers, leaves and containers that are 'medium' sized. Careful thought to the size relationship between *all* the components in the finished arrangement must be given. 'Scale' in flower arrangement design will not end there. Each of the three principles discussed so far – design, harmony and scale – must be related to the setting in which the finished work is finally placed. Between cottage and stately home lie a multitude of buildings, rooms and windows of all kinds. Halls in the more modest-sized houses are small, the living-room as a rule being the largest room, while dining-rooms and bedrooms are proportionately in the medium scale. Where an arrangement is to be finally placed will depend on consideration of size relationship of the plant material and container to the setting.

Balance

The fourth and last basic principle is **balance** (stability). This is perhaps the chief factor separating the work of the experienced and knowledgeable arranger from that of the novice, or from those who think that flowers will look all right if they are just 'put' in a bowl ('plonked' would be a better word for it). In design, balance means *actual* and *visual* balance. Broadly speaking it demands that the finished arrangement must not appear to lean to the right or left, or forwards or backwards. Sometimes poor use of mechanics that allows the stems to fall about, and not 'stay put', can create this effect – even if the arranger knows how to go about making her design. More often, however, it is the result of the arranger not being fully alert to the matter of balance.

What is 'actual' balance? In a nutshell it is equilibrium, a state of equal balance between weights or forces, steadiness. The phrase 'I lost my balance' immediately evokes a mental picture of someone tripping and falling, unsteadiness, lack of stability. Because everything in the world, including human beings, is governed by the forces of gravity, it is disturbing for human beings to see people or objects that have lost their balance. The time-honoured example is that of seeing a picture-frame tipped to one side on a wall. Whether it happens to be in your own home, or in someone else's, the immediate urge is to tip it straight, to restore its balance. Why should this matter so much? The picture is still the same, with the identical frame, but seeing it askew has upset your sense of order and stability. The Victorians carried an admiration for symmetry and and order to excess. Almost all their ornaments and vases came in pairs, and the Victorian mantelpiece with its clock in the centre and two marble urns each end typifies the symmetrical visual balance that was sought after.

Now to visual balance. Assuming there are two kinds of balance how do they differ? If you were to place a one-pound weight of lead (about half a kilogram) on one side of a pair of old-fashioned measuring scales, and a pile of feathers on the other, the amount required of the latter to balance the former would be visually

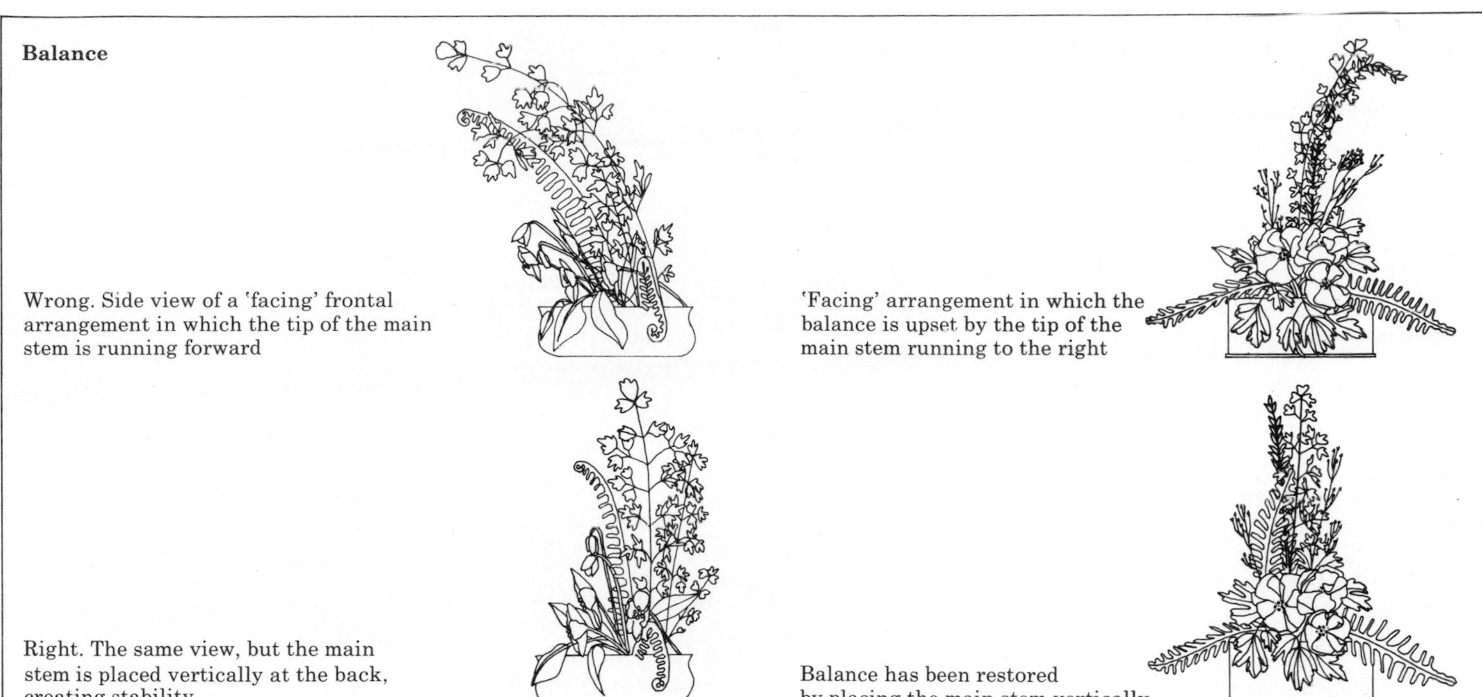

Wrong. Side view of a 'facing' frontal arrangement in which the tip of the main stem is running forward

'Facing' arrangement in which the balance is upset by the tip of the main stem running to the right

Right. The same view, but the main stem is placed vertically at the back, creating stability

Balance has been restored by placing the main stem vertically

disproportionate. In fact, it is doubtful if the quantity of feathers needed would sit on the scale. Here, then, is a simple case of actual balance being achieved, but not of course visual balance. There are other design factors – colour, texture, light, lines – that can have a 'visual weight' quality. Certain flowers *look* different in size just as a one-pound weight of lead and an equivalent weight of feathers are in volume – though actually they may be of more or less identical proportions. A pale pink dahlia may be exactly the same circumference as a dark wine-coloured one. It could have exactly the same number of petals, yet, placed in an arrangement, the dark flower *looks* much heavier. This is why flowers of darker tints and hues should be placed towards the base of a design, and lighter ones towards the top and sides. The heavy, dense colours of the dark flowers would appear to press down on the lighter and more fragile-looking blooms, disturbing the viewer's inborn sense of balance, and provoking a feeling that something is out of order.

Two identical blooms with different visual weight as a result of colour value

Texture too has this quality of visual height. A leaf of rough, nobbly texture looks visually heavier than a smooth-textured leaf of the same size. It will be appreciated that thick or thin stems can also have this quality, which is why they in their turn should be placed within a design with the fine and delicate lines at the top and sides, and the more robust and solid ones lower down. Lines also have to be thought of as creating a response to visual weight. Horizontal lines look heavy, and are connected in the mind with the lying down or sleeping posture. They *look* heavy. On the other hand a vertical line provokes a feeling of vitality and life, and usually lightness. How important it is then that lines are placed well. The use of containers of heavy shape, colour and texture should also be governed by an understanding of and response to visual weight. A matt surface will *look* heavier than a smooth one, and this must be taken into consideration in relation to the finished overall effect.

horizontal

vertical

The lines are the same length, but the horizontal *looks* longer

Moving onward, it must be emphasized that there are in all objects two kinds of 'balance': *symmetrical*, and its direct opposite, *asymmetrical*, which means lop-sided. A mug with a handle is asymmetrical. On the other hand, a drinking-cup of the same shape, but without a handle and with both sides quite smooth, may be classed as symmetrical. And because to the human eye equal lines and measurements tend to look boring, it is asymmetrical designs that, if well carried out, are usually the more interesting.

There are many kinds of symmetrical designs in flower arrangement, the most used and well-known outline being the *facing symmetrical triangle.* The most loved among many asymmetrical designs is the *Hogarth curve* or *Lazy S* (see Chapter 4). The symmetrical triangle is most used because by means of it beautiful and pleasing results can be achieved. Moreover, once the correct scale and placements are known, it is the easiest to execute. The outline consists of a triangle, and the mass of material used to fill it in tends to obscure any misplacements or mistakes. The balance and general appearance are static. This design harmonizes splendidly in churches, large halls and buildings, blending with the proportions of such places. In fact, it fits happily in almost any place and situation.

Why is it necessary to know what constitutes asymmetrical design in flower arrangement? It is because the many varieties all require the use of curves rather than the rhythmic 'flow' of a stem or branch – they give the feeling of movement and create dynamic, as opposed to

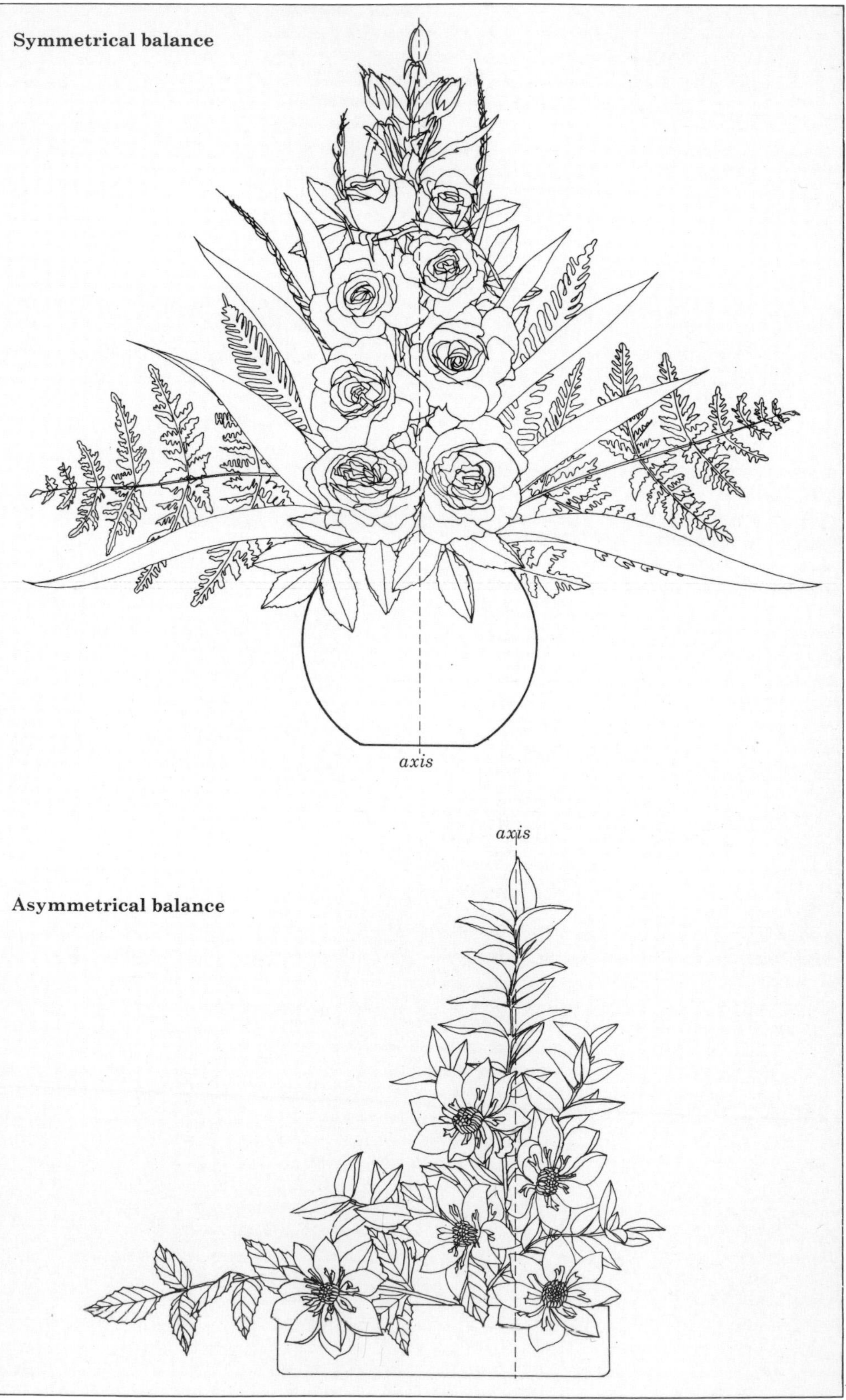

These simple examples show how the addition of a handle changes the visual balance of a container. The drinking glass and the vase have symmetrical balance and the jug and the mug have asymmetrical balance

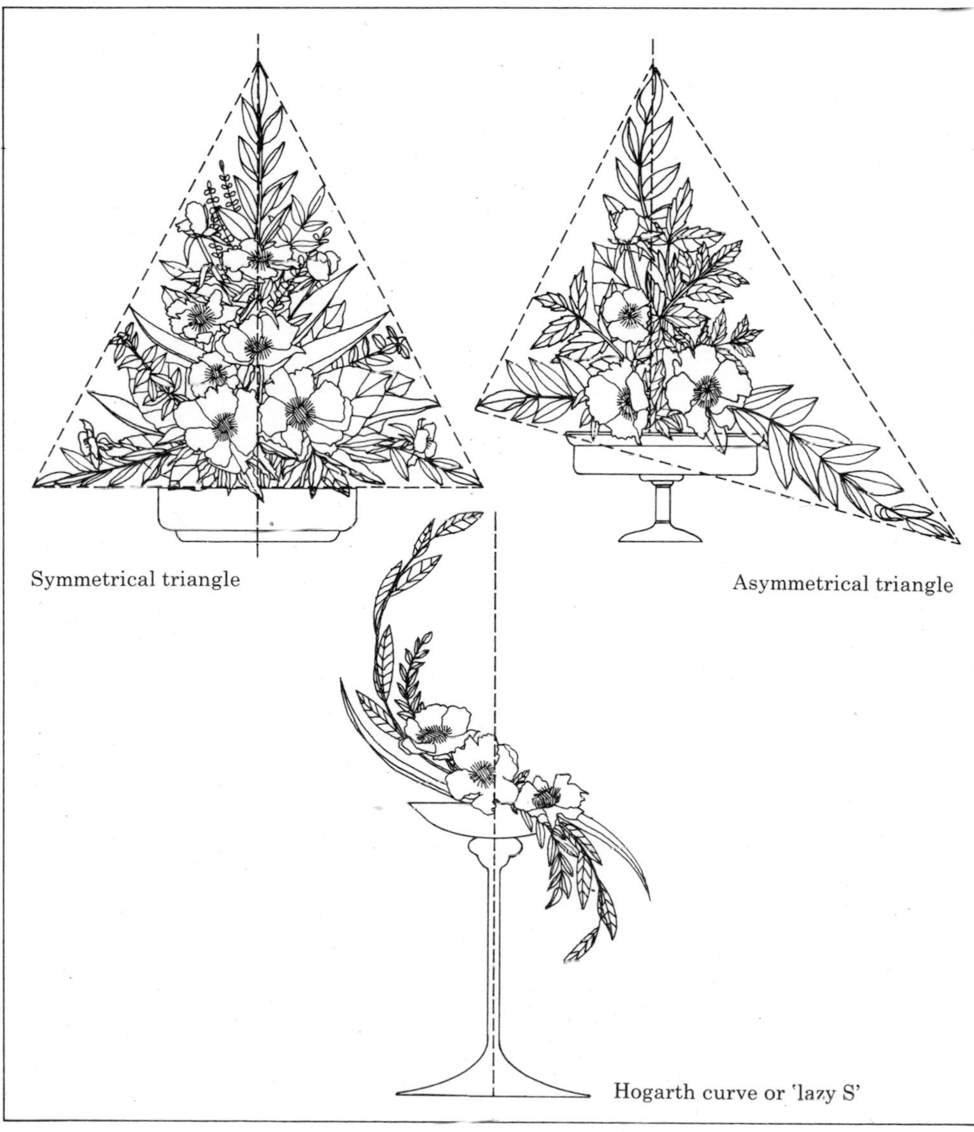

Symmetrical triangle

Asymmetrical triangle

Hogarth curve or 'lazy S'

static, balance. So how can you create such a design, or decide when it is finished whether it has good symmetric or asymmetric balance? It is very simple. You place a real or imaginary line through the axis of the design. The eye should find equal visual balance each side of the line so placed. In a symmetrical design there is 'the state in which two parts, on either side of the dividing line, are equal in size, shape and position'. This does not mean that each flower, leaf and stem has to be identical on each side, but that they will be similar in look and feeling so that they appear more or less the same.. The colours used must also be distributed in such a way that the materials on each side of the imaginary dividing line are consistent in feeling. In a symmetrical design the tip of the main height stem creates (if placed correctly in the centre) the centre tip of the imaginary dividing line running down to the base of the design. In an asymmetrical design the eye should find differing lines and shapes each side of the imaginary dividing line running through the axis of the design. The amount, kind, and colour distribution should visually be in balance on each side of the dividing line.

It will be obvious that more skill and knowledge of design principles are needed for asymmetrical than for symmetrical designs, but with patience and understanding these are not difficult to acquire. Instruction is given in the chapters dealing with both symmetrical and asymmetrical designs how to set about making the correct placements with your plant material.

This chapter has dealt entirely with the four basic principles:
(1) **Design** (form and shape), (2) **Harmony** (mood, colour, setting), (3) **Scale** (size relationship), and (4) **Balance** (stability). They need not be placed in any particular order because they are equally important. It is wise to memorize them, for they will be with you always, in all designs from traditional to abstract. They always apply. A national judge will look for these principles in the most advanced work, and if they are missing from the beginner's arrangements it will be at once apparent. Look for these principles of good design in everything around you, but most of all in your own flower arrangement. The beginner should not attempt to create asymmetrical designs until she has gained confidence through proficiency in symmetrical designs. This should not take her very long, and once she has a good grasp of one technique, her first attempts at the more stimulating asymmetrical arrangements will be made all the more easy.

'The great journey' has truly begun once the four basic principles are known, have been practised and consequently understood at first hand. All the subsequent steps lead to new knowledge and the excitement of discovery.

4. Traditional Design

Flowers seem intended for the solace of ordinary humanity: children love them; tender, contented, ordinary people love them. They are the cottager's treasure; and in the crowded town, mark; as with a little broken fragment of rainbow, the windows of the workers in whose hearts rests the covenant of peace

JOHN RUSKIN 1819–1900

'The Castle Banquet': a competitive exhibit. Cottage and garden flowers are the ones most frequently enjoyed in traditional design. Sometimes, however, special flowers are necessary for the castle setting and the banquet. Here a silver épergne and tray have been set on a rich purple cloth and candles of the same colour have been added. *L. Rubrum*, roses, gladioli and dianthus flowers have been chosen to accord with their rich setting. Fruit – grapes in the épergne and a pineapple at the base – give texture and contrast of shape

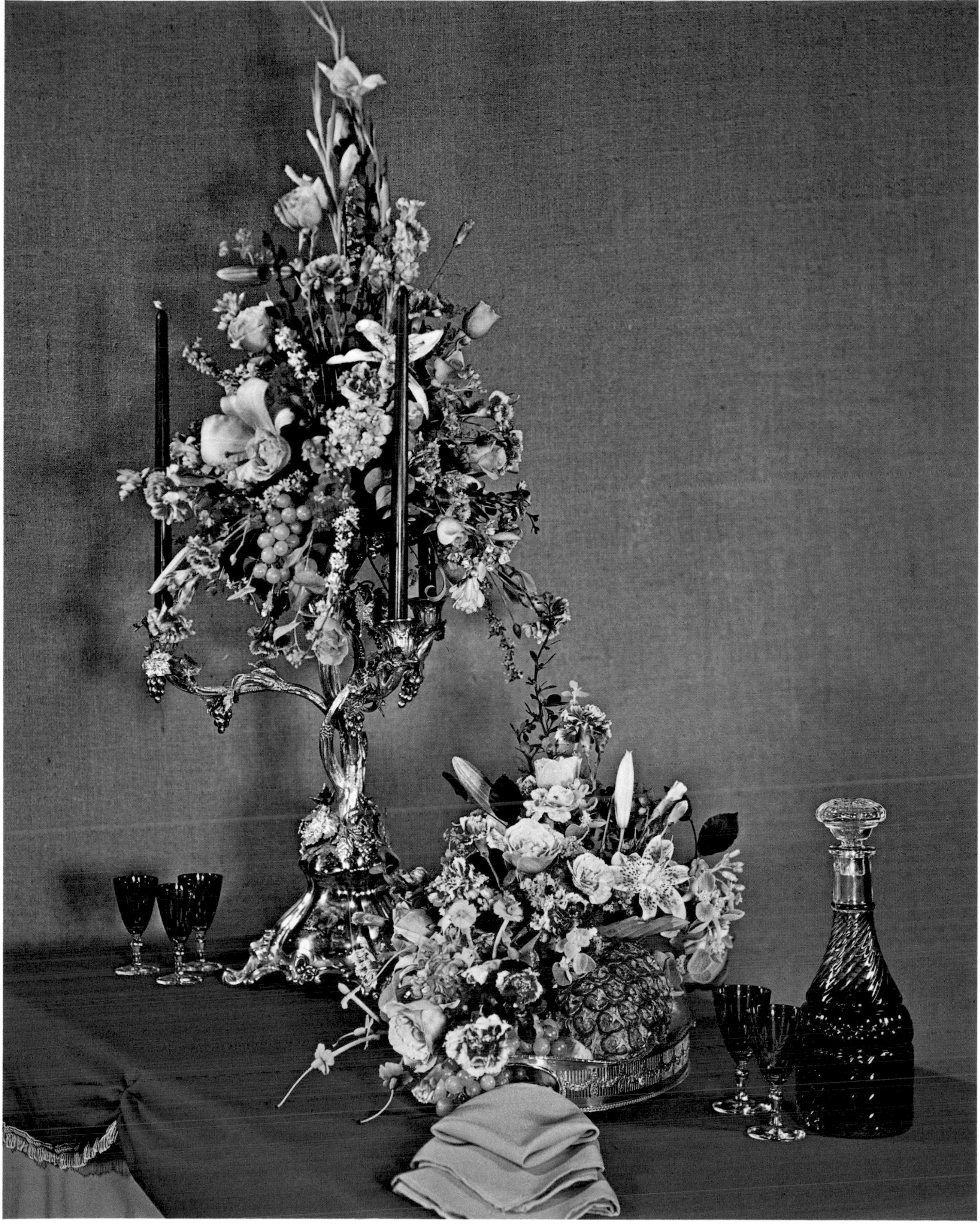

The *NAFAS Schedule Definitions* (1975 edition) describes **traditional design** as 'A style originating in a previous generation based on continuous usage'. **Period** design, on the other hand, 'must be in keeping with the furnishings and décor of a past era'. With **traditional** designs we are only dealing with *a previous generation*, not a *past era*. It is as well to use these two terms, and to know what exactly is required from the design you intend making if the finished work is correctly to fit these descriptions. In exhibition and competitive work it is essential to conform, but even in everyday use, it is good to feel confident that your skills equip you to produce work that is appropriate to any situation. There is a crucial difference between something that is false and that which is accurate, and an appreciation of that difference will ensure that your work looks right. This applies to genuine period furniture or reproduction, or to masterpieces of early paintings, or a copy. However well reproduction furniture or copies of paintings may be constructed or painted, they will lack the distinctive patina of age, and other characteristics. In a period flower design the atmosphere of the period can be recalled only if the flowers and leaves available at that time in history are used, or some that look very much the same. It is also essential that the arrangement is placed against the correct background of the era, and into a container that looks like something that would have been used at the time. All this will be described in Chapter 11.

Traditional designs are those that were used in Edwardian times through to 1945. This style developed in Great Britain and has taken its place amongst the classic designs. It originated in large or medium-sized homes and also from the country cottage. In these backgrounds very large urns, medium-sized containers and quite small vessels held flowers and foliage picked from the garden and arranged with a massed effect, and more or less informally. The outline shape was usually semi-ovoid and the appearance natural, like a bouquet. In the large country houses, some special flowers or foliage in season would be included, because the head gardener would wish his employer to enjoy them. Equally, in the more modest home or cottage, the owner would pick from his garden the flowers in season, and those he treasured most.

As things progressed – and probably because the 'mechanics' were improved – the shapes became much more stylized, ordered and thought-out. Instead of the semi-ovoid outline shape, there emerged the much-used Triangle outline, although the oval semi-ovoid, circle and horizontal, and many variations, are all included in the traditional design. The placings can sometimes be soft, flowing and graceful in outline or very formal and more solid – almost stiff – but all forms and outline

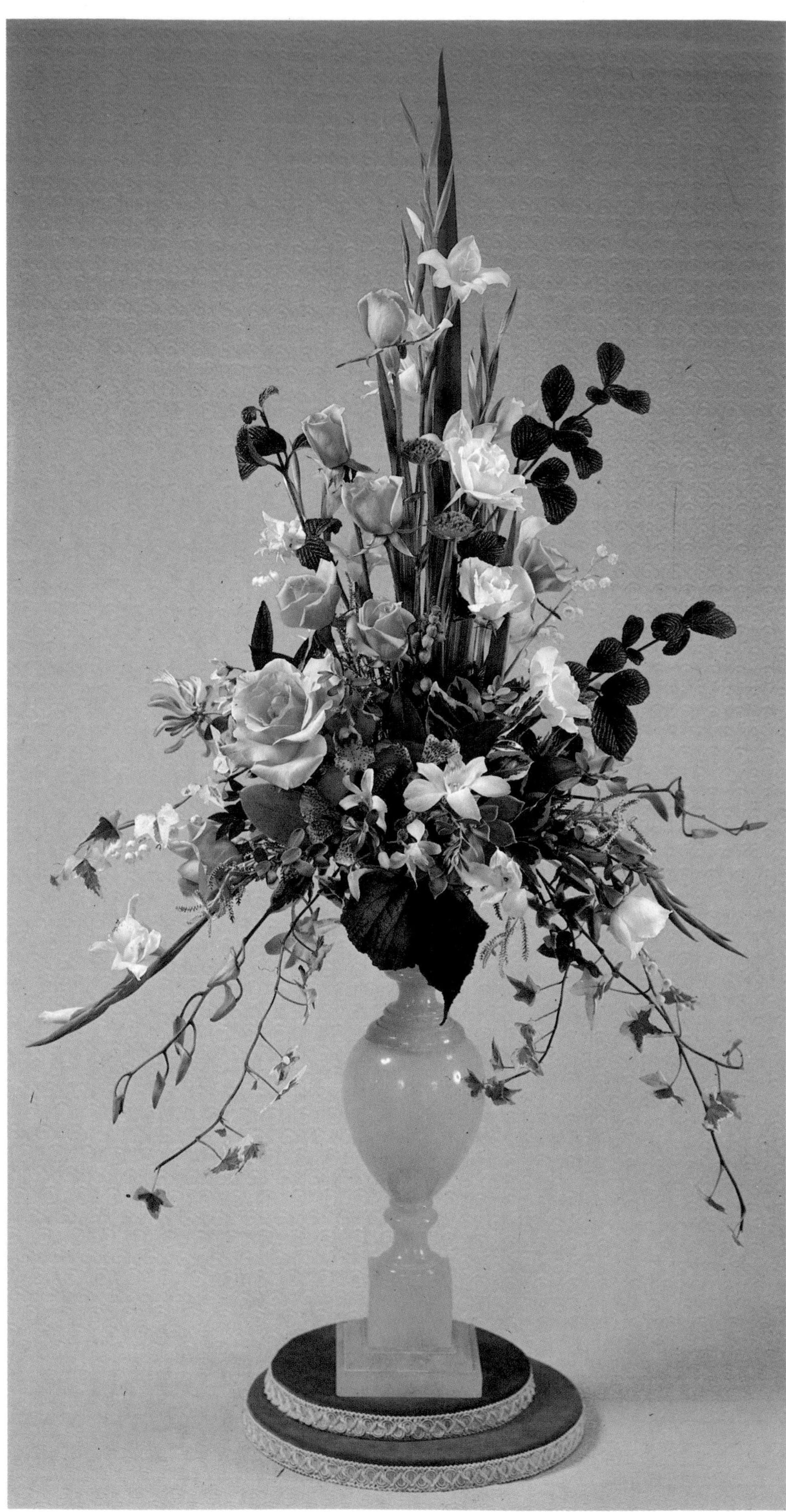

shapes are characterized by a *mass* of plant material, and very little space within the design. The arranger has a free choice of plant material, whether picked from the garden or bought. The flowers in a traditional arrangement are often accompanied by foliage from other plants, which greatly enhances them. Roses and lilies of the valley, however, look best with only their own leaves.

Whatever the appearance of the container, in a traditional design it must hold plenty of water. It is surprising how much water is absorbed by a mass of stems, so the consideration of water depth is important. However, the container must not be 'out of harmony' in choice of texture and type for the flowers used, or the rooms in which they are placed. Nor must it be 'too large, or too small', for the space, if it is to conform to two of the basic principles of design and reach a good standard in the finished work. In the early days the mechanics would be only sand or pebbles, or the stems of the flowers themselves, to make them stand up. Later, there were constructions of wire with tubes in which to place the stems. Then followed a glass dome with holes at regularly spaced intervals which provided support for the stems. These, like the vases with pierced, domed lids or covers, held the flower heads stiffly aloft in stark fashion. Equally unsatisfactory was the method employed by those who, influenced by the Japanese style, constructed bamboo 'wedges' which required a deft hand to put them in place in the smooth neck of a vase. The *style nature* attracted a following, who placed a few flowers casually in a jug or other simple vessel. Stem ginger jars which were imported from China or simple cream jugs of earthenware were fashionable. The painter William Nicholson (1872–1949) painted still life work of this kind.

Flower arrangers owe much in garden knowledge and the arrangement of flowers to Gertrude Jekyll. In one of her books she wrote that galvanized wire-netting should be used 'like scaffoldings, placed in the vase in two tiers, the two tiers being kept in shape by stout wire legs soldered on by any handy village blacksmith'. Despite the disappearance of the blacksmith, wire-netting remains the stand-by of flower arrangers for mass arrangements of flowers although the 'stout legs' are no longer necessary – for the arranger knows how to fold her wire and has acquired the skill of using the cut ends of the wire to help hold and anchor the stems. She knows how to keep the wire firm by threading string or wire through the mesh and round the pot or keeping it in place with adhesive tape. Virtually everlasting, allowing the maximum of water to reach the stems and yet providing a light strong and flexible structure to support them, galvanized wire-netting has not been surpassed or replaced. In addition, a pinholder is now placed at the base of the wire to give extra support.

With this stride forward in basic 'mechanics' the standard of work immediately started to improve and gather better shape. The odd ugly stem sticking out at random became a thing of the past, and the design that now typifies the traditional style is one of ordered and stylized loveliness. Greater awareness of design principles and the practice of better techniques has meant that everyone can, with a little practice, create a thing of beauty with their garden or bought flowers. Rooms have their dull corners revitalized by living flowers, or a picture or *objet d'art* has its colours or shape picked up by a

Left: a facing arrangement in a classic urn-shaped container with velvet-covered bases added for balance. Cream and pink roses, honeysuckle, gladioli and lilies of the valley are arranged with foliage, including variegated ivy, in a symmetrical triangle design. This is the design most favoured for traditional styles. (See p. 48)

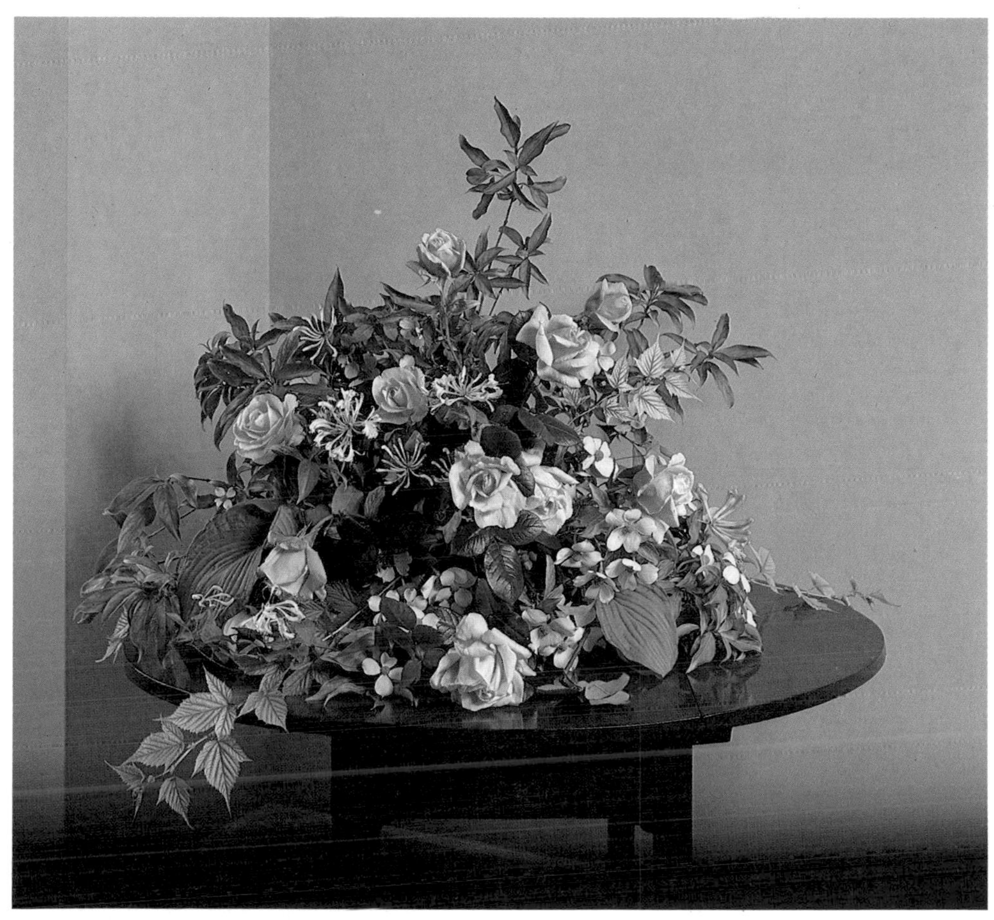

Right: this side-table holds a lovely traditional mass arrangement of apricot-coloured roses, honeysuckle, and *Cornus kousa* with mixed foliage in which *Hosta* leaves and graceful sprays of stephanandra can be seen

Below: an all-round arrangement. Sweet peas are beautiful arranged by themselves so that their fragrance can be enjoyed. The separate colours are grouped for effect. (See p. 48)

design to complement it. Hotels, offices, hospitals and churches see people at work bringing life and colour and loveliness from gardens into the buildings to cheer all those who see them. Arrangers now know that by placing shorter stems to the back of the 'facing arrangement' they create the depth of a third dimension – this prevents a 'flat' presentation and gives the feeling of being able to walk round the design. People do not look at the centre front of an arrangement all the time. They view it from all angles as they move around a room. The arrangement must look good from all sides and there are ways of seeing that this will be the case. It is important to have stem ends of differing lengths so that there is light and shadow in the design and not the monotony of flower faces placed all at the same length all looking at the viewer. The flower face turned in profile gives further interest and a careful placement of fine, medium to dense, and heavy forms at the base of the design creates lines of 'transition' or stepping stones for the eyes of the viewer so that they can happily travel around the whole design, however complex.

Miniature design

The Traditional design comes in all sizes. The smallest is a **miniature**. The *NAFAS Schedule Definitions* tells us this is 'An exhibit not more than 4 ins. overall'. Such arrangements are enchanting in tiny containers such as small snuff-boxes and little shells, even thimbles or the caps of tooth-paste containers used upside down. Minute bases are often added, such as a button or covered coin, and they can bring in a contrast or blending of colour and texture. The miniatures exert the fascination of all small and beautiful articles providing the workmanship is perfect. They can have the quality of a Fabergé creation. *Scale* is all important here: tiny flowers, leaves and stems must be used, not single large flowers taken from a flower cluster that is of large scale. Blades of grass or carnation leaves give height and tiny leaves fill in. Alyssum, scarlet pimpernel, thrift, forget-me-nots and other small scale flowers provide the colour. Much patience and steadiness of hand are needed gently to create the miniature, but the reward is in the exquisite finished work, placed on a shelf or side-table where it can be seen and enjoyed at close quarters.

Petite designs

If a true miniature is too tiny for your tastes, then the next stage is a **petite** which is 'An exhibit more than 4 ins. and less than 9 ins. overall'. This is also lovely and in a small home very useful as well, for it is just right on side-tables, dressing-tables or writing desks. Small boxes and baskets and little decorative bowls and vases make good containers for this design. Of course, these precise measurements only apply to exhibition and competitive work. Any size

Miniature designs
These tiny arrangements must not exceed 4in (10cm) in any dimension for competitive work, but in the home, where exact sizes are not so important the 4in (10cm) rule can be slightly exceeded. Small articles with plant material in scale make excellent decorations for wine- or side-tables
Above: the frame contains thyme flowers and tiny sedums and foliage

Below: in front of the one-inch (2.5cm) plate there is a small crescent composed of mixed flowers, including a tiny rose, daisies, cyclamen and berries
Right: both these designs are arranged in patch-boxes. The boxes hold sprigs of heath and heather with grey foliage. The colours of the plant material pick up the colours of the enamel of the boxes

will do, or any container providing the essential respect for scale and harmony is observed. If you look around you will find that a house has many articles suitable for use as containers such as silver cigarette boxes, now seldom used, or tea-caddies. These would need a lining, easily contrived in these days of plastic containers that can be cut to size. Pansies, anemones and small rose-buds are perfect in such settings though not easy to use in larger containers. If you do not possess such articles, then you can buy simple inexpensive little wicker baskets, with lids or handles, sold with tin linings. The small plastic refrigerator boxes can be utilized and if the foliage is made to flow over the edge sufficiently, the material the container is made of need not show.

'Facing' and 'all round' designs

The average-sized traditional arrangement is often placed in a classic urn-shaped container which looks good in virtually any background of the traditional kind. A footed container makes the design more graceful by adding height. Potters make urns that are not expensive, but if you possess one in finer material you have a great stand-by, for they seem to suit all flowers. There are many versions of a cherub holding aloft a small container, or a dolphin with a shell on its upraised tail. These copies of older designs also look good and of course hold far fewer flowers than the urn. They all are useful in that they take less table space than a conventional bowl or vase.

Almost always the designs in the containers described will be what are called 'facing' or 'frontal'. This will mean that it is constructed so that the main height stem is placed at the back of the container and the design is then worked to the front edge. In an 'all-round' traditional design, however, the main stem is placed in the centre of the container and the plant material radiates round this central placement. In a true period design of a specific era this was the case and the 'bouquet' was composed on all sides. The usual custom was to have tables and some furniture free-standing. Latterly, furniture has tended to be placed against the walls of a room with probably only a low coffee table or the dining table in the room centre. One of the advantages of a 'facing' design is that it takes much less plant material to complete a design. The appearance is also better as the wall usually provides a good colour background. The facing arrangement can be placed close against the wall rather than at a slight distance with the back of the plant material hidden or obscured from view. In this way space on the furniture top is saved – even more so if the container is footed. So it can safely be said that the majority of the present-day traditional designs are likely to be 'facing' rather than 'all-round', for these reasons. This, broadly speaking will

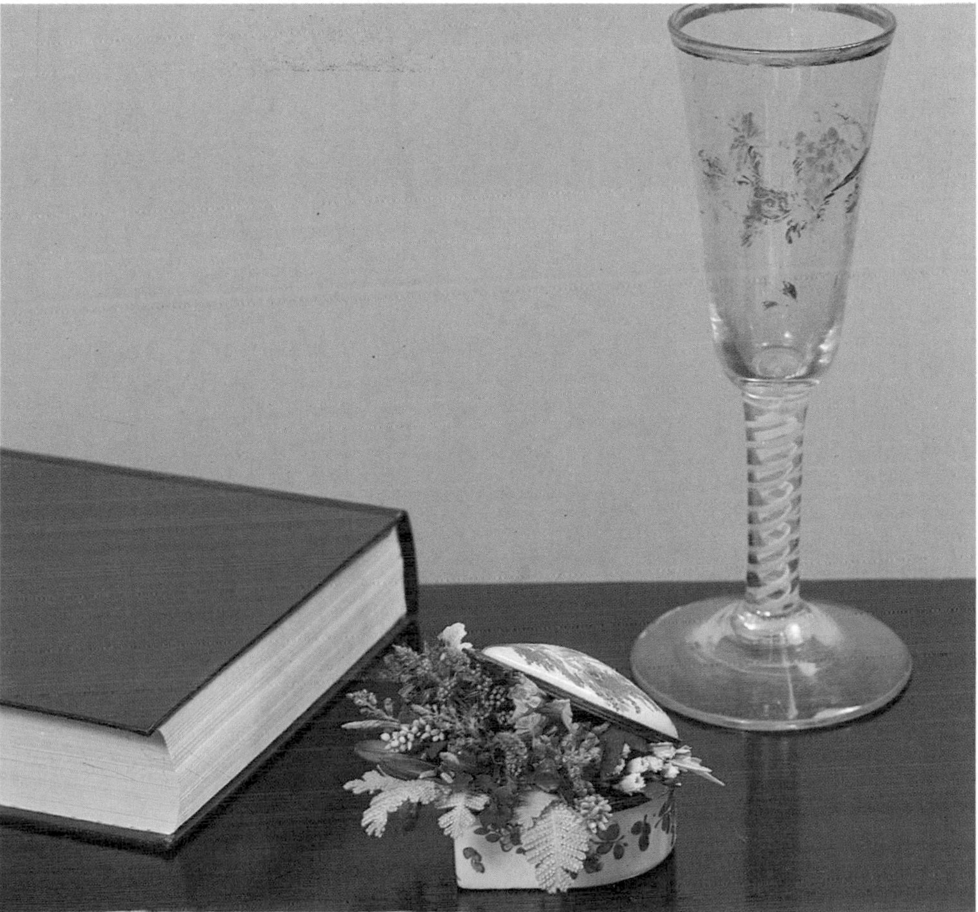

mean that the very important table arrangement (whether it be a dining-table or any other table which is free-standing) will be an exception to the general rule.

Many large buildings such as hotels and the entrance halls of the larger houses do still have a table placed in the centre of the hall or a large room, but it is mostly for a dining-table that a traditional all-round mass design is used. There are so very many possibilities with dining-table arrangements, and so many factors to be taken into consideration, that it will be wiser to go into these in the chapter dealing with flowers about the house (Chapter 7), concentrating here on traditional facing and all-round design.

The important thing is the careful placement of the main stems for height and width. In the facing and all-round design this will mean getting the plant material in proportion to the scale of the container and then placing the main stem to the back of container if facing, and the centre, if it is to be all-round. Then comes the filling in. In the facing design this will mean that these first placements are 'strengthened' by two other stems noticeably shorter and unequal in length to the first placement; then follow the supplementary or filling stems, all placed with care and thought as to their suitability and to the graduation in size of form and shapes. Fine and elegant materials are placed towards the edges of the design, then the medium stems at the mid-way, with the dense and heavy forms at the base of the main stem. It is here that, except in Modern and Abstract designs, the **focal point** (see p. 37) will be found in the shape of the larger or darker flower, the change of colour or texture or form or shape, that you have decided upon. The outline shape will be that of a symmetrical triangle with a serrated edge. This is always aesthetically pleasing when well carried out, for it can never be top heavy and the lower base line gives a sense of security and balance. The height and width of the triangle can be varied according to the needs of the arranger and the occasion. It is of great importance to remember to add the shorter stems and leaves at the sides and back of the design to give a feeling of depth.

The all-round design differs from the triangular mainly in its outline shape, which will be, as the name suggests, a circle or oval. It presents an equally pleasant and visually balanced appearance from every angle. To achieve this equal distribution of shapes, forms and colour it can be a help to place five 'width' stems (if it is a large bowl) radiating from the central main stem placement (or four stems if it is a smaller bowl) to create the correct width. All these will lead to the central stem. These stems should be graceful and curved in feeling to avoid a hard outline. The main stem should be compacted down in height and the width stems increased in length to compensate for this.

Petite designs
For competitive work these designs must be more than 4in (10cm) high but less than 9in (22.5cm)
Right: a petite arrangement of white jasmine flowers and buds contrasted with dark green foliage

There must be more than one focal point at the base of the main stem if the people sitting or looking on all the other sides of the design are to be able to enjoy a centre of interest. Consequently, a focal point should be made at the edge of the design, between each of the four or five width lines.

There must, as always, be some kind of visual balance and interest in the all-round design. If it is decided that (shall we say) a red rose and buds will be the focal points, and you do not have enough for all the centres of interest, then remember to place the red roses and buds in one group on each side of this symmetrical arrangement, and then make different plant material your centres at the other sections. If you have sufficient of the same texture and variety then use them if you wish. It is a formal symmetrical design and your flowers and colours must be grouped, not just dotted about the design.

The Traditional design originated in Great Britain. It fulfils the British love of profuse use of garden flowers and foliage. You will find it in all their homes and churches, and at all their festivals and great stately occasions. This kind of 'bouquet' design could not be written about without paying homage to the name of Constance Spry, loved and revered by everyone who knew and worked with her, or perhaps only read her books and saw pictures of her lovely free use of flowers, foliage and fruit.

Right: pansies arranged in a box with jasmine and viburnum leaves, another petite design. When using valued possessions, make sure they are not spoiled by water: a box like this could be lined with aluminium foil or polythene

Pedestals for autumn and winter
Opposite page left: an autumn pedestal which contains brilliant red carnations, gladioli, *Elaeagnus macrophylla*, *Rosa rubrifolia* foliage, *Sedum maximum* 'Atropurpureum', *Euphorbia myrsinites* and *Euphorbia fulgens*. Such an arrangement evokes a feeling of warmth as winter approaches

Opposite page right: during the winter months even country-dwellers have difficulty in finding sufficient good foliage for a large pedestal design. However, even those without gardens will be able to collect flowers and foliage similar to that used in this pedestal – all the material is either dried or glycerined. The foliage is glycerined beech, eucalyptus and aspidistra, with grasses, *Moluccella laevis* (Bells of Ireland) and hydrangea heads. Combined together, they make a lovely arrangement in soft browns and creams well suited to the alabaster pedestal

Pedestals by Dora Buckingham

An important traditional design that is associated with the Traditional English style is the Pedestal. This is the largest of the traditional designs and requires special skills and understanding of working in a really big scale. It is fitting therefore that Dora Buckingham who actually worked with Constance Spry, and was a personal friend of hers, and who is an accepted master and authority on this specialized Traditional style should write on the subject of pedestal designs in this chapter.

Many arrangers would agree that a pedestal design should be symmetrical or asymmetrical triangle in outline (especially if a pair is being arranged in a church). Hogarth curves and gimmicky shapes do not lend themselves easily to the dignified effect one hopes to achieve. The basis upon which to work is suitability to occasion and background, whether the arrangement is for a special event such as a wedding, christening, one of the Church Festivals, for a competition or exhibition in a flower club, in a hall or just in one's home. There are, however, certain points applicable to all pedestal designs. These are: (1) the choice of container (2) the kind of group (3) the placing (4) the colour scheme and most important, (5) the lighting. Remember that shape, too, is extremely important. The completed arrangement should be clear-cut, simple and unfussy. When flowers, flower branches, foliage and a few flowers stand out in elegant simplicity against a plain background, the result is usually pleasing.

Pedestals are used a great deal in the decoration of churches and large elegant buildings. The placing of the arrangements should be carefully considered. Be restrained in placements: one really good pedestal group or a pair give much more impact than several small arrangements scattered here and there. It is important not to detract from the fine carving in stone or wood that adorns many churches by introducing inappropriate arrangements in the wrong place. The obvious spot for a pair is either side of the chancel steps. A single pedestal might stand by the pulpit or beside the altar, where it can be seen and enjoyed by everyone before and during the service. In the case of a wedding, the guests waiting for the bride and her bridesmaids will get great pleasure from looking at the flowers. Sometimes in a church there is an ugly feature that someone wishes to cover up. It is better, however, to draw the eye away from it by placing a group at a strategic point. In this way an unlovely feature goes unobserved.

Materials

Pedestals may be made of wood, wrought iron, stone or marble. The least appealing of these in my opinion is wrought iron, although the white Vixen Forge pedestal which was used in the Innocents Chapel at Westminster Abbey is exceptional, for it is gracefully formed and looked particularly good with the beautiful stone background. Stone and especially marble are both elegant to use. Wooden pedestals can be used successfully providing they are not too shiny. I have a beautiful Italian carved mahogany pedestal with a cherub, three carved legs and what appear to be acanthus leaves entwined. It really is charming and is only 75 cm (30 in.) high, which is a most useful height. During the Regency period gilt and ebonized wood examples were produced.

Many flower arrangers like to use wrought iron pedestals, challenging though they are as features in a design, and they are widely available. It is a good idea to have a pair of matching pedestals in wrought iron, as they can easily and quickly be repainted matt black or white as the individual design demands.

Stone or marble pedestals are less easy to find these days. The enthusiastic arranger must be constantly on the watch in modern and antique shops as well as auctions and garden centres. There are often good opportunities for buying stone and marble ware in countries like Italy,

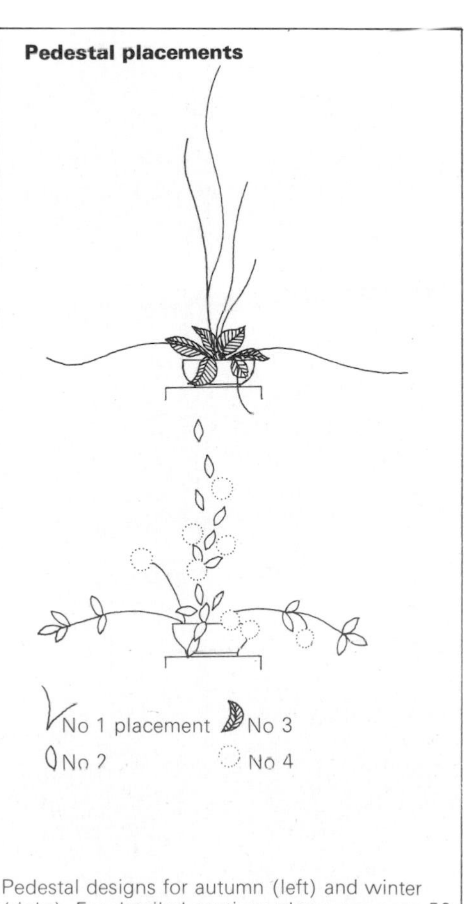

Pedestal designs for autumn (left) and winter (right). For detailed captions please see page 50

Spain and Greece, if you are able to transport it home after your holiday.

Antique carved wooden pedestals are now extremely costly, it is sad to say. Here again it is necessary to explore little antique shops whenever possible. Regency period pedestals can be found, but they are expensive. Sometimes they are sold in pairs, in which case it may be possible to sell one to a friend.

As for the container, use one which will sit on top of the pedestal. A china one 9 cm (3½ in.) deep and 25 cm (10 in.) across has proved invaluable. Small enamel washing-up bowls of similar size with a lip are good. The foliage in the arrangement will hide the bowl and give a much better effect than using an urn-type of holder. Some iron pedestals have their own containers, but these can be restricting and if so you should feel free to replace them.

Mechanics

Time spent on fixing the mechanics is very important and always pays dividends. Wire-netting, pinholders, tubes and water-retaining material (plastic foam) are all involved. Fix two or three blobs of water-resistant adhesive inside the container, and fix a green plastic pinholder to each one. Take a 22.5 cm (9 in.) deep block of plastic foam and cut it into two pieces, one 14 cm (5½ in.) and one 8.5 cm (3½ in.).

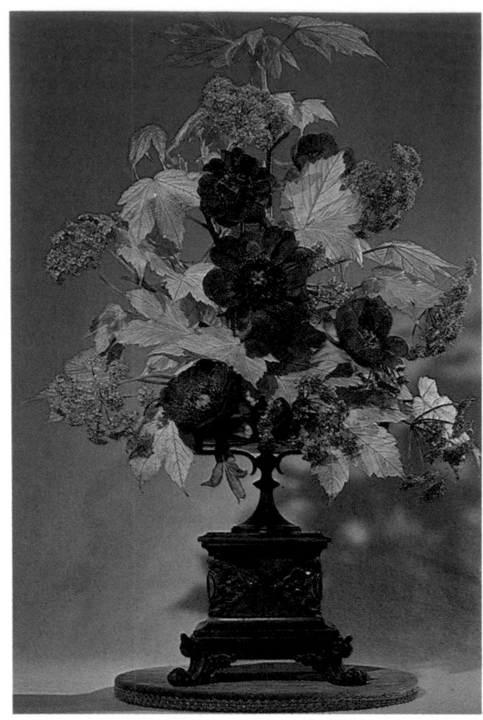

These three examples of the use of urn-shaped containers – in bronze (above), alabaster (below left) and copper (below right) – show that a raised design can be given added grace by a pedestal stem

Place the larger piece at the back of the bowl on to the pinholders, with the smaller piece in front of it. Fix two thicknesses of 5 cm (2 in.) wire mesh over the plastic foam, pushed well down into the bowl, but leaving the wire dome shaped at the top. Leave plenty of space between the plastic foam and the bowl for topping up with water. Tie up the wire and bowl like a parcel, with black or white 6 mm (¼ in.) cotton tape. When all this is finished, one should be able to pick the bowl up and *nothing* should move. This means your plant material will stay where you place it.

To add extra height, tubes or funnels made of metal or plastic and available from florists' suppliers may be used. Now is the time to fix them in. Put them in the plastic foam towards the back of the arrangement. If more than one tube is necessary, you may find it useful to fix them on to a piece of 12.5 mm² (½ sq. in.) wood with adhesive tape. Try not to use more than one tube to get the requisite height. Another useful aid is a small glass tube for a single bloom which has had to be cut off the main cluster of flowers (a lily, for example). Toothbrush tubes, metal cigar holders, glass tubes with a rubber top which has a hole in it can all be used. These single flowers can be placed in the arrangement low down and well-placed foliage will hide them.

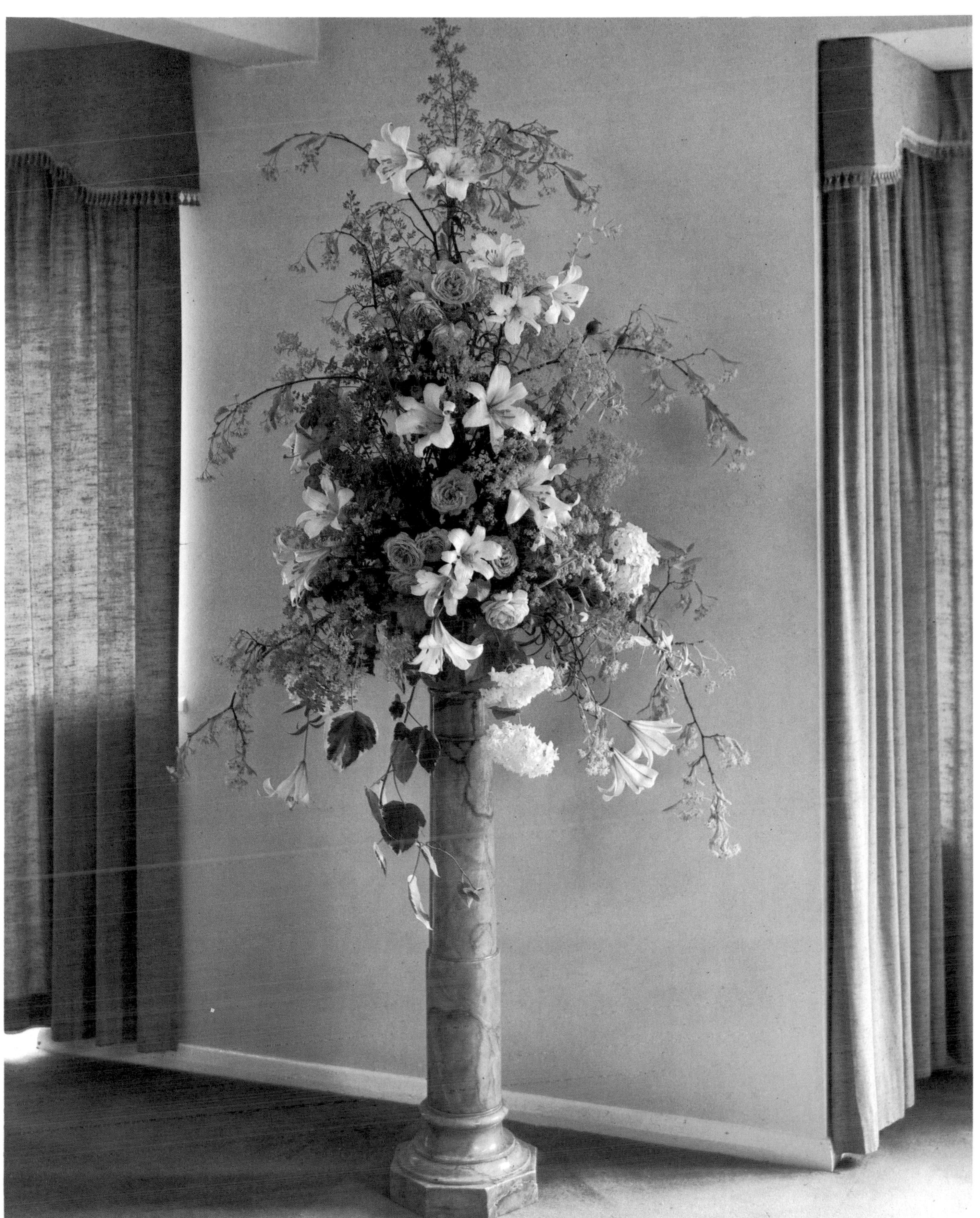

Conditioning of plant material

Pick plant material either in the early morning or when the sun has gone down. Material which flags easily should be placed in a bucket of warm water immediately after picking and then conditioned along with the other foliages and flowers. Although some churches, halls or rooms may be cool, plant material should always be conditioned. The day of arranging may be warm. Transporting by car, necessary handling and maybe the sun shining brightly on to the exact spot where one is going to arrange flowers, all make it imperative to condition. Burn the tips of the stems of all the foliages and flowers for about twenty seconds. Some woody stems require hammering, about 5 cm (2 in.) of the bark removed and the base of the stem cut diagonally. This helps the flowers and foliage to absorb water more quickly. Grey foliage does not last well, especially in plastic foam, but deep water is a help.

Bergenia, Hosta, Arum leaves and all ferns need singeing. If possible plunge them into water all night or for at least eight hours. They can be stored in a polythene bag until it is time to arrange them. Roses, especially florists' roses, need cutting diagonally. Split and singe the stems, and then plunge them under water. It is a good plan to place something over the stems to be sure they are under the water, as they are inclined to float to the surface. After they have had a long drink, pack the flowers in long florists' boxes lined with polythene. Cover the top with polythene and put on the lid. Do not peep inside as this lets the air in.

Suitable plant material

The choice of material is a very personal matter. In flower arranging, however, one must be prepared, as Constance Spry once reminded me, to work with any colour regardless of personal taste. I venture to suggest here some materials that I particularly enjoy working with and which lend themselves to pedestals. First, **foliage**, remembering that the backs of leaves are often as beautiful as the front:

- Beech sprays (fresh and glycerined for winter use)
- *Elaeagnus* × *ebbingei* (gorgeously grey underneath)
- *Elaeagnus pungens* 'Frederickii' (smaller leaves)
- *Stephanandra tanakae* (long, arching rich brown stems)

There are many other suitable foliages, but these four are a good basis.

Foliage to hide mechanics is important:

Bergenia Available all year round, red and yellow in autumn

Hosta Of the very many varieties available, most except the very small leaves may be used in pedestals. They are available from early spring until the frosts come, and they are really beautiful. Perhaps the most useful for pedestals are: *H. sieboldiana* 'Elegans', *H. crispula, H. fortunei* 'Albopicta' and *H.f.* 'Aurea'.

Hedera (Ivy) family. Use three sprays of *H. helix* 'Buttercup', *H. h.* 'Jubilee', *H. h.* 'Silver Queen' or a variety suitable for your colour scheme. Long sprays provide a point of interest at the base of the arrangement.

Ferns too are elegant to use and give another shape. One of the most useful is *Athyrium filix-femina*, a lacy and light fern with fronds up to 60 cm (2 ft.) long.

Of the many **flowers** one can choose from, there is none I enjoy working with as much as lilies. For secondary placements the following is a by no means exhaustive list. As a general rule, try to combine pointed and round material:

- Antirrhinum
- Azalea
- Carnation
- Chrysanthemum (spray)
- *Euphorbia* family
- Gladioli (the butterfly type can replace *Lilium* as the main bloom)
- Hydrangea
- Lilac
- Rose (especially 'Peace')

Quantity of material

The success of an arrangement depends very heavily upon good picking. So many inexperienced arrangers make the mistake of going out into the garden with a pair of secateurs and cutting indiscriminately. For one thing, this is very harmful to your shrubs or flowers. It is most important to pick only what you require to use, and defoliate it. The value of defoliating flowers and foliage cannot be too heavily emphasized. Sometimes I look down at the piece of polythene I have been working on and see up to a hundred discarded leaves. Another point is that your work is lightened a great deal. Study the shapes of leaves and branches *before* picking them. Choose for the central pieces of foliage fairly straight examples on which the foliage growing with a left curve goes to the left side, and the same with the right side. Get the right shapes for sprays of *Hedera*, for example, which may go in on the side front. Pick them so that they will go the same way when arranged, not one pointing to right and another to the left. For foliage to cover the mechanics, pick material the leaves of which are of a suitable size for the flowers. Cut every piece as long as possible.

Main foliage: seven pieces are needed: one for the centre and back of central placement, one in front, two side pieces, one growing to the right and one to the left, and one flowing over the front of the container.

Subsidiary foliage: ten to twelve solid leaves to hide the mechanics.

Flowers: use five to seven pointed flowers and the same number of round flowers, as

Previous page: summer's bounty provides a choice of many flowers and much foliage. In this beautiful pedestal a lacy outline has been created with stripped lime branches. The same fragility is to be seen in the sprays of *Alchemilla mollis* and the plumes of *Macleaya cordata (Bocconia cordata)*. A trail of variegated ivy flows down the stem of the alabaster pedestal and is balanced by the white hydrangea heads placed opposite it. *Lilium regale* provide a rhythmic line of beauty through the centre, where soft pink roses are recessed to give depth

Right: a pedestal of pale pink and cream flowers arranged in the Chapel of the Holy Innocents in Westminster Abbey on the nine-hundredth anniversary of the Abbey. There is a feeling of lightness about the design, which is accentuated by the wrought-iron pedestal. The fresh beauty of spring is suggested not only by the flowers used but also by the design itself. Surprisingly, little foliage is discernible yet each flower is clearly visible. Rhododenron blossom provides solidity at the centre and from there stocks, peonies, sweet peas, carnations and other kinds of blossom flow. There could not be a pedestal design better suited to this position in the Abbey

well as odd bits and pieces of flowering shrubs, or something off-beat in colour for added interest. A typical arrangement might include seven *Alchemilla mollis*, seven *Nicotiana* 'Lime Green' or about five medium-sized pieces of *Helleborus foetidus*. It is more difficult in winter but there are lime green conifers which can help, such as *Cupressus macrocarpa* 'Goldcrest'. These are the main requirements, but depending somewhat on size you may need less or more material. The above suggestions are suitable for a pedestal 105 cm (42 in.) high by approximately the same width. The height of the arrangement commences at the top of the pedestal.

Remember to recess some of the material, and make sure that the sides of the arrangement are correctly finished. Adjust the back of the arrangement so that no mechanics are showing. Spray the arrangement when finished and again daily. A daily top-up with water will help the flowers and foliage to last. Be careful not to damage walls or curtains when adding water.

When you are ready to take off to your destination, you will need all the usual flower arranger's impedimenta, plus a 1.5 × 1.5 m (5 × 5 ft.) piece of thick polythene to work on, one or two pieces of lighter polythene to cover precious furniture, three or four buckets, a watering can and a brush and dustpan. Leave your working space tidy. *Dora Buckingham*

The geometric style (Massed Line)

The lack of variety in the period or traditional mass design, whether oval, all-round or triangle can be rather monotonous. Arrangers felt a need to experiment and create other outline shapes and there evolved the **mass asymmetrical triangle**, not at all an easy design to do really well, and yet bringing more interest to the viewer than the perpetual symmetrical triangle. Instead of the three main lines of the outline shape being of equal visual balance, either one, or perhaps two, of the three main outline stems are of different lengths, care being taken to give equal visual balance on each side of the central axis of the design. The outline of the triangle shape is then filled in with the focal point being placed (as always, except in modern or abstract designs) at the base of the main stem. This variation of the mass symmetrical triangle is satisfyingly different. (See p. 43.)

In the post-war years, a different social climate together with the new awareness of the Oriental use of lines and space within the design led to a wish for change and experiment. It was not a long step from the mass asymmetrical triangle to a **line asymmetrical triangle**. Indeed, this is a direct result of the influence of the classical oriental use of three branches. Perhaps nothing teaches a student used to handling mass plant material how to go about using the minimum of plant material satisfactorily, better than this design. It is essential for a student to learn how to place the three branches correctly. It is an exercise teaching her a discipline that, once mastered, will enable her to make variations in the placement of the three branches, and still achieve good visual balance. The requirements are a flat dish, pinholder and base. The latter is not essential if the container is really long and low, or if a long base only is used with a well-pinholder, or small bowl with a pinholder placed one end of the base. You will need three branches, chosen with great care and an eye for their beauty. Blossom is very desirable, but usually is difficult to acquire except at certain short periods in the year. Happily, any branch with graceful outline and with good and interesting foliage can be used. Those with emerging leaf buds are particularly lovely. However, any branches in full leaf, if suitable in scale and shape provide all you need. Branches with foliage that grows only on the side of the stem (and not all round the stem) make it difficult to convey good visual balance and stability.

Whatever the branch you finally choose, select it with care and remove any insect-bitten leaves, or those that cross other leaves or 'clutter' the stem. A pair of small scissors is good for this removal of unwanted pieces. The branches should, ideally, all come from the same shrub or tree.

Branch 1 must be at least one-and-a-half times, perhaps twice (according to the visual weight of the stem thickness and its foliage), the length of the dish and base, or base, used. It should be tapering and have a slight elegant curve.

Branch 2 should also be curved with a line that follows the same 'flow' as Branch 1. It should be half to three-quarters the length of Branch 1.

Branch 3 should be half to three-quarters of the length of Branch 2. Your pinholder (which should have good strong pins not placed too far apart) must then be put to the right or left of the bowl or base, according to the flow of the 1st and 2nd branches. All stems and branches have a 'flow' to a greater or lesser extent, with very few exceptions, such as a bulrush, or other soldier-stiff material. The latter are good as main stems in symmetrical balance designs, but will not help you in asymmetrical work. One of the useful things to be learned by carrying out this exercise in three branches is the importance of studying the flow of branches and the detail of the foliage growing on them. This flow will come from the growing habit of the tree or shrub, or perhaps the way the light has drawn it, or because of the position in which it was planted.

Place the *base* of Branch 1 on to the pins, having cut the branch end at a slant, so that the pointed end fits firmly between the pins. Then, position the *tip* of Branch 1 so that it is just a few degrees off vertical.

Three branches combined with three arum lilies *(Zantedeschia aethiopica)* are used for this asymmetrical design. Bold flowers such as these need very little accompaniment

Satisfy yourself that the branch looks well from the front of the design. Then place Branch 2. It is *essential* that this branch is placed on the *outside* of the curve of Branch 1. Take care about this; it is surprising how many people place it on the inside of the curve. The tip of Branch 2 should be half-way between vertical and horizontal and have an easy curve away from Branch 1. Now place the final branch. This should have its tip virtually horizontal, but just lifted off the edge of the dish or base. The diagram makes these positions clear. When you are satisfied with your asymmetrical triangle just place the top of your finger on to the tip of Branch 1 and draw an imaginary line from that point to the tip of Branch 2. From there go on to the tip of Branch 3 and then

Placement of branches for the line asymmetrical triangle design

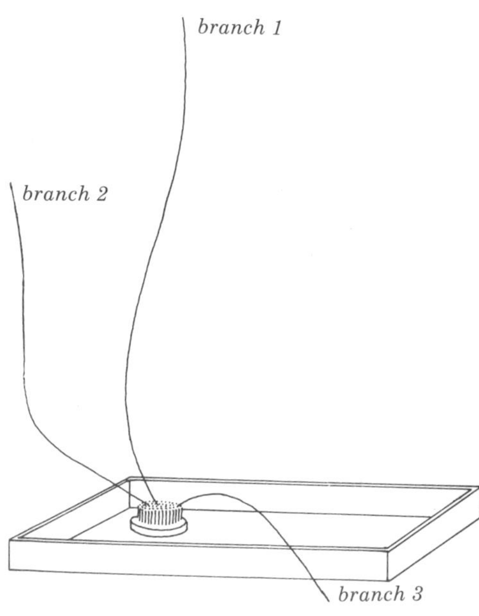

A mass-line 'L' design made by using grey foliage and *Stachys lanata* seedheads combined with yellow 'Water-lily' dahlias in a low black dish. (See p. 58)

A vertical arrangement of tints and tones of pink using *Crinum* x *powelli*, *Cotinus coggygria* and seedheads of atriplex (mountain spinach). (See p. 59)

The horizontal line of the Chinese table is repeated in this flower arrangement which contains mimosa and chrysanthemums. (See p.59)

back with your imaginary line to the tip of Branch 1. You will then be aware of how successfully you have made an asymmetrical line triangle with the three branches. You have not only created a design in space, but also have enclosed space within the branches. Now you have only to place one, two or three flowers, according to your taste and the variety of flowers chosen. Alternatively, another form or shape such as succulents or berries can be used. Now just add the absolute minimum of leaves, perhaps three or four at the base. Guard against stuffing in a multitude of small mixed-up looking leaves, and seek out those that have clear outline and shape.

If you follow the directions with care, you will have acquired a design that will delight you and one that has made you aware of correct visual balance, for your low third branch, and the bottom line of the dish or base, free of the branches and the pinholder, is providing the counterpoise of visual weight to that created by the tall Branch 1. There is no more useful design for an arranger, particularly if she has no garden. The three branches last for many weeks if they have been well-conditioned and chosen for their lasting qualities. In winter or autumn and early spring, three branches of glycerined beech leaves can be used most effectively with up to three chrysanthemums.

When the pinholder is placed either to the right or left hand of the bowl or base (according to the branch' 'flow'), it is essential that the base of the pinholder is firmly stuck with modelling clay or similar substance to the bowl base, and that both are bone dry when this is done. Some firm pressure is required when the branches are placed on the pins and it is fatal if the pinholder skids around on the smooth surface of bowl or base. Some people place an upside down pinholder on the one being used – but they are adding to the mechanics that must be got out of view when the design is concluded. It could be that a very small twist of wire-netting might assist anyone having difficulty at the start to make her stems stay in position, but you can soon learn this and discard the wire-netting. This arrangement looks especially well on low coffee tables but is good in every position.

One final point: all three branches must

Right: an inverted crescent design composed of beautiful spring flowers – narcissi and *Spiraea* – and foliage. (See p. 61)

Below: contrast this mass-horizontal design with the sparse line-horizontal above. Both are equally acceptable. (See p. 59)

emerge from the point on the pinholder where Branch 1 is placed. By observing this rule you create a strong 'source of springing', that is, a sense of vital growth such as we see in nature. The flowers, if used, should be placed with care and with their 'faces' looking up to the stem tip, or out to the viewer, not in dull flat positions. Here is an opportunity to show the interesting side-views – even the back – of a flower head. All flowers have faces, and there is a position in which a flower looks at you, or the ceiling, or to the other side of the room. You can see this best in round-faced flowers such as members of the daisy family. This is yet another way to develop your 'seeing eye' and understand how best to place your plant material.

Now let us consider what are described as **mass line** arrangements. This seems a contradiction in terms. How can there be a design that embraces both line and mass? What is meant by this term is that while the outline shape of the design consists of lines, the amount of material required to construct these designs, quantitively, is a mass. Because space now plays a part as a design element, this amount is considerably less than that used and required in the traditional filled-in outline of oval, triangle and semi-ovoid. Some of the most popular designs are the 'Hogarth Curve' or 'Lazy S', the Crescent, and the Fan (or Inverted Crescent). No doubt this is because the curves employed make them visually exciting and rhythmic. I think it is far wiser for the beginner first to master the mass-line designs that require straight main lines, for they are easier to do and give confidence before moving on to the curving designs. The straight-line designs are the 'L' shape, Vertical, Horizontal and Diagonal, and of course, the many variations on these.

The 'L' Design

The 'L' shape is perhaps the most useful of the outline shapes mentioned because it can be of help to an arranger when making landscape designs or one featuring water. Use a base with a container placed at one end, or a low dish or bowl with the pinholder placed to the left or right, so that this distinctly asymmetrical shape can be best viewed. Obviously the lower part of the 'L' will best be seen from above, but more important is the feeling of stability given if the 'L' is ground-based and not 'perched'. After ensuring that the mechanics are firm, look for plant material that is reasonably slim and straight with flowers that are not too full, but rather of the stemmed variety. Gladioli, narcissus and long stemmed flowers are particularly useful. Do not cut their stems down to next to nothing. Do not lay these naturally tall growing flowers in a horizontal position. It looks awkward because it is contrary to their nature. Large heavy foliage is not needed because it will thicken the design; any larger leaves should be used only at the base.

The main stem should be one-and-a-half to two times the length of the base of the container. Place it at the back of the pinholder. This will ensure you have the rest of the pinholder on which to work. Virtually all 'L' designs are planned on the left side because it appears to accord better with the shape, but occasionally it is worked from right to left of the base or container. The latter may suit a landscape or be needed as one half of a pair of 'L' designs for use on a mantelshelf. After the main stem has had two more stems of unequal length placed to its back and front to provide depth and a highlight, continue down with foliaged stems. All the stems should emerge from the place where the first main stem is placed on the pins. The lower stem should measure half to three-quarters the length of the tall main stem. Because it is placed low and is lying down in the horizontal position it appears to be heavier, so to counteract this you make the stem shorter – how much shorter this will be is decided by the kind of plant material you are using. If it makes a fairly strong visual impact, then make it half the length of the main stem, but if it is delicate in feeling then you can make it three-quarters. Your sense of visual balance will tell you when it is correct. When these two stems are successfully strengthened, add flowers and colour (if you are using them) remembering that they too have visual weight, and place them in the bud, half-opened and bloom sequence. The focal point (as always except in modern and abstract designs) is found at the base of the main stem.

This really is a simple design but very satisfying and effective if done well. Beginners tend to make the elbow of the 'L'

A simple Christmas arrangement in traditional triangle shape: holly leaves and berries and *Helleborus niger* (Christmas roses) with a white candle and red ribbon

An arrangement of roses, carnations, blossom and foliage complemented by two figurines. A lovely grouping for an antique table

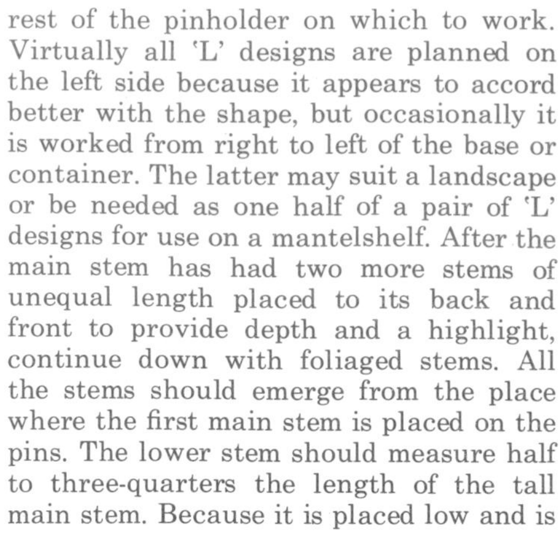

Right: 'The Queen's Piper'. A pedestal class often has an interpretative title. Here the red of the roses, gladioli and carnations is complemented by the tartan accessories

A mass-line 'L' design made by using grey foliage and *Stachys lanata* seedheads combined with yellow 'Water-lily' dahlias in a low black dish. (See p. 58)

A vertical arrangement of tints and tones of pink using *Crinum x powelli, Cotinus coggygria* and seedheads of atriplex (mountain spinach). (See p. 59)

The horizontal line of the Chinese table is repeated in this flower arrangement which contains mimosa and chrysanthemums. (See p.59)

back with your imaginary line to the tip of Branch 1. You will then be aware of how successfully you have made an asymmetrical line triangle with the three branches. You have not only created a design in space, but also have enclosed space within the branches. Now you have only to place one, two or three flowers, according to your taste and the variety of flowers chosen. Alternatively, another form or shape such as succulents or berries can be used. Now just add the absolute minimum of leaves, perhaps three or four at the base. Guard against stuffing in a multitude of small mixed-up looking leaves, and seek out those that have clear outline and shape.

If you follow the directions with care, you will have acquired a design that will delight you and one that has made you aware of correct visual balance, for your low third branch, and the bottom line of the dish or base, free of the branches and the pinholder, is providing the counterpoise of visual weight to that created by the tall Branch 1. There is no more useful design for an arranger, particularly if she has no garden. The three branches last for many weeks if they have been well-conditioned and chosen for their lasting qualities. In winter or autumn and early spring, three branches of glycerined beech leaves can be used most effectively with up to three chrysanthemums.

When the pinholder is placed either to the right or left hand of the bowl or base (according to the branch' 'flow'), it is essential that the base of the pinholder is firmly stuck with modelling clay or similar substance to the bowl base, and that both are bone dry when this is done. Some firm pressure is required when the branches are placed on the pins and it is fatal if the pinholder skids around on the smooth surface of bowl or base. Some people place an upside down pinholder on the one being used – but they are adding to the mechanics that must be got out of view when the design is concluded. It could be that a very small twist of wire-netting might assist anyone having difficulty at the start to make her stems stay in position, but you can soon learn this and discard the wire-netting. This arrangement looks especially well on low coffee tables but is good in every position.

One final point: all three branches must

Right: an inverted crescent design composed of beautiful spring flowers – narcissi and *Spiraea* and foliage. (See p. 61)

Below: contrast this mass-horizontal design with the sparse line-horizontal above. Both are equally acceptable. (See p. 59)

emerge from the point on the pinholder where Branch 1 is placed. By observing this rule you create a strong 'source of springing', that is, a sense of vital growth such as we see in nature. The flowers, if used, should be placed with care and with their 'faces' looking up to the stem tip, or out to the viewer, not in dull flat positions. Here is an opportunity to show the interesting side-views – even the back – of a flower head. All flowers have faces, and there is a position in which a flower looks at you, or the ceiling, or to the other side of the room. You can see this best in round-faced flowers such as members of the daisy family. This is yet another way to develop your 'seeing eye' and understand how best to place your plant material.

Now let us consider what are described as **mass line** arrangements. This seems a contradiction in terms. How can there be a design that embraces both line and mass? What is meant by this term is that while the outline shape of the design consists of lines, the amount of material required to construct these designs, quantitively, is a mass. Because space now plays a part as a design element, this amount is considerably less than that used and required in the traditional filled-in outline of oval, triangle and semi-ovoid. Some of the most popular designs are the 'Hogarth Curve' or 'Lazy S', the Crescent, and the Fan (or Inverted Crescent). No doubt this is because the curves employed make them visually exciting and rhythmic. I think it is far wiser for the beginner first to master the mass-line designs that require straight main lines, for they are easier to do and give confidence before moving on to the curving designs. The straight-line designs are the 'L' shape, Vertical, Horizontal and Diagonal, and of course, the many variations on these.

The 'L' Design

The 'L' shape is perhaps the most useful of the outline shapes mentioned because it can be of help to an arranger when making landscape designs or one featuring water. Use a base with a container placed at one end, or a low dish or bowl with the pinholder placed to the left or right, so that this distinctly asymmetrical shape can be best viewed. Obviously the lower part of the 'L' will best be seen from above, but more important is the feeling of stability given if the 'L' is ground-based and not 'perched'. After ensuring that the mechanics are firm, look for plant material that is reasonably slim and straight with flowers that are not too full, but rather of the stemmed variety. Gladioli, narcissus and long stemmed flowers are particularly useful. Do not cut their stems down to next to nothing. Do not lay these naturally tall growing flowers in a horizontal position. It looks awkward because it is contrary to their nature. Large heavy foliage is not needed because it will thicken the design; any larger leaves should be used only at the base.

The main stem should be one-and-a-half to two times the length of the base of the container. Place it at the back of the pinholder. This will ensure you have the rest of the pinholder on which to work. Virtually all 'L' designs are planned on the left side because it appears to accord better with the shape, but occasionally it is worked from right to left of the base or container. The latter may suit a landscape or be needed as one half of a pair of 'L' designs for use on a mantelshelf. After the main stem has had two more stems of unequal length placed to its back and front to provide depth and a highlight, continue down with foliaged stems. All the stems should emerge from the place where the first main stem is placed on the pins. The lower stem should measure half to three-quarters the length of the tall main stem. Because it is placed low and is lying down in the horizontal position it appears to be heavier, so to counteract this you make the stem shorter – how much shorter this will be is decided by the kind of plant material you are using. If it makes a fairly strong visual impact, then make it half the length of the main stem, but if it is delicate in feeling then you can make it three-quarters. Your sense of visual balance will tell you when it is correct. When these two stems are successfully strengthened, add flowers and colour (if you are using them) remembering that they too have visual weight, and place them in the bud, half-opened and bloom sequence. The focal point (as always except in modern and abstract designs) is found at the base of the main stem.

This really is a simple design but very satisfying and effective if done well. Beginners tend to make the elbow of the 'L'

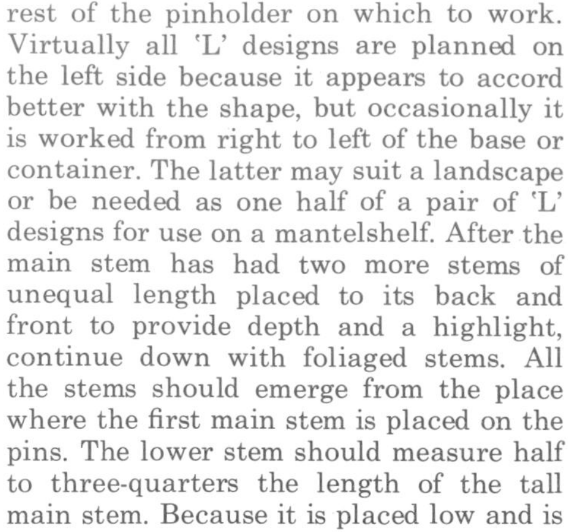

A simple Christmas arrangement in traditional triangle shape: holly leaves and berries and *Helleborus niger* (Christmas roses) with a white candle and red ribbon

An arrangement of roses, carnations, blossom and foliage complemented by two figurines. A lovely grouping for an antique table

Right: 'The Queen's Piper'. A pedestal class often has an interpretative title. Here the red of the roses, gladioli and carnations is complemented by the tartan accessories

A mass-line 'L' design made by using grey foliage and *Stachys lanata* seedheads combined with yellow 'Water-lily' dahlias in a low black dish. (See p. 58)

A vertical arrangement of tints and tones of pink using *Crinum* x *powelli*, *Cotinus coggygria* and seedheads of atriplex (mountain spinach). (See p. 59)

The horizontal line of the Chinese table is repeated in this flower arrangement which contains mimosa and chrysanthemums. (See p.59)

back with your imaginary line to the tip of Branch 1. You will then be aware of how successfully you have made an asymmetrical line triangle with the three branches. You have not only created a design in space, but also have enclosed space within the branches. Now you have only to place one, two or three flowers, according to your taste and the variety of flowers chosen. Alternatively, another form or shape such as succulents or berries can be used. Now just add the absolute minimum of leaves, perhaps three or four at the base. Guard against stuffing in a multitude of small mixed-up looking leaves, and seek out those that have clear outline and shape.

If you follow the directions with care, you will have acquired a design that will delight you and one that has made you aware of correct visual balance, for your low third branch, and the bottom line of the dish or base, free of the branches and the pinholder, is providing the counterpoise of visual weight to that created by the tall Branch 1. There is no more useful design for an arranger, particularly if she has no garden. The three branches last for many weeks if they have been well-conditioned and chosen for their lasting qualities. In winter or autumn and early spring, three branches of glycerined beech leaves can be used most effectively with up to three chrysanthemums.

When the pinholder is placed either to the right or left hand of the bowl or base (according to the branch' 'flow'), it is essential that the base of the pinholder is firmly stuck with modelling clay or similar substance to the bowl base, and that both are bone dry when this is done. Some firm pressure is required when the branches are placed on the pins and it is fatal if the pinholder skids around on the smooth surface of bowl or base. Some people place an upside down pinholder on the one being used – but they are adding to the mechanics that must be got out of view when the design is concluded. It could be that a very small twist of wire-netting might assist anyone having difficulty at the start to make her stems stay in position, but you can soon learn this and discard the wire-netting. This arrangement looks especially well on low coffee tables but is good in every position.

One final point: all three branches must

Right: an inverted crescent design composed of beautiful spring flowers – narcissi and *Spiraea* – and foliage. (See p. 61)

Below: contrast this mass-horizontal design with the sparse line-horizontal above. Both are equally acceptable. (See p. 59)

emerge from the point on the pinholder where Branch 1 is placed. By observing this rule you create a strong 'source of springing', that is, a sense of vital growth such as we see in nature. The flowers, if used, should be placed with care and with their 'faces' looking up to the stem tip, or out to the viewer, not in dull flat positions. Here is an opportunity to show the interesting side-views – even the back – of a flower head. All flowers have faces, and there is a position in which a flower looks at you, or the ceiling, or to the other side of the room. You can see this best in round-faced flowers such as members of the daisy family. This is yet another way to develop your 'seeing eye' and understand how best to place your plant material.

Now let us consider what are described as **mass line** arrangements. This seems a contradiction in terms. How can there be a design that embraces both line and mass? What is meant by this term is that while the outline shape of the design consists of lines, the amount of material required to construct these designs, quantitively, is a mass. Because space now plays a part as a design element, this amount is considerably less than that used and required in the traditional filled-in outline of oval, triangle and semi-ovoid. Some of the most popular designs are the 'Hogarth Curve' or 'Lazy S', the Crescent, and the Fan (or Inverted Crescent). No doubt this is because the curves employed make them visually exciting and rhythmic. I think it is far wiser for the beginner first to master the mass-line designs that require straight main lines, for they are easier to do and give confidence before moving on to the curving designs. The straight-line designs are the 'L' shape, Vertical, Horizontal and Diagonal, and of course, the many variations on these.

The 'L' Design

The 'L' shape is perhaps the most useful of the outline shapes mentioned because it can be of help to an arranger when making landscape designs or one featuring water. Use a base with a container placed at one end, or a low dish or bowl with the pinholder placed to the left or right, so that this distinctly asymmetrical shape can be best viewed. Obviously the lower part of the 'L' will best be seen from above, but more important is the feeling of stability given if the 'L' is ground-based and not 'perched'. After ensuring that the mechanics are firm, look for plant material that is reasonably slim and straight with flowers that are not too full, but rather of the stemmed variety. Gladioli, narcissus and long stemmed flowers are particularly useful. Do not cut their stems down to next to nothing. Do not lay these naturally tall growing flowers in a horizontal position. It looks awkward because it is contrary to their nature. Large heavy foliage is not needed because it will thicken the design; any larger leaves should be used only at the base.

The main stem should be one-and-a-half to two times the length of the base of the container. Place it at the back of the pinholder. This will ensure you have the rest of the pinholder on which to work. Virtually all 'L' designs are planned on the left side because it appears to accord better with the shape, but occasionally it is worked from right to left of the base or container. The latter may suit a landscape or be needed as one half of a pair of 'L' designs for use on a mantelshelf. After the main stem has had two more stems of unequal length placed to its back and front to provide depth and a highlight, continue down with foliaged stems. All the stems should emerge from the place where the first main stem is placed on the pins. The lower stem should measure half to three-quarters the length of the tall main stem. Because it is placed low and is lying down in the horizontal position it appears to be heavier, so to counteract this you make the stem shorter – how much shorter this will be is decided by the kind of plant material you are using. If it makes a fairly strong visual impact, then make it half the length of the main stem, but if it is delicate in feeling then you can make it three-quarters. Your sense of visual balance will tell you when it is correct. When these two stems are successfully strengthened, add flowers and colour (if you are using them) remembering that they too have visual weight, and place them in the bud, half-opened and bloom sequence. The focal point (as always except in modern and abstract designs) is found at the base of the main stem.

This really is a simple design but very satisfying and effective if done well. Beginners tend to make the elbow of the 'L'

A simple Christmas arrangement in traditional triangle shape: holly leaves and berries and *Helleborus niger* (Christmas roses) with a white candle and red ribbon

An arrangement of roses, carnations, blossom and foliage complemented by two figurines. A lovely grouping for an antique table

Right: 'The Queen's Piper'. A pedestal class often has an interpretative title. Here the red of the roses, gladioli and carnations is complemented by the tartan accessories

rather abrupt, so take care to add foliage at this point to create a softer feeling. The straight lines of the main and lower line need to be slim but not too rigid at the sides. The edges should be serrated and not just an uncompromising straight up-and-down. Even though this is a 'facing' design, see that the back of your work is attractive and that all mechanics are concealed from the viewer.

Vertical

A useful design, the vertical takes little ground space compared to most other arrangements. For this reason it is often used at shows where space for staging is limited. In the home it looks very well on small tables against walls, or free-standing. A true vertical will be like a sword blade in shape. Since it is very long and tall, and not wider than the container that holds it, the choice of container is important. Pillar-shaped vases, and those that have greater height than width, are essential if the overall finished work is to have the necessary unity between the container and the plant material. Foliage such as iris, yucca, phormium or *Sansevieria trifasciata* provide the blade-type leaves appropriate to this torch shape. (See p. 35.)

In a competitive show this design must conform to the true vertical, but in the home this can look too severe and tailored and a looser design, though still with good transition of shapes and forms, is more suitable. These are usually called 'upright' designs, and they lend themselves very well to tall slim oriental vases or to church vases. It is wise to half or three-quarter fill such containers with sand or pebbles, so that you do not have to reach down to the base. This device makes it easier to gain the necessary height with your plant material. In the early stages of constructing a true vertical it can help to use a fine wire to link the main stems together once at the base and again about a third of the way up the stems. Do not bind them too tightly, but firmly enough to give a secure foundation to the foliage and flowers that will be added to the stems. In a slim tall stylized design, stability is essential. In the vertical design the main stem should reach the maximum for artistic acceptance. (See diagram on p. 35.)

Horizontal designs

This is the shape most used in table arrangements. An oblong container or base is a basic requirement. There will be two main stems, which will create the low long lines required to give the necessary length to the design. The centre stem, in this symmetrical design, will be lowered from the usual height to what is right visually, both to balance the long low stems and also (if on a dining-table) to the height suitable for the diners to look across the table and converse. After stabilizing these height and width stems, see that there is a soft flowing line reaching

Above: a limited number of well chosen leaves and flowers can have an advantage over the traditional mass design, which uses a large number of expensive flowers. Here the wooden table, rough pottery container and orange curtain are a perfect foil in colour and texture to the simple green arrangement. Six *Hosta* leaves, four fern leaves and their fronds and a few iris leaves with green *Helleborus foetidus* flowers in the centre make a very pleasing and inexpensive arrangement

Right: a Hogarth curve arrangement of *Crocosmia x crocosmiiflora (Montbretia crocosmiiflora)*, dahlias and *Cotinus coggygria* foliage in an ornate silver candlestick

out at each end of the arrangement. (See p. 35.) This is a lovely design if well done but can be ruined by stiff angular 'arms' at the extremities of the design.

The other straight massed-line designs all follow the patterns described in their construction. The arranger can suit her guide lines to her requirements. These geometric outlines can be true 'line' – requiring the minimum of material, like the Asymmetrical Triangle described – or 'mass-line' which calls for a rather greater quantity of plant material to create the effect required while retaining a clear geometric shape.

The crescent

The crescent is foremost among the more stimulating curved geometric mass-line designs. When finished, it should have the clean-cut lines of new moon sickle. It is essential to keep the scooped-out centre between the two pointed tips at each end. The crescent may be asymmetrical or symmetrical in balance, the difference lying in the height and length of the stems and the position of the focal point. In an asymmetrical example, the high curve will be decided by the usual measurement of the container. The lower curve will be half to three-quarters the length of the higher curve in the asymmetrical crescent. As the focal point is always found at the base of the main stem (except in modern and abstract) the focal point will be a little off-centre in the asymmetrical design. Because of the use of less plant material in mass-line arrangements than in traditional designs the focal point area takes on greater importance. It should not reach higher within the centre of the design than one-third the height of the main stem. Most crescent designs are spoilt by the precious half circle being filled in too heavily in the focal point area, so that the flow of the curve is lost. Be restrained.

Crescents can be inverted – when they then take on the outline at the top of an opened fan. Because of the sweep of the lower curve a footed or raised container is required. This design looks very well in a candle-cup container on a candlestick. The curved stems are an essential, so forget all straight stemmed branches and flowers and do not try and contort them into curves if they have not grown that way. Broom will allow itself to be flexed into curves between the fingers or to be coaxed into perfect curves if it is tied into flowing lines and left immersed for some hours. This is an exception, however, and it is far better to find natural curves in growing plant material. Rosemary will sometimes have curved stems and it is just a case of searching them out in other shrubs and plants. This exercise trains your 'seeing eye'. Very little plant material is needed for the Crescent, the Hogarth or 'S' design. Stems on shrubs often curve best when they are growing at the base of the plant.

The Hogarth curve

This design is named after the eighteenth-century English painter William Hogarth, who called flowing curves 'The Line of Beauty'. His paintings had this asymmetrical flow through their composition. This shape is often called the 'S' design or the 'S' lying on its back – because of the asymmetrical visual balance. (See p. 43.)

Again, a raised container will be necessary, to allow for the flow of the lower curve. It can flow from right to left of the design or vice-versa. This will be decided for you by the flow of your stems. When placing your main height stem see that the tip does not cross the imaginary vertical line passing through the axis of the design. Your curve can lie back as far as you wish, but you will get a livelier effect if it is reasonably upright at the tip. Then position the lower curve keeping it in feeling with the top curve. The effect should be that the lower and top curve are created from one rhythmic line with no join at the centre. Of course this cannot in reality be so, but if you take pains to see that the stem ends do meet on the pinholder and that the stem tips are positioned correctly, you will achieve this feeling. The lower curve should flow towards the viewer. All flower arrangers are keen to achieve excellence in this design when they have reached the stage of having more confidence, knowledge of design, and of handling their material.

In spite of the loveliness of the traditional mass bouquet style there was a wish to break away and experiment that resulted in the establishment of the geometric styles. Arrangers used them with more enthusiasm in the early days than they do now that the break with 'mass' has been achieved. This experimentation led to further creative thought and work. Arrangers felt free to work on other new ideas: designs that emphasized texture by using metals or fabrics within the design, interpretation of ideas and moods, and countless other subjects using figurines, or incorporating objects. Once the concept of lines rather than the filled-in mass had been absorbed, and it was understood that space could be brought in to play a part in the creation of a design, the now experienced arranger was ready to study another style – Free-Form and Modern. The chapter which is devoted to this exciting form of arrangement has been written by an international expert and specialist in this work, Marion Aaronson.

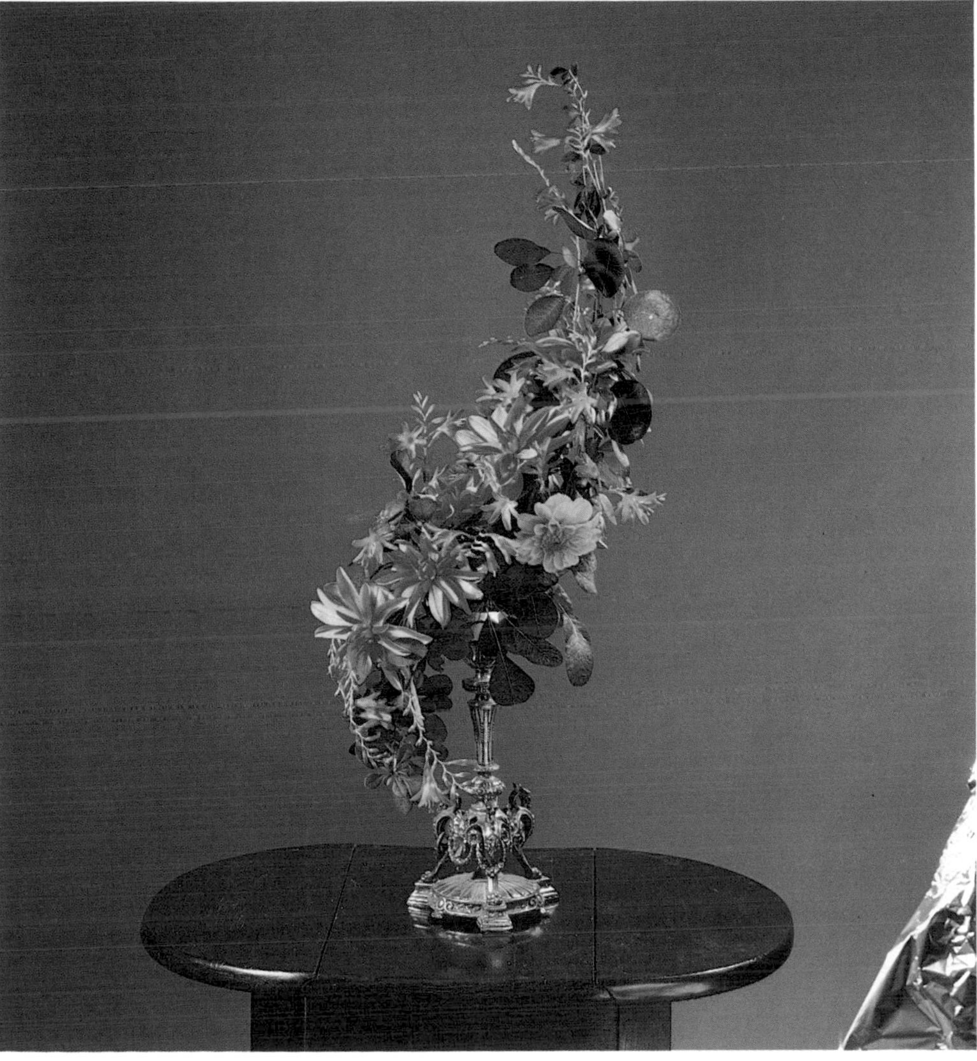

5. Categories of Design

I believe a blade of grass is no less than the journey-work of the stars . . . and the running blackberry would adorn the parlors of heaven.

WALT WHITMAN 1819–1892

Hans Christian Andersen, the Danish fairy-tale writer, delighted in making small posies for his friends. The posy illustrated is a copy of one made by him. The unusual white paper frill of charming little cut-out figures adds his individual touch

As your interest in making flower and foliage designs grows, you will begin to feel the need to experiment and to extend your skills by creating new designs. Do not think in terms of 'trying to be different' or be drawn into the realms of gimmickry, for nothing degrades the art of flower arranging more rapidly than the loss of good design sense, sensitive artistry, and restraint. On the other hand it would be very dull to be content with endless repetition of the same outline shapes, in the same containers in the same places.

Still life

An arranger who feels she would like to branch out a little, might start by exploring the many possibilities offered by combining plant material with other forms and shapes to give more interesting results. She will accentuate as design features the lines or colours of the other objects being used. There is nothing specially new about this kind of design or way of thinking; everyone is familiar with the 'still life' paintings of the Dutch masters. Supreme in their painting of petal sheen and texture, they also delighted in incorporating other forms and shapes and colours that were non-plant material. The finished design was always pleasing to the eye as it travelled through the various components, perhaps to see new beauty in different forms and shapes contrasting and at the same time complementing the finished composition. This kind of work, still life, is much used in art instruction and helps the student become aware of outlines, textures, proportion and colours and how to go about putting them together pleasingly.

You will seldom require many flowers –

Associated Groupings (p. 66). The decorative lid and the fruits at the base of the urn are associated with the flowers

for if a quantity were used, then it would become a 'flower piece' and not a true still life. Find an attractive object such as a pewter plate, or mug, a bottle encased in basketry or an old slip-ware jug. Lovely textures and shapes can be found in modern pottery, and some kitchen equipment. With all these articles you can select what will suit your needs and then start thinking about the plant materials that will be in harmony with them. Edible plants and herbs have a natural affinity with such things, and new design opportunities will be discovered when you set a purple aubergine (egg plant) with the soft grey of pewter. The bland feeling of these two textures might be offset by the addition of a savoy cabbage with its rough-textured purplish leaves that carry the same tinges of colour. Contrast of colour will be provided by the addition of a lemon and a variegated leaf of some kind. One or two magenta shrub roses could be added or some purple honesty flowers put in the pewter mug. The variations are endless, and each one is a personal discovery and a pleasure.

An important aspect of these designs is that the various components must be linked visually. It is no good putting them down like a row of soldiers. The eye must be led from the highest point of the design through all the different elements to the focal point. This linking can be achieved in several ways. It can be by choosing a base of wood, stone or fabric composition upon which all the items are placed to help the feeling of unity. This is not sufficient by itself, and the actual components, either by their grouping together, or placement, must lead the eye through the overall design. This is where vines of all kinds are so wonderfully useful, and, of course, why they play such a prominent part in the old Dutch paintings. They not only draw a thin, tenuous, but graceful line lightly clothed with leaves, leading the viewer's eyes from one feature to another, but their beautiful curves and tendrils provide great rhythm and movement. The vine family is a very large one and easy to come by, apart from the obvious grape vine. Ivy, honeysuckle, old man's-beard (wild clematis) and many other climbers offer similar design opportunities. Condition them by immersing in water overnight or for some hours with the cut ends in water or water-retaining material when arranged. This, of course, applies to any cut flowers used. It is quite easy to conceal a small pot or phial amongst the fruit or vegetable shapes or behind any non-plant objects used. A small fragment of marble, perhaps with a shell, and a grouping of leaves, fruit and a flower or two, could be a refreshing (and economical) design for a dinner table.

The kind of still life described here is rather robust in feeling but you are free to use more sophisticated and elegant objects such as a long, slim, coloured glass bottle or a Dresden figurine. The essential is to keep all the components in harmony, choosing plant material, colours, base and other features so that the finished work is not only a delight to look at but also to study. Do not clutter up the work; every item used must be there because it plays an essential part. Still life classes are often written into show schedules, and are much enjoyed by the show visitors.

In this Still Life, the arranger has brought together fruits and flowers against a background evocative of the style of the Old Masters

Still Life in the Flemish Manner

Still life offers countless possibilities for the grouping of varied plant materials with allied objects. The setting will dictate the style from a simple homespun composition to the elaborate and carefully constructed period piece. The major factors to consider are that all items are relevant to the whole and co-ordinated as to theme and interpretation, most especially when assembled in an antique setting.

Colour, form and texture are the basic ingredients of all design and the juxtapositioning of each object should lead to an overall harmony. My example was prompted by splendid tapestries in a stone vaulted room at Hovingham Hall, Yorkshire, a house in the Palladian style. The furnishings of the Tapestry Hall predate the room by a century, the dominant feature being a massive oak refectory table. This forms the basis of the still life arrangement in the seventeeth century manner evocative of the Flemish and Dutch Schools of painting; the tapestries, with their borders of fruits and flowers in the Gobelin style, are themselves suggestive of a still life arrangement.

The plant material is arranged in a large copper fish kettle held in place by crumpled wire-netting mesh over a large pinholder. A massive plant of *Onopordum arabicum*, a silver-grey thistle, forms the background together with sprays of *Cedrus atlantica* 'Glauca' in young leaf. Blue grey *Hosta sciboldiana* 'Elegans', berries of *Mahonia japonica* and clipped palmetto palms echo the elusive blue grey of the hangings. Crimson flowers add a note of richness and include carnations, amaryllis and *alstroemeria* to match the cranberry-red fragrant candles. These are set on ornate ormolu candlesticks from York Minster. A vibrant note of orange is lent by 'Enchantment' lilies, 'Belinda' roses and pincushion *Leucospernum proteus*. Cream orchids and alabaster-coloured iris pick up the parchment music and stone vaulted roof colour.

Fruits grouped on a copper platter convey opulence. They include half a water melon, bottle gourds, cherries, oranges and dyed okra pods. A cleaned and reassembled lobster adds colour and a touch of the bizarre, so beloved of still-life painters. The elongated cone-like fruits are seed vessels of the giant Brazilian water plant *Gunnera manicata*.

Movement and textural interest are maintained throughout from the elegant pink water grass to the embroidered ecclesiastical stole of coral silk and gold. A soft drape of red silk and the ribbon on the lute echo the hanging lantern glass. Thus the eye is led gently back and forth within the strong horizontal and vertical lines of the table and candlesticks, which in turn create a frame containing the elements without constriction.

Few of us have access to such a splendid setting or to so many precious and original items. Yet no matter what the effect, quality in all elements will always pay dividends. Try to avoid overworking the grouping and allow each object to be seen. The individual architectural quality of the plant material must be allowed space to be identifiable. Depth is also important. The lute on the bench, the table and tapestry are all additions to creating a strong three-dimensional effect. The exaggerated height of the grasses repeats the roof vault whilst the hanging lantern appears much larger because of its proximity to our eye.

George Smith

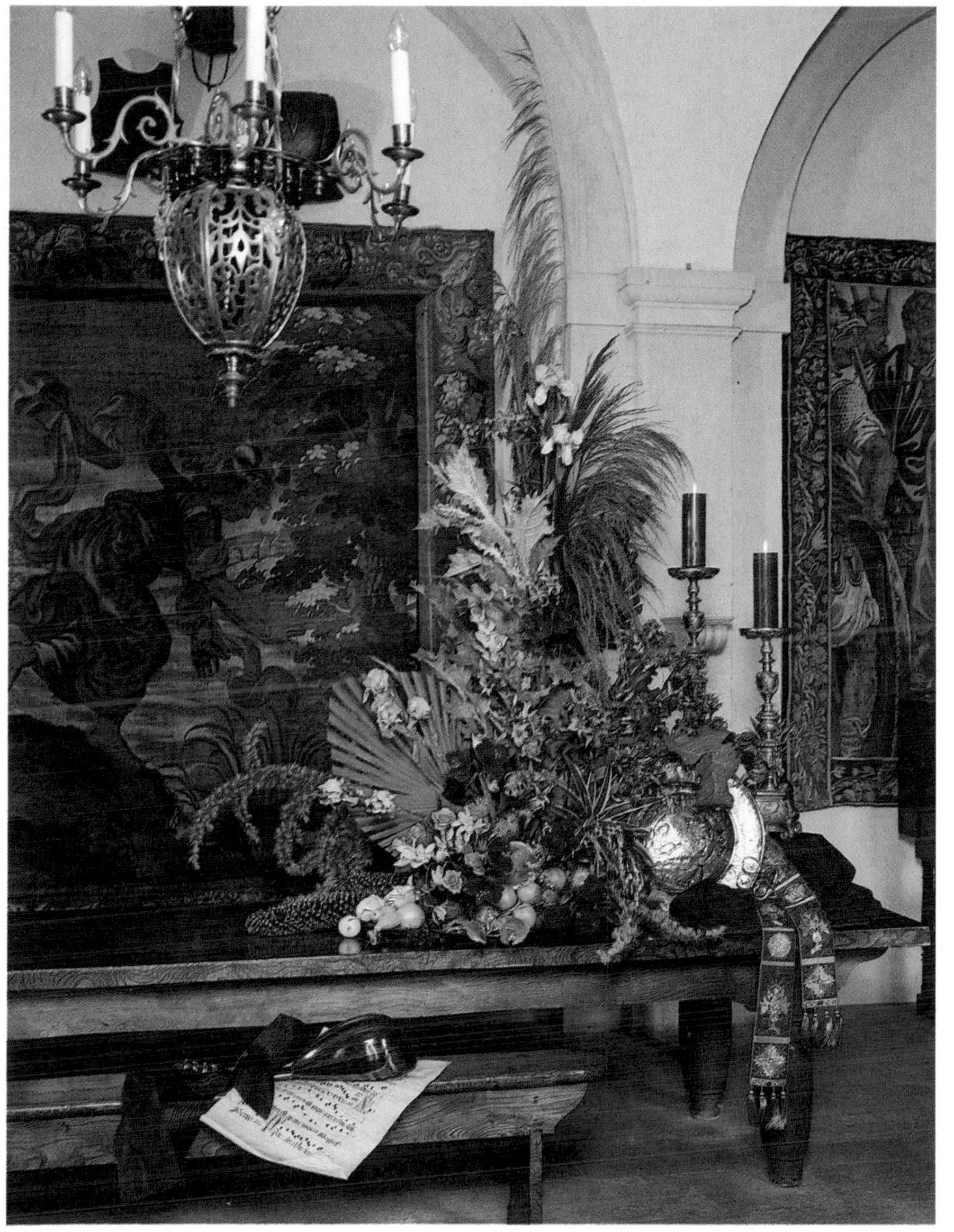

This still life arrangement in the Tapestry Hall at Hovingham Hall, Yorkshire is described above

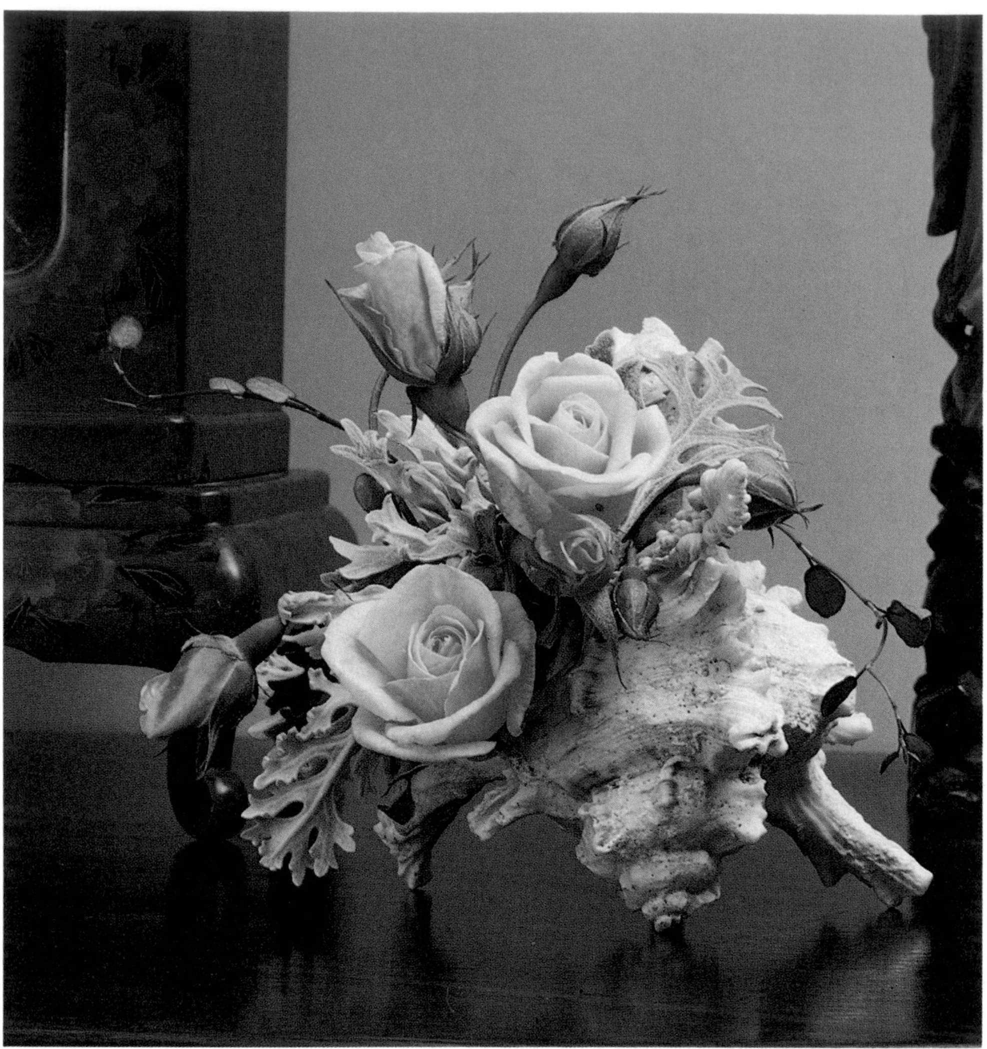

have great possibilities if the mechanics are sound. Ready-made plate stands are available, but can be home-made from wire bent into shape. Such lovely possessions as fans that lie unseen in a drawer, can be brought out from obscurity and used half-open, their colouring picked up or contrasted and their lovely crescent shape emphasized by the repetition of the curve in the flower design. A small driftwood clamp will hold the fan, or the base of the fan could stand on a blob of modelling clay.

Basing a design on a picture

Many homes have a print or painting that is a focal point in a room. A plant material design placed on the surface of a table or other piece of furniture below it has great possibilities. Clearly, the *kind* of painting will be the arranger's starting point and from there the variety is infinite. Your design should go along with the style of the painting, whether it is period, traditional, free form or abstract.

A sea shell positioned so that its tip and two other points act as support for a simple arrangement of roses and grey foliage. The rough texture of the shell is echoed in the serrated edges of the leaves

Below left: white and cream flowers are used to harmonize with the uniform facings in the portrait

Far right: an associated grouping as a show exhibit; class, 'Cries of London', interpretation, 'Buy my sweet flowers'. Here a figurine and miniature basket are incorporated with the flower design and placed against an impressionistic painted background of London

Associated groupings

Another much favoured design that is requested by show schedules – but also can be very decorative in a home – is an arrangement 'in association with' a named object, such as a fan or picture – or it may just say an 'objet d'art'. Whichever it is, and whether it is for enjoyment in your home or for competitive work, the same principles apply.

Staging in such designs is all important; that is, the presentation of your foliage or flower arrangement and your selected objects as a complete, pleasing and easily-perceived whole. Great care must be taken to see that the chosen object really is 'in association with' the plant material. It is no use at all just putting down the chosen object and putting the flower arrangement next to it. Each must complement the other but also clearly link with the other in the viewer's eyes and thoughts. Much can be done by raising the height of a figurine or object and letting the plant material flow from the base of the figurine to the bottom of the design – or vice versa, the flowers raised and the figurine or object at the base. Alternatively, the object can be placed actually *within* the plant material. This is often done very effectively in modern designs with an interesting piece of metal or some other similar non-plant material to which is added spare but strongly formed stems and leaves. As these objects will be free-standing, you can work *behind* them if needed, or flow from the left or right side. Fine or interesting plates

Colour is the second important factor, both in overall colour choice, and colour used for accent. The scale of the picture and the room must also be thought about. Very often in a stately home a large painting is well complemented by a pedestal design beside it, or even two designs flanking it on either side. In show work, space is usually very limited, so the picture will probably be small. If this is so, then keep your design in scale; otherwise, just interpret the feeling and atmosphere of the picture subject.

Using baskets

Probably because they are made of plant material, baskets have a natural affinity with all kinds and varieties of flowers, berries and leaves. Useful all the year round, they come into their own in spring

Small pink shrub roses in a Victorian porcelain basket. A tiny wicker basket arrangement may also be seen in the large illustration (right)

and autumn. Spring flowers – mostly bulbs and blossom – are not easy to arrange well with their stiff stems and uncompromising shapes, but they look wonderful with foliage in baskets.

Baskets come in all kinds and shapes. There are some with handles or without, with or without lids, simple baskets or sophisticated ones – the variety is endless. What must be remembered when you plan your design is to study the type and form of the basket and as it is definitely part of your finished overall design you must work accordingly. This will mean that whether the basket has a handle that is placed *across* the basket or from *end to end* you must design accordingly. Is it a high or low handle? It is best to think in terms of the handle forming the 'main stem' of your design. If it is high then you will have a semi-ovoid outline, but if the handle is low then your outline shape will be horizontal. Baskets must be symmetrical in shape in order to be useful, so the focal point should be placed centrally each side of the handle and flowing over the edge of the basket. All the stems should flow gracefully from the central placement. The top of the handle should be left reasonably free of plant material so that if necessary, the basket can be lifted to be carried, but not so much so that the handle stands bereft and aloof from the rest of the design. Children's baskets are very attractive filled with small flowers of spring – primroses, forget-me-nots and, of course, pansies.

Baskets with lids have to be thought of in a different way. (Incidentally, small boxes or tea caddies with lids are similarly arranged.) This will be a 'facing' or frontal design as opposed to the 'all-round' design of the handled basket. Whether large or small, handled or lidded, baskets can be arranged asymmetrically or symmetrically, 'facing' or 'all-round' but with the lid then inevitably it must be 'facing'. First raise the lid and then place a small stem in the basket, centre front and sloping back to the lid which it will support open, at the angle you wish it to be when the design is finished. The lid should be about three-quarters open. If it is too low, the flowers will look crushed and as though they are struggling to get out; too high, and the lid no longer looks a part of the design. Then open the lid fully so that you can arrange the flowers without difficulty, pausing from time to time to lower the lid down on to the supporting stem to see that it is taking shape as you wish.

For an asymmetrical design, place a fine foliage stem to right or left (whichever you prefer) for height, and a shorter lower stem on the opposite side to the main one. The focal point will be at the base of the main stem, which will be slightly off-centre. The basket with no lid or handle is, in effect, a bowl container and will be arranged accordingly.

All baskets will need linings of course, even if a plastic foam brick is used, for the latter will have to be kept moistened. Autumn leaves and sprays of berries and chrysanthemums are particularly suited to arrangement in baskets, but all the year through baskets and flowers are a pleasure to look at and to arrange. In a class in competitive work calling for 'baskets' a basket must be made of natural plant material. For ordinary use there are many charming small- and medium-sized baskets made from porcelain and glass to be found. They are usually Victorian for the basket shape was much admired at that period.

Shells

Shells are beautiful natural objects of delightful shapes and forms. Like baskets, they are functional objects. The shell will have housed a sea-animal. It is as well to bear this in mind from the beginning and to turn your shell into the 'walking' position, for there is a small drainage channel from which the water for your

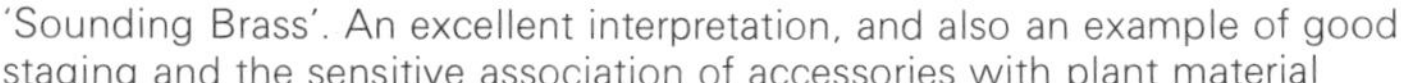

'Sounding Brass'. An excellent interpretation, and also an example of good staging and the sensitive association of accessories with plant material

A 'nocturnal' arrangement of very muted colours, mainly blues and deep purples, which includes a figurine of Hebe

flowers may syphon if you are not aware of it. Fill it up, if necessary, with plaster that will harden. Few shells stand well without some kind of support when they are upturned so that their cavity can be used for flowers. A blob of modelling clay under them as you hold them in the position you want them to stand will usually suffice. If you want a more permanent fix you can use a small base of hardboard and put on it a covering of plaster of paris or similar material. Raise the shell on this at the centre and then use small shells or pebbles to decorate the base. If done with care this can look very attractive. Plastic foam is the best mechanic for shell arrangements because the shell aperture is small and usually slanting so there are problems of space and water spillage.

Because of the natural slant a *diagonal* line is good for the flower design. Few flowers are needed; two varieties that look especially good are sweet peas and nasturtiums. A few flowers in a shell are a lovely decoration. Some shells, in particular the variety that have a beautiful mother-of-pearl lining and are 'open' in shape like a low bowl, look exquisite with a few baby cyclamen or violets or other delicately hued small flowers in a tiny container placed in their centre so that the lovely pearl surface can be seen to advantage.

Glass

As it is a man-made substance, glass poses difficulties of texture when placed with plant material. It may be transparent or opaque, coloured or cut. Its reflecting quality may distract from the flower design but in spite of these pitfalls glass has a very special attraction.

A glass lamp is used for this interpretation in an 'Alfresco Luncheon' class

To avoid showing a confusion of crossing stem ends in clear glass, wind a fern leaf around the edge inside the vessel – the natural leaf conceals everything. Wine decanters will make quite good containers if they are filled with water which is coloured with a little red ink or other colouring and a 'candle cup' container placed in their necks and made firm with modelling clay. These 'candle cup' containers are easily obtainable and are meant for use with candlesticks. Coloured glass is usually sufficiently opaque for stems not to show and if plastic foam is used for mechanics this is not very obtrusive. Modern glass is often made in strong primary colours. If so, grey foliage usually looks better than green. Repetition of the glass colour in the flowers used is effective but if the modern glass is of the smokey grey or black variety good dramatic effect may be achieved with a piece of fine black driftwood or a branch and a few scarlet or gold flowers or something similar. Consider the texture of the plant material, ensuring that the glint and reflective qualities of the glass do not predominate. Shining and reflecting leaves could be used, with a contrasting accent of matt texture. Each glass container will have individual qualities that must be taken into consideration by the user. Wine glasses and goblets make excellent holders for side-tables and writing desks. See that their sparkling quality is maintained. Should there be a water mark as a result of using them for flowers, then treat the glass with some of the powder sold for cleaning dentures.

Landscape designs

The *NAFAS Schedule Definition* describes landscape designs as exhibits portraying a natural scene. They are much enjoyed because they bring the outdoors into the home – or the exhibition. A scene in nature could be in woodland or garden, on a moor, or by stream, river or the sea. All are beautiful and evocative of things we have seen and remembered. The choice for the arranger is wide and the success of her work will be dependent on the accuracy of her 'inner eye' recording in her mind scenes in their natural setting. Wood, slate, stone and lead bases help to set the picture, but low flat bowls or containers may be used. The whole scene will be impressionistic and the minimum of plant material used to convey the atmosphere. A carefully chosen branch or piece of driftwood will emulate a tree, and smaller material at its base will represent the bushes or smaller trees growing round it. Ferns and leaves that are found in the wild can then be added, unless it is a garden scene, when cultivated plant material is used. Rushes, grasses or thrift and coastal plants would be appropriate for seascapes. It is quite certain no cultivated flowers would be found in such settings, and such leaves and stems that live by or in the sea grow in ways characteristic of their environment. If a lush green waterside scene is attempted, then the water in the container should play a decorative role. Seaside plant material is sparse by comparison and often contorted by gales and salt winds. It is wise to remember in seascapes that seaweed is plant material but that sea fern, sea fan and coral are animal.

Above: a fine glass flask in pink and emerald centres and focuses a design of pink roses
Right: a Landscape design in which teazels and ferns are combined with driftwood
Below: Landscape. Foxgloves, ferns, ivy and an alder branch are placed naturalistically in a low lead container, with a second placement for balance. The whole is surrounded by mossy stones

The moors have granite boulders or tors with windswept stunted trees, heather and gorse; some rushes, lichen branches, small ferns, mosses and rushes are found near the streams. In order to achieve a realistic effect, you must be familiar with the landscape you are trying to represent: you will have walked in the wild places and seen for yourself what plant forms thrive there and in what combinations. Almost always an asymmetrical design is best, with a high placement either to the right or left.

A garden scene will, of course, make a feature of cultivated flowers and leaves. The 'landscape' garden designs using early spring flowers – often growing on their roots – (with the earth washed away and then placed in water to be replanted later) are very charming. Moss placed between the small fresh flowers, ferns and leaves and a blossom bough, or one in new spring leaf, are a special joy to gladden the eye after the dreary winter months. Very large meat dishes or a small tray can be used for this kind of work, which looks specially good on a dark oak chest or something similar. Driftwood is very useful in many of the landscape designs and makes a good strong starting point. Tree-shaped pieces are used for giving height, and primroses and ferns nestle happily in an old gnarled tree root.

Colour arrangements
These can be very stimulating if there is an occasion where a certain colour is required to convey a message. Golden weddings are rightly celebrated with special parties. Gold-coloured flowers will be enhanced by gold foliage such as golden privet. The same would, of course, be true of red arrangements. With blue colours, then use grey or glaucous foliage. Green is cool in feeling, and will therefore reduce the impact of pure colour – lovely as it is, used as a foil with all colours. A blend of one colour going through all the tints and shades is always beautiful. Remember the container should be of the same colour chosen, or neutral (that is, grey, black or white). More colour can be brought in by the choice of base which can be painted or covered in fabric.

One-colour arrangements are exciting but never have the charm of mixed, or blended colours. There are, however, occasions when they are asked for at certain celebrations and club dinners. In competitive work they are the most difficult to design – and to judge! *All* components must then conform to the stated colour, or else be neutral. This strict rule does not apply to stems and stamens but it *does* to foliage. It makes life a little easier – though not much – if the schedule allows artificially coloured or painted plant material.

Above left: interesting use of shapes, texture and opposing, vibrant colours

Above right: muted colours in a historically-evocative interpretative design

Below: a grouping in which an antique work box is associated with mixed 'old-fashioned' flowers

Foliage only arrangements
These are some of the most loved and beautiful of all plant material designs. The more advanced arranger turns to them with increasing pleasure and interest as she progresses. Her eye has learnt to observe great serenity and restfulness in the lovely forms and shapes of leaves and in the textures of the surfaces, whether shiny and reflecting or matt or even woolly. The possibilities of these subtle design elements begin to mean more than just the use of colour, in spite of all its beauty and excitement; but of course foliage abounds in colour. Apart from forest and leaf greens there are many tints and shades. Blue-green is provided by glaucous green foliage; yellow-green and lime green do wonderful things for flowers and foliage in mixed designs. There are green and white leaves, grey and silver leaves, and red and bronze leaves in abundance.

House plants yield lovely leaves and the lucky ones with gardens can easily increase their leaf colour range by striking hardwood cuttings. In form and shape there are leaves that are good for outline material, there are trailing and curved sprays of leaves, leaves useful for 'fillers', larger leaves and the really bold and sculptured leaves. Nature is lavish in her provision of the plant. Use only perfect leaves free of insect or weather damage. Immerse them overnight or for several hours. Never immerse grey foliage, however, for it will go soggy and lose its silver charm. Just give it a long deep drink. Do not use too many varieties of leaves in an all-foliage arrangement. This causes a confusing muddle of foliage in which individual beauty of shape and form is lost. Three different varieties of leaves are sufficient.

In show work a foliage arrangement is one of 'leaves and unopened buds not showing petal colour'. The scope of just this material is tremendous. Choose for your focal point leaves that tend to grow in rosette form such as London pride,

succulents and *choisya*. Otherwise just follow the same design principles as in other arrangements remembering you will be using **texture** and **form** and **shape** contrasts for your design interest rather than colour. Containers, if they show, are best in earthy browns or sludgy greens. Wood is good in containers or bases. Pewter and some other metals accord well – once more, natural materials used together will have an unforced affinity.

The use of figurines

A figurine is a small statuette. Although most of these statuettes are of human figures, a number of them are of animals, birds and other creatures. People either like them a lot or positively dislike them when used in flower decoration. Probably much of this active dislike has been aroused by a misuse of the figurines. Some classical statuettes in bronze or alabaster used with understanding and restraint can contribute to the design, but sadly many figurines are of poor design and inferior materials and are not used well. The most sought-after are those that were intended as candlesticks or Victorian mantelpiece ornaments – the latter are usually made in pairs. The figures are usually one male and one female and vary in design from shepherds and shepherdesses to Egyptian couples. Nearly all have one arm raised, holding a crook or torch. This raised arm provided the holder for the candle but will now hold the candle-cup container for the flowers and leaves. This means the flower design looks best with the same visual weight as the maker of the figurine intended, flowing asymmetrically from left to right or vice versa.

A common mistake is to overfill the container so that the flower design is out of proportion to the figurine. Appropriate plant material must be chosen. For example, while the shepherdess will need simple flowers, the Egyptian figure needs plant material of a more specialist variety.

Some free-standing figurines were made just as decorative objects and many, such as the Dresden figures, are very lovely.

Quantities of pottery cherubs, dolphins and other statuettes have been mass-produced. They can be graceful and lovely if well-arranged, but often the unfortunate cherub seems to be staggering under the massive arrangement it is supporting.

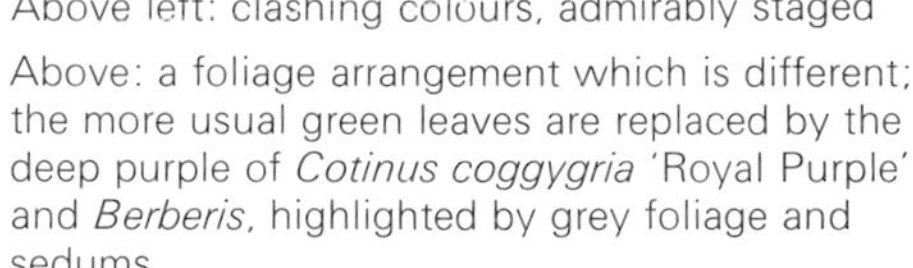

Above left: clashing colours, admirably staged

Above: a foliage arrangement which is different; the more usual green leaves are replaced by the deep purple of *Cotinus coggygria* 'Royal Purple' and *Berberis*, highlighted by grey foliage and sedums

Below left: the colours of the mixed gold flowers reflect the warmth of copper accessories

Below: many shades of green and variegated leaves in an all-foliage arrangement

The arrangement in the bronze figurine container is balanced by its stone base

An expert interpretation of the theme 'The Magic Carpet'

Interpretation

In competitive work 'Interpretative Classes' are very attractive to both exhibitor and the visiting public. In this context interpretative means 'the relation of the exhibit to the class title' (ie the general theme which competitors are set to interpret, using plant material and sometimes accessories to 'tell a story'). Arrangers worry far too much about doing interpretative work. There is no real need to be anxious; after all, in one sense *every* arrangement is interpretative. It could be of a season, for example; in spring, daffodils would be used, in summer, roses play their part, in autumn, berries and coloured leaves are brought together and in winter a bare branch and preserved and dried materials are used. Landscapes, too as described on p. 69, are interpretative of a scene in nature.

If a class title is 'A foreign country of your own choice', think of Spain or Italy and you will know that the use of warm, advancing vibrant colour, and Mediterranean plant material and fruit would be

Foliage for Flower Arrangers

This chart is reproduced from the NAFAS leaflet *Foliage for Flower Arrangers.*

Shape/Colour	Green	Yellow and Lime	Green and White	Grey ar
Outline	*Crocosmia* (Montbretia) *Cytisus* (Broom) Ferns and grasses in variety *Iris foetidissima* *Ligustrum* (Privet) *Phormium tenax* (New Zealand Flax) *Pittosporum* *Stephanandra tanakae* *Taxus* (Yew)	*Elaeagnus pungens* 'Maculata' *Iris pseudacorus* *Ligustrum ovalifolium* 'Aureo-marginatum' (Golden Privet) **Sansevieria trifasciata* (Mother-in-law's Tongue) *Weigela florida* 'Variegata'	*Cornus alba* 'Elegantissima' *Iris foetidissima* 'Variegata' *Ligustrum sinense* 'Variegatum' (Silver Privet) **Sansevieria trifasciata* (Mother-in-law's Tongue)	*Artemis* *Cotonea* *Eucalyp* *Rosmar* (Rose *Senecio* *Sorbus*
Trailing and curved sprays	*Cotoneaster salicifolius* *Escallonia* in variety Ferns in variety *Hedera helix* (Common Ivy) *Lonicera japonica halliana*	*Hedera colchica* 'Dentata Variegata' (Yellow variegated Ivy) *Hedera helix* 'Gold Heart' *Lonicera japonica* 'Aureo-reticulata' (Japanese Honeysuckle)	*Euonymus fortunei radicans* varieties *Hedera canariensis* 'Variegata' (Silver variegated Ivy) *Hedera helix* 'Glacier' *Vinca major* 'Variegata' (Variegated Periwinkle)	*Ballota* *Helichry*
Fillers	*Buxus* (Box) *Choisya ternata* *Cupressus,* various *Hydrangea* *Mahonia aquifolium* *Skimmia* *Viburnum tinus* (Laurustinus)	*Cupressus,* golden varieties *Elaeagnus pungens* 'Maculata' *Euonymus japonicus* 'Aureo-pictus' *Hebe armstrongii* *Ilex altaclarensis* 'Golden King' (Golden variegated Holly) *Lonicera* 'Baggesen's Gold'	*Euonymus fortunei radicans* 'Silver Queen' *Ilex aquifolium* 'Silver Queen' (Silver variegated Holly)	*Cinerar* *Cupress* *Hebe* 'P *Helichr* *Ruta gr* *Santoli*
Larger leaves	*Alchemilla mollis* *Arum maculatum* (Wild Arum) **Aspidistra* *Bergenia,* various *Fatshedera lizei* *Hosta fortunei* *Magnolia* *Tellima grandiflora*	*Aucuba japonica* (Spotted Laurel) *Hedera colchica* 'Dentata Variegata' (Yellow variegated Ivy) *Hosta fortunei* 'Albo-picta' *Pelargonium,* zonal types (Geranium)	*Hosta undulata* *Hosta albo-marginata* *Arum italicum pictum* *Hedera canariensis* 'Variegata' (Silver variegated Ivy) Kale, ornamental	**Begon* *Hosta s*
Bold for pedestals and moderns	**Aspidistra* *Fatsia japonica* **Monstera deliciosa* (Swiss Cheese Plant) *Phormium tenax* (New Zealand Flax) *Yucca gloriosa*	**Sansevieria trifasciata* (Mother-in-law's Tongue)	*Aralia elata* 'Variegata'	*Boccon* *Cynara* (Arti *Onopor*

* denotes houseplant

right. If you want to use them, add suitable accessories and you have evoked the atmosphere and feeling to be found in these countries. If you were to choose Norway or Finland instead then work in muted colours: sage greens and browns with bare but strong outline material reminiscent of the Nordic landscape. With suitable accessories and containers or bases, you would again create the right visual and mental reaction in the viewer.

Suppose the title were 'A mood'. Well, moods can be grave or gay and you can summon up colours, shapes and forms that evoke either feeling. The correct kind of plant material should be selected, nevertheless, for the judge will be looking to see if the type chosen is right for the class title. A 'gay and happy' mood would call for light rhythmic material and flowers of a warm colour. The 'grave or sad' mood would want plant material of subdued colour and more rugged in structure. Do not depend on accessories; however good and well-chosen they are it must be the plant material that tells the story.

	Red and Bronze
	Berberis thunbergii 'Atropurpurea' *Prunus cerasifera* 'Pissardii' *Rosa rubrifolia*
ius m	see above
)	*Cotinus coggygria* 'Royal Purple', etc. (Smoke Bush) *Hebe* 'Autumn Glory' *Mahonia* *Weigela florida* 'Foliis Purpureis'
	**Begonia rex* *Bergenia* 'Evening Glow' and others redden in winter **Dracaena terminalis* *Tellima grandiflora* 'Purpurea' *Vitis coignetiae*
oy) oon) istle)	Canna lily *Ricinus* (Castor Oil Plant) *Senecio clivorum* 'Desdemona'

The use of colour and texture in bases, containers and drapes is important. The fabric used in drapes should not only be of suitable interpretative colour, but also the right texture: light and fine for the gay and happy mood, and much heavier and sombre for the grave and sad mood. Keep drapes to the minimum. They should only be included to help to lead the eye through the design, to give contrast or harmony in texture and colour, or as a base or background. Take care to see they flow gracefully and that they are not dominant. They can always be used in competitive work – without the schedule saying so – as can a base or background. Backgrounds added can be lightly painted if desired – with stylized masts of ships, for instance, in a harbour scene – but as always, they must be skilfully executed if they are to succeed. If you are not confident that you can carry them out well they are perhaps best left alone.

Figurines of many kinds, human or animal, are often used in this kind of work, but once again a word of warning: take care that the *scale* is right for the size allotted and the design. A lovely landscape depicting the countryside can be ruined by the addition of a large horse or lamb that destroys the whole scale and can look ridiculous. If the accessory is not the right one in scale or texture or harmony, better leave it out altogether and let the plant material tell the story for you.

Arrangers seem to fall into two camps when faced with interpretative work – those whose imagination is fired with almost too many ideas, and those who, almost stunned by the enormity of the problem, just cannot get started. For the latter there are two excellent ways to get inspiration. One is to go to the dictionary and look up the subject or word indicative of the class title. There you will find the *essence* of the word described for you. The second way is to write down the class title, then write below it all the words that spontaneously come to you, (suggested by your subconscious) by the particular title. You will be surprised by the leads this exercise will give you. The class could be anything from a 'sport' to an 'industry' or a 'precious stone' to a 'metal'. All these things evoke a certain kind of mental and visual response in you connected with particular colours, shapes and forms. Select the ones that you feel are the most suited to the subject and then relate it to the plant material, its colour, form and shape, that you will use. Flower designs of all the varieties described, give you unlimited scope and nature provides a palette of colours and forms and shapes of all kinds. The rest is up to you.

In the main, success is attained by three factors. First, use plant material suitable for the subject being portrayed. Second, increase your awareness of the form and shape of plant material, which can be light and rhythmic; solid and heavy; vertical, giving quick eye movement, or horizontal, suggesting a more relaxed reaction. Lastly, remember the evocative quality of colour. The often-heard expressions 'I am in the pink' meaning 'in fine spirits' and 'I am in a blue mood', meaning depression, convey how much the average person is affected by colour. Be aware of this characteristic in human beings and it will help you greatly in your work and the interpretation of subjects.

Interpreting 'Christmas' with fresh material in colours both vibrant and harmonious

Below: sensitive interpretation, fine staging and appropriate figures in this design 'Churchill's People'

NAFAS International Affiliates
Several distinguished NAFAS associates from other countries have most kindly supplied illustrated examples of arrangements particular to their climates, taste and available material. Contributory countries are listed in alphabetical order:
Australia
The Floral Art Society of Queensland
Canada
France
Societe National Horticulture de France
Italy
Garden Club di Bologna
New Zealand
The Floral Art Society of New Zealand
United States of America
The National Council of State Garden Clubs, Inc.

Below: Italy. A fine festive table ensemble consisting of two candle arrangements and a centrepiece. Variegated holly, carnations, cones, skimmia berries and *Symphoricarpos albus* (snowberries)
Far below, left: Australia. An impressive abstract using cork bark, Mexican daisies and one cycas palm leaf
Far below, centre: Australia. Stark and monochromatic, this abstract includes white painted foliage, reeds and vines. The white balls denote skiers; the vines are their tracks in the snow
Right: Canada. A mellow colour-linked arrangement of fruit and cones with snowberries providing a lighter motif
Right, below: USA. A striking all-dried arrangement in sculptural weathered wood and the mullein which grows, in odd shapes, wild in north-west USA. The heavy pottery container stands on a Japanese camphorwood base
Right, far below: New Zealand. This sensitively-toned arrangement from Auckland is of *Leucodendron argentinium* cones and dried fan palms

Right: USA. In a hand-formed pottery container, this fresh and dried arrangement is composed of bleached, weathered wood. Umbrella plant gives refreshing textural and colour contrast

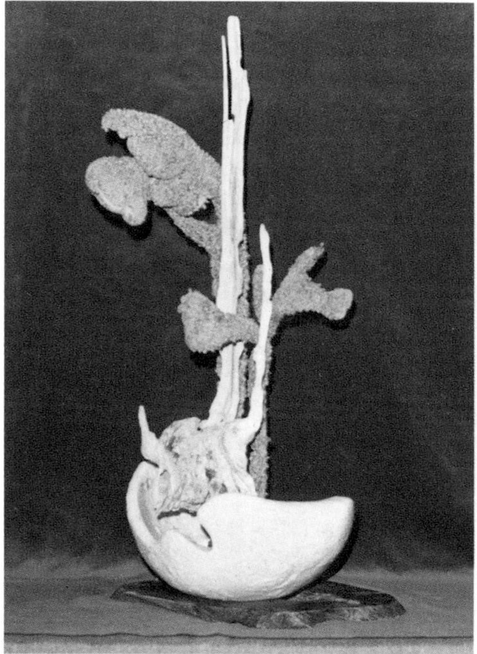

Below left: Australia. An imaginative sta-mobile; the stabile is composed of one birdlike piece of wood 'perched' on another. The mobile is of suspended dried seedpods in autumn tonings. *Asparagus retrofracta* and seedpods in the same tones on the stabile lend unity. (See pp. 204, 207)

Far below: France. An elegant, cool arrangement of dark aspidistra leaves and pale cream tulips on a curving glass dish. The delicate colouring of the flowers is admirably displayed against the blue, green and cream of the base and background

Below right: Italy. A magnificent della Robbia garland (after the Italian Renaissance sculptor). Seasonal cones, variegated holly and assorted fruit are admirably combined on a fir background and decorated with satin ribbon

Right: New Zealand. *Anthurium andreanum*, dried cycas palm and *Pelargonium tormentosum* (peppermint geranium) leaves are sensitively arranged to stress shape and movement

6. Drying and Preserving Foliage and Florist Flowers

These flowers, as in their causes, sleep.
THOMAS CAREW *c*1595–1640

This freeze-dried arrangement of spring flowers, which commemorated the Silver Jubilee of Her Majesty Queen Elizabeth II, was lodged by NAFAS in the East Cloister of Westminster Abbey on 9 November 1977. (See also page 84.)

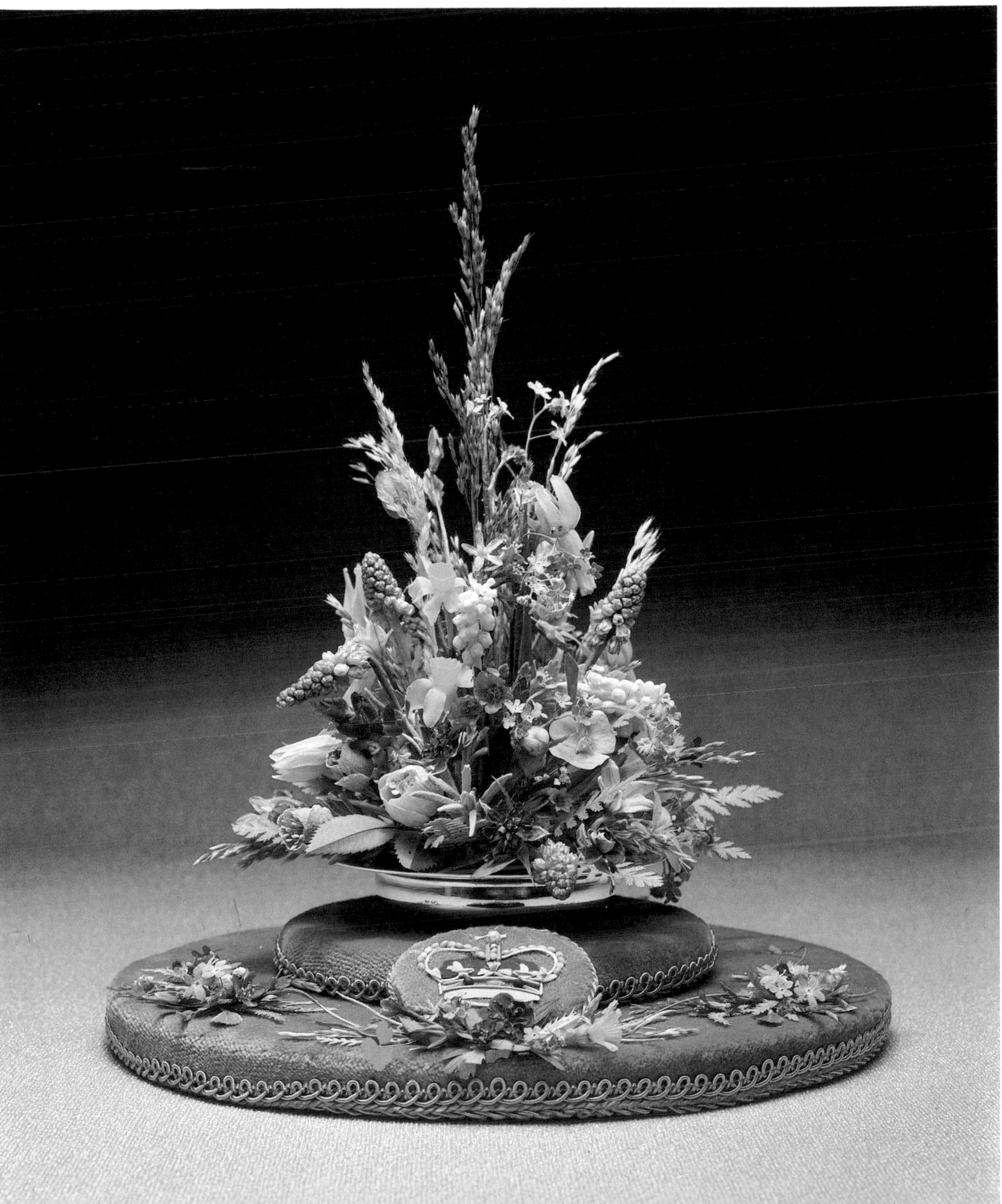

There is nothing very new about drying and preserving plant material – indeed, it was an obsession with the Victorians who made quantities of small and large arrangements of mixed seedheads for all the rooms in the house. In particular, bulrushes, teasels and Chinese lanterns were great favourites. They turned not only to the gardens and hedgerows for their materials, but to the sea-shore as well, picking up shells and sea-weeds. They became very expert in drying sea-weed, washing it in many changes of fresh water to eliminate all the salt, and then pressing it between sheets of blotting paper. Delightful pictures were made of 'forests' using the branching sea-weeds, and the colours of the different weeds were very skilfully contrasted.

For several reasons, there has been a tremendous upsurge of interest in drying and preserving garden and wild plant material in the last few years. One of the most obvious advantages in dried material is that it provides very interesting arrangements during the bleak months of the year when fresh flowers and foliage are hard to come by. They are virtually everlasting, if they are well prepared, and carefully stored when not in use. Since the seedheads and other forms available can be easily gathered from the wild, as well as from the garden, the cost is usually nil or very low. Some very exotic dried material is now being imported from Africa and other tropical places to provide us with new shapes and forms. Inevitably the cost of freight and labour means that some of these new varieties are expensive, but one needs very little and some of the material is very attractive. There is no special need to use this new material but it is interesting to see what is available and ponder whether some particular piece might not give a fresh form or shape to experiment with in your arrangements.

Central heating has become almost universal in the last few years and although adding great comfort in the colder months it works havoc with fresh flower arrangements. Constant replacement is demanding in time, and can be very expensive. Probably the best compromise is found by using a framework of glycerined leaves into which are placed a few fresh flowers. Although dried and glycerined plant material is good and useful in this way, there are a few drawbacks. One is that if you wish to have a good variety of material shapes and forms – and obviously you do – rather than plodding along with just one or two arrangements, then storing the material does take up quite a bit of space. Cardboard dress or flower boxes are very useful for this purpose as they are rigid and give sufficient length for the stems. Providing your roof-space is dry, this is an excellent place for storing the boxes in the summer months. The tops or floors of cupboards can be used, and another favourite place is under the spare-room bed! But none of these places are ideal, for you really need a place where you can open your box and select what you want without clambering about. If you are lucky enough to have a room that you can use as a studio or work-room then you have no worries – but not many people are able to have this space available. Do not let this minor difficulty deter you for you will find space for your box, if you look around, and you can then vary your designs constantly.

The muted colours of the dried sea-weed in this Victorian picture are complemented by the golden basketwork, which represents the container

This is important as it is very monotonous to depend on one or two only, instead of ringing the changes. Small boxes are needed for storing the finer, small varieties of plant material and it is quite a good idea to use some plastic cling-film as a lid because it enables you to see the contents without having to remove the top. All storage boxes, large or small, should be clearly labelled at one end – not the top – so that you can reach for the one you want without disturbing all the others. Do *not* use plastic bags; condensation will cause mildew. Alternatively, the plant material may be hung up in bunches in a dry airy place.

This will be a year-round interest because each season provides different materials for you to work with in the winter, when you can gather up all the different shapes and forms to use in the house or elsewhere. 'Elsewhere' could mean in offices or hotels or perhaps, most useful of all, in a church, in the difficult months when flowers and foliage are so hard to come by. Equally, in very hot climates where flowers and leaves last but a day, preserved and dried flowers and leaves are a great stand-by.

While it is possible to explore this subject in great depth, as whole books on the subject have done, this chapter aims to give the average flower arranger a sound basic knowledge about drying and preserving for her own needs. She will then be equipped to vary her 'fresh only'

A miniature arrangement using pastel-coloured, desiccant-dried flowers

The plant material used for this plaque has been dried using silica gel and includes pansies, roses, mimosa, willow catkins and variegated leaves. (See p. 127)

A striking modern arrangement of dried material in a tapered, rough-textured, glass container: the skeletonized hydrangea heads have been mounted on false stems to give extra height. Two circles of phormium provide contrast

arrangements, or to call on the preserved material when she has little leisure or fresh flowers available – or maybe for economy, if she has to buy from florists all the time.

Those who are critical of dried arrangements often describe them as colourless and dull, and this could be fair comment some long time ago. Now, however, the whole picture has changed dramatically. New techniques mean that colour is far from absent, and that the variety of shapes and forms that can be used is infinite. It is true that often the colours are pastel or muted, but this is in fact one of the greatest charms of dried arrangements. Those who enjoy the honey and straw colours that are found in different varieties of wood and basketry will love the quiet serenity conveyed to the viewer by a good arrangement of preserved material. There are tremendous variations in tones and shades, from soft sage greens and almost black toffee browns to warm scarlets, blues and yellows. Even if your personal taste is for the vibrant colours found in living plant materials, you cannot help but find these designs interesting and restful and they

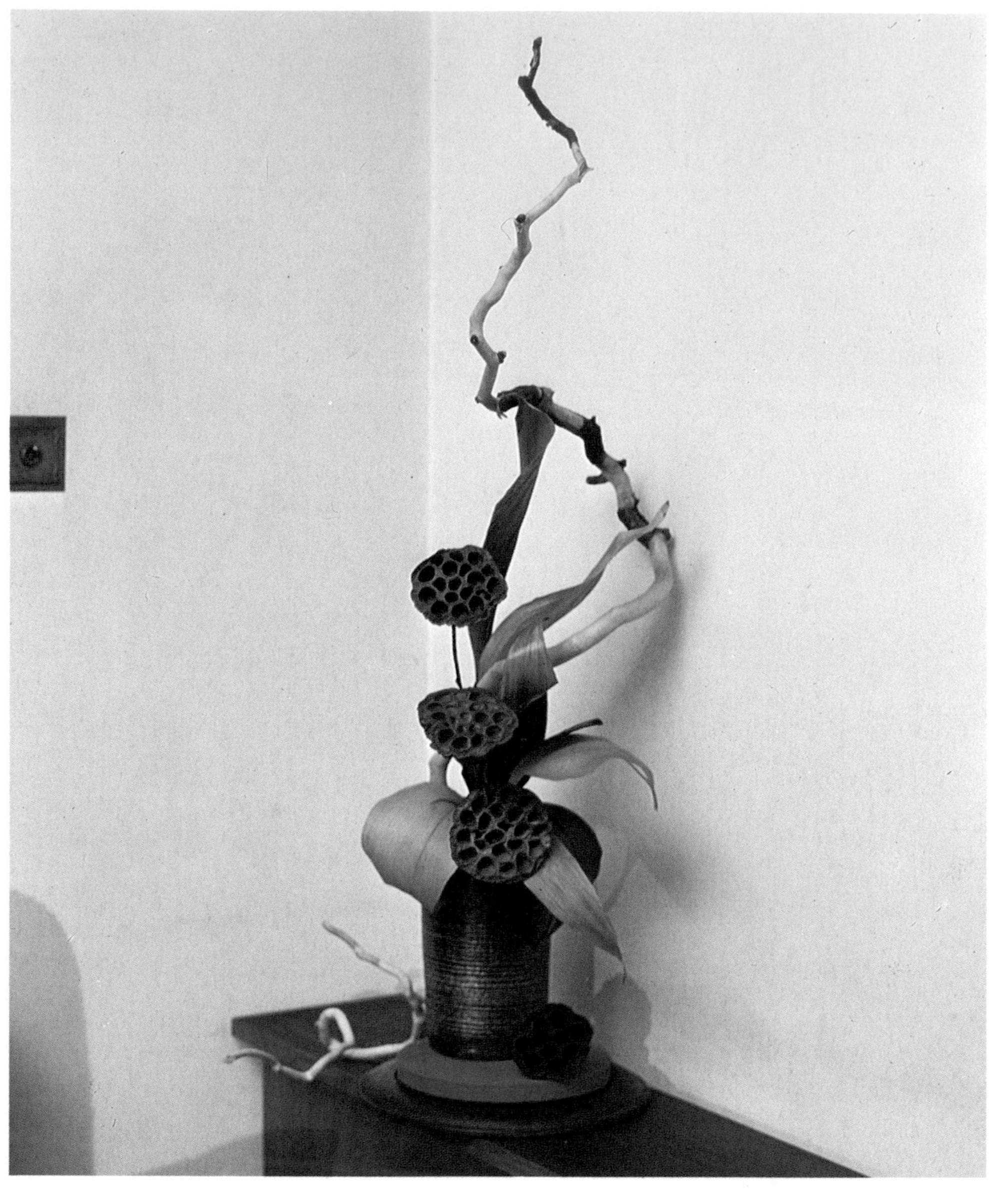

Here a rhythmic line of driftwood is combined with lotus seedheads and aspidistra leaves in a ceramic pot. (See pp. 122–5)

The figure, seemingly carved from ivory, consists entirely of dried plant material

once again develop your 'seeing eye' in quite a new direction in decorative work.

You will become tremendously aware of plant structure and texture. When the sap is dehydrated and the 'bone structure' is revealed, you have another dimension with which to work and one that reveals the beautiful and fragile structure of leaf veins and the tough fibrous 'ribs' that support the plant stems. A deciduous tree presents us with two faces of beauty – a full canopy of summer foliage, and in winter, a filigree of branches with tracery outlined against the sky. Perhaps these two kinds of beauty could be likened to a sumptuous colour painting, or a sculpture of fine lines and shapes. Though visually very different, both provide us with another dimension of experience in our lives. By not appreciating both, we are missing an aesthetic pleasure and experience, and limiting ourselves and our perceptions, which can only be sad.

Preserving plant material

This is a simple and easy process with such quick results that there can be few flower arrangers who do not constantly use the method. 'Constantly' because once the solution is correctly mixed it can be used over and over for totally different plant materials. The object of the process is to replace the water content of plants with a fluid which will not evaporate and which will keep the plants naturally firm. You will need a jar or other transparent container so that you can check the depth of the glycerine solution as time goes by. The solution should be at least 5 cm (2 in.) deep. Use tall and narrow vessels for long branches so that they are supported by the sides of the container. Jam jars or other small pots serve for any shorter pieces. You also need a low shallow dish or pan so that you can immerse in the solution certain leaves that do not absorb too well from their stem ends.

Make up the solution with 1 part glycerine to 2 parts very hot water, directly in the container you plan to use. Put the glycerine in first and then add the hot water. The object of the very hot water is to ensure a good 'mix' between the water and the oil which in the normal state do not blend well. Using a wooden spoon, give the liquids a really vigorous stir. Glycerine has become expensive, but you will not need a vast quantity and the mixture lasts a long time. It is cheaper bought in bulk, so you can save money by buying from a large chemist's shop and sharing the cost of supply between friends. The glycerine must be that sold by chemists or druggists to get the best results. Many flower clubs buy a large quantity and bottle it up in smaller portions to sell on their sales tables.

Because the stems take up the warm solution very easily, the mixture can be used at once, so you can start your preservation immediately if you wish. There is no waste with the mixed solution. Between use, it can be stored in an air-tight container. Eventually, the mixture will darken, but it is not impaired. If mildew forms, the mixture should be poured through a strainer. If the depth in your jar falls below the necessary 5 cm (2 in.) you can add more of the same mix. Never let the cut ends of the stem dry out by leaving them out of the solution. The stems may need to stay in the solution from three days to six weeks, depending on the species. See Table on page 84. When the leaves and stems are ready to be taken out and to be used; others can be processed in the same solution. If the container is sufficiently large, then you can add various kinds of plant material, just taking them out when they are at the correct stage of preservation. The progress of the glycerine up into the leaves is visible, and so it is not difficult to determine when the process is finished. If the tips of the branches have sagged, then hang them upside-down for a few days to allow the glycerine to reach the tips of the branches. Leave them in this position for a few days or until you need to use them. Spraying the leaves or moistening them in the glycerine solution, before putting the stems into the mixture, will also help absorption. 45.5 cm (18 in.) is about the maximum length of a branch for success.

Most leaves change to a soft toffee brown, but colours vary according to variety. Some become a soft golden colour and are supple to the touch. Do not let them stay too long in the solution, or beads of moisture will appear on the leaves and their appearance will be 'oily' and limp. Sometimes this will happen with one or two leaves before the whole stem is ready to be taken out of the solution. If this occurs then just mop it off with a tissue.

A colourful abstract: driftwood, seed-cases, maple, laurel and painted bean-pods

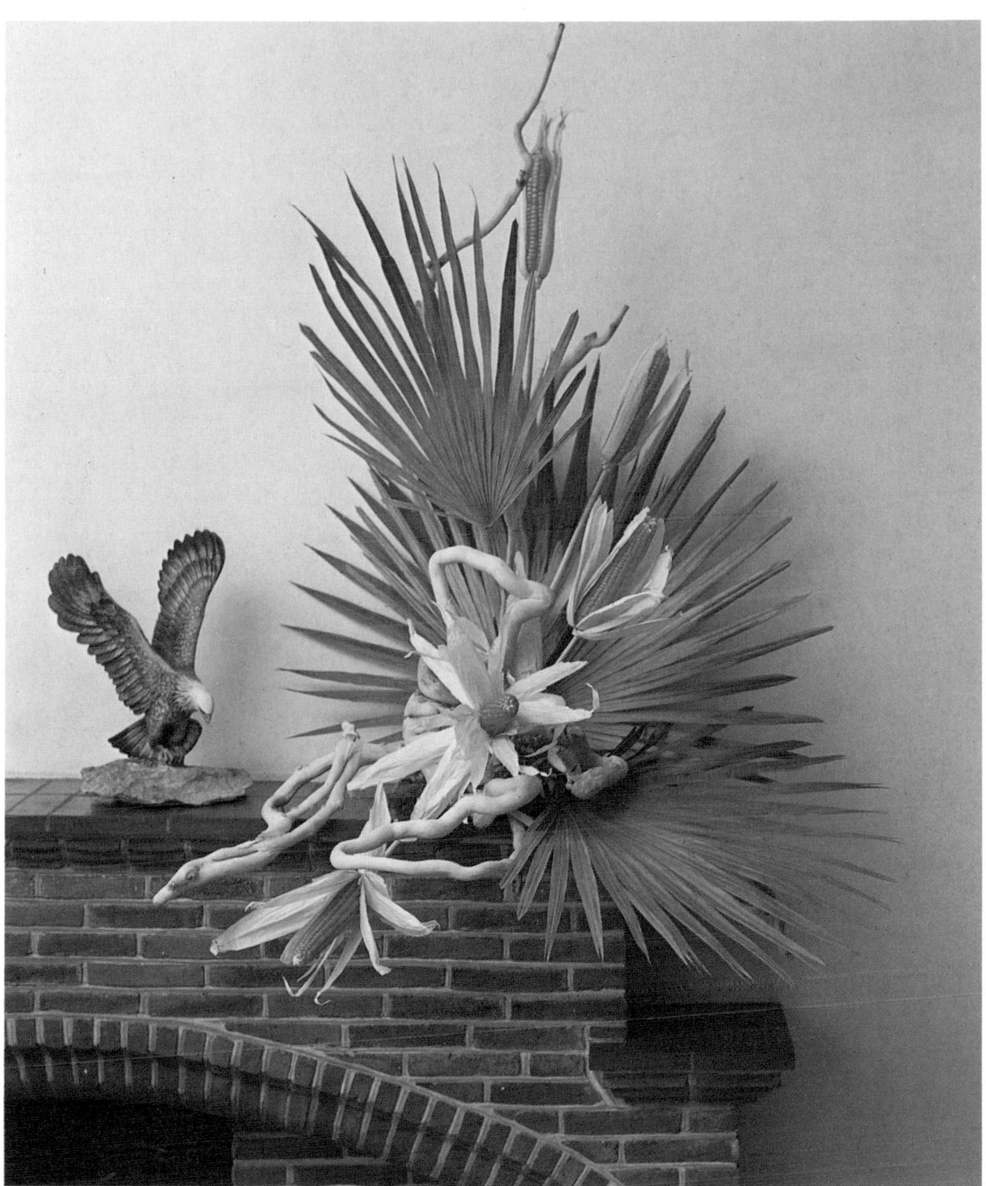

The colours of the fireplace are echoed in the combination of dried palm leaves, corncob heads and driftwood, which stands on the mantel-shelf

Watch the progress of your stems and leaves with care to get the best results, for the time required varies from plant to plant.

The experienced flower arranger knows that lovely as they are, young fresh leaves flag and wilt almost immediately; this is because the structure of the leaf is incomplete. Still soft, the flesh of the leaf lacks supporting veins and fibres. Those who set out to preserve foliage must, therefore, use leaves that are mature. High summer, July and August are the best months in Great Britain or the United States. Wherever she lives, the arranger should wait for the leaves to be at their peak of development. When the sap is receding from the leaves then the leaf is past its best and, (if deciduous) preparing for the chemical changes which cause the superb autumn colouring, and the eventual miraculous severing by the tree of the leaf stem that ensues at leaf-fall. Clearly, a leaf preparing for this termination of its life cycle is useless for preservation. Evergreen trees – contrary to what many people imagine – also shed their leaves at different times of the year. Take the trouble to find out when this happens in a plant encyclopaedia, or just observe it for yourself (yet another way to develop your 'seeing eye'), and avoid that particular moment in the life of your evergreen tree.

The preparation of stems and leaves begins by selecting your material. Walk around and mark down the branches and leaves that will suit your needs. Obviously you require well-shaped branches; all leaves must be free of insect bites, for these show up alarmingly when arranged. Beech leaves are a favourite variety to preserve but are plagued by puncture holes if not picked with care. With observation and luck you may escape this problem but if some leaves are scarred, then trim them away before you put your branch into the solution. At the same time cut out any crossing or cluttering leaves that spoil the line of the branch. If you leave them on, you will be wasting your precious glycerine solution when you snip off the unwanted leaves from the branch later. When you are scrutinizing the leaves for defects, study the 'flow' of the whole branch. If the tip has a graceful curve to the right then you do not want an angular branch below it jutting out to the left or right and preventing the eye following the natural line down to the base of the branch. Do not, however, denude the stem of every interesting branchlet or leaf. Practically all branches need a little judicious thinning to be seen at their best. Ideally you should be able to select and pick branches that are more or less the shape you want, and with practice this soon becomes easy. An experienced flower arranger is able to choose exactly the stems and branches she needs.

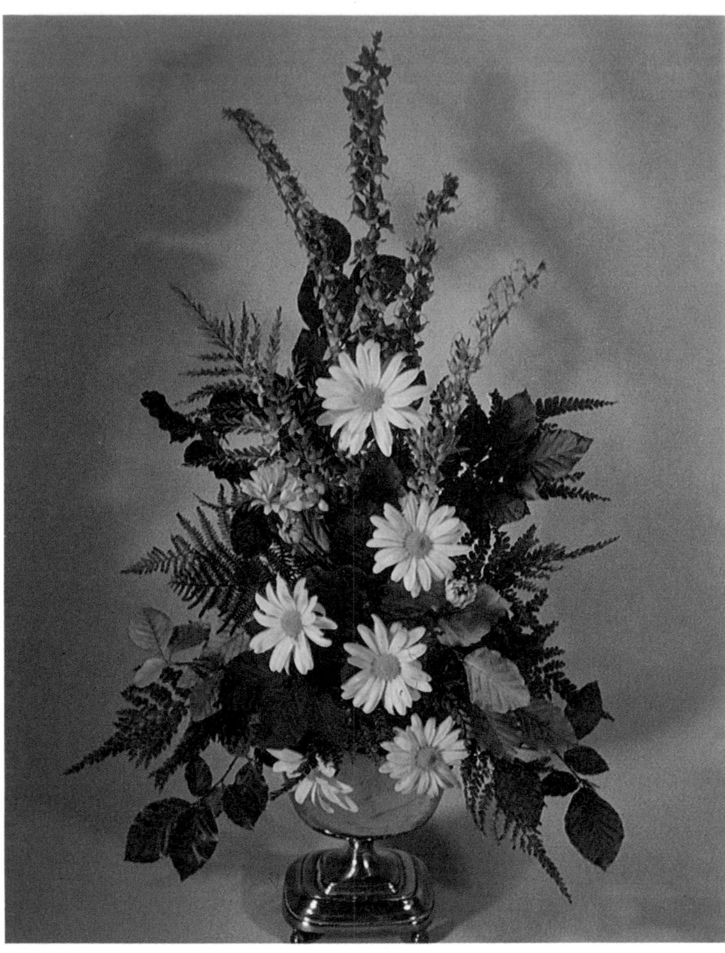

An ideal design for the arranger with no garden. Half a dozen fresh chrysanthemums are arranged with a mixture of dried material

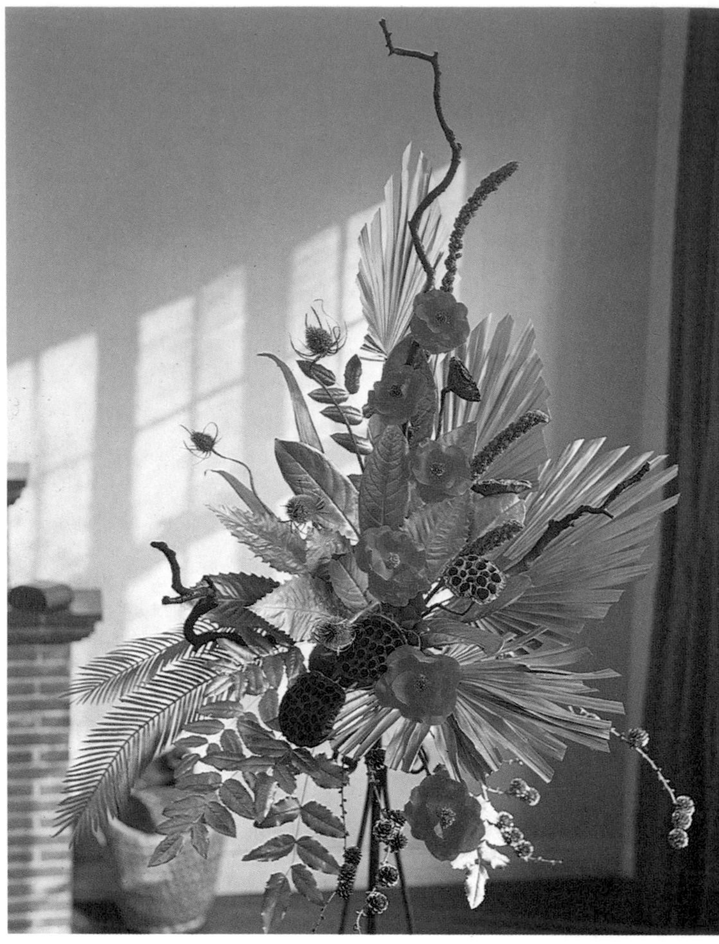

Material for this Christmas pedestal – lotus seedheads, driftwood, gold-painted leaves, contrived flowers – is prepared in the autumn

Glycerine turns leaves brown as it replaces the water they once contained. Not a uniform dull brown, but all kinds of tints and shades, can result, from pale biscuit and golden shades to rich mahogany and even almost black. One kind of leaf can take on varying shades according to the time it is picked and its maturity. If you do find your beech or other leaves lack variety in their colouring, stand some branches by a window in strong sunlight, and this should make them paler. Glycerined leaves feel almost the same as they did before treatment. They are glossy, and flexible rather than stiff and unnatural. If you should put them in a position where they collect some dust (but do not let them collect dust from just being forgotten and staying around too long), then the preserved plant material may be washed in warm soapy water, thoroughly dried and then either used again, or stored away. Nothing could be better-tempered than preserved plant material providing it is treated with the respect it deserves! Store it carefully and inspect it often, for it is attractive to moths and mice.

Leaves of a transparent texture will need less time in the solution than thicker kinds. Ivy or *Fatsia* and similar thick leaves need immersing in the mixture. Larger leaves, such as aspidistra and other coarse-textured species should be dabbed all over their surfaces with cotton wool or a similar substance soaked in the mixture *before* the stem is placed in the glycerine mixture. This prevents the tip of the leaf from drying out. It would, of course, be better to immerse them but their size prevents this. Before putting the stems finally into the glycerine mixture, and after you have cut away all unwanted leaves, cut the stem ends on a slant in order to expose a wider area to absorb the glycerine. Scrape off the bark from hard woody stems and split them upwards for about 5 cm (2 in.) to allow the glycerine to be absorbed more easily.

Do not use water when arranging preserved materials. Should you wish to arrange them with living flowers then either put the flowers in a separate water-filled container inside the container used for the completed arrangement, or, if you fill the bowl used with water, then you must protect the stem ends of the preserved material with nail varnish or melted candle-wax. If they are to be left in water for a long time this action will prevent the stems going mouldy. As your mechanics you can use a pinholder, wire-netting, dry plastic foam or sand. It is best not to use plaster of paris or modelling clay for temporary arrangements because the stems ends will be damaged when the arrangement is dismantled, and the clay makes them messy. Hard substances like plaster of paris are fine for the kind of 'perpetual' design under a glass dome such as the Victorians used. This is not a general practice now.

The base or container chosen for the preserved plant material should, of course, be 'in harmony' with it. Natural materials

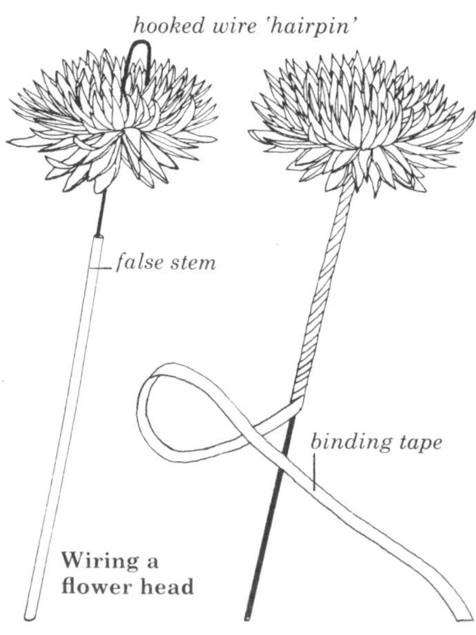

Wiring a flower head

such as wood, stone and basketry succeed best because their muted earthy colours and textures are in accord with the plant material. As long as it is not patterned or highly coloured, pottery also looks good and so do some metals, such as brass, copper or pewter. Your choice must be guided by the design you choose to make and where you will place it.

A surprising number of plants accept preservation very successfully and experiments can be worthwhile. Grasses, for example, can be preserved in glycerine with very pleasing results. If picked at their prime they will develop a beautiful silken sheen and will be very supple. Glycerining the grasses makes them develop a rich golden hue rather than the pale straw colour of grasses preserved by air-drying. A combination of the two methods for different grasses provides a charming contrast of colour. The fine grass forms have great delicacy and interest in all arrangements. If the larger leaves seem a little lacking in curves and rhythm it is very simple to place a stub wire down the reverse of the leaf and cover the wire with sellotape You can then gently curve the leaf into the shape you wish. This is the best method, but if preferred you can thread a stub wire up the leaf stem and around the rib of the leaf on its reverse and then manipulate the leaf into the position you want. Another great help to the arranger is that the stem length can be easily raised by either inserting it into another hollow stem, or wiring it on to a second stem. With live material stem lengths can be a problem but with preserved material free of the need for water this is easily remedied.

Wiring dried flower heads

Dried stems can become so brittle and weak at the neck of the flower that it is wise to provide an artificial stem, made from stub wire and wrapped around with florist's tape. Use 26 gauge wire for delicate subjects like violets and pansies, 22 gauge for medium-sized flowers and 18 gauge for large and heavy-necked flowers. Cut the wire to a suitable stem length for the flower being treated, leaving about 1.5 cm (½ in.) of natural stem under the flower head. A total length of approximately 10–15 cm (4–6 in.) is usually sufficient. Bend a hook in the end of the wire, then insert the long straight end through the flower centre and pull down through the flower neck so that the hook keeps the wire in place. If the stem is hollow, the wire should be pushed down through its length. It may be drawn parallel to a solid stem end, and they can both then be covered with tape. Draw the hooked end of the wire down firmly until it is embedded in the flower centre and cannot be seen. (See diagram opposite.)

It is wise to wire flower heads before drying them if they require artificial stems. The flower heads can then be placed in more graceful curves, whereas their own stems can appear stiff and are fragile.

Grinling Gibbons' magnificent carving in St Paul's Cathedral, London, is perfectly complemented by this swag of dried plant material. (See p. 126)

Drying plant material

This is the alternative method of preserving plant material so that its use is prolonged indefinitely. The process is really the reverse of the glycerining method. Instead of replacing the water in the plant material with glycerine, the object is to eliminate all the water content. Inevitably this makes the material far more fragile and brittle than is the case with the turgid material preserved with glycerine. There are three main ways of going about the drying process: (1) air-drying (2) pressing, and (3) with desiccants. Although these three methods are totally different in practice, the care and preparation of the flowers and seedheads are the same, which simplifies what must be learnt and remembered. It is common sense to select only perfect material and to discard any material that is not of the first quality. Time and effort will be wasted on poor, badly formed specimens. Take care to pick your flowers and seedheads *just before* they reach their peak of development. Do not leave them until they are about to disintegrate or they will

Plants suitable for preservation with glycerine

Foliage	*Weeks*	*Comment*
Aspidistra	12	mop, beige
Atriplex	½	beige
Beech	1–2	green beech more successful
Bergenia	3–4	immerse
Box	3–4	beige
Broom	2	almost black
Camellia	4	dark brown
Choisya	3	light beige
Cotoneaster	2–4	colour varies with type
Elaeagnus	4–6	variegation is lost
Fatsia	2–6	mop or submerge
Ferns	2	pick when spores show
Grevillea	2	colour varies
Ivy	2–3	mop or submerge
Hellebore	2–3	light brown
Laurel	2–3	very tough, dark brown
Magnolia	3–4	tough, dark brown
Mahonia	2–3	medium brown
Oak	2	light brown
Pittosporum	2	medium brown
Rhododendron	2	single leaves better
Rose	2	use woody stem, dark green
Rubber plant	4	mop or submerge
Solomon's seal	1–2	treat after flowering
Spotted laurel	3	variegation lost, dark brown
Sweet chestnut	1–2	single leaves better
Whitebeam	2	brown with grey underside
Garrya elliptica catkins	3	treat in Spring

Other plant material	*Weeks*	*Comment*
Hydrangea flowers	2	use woody stems
Iris seedpods	2	useful shape
Lime flowers	2–3	remove leaves
Old-man's-beard	2	treat before flowers open
Pussy willow catkins	2	treat when silky
Sea-holly flowers	2–3	light brown
Teasels	3	treat when green

The times given are only a guide. Weather, time of picking and temperature may all affect the process. This NAFAS leaflet can be obtained from the address in the list of stockists at the end of this book.

This stone, in the East Cloister of Westminster Abbey, marks the place where the freeze-dried arrangement illustrated on page 77 is lodged. NAFAS has been responsible for the decoration of the Abbey for many festivals and special occasions, which has led to a close association with the Abbey authorities

Freeze-drying

Freeze-drying consists basically of dehydrating tissue while it is frozen. Whereas biological tissue dried from the non-frozen state becomes distorted and shrunken, tissue dried from the frozen state retains its original appearance. If tissue is first frozen to give it mechanical rigidity and the water is removed by sublimation (conversion from a frozen state to a vapour, by-passing the liquid phase), it can be dehydrated without any apparent physical change. Sublimation begins at the outer surface and proceeds towards the centre during the drying process. One of the problems of flower drying has been the presence of cellulose cell walls, which have tended to resist the sublimation effect. However, with the use of liquid nitrogen during the initial freezing, this problem has been virtually eliminated. Depending upon the season and the age of the flower being treated, in most cases satisfactory drying has been obtained.

Research into the process of freeze-drying began at the British Museum (Natural History) in the late 1950s. After some setbacks suitable apparatus was developed and at the present time a full service of freeze-drying for both plant and animal material is provided

Department of Zoology
British Museum (Natural History)
May 1977

lose the crispness of their appearance. Finally, wait for a fine dry day to do your picking. This again is common sense. You are seeking to dehydrate the petals and leaves so it is a good idea to let the air and the sun help the process along. Material wet with rain will not have the same results and will not give you the same good colour retention. The sooner the dehydrating process is completed, the greater your success will be.

Air drying

This is the easiest and most popular way of drying plant material. After picking, your flowers and seedheads are suspended by the stems in a dry airy place. A garage, outhouse or spare room that you can hang a line across or have some other means of suspending the bunches, and which is very dry and airy, is excellent. Though airing cupboards are often used they are seldom well enough ventilated. A room near a boiler may be better if there is more air movement. However, hydrangeas and delphiniums, which require only a few days to dry, retain their colour better in the greater warmth of an airing-cupboard. Hang them upside-down to dry.

Prepare the material by removing all leaves from the stems, for they delay dehydration and in any case will shrivel up and look unsightly. Make the flowers or seedheads up into bunches small enough not to

Plants suitable for air-drying

Flowers
Acroclinium roseum
Globe artichoke (*Cynara scolymus*)
Bear's breeches (*Acanthus*)
Delphinium
Globe thistle (*Echinops*)
Helichrysum (Everlasting flower)
Larkspur (*Delphinium consolida*)
Lavender (*Lavandula*)
Love-lies-bleeding (*Amaranthus caudatus*)
Pussy willow (*Salix*)
Pearl everlasting (*Anaphalis*)
Helipterum (syn. Acroclinium roseum)
Sea holly (*Eryngium maritimum*)
Statice (*Limonium sinuatum*)
Yarrow (*Achillea*)

Seedheads
Allium (onion and related plants)
Bulrush (*Typha*)
Chinese lantern (*Physalis franchettii*)
Clematis
Cow parsley (*Anthriscus sylvestris*)
Dock (*Rumex* family)
Honesty (*Lunaria annua*)
Iris
Love-in-a-mist (*Nigella damascena*)
Pampas grass (*Cortaderia*)
Oriental poppy (*Papaver orientale*)
Rushes, sedges, cereals, grasses
Teasel (*Dipsacus fullonum*)

Above: pressed flowers in a simple line design. Right: the owl collage uses driftwood and honesty seed-pods. (See p. 89)

damage or crush the heads. These bunches must be *hung upside down* so that the sap runs down the stem. Failure to hang them up in this way will mean the neck of the flowers or seedheads will shrink before the drying process is completed. You then leave your bunches suspended until the material feels papery and crisp to the touch.

Some flower heads or bracts dry better if their stems are placed in about 1 cm (½ in.) of water. This applies particularly to hydrangeas, which are especially useful for decoration with their large heads and their varied colours, ranging from steely blue to soft pinks and deep crimson. Do not pick hydrangeas until they feel just papery, which means they are beginning the process of drying. Leave the stems in 1 cm (½ in.) water until it evaporates and the flower heads are really papery. Bells of Ireland *(Moluccella laevis)* and heathers all dry well in this way.

Strong sunlight eventually drains dried flowers of their colour, so place them out of direct sunlight. If your dried plant material is crushed it can easily be reshaped by holding it in steam from boiling water for a few seconds, and then gently stroking it into the shape you need it to be.

Pressing

This method is used chiefly to prepare plant material for incorporation into pressed flower pictures. The flowers to be pressed *must be dry*, at their prime, and stripped of their leaves. Pick the flowers on a dry day, and do not condition them (unless they have travelled a long distance). Probably you will pick from your garden, but if you have to visit another garden to get material or are getting it wild, then you can take with you a block of plastic foam which has been soaked in water. Keep the flower stem in this until you reach home again. Some enthusiasts keep in their car an old thick telephone directory or out-of-date wallpaper sample book equipped with blotting paper sheets, and start the pressing process right away. Flowers and leaves with thin tissue will give the best results. Succulents and heavy-textured fleshy flowers that consist predominantly of water are best forgotten. Experience is the best tutor, but it is interesting to note that whereas the white daffodils tend to get 'papery' and faded, the ordinary yellow and bi-colour varieties press well and keep their colour. Remember conservation principles when picking in the countryside, for many wild flowers are in danger of extinction.

The stems and leaves required are pressed separately. Stems must be picked with 'outline' in mind, choosing some straight ones and others with interesting curves. Keep them in place on the paper with strips of gummed tape. Clematis and buttercup stems are good for pressing purposes. Pure colours rather than the more subtle shades or bi-colours dry best. The pure hues of yellow and orange are seldom affected by the drying process. Iceland poppies, celandines, buttercups and marigolds retain their colour very well. Blue tends to fade but happily delphiniums and lobelias remain a good colour. Pink is usually good but reds and purples tend to take on a brown shade. White tends to become pleasantly creamy. Many white flowers, including daisies, cow parsley and hellebores press well. Green leaves give differing shades of colour. Grey leaves are usually very successful. Leaves picked in autumn usually retain their lovely colouring, probably because nature has started the dehydration process.

The method of pressing is very simple.

Silver leaves add luminosity to this design

First cut off the stems. Have ready either a flower press or heavy book and very carefully place your flowers or petals between two sheets of clean blotting paper. There must be no creasing or over-lapping if a good standard of pressing is to be achieved.

Flower presses can be bought, but are easily made, with 2 pieces of thick plywood or chipboard about 30 cm (12 in.) square; 10 sheets of thick card, 18 sheets of blotting paper of the same size; and 4 bolts with wing-nuts 10–12.5 cm (4–5 in.) long. Drill holes to take the bolts at each corner of the two pieces of wood. Cut the corners off the sheets of paper and card and place them with 2 sheets of blotting paper and one of card alternately. Start and finish with card. Place these between the two pieces of wood and insert the bolts from the bottom with the wing-nuts on top. The advantage of using a flower press is that the plant material does not wrinkle. If the wing-nuts are tightened daily for the first ten days of pressing the plant material becomes tissue thin.

Label each layer with the types of material they contain, whether flowers, petals, stems, centres or leaves. Many compound flowers such as roses are better taken apart, and pressed as separate petals. It is possible to halve a daffodil and then press each piece, making two flowers for use in picture-making. Separated petals can be reassembled with their own centre or other smaller flowers can be placed to make a new centre. There is no limit to the possibilities of such variations. The plant material must remain in the press or book for at least three months, but it is less likely to fade when exposed to light if it remains in the press for six months to a year.

Large and heavy leaves unsuitable for pressing in a book or press may be placed between sheets of newspaper and put under a carpet or large rug. Bracken and ferns are examples. They must remain there for three weeks or longer until quite dry. In addition, large flat leaves may be placed between two pieces of newspaper and pressed firmly with a warm, not hot iron. This speeds up the drying process. Place them under a carpet between sheets of newspaper for a week or so to complete the drying process. If they appear to wilt when ironed they usually stiffen as they dry.

Preserving with desiccants

The flowers and plant material that cannot respond or are not suitable for preservation by the glycerine and water method, or for air-drying or pressing can be dried in a desiccant. Briefly, this means burying the plant material in a substance which will draw all moisture from the plant. The great advantage is that, thus treated, they retain their natural forms and shapes and, often their colouring too. The desiccant materials most often used to withdraw and retain the water from plant material are: alum; borax; sand, and silica gel. Choose the grain suitable for the kind of flower being treated, bearing in mind that petals must be supported, but not crushed, by the weight of the desiccant. All desiccants need to be dried after use in order to ensure that they will take up moisture again. To do this, spread the used desiccant on a baking tray and place in a slow oven for about an hour, stirring occasionally.

Alum and borax are bought from chemist's shops and are not expensive. They are suitable for delicate petals but do not support heavier flowers. Borax has the disadvantage of clinging to the plant material. The fine alum granules do not penetrate too well into the petal crevices. Flowers dry in seven to ten days.

Silica gel crystals are the most expensive. Fine crystals are supplied by proprietary brands,. but those bought from the chemist can be crushed to make them into a finer grain. Because it is the most rapid dehydrant it provides tremendous value, for the more rapidly water is withdrawn the better the colour retention. However, if flowers are left in too long they will become very brittle. Flowers take from one to three days to dry out.

Sand is the heaviest and slowest desiccant. It supports flowers well and is easy to pour into flower heads. Mixed half and half with borax it makes a good general purpose desiccant. Sand requires cleaning before using it for the first time. Fill a bucket three-quarters full of sand. Top up with water. Stir, then allow to settle. Pour off any floating pieces. Repeat this several times with clean water each time. Dry sand in slow oven for several hours. When dry, sift the sand. Flowers take fourteen days or more to dry out but can be left in the sand indefinitely without harm.

You will require an air-tight tin, or plastic or cardboard box (these can be sealed with sticky tape), stub wires, a meat or

This ring is made from a hogweed flower

Victorian Jewellery

These exquisite examples are based on Victorian designs.

Method: the design is worked out on plastic foam or modelling clay; selected items of plant material are covered with several layers of gold or silver paint and when dry are applied to the base. This can be either clay or a commercially-produced gilded disc. When clay is used, one must work quickly to position the items before the clay hardens. Non-stringing glue is used to apply material to the gilded disc. Texture and shape is provided by minute plant material such as seeds, grains and calyxs. Tendrils from climbing plants are excellent for outlines.

Such intricate and delicate work requires great patience and skill as well as an understanding of design principles

Curving tendrils balance gold-painted plant material, including seeds and foliage

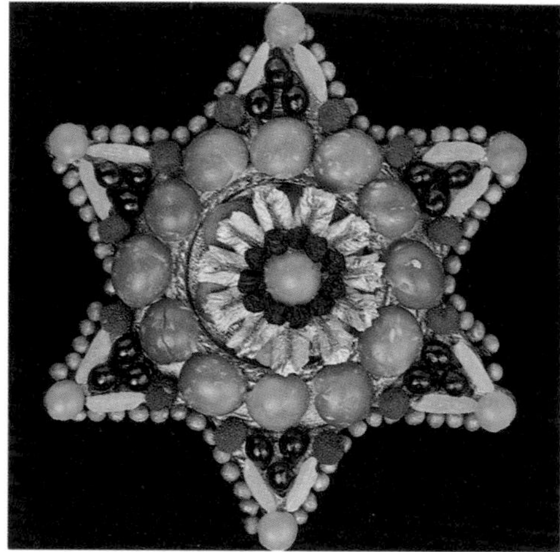

Gold-painted leaves, split peas, rice and other tiny seeds are used in this brooch

An ivory-coloured brooch with a tiny spray of ivy: a cross entwined with ivy was an emblem of Christianity and was often used for mourning jewellery

The lentils used in this brooch have the colour and texture of coral – a favourite in Victorian jewellery. The feather-like top feature is made from mimosa leaves

Above: the use of amethysts and small pearls adds realism to this brooch

Below: this design is given perfect balance by the pendant drops

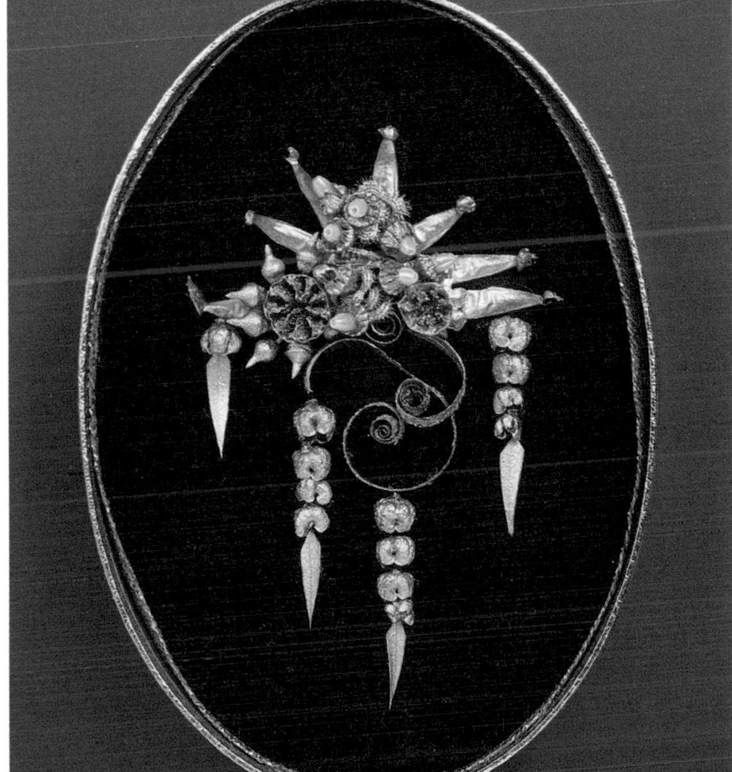

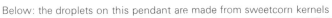

Above: the designer of this brooch has used spiralled passion flower tendrils

Below: the droplets on this pendant are made from sweetcorn kernels

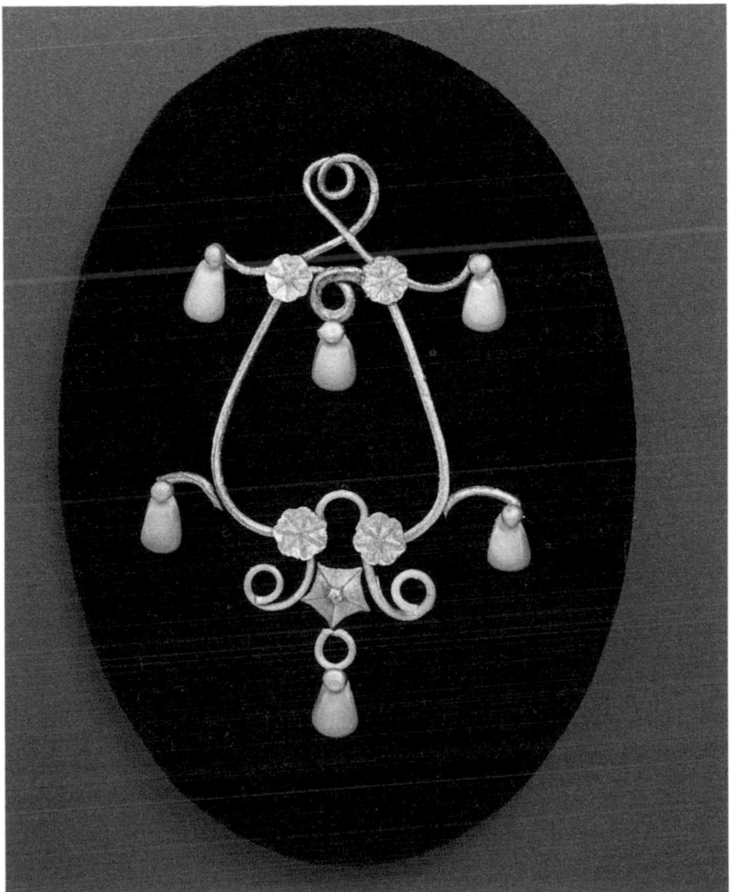

The absence of glass allows greater depth of design: this dried arrangement uses seedheads, cones, glycerined leaves, nuts and artificial flowers made from seedheads and dried leaves.

other pointed skewer, a fine paint brush and the desiccant of your choice. The plant material you are to work on must be in perfect condition and bone dry. Cut off most of the stem, and push a stub wire down through the head of the flower (or through the stem end). If you push it in from the flower, then coil the wire under the head so that it is out of the way. The flower head is easier to wire at this time. Pour a 2.5 cm (1 in.) layer of desiccant into the box or tin used and lay the flower head on this. Then gently sift the desiccant over the petals of the flower. Great care should be taken to see that the grains fill all the crevices, so that the petals are well-supported. Use a skewer or other pointed article to help the guiding of the crystals and to put the petals in place again. Shake the box gently from time to time to help the distribution of the desiccant. Continue pouring and shaking gently until the flower is covered by 1 cm ($\frac{1}{2}$ in.) of the granules. Then put on the box or tin lid and seal. Affix a label bearing the date and a description of the plant material.

When the drying period is concluded, slowly pour the desiccant through your fingers until the flower falls out gently into your hand. It should feel dry and papery. (If it does not, then it is not thoroughly dried out and you must put it back in the desiccant and the tin.) Using a soft small brush, remove any remaining granules. If any petals come away, put them back into position with a touch of clear glue. Flowers dried with desiccants are very fragile and must be handled with great care. They must not be arranged in water or used in any but very dry atmospheres as they can re-absorb water and moisture

These flowers, which have been dried using a desiccant, include primulas

from the air. The delicate colours will fade if in strong light so care must be taken to avoid sunlight. When not in use, store in a dry place in a container containing a little desiccant. The wire stem of the flower can be pushed into a piece of dry oasis placed in the box so that the flower head is not damaged. The wire can be covered when the flower is arranged with florist's tape or with a hollow dried stem.

Flowers dried in this manner are exquisite and are as near to a live flower in colour and shape as one could hope for. They look very beautiful in dried arrangements, garlands, swags and plaques or in flower pictures that have their glass raised a space from the background. Daffodils, hellebores, mimosa,. narcissi, primroses and tulips are spring flowers that dry well in desiccants. Try carnations, clematis, delphiniums and hollyhocks (dry florets singly), pansies, poppies, pinks, marigolds and roses in summer, and dahlias and zinnias in late summer. There are very many other possibilities – so experiment and discover.

Flower pictures To make a flower picture you need, first of all, a picture frame, preferably a lightweight one, of the size and variety you prefer. The glass must press firmly against the material. It is usually best to choose the frame before planning your design so that both will be in harmony and in scale. Consider whether you need ordinary or non-reflecting glass. The latter is more expensive and a little opaque.

The backing of the picture can be hardboard or Daler-board (sold for oil painting). It must be rigid and thick (3 mm ($\frac{1}{8}$ in.) or more). Any softer material is no good, although strawboard or cardboard, if rigid and thick enough, can be used. A smooth-textured finish is advised – use paper, fabric or matt emulsion paint. A latex glue

These two very different pictures composed of preserved flowers and foliage incorporate plant materials that have been dried in various ways: dehydration, silica gel, borax, sand, pressing and air-drying. The backgrounds have been chosen to complement the colours of the plant material used. The soft blue velvet (above) is a perfect foil for the predominantly gold design; the deep green (right) provides a restful background for the white, silver and green plant materials, which are highlighted with touches of gold. Among the flowers used are hellebores, pansies, fuchsia, crocus, summer snowflakes and *Helichrysum*. Extra interest is supplied by skeletonized poppy heads, grasses and seedheads, to which are added contrived flowers made from honesty seed-pods centred with a dried flower. In both designs foliage plays an important part, providing excellent outline materials and contrast in form, shape and colour – both brilliant and muted

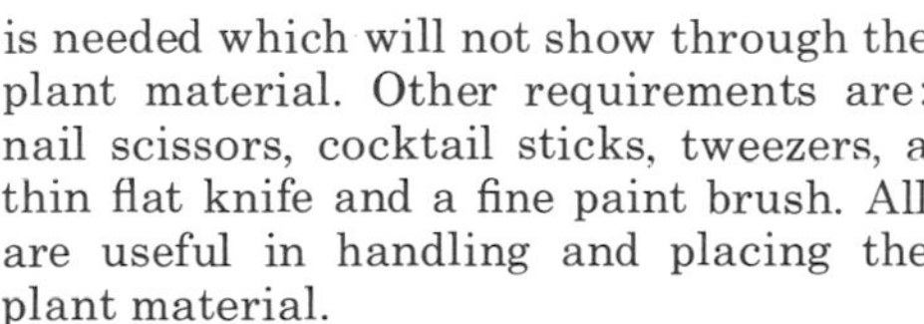

is needed which will not show through the plant material. Other requirements are: nail scissors, cocktail sticks, tweezers, a thin flat knife and a fine paint brush. All are useful in handling and placing the plant material.

With the frame, backing and pressed material all prepared and at hand, plan the design. Lift plant material gently with the knife and tweezers. When satisfied with your design pattern, just touch the pieces of plant material with one or two spots of glue. As it is a two dimensional medium, depth can only be suggested. If you cannot complete the picture at one session, place a piece of glass over the incomplete design until you can continue. When you have finished, make sure that the glass on the inside is immaculate as it cannot be cleaned afterwards. Put the glass and picture into the frame and pad the back with more cardboard or paper to ensure a really tight fit. *This is essential* so that the glass presses down on the leaves and flowers and prevents any wrinkling or curling. Complete the picture by covering the back with brown paper, sealed all round with masking or brown-paper tape. Put in screw-eyes for hanging the picture.

Collages

A collage is a collection of materials, not necessarily joined, attached to a visible background and made to hang or stand. Plant material must predominate if it is to be entered for a show. In a way, a collage is really an extension of making pressed flower pictures. They can be made of pressed plant material or can have the addition of dried and preserved materials, shells, cork and other non-plant material all assembled on a background to create a pleasing picture. While the flower picture as a rule, draws on nature for inspiration, the collage offers artists and designers an opportunity for more impressionist and abstract interpretations.

Backgrounds will vary in colour and texture according to needs and tastes. With the addition of more solid materials such as cork, shells, beans and other forms and shapes, the question of framing arises. If a glass front is required then the frame must be sufficiently deep to allow space for these items. Probably for this reason many collages are not framed in the conventional way, and have no glass.

Whether the collage is to hang or to stand when completed is up to the individual. Given the wide choice of suitable materials – pieces of bark, stitiching or other pattern making shapes – and the variety of subjects – landscapes, abstract patterns, or a play on plant structure – the opportunities are limitless. Chapter 15, p. 204 gives useful points on collage design.

7. Favourite Flowers and Designs in the Home

She has a touch with flowers; a way
To make the severed blossoms whole.
And plan them so that we may
Observe a field within the bowl.

Removes some, moves some to the edge.
Adds foliage – so that we see
Confettied summer in the hedge
Or burst of bluebells by a tree.

Grants country thoughts a longer lease
And with deft hands creates at will
A meadow on her mantelpiece,
A wild wood on her windowsill

MARGARET CALLAWAY

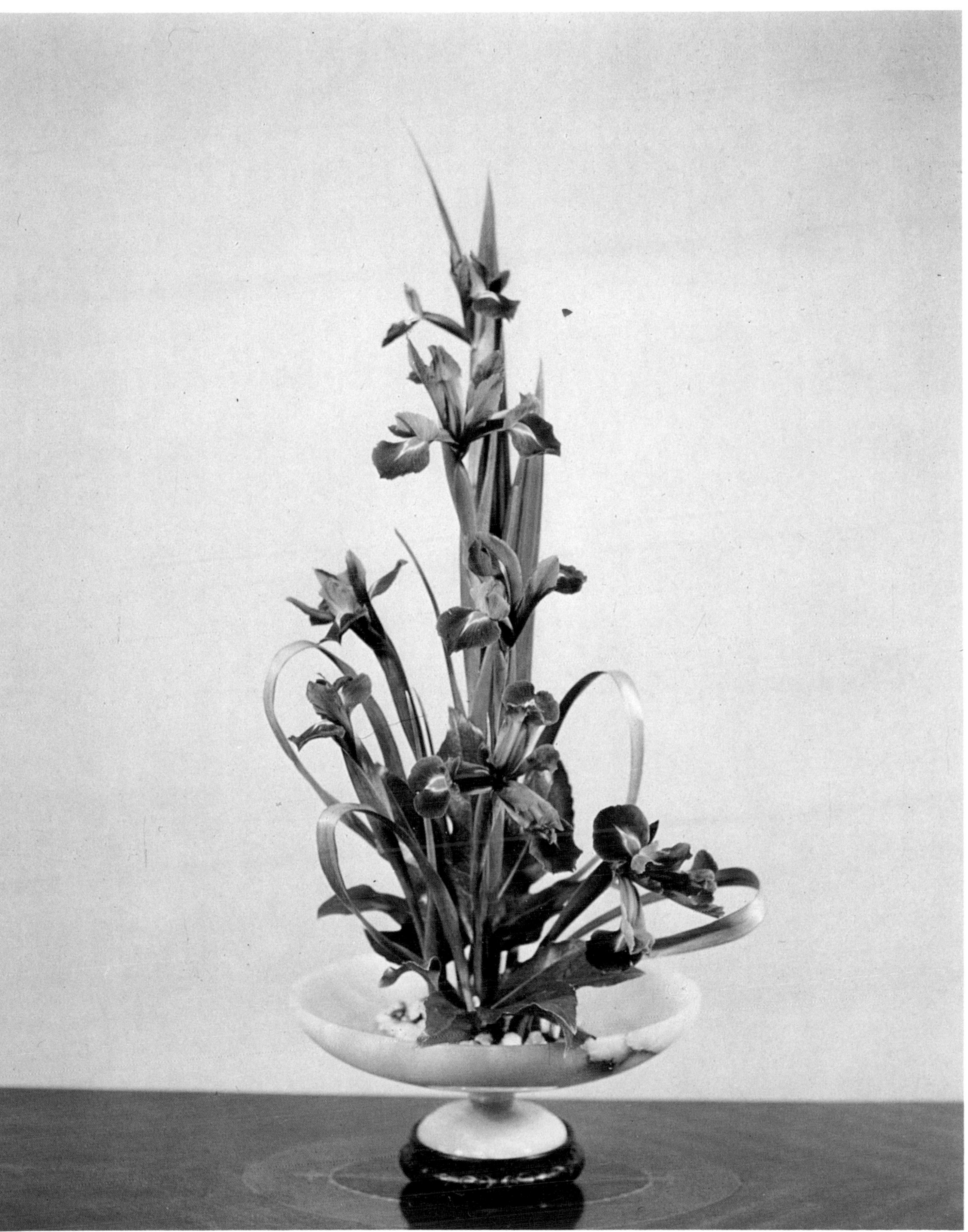

'Most roads lead men homewards' wrote John Masefield, and there can be little doubt that both men and women see their home as the centre of their existence. Homes will be as varied as the people who inhabit and plan them, but although they vary from the modest two-room flatlet or the country cottage to the really large and luxurious houses, they are all 'home' to someone. They are the places where we spend at least half our lives.

It is impossible to cover all the different backgrounds, rooms and lifestyles, so let us think about the average home which, though it may differ in appearance, will be similar in size one to another. It should not be difficult for those with either smaller or larger homes to increase or reduce the scale and needs accordingly. It must be borne in mind, however, that wherever flowers are placed in the house they must be arranged in the position they are to stand. It is impossible to achieve correct scale and appearance away from the final setting.

The entrance hall

From the flower arranger's point of view, this is perhaps one of the most important places in the home to have some kind of decoration. The entrance door of the house will lead everyone through this area, whether they be the members of the family, guests, or the casual caller. This is where important first impressions will be made. Much more important is the aesthetic effect on those who enter. They will either feel a warm welcome and a lived-in atmosphere, or cold and rejected as if just passing through a functional and dreary area leading to the main rooms.

The entrance of a house is, of course, a functional place. Hats and coats have to be removed and gloves, parcels and dog leads put down, so space is at a premium here. It would be inviting disaster if the flowers were in the way, or in danger of being knocked and damaged. Generally, there is a small table against the wall and perhaps a mirror for checking appearances of those going out. This will mean that the facing vertical style arrangement described in Chapter 4 will almost certainly serve you best in this position. It takes very little plant material and requires an upright or pillar vase, or a footed container, well pinholder or small bowl. If you choose long-lasting foliage you need probably only four or five flowers which can be replaced if they droop, while the framework of foliage continues longer. City apartment dwellers can use their house plant foliage, for so very little is required. A framework of glycerined beech leaves would last for ever, if anyone wants them to! Dip the stem ends in melted candle-end wax so that they do not go mouldy in the water the flowers must have.

Alas, halls can be draughty even if the front door has draught proofing. The door must be opened at intervals and in comes the wind. The worst destroyer of plant material is draught. Cold winds 'scorch' leaves and petals growing in a garden or hedge. Try to position your flowers strategically to avoid draughts whether from the front door or up and down the staircase. If the hall has reasonable space then a chest gives a roomier surface and a more generous bowl of flowers looks lovely on

Right: a vertical design of great elegance, well suited to the furnishings. Delightful *Lilium martagon* (Turk's cap lilies) and *Allium* seedheads are arranged with aspidistra leaves and *Maranta*, a house plant with striking foliage

Opposite, top left: a warm welcome in the entrance hall is given by a copper bowl of red gladioli, foliage and *Macleaya cordata (Bocconia cordata)* seedheads

Opposite, top right: a white pot full of single white chrysanthemums placed on a small painted table looks crisp and clean. The visual impact of this fashionable style is provided by the solidly-packed flower heads and their yellow centres. (See p. 96)

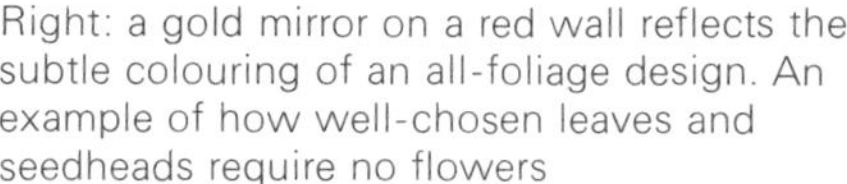

Right: a gold mirror on a red wall reflects the subtle colouring of an all-foliage design. An example of how well-chosen leaves and seedheads require no flowers

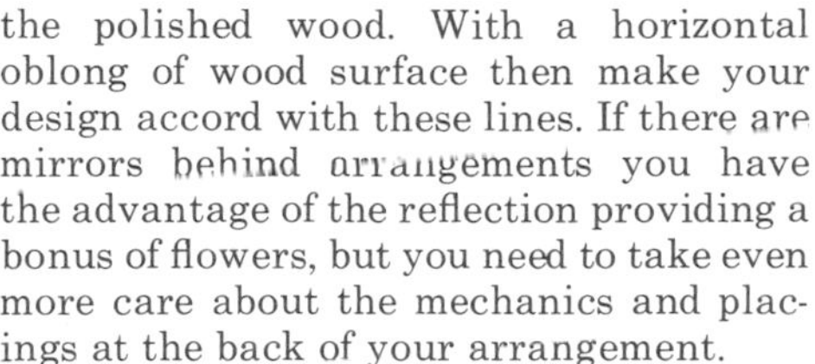

the polished wood. With a horizontal oblong of wood surface then make your design accord with these lines. If there are mirrors behind arrangements you have the advantage of the reflection providing a bonus of flowers, but you need to take even more care about the mechanics and placings at the back of your arrangement.

Time, resources and life-style will dictate what is best for your hall and your needs. Should you have leisure, some space and a garden then a basket - long and low with a liner inside it - and filled with spring flowers, or in summer with roses and honeysuckle, not only looks lovely and is seen by everyone but also fills the house with its scent. If you have only a small garden and hall and resources then the upright arrangement described will still bring colour and life. If you have little time to spare, not much space and few resources, house-plants in an attractive container might be the answer. Small copper preserving pans are especially good and their warm reflecting surface makes the hall welcoming. Place polythene inside as a liner, and some pieces of charcoal to keep it 'sweet' (as there is no drainage) and then place in it two or three house-plants with interesting foliage, of varieties that look good together and are not temperamental. Many pot plants are very good-tempered but others are fickle. Your florist will advise you and details are given in Chapter 9 where making *pot-et-fleur* designs is described. Into this group of pot plants place a small tube or funnel type holder which is concealed by the plant foliage and then add a few cut flowers. The flowers can be changed - or even left out if you are especially rushed - but they do make all the difference.

The living room

This will be the room where flowers will be looked at and enjoyed for the longest period of time. It is worthwhile to seek out a position in the room that lends itself well to this purpose. If possible, choose a wall with a good plain background colour, because a wall-paper or curtain pattern may confuse the pattern of your flower design. Should your walls be patterned, then you must give careful consideration to this factor. Sometimes one wall or alcove can be of plain colour in a room that is otherwise patterned, where it provides a good contrast. Neutral or pastel colours make superb background colour against which the flowers can be enjoyed without the conflict of patterns. Mirrors have their uses if the arranger is aware of certain challenges they provide, but they do have the advantage of reflection and a reasonably plain background, rather than a patterned wall.

Select a piece of furniture on which to place the arrangement. It need not be a table: a shelf or alcove is equally useful. Wherever it stands it is wise to have a piece of plate glass cut and levelled to fit the top exactly. If you cut out a template in newspaper the glaziers will cut the glass to fit your surface. This pays dividends, for you will have no worries about water or pollen dropping on to precious furniture. Black plate glass is available and looks good on oriental wood. If you do not follow this advice take great care to place a cork or rush mat under your arrangement so that the furniture surface is safe. The mat should not be visible unless it provides a base suitable in texture and shape, or if it provides visual weight at the base.

Right: branches of creamy-green cherry blossom *(Prunus x yedoensis)* contrasting with the stone mantelpiece

Below right: spring flowers arranged as a graceful adjunct to a buhl clock bracket

Below: a bronze figure in an alcove holds a bouquet of roses, their foliage flowing down gracefully on each side

In modern rooms, pottery containers are often used. They look fine, but since pottery is porous you can find an unwanted circle on your wood furniture unless the base is stood on a mat or on plate glass. Should this misfortune happen, metal polish rubbed in the wood may remove it, or there are some proprietary polishes available to eradicate the mark. A circle of baize or felt glued under the pot is a wise precaution. The facing arrangement against a room wall can be line, massed-line or mass in outline. The containers can be modern, contemporary or period. These will be chosen according to your room and personal tastes. There is sound advice and guidance on these points in other chapters.

Where in a sitting room other than against a wall do flowers look attractive? Some modern houses are built without fire-places, but the open fire is returning to

Above: a flowing design for the end of a mantelpiece
Above right: single chrysanthemums and yellow berries placed in a fine bronze candelabrum which flatters their colouring
Right: interesting possessions such as this 'Nubian' figure, if well incorporated, give impact to a slightly exotic design

popularity. The majority of houses still have mantelpieces even if the space below no longer houses a real or simulated fire. A mantelshelf is perfect for flowers, providing no drying ripples of heat are wafting up from a fire below. If they are, then decorations must be confined to dried and preserved plant material. Such conditions will suit them, but will kill fresh flowers. With the advent of central heating many fireplaces have been sealed over. The mantelshelf above is perfect for either a central symmetrical placement or two asymmetrical ones placed each end of the shelf. For a special occasion, and if the shelf is sufficiently long, all three could be used. Because the mantelshelf is raised it is a particularly good place for your flowers.

Do not put your flowers at ground level in the actual fireplace. If the aperture is not filled in, a fierce draught is being drawn up or blowing down the chimney itself. Flowers do not really look right in this position, where they are at ground level and probably hidden by people standing on the hearth. The Victorians and some of their predecessors loved to fill the fireplace with ferns, bulrushes, Japanese fans and anything else that fitted in, but this probably was caused by an excess of zeal in seeking to decorate any open place left in the room. Rather find some lichen-covered logs or pine cones, and put them in the actual fire-basket or a wicker basket if you want to decorate what looks to you like an over-bare hearth. Flowers never seem to look happy there and would almost certainly give more pleasure elsewhere in the room.

Room proportions will dictate whether a small elegant sparse pedestal can be put in a suitable corner or space. If it can, and if it is arranged lightly and in no way 'stuffed' it can be very pleasing indeed. The flowers once more gain grace by being elevated, and can be seen and enjoyed from all parts of the room. Lilac blossom or sprays of roses look really superb in this position, particularly on the wood column or torchère type of stand on which oil lamps were placed in times past. Regency Nubian figures holding flat bases on which a tray was placed are marvellous for rich fruit and flower arrangements – but such possessions are rare indeed! Light wrought iron pedestals, however, are not expensive and can very often be adjusted to several heights. Very decorative alabaster and marble pedestals are being imported but, of course, are more expensive.

Few people seem to realize the possibilities of a small round table, or other small

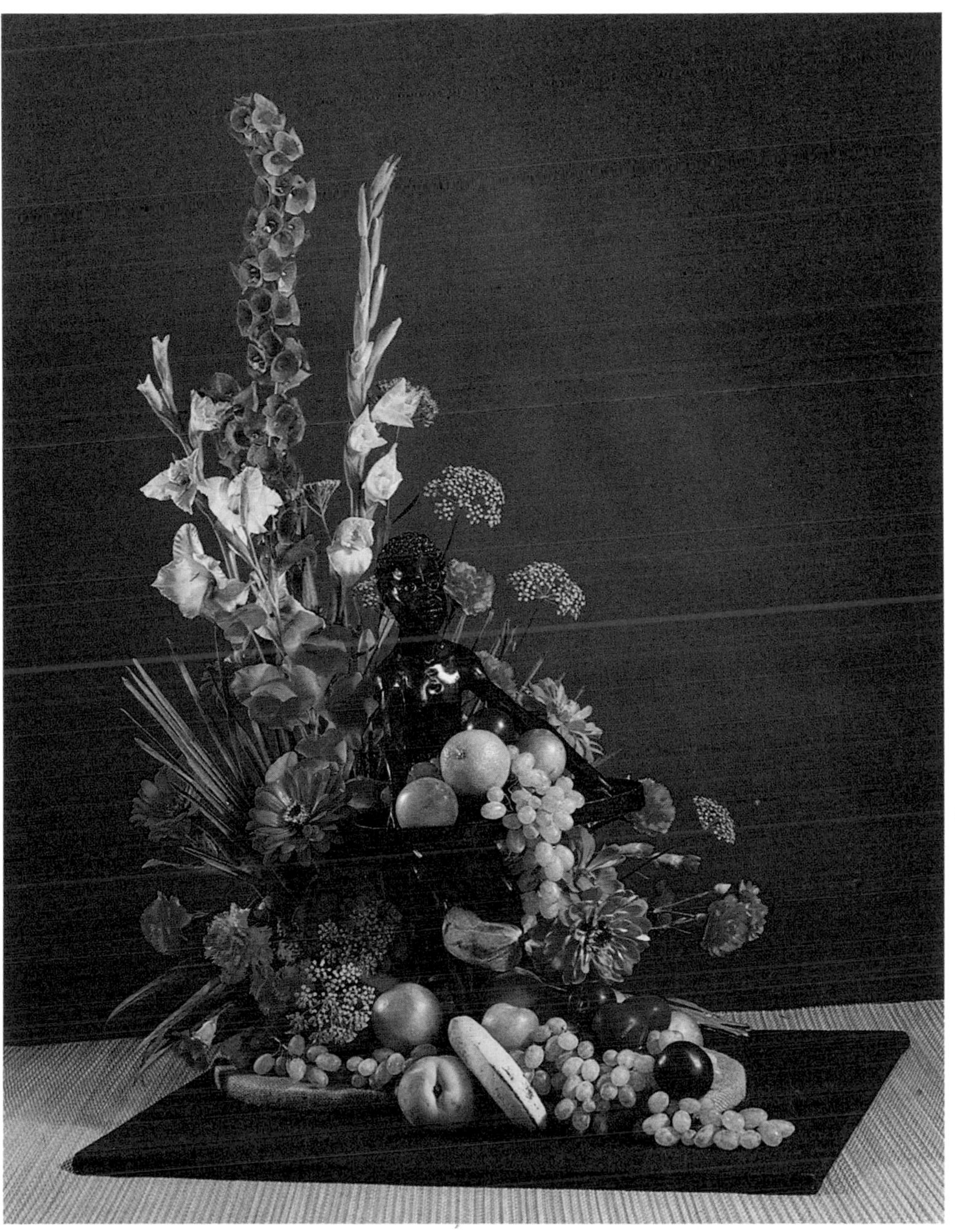

occasional tables for holding what is, in effect, a small pedestal arrangement. They look very lovely, do not take a large amount of flowers to complete and they give great scope for sprays of foliage or blossom to flow down gracefully. For the modern living room, low oblong coffee tables offer scope for modern or abstract designs in chunky or rough textured modern pottery. An interesting piece of driftwood if well-placed can be as decorative as a piece of modern sculpture – which, after all, is what it really is. It could be free-standing and making its own statement, or if you wish to introduce colour then one or two flowers strong in shape and form or fruits or foliage could bring further visual and textural interest.

Currently in favour is the taste for using a collection of one kind of flower – daffodils, single chrysanthemums or similar flowers – cutting their stems at about the same length, and then packing all the flower heads tightly into a square white pot or something similar. The result is exciting from the point of view of the impact of sheer vibrant colour and creates a sort of exclamation mark in the room, as a bright cushion, picture or some specially striking *objet d'art* might do. See p. 93, top right. It is a matter of personal taste whether you care for flowers placed in this way. No skill or mechanics are required, so that is in its favour. It is not inexpensive, however, for to get the impact quite a quantity of flower heads are required and with the present price per purchased bloom, one filled pot could be costly. Those who love to see flowers individually and with leaves might well prefer a single flower with leaves in a stem vase. Those who grow their own flowers might not want to cut a whole bed of perfect flowers to achieve the necessary effect. But this is certainly a dramatic way to make an impact with living colour, and it would be a dull world without stimulating differences in personal tastes and styles.

This unusual quadruped Victorian container, used on small pieces of furniture, allows four roses to be enjoyed individually

Below: two wall vases hold flowers which suit their differing qualities and appearance. The strong colours and graceful foliage of nasturtiums complement an ancient bronze Chinese basket, whereas the more delicate gilded ceramic holder needs material lighter in colour and form

The striking free form modern designs seem to be a half-way house and a happy compromise between the more conventional flower arrangements and the abstract designs of plant material or flowers used as a decorative mass colour design element.

Writing desks and side-tables give opportunities for small bowls and posies arranged to give pleasure in more detail to those who look at the flowers. It will be in these arrangements that the detail of the markings in the petals of such flowers as pansies or salpiglossis will be enjoyed, or the lovely 'flight' pattern of sweet-peas, or the perfume of lilies of the valley, daphnes or violets. Two or three fresh rose-buds or a china-blue patch of forget-me-nots would

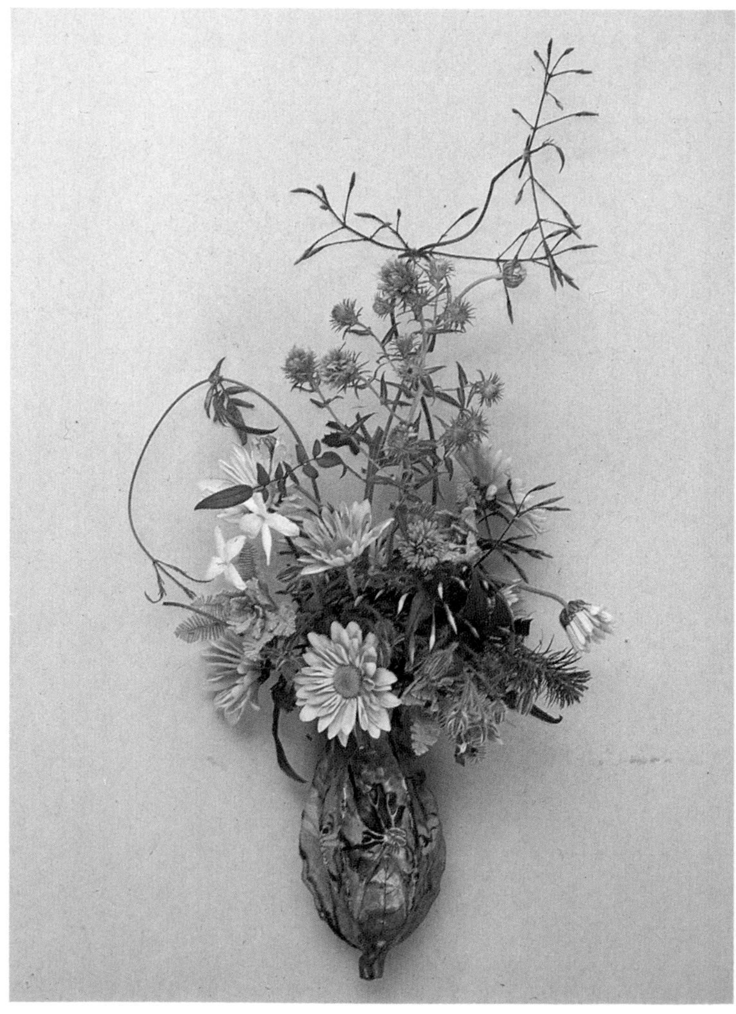

also be charming. An interesting lichened twig with small cones with some leaves of interesting muted texture and colour, will be just as absorbing as fragrant flowers and pleasing to view at close quarters.

Surprisingly few people think about the possibilities of wall vases. Although it is now difficult to find interesting vases and bowls, it is still possible to pick up Victorian wall vases that have great decorative appeal. A favourite porcelain design was that of the nest of a humming-bird made in a three-cornered envelope shape with simulated stitching of the vines which the bird used to fix the leaves together. Many of these vases have a velvet oval behind them to prevent water and flowers staining the wall. Chinese bronze hanging baskets lend themselves to a few flowers and some flowing vines and tendrils, which look lovely outlined against the background of the wall. Because the living room is almost certainly the largest room in the house its decoration requires great restraint. Careful planning of what kind of arrangement of flowers will best suit the room is essential. In almost every room of this kind – unless it is a very special festive occasion – one lovely design in a position where it can be seen by everyone and enjoyed without complicating the use and life of the room, and one smaller arrangement for close-quarter viewing, is about all that is needed at any time. Lots of pots of flowers dotted about look fussy and cluttered, however lovely the flowers may be in themselves. You want quiet relaxing music in much-used rooms rather than the cacophony of a brass band, which requires an out-of-door or very large setting. Let your flowers enhance the setting you live in without overpowering it.

The dining room

Every meal is more stimulating with some flowers to look at as you eat, whether it is a boiled egg or something very delicious and exotic. In the course of a day there may be many different occasions at your table. Flowers will be looked at closely in this situation, so whatever the occasion see that their condition is crisp and positive. For the everyday meal few things can equal a bowl of nasturtiums with their warm and vibrant colours, interesting 'umbrella' leaves and quartered seedheads. A bowl of roses or field daisies would be just as pleasing. There is something forthright and invigorating about the simple things of life that no complicated and exotic affair can match.

The everyday family or bachelor meal is best not complicated in presentation of food or flowers. The presentation is important none the less, as flower arrangers and good cooks would agree. It is rare that these two skills do not go together in the same person. Both work with impeccable natural material, in the sensitive treatment of which lies the difference between excellence and failure. However painstaking the preparation of food or flowers, the effort will be wasted if the precious raw materials are not also presented with delicacy and flair. Care must be taken, time and thought given and specialist knowledge acquired, if a simple meal or a bowl of marigolds are to be memorable in their different ways. When a more sophisticated meal is being presented, the flowers provided for the occasion should complement with restrained embellishment food that has been prepared with great expertise.

Here is one of the four basics in action, **harmony:** if the situation is simple, so too should the presentation be, and vice versa. For boiled eggs and honey, perhaps a blue and white check breakfast cloth and a brown pottery bowl with marigolds would adorn the table. As times and social conditions have changed, many families now live and eat in their kitchens, and entertain their guests on a scrubbed stripped pine table. Simple flowers look fine in these surroundings. Nothing could better a wooden bowl or old kitchen mortar, filled with all the lovely mixed herbs that are so easy to grow, even if you only have a window box. Bowls of fruit with glossy laurel leaves tucked amongst them are reminiscent of the sunny Mediterranean or Greek islands. Wayside ferns and grasses look fresh and good in such circumstances. For the carefully planned meal with fine cuisine then thoughts turn to porcelain plates, silver, glass and candles. More stately flowers will be appropriate – perhaps camellias or roses in silver or glass, in harmony with the fine food and its presentation, and a relaxed social occasion in which all the components will be enjoyed.

Polished wooden dining-tables, or those of plate glass or marble need special treatment. All these tables will have differing textures, colours and shapes that must be taken into consideration. The round table will look best with an all-round arrangement in the centre, the refectory table with an oblong design. Variations on these shapes should follow their table outline, in the container chosen to be used. The texture of the wood or table surface is important, with such wide

'Frencham' roses and ivy berries combine to make an arresting table decoration

Delicate and elegant table decorations whose contrived colours complement those in the china

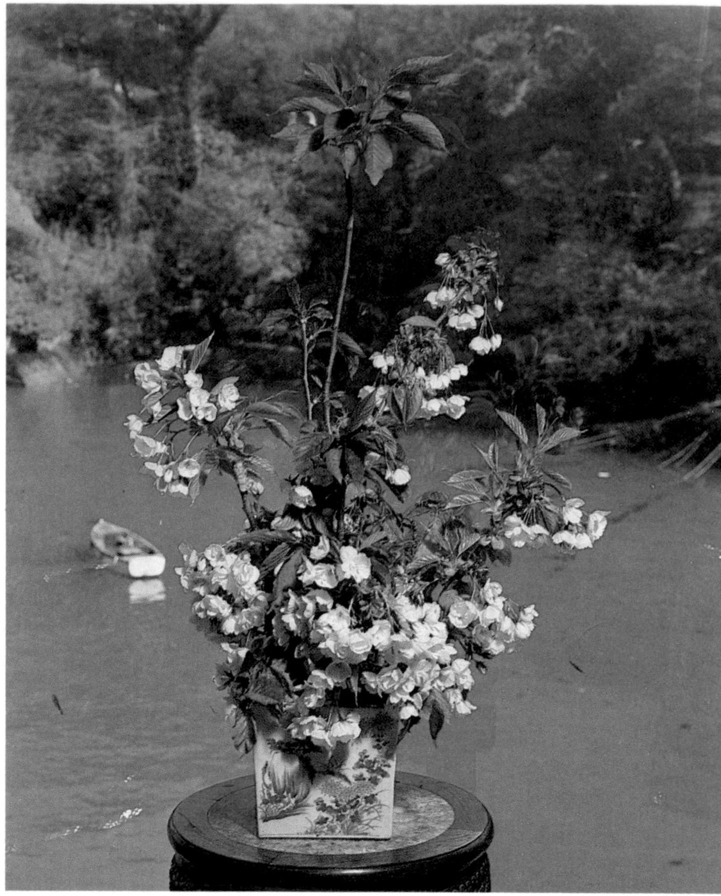

Below: pestle and mortar filled with fragrant herbs, a cool, simple and harmonious combination, suitable for a kitchen or a cottage room. Above: Backgrounds which at once emphasize and complement the arrangements placed against them. The pink blossom echoes that in the Chinese print, and the white is strong enough in character to stand out against the water beyond

Right: the *Papaver somniferum* 'Pink Chiffon' poppies provide repetition of the rose colour in the medallion above. Poppies last well if conditioned (see Chapter 2)

differences as shadowed black polished wood or scintillating plate glass. The dark wood calls for more solid flowers and foliage in rich colours, and the glass, for plant material more delicate in feeling.

Colours and patterns (if there are any) in the china, place mats or table cloths must be considered and the flowers chosen either to blend or contrast in colour. Remember that artificial light changes colour values and that blue will look dead, whereas soft pinks look their best. Yellows, surprisingly enough, lose the luminous quality they have in daylight. The occasion, and even the season of the year must be given thought. Choose cool greens, white and cream on a sultry summer evening, but colours that give a warm feeling in the cold months. An evening or event which has been carefully planned will give lasting pleasure. The hostess can have much fun working out the details of such an occasion as deciding what dress to wear and it really demands very little more effort than that.

In warm summers much entertaining is done on patios or by swimming pools. Simplicity is the keynote for informal occasions out of doors. Fun decorations for a special party could be used, such as an old wooden wheelbarrow filled with geraniums, or a wicker log basket with tall summer grasses and seedheads.

Bedrooms

There should always be flowers in your guest bedroom. Nothing elaborate is called for; a posy on the dressing table or chest will suffice. If possible, pick something sweet-smelling from the garden but if you have to buy them choose flowers that are pastel in colour and welcoming in spirit. If your guests are staying longer than the life of the flowers be sure to replace the posy or else whisk it away. Nothing could convey the message of a welcome out-stayed more than some withered flowers!

Do not forget your own room. A stem vase with one lovely flower would give a lift to the start or the end of the day and smooth away some of the rough edges of present-day living. 'Home is where the heart is' we are told, and there are few people whose hearts do not beat a little more happily if they can see a few flowers around them. Let flowers play a part in the pattern of daily life in your home. They will remind you of uncomplicated country things and will help you and everyone else who sees them to accept the complexities of life outside your own four walls.

Around the house

Kitchen and bathroom window-sills make good homes for pot plants that provide such useful foliage for those without gardens. Many staircases provide space on a turn or bend for a dried or preserved arrangement in a tall pot on the floor or even on a small three-legged table – but *only* if there is ample space. The top of the staircase is a good place to hang a home-made mobile of strange bird outlines or butterflies made from dried stems and leaves. Children will be fascinated as the draughts on the stairs send the small shapes whirling around.

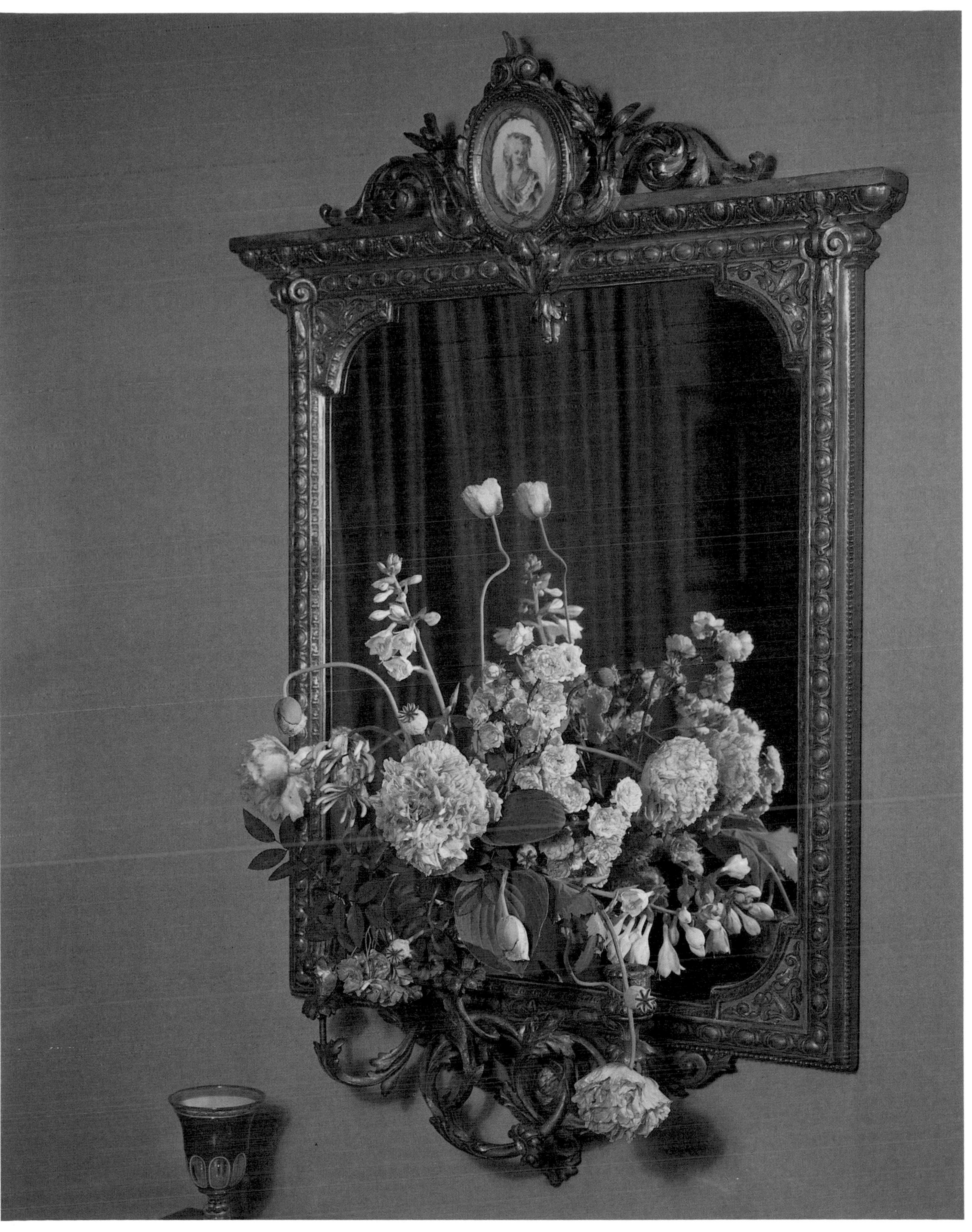

8. Special Occasions

Formal Special Occasions
Eve Taylor

Informal Party Flowers
Richard Jeffery

Beauty itself does of itself persuade
The eyes of men without an orator.
WILLIAM SHAKESPEARE 1564–1616

An example of the continuing importance of foliage and flowers to any celebration or notable event. These Christmas preparations are a detail from a Victorian painting by G B O'Neill

Formal special occasions

Formal occasions do not demand clever flower arrangements. The aim should be to welcome guests, help them relax and perhaps give a talking point to stimulate conversation. When planning the flowers for any party, the overall effect should be considered. In general, one or two large arrangements are better than several small ones. If guests are to stand, as at a large cocktail party, the flowers should also be raised. The mantelpiece is a particularly good place for flowers, for guests always gravitate to the fireplace, even when there is no fire, and on entering the room flowers on the mantel invite one to come closer to enjoy them. In the home, the flowers should harmonize with the interior and be elaborate or simple according to the furnishings. Proportion is important, and whilst there are no hard-and-fast rules when arranging flowers for the home, rather than for shows, nevertheless following basic principles as regards scale, balance, unity, rhythm and transition will help the general effect. This applies whether flowers are being arranged for a party in an average home, or for a large reception in the ballroom of an hotel.

The formal dinner party

The formal dinner party, where several wines are to be used, calls for more sophisticated flowers than those for a family luncheon. Highly scented flowers, such as hyacinths, are to be avoided if vintage wine is to be taken with the meal. The acute scent of the hyacinths would spoil the bouquet of the wine, and they should be used in another situation, away from food. Generally one-sixth the table size is a good proportion for the arrangement – a round centre-piece for a round table looks best, and an oblong arrangement for an oblong table. Height depends on the seating of the guests; they do not want to have to peer round the flowers to see each other. A low arrangement, not more than 30 cm (12 in.) high, is usually right; and as the guests will be looking down on it, it is better arranged on the table, where it is to be used.

Flowers should harmonize with china, cloth and napkins and not clash with the dining-room as a whole. Nothing gives a party feeling better than candlelight, but when using candles for a dinner-table take care that the colour does not dominate.

In winter-time, when flowers are scarce, a combination of fruit and foliage can be sophisticated or simple, according to the container used and the table appointments. For the flat-dweller it is a happy solution to the 'no flowers' problem. A few leaves spared from pot plants, together with some fruits, makes a long-lasting and elegant centre-piece, especially if the china used has a design of fruit. The colour plate above shows an arrangement for the side-table in a small dining-room, to link with the Royal Worcester 'Evesham' design on the porcelain. More impact is given by the painting of fruits above the arrangement. Late autumn foliage of *Vitis vinifera* 'Brandt', together with foliage of rhododendron 'Fabia' showing its brown fretted underside, and of camellia 'Adolphe Audusson', combine with rosy apples, greeny brown pears, purple grapes, an aubergine (eggplant), a few cherries and a pineapple, on a terracotta marble and ormolu perfume burner. The pineapple never fails to give an opulent feeling to any arrangement, and in time, when its scent warns that it is well and truly ripe, it can be the basis of a delicious fruit salad for the next party!

Autumn fruits and foliage make a centrepiece which echoes the design on the china. Leaves of rhododendron 'Fabia' contrast with the polished fruits, and link with the pineapple's texture

Buffet parties

Grapes were used also in the buffet party arrangement shown, to celebrate a golden wedding in winter-time. Here 'Harvest Moon' and 'Florida' carnations were used, with foliage of *Hebe armstrongii*. Invaluable for the flower arranger, this foliage lasts weeks in water, and its subtle dull gold colour tones with everything. Another form of leaf was needed to make the transition between the carnations and spiky form of the Hebe. A few gilded leaves made the whole arrangement look tawdry, so instead bleached leaves of preserved *Magnolia grandiflora*, replaced those of the gilded ones, and the effect of the gold and cream flowers, with the grapes, also more gold than green, became elegant and fitting. The container used, an antique gilt compote of French origin, had complementary twin candelabra of gilt and ormolu at each end of the buffet-table, and white gilt-edged china.

Normally, guests at a buffet supper party are prepared either to stand, plate and glass in hand, or sit wherever a few feet of space can be found, since the party is designed to feed more people than can be seated at the dining-table. At a party where older guests are to be present – and after fifty years of marriage most of the friends of the couple will be in their

Cream and gold flowers, foliage and grapes for a Golden Wedding buffet party

A winter party: stems of dried *Hosta* seeds, bleached to a pale cream, give height to 'flowers' made up from blue-green hydrangea petals and alder cones and 'roses' of beech leaves

seventies – it is wise to prepare enough small tables and chairs for everyone to be seated. It is not easy to rise from the floor, to enjoy the pleasures of the buffet-table, when you are no longer young. A small arrangement can be made for each table to tone with those on the buffet; cloths can be cut from inexpensive material, some dull gold, some ivory. Pinking scissors will avoid having to hem the edges. The food itself can reflect the golden theme. An orange mousse looks well as a 'golden' pudding, and it is not difficult for the older guests to eat.

Cocktail, sherry and drinks parties

The cocktail party is another way of entertaining more guests than could be asked in for a meal. The cocktail shaker is once more in evidence, having been out of favour for some time, and a 'White Lady' or wine spritzer will relax the most shy of guests. Flowers for the cocktail party should be kept rather tall, as most of the guests will remain standing throughout the party. Dried flower arrangements will always start a conversation – some people love them, while others dislike them intensely. It is true that at one time dried arrangements could be colourless, dusty, poor relations, but today's preserved flowers and foliage are grand enough to take to any party. The room for the cocktail party shown below was designed as a setting for a collection of early nineteenth-century marine paintings, the decorations being mainly soft blues and greens and milky browns. The Edwardian figurine, to one side of the drinks table, holds aloft an asymmetrical arrangement of creamy glycerined foliage of *Elaeagnus ebbingei* and Solomon's seal (*Polygonatum japonica* 'variegatum'), the small leaf variety. 'Contrived' flowers from honesty and hydrangea add colour and interest. The honesty petals were dyed dusty pink with a cold-water dye and then dried. A button, or cardboard disc, is wired to a firm stem or wire, and the 'petals' then glued with a clear quick-drying gum in two circles overlapping on the centre support. When dry, a 'stamen' centre is added and the back is neatened with extra petals. Stamens can be dried ballota, which must be picked in June to retain a good green colour, or ivy berries dried in the airing cupboard, or, as here, flowers of the fatshedera, picked as soon as they form and dried in the airing cupboard, when they shrink a little but retain a good green colour (see drawing on p. 117).

Garrya elliptica, the dusty pinks and blues of hydrangea and the grey-green of *Olearia ilicifolia* blend into the colouring of the hanging silk Persian rug

Contrived flowers from honesty and hydrangeas, with glycerined foliage of *Elaeagnus ebbingei* and Solomon's seal

An arrangement in the alabaster container was designed to go under a pair of marine paintings on a side-table in the corner of the room. Here height was given with *Hosta* seed-pods, picked at the end of the year in their dry state, and immersed overnight in a mixture of two cups of domestic bleach to 4.5 litres (1 gallon) of cold water. A little detergent added to the mixture assists the process. As soon as they reach the necessary colour, stand in a block of old plastic foam, and allow to dry in a warm place.

The large leaves of the American oak were collected in their dry state and treated in the same way. After a good colour was reached, they were dried between sheets of blotting-paper and then mounted on wire stems. Leaves of the poplar *P. candicans* 'Aurora' were also preserved in late autumn, and then mounted to add another form in this arrangement. The small green flowers are petals from dried hydrangeas, tipped with glue and inserted into an alder seedhead, this having first been firmly mounted on to a wire. In turn, this may be bound to a false stem of the required length.

The 'roses' are pressed beech leaves mounted and bound to a curled centre leaf and used to link with the brown sails in the fishing-boats in the painting above. Details of these 'flowers' are shown on pages 117–19.

The decorations for this party were completed by a large grouping in the hall, where the guests removed their coats. A chest in front of a Persian rug called for muted colours, and the hydrangea was used again here dried on its own stems, to soft blues and dusty pinks, quite naturally by standing it in a very little water and allowing it to dry out. *Garrya elliptica*, with its greyish-green catkins, was at its best, and made an interesting background for the hydrangeas, *Olearia ilicifolia* × *lacunosa,* carrying through the grey-green background and causing the guests to delay their chance of a drink by stopping to discuss it.

Christmas party time

Christmas is a time when everyone likes to entertain, whether it is for a family gathering or a larger party. The dinner-table opposite is set for a small dinner party, with a traditional red-and-green colour scheme. The centre-piece is on a narrow, oblong silver tray, to prevent the syphoning of water on to a precious antique top. Norway spruce, variegated holly, and holly berries, with red ribbons for added colour, made a background for Christmas roses. There were no fresh ones to be had, and so crêpe paper ones dipped in wax were made as a substitute. Silver candlesticks with red candles gave a festive feeling, and at each place setting lay a gift in shiny red paper, tied with green ribbons and decorated with a Christmas rose and leaves for the women guests and with small fir-cones for the men. The traditional Christmas colour scheme was carried through in the drawing-room by a large grouping of evergreen foliage placed on a French commode before a gilt mirror, the value of the arrangement enhanced by its reflection there. Care must be taken that the plant material, although more flat at the back, should be as interesting as that shown in front of the container. The mirror will reflect and emphasize a badly filled-in rear view.

'Portugal laurel' (*Prunus lusitanica*), invaluable in winter-time, was used for height, with branches of Norway fir and superb pieces of the variegated holly, 'Golden King', variegated rhododendron foliage 'President Roosevelt', (so useful for giving colour in winter foliage arrangements), large fir-cones, and branches of *Hydrangea quercifolia* leaves, as a background for artificial poinsettias. A red shiny ribbon accentuates the colour, and links with the texture of the 'flowers'.

Any red, even at Christmas-time, would be a disturbing, rather than decorative feature, in the small quiet sitting-room where a log fire burns in winter. The pine surround and mantelpiece with a marine painting above set the scene for an arrangement in a low dish to one side of the mantel which held a branch of lichen, fir and holly (the variety 'Argenteo-marginata'), with browny twigs of tiny fir-cones.

Dances—large and small

The dance gives scope to the flower arranger's imagination, whether in an hotel, large hall or a private house. At one very successful New Year's Eve party a tall white reeded plaster column was placed at the entrance to the room in which the dance was held. A revolving cheese-board covered the top of the column, in the centre of which was placed the bust of a handsome young man. A mask for this

Above: the table centrepiece holds Norway spruce, variegated holly and berries, pine cones and red ribbons. A few helleborus leaves give a more realistic look to the wax Christmas roses

Below left: Portugal laurel, variegated holly 'Golden King', variegated rhododendron 'President Roosevelt', large pine cones and red silk poinsettias

Below right: ivy, variegated holly, fir, lichen and pine cones look festive but tranquil

Opposite: Adam style mirror wreathed with sprays of ribbon roses and leaves to decorate a St Valentine's Day dance
Opposite below: daffodils, Norway maple and lenten hellebores around a bronze figure at an Easter christening party

was made from papier mâché, decorated with long, drooping grey hair, beard, moustache and eyebrows – the latter being extra bushy to obviate the need for eyes! First the young man was given a garland of camellia foliage and a circlet on his head. White silk camellia flowers were tucked in at intervals. Then the column was revolved and the mask of the old man was lightly fitted to the back of the head of the bust. Some camellia foliage sprayed with 'snow' linked the division and this side of the column was decorated with a bare branch, wild polygonum (old man's beard) a small discarded bird's nest, and an old wooden egg-timer with the sand run through. A sickle, made from thick card, painted silver, completed a picture of greyness and tiredness. Diffused light helped enhance the feeling and, incidentally, cover any defects in the mask.

Hey presto, a few seconds after midnight a touch of the finger turned the old man into a young one, amusing and delighting the guests as they passed him on their way home.

On this occasion, the only decorations in the ballroom were high mantels banked lavishly with camellia foliage, white artificial camellias being interspersed here and there. In mid-winter, with no strong light in the room, the effect was very fresh and beautiful.

Engagement party or St Valentine's Day dance

An engagement party, or a dance for St Valentine's Day, also gives scope for handicraft, added to flower arrangement, to decorate a large room when flowers are scarce. Above, we see a mirror decorated for a St Valentine's Day dance. Ribbon 'roses' are bound to sprays of leaves, then mounted to form a colourful decoration on elegant Adam mirrors. The effect is enhanced by the light from grey-green candles which pick up the colouring in the painted mirrors. Red candles to match the roses would have given too Christmassy an effect. The buffet-table was draped with inexpensive grey-green taffeta lining material, and swagged with the trails of roses. More candles on the table gave the romantic effect essential to this occasion.

Christening parties

Lucky the child to have a christening party at Easter-time. The florists' shops and the gardens are bursting with glorious spring flowers, and the flower arranger's ingenuity is no longer needed, with so much from which to choose. For the christening tea, small dainty flowers are needed, usually pink, or pink and white for a girl, and blue and white for a baby boy. Because it is Easter-time, we have used pale yellow, cream and white flowers for the table seen below. To greet the guests as they arrive from church to toast this little girl, a 2 m (6-ft) high arrangement grouped around a bronze child figurine shows Norway maple (*Acer platanoides*) for height, with flowers of lime-yellow daffodils 'Spellbinder' and 'Binkie'. Bronzy green epimoides leaves are recessed, to give transition between the little girl figure and the lime-yellow daffodils. Her basket holds, of course, eggs. Guests can never resist touching these small hen's eggs, so for safety they are carefully blown, washed in detergent and bleach, allowed to dry thoroughly, then grouped on to a piece of felt the colour of the bronze. This in turn is attached by a fine wire to the handle of the basket. Stored away after the festival, in a cotton wool lined box, they are as much part of the Easter decorations here as are the handed-down Christmas tree baubles. As with the baubles, each year there are a few casualties, and they are replaced by other small blown eggs as necessary.

The early spring luncheon gives scope for massing primroses and other small

flowers in baskets, for which a white fringed yellow or lime-green linen cloth makes a fitting background.

Weddings

Perhaps the wedding gives more scope to the flower arranger than any other special occasion. All the world loves a wedding, but first and foremost it is the bride's day. Even if her wishes are not to the taste of the decorator, she should have them carried out, although sometimes it may be possible to guide her away from the more bizarre effects.

The flowers should make a beautiful setting for the bride and her attendants. Colours should be chosen to link with the

makes spectacular wedding decoration material.

Later still, *Philadelphus* in all its varieties gives effective background for white peonies, delphiniums and roses. All should have a place in the garden of anyone called upon to arrange flowers for special occasions at frequent intervals. In summer, when garden roses are plentiful, a charming colour scheme is that general favourite, apricot and cream.

Opposite is a pedestal intended to stand where the bride and groom will greet their guests. The bride's gown is of heavy cream silk, with a parchment lace veil, and her attendants are dressed in apricot coloured silk.

Opposite above: designed for a reception in early summer, sprays of *Elaeagnus macrophylla* make a graceful outline on a reeded column for Regale lilies, gladioli and pink roses 'Royal Highness' and 'Michelle Meilland'

Below left: primroses for a spring christening party, arranged in a white ceramic container
Below right: when they may be picked in quantity, primroses massed in a rustic basket look their best for a country or garden setting

gowns of the bridal party and in consultation with the florist who will make the bouquets, so that they will complement the flowers chosen to decorate the church.

Bouquets should not be attempted by the amateur. Long training goes in to the art of the wiring of flowers. A well-made bouquet will have taken into consideration the height of the bride and will be light and well-balanced. A badly made one will spoil the effect of the most exquisite wedding gown. A friendly florist will often be willing to buy in the flowers, and give a discount, if she is doing the bridal party flowers.

If the gown is to be white, nothing looks more lovely than all-white flower arrangements. Alternatively, even in winter-time a white-and-green combination looks fresh and bridal, and in springtime, when large shrubby material such as azalea 'Palestrina', white lilac, and the double peony-flowered tulip 'Mount Tacoma' are available, then it is superb.

A little later the ornamental cherry blossom *Prunus* 'Ukon', with its greeny white blossom, combined with rhododendron 'Carita Cream' or 'Jersey Cream' and late tulips of the lily-flowered variety,

Another suggestion for a wedding pedestal is to use long sprays of *Elaeagnus macrophylla,* grown in partial shade where it will throw long spindly growths. This makes an ideal outline for flowing pedestals, the silvery foliage providing a foil perhaps for sprays of lime, stripped of foliage, and cream stocks, together with the rose 'Apricot Nectar'. The texture of the stocks would look well with the silk of the gowns.

Small children attendants at a summer wedding were little girls in apricot organdie dresses who carried ribbon-hung balls of tiny cream roses. They were escorted by small boys in satin trousers of duck-egg blue with cream shirts, the colour of the bride's gown. Pedestals for the reception held 'Apricot Nectar', 'Apricot Silk' and 'Elizabeth Harkness' roses, with creamy lilies. The duck-egg blue was introduced by hydrangea plants from a specialist grower, removed from their pots, the soil being gently washed away and the roots wrapped in polythene, which provided bold patches of colour in the large arrangements.

The round table which held the cake was covered with a draped cloth of the same blue silk and was overlaid with cream organdie. Lover's knots of matching blue ribbon were interspersed with light swags of apricot roses. Behind the cake-table a complementary pedestal made a harmonizing background for photographs of the cake-cutting ceremony.

Silver wedding

The celebration of a silver wedding is another occasion when *Elaeagnus macrophylla* or its near relative *E.* × *ebbingei,* can be used to advantage. Even in the darkest days of winter this foliage is there for the cutting. Surplus leaves throughout the year may also be pressed between blotting-paper and saved for this decoration. When wired and mounted into sprays they make an excellent foundation for the palest pink flowers, when fresh *Elaeagnus* is not available.

On p. 108 is shown a buffet-table for a silver wedding party. The tall silver centrepiece holds blocks of florist's foam wrapped in foil. Pale grey candles are mounted firmly on cocktail sticks to hold them above the waterline, so that the candle wick does not absorb moisture and make them impossible to light. The foliage is inserted into the foam, with pink-tipped jasmine and the roses. Smaller flowing groups, placed in attractive silver dishes to complement the candelabra and emphasize the theme of the evening, may be grouped around the centrepiece. Similar flowers and foliage could be used, and the whole displayed on a silver-grey organdie cloth.

Ruby wedding

Forty years of marriage calls for flowers in ruby red colouring. The effect can best be obtained by using very little foliage, as green lessens the intensity of the colour, and a mixture of reds. Exclude the very orange reds, and keep to the blue and pink ones.

In summer-time the rose 'Fragrant Cloud' is a favourite and gives off a lovely but not overpowering scent. The florist's rose 'Garnet' and the long-stemmed 'Ilona' is a good choice also. If a few heads of rhododendron 'Moser's Maroon' can be found in late spring these give a deep ruby colouring amidst the collection of reds. What could be more attractive than a table laid for a ruby wedding dinner party with a pyramid of flowers on a dessert dish, matching plates and ruby glasses.

Banquets

Big receptions and banquets demand flower arrangements on a large scale. First the colour scheme must be thought out, and if any particular colouring can be applied to the event, it is courteous to incorporate this in the scheme. Perhaps the most difficult to employ is the red-white-and-blue theme. Unless the flowers are used in bold bands, the effect will be 'spotty', so the colours should be arranged in blocks of colour.

Red and white flowers can be obtained easily throughout the year, but frequently the dark-blue colour is hard to come by. A box of dried dark-blue delphiniums is a useful standby. The delphiniums need to be picked when at their best, and hung upside-down by a cord in a cool airy place until fully dry. Extra false stems may be added to give height for important groups, but all stems of dried material should be kept out of water.

It is also possible these days to find good quality 'fake' flowers, and where it is essential to work to a set scheme, these can well be incorporated to provide the missing colour range. It is best to keep these out of reach of the guests where possible, for some will most assuredly want to feel them to see if they are real. However, it is preferable not to use them unless they are absolutely necessary to the scheme.

For a large banquet a great many flowers will be required, since it means multiplying the dinner party table many times over. This is a good way of deciding how much material to order. The choicest flowers should be kept for the top table and arranged fairly low in front of the guest of honour so that guests seated

Below: the Italian wall vase holds *Magnolia soulangiana*, *Amelanchier canadensis* and palest pink carnations at a spring reception

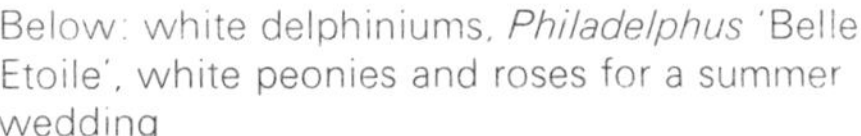

Below: white delphiniums, *Philadelphus* 'Belle Etoile', white peonies and roses for a summer wedding

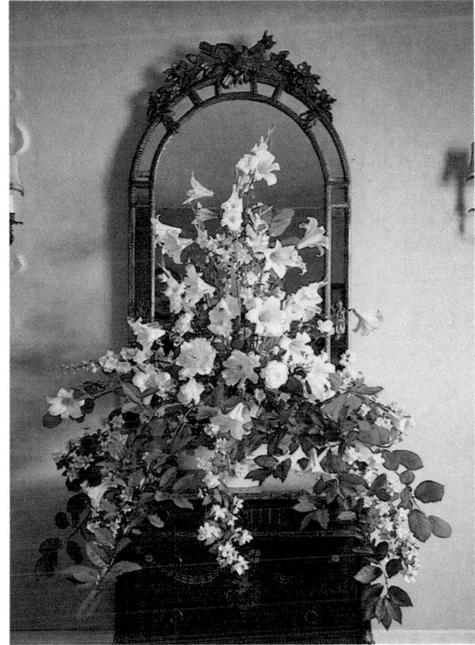

'Tiara' roses, jasmine and *Elaeagnus macrophylla*

elsewhere can see, as well as hear, the chief guests as speeches are made and toasts drunk. Low arrangements will probably be interspersed with tall candelabra and many candles.

Sometimes candlecups are used on top of candelabra to hold the flowers, but usually it is better to keep the flowers separate from the candles for large events. The smell of scorching leaves or flowers could prove most discordant to an important event, so this way of using candelabra is best saved for less important occasions.

If no special colour scheme is demanded, then the flower arranger might look for some decorative scheme in the room where the banquet is to be held with which to link the floral decorations. Where men are present, very often the most successful decorations are those in which lots of colour is used. A mass of red, or of orange colouring, has a stimulating effect for very large dinners, used on damask table-cloths. For all-male dinners, red roses and carnations are guaranteed to please, men being much less impressed by a subtle colour scheme, whereas at a mixed gathering, the chief lady guest will be delighted to find the flowers have been chosen to complement her own gown. This choice would not be wise, however, if the gown is blue, for blue flowers do not stand out well in artificial light. Instead, other blending colours can be used.

Candlestick and candlecup holders

While it is better to keep flowers rather low and spreading for the top table, if the candelabra are tall, it will be possible to see from the lower tables quite well beneath the arms which hold the candles. Generally the top table will take up most of one end of the room and subsidiary tables will lead from it to hold the rest of the guests. It is better to place the arrangements at the same spacing all the way down the tables to give a tidy and balanced effect. One arrangement for each 2.5 m (8 ft) of tabling should be right. For a very large banquet, every second or third arrangement can be raised so that there are three decorative levels. In front of the guest of honour, the arrangement can be larger than elsewhere, or three arrangements be used close together.

These arrangements should be made well away from the tables in order not to obstruct the catering staff, and while sufficient water must be used to last out a long evening, care should also be taken in topping up that the containers do not overflow, or syphon out on to the table-cloths. Care must also be taken when transporting arrangements from the working position to the tables themselves. Drips of water on highly polished floors could cause an accident, and this should be guarded against by carrying the arrangements on a large tray or other support.

A pedestal where the guests are received will set the scene for an evening in the grand manner. If there are mantelpieces, these could also be banked with toning flowers, high enough to be seen by the guests, who will be seated the greater part of the evening.

At a banquet where many courses and wines will be served, it is best to keep the flowers loose and light, to avoid a heavy appearance.

Balls

Decorating for a ball has many of the problems of the special dinner or banquet. Floral decorations need to be large, kept to the sides of the room, or else high up, so as not to impede the dancers.

A charity ball, where off-white walls, picked out with gilt and with gilt chairs around the room, was successfully decorated at a difficult time of year with 'Sonia' roses. 'Sonia' may be obtained from the florist all the year round.

Order the roses for arrival three days

Camellia 'Nagasaki', *Euonymus* foliage and grapes

before the event. All the lower leaves and thorns should be removed and the base of the stem trimmed and slit. Then a long drink for forty-eight hours in a cool place will bring them to perfection for the night. Again, massed rather than distributed colour will have much more impact.

For civic occasions quite often the Parks Department will supply pot plants on loan to assist the required massed effect. If the superintendent is asked in good time, he may also be persuaded to send a supply of interesting foliage for use as background to the arrangements. From time to time the gardener-flower arranger gets a bonus to what is normally available. Wandering disconsolately round the garden on a cold February day, despairing of finding anything to give a boost to the iris, tulips and daffodils available from the florist, the shrub *Sycopsis sinensis* was found in

'Sonia' roses, chrysanthemums, rhododendron and garden foliage

bloom. Stripped of its foliage, which hid the star-like yellow flowers, not unlike the witch-hazel, the long branches were just what was needed for the pedestal to decorate a charity fashion show.

This happened just before Easter, when the yacht club had to be decorated for a fitting-out dance. There simply was nothing big enough to support the daffodils available. Then a telephone call came: a mimosa tree had broken a limb from the weight of bloom. First aid required amputation of the branch – could it be of use? The 'branch' turned out to be of tree size. Suitable pieces were removed, the tops tied in large polythene bags and the stems put in deep lukewarm water for two days prior to the dance. They emerged beautifully fluffy, and gave great pleasure, and a romantic setting to the dancing, lasting well over the Easter week-end.

On another occasion in late July, white material was needed for a wedding and nothing unusual seemed to be available. An invitation to a private garden produced divine branches of *Hoheria glabrata*. It looked, when bereft of some of its foliage, like spring cherry blossom, so cool and delicate for the hot summery day. One September when white material was needed, generous quantities of the shrub *Eucryphia nymansensis* were offered, just when everything seemed to be flame coloured or orange.

Marquees

Decorating a marquee for a special occasion is a challenge; in addition to the lack of decorative features in the surroundings, the elements must be considered.

Decorations made on a balmy June day for a wedding can be ruined overnight by a summer gale. Pedestals may be thrown to the ground by an agitated tent-flap, and next morning the flowers will be found mangled on the ground. Usually coconut matting is used to cover the grass in the marquee, which may also conceal unknown slopes, bumps and bulges – a real hazard. Therefore pedestals of strong material such as wrought iron should be used, and lashed back to tent-poles for added support. Generally the tent-poles will have been covered in the fabric used to line the marquee, and unless the tent is a very new one, nails and hooks will have been left in them on some previous occasion. The tent-pole is always the major problem, but garlands of greenery made in advance can be interspersed among them with small blocks of plastic foam wrapped in film. Once the garlands are in position, the foam is filled with flowers and effectively cloaks the tent-poles.

Flowers for the buffet-table may be kept in a safe place until just before the guests are due and put in place after the caterers have completed their work. Usually, caterers prefer not to have too many flowers on the buffet. The cake may have to have the premier position.

Sometimes the flowers carried by the bride and her attendants are placed around the cake during the reception. Perhaps garlands across the front of the table are all that will be wanted if this is to be done. Looped up and pinned to the cloth, they will look well and yet not disturb the most temperamental caterers. Garlands should be prepared well in advance and put in position when the catering staff are absent.

Good relations with caterers should be nurtured. They have the same aim: to put on a successful event. Most hirers of marquees keep swatches of the tent linings and will, if asked, allow a sample for whoever is to do the flowers.

On one occasion for the grandest wedding the marquee had a pink-and-white striped lining. There was an annexe attached as a ladies' powder-room, complete with rose chintz covered dressing-tables. Massive crystal chandeliers hung from on high, with wall light brackets of crystal attached around the sides of the marquee. It seemed the simplest possible matter to order quantities of pale pink and white flowers and devise wall vases from loaf tins, sprayed with pale pink paint, wrapped around with chicken-wire, after foam had been inserted. Loops of strong wire were used to bind and for hanging at intervals between wall lights.

The marquee was in position some days before the wedding and a visit to the site gave the feeling of an enormous ice cream. Horrors! Pale pink and white flowers would only add to the insipid effect. A hasty telephone call to the suppliers changed half the flowers ordered to red, and the finished effect of red and pink flowers, lit by hundreds of twinkling crystal lights, was quite unforgettable, and most dramatic.

This was one of the occasions on which a change of mind midstream turned out well – and how fortunate the team doing the decorating had confidence in their leader and allowed the scheme to be changed at the last minute. The bewitching French bride must have led a charmed existence, for not the slightest wind disturbed all the lights and flowers and the celebrations went on the whole week-end. On second thoughts, the crystal must have been plastic – but it was most effective. The final touch of grandeur were 'Georgian' french doors at each end of the marquee! Normally such conditions do not prevail and it is the flower arranger's task to draw the eye away from tent-covers that have seen better days.

For a charity ball a stately country home was loaned for supper, sitting out, and a bar with dancing in a marquee in the grounds. The marquee, which was to have a temporary dance floor and a covered way to the house, was brand new, bought specially for the event. In due course, swatches of the lining material arrived. These were not at all the pale cream and blue that had been planned, but a very harsh kingfisher blue with yellow stripes.

Only white flowers seemed possible set against the crude colouring, or lime and green, to tone it down. Then, thumbing through old flower-arranging books, the 'flowerpot' theme came to mind. Large flowerpots were painted white and 2 m (6 ft) dowelling set in concrete. Quantities of moss covered the concrete, and stayed green for some weeks. From crêpe paper,

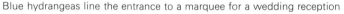

Blue hydrangeas line the entrance to a marquee for a wedding reception

hundreds of roses were made, together with buds and leaves, and bound to the top of the dowelling, which was covered with strips of green crêpe paper. Fortunately double crêpe paper, which matched exactly the harsh coloured stripes of the lining, was found. Some weeks of work produced enough 'rose trees' to decorate the raised dais on which the band were to play, and for a guard of honour along the covered pathway leading into the house. Paper roses of one colour only to each vase were used. The yellow ones had a bow of the kingfisher blue ribbon, and the blue had yellow ribbon. Garlands were made to match and used to decorate the tent-poles and along the walls of the marquee. The final effect, which took a great many hours to achieve, was rather Alice-in-Wonderland like, and it fascinated the guests.

Next morning when the lorry that had been engaged to collect the trees and garlands arrived, to store them for another event, there was not a tree in sight. The elated overnight gathering had taken the trees home with them as souvenirs. Fortunately the garlands remained, and these were stored and used for two other parties for young people, eventually being sprayed with gold paint for a Christmas ball at a guild hall.

It is important to decide *before* a very large event what is to be done with the flowers afterwards. Someone should be made responsible for seeing that they are not dismantled by irresponsible people but carefully taken down the next day, and delivered to hospitals or wherever the committee have decided they should go.

Sometimes, as at a guild hall, there may be other civic occasions during the ensuing week, for which the same flowers can be left *in situ*. A telephone number should be left with the authorities so that they can inform the team leader when the flowers are to be taken down, unless other arrangements have been made. The manner of assembling and dismantling in stately rooms is of great importance, for pools of water or scratches from branches on floors inadequately protected during these operations will not endear one to the owners or caretakers. Therefore a team for large special occasions should be chosen with care, almost as much for their expertise in handling delicate situations as for their talent in flower arranging. We all have friends guaranteed to behave like the proverbial bull at most inopportune moments.

Flowers for invalids and hospitals

Here is an opportunity to use all the charming small flowers, too intimate for the large special occasion group.

A stay in hospital nowadays does not necessarily mean a private room, with space to display large baskets and bowls of flowers. Today patients are much more likely to be in small rooms, with shared facilities. Stability is of great importance. The container's base must be wide enough to stand firmly on the bedside locker or table. A small lidded basket, with leak-proof liner, is ideal. Filled with plastic foam and arranged with small long-lasting flowers, it will give pleasure for many days with no attention needed. However, when visiting a friend in hospital, attend to her flowers' thirst and remove fading blooms.

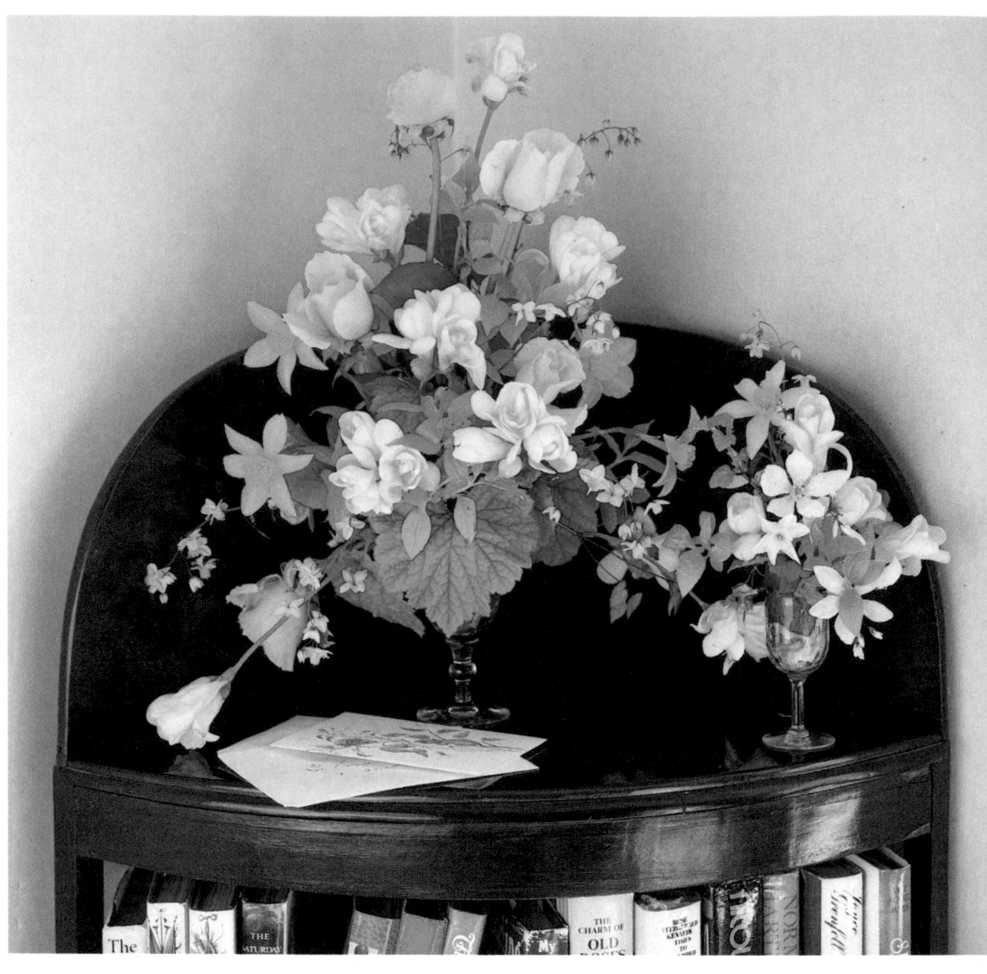

Pale yellow freesia, narcissi, tulips and roses for a new mother and baby

Pastel-coloured flowers are best for sick-rooms, but a man might prefer stronger colours. 'Orange Belinda' roses, which can be obtained from the florist all the year round, are colourful and long lasting, and they do not fail to please. Red and white flowers together should never be sent to hospital, for the nursing profession consider the combination unlucky and have been known to banish them from a hospital ward.

Sending flowers to congratulate a new mother can be fun for both donor and recipient. An arrangement for mother, with an identical miniature for baby, never fails. Again baskets in two sizes may be used; and wineglasses too make excellent containers, providing they stand firmly and their stems are not too slender. First, line the bowl of the glass with long-lasting leaves, such as variegated ivy. Then insert plastic foam. The ivy will prevent stems and foam showing through glass. A drop of antiseptic solution in the water will help prevent decay, and in fact this is a good preventive at all times. Above, two such arrangements are shown, ready to congratulate the parents of a new baby.

The gardener-flower arranger can grow material ideal for such a scheme. By growing for example floribunda roses, and miniature roses in the same colour range, together with side-shoots of plants such as delphinium, flowers can always be kept to hand for such a scheme. 'Cecile Brunner' is a delightful miniature rose, easy to grow and prolific in flower.

In the home, flowers for an invalid should not be too easily overturned, and specimen vases should be chosen with heavy bases so that the patient is not distressed by them spilling water over her tray, as she moves to reach for something.

Small children in the sick-room will appreciate animal shapes of plastic foam, well soaked then wrapped in thin polythene. Teddy bears are firm favourites. The shape is studded all over with long-lasting flowers, such as a spray of chrysanthemum heads. When all excess water has ceased to drip, a ribbon round the neck completes Teddy and will be very well received. A rabbit is also easily made and would be good at Easter-time. *Eve Taylor*

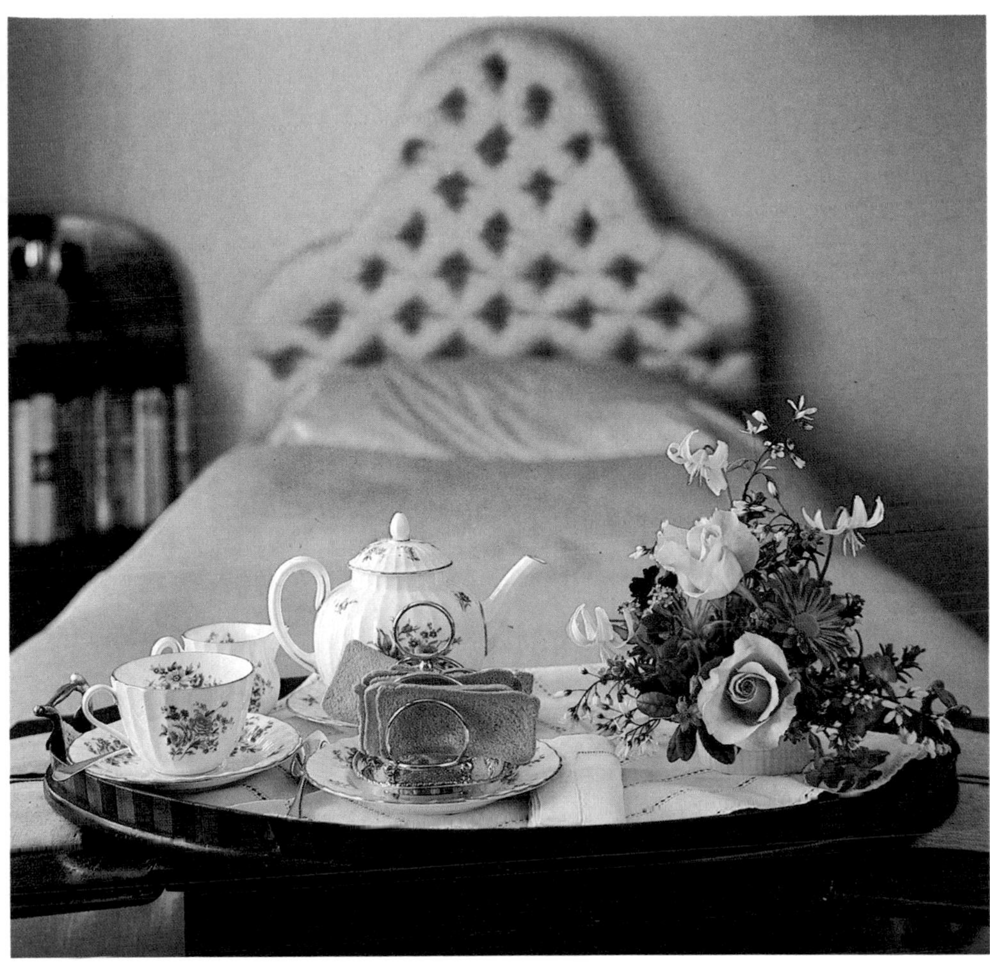

Tiny rosebuds, forget-me-nots, gentian and *Anemone pulsatilla* on an invalid tray

Informal party flowers

Flowers are indispensable as part of the grace and elegance of any formal occasion; but they can add charm, excitement or beauty to the most unpretending of our gatherings and should never be neglected.

Entertaining today

As living styles and standards change, large formal occasions have given way to informal gatherings that require a new approach to all aspects of hosting parties. Restrictions on staff, with the host or hostess having to do all the preparations, the financial limitations and the lack of space in the modern home all help to influence the style of these present-day occasions. Apart from normal replenishing the day of the party should be free for the preparation of the food and not for arranging flowers, which should be picked or purchased in advance to be at their best on the night. If the flower arrangements are created a day or two in advance, the hosts can receive additional pleasure from them, for the heat of the evening will help to shorten the lasting qualities of even the best conditioned flowers. Experience will tell you how soon in advance the arrangements can be created, as so much will depend on the time of the year and the weather. Those flowers with a short life cannot of course be arranged too far in advance if they are not to fade on the night. The need for good conditioning and choice of plant material to be used is, as always, most important.

For normal day-to-day living the colour of the various arrangements may be chosen to blend with the décor of the room, but now it is possible to change these colours to suit the occasion. Paper napkins, which are cheap and available in many colours, and the colour of the table covering, may be the guiding influence with advancing or receding colours being used effectively to set the mood of the evening. It should be remembered that the arrangements will be seen under artificial light, and while this can be used to emphasize the presence of flowers, the effect on the colours must be borne in mind. Containers are often improvised with the formal 'pedestal' and other attractive containers giving way to shallow dishes only large enough to hold a piece of wet foam.

The placement of the finished arrangement may have to differ from the usual favourite spots, depending on the particular evening and the number of people expected. Guests may be serving themselves from a side-table and eating either standing or from their laps. This table then becomes the focal area and it is an ideal place for an arrangement. It is important that the plant material does not become entangled with the food, and unless there is ample space it may be advisable to use a stemmed-type container, which also allows the guests to view the arrangement if they are to remain standing. With first impressions being important, an arrangement placed in the hall can set the scene for the evening, but in all cases flowers should be seen and enjoyed and not knocked over.

The variations of each occasion and season of the year call for individual treatment and the following advice is given only for inspiration, as so much will depend on the size of the occasion, location and availability of plant material at the time.

New Year's Eve

Overflowing into the new year, 'hogmanay', to give it its true Scottish name, is the last day of the dying year. The Scottish influence, and other traditions like the carrying into the house of coal after midnight, not forgetting 'Old Father Time', the hour-glass, and bells, can be incorporated in the arrangements. The whole evening revolves around the clock, waiting for the hands to reach midnight, and then comes the raising of glasses to the new year.

While it may not be possible to include a real clock, a mock face can easily be made by covering a cake-board with fabric and either drawing on the figures or cutting them out of card and fixing them with the hands just before that final hour. This can be brought into the arrangement with the plant material designed around it. Since this will become a focal area it should not be too dominant, and therefore its colour must be chosen with care. If a base is to be used under the arrangement, to help to link the accessories as well as to protect the furniture, then it can be covered with a piece of tartan material. Alternatively, the table covering could be of tartan.

The plant material needs to be chosen with equal care; some to depict the old year and some the new. A lichen-covered branch will give height whilst being a very good choice for the 'dying' year. Alternatively, any dried plant material can be substituted. Fresh plant material needs to be placed at the base of the arrangement, representing the emergence of the new year. Suitable material could include the white tree heath, *Erica arborea*. Providing the soil does not contain lime, plant can reach heights of up to 3 metres (10 ft), and in sheltered gardens will be in flower at this time of the year – as will *Erica carnea* 'Springwood White'. Those gardens which can grow heathers may also have *Rhododendron nobleanum*, 'Christmas Cheer', in flower. In some situations these flowers appear as early as October or November. Two flower trusses are all that is required to give the necessary 'weight' at the base of the arrangement.

If these are not available then a bunch of the 'pre-cooled' or glasshouse daffodils, or other spring flowers which begin to appear in the florist's at Christmas, can give the desired effect. Alternatively, a 'fir' and cones, with heather which has been dried earlier in the year by being left standing in shallow water until the water is fully absorbed, can be used.

St Valentine's Day

On 14 February red roses may be given and, as they are very expensive at this time of the year, may be few in number. A container with suitable foliage, as nothing apart from possibly a piece of fern may have been included by the florist, needs to be ready for this 'surprise'. If just one rose is given in a presentation box then a specimen vase, with the rose stem recut and placed into boiling water, may be all that is required. A larger arrangement can be created out of two or three roses by placing them on a pinholder with an interestingly shaped branch used for an outline, a few large leaves or stones being used to cover the mechanics.

A heart-shaped base cut out of stiff card or a board, and covered with red velvet, can add to the occasion with smaller hearts made in the same manner, placed on false 'stems' and brought down through the centre of the arrangement. Many variations can be made around the heart theme: for example, an old metal coat-hanger can be bent into a heart shape, with the hook bent at right angles at the base to keep it in an upright position. Bind the wire with cotton wool or material to make it a little thicker and finish it by stitching on a frill of red net or ribbon. This can then act as a frame with an arrangement of plant material flowing through the open heart.

Easter

Depending on beliefs Easter, like Christmas, can have two meanings and both can easily be incorporated in an arrangement. The Bible reminds us of the suffering and then the Resurrection, whilst to others Easter eggs and chicks are the first things that Easter brings to mind.

The pure white trumpets of *Lilium longiflorum* or the majestic flowers of the Arum lily on their long, fat stems, which can gently be coaxed with the hand into a gentle curve, are the principal Easter flowers. As these can be very expensive it may be an idea to plant some roots of the Arum in large pots and bring them into the greenhouse for early forcing.

Christ's crown of thorns can be depicted with many varieties of bare stems. Blackberry bent into shape whilst still green and left to dry is but one variety. Red carnations will suggest Christ's blood.

Spring is associated with new life. As the countryside awakens after its winter rest so lambs, young birds and baby chickens emerge. Felt models of these creatures are often incorporated into the traditional arrangements. After the dullness of winter come the bright yellow colours of daffodils, tulips and forsythia, to mention but a few, which go to make up the dominant colours of the arrangements. The style is very informal, often a landscape, with a branch of lamb's-tails or catkins for outline and a bunch of daffodils arranged on a pinholder at their base and covered with moss. If a bird's nest is to be used, do not take a real one but make one yourself out of dried grass and place

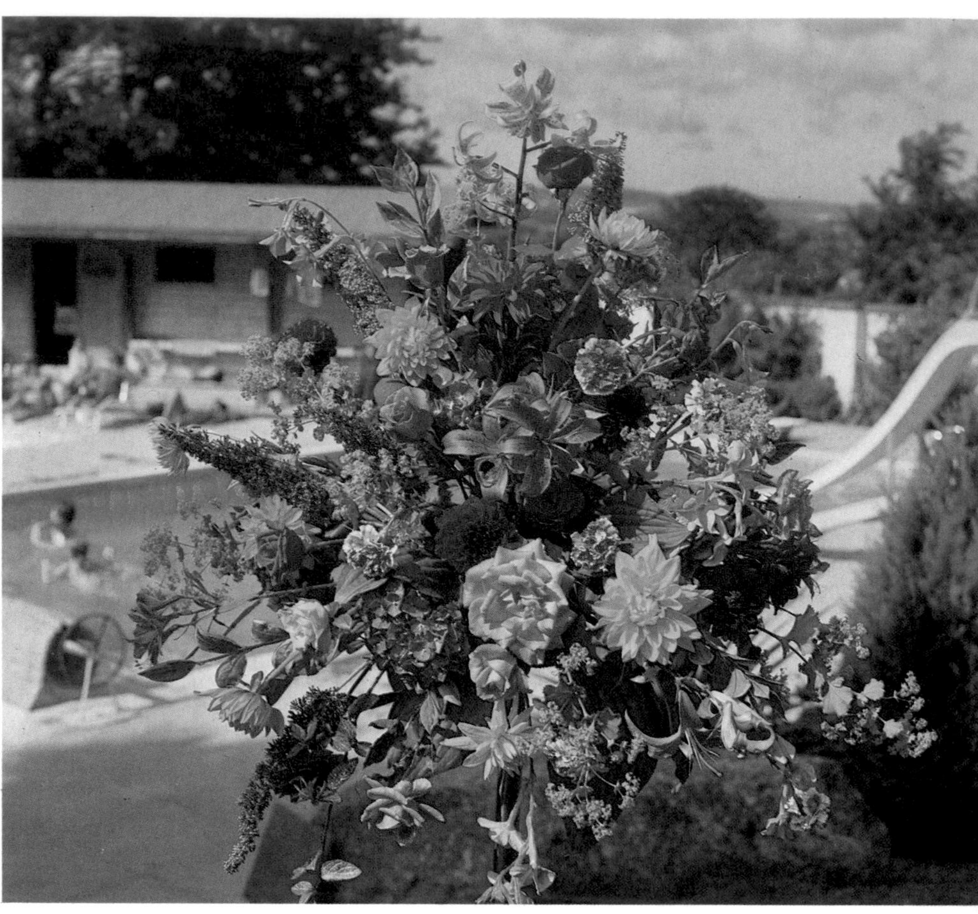

Above: brilliantly coloured roses, dahlias, buddleia, hydrangea, lilies and pinks with golden privet and *Hosta* leaves in the form of a topiary tree at a swimming pool barbecue or outdoor party

Below left: at a Harvest Supper, pampas grass gives height to gladioli, chrysanthemums and dahlia, with foliage of preserved beech and magnolia leaves, *Elaeagnus pungens* 'Maculata' and ears of wheat

Below right: plant material for 'Hallowe'en' includes *Salix sachalinensis* 'Sekka', painted onion and poppy seedheads, rhododendron and aspidistra leaves. Green fatsia leaves and red dahlias complete the arrangement

marzipan eggs in it. Likewise, place a basket in the centre of an Easter arrangement for the children's chocolate Easter eggs in the same way that the Christmas Tree is used at Christmas-time as a focal area for the presents.

Harvest

The autumn, or fall, celebrates the gathering of harvest. The churches and chapels overflow with fruit and vegetables, sheaves of corn – now sadly disappearing with modern farming techniques – and a loaf of bread baked in the shape of a sheaf of wheat by the local baker, taking pride of place at the altar. It is often felt that a more organized grouping of these items would be desirable, but whilst a row of jam jars may seem unsightly around the base of the pulpit, it should be borne in mind that they will have been placed there with the same loving care as the pedestal at the side of the altar.

Outside the church the completion of the harvest is celebrated on the farms and in the village halls with the traditional harvest supper, a very informal occasion. Frequently, long trestle-tables covered with white sheets are laid end to end, and the girl members of the local young farmers' club serve salads and cold sweets to the parents and friends assembled in the village hall. However, in the corn-growing areas their suppers are held in the barns of the large farms and are given by the land-owner and his family for the workers. The location of these suppers, and the fact that they are often followed by a dance, limits the position of any flower arrangements. While the tables are the first choice, the arrangements are soon lost in the vastness of the building. Here it is possible to forsake the low arrangements on the main table and place two large ones at each end. These are then seen by all attending and also help to locate the host's table. This table can be left in position when the others are removed for the dance. Blocks of wet foam wrapped in thin polythene and then wire-netting can be fixed to the walls to take large groups of informally arranged branches of autumn-tinted foliage and sprays of hawthorn berries for outline, with dahlias and chrysanthemums also in the autumn shades for filling in. The British Harvest Festival can be compared to the New World's Thanksgiving; an arrangement for this occasion may be seen on p 116.

Hallowe'en

Tradition has it that the evening of the last day of October is the time when witches make their appearance, and here is an excuse to design an arrangement as vivid as the imagination will allow. Black cardboard cut-outs of cats, moons and witches on broomsticks can be included in the decorations. Swedes or mangolds or pumpkins hollowed out and with spooky faces cut into the sides and a lighted candle placed within can be used around the house and garden to keep the witches at bay. Only a few simple red flowers need to be incorporated with any weird-looking plant material that you have, dried or fresh. A suitable container may be used to represent a witch's cauldron.

Cheese and wine party: short stems of *Alba Simplex*, white camellia, *Erica arborea*, flowering *Skimmia*, *Helleborus corsicus*, leaves of *Hedera canariensis* and grapes inserted into a cone of wet plastic

Guy Fawkes' Night

In England, a few days after Hallowe'en comes Guy Fawkes' night, and after the bonfire and firework display in the garden the guests can be welcomed into the house with steaming hot potatoes baked in their jackets. A 'bonfire' arrangement can be designed around twisted black-painted driftwood with red, orange and yellow flowers as the flames. The children can make their own miniature 'Guy', which may become the focal point of the arrangement, and will add to their pleasure.

A more ambitious idea is to make mock 'fireworks' (never using real ones in the house) out of seedheads and grasses. These would be in the abstract manner, brightly coloured and hung around the room as mobiles.

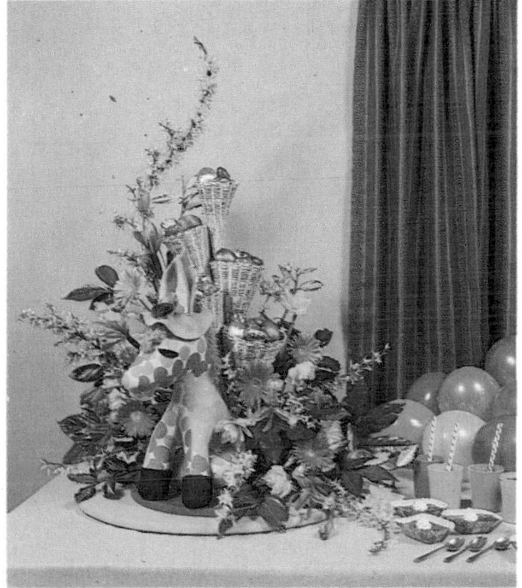

Children's Easter party: a felt donkey, eggs forsythia, 'Wedgwood' iris, narcissus 'Golden Ducat', and orange gerbera, with foliage of fatsia, camellia and *Elaeagnus pungens* 'Maculata'

Christmas

This is the time of the year when most people will make that extra effort to create their own arrangements. (See p. 104 for more formal ideas.) Tradition has not faded, with angels, stars and cribs taking pride of place. Carols, pantomimes and all the other trimmings that go to make up Christmas can set the mind working overtime with ideas. Choose one theme or colour scheme and use this throughout the house for the greatest impact rather as the large stores use an overall theme for their windows and departments.

While space does not allow many ideas to be discussed here in detail, it should be remembered that the techniques used are the same as for the rest of the year. It is only the plant material which changes, with red, white and gold being the most popular colours. Evergreens have been used to decorate houses for centuries with the traditional tree as the focal point, but even this in past years has given way to plastic! So also has a good deal of the material used in Christmas arrangements. This has now become big business for the suppliers, with new colours being introduced each year. There is no reason why plastic material should not be used, but it must be selected with the same attention as fresh plant material. Pointed, finer shaped items are needed for the outline, with the larger, bolder material used in the centre, and these need to be linked with carefully chosen transitional material.

There are many colours to choose from, but for the best returns on the outlay – for this material can be expensive although long-lasting – choose a colour that is not limiting and does not require a lot of skill in the changing of colour combinations from one Christmas to the next. This can be done by incorporating home-made artificial flowers of ribbon, crêpe paper or old nylon stockings, in blending or contrasting colours.

Containers need to be chosen with equal care and should be harmonious. Only the very skilful will succeed with using plastic material in an antique container. A safe guide-line is to make 'fun' arrangements by incorporating the material with crackers, baubles and the like.

Since the Christmas festivities now extend over many days, with many parties given or attended, less time is available for flower arranging. There is a proportionate increase in the use of plastic material. The heat of the rooms also calls for long-lasting arrangements, and this is another reason why plastics have increased in popularity. It also means that the arrangements can be created a week or two in advance and stored until required. If used from one year to the next the material will require washing in soapy water to remove accumulated dirt and dust before being reused.

To a true gardener nothing can replace even the smallest arrangement of carefully chosen evergreens, which will last the full twelve days if not longer. Condition them well, always keeping the container topped up, and if possible spray twice a day with a fine mist spray to replace the moisture lost in the dry atmosphere of the room. Removing to a cooler room at night and bringing the arrangements back to their original positions just before the guests arrive is another means of extending their life.

By planning a garden in advance the appropriate foliage can be made available at this time of the year. All but the smallest garden can support one of the variegated hollies such as *Ilex aquifolium* 'Golden King' or 'Silver Queen'. These hollies, together with golden cupressus and ivy trails, are but some of the foliage which can be used in the arrangements. A few red carnations, or a stem of spray chrysanthemum cut down and graduated through the centre of the arrangement, can be added – and can easily be replaced when they fade without disturbing the rest of the arrangement.

A welcoming wreath on the front door can be made around a wire frame wrapped in deep moss with the stem ends of evergreens bound into it. Cones, Christmas roses and plastic fruit, and ribbon which is water resistant, can all be added for decoration. The outside air should be sufficient to keep the arrangement fresh without any further attention. Garlands made in the same way can also be used in the house, but for these constant spraying is required. In this case the moss should first be wrapped in polythene strips to protect the wall and to retain the moisture.

Candles can give height or focal areas to arrangements when other material is in short supply. Never cover them, always allowing at least three-quarters of the candle to show, especially if it is to be lit.

Dried plant material sprayed or painted with gold, silver or bronze, or a combination of two, with glitter added (by placing it, whilst still wet, in a paper bag containing glitter and shaking it) can be just as rewarding, if not more so than plastic material, and will last just as long. It is cheaper too, especially if it has been dried or preserved by the arranger, and is also useful for disguising marked items, for as long as the shape is perfect the paint will cover any surface blemishes.

Having dealt with the seasonal events of the year, a closer look may now be taken at some of the many other occasions which

take place. The plant material will depend on availability, and in the winter months the use of dried and preserved, or a combination of dried and fresh material, should not be ignored.

Cheese and wine party

Here an arrangement can take pride of place in the centre of the table with the wine, cheese, dips and other items of food placed around it. These occasions are often an excuse to use a new recipe or try a new wine, and they can at the same time be an opportunity to introduce a new colour scheme or style of arrangement. Empty bottles, grapes and vine are appropriate accessories, but do not be afraid to use or do something a little different. It could become a talking point, and therefore invaluable as an ice-breaker.

Barbecue

There is no reason why there should not be a flower arrangement in the garden for a barbecue party, especially if the garden is a small one, is paved, or is lacking in colour at that particular moment. Tubs of bedding plants and geraniums are useful, but these are often too low down to be effective. Use a tall urn, stone pillar or even build a pedestal of loose bricks on which to place the arrangement.

Unless it is possible to position the arrangement under a floodlight, the only lighting available will be from the fire or a string of coloured lights erected for the occasion. With this limited lighting the colours of the plant material used need to be bright; a clashing scheme of advancing colours being very exciting. Large, strongly textured garden material is an

Left: Disco party. Painted stripped ivy supports two sprayed heads of *Allium schubertii* with multi-coloured glixia flowers stuck to the seed cases

Right: an oriental setting for a curry party has dried palm and aspidistra leaves with brightly coloured flowers of anthuriums and orchids

Below: 'Sub-aqua Club' Sea-fern and coral, driftwood and a fishing net back camellia, *erica australis*, grape hyacinths and *helleborus orientalis*

Below right: a 'Horse Show' party has wild sycamore, ferns and cow parsley together with 'bronze' *Bergenia* leaves and hedera 'Goldheart'

ideal choice, with the lesser use of transitional material, to make the arrangement more dominant.

Children's parties

There is no reason why each member of the family should not share the flower arrangements, especially the children. A parent who has brought a young guest and is staying on to help out will also appreciate the efforts. As before, it is the occasion that dictates the arrangements and none more so than this kind.

Inspiration can come from a child's book, where it will be noticed that the colours are bright and the pictures often lack detail. In the case of a birthday, age can lead to other ideas. It is common to incorporate figurines into arrangements and here is a good opportunity to do so. Do not use one of bronze or china, but one from the toy cupboard. A felt animal from a popular television show would be an appropriate choice, or an old toy drum turned into a container or used as a base for an arrangement is another idea. There are many toys that need little improvisation to transform them into containers. The plant material should be bright but simple with bold outlines, and use can be made of flowers which the children have gathered themselves.

Disco party

As the children grow up, they will want to give their own parties. Times change and so therefore will the style of parties from those given by past generations. The music will be louder and the lights may start to flash! Maybe even some of the walls would be black if the young had their way!

A different approach to flowers is needed, abstract shapes being the most effective. These will bring their own challenges, use being made of the reflections of the differing coloured lights. Use them to play on the white-painted branches and shining textured plant material, the shadows thrown on to the background giving depth.

If lack of room prohibits an arrangement being placed against a wall, hang a collage of luminous-painted material on a wall with 'black' light focused on to it, or mobiles of strongly textured and coloured plant material from the ceiling. These will 'move' either on their own or with the aid of the shadows, and so add a new dimension – and desirable originality.

International parties

An informal party can be given identity by choosing a particular menu or style of food such as Indian curries or Italian pasta dishes. A holiday to a foreign country may also give inspiration. These evenings can be very rewarding: a little research is needed in libraries, and travel agents can be a useful source of information. Flowers can help to create the atmosphere required, and accessories do not have to be so authentic as in show work.

If subtropical plant material is not available from the garden, appropriate imported, dried material, with the addition of a few fresh flowers, can be used. These flowers could include anthuriums, gerbera, strelitzia, protea, orchids and the like, which are not as expensive as is often thought and will last longer than a number of traditional flowers. Fruit is also an interesting addition, especially the more exotic types, such as pineapples, gourds, squashes or figs.

Sporting occasions

These occasions can include fishing, golf, equestrian events, shooting or even football to mention but a few, with your friends invited back home after the day's enjoyment.

To tie in the arrangement with the occasion, the supporting teams' colours can be used in many cases. A water scene with reeds and other water-loving plant material would be suitable for a fishing expedition, whilst coral and sea fern used as a background to the arrangement would be appreciated by a diver. These arrangements need not be large, and they will add a personal touch which will be appreciated.

It is hoped that some inspiration can be found from the foregoing suggestions to add to the enjoyment of hosting parties. A house is not complete without flowers, and an added attraction is to plan the party around them. They will probably become a talking point, not only on the day, but for days to come. *Richard Jeffery*

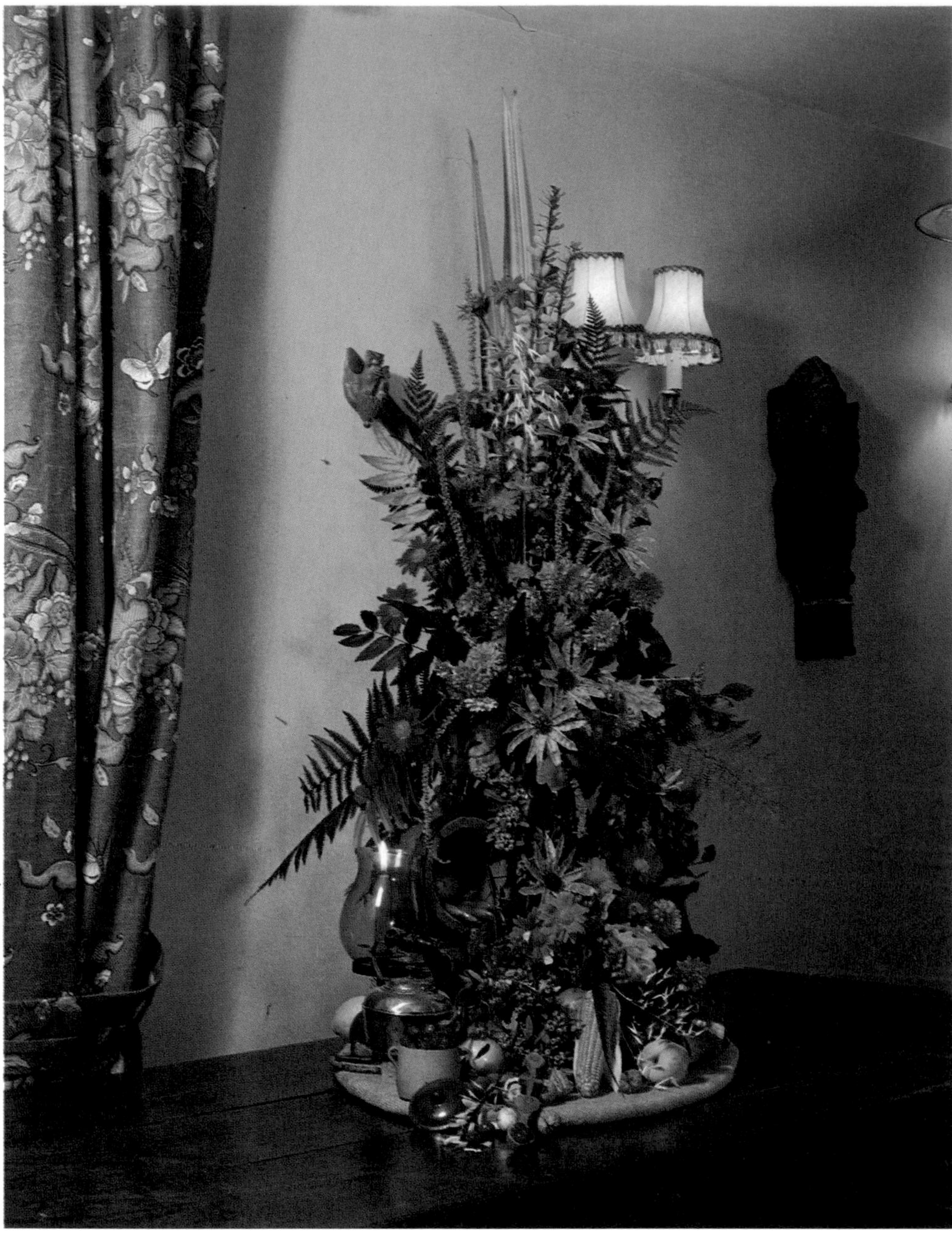

Thanksgiving is celebrated on the second Monday of October in Canada and on the fourth Thursday of November in the USA. An arrangement of this scale is intended for a large party. The colours, however, are those that would be used in an arrangement of any size and the materials could easily be adapted to make a centrepiece for the smaller family celebration.

Thanksgiving by Iris Webb

Thanksgiving is a very special social and family occasion in the USA and Canada, when colourful harvest-time designs of flowers, fruit and foliage are called for. The style of the arrangements can be either casual or simple for a small family party, or more formally elegant and bountiful for larger gatherings. In either case, the colours and materials used should be rich and warm, and have the textures associated with the harvest season. The design should be traditional mass or mass-line, incorporating fruits, berries, vegetables and nuts, as well as suitable flowers, leaves and grasses.

Simple accessories, such as cranberry pickers, rustic wooden bowls or domestic items made of brass and copper give a warm accent of colour and the added dimension of reflection. Other ideas of plenty and prosperity could be suggested in such a motif as that of the game-bird; actual tail-feathers, for instance, could be incorporated. Ceramic or metal birds such as turkeys or ducks are sometimes included. 'Pilgrim Father' figurines can serve as a reminder of the early settlers' rejoicing and thankfulness for their first harvests. The choice of such accessories will be an individual and personal one; the fine colours, plant forms and contrasting textures provide a rich picture by themselves.

It is wise to use a base which will be large enough for a tall arrangement with placements of fruits, nuts and berries at its foot. Accessories are then also more easily incorporated. Brass, copper, wood or basketry trays are suitable for this purpose. Alternatively, bases may be covered with a simple fabric, such as hessian or coarse linen, as in the arrangement shown. Not only do all these base materials combine well with the plant material used, but they provide a practical way of giving unity to the overall design with its several placements. Smaller trays and bases serve the same purpose in an arrangement reduced in scale for the dinner table.

Red or gold candles in glass hurricane holders could be used to provide highlights on polished apple skins and gleaming copper. They will also throw a mellow golden light on the abundance of the harvest, and serve to underline the thought which lies behind Thanksgiving.

Ribbon Roses and Leaves

Roses

Use 1 m red ribbon per rose, 4 cm ($1\frac{1}{2}$ in) wide

1 Attach ribbon to strong wire and fold to make half width
2 Roll to form centre of rose
3 Coil ribbon round stem to form rose, twisting to form rounded petals
4 Hold with a little glue and/or fine wire to prevent slipping. Glue tail of ribbon underneath rose. Neaten with florist's tape
5 Make bracts from 'leaf' material and glue under rose

Leaves

Use 1 m transparent adhesive plastic and 1 m green taffeta or velvet (depending on the texture required)

1 Place green material on adhesive side of plastic. Cut out leaves, using a rose leaf as pattern (ivy leaves may also be made in the same way)
2 Bind wires with green florist's tape
3 Fasten with plastic to the leaves to make stems and midribs
4 Trace veins with the back of a knife
5 Mount in groups of five

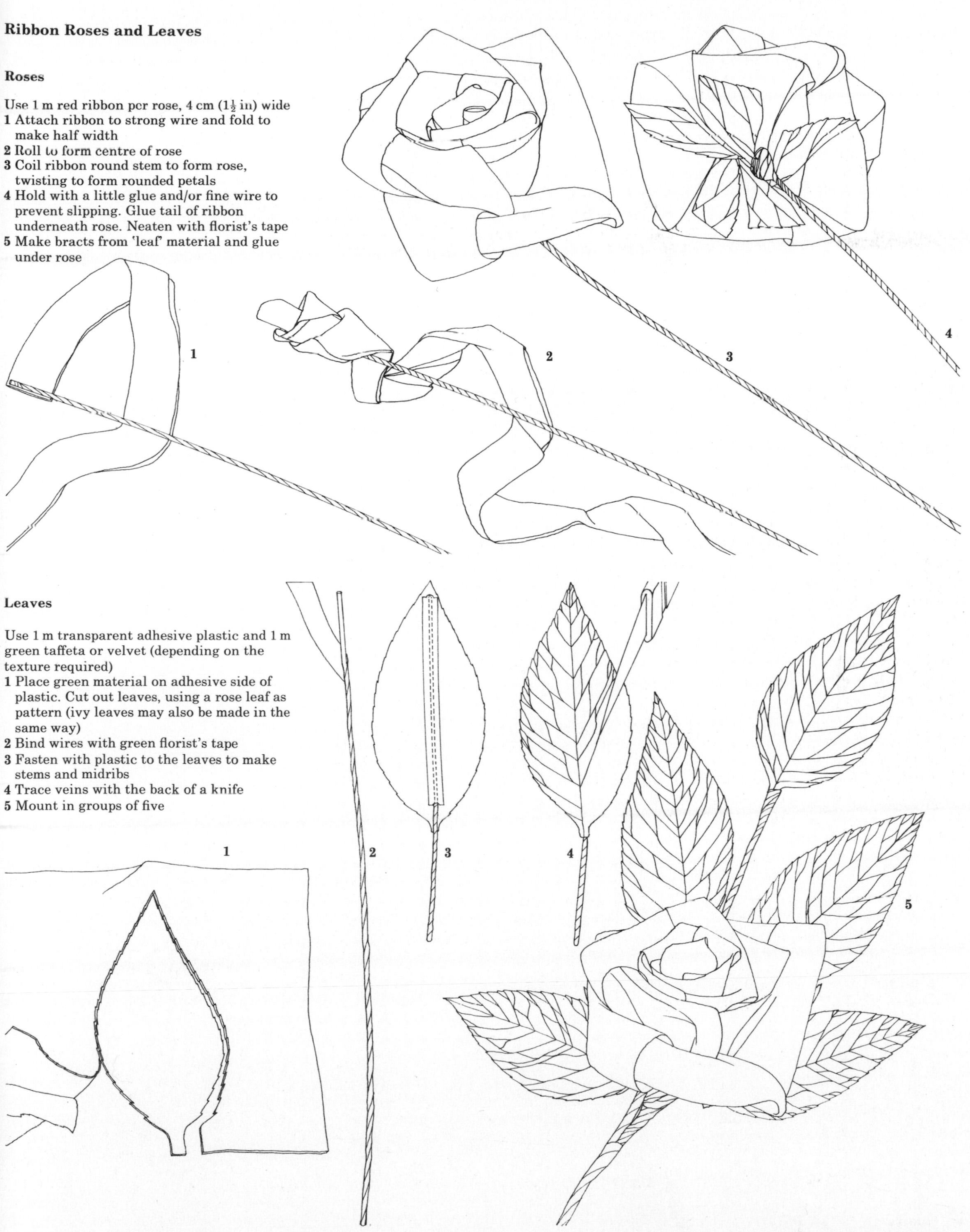

Tissue paper 'roses'
1 Bind stub with florist's tape to make stem
2 Make or buy stamens. Bind to stub wire with florist's tape
3 Cut petals from tissue paper, about twenty for each rose
4 Bind with fine wire round stamens, taking care to bind wire over the same area so that it does not slide down the stem
5 When sufficient petals have been added, place a touch of glue at base of flower; when this is dry, tape stem
The 'roses' may be used for garlands, or bound in sprays to strong dowelling (or a broom handle) to make 'rose trees'. Crepe paper may be used to make them the same way

'Rose leaf' spray
1 Cover medium weight stub wire with narrow strips of brown crepe paper or gutta percha, glueing to finish it at top and base
2 Cut out large (5–7 cm) and small (3–4 cm) leaves from taffeta or cotton placed on adhesive plastic
3 Using short lengths of wire, make five small leaves and four larger leaves
4 Bind small leaf to end of wire
5 Make up spray by binding the leaves in pairs (same size opposite each other) to the main wire stem
6 Make sprays into required length, binding in a paper rose at intervals

Rose trees
1 Cover dowel stick (or broom handle) with brown crepe paper
2 Mix plaster of paris, pour into urn or pot of 25 cm (10 in) diameter, and allow to partially set
3 Insert dowel stick, and hold or wedge to keep upright until set
4 Attach required number of rose sprays firmly to top of stick, cut off surplus wires, then bind again with crepe paper to neaten

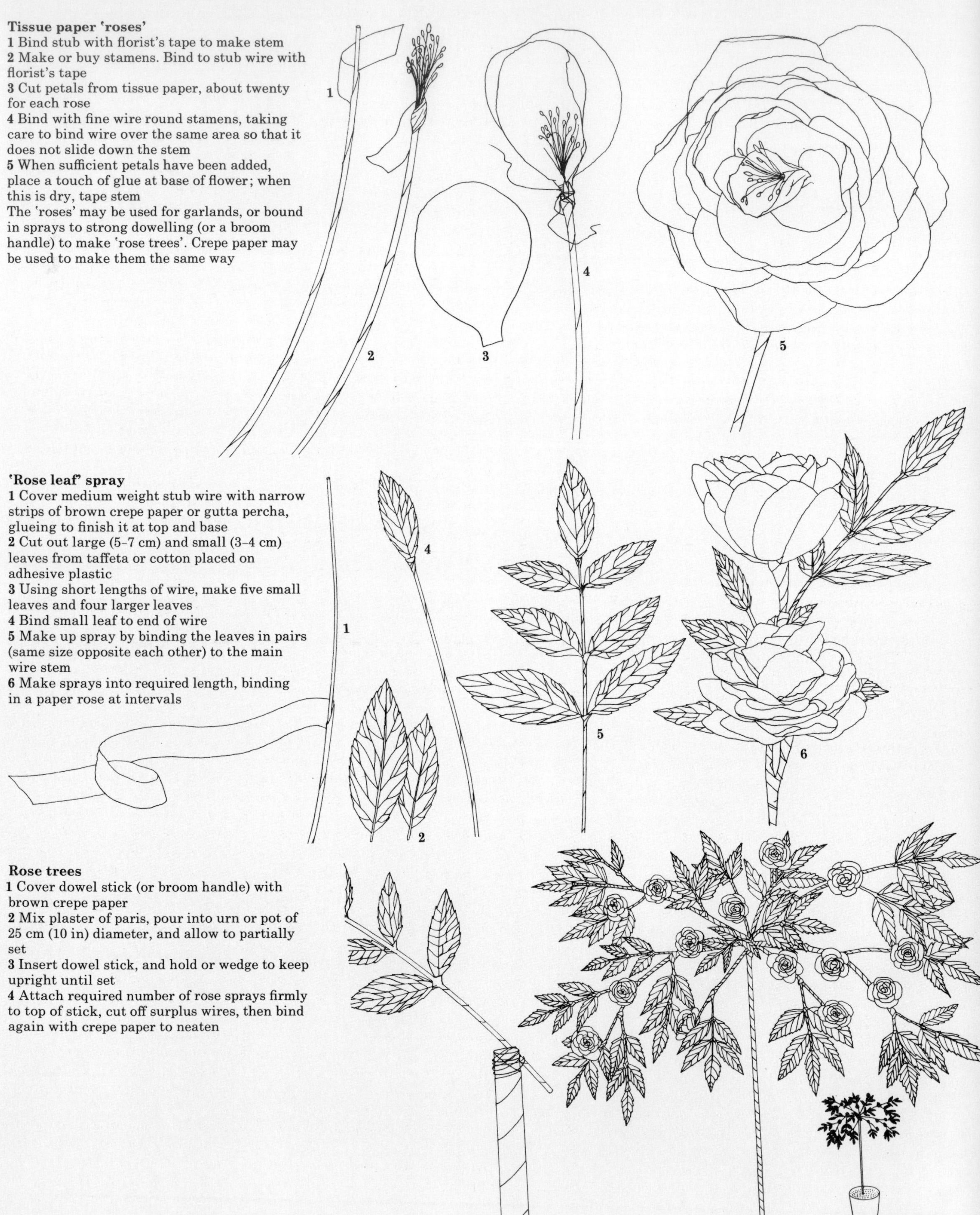

Honesty pod 'flowers'

1 Skin honesty pods to reveal silky inner petals (Dye if desired with cold water dyes)
2 Cut discs of thin card about 2 cm (⅔ in) in diameter. Alternatively, use a button of similar size
3 Pierce centre of card in four places, making very tiny holes. Thread through fine wire to attach firmly to strong stub wire. Bind stem with gutta percha for a neat finish
4 Attach petals with adhesive in overlapping circles on the card, repeating the process on the back
5 Glue 'stamens' to the centre: bracts of dried ballota flowers, fatshedera or ivy flowers

Hydrangea and alder cone *'Ranunculus'*

1 Spray of dried round alder catkins
2 Remove alder catkin and attach to a firm stub wire (for a larger flower, a small fir cone gives the same effect)
3 Neaten stem with gutta percha or crepe paper
4 Insert dried hydrangea petals, touched with glue, into the base of the catkins to form a circle. Approximately fifteen petals give a good form
5 The flowers may be used singly, or may be grouped to form sprays for larger arrangements

Copper beech or *Eleagnus* 'roses'

1 Collect beech leaves as they fall in autumn Press slightly and treat with glycerine for suppleness
2 Take a firm stub wire and attach a tiny wad of cotton wool to its tip. With a fine fuse or reel wire, bind leaf over cotton wool to make centre. Tape stem to neaten
3 Fold another leaf in half, and with fine wire bind point to base
4 Bind on the leaves around the stem until the required size of 'rose' is achieved; some full-blown, some buds. An average flower will need 10–11 petals. Tape again to neaten top of rose

9. Designs Requiring Special Techniques

Fine art is that in which the hand, the head and the heart of man go hand in hand.
JOHN RUSKIN 1819–1900

In this painting of the Virgin and Child in glory, Peter Paul Rubens (1577–1640) has used a magnificent floral wreath – as a fitting framework for the divine, and as a thing of beauty in its own right

Although most people who enjoy flowers in their homes find little difficulty in arranging simple bowls and containers suitable for their needs, there are some interesting methods of creating designs that demand a little more expert knowledge and technical skill. These are specialist designs and some information and instruction is required to achieve success.

Driftwood

Driftwood is one of the most useful materials that an arranger can acquire. It not only brings a new element of design into a flower arrangement – previously consisting of just flowers and leaves – but it also provides a dynamic shape and form difficult to achieve in quite the same way with other plant material. In show work it is classed as 'dried plant material' and of course this is just what it is – because driftwood is an umbrella term for dried roots or chunks of wood, branches, stems and even pieces of bark. It can describe any part of a growing tree which has become a separate entity.

Although some wonderful pieces of driftwood are washed up on the beach (particularly after a gale), the majority of 'finds' are made in the woods and hedgerows and on river banks. Clearly, tree wood will not be found in the sea unless it is near an estuary from where it has been washed down after storms. So those living far inland need not be discouraged, for lake sides, streams and moors yield splendid examples. Most of us are beachcombers at heart, and this driftwood collecting not only develops the 'seeing eye' but also adds some new purpose to a country walk. Autumn gales bring down branches, but it is sad that many hedges are being removed, for interesting roots (particularly hawthorn) can be obtained from this source.

Bought driftwood, though convenient, can never give as much satisfaction as the piece you found and prepared yourself. The wood should be hard. If it is soft and rotten it will continue to disintegrate and is not worth collecting and working upon. When you have found an interesting piece give it a good scrub with detergent and then let it dry out. It usually has mud and dust and some insects lurking about, and scrubbing the debris removes this. Then scrape away any soft bits, and finally give it a good firm brushing with a wire or hard brush. As a rule the wood looks best left in its natural colouring but if you prefer it with a slight polish then brush on *colourless* wax polish of the kind used for furniture or shoes. Leave overnight and then polish well. This waxing will improve some pieces and will also give some protection. Some of the bought pieces are sand-blasted but although they look very professional somehow their texture loses its special quality. Sometimes varnish is painted on. Matt varnish looks better than the shiny kind, but all varnishing tends to give an artificial look.

It is possible that your piece of wood

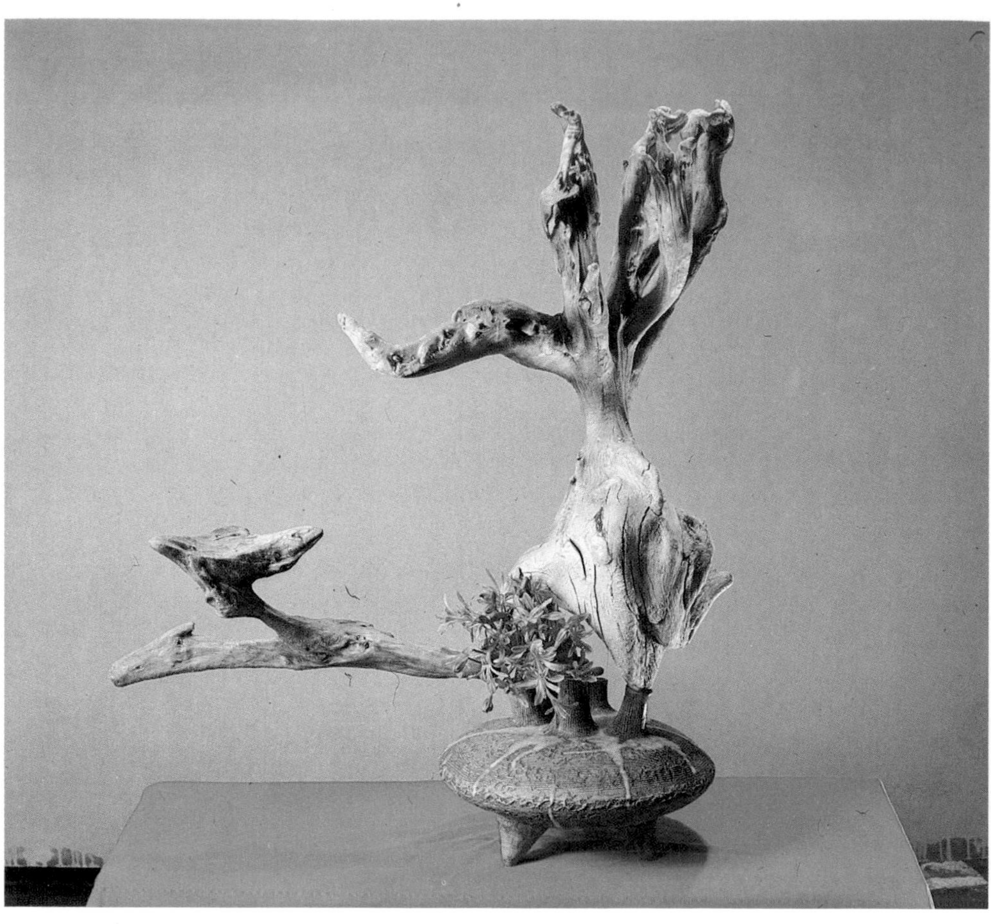

Above: interesting movement is created by two pieces of driftwood placed in a stoneware pot chosen for its affinity in colour and texture

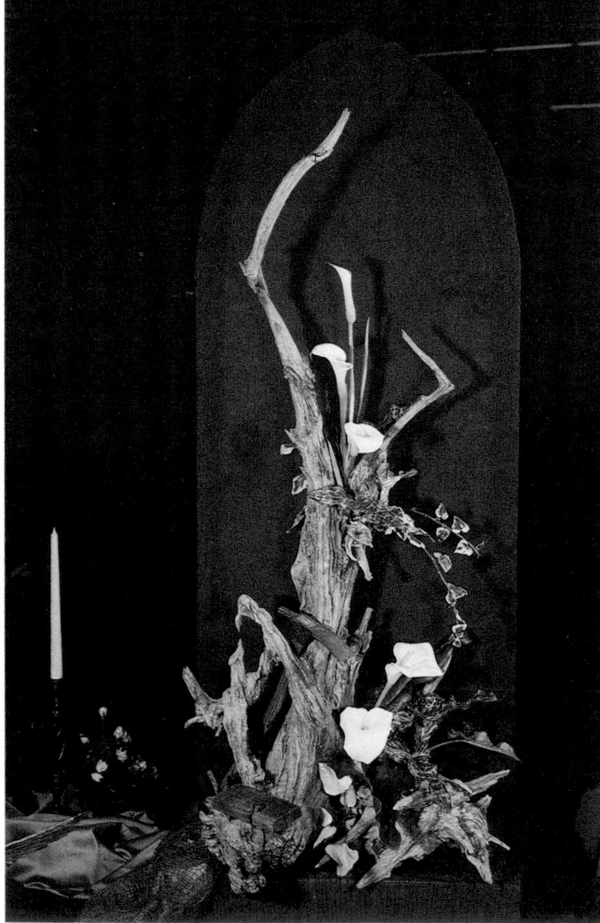

Left: the striated texture and angular shape of the wood contrast well with the smooth surface texture of the lilies and the foliage

Left: an unusual piece of driftwood has been combined with fruits and pastel-coloured flowers which harmonize well

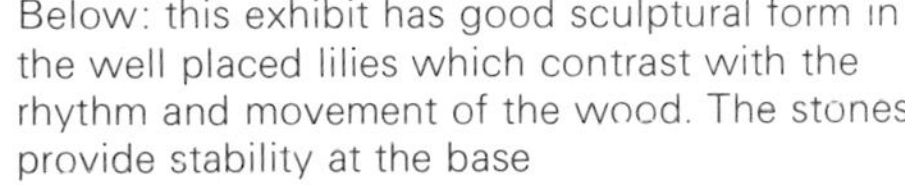

Below: this exhibit has good sculptural form in the well placed lilies which contrast with the rhythm and movement of the wood. The stones provide stability at the base

looks rather negative in colour, or that you wish to accentuate a particular shade or tone. Subtle colouring can be added by judicious use of wood stain or coloured shoe polish wax. If you need other colour effects then matt emulsion could be used. The wood can be bleached by adding half a bottle of ordinary household bleach to a bucket of water. All this alteration of colour needs an artist's eye and hand, for if it is overdone it can look brash instead of beautiful.

After preparing your wood you may find it difficult to make it stable in an arrangement. Time and care must be taken to see that the wood stands firmly and does not fall over or even give a feeling of its instability to those who view the finished arrangement. Real care about supports and mechanics pays dividends. If your branches are very light and slender or of a very soft texture, then they would probably fix directly on to the pinholder pins, or into your plastic foam brick. The base of the wood branch should be cut at a slant so that the pointed end will go easily between the pins or into the foam.

If the wood is more robust and heavier then use the special driftwood clamps that can be bought. These have adjustable screws so that you can angle your wood into the position you want and have it held there. Some of these clamps are fixed on an upside-down small pinholder that you sit on the teeth of the pinholder holding the flowers and foliage, or on to another one placed specially to hold the clamp. You can use the small carpenter's clamps available from hard-ware shops. The slight disadvantage is that all these mechanics take up some space. But if the wood is large enough to require these additional mechanics then the arrangement will be of a reasonably large scale anyway and there is probably ample space.

A good way with a chunky piece of interesting shape is to find the best position for it to stand and then either glue on, or burrow out little holes, into which small 'legs' made from dowelling – rather in the manner of a three-legged milking-stool – are fixed. This is a very satisfactory method. Another good way is to use a small base and screw up through this base and into your driftwood. It is essential to use screws, for nails will split the wood. Two permanent ways of fixing are (1) a lead base with a screw projecting upwards which can be bought, and the wood screwed on to it (2) very large heavy pieces can be set into a mixture of two parts of plaster of paris (bought from a chemist) to one part of cold water, adding the water to the powder. Work quickly for the plaster sets immediately. Working on a polythene base, make it into a suitable lump. Put the wood into the plaster of paris and hold it until it has set. Allow to set and dry thoroughly and then paint or varnish it to seal it. It probably does not matter too much about a really large piece whose position you would not want to change, but

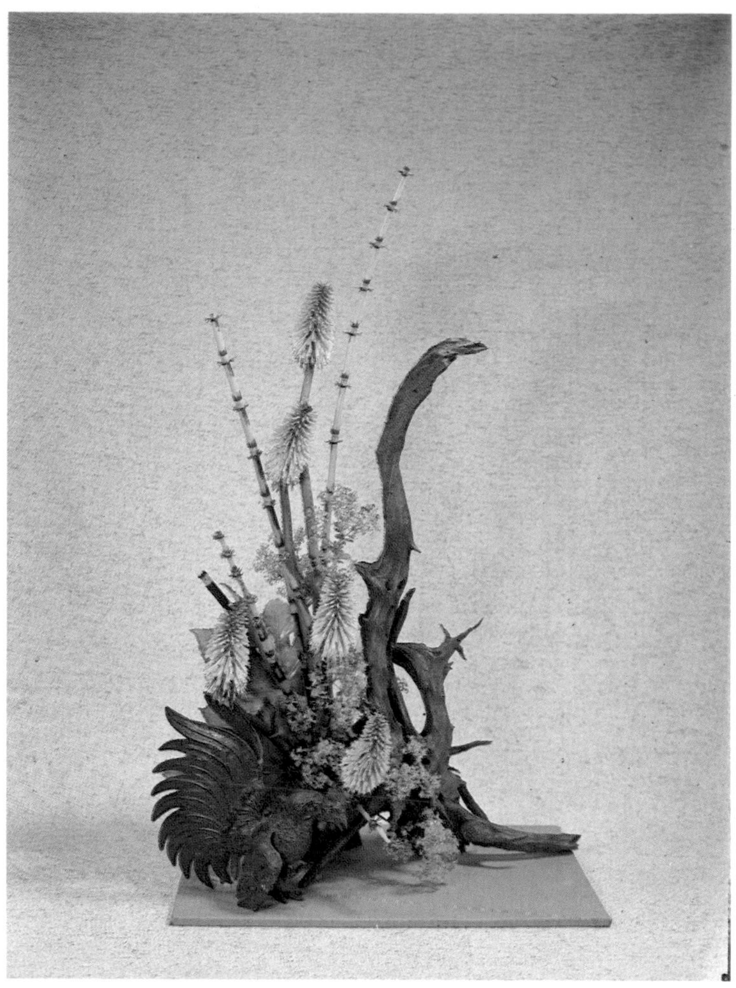

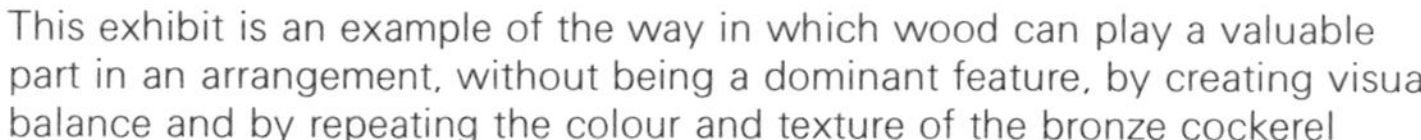

This exhibit is an example of the way in which wood can play a valuable part in an arrangement, without being a dominant feature, by creating visual balance and by repeating the colour and texture of the bronze cockerel

Here the piece of wood serves to raise the flowers and foliage above the water scene and figurine at its base

the pity is with these two methods that the fix is more or less permanent. Almost every piece of driftwood has many possibilities of placement – many look good on their sides, or reversed. With clamps you can change the positions very easily but a permanent fix means only one position.

Great possibilities lie in joining together two or three interesting pieces of wood. If carefully joined they really do look like one and you can create splendid lines. It is interesting to use a piece of wood that curves down the front of a tall pot and this can be done by fixing to it a piece of dowel wood that is put inside the pot, and holds the driftwood. The smaller pieces of bark are most useful for hiding mechanics at the base of an arrangement. They fit in naturally with the plant material as do small stones or pebbles.

Perhaps the most useful part driftwood plays is in landscape designs 'portraying a natural scene'. The driftwood might be placed on a slate or wooden base, with the addition of a branch, some ferns and simple foliage and flowers. There are countless variations, all of them very restful and full of charm. On the other hand a curving piece of a dark or almost black coloured branch, with two or three scarlet tulips and their leaves arranged on a dark wood base can look very dramatic and striking. Driftwood has given another dimension to flower designs. It is worth finding (or buying) one or two or more pieces for they last forever. Those lucky enough to have holidays on tropical beaches can bring home pieces of driftwood that have been bleached a lovely silver colour by the sea salt and the sun. If you find such a piece, wash and brush it very gently in order to preserve this lovely patina, for it is only on the surface.

When first found, most pieces of wood require shaping. Study the wood carefully from all angles and saw off or cut off any awkward bits that spoil the look of the piece or make it difficult to stand up. A good way to find how best to shape the larger wood so that it will stand as you wish it to, is to lower it into a tub of water holding it in the position you want it to stand. The water-line mark will show you where to work with your saw or tools. Do as little as possible and only what is necessary, as the saw-marks remain and are not easy to disguise. When doing this kind of work and when joining pieces, use quick-setting epoxy-resin type adhesives or wood-working adhesive.

Perhaps the wood most often used for average-sized arrangements is tree-ivy. This grows in fascinating twists and curves and is very easy to obtain. Trees in woods or by roadsides usually have the ivy clambering up them and a length can be dislodged easily. Smaller pieces come off without effort after a wet day if a knife is put behind the stem to lift it. Take with you a small pruning saw and you can cut each end of the tree ivy. It is courteous to get permission for cutting and not to trespass, although most tree owners are glad to be rid of ivy growing up their trees. The tree-ivy is, as a rule, stripped of its bark, which is not very interesting or attractive. Use a sharp knife and you will find white wood underneath that mellows in time to a cream colour. If the ivy bark is very tough then soak it in water several days and it will then peel more easily.

Driftwood looks good with all kinds of plant material fresh or dried, with flowers or fruit. It blends happily with natural wild plants or sophisticated exotic flowers and leaves. Driftwood is its name but it is also 'treasure trove' for an arranger.

Making garlands of fresh or dried and preserved flowers and foliage

There is something very gay and festive in the very word 'garland' - probably because it is connected in the mind with happy processions of maidens 'garlanded' - with wreaths of flowers in their hair and carrying what were described as 'scarves' of flowers as they went on their way to a festival or feast. The garland has persisted through the ages from the days of the ancient Greeks and Romans and appears again gloriously in the paintings of the masters. The Dutch painter Pieter Brueghel set wide garlands of fruits and flowers round the Virgin and Child and they can be seen also in the Della Robbia plaques. Garlands survive today in May Day celebrations and are hung round the shoulders of victorious motor-racing aces.

The form has long delighted sculptors and wood carvers whose work we see in the architecture and interiors of most classical buildings. For some years now, garlands have been used by flower decorators at Christmas, at dances and balls and also along the front of buffet tables. Perhaps their most frequent appearance in recent years has been in the decoration of pillars or walls at church festivals, either sumptuous with fruits and flowers in great cathedrals or more simply in smaller churches for their Christmas, Harvest or other festivals.

There are several methods of making garlands. After many years of experience and trying many different methods, the best one, in my view - for fresh material - is the following: take a length of 1-5 cm ($\frac{1}{2}$-2 in.) mesh wire-netting and cut it to the required length. If you want the garland to loop very low down in the centre then make allowances for this in your wire measurement. For an average width garland then cut the wire 20-22.5 cm (8-9 in.) wide. Lay the wire on a trestle or similar table. Should your length of wire be too short it is easy to join a second or third strip of wire-netting to it by entwining the cut snag ends of the wire together. A small sack of sphagnum moss is needed for the filling. This is the moss used by florists for the base of wreaths and by gardeners for lining hanging baskets, and it is not very expensive. It grows on boggy land and at stream edges and is easy to collect if you live near such places. With a 'spring-bok' or garden rake it is easily scraped up. The joy is that once you possess some of this moss it will go on for ever, if you keep it in a plastic sack in a cool place. Do not confuse it with what is called 'bun' moss, the green velvety variety with an earth back. Sphagnum moss is quite clean to handle and has the consistency of a kind of cotton waste.

To insert the filling, lay down the centre of your wire a good 'backbone' of the moss,

Above: a large swag of colourful dried and preserved materials is flanked by four smaller ones to make an interesting group (see p126)

Below: a table garland of fresh roses and foliage suitable for a party

When flowers are difficult to find, a swag can be made using silver-sprayed dried material, here complementing a few *Helleborus niger* (Christmas roses)

along all its length. It should be fairly moist and cling together so that you can then hook up the cut wire ends on both sides of the moss so that it is buttoned into the wire like a corset. This takes very little time and your garland then is turned over with its joined side on the table top. The wire-encased moss backbone should be about 7.5 cm (3 in.) thick for general purposes, but will vary according to your needs and the place and occasion. For instance, it could be about 12.5 cm (5 in.) for a cathedral wall, or a 2.5 cm (1 in.) cord for delicate designs. Then press the wire down so that the back is flat, and the sides and top are half rounded – rather the shape of the outer cover of a bicycle tyre. The moss should be firmly packed, but if it is too tight it will be difficult to make the plant stems enter the moss. The 'carcase' is now ready for filling. Without doubt a fine-leaved foliage such as box, macrocarpa yew or *Pittosporum* looks best as it is light and elegant. This foliage is only providing a background for the flowers and/or fruit to be placed on it. The branchlets are stiff enough to push into the moss with ease, and the leaves should overlap. Naturally scale must be taken into account when planning such a scheme, and if the swag is to be in a large-scale setting then more substantial foliage such as laurel, ivy and other evergreens can be used.

Whatever foliage is chosen it is essential that it is first cut into fairly small lengths of 5, 7 or 10 cm (2, 3 or 4 in.) according to the scale. Large pieces disturb the clean sculptured look that such a classical design requires. Mark the centre of your garland and then start clothing the wire framework by pushing the stem ends through the wire and into the moss. This becomes easy with a little practice, although it does take time. The object of marking the centre is to ensure that all the left hand side leaves point down to this centre and all those on the right hand side also do so. This will mean beginning 'stem filling' at the ends and working towards the centre, seeing that all the leaf tips point to the centre as you proceed. Some may think this a refinement; you can, of course, work just straight from one end to the other end, but the finished result will not be as satisfying, for the leaves change colour and appearance as the light catches them. You will soon acquire the knack of fixing the stems in the moss so that they remain firm. If you need to get a more tailored look, cut stub wires into lengths and bend them into hair-pin shapes, push them over the awkward stems, *through* the moss, and turn the ends of the hairpins flat, on the *back* of the garland. This makes them absolutely firm, and a little grooming with scissors will trim off any wayward leaves.

You are now ready to decorate the garland. Remember that the focus or centre of interest will be at the low centre of your garland, from which point the other placements should be equidistant. The garland is a classical design, and therefore there should be symmetrical placements each side of the centre. Should you wish, your garland can be a solid rope of flowers. You should still give thought to this careful repetition of pattern, form and colour. Wire-netting and moss is flexible, so after making the back of the garland flat (to go against the wall), squeeze the wire and moss so that they taper towards each end of the garland. The water-retaining moss keeps the foliage and flowers fresh and lovely for days. If you wish you can put single lily heads or roses or other flowers in small tubes with rubber caps to hold water and stems, but if conditioned beforehand, the flowers should last perfectly. Fruits are heavier and their round forms are difficult to absorb into the design. Some can be cut in half to reduce their size and the cut side covered in clinging plastic film or foil, as long as it does not show.

To fasten both flowers and fruit to the garland carcase use stub wires. You may need an 18 gauge stub wire for heavy placements, but use the finer gauge for the 'hair-pins'. Such a garland is not tremendously heavy when completed, and the two ends can be hung on a screw plugged into the wall. Nor are they especially costly, for every flower shows more or less individually. If you then spray the garland the moss will absorb the fine mist, and everything remains remarkably fresh. A strip of polythene cut to size, and not to show, will prevent damp on the wall if it is fixed behind the garland.

The same method can be used to make a circle of flowers and foliage, but in this case the wire and moss should be the same width all round the circle, rather than tapered. Another method, much used, employs polythene tubing, or polythene stitched into a long tube 20 cm (8 in.) wide and up to 3.4 m (12 ft) long. Cut plastic foam bricks into four lengthwise, and push

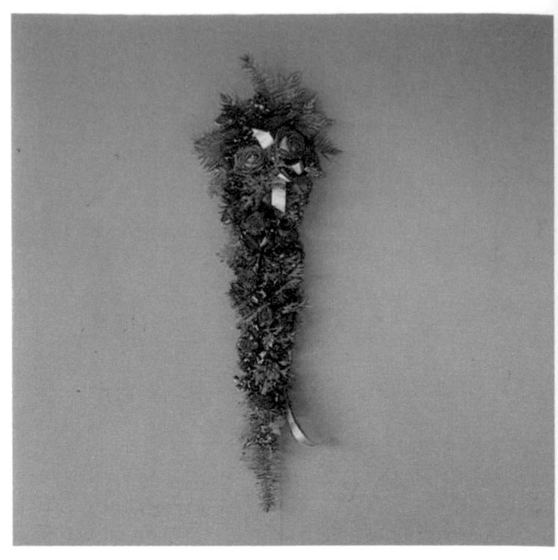

The seasonal colours of the roses, carnations, variegated holly and fresh evergreen material make this swag suitably festive

them into the tube – wiring between each section, but with sufficient space between to keep them flexible – like a string of sausages. The plastic foam must have been soaked beforehand. Then enclose the 'sausage' in 2.5 cm (1 in.) wire-netting. The snag is that the plastic foam is not cheap and cannot be used again if it dries out, and that unlike sphagnum moss, plastic is resistant to the stems. Constance Spry used to advise – for a quick result for a party – gathering a full double page of a newspaper widthways from side to side into a paper baton and then winding string around this with evergreens and joining on further 'batons' until the required length is reached. This is quick and effective but, of course, is not up to the more 'finished' work to be viewed at close quarters. Another way is to use a length of rope for the base, cover it up with moss and wind fine string or wire around it. This sounds the most obvious method but in practice, the rope garland tends to twist when it is hung up so that you do not get the good effect of a 'straight run' of foliage.

Dried or preserved garlands and drops

Drops for garlands – used at each end of the horizontal loop – are made in the same way as described for the loop garland, if living fresh plant material is being used. To make a garland and drops with dried or preserved materials different mechanics can be employed. In my opinion there is still no better method than the sphagnum moss and wire-netting method for use in churches and large buildings – only now it is not necessary to have the moss saturated but merely moist or even dry. The moss-and-wire fixture makes much easier one of the most tedious things about making swags and garlands – the putting in of countless small sprigs of greenery or dried material. The moss-and-wire is wonderfully pliable compared to the other materials which are quite rigid in comparison and give resistance when the sprigs are inserted. Indeed, it is often necessary to use a skewer or other firm pointed tool to make a hole for the stem end before it will slip in. Other techniques that can be used for dried and preserved material include cutting a piece of pegboard to the desired length and width, and then wiring the dried material to this base through the pegboard holes; or the materials can be glued into place with a strong adhesive or stuck into a plaster of the kind that can be bought at art shops. There is a special harder plastic foam that is made for use with dried and preserved materials but it is very tough for the stems to penetrate. Ordinary plastic foam can be used but must be enclosed in 2.5 cm (1 in.) wire-netting or a fine mesh fabric netting such as that in which fruit is sold.

To make elegant dried swags and drops for more permanent use in a house then extra care in construction is required. When constructing a loose garland use cord as a base, but substitute wire for a stiffer style. These bases must be covered with tape. Each piece of plant material should be wired separately and the wire covered with florist's tape. They should then be bound to the covered base cord or wire with black or silver reel wire. Graduate the plant forms into the graceful design you require. Very fragile leaves can be strengthened by 'stitching' fine silver wire through them. It is worth taking extra care with such swags or drops for they last for years; they will collect dust in time which blown air will remove, or they can be sponged clean. The use of steam, or a warm iron, will restore 'tired' preserved or dried plant material. Glycerined material can be refreshed by washing it in tepid water.

Plaques

Plaques are used chiefly to decorate walls. They can be round, oval or shield shape. The background can be made of hardboard and either painted with matt paint to the colour required or else covered in furnishing felt or other matt texture fabric. In this case the background is meant to be part of the decoration and to be visible.

On to the hardboard will be wired – by making holes through the board – a brick of wet plastic foam wrapped in a thin plastic bag if fresh material is to be used. A *dry* brick or circle of harder foam (available from florists or club sales tables) encased in wire is substituted if dry plant material is used. Into these bricks, after they are firmly fixed on to the background,

Reminiscent of a Victorian dried flower picture, this interestingly conceived plaque is full of colour. The lattice basket represents a container

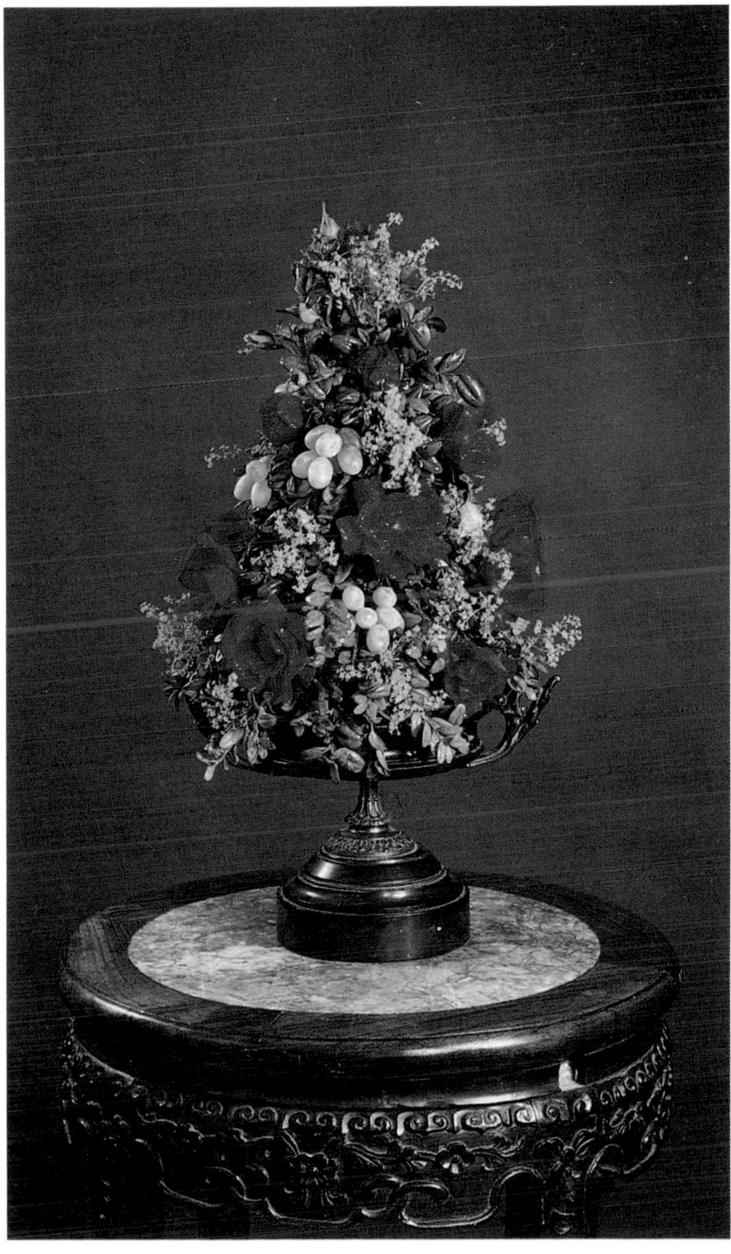

A cone (see p128) made of sphagnum moss in wire-netting decorated with red 'Frensham' roses, *Alchemilla mollis* and green grapes

the leaves and flowers, or whatever is the choice of plant material, are placed, usually radiating round the plastic brick with the important focal point placed in the centre. Alternatively the design can be worked from top to bottom if preferred and if dried material is chosen then again plaster can be used, or glue, to fix the material on to the background. The special, hard plastic foam brick is usually the best method.

These plaques can be very effective if the colour used on the background is chosen either to blend or contrast with the colours chosen for the plant material. They can be very useful in the decoration of rather bare institutional kinds of building with tall bare pillars or with a very bare gallery running round the hall. If a fabric cover is made then it can be glued on to the base, but an elastic rim means the cover can be slipped on or off with ease and used again. Oval shields covered in this way can have scarlet or green covers for use at Christmas and one of a soft green colour to set off midsummer flowers, according to the need and the season. It is always wise to cover the foam brick with small close foliage to cover the mechanics and make a good base for the main flowers and foliage. They can also provide decoration on walls or be used as fire screens.

Cones

Swags, plaques and garlands come to us from the Romans and Greeks; the cone design we owe to the Byzantine period. They can be of any size, from one placed in a goblet for using on a Christmas or other dinner-table occasion, to one a metre high placed in a container the size of a garden urn. The method of construction remains the same, broadly speaking, whatever the size, and is as follows: cut a piece of wire-netting into a triangle shape of the size required and then roll it to a point at one end. Fasten the cut wire snag ends together to make a good 'carcase' shape that will fit the diameter of the container in question. Pack the cone-shaped wire with sphagnum moss and then make a flat base of wire-netting so that the cone will sit on the top of the urn or container used, preventing the moss from slipping down into the container. A plastic brick can be used instead of moss, cut into shape and covered with wire-netting to stop it crumbling. A very large cone can be constructed with a centre of damp crumpled newspaper with an outside of moss (if moss is hard to come by). Whatever its construction, the cone is first covered with the greenery and then decorated at regular intervals or in a spiral of decoration. These cones always look decorative, are interesting to do, and take surprisingly few flowers and fruits to complete, compared to their size. Small cones look beautiful on a dinner-table decorated with roses and grapes or other flowers and fruit from classical motifs.

Remember that with all these designs – garlands, swags, plaques and cones – you are making an outline that you will dress with foliage, flowers and fruits. Consequently the finished design will end up by being very much thicker than the shape of the carcase. With this in mind, make your wire frame much slimmer than the finished design you envisage. Otherwise you can end with an undesirably over-blown look.

Christmas door wreaths

A small wreath frame can be bought from a florist. Attach to it a base of sphagnum moss bound on with fine reel wire wound over and over. Follow the same methods as for garlands, covering the moss with a ground base of foliage and then placing the decorations on the wreath as follows. The decorations are fixed by the 'hair-pin' method of using stub wire as previously described. The top and bottom of the wreath should be marked, and the foliage flow from top to bottom, from top centre to base, with the largest decorations at top centre and bottom centre, and a lesser feature of interest mid-way on each side. Red and green ribbons of florists' water-proof material add a festive note, as do suitable decorations such as small bells or baubles. The material could be sprayed with gold or silver paint, or with other colours. Dried and preserved material may also be used either alone or with fresh foliage.

A topiary tree

Begin by setting a dowel stick or a broom handle in cement or similar setting material in a flower pot, the size of which will vary according to your needs. Tiny trees in tiny pots are lovely on a children's party table, while trees of the stature of a clipped bay tree are splendid placed down an aisle, or up steps at a wedding or party. Make a small round ball of moss contained in wire-netting for the large trees. For tiny trees small potatoes could be used, or foam in wire. Potatoes are excellent used as water-retaining material for stems and they can be sprayed with silver or gold. Once again, make the foliage base and then decorate. Single white chrysanthemum flowers look fresh and lovely against the green and last well. If the flower pot complete with 'tree' is placed in a decorative plastic or fibre-glass garden urn, and the tree stem either painted or ribbon wreathed it makes a worthwhile contribution to the party scene.

If you are aiming for a freer arrangement than the clipped foliage design, then screw a pie dish on top of the broomstick end, place a brick of plastic foam well soaked on a holder, and then arrange with flowers and light flowing sprays of foliage. Ribbons can be added for a wedding if you like them.

Large scale tall arrangements

The same principle used for topiary trees, of a fixed wooden batten or thin pole, can be employed to make really tall arrangements up to 3.5 m (about 12 ft). Thin water, gas or conduit pipes are rigid but are heavier to transport. Naturally due consideration must be given to stability the higher you go. There must be a container at the base sufficiently weighted with concrete or plaster of paris to keep the pole or pipe quite firm. If the stem is to be over 120 cm (4 ft) then it is best to have two sections – say 120 cm (4 ft) each or whatever height you require – firmly joined with screws at the centre. Otherwise you can make the stem so that one 120 cm (4 ft) end fits inside the top of the bottom one and so gain your 2.4 m (8 ft) height – or more. Wrap wire-netting or moss round the stem using fine black reel wire to make it secure. Then clothe the stem with foliage and fix funnels on alternate sides at intervals in which water can be poured and into which flowers and foliage can be placed. Conceal the funnels with extra foliage. These tall slim designs look splendid if well done and can be seen by everyone in crowded halls. They provide an excellent means of effecting a strong visual impact with few flowers.

Tall arrangements can also be made by using an upright saucepan-stand. Place containers on each saucepan space and let the foliage mingle with the arrangement directly below it to make a stand of flowers that is pretty and elegant. Such designs look good in pairs flanking a doorway. Large pillars can support tall arrangements, contrived by the juxtaposition of a pedestal, below that a small table holding a container, and finally a low stool holding a third container. Each of the three containers must be arranged so that the materials flow down one into the other in a single unbroken line. This is not difficult if foliage and sprays are used that have a natural downward line.

Another way is to place a washing-up bowl at the base of the column. Fix a plank 10 cm (4 in.) wide. Knock nails through at 7 cm (3 in.) intervals and impale foam bricks upon them. Wrap plastic and wire netting around the bricks. For a tall pyramid design, use a washing-up bowl once more with a 5×5 cm (2×2 in.) rod securely fixed in it. Fix shelves at about 90–120 cm (3–4 ft) intervals with one at the top and base, held by brackets. Each shelf should hold a container with arrangements that will, when filled, create the tall pyramid outline. Put screw eyes in the wooden upright so that wires can be tied around the pillar against which the design stands to give stability.

Hanging designs

Hanging flower baskets can be lined with moss or greenery, then filled with polythene and plastic foam bricks before being decorated all round – that is, *under* the basket as well – by pushing stems through the flower basket wires. These baskets look well hanging from the rather difficult balconies found in large halls. Pew ends or sloping window sills can be decorated with plastic foam bricks wrapped in plastic suspended from the top of the pew or the window frame. An alternative for the pew

Left: a large scale cone-shaped arrangement in which funnels holding water make it possible to use fresh flowers several feet above the base

Below: two examples of mobiles using arresting configurations of contrasting dried materials. One is supported from the base and the other is suspended from above. Both are sufficiently light to be continuously moved by air currents and are a constant visual challenge. See Chapter 15, *Modern and Abstract Design*

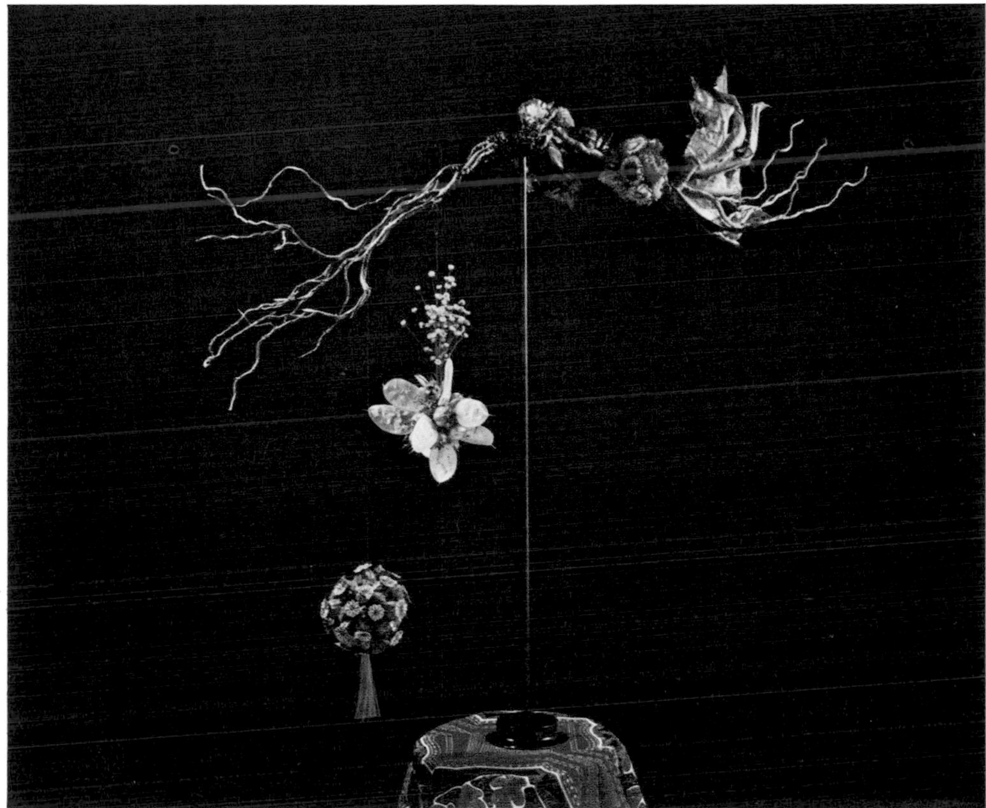

end is to work from ground level. Fix a small wooden board in a container and attach either moss or plastic foam (as described for the larger designs) to it. Dress the board with small foliage and then decorate as desired. If foam bricks are used on top of each other to a considerable height, place a plant stick (or broom-stick according to height) through the bricks and wire-netting around them to give firmness. A funnel placed in the top gives further height without the need for an extra foam brick.

Constructing a pot-et-fleur

This is a group of growing plants combined with cut flowers, all in one basic container. Because this decoration will be used indoors you will require a container that will hold water. Furthermore, the container must be sufficiently deep for the earth to be at least 2.5 cm (1 in) below its rim, so that watering can be carried out safely. Ensure that there is sufficient depth in the bowl to contain the roots of the plants without overcrowding. Victorian bedroom washbowls, brass and copper preserving bowls, lined boxes and baskets and specially made plant containers are all suitable. You will need broken crocks or gravel to provide drainage and some charcoal to

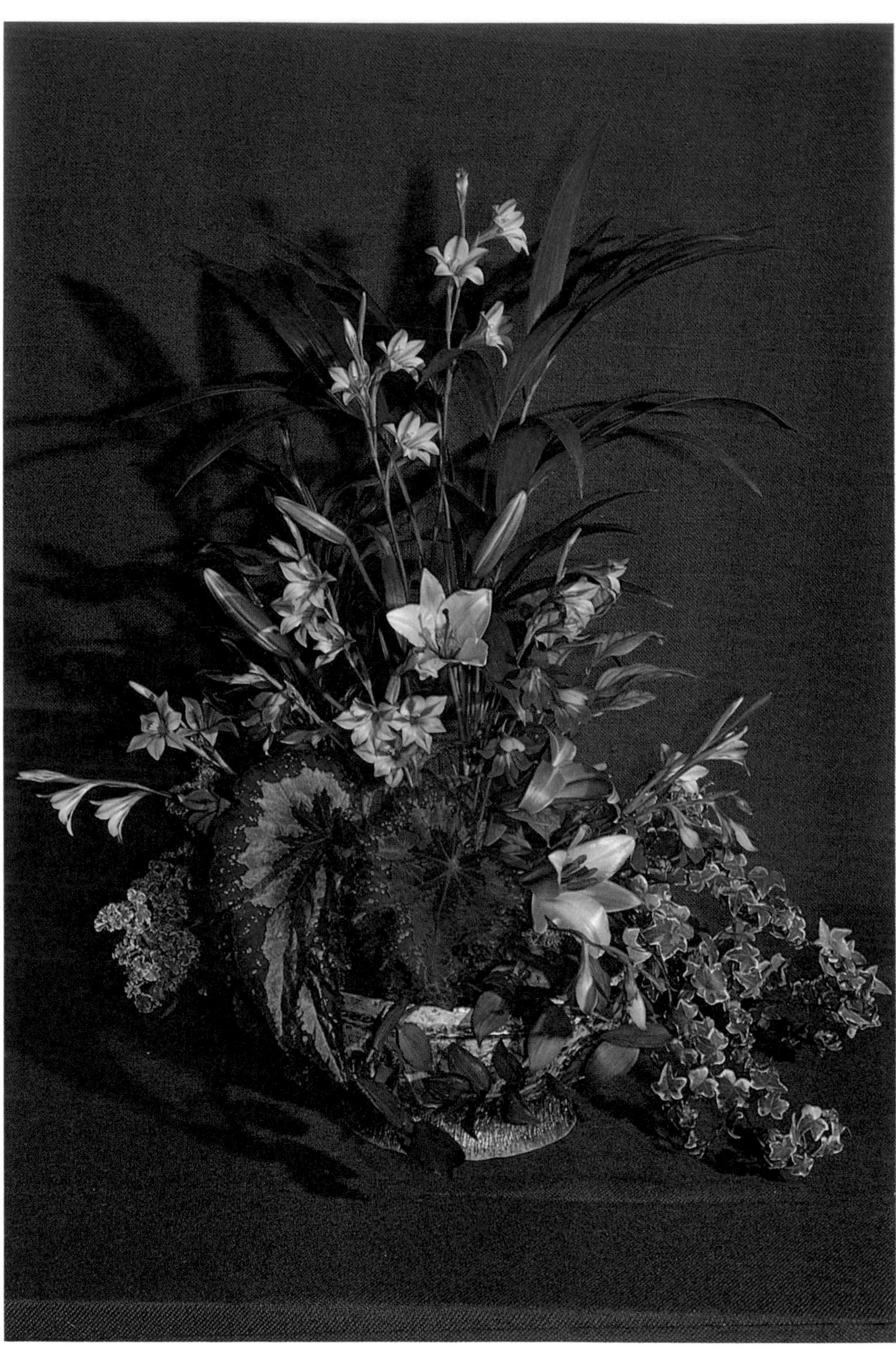

Pot-et-fleur—an award-winning exhibit. The growing plants have been placed in the container with due regard for colour harmony and contrast of shape and form. Height has been achieved and colour been taken to the top of the arrangement by blending a few cut flowers with the growing foliage

keep the water 'sweet'. Put into the bowl a 2.5 cm (1 in.) layer of crocks or gravel and a few bits of charcoal, then a loose 5 cm (2 in.) layer of John Innes No. 2 compost which you can get from a garden centre or shop. Then take your chosen house plants from their pots and arrange them on the layer of compost, and position the small container that will hold the water and your cut flowers. Firm the plants and container and add more compost until you reach within 2.5 cm (1 in.) of the rim. It is possible to use plants in their own pots with peat packed around them and the flower container. This method is cumbersome, however, and the pots take up a great deal of room. The plants do not mingle as well if they are not all buried in the same growing medium.

Consider carefully where in the room to place the *pot-et-fleur*. It is necessary to take into account whether it is in full sun, or in rather a dark north-facing corner and what the normal temperature of the particular room is. In cool, dark rooms ferns and ivies will flourish but a sunny hot room would suit plants like *Echeveria* and *Sansevieria trifasciata* (mother-in-law's tongue). The attractive variegated plants need really good light, so assemble a group that has similar cultural needs. Most house plants are sold with a label giving their name and their needs. Think about arranging these plants as you would about making a flower arrangement. You will need height at the back which, at least one-and-a-half times the width of the container, will mean quite a tall plant. The next requirement is medium-sized plants, and finally trailing plants to flow over the edge of the container. Variety in forms and shapes of leaves and contrast in leaf textures is important. Choose plants carefully for their own colour and also to harmonize with the bowl. If you can link up the plant and container colours and texture, so much the better.

The shades of the cut flowers that you add are of course of equal value, whether they contrast or blend with the other components. Be watchful of the danger of over-watering – fix a particular day for this task at a suitable interval dictated by the plant variety. Feed the plants as recommended by the proprietary brands, and *only* at the correct times. Spray the foliage regularly, for the plants will miss the outdoor rain and will look their best if the leaves are fresh and shiny. The cut flowers can be placed in their container with a pinholder or a narrow funnel can be used. This indoor garden arrangement is the answer for the flat-dweller with no garden and there is no better way to use but a few cut flowers to maximum advantage.

Should you enter a show class judged by *NAFAS Schedule Definitions* (1975) do not include *cut* foliage in a *pot-et-fleur*. Driftwood, moss, stones and accessories may be added if wished and if the show schedule allows.

Far right: an interesting grouping of growing plants in which gerberas are combined with driftwood

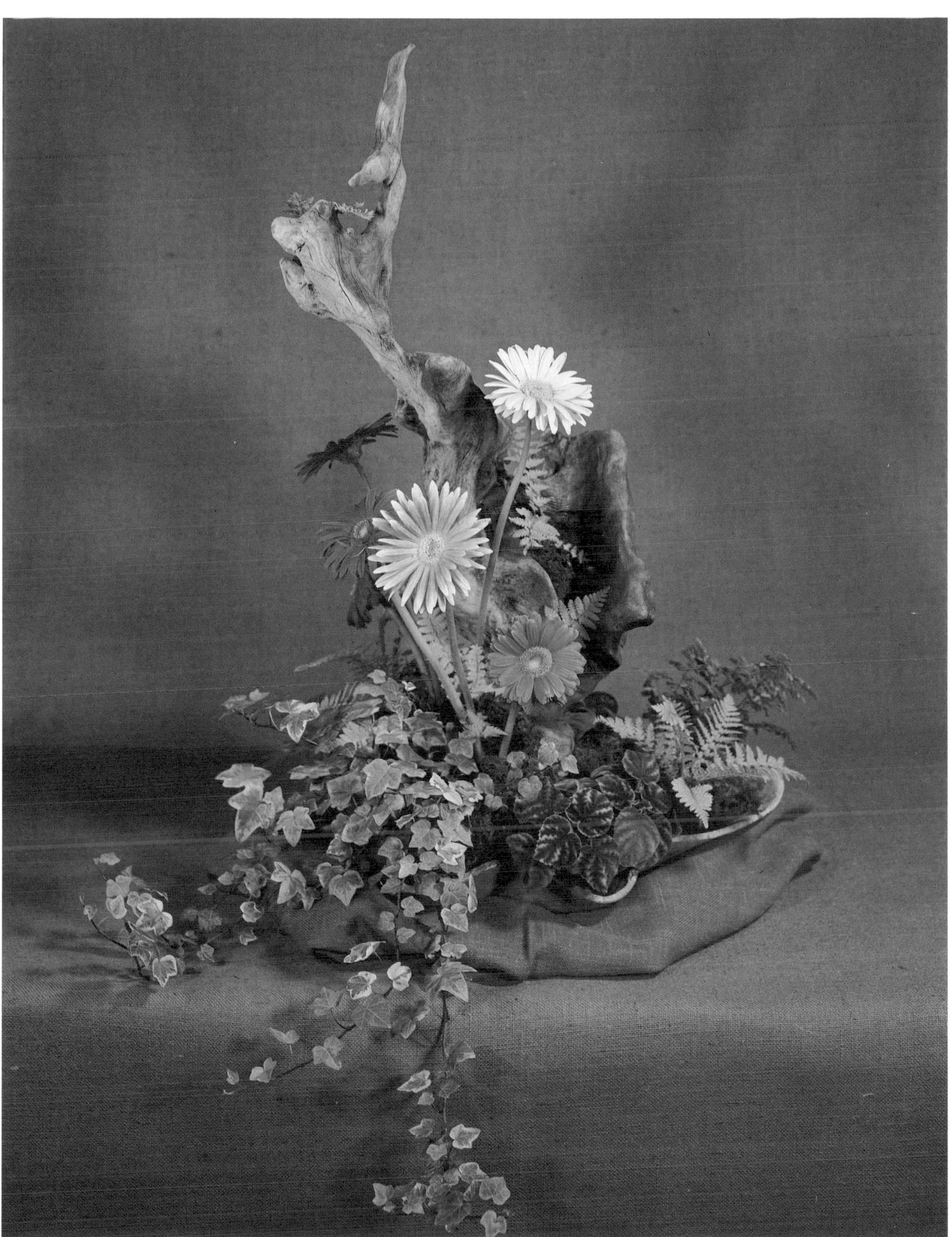

10. Plants for the Flower Arranger's Garden

George Foss

God Almighty first planted a garden; and, indeed, it is the purest of human pleasures.
SIR FRANCIS BACON 1561–1626

Before making suggestions regarding plant selection, I should like to make a few observations about flower arrangers' gardens in general. In the first place, without seeing the site, it is impossible to make a plan for any particular type of garden, as size, shape, situation, aspect and soil all have to be taken into consideration. The winter is probably the best time to look for a site or buy another house, for if the place appeals to you then, it will do so all the more in the summer.

When creating my last garden I did away with a straight path that ran the entire length of it. Most of this path became a border, and although things grew there afterwards, one or two of the flowering shrubs forming part of the border never really looked happy. This was undoubtedly the result of lack of attention during excavation of the old path. The moral is that thorough preparation of borders and beds is essential, subsequent success depending on the amount of thought – yes, and hard work – that are put into it.

If possible, arrange to have a paved area near the house, making it large enough to entertain your guests.

When planning, subsequent upkeep is of paramount importance. There are two ways which will greatly minimize labour. The first is to edge lawns with brick or stone. In the case of a large lawn this can be expensive, but if you are your own labourer then of course the cost is more than halved. The edging or narrow path (in my case four bricks wide) eliminates edging and enables planting to be carried out much nearer the front borders. I dislike the gap which so frequently appears between border and lawn. The second aid can be attained by choosing plants which do not require staking and tying, for this can be a lengthy and rather dreary job. There are, nevertheless many plants which no arranger should be without, and which more than compensate for the labour involved.

Where borders are wide, it is an advantage to leave a narrow path at the back. This will be completely hidden when plants have grown.

I would also suggest round paving stones placed a stride apart through the border, which enable one to gather flowers with greater ease. These can easily be obtained, are about 23 cm (9 in.) in diameter, and being round they take up the minimum of space and are soon practically hidden by surrounding foliage.

A garden created by George Foss shows the value of brick path and edgings

Flowering trees

It is extremely difficult to make a choice among the many beautiful flowering trees. If, however, the garden is small or of medium size, it is important to choose from those which are attractive not only in bloom, but throughout the remainder of the year.

The first two mentioned in the list given below are not strictly flowering trees, although they do have insignificant flowers. For ease of reference, this list has been put in alphabetical sequence.

Acer platanoides 'Dummondii' Origin: Europe. Variegated green leaves edged in cream. Maple family. 6 m (20 ft).

A. 'Goldsworth Purple' Good dark purple foliage during summer. 7.5 m (25 ft).

Betula pendula (syns. *B. alba, B. verrucosa*) Origin: Europe. Silver birch. 7.5 m (25 ft). Put a group of three in a little glade with spring bulbs planted beneath.

Plants break the formality of the paving

B.p. 'Youngii' (Weeping Birch) Branches sweep to the ground, suitable for small garden. 3.6–4.5 m (12–15 ft).

Cercis Siliquastrum (Judas Tree) Origin: S. Europe. It is surprising that this most attractive tree is not more widely grown. The flowers, which appear in May, are an unusual bright purple magenta, and some of them grow out of the main branches. It is a slow growing tree, and in cold districts should be planted in front of a south-facing wall. *C.s. alba* bears white flowers.

Malus floribunda Origin: Japan, China. As its name implies, this malus is smothered with flowers, which are pale pink. Crab-apple family.

M. 'Golden Hornet' Rather erect habit: yellow fruit which stays long on the tree. 6–7.5 m (20–25 ft).

M. 'John Downie' Graceful shape, full of movement, excellent orange scarlet fruit, the size of a crab-apple. (Both this one and the Golden Hornet make excellent attractively coloured jelly.)

Prunus sargentii (syn. *P. sachalinensis*) Origin: Japan, Korea. Flowers very freely in April. Flowers pink, followed by attractive bronze foliage which turns a brilliant deep red in autumn.

P. subhirtella 'Autumnalis' (Autumn cherry) Origin: W. China. A small de-

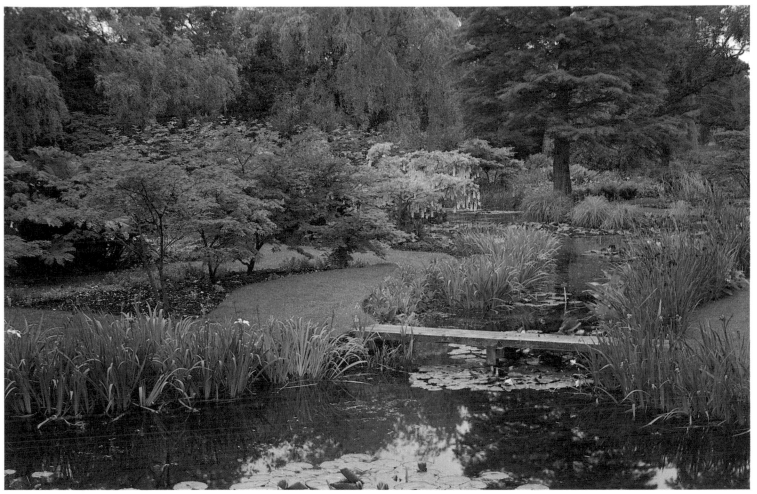

A restful vista in which acers and white wisteria provide a feature with the usual water-loving plants

ciduous tree of rather spreading nature, flowering intermittently in autumn and winter. Pinkish white. 6–9 m (20–30 ft).

P. yedoensis (Yoshino Cherry) Japan. A graceful tree with arching branches. Flowers pink in the bud, opening to white.

Robinia pseudoacacia Origin: U.S.A. Robinia is fast growing, with bright yellow foliage which retains its colour throughout the year, turning an even more glorious colour in autumn, when it is like reflected sunlight. 6 m (20 ft). The variety 'Frisia' bears leaves which are golden-yellow on opening and turn pale green-yellow as they mature.

Brick path softened by low-growing plants

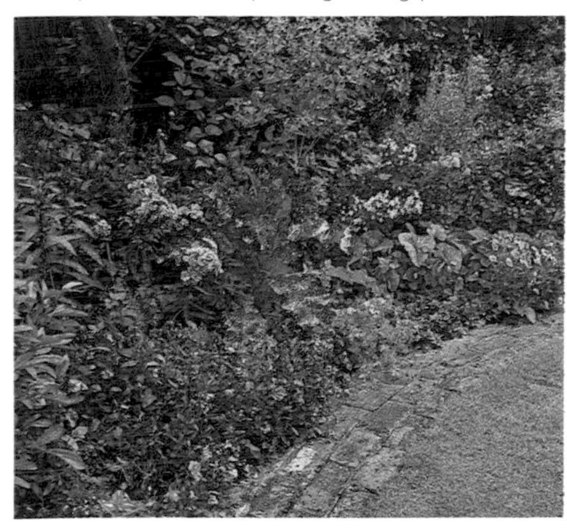

Sorbus vilmorinii (Mountain Ash) Origin: W. China. Light feathery foliage and red berries in autumn.

The acers and robinia do not last well in water. The other species would only be cut to improve the shape. There is nothing easier to achieve and more lovely than silver birch branches heavily glittered for a Christmas decoration. *Sorbus Aria* (whitebeam) will take the solution of glycerine and water and makes an excellent winter decoration.

Evergreen trees have been deliberately excluded from the above list, since they are not as fast growing and it takes many years before they can be cut for decoration. They should not, however, be left out on this account, as they are invaluable during the winter months.

The species *Ilex* includes innumerable varieties of great value to the flower arranger. Amongst them is *I. Aquifolium*, the common Holly, with dark glossy green leaves. Many varieties bear gold or silver variegated leaves, notably *I. argentea marginata* (silver) and *I.* 'Golden King'. Other evergreen trees worth cultivating are *Cupressus* (Cypress), *Chamaecyparis* (False Cypress) and *Taxus* (Yew).

The season for planting is from late autumn to very early spring. Prepare holes 60 cm (2 ft) deep by 1 m (3 ft) diameter or larger. Break up subsoil, spread out roots, and add damp peat and well-rotted manure, replace topsoil and firm well. Place stake in position before planting tree and secure with special tie. Do not plant too deeply, by observing the mark on the stem where previously planted.

Flowering shrubs

The borders of the future may well consist of flowering shrubs and decorative flower-

A rhododendron in full bloom

ing foliage plants. This is just what the flower arranger requires. Many flowering shrubs should be pruned immediately after flowering so that all the vigour is built up for the next year's bloom. So, do a little pruning during the flowering period by cutting some flowers. One must not be too impatient, however, as it takes about three years for a shrub to develop sufficiently to allow for cutting, although container-grown plants are often well developed and can be cut sooner. During this waiting period the space around the newly planted shrubs could be filled with annuals or biennials.

The measurements given are approximate, for an eight- to ten-year-old shrub. Under favourable conditions they may be larger. I have seen Garrya on a north wall 3.5 m (12 ft) high and nearly as wide. In order to condition the cut shrubs for a decoration, simply remove any surplus leaves and side-shoots. Hammer the stems, lighter on new wood than old, and place overnight in deep water.

Berberis – deciduous varieties

B. atropurpurea Marvellous bronze foliage, very useful for colour contrast. Fairly spreading habit 1.8 m × 1.2 m (6 ft × 4 ft). To prune, just thin out overcrowded branches, although in all probability this will not be necessary. Gloves required.

B. rubrostilla Delightful arching sprays, white-red translucent fruit in autumn, flowers in early summer 1.8 m × 1.2 m (6 ft × 4 ft).

Berberis – evergreen varieties

B. darwinii Rich orange-yellow flowers, late spring. Purple berries covered with bloom in autumn. The foliage is particularly useful. 1.8 m × 1.2 m (6 ft × 4 ft).

B. linearifolia 'Orange King' Deep-orange flowers in spring, purple berries with greyish bloom. Prune as for deciduous varieites. 1.8 m × 1.2 m (6 ft × 4 ft).

B. stenophylla Arching branches of yellow flowers in late spring. Makes a very good hedge. 3.5 m × 1.8 m (10 ft × 6 ft).

Callicarpa giraldiana

Origin: China. If you live in a mild climate and can give this shrub full sunshine against a south wall, then it is a must. Flowers in late summer, but it is for its violet berries that it is grown. Prune previous year's growth fairly severely at the end of the winter.

Camellia

Origin: China, Japan. It may be several years after planting before it is possible to cut lengthy branches, and then only to improve the shape, but being evergreen camellias are very useful. They are delightful grown in pots for the terrace. After flowering, these can be moved to another part of the garden and other flowering plants put in their place. They dislike lime and chalk. If grown in a pot use a mixture

Brilliant azaleas in a green landscape

of equal parts of good loam, peat and leaf-mould, with the addition of some sharp sand. Plant where the morning sun does not reach.

C. japonica. Many varieties.

C.j. 'Mathotiana Alba' Large double white, free and vigorous.

C.j. 'Adolph Audusson' Semi-double large blood-red, yellow stamens.

C.j. 'Lady Clare' Large semi-double pale pink flowers, rather drooping habit.

C. × *williamsii* An outstanding group of hybrids. Named varieties include 'Donation', with semi-double silver-pink flowers up to 10 cm (4 in.) across; 'Inspiration', a deeper shade of pink, and 'J. C. Williams', with large blush-pink flowers with yellow stamens.

Carpentaria californica

This evergreen native of the U.S.A. was introduced into Britain in the latter part of the last century. It flowers in summer, producing pure white, fragrant flowers 5–7 cm (2–3 in.) across, with a cluster of yellow stamens in the centre. It does best in a light, loamy soil and in colder districts prefers to have south-facing wall site in full sunshine.

Camellias, with their fine glossy foliage

Chaenomeles lagenaria, syn. Cydonia japonica

Origin: Japan. I still like to think of this quince as Japonica, partly because that is less difficult to pronounce. Besides, this popular name suggests Japan, from where so many of them came. They are completely hardy, are quite happy in any soil or site, and if given the protection of a wall will flower very early in the year. Not only do they have very beautiful flowers to delight one during the dreary days, but their fruit in the autumn makes excellent jelly. The ripe fruit has a delicious scent, and can be gathered in a bowl for indoor use. A small branch with the addition of early flowering bulbs is charming.

C.l. Moerloesii Apple-blossom pink, white within, arching habit.

C.l. nivalis This pure white variety is rather larger than the others, reaching a height of 3 m (10 ft).

C. × *superba* 'Knap Hill Scarlet' Salmon-scarlet, very free flowering. 1.2 m × 1.5 m (4 ft × 5 ft).

Choisya ternata

(Mexican Orange Blossom) Origin: Mexico. A good evergreen plant, flowering in early summer and spasmodically at other times throughout the year. It is not particular regarding site, except in cold districts. It will take the solution of glycerine and water, the leaves going a lovely pale ochre. 2.1 m × 1.8 m (7 ft × 6 ft).

Clerodendrum trichotomum

Origin: Japan, China. The white star-like flowers which appear in late summer are followed in the autumn by clear-blue berries surmounted by a deep-red calyx. It prefers a well-drained soil in full sun. 2.4 m × 2.1 m (8 ft × 7 ft).

Cornus

A group of very hardy trees and shrubs that grow in any soil of good quality.

C. florida rubra Origin: Eastern U.S.A. Has bright rose-red bracts 5–7.5 cm (2–3 in.) across, lovely autumn foliage. 2.4 m × 1.5 m (8 ft × 5 ft).

C. kousa var. *chinensis* Origin: China, Japan. Free-flowering creamy white flowers. 2.4 m × 1.8 m (8 ft × 6 ft).

C. Mas Origin: Europe. More like a small tree, this variety flowers in very early spring. If branches are brought indoors it will flower in late winter, bearing innumerable small greeny yellow hamamelis-like flowers. It sometimes bears small deep-red fruit.

Corylopsis spicata

Origin: Japan. A delightful early flowering shrub, having pendulous spikes of scented primrose-yellow flowers on bare branches. It thrives in a sheltered spot with peat or leaf-mould. 1.8 m × 1.8 m (6 ft × 6 ft).

Corylus avellana 'Contorta'

Origin: W. Europe, W. Asia, N. America.

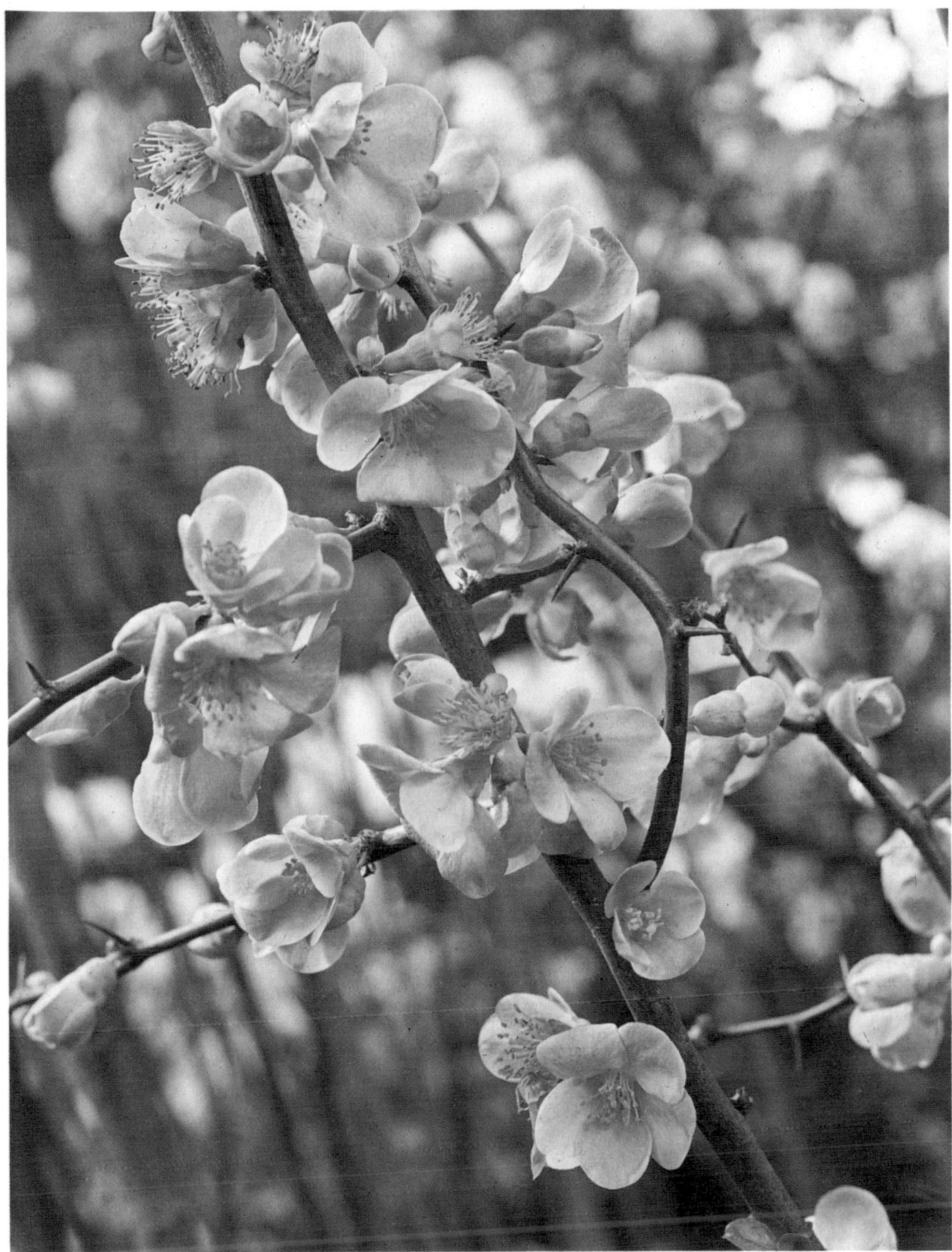

Chaenomeles lagenaria provides beautiful blossoming branches for decorative work

Known as the 'corkscrew hazel' this shrub is most attractive for arrangement. 2 m × 1.5 m (7 ft × 5 ft).

Cotinus, formerly **Rhus cotinus**
Origin: Europe. When well-established this shrub has a cloud of tiny, wispy flowers which gave rise to the popular name 'smoke tree'. It does not take water well when young, but will do so when mature. It is very well worth having in the border for its colour.

C. coggygria var. *atropurpurea* Deep burgundy colour. 1.5 m × 2.4 m × 1.5 m (5 ft × 8 ft × 5 ft).

Cotoneaster
Origin: China, Himalayas. A most useful shrub which will grow well in almost any situation and in any soil. A branch of the horizontal varieties makes a wonderful background for a line arrangement.

C. divaricatus A fast-growing variety with crimson berries in autumn. 1.5 m × 1.5 m (5 ft × 5 ft).

C. horizontalis Distinguished by its herring-bone-like branching. 1.2 m × 3.5 m (4 ft × 10 ft).

C. lacteus Evergreen. The fruit, which is orange-red, lasts throughout the winter. Good for hedging. 3.5 m × 2.4 m (10 ft × 8 ft).

C. variegatus Leaves edged with white. (2 ft × 6 ft).

Cytisus
Origin: Morocco. Generally, broom does not seem to last well in water, but as it is so decorative in the border and gives an entirely different shape in a flower arrangement, you may like to try a few.

C. battandieri Fast-growing shrub from Morocco which has a lovely, almost cone-like yellow flower with a scent not unlike pineapple. The foliage is covered with a silvery down. It can either be grown against a wall or as a standard.

Daphne
Origin: Europe. Most people know Daphne, with its delicious scent. It is not the easiest plant to grow well, for it requires a cool, moist but well-drained position in semi-shade.

D. mezereum Origin: Europe, Asia Minor, Siberia. Erect branches of purplish-red flowers. 1.2 m × 1 m (4 ft × 3 ft).

D. odora variegata Origin: China, Japan. This is evergreen with a most delicious scent. Give it a spot free of lime and sheltered from north and east winds. (4 ft × 5 ft).

Deutzia
Origin: Japan, China. An easy-to-grow shrub with graceful, arching branches full of numerous flowers.

D. × hybrida 'Magician' Large clusters of rich lilac flowers, tinted pink, appearing in summer. 1.8 m × 1.2 m (6 ft × 4 ft).

D. setchuenensis var. *corymbiflora* Late flowering shrub with myriads of small, white, star-shaped flowers; slow growth. 1.8 m × 1.2 m (5 ft × 4 ft).

Dipelta floribunda
Origin: China. Not unlike Weigela; abundance of pink bell-shaped flowers. 2.8 m × 1.5 m (9 ft × 5 ft).

Elaeagnus × ebbingii
Origin: Japan, China. The first of two evergreen shrubs, it has dark-green leaves overlaid with white down, the underpart being silver. The foliage lasts extremely well in water. The arching sprays are very useful for pedestal design. 3.5 m × 2.4 m (10 ft × 8 ft).

E. pungens 'Maculata' (syn. *aurea variegata*) Origin: Japan, China. Golden variegated, useful during the winter months; rather dense and slow growing. Foliage also lasts well in water. 1.5 m × 1.8 m (5 ft × 6 ft).

Enkianthus campanulatus
Origin: Japan. This plant grows best in semi-shade. In late spring it bears charming, pendant, bell-shaped flowers which are a pale cream edged with red. The flowers are borne on the bare branches. In autumn the foliage shows very bright colours. The plant demands lime-free soil. 1.8 m × 1.2 m (6 ft × 4 ft).

Escallonia
Origin: S. America. An easy, quick-growing family of shrubs which are semi-evergreen. They do not mind lime, but require the benefit of a wall in the north. They make a very good flowering hedge,

and should be trimmed back after flowering. The arching branches are excellent for decoration. Full sun or semi-shade.

E. × 'Apple Blossom' Branches covered with pink/white flowers, light-green foliage. 1.5 m × 1.5 m (5 ft × 5 ft).

E. × *edinensis.* Bright rosy pink. 1.8 m × 1.5 m (6 ft × 5 ft).

E. × 'Slieve Donard' This evergreen variety has long arching branches of large apple-blossom-like flowers. Makes a very useful hedge or single plant. 2.1 m × 1.5 m (7 ft × 5 ft).

Eucalyptus
Origin: Australia, Tasmania. These can used as specimen trees in sheltered places, including some exposed districts. For flower arrangers they are better grown as standards. Grow to the desired height, pinch out, and cut branches back to within 23–30 cm (9–12 in.) Large plants do not transplant well. Protect for the first two winters.

E. gunii Glaucous blue in colour, and although the young leaves are rounded, the older ones are sickle-shaped. Takes preserving mixture well.

E. perrinianna Most attractive when young. The leaves are round, with the stem growing through the centre of the leaf. Later the leaf divides. If cut back each year, new growth will persist, and you will always have the most attractive part of the tree.

Eucryphia × nymansensis
Origin: S. America, Australia, Tasmania. This magnificent evergreen flowers in August, bearing large, single white, scented flowers with gold stamens. Growth is pyramidal in shape. It prefers a cool, moist loam, and will tolerate lime. 2.8 m × 1 m (9 ft × 3 ft).

Euonymus
Origin: Japan. Two evergreens are selected as being very useful during the winter. Slow growing.

E. japonicus aureus Golden variegated foliage. After a few years can be cut freely. 1.2–1.5 m × 1 m (4–5 ft × 3 ft).

E. radicans variegata 'Silver Queen' Leaves edged white. 3 × 2 m (10 ft × 6 ft).

Exochorda racemosa (syn. grandiflora)
Origin: China. This lovely pearl shrub flowers in early summer, to produce long arching branches of white flowers in short spikes. Full sun is its best position. 3.6 m × 2.4 m (12 ft × 8 ft).

Fatsia japonica
Origin: Japan. Large glossy green palmate leaves makes this plant very useful. As it will grow in shady sites fatsia is a good town plant. I have seen fatsia covering a south-facing wall 4.5 m high by 3.5 m (15 ft × 10 ft). It produces small white flowers in November followed by jet-black berries, rather like large ivy berries.

A simple arrangement of apple blossom

Recently crossed with *Hedera* (ivy) to produce the hybrid *Fatshedera.*

Forsythia
Origin: China. Everyone knows this glorious early-flowering shrub that is so easy to grow and propagate. Branches pruned in winter and brought indoors will quickly flower.

F. × 'Beatrix Farrand' Recently introduced from America, this variety has a symmetrical growth and large deep-yellow flowers with orange throat. 2.4 m × 1.5 m (8 ft × 5 ft).

F. × 'Spring Glory' Bright yellow flowers smother the branches. 2.1 m × 1.8 m (7 ft × 6 ft).

F. suspensa Has long trailing branches which can be trained to cover an arbour or a north wall. Train branches up and side-shoots will tumble down, forming a curtain of colour in the spring.

Fothergilla major
Origin: U.S.A. The creamy-white cone-shaped flowers of spring are followed by spectacular autumn colours. It needs a sunny site and no lime. 1.8 m × 1.2 m (6 ft × 4 ft).

Garrya elliptica
Origin: California. A delightful hardy evergreen shrub. Can be grown either on the north side of your house or in the open, but if the latter some training is required. Huge 7.5–19 cm (3–4 in.) grey-green catkins appear during the winter from male plants. 1.8 m × 1.8 m (6 ft × 6 ft).

Halesia carolina (syn. H. tetraptera)
Origin: N. America. Spreading branches hung with creamy bell-shaped flowers in May. It flowers on almost bare branches and dislikes lime. 2.4 m × 1.8 m (8 ft × 6 ft).

Variations of colour in hydrangea heads

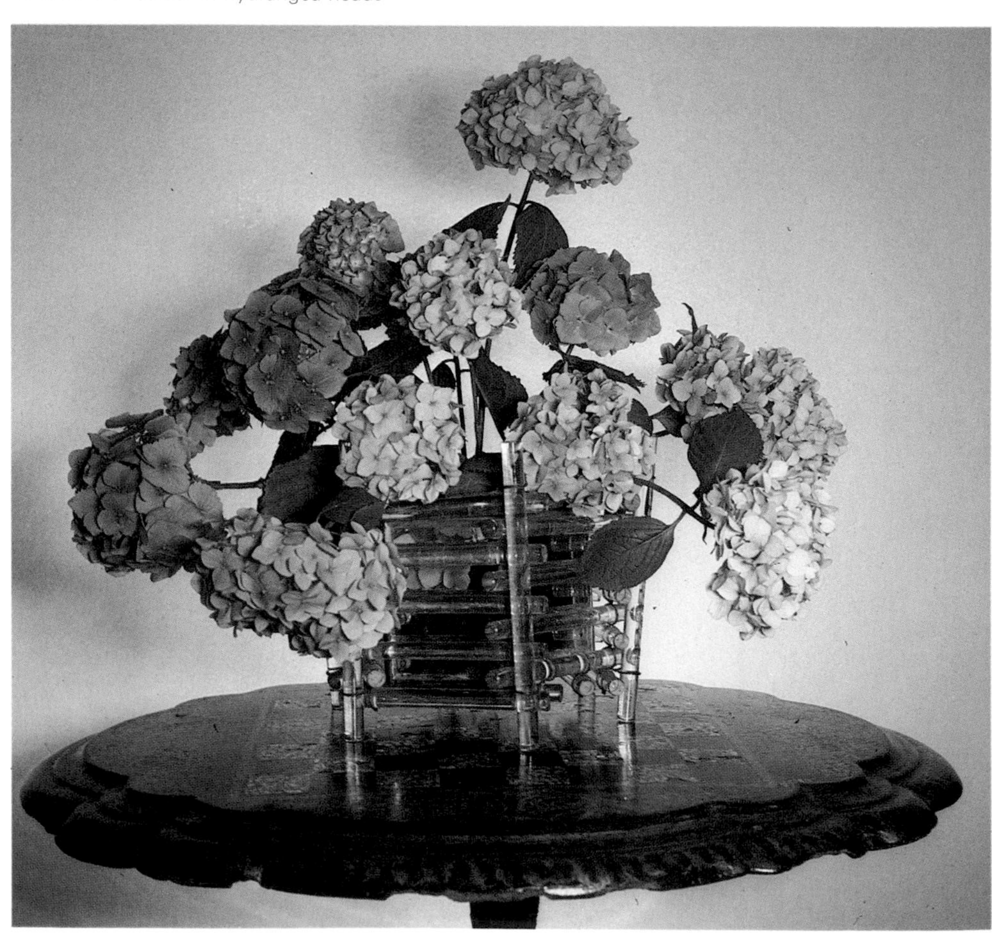

Hamamelis mollis (Witch Hazel)
Origin: China. Whether one grows hamamelis or the more vigorous *Chimonanthus* (Winter Sweet) depends greatly on the size of one's garden. Both are fascinating; the former for the attractive shaped branches with its curious flowers, while the scent of the latter rivals that of *Daphne odora*, although when not in flower it is not very attractive. 2.1 m × 3.6 m (7 ft × 12 ft).

Hoheria lyalli glabrata
If you have a sheltered site then try Hoheria. It is from New Zealand, grows to some 4.5 m (15 ft), has arching branches of white flowers not unlike *Philadelphus* (mock orange) in summer and silvery grey leaves. It benefits from full sun and will grow in chalk.

H. sexstylosa This is evergreen but not as hardy as *H. lyalli*. In a sunny, sheltered position against a south wall, however, it would look magnificent.

Hydrangea
I shall deal only with what I call florist's hydrangeas. These are the ones which are most useful. Some floral arrangers experience difficulty in making the flowers last in water, but if the following method is used they will last well. Pick mature flowers with about 5 cm (2 in.) of the old wood, strip the leaves, hammer the stems and submerge all in water overnight. Shake off superfluous water and add a teaspoonful of alum to the water in which you arrange them. Those who would like to use them dried should pick flowers at the end of the summer or early autumn, when papery to the touch. Plunge all under water overnight, shake off superfluous water and stand hammered stems in a jar of warm water. Place in warm spot until heads are dry.

H. acuminata × 'Preziosa' A new introduction with rounded heads and salmon-pink flowers turning red. 1.5 m × 1.2 m (5 ft × 4 ft).

H. arborescens 'Grandiflora' Origin: Eastern U.S.A. A most useful and decorative hydrangea which can be used in its early green stage, later in flower (creamy white), and yet again when the flower-head has turned brown. 1.8 m × 1.5 m (6 ft × 5 ft).

H. macrophylla (syns. *H. hortensis*, *H. opuloides*) Origin: China, Japan. The flowers are blue on acid soils, red or pink on lime. The soil should be well drained and it may be watered during the dry season. Leave old flowers on plant until spring but remove some of the old wood when necessary. Old plants can be renewed by this method. Never cut to the ground each year. The lace-cap variety is attractive but not for decorative purposes. 1.8 m × 1.8 m (6 ft × 6 ft).

H. paniculata 'Grandiflora' Origin: China, Japan. A very handsome plant, most useful in the autumn, bearing creamy white panicles that fade to pink. Can be grown as a bush or standard. 1.8 m × 1.8 m (6 ft × 6 ft).

The silken petals of the tree peony which is hardier than is generally supposed

Hypericum
Hypericums are not particular as to site and are most useful both in flowering stage and later with berries.

H. elatum 'Elstead' Origin: Canary Islands. Yellow flower with deep rose berries. 1.2 m × 1.2 m (4 ft × 4 ft).

H. patulum 'Hidcote' Origin: China, Japan. Large golden flowers, makes a good bush. 1.5 m × 1.2 m (5 ft × 4 ft).

Kalmia latifolia
Origin: N. America. If you have lime-free soil, this is an attractive, slow-growing evergreen shrub, forming a neat bush with charming clusters of clear pink flowers. 1.5 m × 1.5 m (5 ft × 5 ft).

Kerria japonica
Origin: China. A charming, easily grown shrub which will tolerate half shade. It has single yellow flowers on slender pale green stems. 1.2 m × 1.5 m (4 ft × 5 ft).

Leycesteria formosa
Origin: Himalayas. The pendulous, burgundy coloured bracts and green stems of this shrub are useful in winter arrangements. It can be cut to the ground each year. 1.5 m (5 ft).

Mahonia aquifolium
Origin: Western U.S.A. This most useful plant, an evergreen with leaves which turn to purple and red in winter, will grow in any soil and on any site. Golden yellow flowers in spring are followed by black berries. 60 × 120 cm (2 × 4 ft).

M. bealei Origin: China. Charming scented clusters of yellow flowers in the winter, with handsome foliage, make this a notable plant. 1.2 m × 1 m (4 ft × 3 ft).

Osmanthus delavayi (syn. Siphonosmanthus delavayi)
Origin: China. The branches with their small dark-green leaves are covered with very sweet scented flowers. It is best grown against a wall. It flowers in April and will grow on chalk. 1.8 m × 1.5 m (6 ft × 5 ft).

Paeonia (Tree peony)
These prefer good, rich, deep soil and are rather slow in growth, except perhaps the hybrids. The flowers last well and the foliage is most decorative. Do not disturb established plants by transplanting – they may never recover.

P. lutea Origin: N. Asia. White with streaks of purple. 1.2 m (4 ft).

P. ludlowii Origin: China, Tibet. Single bright yellow flowers. 1.5 m × 1 m (5 ft × 3 ft).

P. moutan (syn. *suffruticosa*) Double or semi-double, white, pale, pink to rose and purple. Up to 1.8 m (6 ft).

P.m. 'Comtesse de Tudor' Shell-pink enormous flowers. 1.5 m × 1 m (5 ft × 3 ft).

Pernettya
Origin: S. America. Because pernettyas are intolerant of lime they require a good loamy soil, or one to which peat and leaf-mould have been added. They are evergreen and the leaves last for a very long time. In order to get the berries, a male plant is required.

P. mucronata 1 m (3 ft) spreading. 'Bell's Seedling', large dark-red berries; 'Davis's Hybrids', all shades of pink, 'Alba', white berries as the name implies.

Philadelphus
This is mock orange, sometimes confused with *Syringa* (lilac). It is one of the loveliest and most fragrant of spring flowering shrubs.

P. coronarius 'Aureus' Origin: S. Europe. This is enchanting in spring and retains its lovely greenish leaves well into summer. A little light shade will prevent the leaves getting scorched by hot sun. The flowers are sweet scented and compact. Height 1.8 m–2.5 m (6 ft–9 ft), spread 1.8 m–2 m (6 ft–8 ft).

P. microphyllus 'Beauclerk' Origin: South-West U.S.A. This has a very sweet-scented large white flower splashed with pinky-violet at base, and lovely tumbling branches, just right for the front of an arrangement. 1.5 m × 1.2 m (5 ft × 4 ft).

P.m. 'Belle Etoile' Origin: South-West U.S.A. An equally lovely variety with fringed petals and semi-arching habit. 1.8 m × 1.2 m (6 ft × 4 ft).

P.m. 'Virginal' Origin: South-West U.S.A. A magnificent plant with semi-double strongly scented white flowers, which is rather apt to get out of hand unless firm measures are taken. It flowers on the previous year's growth so remove stems after flowering to allow current growth to develop fully. When using for decoration, remove some of the leaves, for the flowers will last longer if helped in this way. There are two small varieties which do not exceed 1 m (3 ft).

Physocarpus opulifolius lutea
Origin: N. E. America. Flat flower heads of white, tinged pink, appear in summer. The leaves are golden yellow when young, slowly turning pale green. Height 2 m (6 ft) or more.

Rhododendron, including **Azalea**
If you have suitable conditions, peaty lime-free soil, then of the many spring flowering shrubs, these are perhaps the most notable. At the other end of the scale is 'Polar Bear', flowering in summer and scenting the surrounding air at The Savill Garden, in Windsor Great Park, Berkshire, England where they grow magnificently. So great are their powers of rejuvenation that they can, when quite old, be cut to the ground. Suffice it to mention a few of the species.

R. Augustinii Origin: China. The large pale-deep mauve flowers seem to perch on the branches. Plant in a sheltered place where the early morning sun will not reach. 1.8 m × 1.5 m (6 ft × 5 ft).

R. campylocarpum Origin: Himalayas. Bell-shaped yellow flowers, the glossy leaves silver beneath. 1.5 m × 1.5 m (5 ft × 5 ft).

R. lutescens Origin: China. Primrose yellow flowers and willow-like leaves. Flowers in spring. 1.2 m × 1 m (4 ft × 3 ft).

Rhododendrons now include the deciduous varieties previously known as Azalea, as well as the Japanese or evergreen varieties. Do not attempt to grow them unless you can provide the right conditions.

Ribes (Flowering currants)
R. aureum Origin: North-West U.S.A. Sometimes erroneously called *R. odoratum*. The bright yellow flowers of *R. aureum* (the name means 'golden') are like patches of sunshine in the garden. The strong smell of cats soon wears off once the branches are arranged. Can be brought indoors to force as soon as growth appears. 1.2 m × 1.5 m × 1.2 m (4 ft × 5 ft × 4 ft).

R. sanguineum 'Pulborough Scarlet' Good deep-red flowers, vigorous and erect rapid grower. 2.4 m × 1.5 m (8 ft × 5 ft).

Ruta (Rue)
I dislike the acrid smell of rue, but, for its appearance, would never be without this blue-foliaged plant. It is so easy to strike, as every piece seems to root. Cut it back in late winter. Useful as a low hedge; the individual leaves are ideal for small arrangements or sprays.

R. graveolens 'Jackman's Blue' Origin: S. Europe. Prefers a light soil in sunshine. The flowers are yellow-green but of secondary consideration. 60 × 60 cm (2 ft × 2 ft).

Santolina chamaecyparissus
Origin: S. France. A plant with small, feathery, grey evergreen leaves useful for small arrangements. It does best in light sandy soil. 75 × 60 cm (2½ ft × 2 ft).

Senecio
This family of plants is an important addition to the arranger's garden, for their unusual and distinctive foliage enhances any arrangement.

S. cineraria (syn. *S. maritima*) Origin: Mediterranean. This species has attractive soft, lobed foliage covered with white down, and should be planted at the foot of a south-facing wall in spring. Height 60 cm (2 ft).

S. laxifolius Origin: New Zealand. Hardier than cineraria, with yellow daisy-like flowers in summer. 1 m × 1.5 m (3 ft × 5 ft). Often confused with *S. greyi*.

Constance Spry first discovered the pleasing impact of a mixture of reds

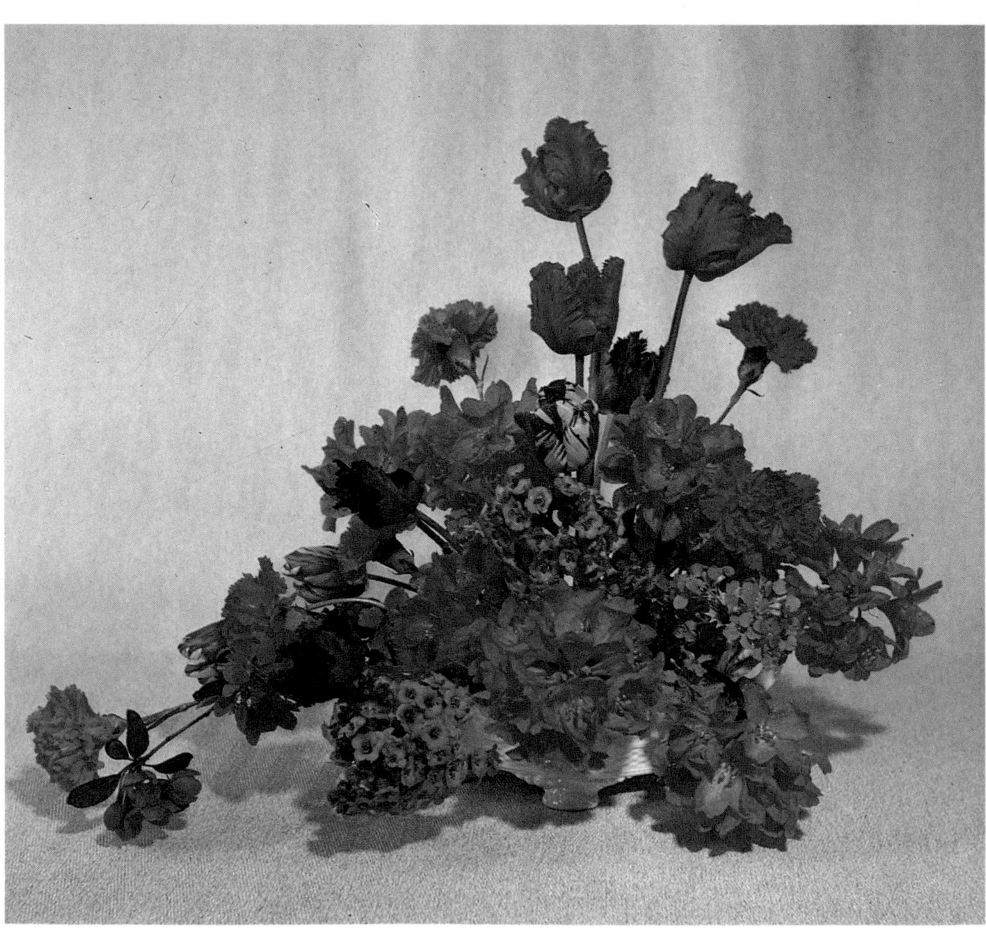

Skimmia
Although rather slow growing, a group of these would be welcome, both for flowers and berries. Two forms are needed, male and female, to produce berries. One male will pollinate three females.

S. japonica (female) Origin: Japan. Pale-green leaves enclose a cluster of creamy flowers, followed by scarlet berries. It should be grown in semi-shade in a soil containing loam and peat. 1.5 m × 1.2 m (5 ft × 4 ft).

S. rubella (male) Origin: China. Scented pink flowers in spring. 2.1 m × 1.5 m (7 ft × 5 ft).

Spiraea × arguta (Bridal Wreath)
Origin: Japan. Myriads of small white flowers on arching branches in late spring.

S. opulifolius var. *aureo-marginata* See *Physocarpus*.

S. × *Vanhouttei* Perhaps the best of the spring spiraeas with arching branches, simply smothered with pure white flowers. It makes a lovely hedge. 2.4 m × 1.8 m (8 ft × 6 ft).

Symphoricarpos
Origin: N. America. This group of hardy berry-bearing shrubs are suitable for planting in shade. They are popularly known as Snowberry.

S. albus Origin: N. America. Leaves pale to mid-green with a grey tinge. Small pink flowers of summer are followed by glistening white round berries. 1.5 m × 1.5 m (5 ft × 5 ft).

S. × 'Constance Spry' A heavily berried variety, named after Mrs Spry who grew and used this splendid shrub. Very easy to grow in shade or semi-shade.

S. × 'Mother of Pearl' A lovely smaller variety with white, pink-tinted berries.

Syringa (Lilac)
Origin: E. Europe and elsewhere. Lilacs, as undoubtedly we shall continue to call them, love the sunshine. There are so many varieties, both single and double flowered, that it becomes difficult to make a choice. It may be compact, bushy, or tall and luxurious. Syringa is not particular regarding soil, providing it is well drained. Dead heads should be removed after flowering. Pruning can be achieved simply by cutting for decoration to keep the bush in shape. 3.5 m (10 ft).

In my last garden there were twenty lilacs in all which in a small space was rather overdoing it. In the garden I am now creating, I hope to have the following six, all of which may reach 3.5 m (12 ft) in height.

S. Vulgaris 'Edward J. Gardner' Raised in the U.S.A. Semi-double, light pink, mid-season.

S.v. 'Katherine Havemeyer' Deep purple lavender, gorgeous scent, mid-season, fairly open bush.

S.v. 'Maud Notcutt' A variety with pure white, exceptionally large flowers and an upright habit. Cut branches last well in water.

S.v. 'Primrose' A very free-flowering compact bush with primrose yellow flowers.

S.v. 'Souvenir de Louis Späth' Deep burgundy, scented flowers. Strong growth, spreading habit.

S. × *prestoniae* 'Isabella' One of the so-called Canadian hybrids, vigorous and disease-free. Long panicles of mallow-purple flowers.

Viburnum
Origin: North America, Japan. An extremely useful and popular family of shrubs.

V. burkwoodii Origin: China. Evergreen. Produces delightful, sweetly scented white flowers, from pink buds in late spring. 1.8 m × 1.5 m (6 ft × 5 ft).

V. opulus 'Sterile' (snowball bush) Origin: China. Deciduous. Long-lasting sterile flowers, like snowballs, that can be used in the green stage. Often depicted in Dutch and Flemish paintings, the flowers are the size of a golf ball.

V. tinus (laurustinus) 'Eve Price' Origin: S.E. Europe. Winter-flowering evergreen. Carmine buds, pinky white flowers, dense bush. Good for tubs. 1.5 m × 1.5 m (5 ft × 5 ft).

V. tomentosum 'Plicatum' Known as the Japanese snowball, this variety has long-lasting round white flowers. Deciduous, it may reach 3 m (10 ft) in height.

Weigela
A quick-growing valuable shrub for the border. Flowers resemble small foxgloves and grow in clusters. Does not last particularly well in water but worth growing for its long, arching branches. Removal of leaves will prolong the life of the flower. Now more properly known as Diervilla. The two free-flowering hybrids listed below are crosses between *W. florida* and other Asiatic species.

W. × 'Bristol Ruby' Origin: Japan, China. Branches thickly covered with ruby red flowers. 1.5 m × 1.5 m (5 ft × 5 ft).

W. × 'Conquete' Rose pink, loose and spreading. 1.5 m × 1.8 m (5 ft × 6 ft).

W. florida 'Variegata' Has golden variegated foliage, retaining its attraction into summer. Flowers rose pink. Slower growing, as so many of the variegated plants are, but worth waiting for. Provides useful foliage. 1.2 m × 1.2 m (4 ft × 4 ft).

The glorious rose

No garden should be without the glorious rose. Roses are superb for decorating, not only for their scent and colour, but for a special quality that few other flowers can impart. It is in full bloom, not in bud, that they need to be enjoyed, and

'Just Joey', a fine yellow hybrid tea rose

it is within the last 20 cm (8 in.) of the stem that their beauty lies.

I shall deal here only with floribunda that I have grown. Planted in groups of three, they well lived up to the name, flowering prolifically. They were Anna Louisa (pale pink), Chanelle (creamy pink), Daily Sketch (silvery-pink), Dearest (rosy-salmon), Golden Fleece (yellow), Golden Jewel (yellow), Iceberg (white), Lilac Charm (pale mauve), Lilli Marlene (scarlet), Magenta (rosy-magenta), Rosemary Rose (bright carmine), Sambra (orange), Saratoga (white), Sir Lancelot (apricot-yellow) and Violet Carson (peach pink). They were grouped on the basis of size and colour, and gave me a wide variety from which to cut.

The climbing roses, some of which I allowed to ramble through old apple trees, were as follows: 'Caroline Testout', that lovely fragrant pink delight. With her grew the double white clematis 'Duchess of Edinburgh'; 'Zephirine Drouhin' (mistakenly planted with 'Lady Sylvia' for the soft pinky apricot of 'Lady Sylvia' was not a happy complement to the sweet-scented, thornless, carmine pink of 'Zephirine Drouhin'.) A truly happy partnership, however, was that of the pale flesh pink 'New Dawn' and clematis 'Comtesse de Bouchard'. What a charmer New Dawn is, soft shell pink with a wild rose scent. Having climbed to the top of the tree, it cascaded to the ground. With the clematis, cyclamen pink in colour, flowering at the same time, it was an unforgettable sight.

Sweet-scented 'Albertine' covered an arbour; coppery chamois, it fades to salmon pink, and needs ample space.

Although, through lack of space, I have not grown 'Peace' and 'Queen Elizabeth', both these are outstanding for decorative purposes. Lime branches stripped of their leaves, partnered by Regale lilies, *Hosta* leaves and 'Peace' roses, make a decoration which would grace any occasion.

I found space for but five of the old shrub roses, but what pleasure they gave: 'Madame Hardy' (white), 'Fantin-Latour' (pink), 'Madame Pierre Oger' (creamy-rose pink), 'Tour de Malakoff' (magenta), and 'Nuits de Young' (deep maroon-purple) – all enchanting. The best way to support these rather lax-growing roses is to encircle each with a ring of chestnut-paling. Two roses I could never be without are the beautiful bloom named after Constance Spry, a clear pink, many petalled new shrub rose, having so many of the qualities of those from the past and in addition the scent of myrrh. This was introduced by David Austin a few years ago, and quickly became extremely popular with all arrangers. The other is my favourite, 'Paul's Lemon Pillar', alas, now difficult to acquire. This beautiful pale lemony-white rose, with its faint citron-like scent, is lovely in shape, and soft in the hand. If I could have but one rose, this would be my choice.

A profusion of 'Vespa' floribunda blooms

'Compassion', a beautiful climbing rose

Climbers

Apart from roses, the climbers which are most useful are clematis. Here the choice is wide. I find the larger varieties last better when cut. This is because the stems are thicker, and the flower is thus able to absorb the water. Pick them, scrape the lower part of the stems, then slightly smash them and stand them in deep water overnight. An exciting one is 'Vyvyan Pennell', with double lilac-coloured flowers with streaks of cream and green, blooming in early summer. Later in the year when it again flowers, the flowers are single. Another favourite is the species *C. tangutica*. Its seed-heads make a delightful winter arrangement.

We miss so much beauty through not clothing the walls of our dwellings. Most walls can be smothered with climbers, though one naturally has to be a little restrained when considering the façade of a lovely old Queen Anne or Georgian house. A rose or clematis can only enhance

Clematis seen to advantage with *Hosta* leaves and flowers and Candidum lilies beyond

its charm, and do no damage. Care should be taken not to plant too near the walls, and below the level of the damp-course. I once grew *Actinidia chinensis*, and although I never managed to get it to flower, it proved to be an interesting quick-growing climber. The leaves and stems are hairy, the flowers are cream, grown in clusters. The fruit is brown and oval, about 5 cm (2 in.) long.

Actinidia chinensis (Chinese Gooseberry)
Origin: E. Asia. For the south or west aspect. Probably it requires pruning to make it flower and fruit. Height 9 m (30 ft).

A. kolomikta Origin: W. China. An elegant plant with coloured foliage: large, heart-shaped leaves, starting green, then streaked with white, and later turning-turning pink to pearl-white. Grow on a sunny wall. 1.8 m × 3.5 m (6 ft × 10 ft).

Campsis grandiflora (syn. C. chinensis) (Trumpet Vine)
A deep-orange, trumpet-shaped flower, long and wide in clusters, for south or west aspects. Since it flowers on the current season's wood, it should be pruned hard in late winter. Up to 6 m (20 ft).

Hedera (Ivy)
Ivies, being evergreen, are very useful the whole year round. On sound walls they do no damage, and make excellent cover.

H. canariensis 'Variegata' Olive-green leaves, silver and white edging.

H. colchica dentata 'Aurea' Large shiny leaves, soft green with deep-yellow variegation.

H. helix 'Jubilee' Gold and green leaves. Also useful for sprays.

H. helix 'Buttercup' Small bright golden leaves. Useful for sprays. Needs to be in full sun to keep its colour.

Jasminum nudiflorum (winter-flowering)
Origin: China. This well-known jasmine is vigorous and easy to grow. Tie in main shoots until the desired height is reached. It should be pruned after flowering.

J. grandiflorum Origin: Persia, Kashmir, N. China. Bears sweetly scented white flowers in summer. Needs protection. Can form a tangled mass if not well-trained.

Lonicera periclymenum
Origin: Europe (Gt. Britain), Asia Minor. The much loved honeysuckle. Two varieties are commonly available, both of which are very fragrant.

L.p. 'Belgica' (early Dutch honeysuckle) Bushy in habit, bearing red and yellow flowers in late spring/early summer. Height to 6 m (20 ft).

L.p. 'Serotina' (late Dutch honeysuckle) Bears flowers all summer, red-purple on the outside, cream-white within.

'Nellie Moser', a favourite clematis which invariably gives a large number of blooms

Magnolia grandiflora var. 'Exmouth'
Origin: South-eastern U.S.A. If you grow this magnificent magnolia, you will be twice blessed. Each year it drops some of its leaves, which are tough and turn mahogany in colour, and are useful mounted on branches during the winter. In time richly scented goblet-like flowers, cream in colour, will reward you.

Passiflora (Passion flower)
The flower which, with its three stigmas, five anthers, coronal rays, digitate leaves and ten parts of the perianth, has been adopted as the symbol of the Passion of Christ. On a warm wall facing south, it will grow vigorously, and after two years flower profusely. The flowers are followed by equally decorative orange fruit.

P. caerulea Origin: Brazil. Purplish-blue, flowers from June onwards. 'Constance Elliott' is an ivory-white variety.

Solanum crispum 'Glasnevin Variety'
A good free-growing form of the Chilean potato tree with very attractive clusters of purple-blue flowers with orange-yellow stamens.

Perennials

The choice of perennial plants determines the difference between an arranger and a non-arranger, for the former perhaps is more concerned with the value of the leaf, while the latter concentrates on the beauty of the flower. *Hosta* and *Bergenia* are good examples of perennials that satisfy the needs of both. Both have attractive flowers, but it is for the usefulness of the leaves that they are included in the flower arranger's list given below. This list comprises plants which either I myself have grown, or seen growing in the late Constance Spry's garden. Some of these flowers are so well known that a description of them is hardly necessary, and where practicable the common name as well as the correct Latin one are given.

The conditions under which these plants can be grown will of course differ greatly according to soil and locality, so cultural instructions are not included. Many catalogues give excellent instructions on whether a plant needs full sun, partial shade, or will thrive in full shade. It may be that these days few of us have time to devote to the maintenance of the old-fashioned herbaceous border as such. The concept of the border will, I believe, be modified to include flowering shrubs and bold plantings of perennials. Make it a rule to buy three plants of the same variety, in order to make an immediate effect. For a larger border buy five or even seven plants. When planning and planting a border, consider its width in relationship to the height of plants. Subjects like Bowles Golden Grass or London Pride (*Saxifraga × urbicum*) can be used to divide groups of bolder plants and make a border look less hedge-like. Island-beds are also attractive, though for these even greater care must be exercised in the selection of plants, which must have good foliage and retain their vigour for the entire season. To minimize work, avoid plants that need staking.

Acanthus
Renowned as an inspiration to the great architects, with its handsome foliage and tall spikes of flowers 1–1.2 m (3–4 ft) high. The leaves unfortunately do not last when picked. Cut flowers only when the stems are fully extended, in other words when every individual flower is out. To dry for winter use, simply cut stems when the plants have gone to seed, and hang them upside-down in a damp-proof place.

A. mollis latifolius 1.2 m (4 ft).

A. spinosus Leaves are smaller and more deeply divided than *A. mollis.* 1 m (3 ft).

Achillea (Yarrow)
A. filipendulina 'Gold Plate' Has rigid stems with golden yellow heads. It is excellent for winter use and should be cut when fully developed on a warm sunny day and hung in bunches. 1.5 m (5 ft).

A. taygetea 'Moonshine' A smaller variety with pale yellow flowers. 45–60 cm (1½–2 ft).

A. serrata (syn. *A. decolorans*) 'W. B. Child' Open heads of pure white flowers which are useful for small arrangements. 30 cm (1 ft).

Aconitum (Monkshood)
Resembles delphiniums, but there is no need to stake this plant. All parts of the aconitum are poisonous.

A. napellus 'Blue Sceptre' Blue-and-white flowers. 60 cm (2 ft).

A.n. 'Bressingham Spire' Violet blue flowers. 1 m (3 ft).

A.u. 'Ivorine' A variety with ivory white flowers and attractive foliage. 1–1.5 m (3–5 ft).

Agapanthus
These used to be grown in pots and covered during the winter, but are hardier than is realized. I have grown and flowered them from seed in two years.

A. 'Headbourne Hybrids' Has pale to deep-blue flowers. 60–90 cm (2–3 ft).

Alchemilla
A. alpina A plant making a silvery ground cover, bearing small buff flowers. Height 15 cm (6 in).

A. mollis An absolute must for all arrangers, with feathery lime-green flowers which enhance any arrangement. It will grow almost anywhere, and the foliage is most delightful after rain. 45 cm (1½ ft). Commonly known as Lady's mantle.

Alchemilla mollis makes a good ground cover

Anemone japonica, flowers of classic simplicity

A pleasant corner in George Foss' garden

Alstroemeria
Although this can be bought as a young plant, it is more satisfactory to grow from seed. Seeds should be sown in spring in a trench about 15 cm (6 in.) deep; as the young plants grow, gradually fill in trench.

A. aurantiaca A variety which bears showy rich orange flowers. It will take a little time to establish but is worth the trouble as it is very long-lasting. 1 m (3 ft).

A. ligtu The hybrids of the group bear flowers of pink coral to salmon. Avoid heavy soil when planting. 60–90 cm (2–3 ft).

Althaea (Hollyhock)
Everyone knows the stately hollyhock, which can be single or double and in various colours, deep crimson, pink, scarlet, white, yellow and violet. May also be grown as an annual. 1.8–2.4 m (6–8 ft).

Anaphalis
A. margaritacea A plant with silver-grey foliage and heads of small white everlasting flowers. 45 cm (18 in.).

A. triplinevis Slightly smaller variety than above. 30 cm (12 in.)

Anemone × hybrida (Japanese anemone)
A most useful late summer/early autumn flowering plant. The flowers range from chalk white to deep burgundy colour. The leaves are most decorative, and the plant does not need staking, although it may reach 1 m (3 ft) in height.

A. × 'Lady Gilmour' Pure pink, almost double.

A. × 'Louise Uhink' White.

A. × 'Profusion' Deep heather pink.

Angelica
This plant, the stems of which are candied and used in confectionery, grows to 1.5–1.8 m (5–6 ft). The seed-head is most useful for a large group and should be cut when the seeds are formed, the hollow stem then being filled with water and plugged. The main plant dies after flowering, but side-shoots grow from the base.

Anthemis tinctoria 'E. C. Buxton'
Primrose yellow flowers. 75 cm (2½ ft).

Aquilegia (Columbine)
Planted in bold clumps these graceful plants are most effective. They are all easily grown from seed. The foliage of *A. vulgaris* (granny's bonnet) is superior to that of the long-spurred varieties. 45 cm (18 in.).

A. alpina Clear blue. Suitable for rock-garden. 30 cm (1 ft).

A. flabellata 'Nana' Shorter stems, deep-blue flowers. 15–20 cm (6–10 in.). 'Alba' is a white form.

A. vulgaris 'McKana hybrids' Large flowers in many shades and colours, useful and distinctive foliage.

Artemisia
A. lactiflora Green leaves, erect stems, plumes of ivory heads. 1.2 m (4 ft).

A. absinthium 'Lambrook Silver' Bright foliage, sprays of grey flowers. 75 cm (2½ ft).

Arum italicum 'Pictum'
This Arum bears dark, glossy-green spear-shaped leaves veined with ivory, which appear in late autumn and continue to spring. A very desirable plant for the flower arranger. 30 cm (1 ft).

Aruncus sylvester
Also known as *Spiraea aruncus* and goat's beard. It is very imposing at the back of the border with its massive plumes of creamy-white flowers. Good also when the flowers are over. 1.2 m (4 ft).

Aster (Michaelmas Daisy)
There are both species and hybrid asters, all of which are useful for autumn decoration. Most nurserymen list about twenty varieties of the hybrids. They need space, and a good current of air, as they are very susceptible to mildew.

Astilbe
A. 'Bronze Elegance' Rose pink, most delightful. 22 cm (9 in.).
A. 'Fanal' Dark crimson flowers. Good plants to grow in damp ground. 60 cm (2 ft).
A. 'Ostrich Plume' Arching sprays of clear pink. 1 m (3 ft).
A. 'Professor Van der Wielen' Elegant white. 1 m (3 ft).

The marbled leaves of *Arum italicum* and early spring flowers in a soapstone vase

Astrantia
A. major A most attractive subject which will mix with most other flowers. Star-like greenish-pink flowers appear in summer. It grows in shade and seeds freely. 60 cm (2 ft).
A. maxima Has strawberry-pink flowers. 60 cm (2 ft).

Ballota pseudo-dictamnus
Has curving stems covered with grey-white down, small pale yellow flowers. 45 cm (18 in.).

Bergenia
Formerly known as *Megasea* or *Saxifraga*, this is without question one of the most useful plants for arrangers. They flower during the spring, but it is for the leaf form that they are most valued. Being evergreen they can be gathered at any time. Height 30 cm (12 in.).
B. × 'Ballawley' Cherry red flowers, and magnificent leaves which colour like old leather in the autumn. 45 cm (18 in.).
B. cordifolia The hardiest of a hardy race, with large heart-shaped leaves and deep-pink flowers.
B. crassifolia First to bloom, in spring, and carries pale-pink flowers.

Campanula
C. alliariifolia 'Ivory Bells' Neat growing arching stems of creamy-white flowers.
C. lactiflora Light blue. 75 cm (2½ ft). 'Loddon Anna', lilac pink, 1 m (3 ft), is a good variety.

Catananche caerulea
The flower is a lavender blue, dark-eyed daisy enclosed in a papery calyx, on stout stems, appearing in summer. Dry sites suit it admirably. 45 cm (18 in.).

Centaurea
C. macrocephala Large golden flowers on strong stems, very useful in a border. 1.2 m (4 ft).
C. moschata (Sweet Sultan) Scented summer flowers; yellow, white, pink and purple. Height 60 cm (2 ft).

Chrysanthemum maximum (Shasta Daisy)
Numerous white varieties. Height 75 cm (2½ ft). 'Cobham Gold' is double, yellow flushed. 'Wirral Supreme', white with 'anemone' centre, is an excellent plant for border and cutting. 1 m (3 ft).

Convallaria (Lily of the valley)
Beloved of all, nothing gives greater pleasure than a bowl of lily of the valley. It used to grow wild in Derbyshire dales.
C. 'Fortin's Giant' An excellent variety which will grow in any shady place. Top dress during winter with leaf-mould.

Crocosmia masonorum
Orange flame trumpet flowers, and useful seedheads. *C. masonorum* has now been crossed with Montbretia, and interesting hybrids produced. 60 cm (2 ft).

Cynara scolymus (Artichoke)
Although a vegetable, the flower, seedhead and leaves are most useful in decoration. Do not be tempted to cut the leaves when young (and do not cut too many). 1.5–1.8 m (5–6 ft).

Delphinium
A magnificent plant in the border and for large groups. The Belladonna group is more useful for smaller arrangements. It is well worth buying seeds of the Pacific Giants and raising these, for some interesting colours may result. Slugs are its great enemy, so place a tile or slate with slug-killer near a clump. After dark a tin of salt provides a sure remedy.
D. elatum group: 'Maz Samule', deep blue; 'Pacific Galahad', pure white; 'Startling', deep violet, white eye. 1.5–1.8 m (5–6 ft).
Belladonna group: 'Blue Bees', clear blue; 'Pink Sensation', clear pink. 1.2–1.5 m (3½–4½ ft).

Dianthus (Pinks)
D. 'Mrs Sinkins' A great favourite for its lovely scent and white double flowers.

Dianthus (hardy hybrids)
These are long flowering, and love the sun and limy, well-drained soil.
D. 'Doris' Shrimp pink with darker eye, scented.
D. 'Ideal' Creamy with pink eye.

Dicentra spectabilis (Bleeding heart)
This variety bears deep pink heart-shaped flowers in early summer. It dies down completely after flowering.

Digitalis (Foxglove)
These are the perennial foxgloves which bloom later than biennial ones. Being smaller they are useful in the border. 75 cm (2½ ft).
D. ambigua Primrose yellow. 45–60 cm (1½–2 ft).
D. mertonensis Pink. 60 cm (2 ft).

Doronicum cordatum
A very early charming yellow daisy-like flower. 15 cm (6 in.).

Echinops ritro
Blue-headed globe thistle. 1 m (3½ ft).

Euphorbia (Spurge)
Another must for all arrangers. The lime-green flowers, which most of them have, are excellent with many other colours.

E. epithymoides Sulphur yellow in spring. 45 cm (18 in.).

E. palustris Large greeny-yellow heads. 1 m (3 ft).

E. sikkimensis Purple-red shoots, leafy stems topped with yellow heads. 1.2 m (4 ft).

E. wulfenii A most handsome plant which, over the years, forms a large clump of a dramatic nature. 1–1.2 m (3–4 ft).

Gyposophila (Rosy veil)
It should be planted where the masses of small pale-pink flowers can tumble for best effect. 30 cm (1 ft).

Helenium
Easily grown, showy, good for cutting. Summer/autumn. 60 cm–1 m (2–3 ft).

H. autumnale 'Moerheim Beauty' Bears mahogany red flowers. 1 m (3 ft).

H.a. 'Wyndley' Large, brown and yellow. 60 cm (2 ft).

Helianthus decapetalus 'Loddon Gold'
Must be planted in full sun at the back of the border. 1.5 m (5 ft).

Helleborus
They have a very long period of blooming and are equally useful when they have gone to seed.

H. foetidus Light-green flowers on 1 m (3 ft) stems. Very useful side-shoots and foliage.

H. niger (Christmas rose) It is a joy to behold this perfect flower in the winter months. Cover it with a cloche when flowers appear, as this will keep the blooms clean and lengthen the stem. 30 cm (1 ft).

H. orientalis (Lenten rose) A wide variety of colour, from white to burgundy. 30–45 cm (1–1½ ft).

Heuchera
H. sanguinea 'Coral Cloud' Produces sprays of dainty coral-red flowers on slender stems. 45 cm (18 in.).

H.s. 'Greenfinch' Curious but striking sulphur-greenish flowers. 75 cm (2½ ft).

H.s. 'Pearl Drops' Near-white, graceful arching sprays. 45–60 cm (18–24 in.).

Hosta (Funkia)
There is still uncertainty about the nomenclature of these plants, but like the bergenias they are quite invaluable to the arranger. After a few years the clumps of leaves are weed-proof. Most have lilac-coloured flowers of varying heights. The leaves vary in size and colour, so a good assorted collection is desirable. They are not particular as to site but prefer a moist situation.

Hosta leaves with a distinctive border

H. fortunei albo-picta Large glaucous leaves, marbled in yellow, primrose, or soft-green. Height up to 1 m (3 ft).

H. 'Aureomarginata' In spring young leaves are butter yellow, later turning green.

H. plantaginea Fine leaves of bright green which retain their colour. Late in season, white scented flowers. Height 60 cm (2 ft).

H. sieboldeana (syn *H. glauca*) Grey-green foliage. 60 cm (2 ft).

Iris
I. chrysographes 'Black Knight' Almost black flowers. 60 cm (2 ft).

I. 'Evergreen Gladwyn' For dry shade; scarlet seed-pods in autumn.

I. foetidissima Grown for its seed pods rather than its flowers. 50 cm (20 in.).

I. kaempferi The gorgeous Japanese iris for moist but lime-free soil. There are numerous, and most beautiful, iris of the species *I. germanica* or bearded iris, which if more difficult to grow, have much to offer. Little wonder that they are called 'the poor man's orchid'.

I. variegata Striped foliage.

Grey foliage useful as a restful contrast
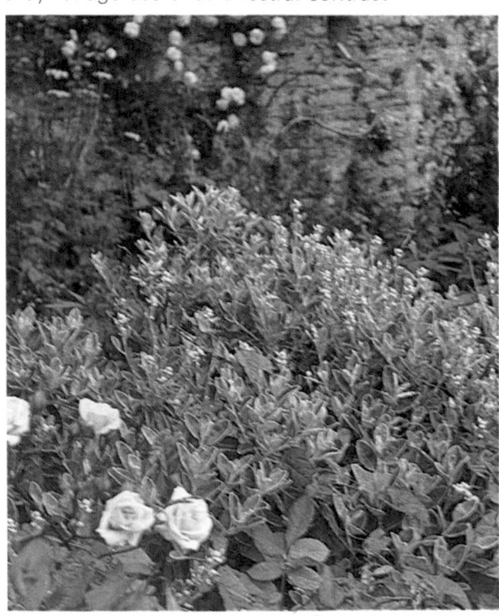

Kniphofia (Red Hot Poker)
These are no longer simply 'red hot', as as they can now be obtained in a variety of colours and sizes. They come easily from seed.

K. 'Green Jade' Pale-green tubular flowers. 1 m (3 ft).

K. 'Maid of Orleans' Most beautiful slender stems, creamy-white flowers. 1 m (3 ft).

K. nelsonii major Deep orange/flame. 75 cm (2½ ft).

Lupinus (lupin)
The Russell varieties are mixed hybrids with interesting colours and can be grown easily from seed. They should be treated the same as delphiniums.

Lysimachia clethroides
With slender arching spikes of white, this variety is not as rampant as the yellow *L. punctata*. 1 m (3 ft).

Macleaya
M. cordata (Bocconia) It is a graceful tall subject for the back of a border. Leave for cutting until fully developed.

M. microcarpa 'Coral Plume' Tiny flowers but effective. 1.2–1.5 m (4–5 ft).

Paeonia (Peony)
Peonies take a few years to settle down and give of their full beauty, but having done so are splendid. They demand no staking, are weed suppressing and need no periodic dividing. They produce magnificent flowers which last well with good foliage. What more could one ask? They require a good rich soil and sunshine. 75 cm–1 m (2½–3 ft).

Double varieties, summer-flowering: 'Duchess of Teck', white with cream centre; 'Felix Crousse', brilliant red; 'Queen Wilhelmina', vivid pink; 'Marie Lemoine', white with cream centre; 'Sarah Bernhardt', apple blossom pink.

Papaver (Oriental Poppy)
Poppies should be picked when the bud has just split to reveal colours. You should then burn the end of the stem, and stand in deep water for several hours before arranging, to lengthen the flower's life. Although the foliage is rather untidy after flowering, the poppy is outstanding in the border and for decorating.

P. orientalis: 'Lady Haig', glowing scarlet; 'Marcus Perry', orange-scarlet with black blotch; 'May Sadler', salmon pink; 'Perry's White', white tinged with blush pink.

Phlox paniculata hybrids
Phlox last longer than expected when cut,

if you lightly hammer the stems and remove unwanted leaves before giving them an all-important long, deep drink. Give a shake to remove dead flowerlets before arranging. They require no staking and last extremely well in the border. A wide variety is listed in most catalogues, but attention should be drawn to one named 'Norah Leigh' which, although not particularly floriferous, has fine variegated green-and-white leaves. Phlox are helpful in the border and for cutting. Full sun, rich soil. 75 cm (2½ ft).

Phormium tenax (New Zealand Flax)
Tough fibrous leaves growing 2.4–3.5 m (8–10 ft) in length. 8–10 cm (3–4 in.) wide. Excellent for modern design. Bronze-leafed and variegated sorts can also be obtained. Good for moist soil in mild climates.

Physalis alkekengii (Chinese Lantern)
Valuable for winter decoration. 60 cm (2 ft). *P. franchettii* is a larger growing variety with deep orange fruits.
Polygonatum multiflorum (Solomon's Seal) Produces graceful arching stems with small bell-shaped flowers beneath, and will thrive in quite dense shade.

Primula auricula
These charming, old-fashioned flowers, so often seen in the old flower paintings, can be obtained in a range of beautiful colours. The stems and blooms are covered with mealy powder. They should be planted in rich soil in a shady border. Height and spread 15 cm (6 in.).

Rudbeckia
Popularly known as the Coneflower. *R. hirta*, the black-eyed susan, grows to 1 m (3 ft); the varieties are golden-yellow and bronze. 'Goldsturm' is a perennial hybrid reaching 60 cm (2 ft).
R. nitida The species has been replaced by the variety 'Autumn Sun' with single yellow flowers. In rich moist soil it may reach 3.6 m (12 ft) in height.

Scabiosa (Scabious)
S. caucasica 'Clive Greaves' Violet-blue flowers on long stems. 60 cm (2 ft).
S. 'Miss Willmott' Creamy-white flowers. 60 cm (2 ft).

Sedum (Stonecrop)
This family, which is tolerant of dry conditions, is beloved of the bees and butterflies when in flower.
S. × 'Autumn Joy' Salmon pink changing to a deeper colour. Height 60 cm (2 ft).
S. maximum 'Atropurpureum' A handsome plant with deep reddish-brown stems and leaves, the flowers of which are deep mushroom pink. Lovely with clear pink and lime green. 60 cm (2 ft).
S. 'Ruby Glow' Colour of rubies; needs a position where it can tumble. 25 cm (10 in.).
S. spectabile 'Brilliant' Large heads of deep rose. Height 30–45 cm (12–18 in.).

Senecio przewalskii (syn. *Ligularia przewalskii*)
If you have a moist sunny spot in the garden, this is an interesting plant to grow. Bright yellow flowers with shiny black stems, like a small Eremurus. 1.5 m (5 ft). 'The Rocket' has darker yellow flowers.

Smilacina racemosa
A plant for shade, having a growth not unlike that of Solomon's Seal, but with a tassel of cream flowers at the end of the stalk. 75 cm (2½ ft).

Solidago (Golden Rod)
Grow 'Garden Hybrids' rather than the species. They are vigorous in growth but less invasive. As well as the flower plumes, it is useful in its early green stage.
S. × 'Golden Gates' Large sprays of rich yellow. 75 cm (2½ ft).
S. × 'Goldenmosa' Yellow leaves and flowers. 60 cm (2 ft).
S. × 'Lemore' Branching heads of primrose yellow. 60 cm (2 ft).

Tellima grandiflora 'Purpurea'
Bronzy purple-green foliage, graceful spikes, numerous pink fringed, green bell-like flowers 1 cm (½ in) long. Good ground cover for shade. 45 cm (18 in.).

Thalictrum
T. minus (syn. *T. adiantifolium*) Foliage like maidenhair fern, useful for smaller arrangements. 60 cm (2 ft).
T. flavum 'Illuminator' Erect stems, loose head of sulphur yellow flowers. (Growing head can be picked out to save staking). 1.5 m (5 ft).
T. dipterocarpum 'Hewitt's Double' A charmer, with tiny double-lilac flowers like jewels. Requires good rich loam. 1 m (3 ft).

Veratrum
V. album Greeny-white summer flowers. 1.5 m (5 ft).
V. nigrum A handsome plant, tall and erect, large pleated leaves, purple flower almost black. 1.5 m (5 ft).

Verbascum (Mullein)
V. hybridum 'Gainsborough' Spikes of sulphur-yellow flowers. 1.2 m (4 ft).
V.h. 'Pink Domino' Deep rose pink. 1.2 m (4 ft).
V.h. 'Mont Blanc' Branching spikes of white, felty grey leaves. Height 1–1.2 m (3–4 ft).

Hardy annuals for cutting

The easiest and best way to grow annuals is to sow the seed thinly in rows. They will then be easy to weed and to gather. Listed below are some that can be sown directly in the open.

Amaranthus (Love Lies Bleeding)
Crimson and green flowers. 1.2 m (4 ft).

Atriplex (Red Mountain Spinach)
Sow where intended to flower. It has very useful foliage and will seed itself. 1.2 m (4 ft).

Chrysanthemum (Hardy annual varieties) Sow in open ground in early spring.

Euphorbia marginata (Spurge)
Sow in late spring. The stem has a milky sap which *must not* be allowed to come in contact with eyes, mouth or an open wound. 60 cm (2 ft).

Godetia Choose mixed seeds of the variety *G. grandiflora*. 30 cm (12 in.).

Grasses, ornamental Some seedsmen offer selections of the most useful varieties. Sow during spring. They are useful either

Mimosa growing outdoors in S.W. England

Green hellebores used for central interest

fresh, or dried for winter.

Helianthus (Sunflower) These large flowered hybrids with a wide colour range are magnificent for autumn. Sow in spring. If earlier flowering is required, sow inside in individual pots, then transplant.

Helichrysum Extremely good everlasting flowers reaching up to 1.2 m (4 ft). Cut for drying before fully open. Sow during spring.

Lathyrus (sweet peas) There is a great variety of these. Sow in very early spring in a heated greenhouse of 15–20°C. (60–68°F.) in open ground after the frosts or in autumn in a cold frame to over-winter.

Nicandra physaloides (Shoo-Fly) Can be grown in a heated greenhouse or in open ground. It has interesting seed-pods which can be remounted for winter use.

Nigella damascena (Love-in-a-Mist) The mixture Persian Jewels gives a range of colours. Sow during spring. Good seed-pods. 60 cm (2 ft).

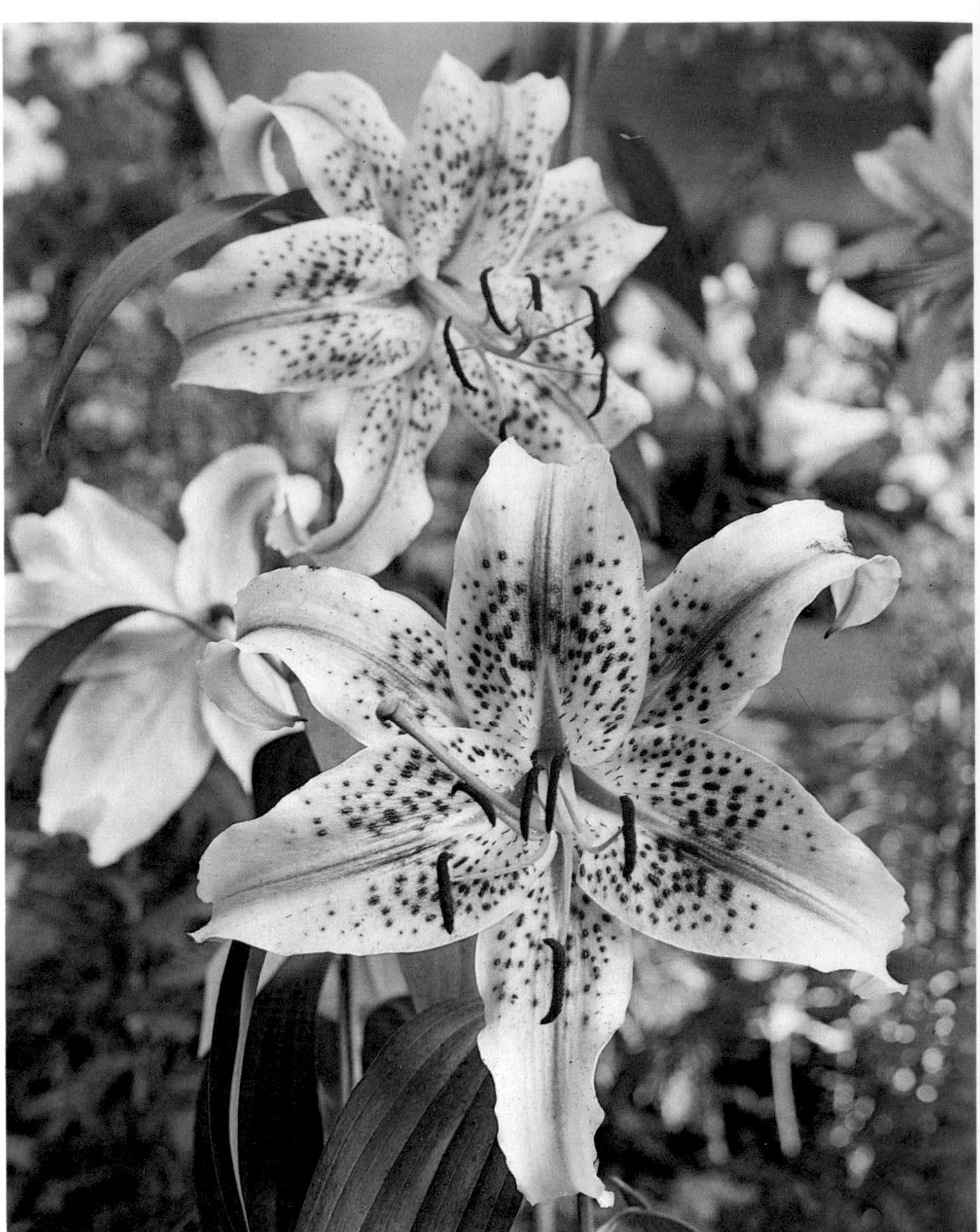

Lilium speciosum 'Rubrum'. All lilies are of great decorative value in large formal groups

Nicotiana, a long-lasting cut flower

Rhodanthe helipterum Daisy-like everlasting pink flowers which can be dried for winter arrangements. Sow in a sunny position. 45 cm (18 in.).

Biennials

Biennials are plants which are sown one year to flower the next. Who would be without foxgloves, honesty, Canterbury bells and others that seed freely and make good winter ground cover. Grow self-colours, so that, when the autumn transplanting is done, you can plan a colour scheme in the border. Such a planting will furnish the border until the flowering shrubs are established.

Campanula medium (Canterbury Bell) Sow in spring in a shady spot and transplant to a border in the autumn.

Cheiranthus × allionii This wallflower from Siberia is a hardy perennial which is usually grown as a biennial. It should be sown in open ground during summer and transplanted to the flowering site in the autumn.

Cheiranthus cheiri (Wallflower) Sow in summer in open ground and transplant in rows as soon as the plants are large enough. Plant in the flowering site in the autumn. It should be given a dressing of lime. The flowers last well in water if cut no longer than 12–15 cm (5–6 in.), and if unwanted leaves are removed.

Dianthus barbatus (Sweet William) Sow in open ground during early summer. Transfer in the autumn.

Digitalis purpurea (Foxglove) Sow in a cold frame during early summer and transplant in early autumn.

Lunaria (Honesty) This plant is grown for its seed-pods, but the leaves are good for decoration during the winter. Sow in open ground in summer.

Half-hardy annuals

Antirrhinum (snapdragon)
Sow under glass, prick out, and plant out after the frosts. 'Madam Butterfly' has a marvellous range of colours, is tall and lasts well in water.

Arctotis (African Daisy) Sow during early spring in a heated greenhouse. Plant in a sunny position in late spring.

Aster Grow as arctotis: 'Ostrich Plume', large loose feathery heads; 'Duchess mixed', chrysanthemum-like incurved flowers; 'Super Sinensis mixed', large single flowers.

Cabbage – *decorative cabbage or kale* Very useful during the winter. The colour improves after frost. Sow during spring in a heated greenhouse at 10–15°C. (50–60°F). Transplant in mid-summer.

Carnations (treated as annuals) Choose 'Chabaud Giant mixed'. Sow indoors in winter and harden off before planting out in spring.

Chrysanthemum (for open border) Korean Suttons Hybrids. Many will continue as perennials if the conditions are good. Culture as for carnations.

Cobea Scandens (Cup-and-Saucer Vine) A rapid climber for a sunny wall, which will scale 6 m (20 ft) in a year. A perennial from Mexico, it is grown in Britain as an annual. It is most decorative both for its flower and seed-pod.

Moluccella (Bells of Ireland) This most attractive plant is sometimes slow in germinating. Sow in a heated greenhouse of 15–20°C. (60–68°F.). Prick off, then plant out, taking care not to disturb the root. It is excellent for drying.

A basket of mixed spring flowers

Nicotiana (Tobacco Plant) There are several colours, the popular one being lime green. Sow in heat of 15–20°C. (60–68°F). Prick out in boxes and plant out in early summer. It will sometimes survive the winter.

Gourds Sow in individual pots in a cool frame. Plant out in rich soil in early summer, and do not gather until fully ripe.

Zea (maize) Sow late spring in heat of 15–20°C (60–68°F.). Plant out when the danger from frost is over. It can be grown for its elegant foliage.

Zinnia Sow during late spring in a heated greenhouse of 15–20°C. (60–68°F.). The seedlings resent check, so plant on into larger pots. Green *Zinnia elegans* 'Envy' is a must. 'Persian Carpet' has all the colours found in oriental carpets.

If you have no means of raising half-hardy annuals, try contacting a local nurseryman. Suggest that he raises your seed and that you then take an equal amount. Such an arrangement can work very well.

Bulbs, corms and tubers

Lilies are a great source of beauty in the garden, adding grace and grandeur to the flower arranger's art. Many are far hardier than one is led to believe and, although you may not have an ideal situation for them, much can be done to encourage their growth. I have never had the good fortune to garden with an agreeable soil; it has always required improvement. When planting lilies in the open ground, excavate a hole 45 cm (18 in.) in depth and 45 cm (18 in.) wide, making sure that the ground below is well drained. Fill it with a mixture of equal parts of good loam, leaf-mould and peat. Add a shovelful of coarse sand and mix well. Now, five bulbs can be planted, and they will remain where you have put them for several years. Plant to a depth of 12 cm (5 in.) with a handful of sand at the base of each bulb.

Madonna lilies, which are lime-tolerant

My own greatest successes have been with *L. regale*, *L. speciosum* 'Rubrum', *L. pyrenaicum* (a lily for the garden only, its perfume being far too strong indoors), *L. martagon* (both purple and white), and *L. henryi*, which flowers late in the year. I have not been successful with perhaps the loveliest of all – *L. candidum* (the lily of the Madonna). It loves to be baked by the sun and left undisturbed. It can be grown most successfully in the vegetable garden, and this is where one often sees it flourishing. A word of warning regarding all lilies grown for cutting: leave a good 45 cm (18 in.) of stem after cutting in order that the bulb can build up for the following year.

The more unusual and the more expensive lilies I grow in pots, using the same mixtures, where I can keep an eye on them. One of their advantages is that, when one requires a little glamour, they can be moved when flowering to any part of the garden. During the winter I move pots to a sheltered spot and cover with polythene, thus preventing excessive damp during this season. Try 'African Queen', 'Green Dragon', 'Limelight', 'Royal Gold' and, if you can find it, the enchanting *L. rubellum*. You will hesitate to cut these, and who could blame you. So much beauty should be preserved.

One other lily, which has been by far the most successful for me, needs mentioning. Imagine a large pot 45 cm (18 in.) across containing twenty-five golden lilies 75 cm ($2\frac{1}{2}$ ft) high, each stem bearing nine to twelve blooms. This was 'Sutters Gold', the result of five bulbs planted three years ago. Truly magnificent.

If you want something a little out of the ordinary, plant *Eucomis*, the pineapple plant. This is so-named because the spikes of greenish-white flowers end with a tuft of leaves not unlike the top of a pineapple. The bulbs come from South Africa. It would be wise to plant it at the foot of a south wall, rather in the same position as one would Belladonna lily. The very strong scent from it is quite objectionable until it has been pollinated by flies. Once this has occurred all is well, and the result is an intriguing greenish flower ending with a tuft of leaves, particularly suitable for an arrangement of fruit and flowers. The leaves are about 30 cm (1 ft) long and strap-like.

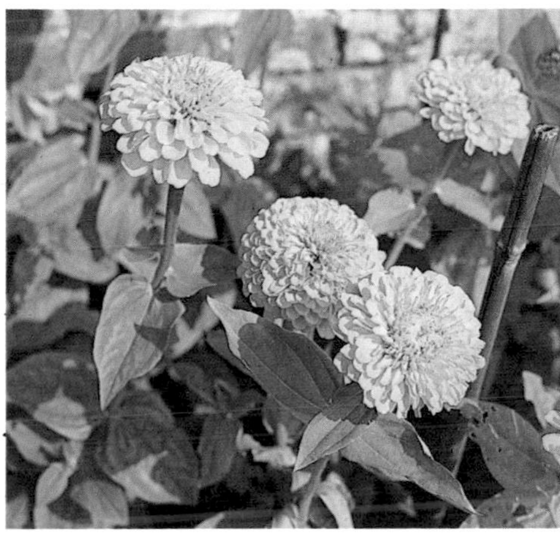

Zinnia elegans 'Envy', a favourite green flower

Acidanthera murielae
A graceful, bulbous plant which grows to a height of 60 cm–1 m (2–3 ft). It is a little gladiolus-like but the individual flowerlets are farther apart, the stem thinner and more graceful. The flower is white and scented, with a purple blotch in the centre. Plant 7 cm (3 in.) deep in late spring. Flowering is in autumn.

Camassia
The camassia deserves to be more generally grown; it is hardy and easy to grow. *C. Cusickii* is pale blue; *C. Leichtlini alba* has large spikes of white flowers; *C.*

Leichtlini caerulea is deep blue. Plant in the autumn 12 cm (5 in.) deep and 10 cm (4 in.) apart in well-drained soil.

Cyclamen The first and the third of the following are autumn flowering and are delightful beneath trees. All will tolerate lime.

C. cilicium Charming light pink with carmine eye, deep-green foliage.

C. Coum hybrids Light to deep pink, flowering in the spring.

C. neapolitanum The ivy leaf cyclamen, with rose-pink flowers.

Dahlia tubers

These are divided into four main groups: decorative, pompom, cactus and the double orchid varieties. No flower has quite such a wide range of colour. The choice is wide both in size and shape. They flower over a long period, sometimes well into late autumn, and can also be raised from seed with interesting results.

Fritillaries

What mysterious, elegant little flowers the *Fritillaria meleagris* are. They seem to hide away in the garden and yet, when added to a little spring group, stand out with great distinction. Their names too are distinctive: 'Aphrodite', 'Artemis', 'Poseidon', 'Sulphanus'. Oh that one could grow great drifts of them! The one that I grow is the legendary stately *F.* 'Crown Imperial' which is always given pride of place in the paintings of the Dutch Masters.

Galtonia candicans (Giant Summer Hyacinth)

A hardy bulbous plant, which flowers in August. The tall stems at 60–75 cm (2–2½ ft) carry bell-shaped white flowers on shorter 5 cm (2 in.) stems. It has much grace and adds distinction to a group of white flowers.

Gladiolus

I particularly like the Primulinus Hybrid Seedlings, which are about two-thirds the size of the large stately ones, and are consequently the size required for the average arrangements. However, in your order do include a few 'Green Woodpecker', 'Peter Pears', 'Forgotten Dreams' and 'Mabel Violet'. This is how the catalogue describes 'Forgotten Dreams': 'Creamy buds tipped red open to large smooth petalled flowers, outlined rose red, making an attractive picture with the soft jasmine yellow petals, faint rose blush suffuses flower as it ages. Long strong spike with many flowers out at once.' A tempting description!

The question is, where does one plant gladioli? One good place is in a row in the vegetable garden or some out-of-the-way corner, for they seem essentially a flower for cutting. Nothing looks more dreary in a border than a tall spike with the last few shaggy flowers swinging in the wind. Plant in well-manured soil 10–12 cm (4–5 in.) deep and 12 cm (5 in.) apart. To prolong the flowering period, plant at intervals. As cut flowers, they provide valuable pointed material and are remarkably long-lasting.

Leucojum aestivum (Gravetye variety)

This is the finest form named after the home of William Robinson, the famous gardener.

One could continue to suggest bulbs suitable for spring arrangements indefinitely. *Scilla campanulata* – in white, pink and blue – can be planted at the back of the border in clumps of self-colour. Cut the

Daffodils and forsythia with *Iris stylosa* which surprisingly flourish in warm starved soil

White tulips and green hellebores are arranged with graceful branches of alder catkins

A lovely vista framed by the hanging red blooms of the Chilean lantern bush

stems about 12 cm (5 in.) long, wrap in paper and give a long drink before arranging. It does not last well if cut its entire length. Then there are *Galanthus* (Snowdrops), *Muscari* (Grape Hyacinth), and *Chionodoxa* (Glory of the Snow). Mention, too, should be made of *Hyacinthus* (Hyacinth) – not because of its culture for pots, but rather as a cut flower. If, as sometimes happens, you are able to buy bulbs cheaper at the end of the season, box them up and put them into cool frames to grow on, entirely for cutting. This is rewarding, for the plants can be cut just when they are beginning to show colour, and in shallow water they will last extremely well. Second quality, unprepared bulbs are quite suitable, and if you can obtain 'City of Haarlem' or 'Lord Balfour', you will find they throw two, and sometimes more, stems suitable in size for arranging.

With the return of many somewhat neglected flowers, let us hope we shall see more of the double-flowered varieties such as 'Chestnut Flower', 'General Kohler', 'Madame Sophie', and others.

Narcissus

The genus is enormous and includes those which we call daffodils, as well as the charming little *N. bulbocodium*, *N. cyclamineus, N. triandrus* and many other small varieties. 'Moonshine' and 'Niveth' are good growers. An excellent small but not miniature daffodil is 'W. P. Milner'. A very early flowering one is 'February Gold', blooming over a very long period. Others to be recommended are 'Hunter's Moon', 'Beersheba' (white trumpet), 'Geranium', 'Kingscourt' and 'Pheasant Eye' – the last being late to bloom and having a delicious scent. These are but a few of the vast range of these glorious spring flowers.

Ornithogalum nutans

A bulbous plant with spikes of its starlike flowers of greenish-grey, 30–45 cm (12–18 in.) long. It will increase rapidly in favourable conditions, and is a welcome addition to a green-and-white vase.

O. thyrsoides 'Chincherinchee' This is imported in bud from South Africa at Christmas-time. Bulbs can be grown outside in Britain. Plant as above in spring.

Tulips

The same could be said of tulips as of Narcissus, there being a wide range of colour and types. Many of the species flower well and do not require annual moving, for example: *T. praecox*, a tall red tulip from northern Italy; *T. clusiana*, with its red-and-white marking on the outside of the petals; *T. kaufmanniana*, the seedlings of which are now the huge scarlet crosses; and *T. viridiflora* which, with its hybrids, is welcomed by all arrangers. The others make such a rainbow of colour it is almost impossible to choose between them. The pointed petalled ones – 'Moonlight', 'Maytime', 'White Triumphator' – are personal favourites. The doubles too are extremely useful, being as effective as peonies in a large arrangement. 'Mount Tacoma' is a very good, long-lasting white, then there is pink 'Eros' and mauve 'Lilac Time'. Each year more lovely varieties are bred. Among those of recent years is 'Artist' (an exciting one to use) and the lovely, soft-coloured 'Apricot Beauty'. Finally leave a spot for a few 'Bizarres', quite indispensable for the Flemish group.

Suggestions for planting

Several years ago I planted a bed some 9 m × 4.5 m (30 ft × 15 ft) with several varieties of hostas and lilies, and as a golden carpet beneath them *Lysimachia nummularia* 'Aurea' (the golden creeping jenny). To prolong the period of flowering I introduced *Galtonia candicans*, and a white Cosmos which I raised from seed saved annually. In the spring this bed was a blaze of red 'Bartigon' tulips. These were never taken up and increased with every passing year. It was in this wide bed that, at a stride apart, I placed round stepping-stones. Here then was a bed glowing with brilliant tulips in the spring, followed by the fresh young growth of hostas which effectively covered the dying tulips. The lilies followed with the ever-increasing beauty of the hosta leaves and flowers. To prolong the display came Galtonia and Cosmos.

Should you be planning a bed in a semi-shady position, try Helleborus, and with them plant Aquilegia and Astrantia or Alchemilla. At the back could be *H. corsicus* in a group of three or five; also *H. foetidus*, with *H. orientalis* midway. No staking should be required.

The stately Acanthus makes a foil for Bergenia, and with the addition of *Iris foetidissima variegata* one has a combination of colour, shape and texture. The bearded Iris are best grown in a bed by themselves, though unfortunately the glory is soon over. For the first year or so one could help to prolong it by planting Gladiolus or Acidanthera, their foliage being similar.

Peonies planted with Kniphofia and Hemerocallis, with Heuchera in the foreground, would make an interesting group, the foliage being attractive at all times.

In this chapter very many beautiful and worthwhile plants have necessarily been omitted, such as Romneya and the garden Geranium. These among others do not, as arrangers say, 'take the water well', but this should not stop you growing them. Romneya is glorious, and *Geranium endressi* and *G.* 'Johnson Blue' can be used effectively as an underplanting for roses. Indeed they all contribute to the glory of the garden.

II. Historical Background

And time remembered is grief
forgotten
And frosts are slain and flowers
begotten

ALGERNON SWINBURNE
1837–1909

Portrait of the family of Sir Thomas More by Hans Holbein (about 1530)

Fascinating and absorbing as is the study of the historical development of flower arranging against the social and political background, it would be out of place in a practical handbook for the modern reader, apart from those requiring details for formal study courses. But some understanding of past practices, the factors that influenced them and the reasons why they have survived to become the recognizable styles of the present day is both relevant and of great value to today's flower arranger. Although the student needs to become proficient and knowledgeable about designs which she hopes to use in the present day, yet much can be gained from giving thought to the achievements of earlier periods. For one thing, many of the buildings and rooms still in frequent use were designed in other centuries and include contemporary furnishings. Everyone is familiar with the great elegance and beauty of the French chateaux, the large Paris houses, and the exquisite furniture that embellished them. In England, many examples of the Georgian and Regency period of dignified architecture and gracefully proportioned furniture remain, the work of Chippendale, Adam and Hepplewhite. America boasts many fine houses with rooms that contain examples of work influenced by the French and English periods as well as Dutch, Italian and German and other European period furniture. These furnishings and décor evolved into the American Colonial style, which is as distinct from present-day American flower designs as the styles used now in the United Kingdom are from Georgian or Victorian designs.

Not everyone is fortunate enough to live in period houses with rooms such as these. There are, however, very many occasions when flowers are placed in such rooms, for they often provide the setting for important social occasions and for formal entertainment. Even when these impressive buildings are still used as private homes, it is usual for the rooms and corridors and entrance halls to have large and elegant bowls of flowers complementing the fine tapestries, pictures and furniture. It is surprising how often a flower arranger is given the opportunity of working in such surroundings. In Britain, almost every member of NAFAS is given the chance. Since many fine public and private houses need to be decorated for charitable causes or important social occasions, it is very necessary that an arranger is aware of the kind of style or design, the containers, flowers and colours suitable to certain periods, so that her decorations will be authentic in relation to the décor and background in which she is asked to work. Flower arrangers working for professional florists (and more and more men and women are finding employment in arranging flowers) are constantly expected to work in the environments described, or in embassies, hotels or official buildings where the staff may not have any flower decorative experience. Flower arrangers must have this specialized historical knowledge if they are required to work in such settings, or in large private homes with fine antique furniture.

The seventeenth century bedroom of the Marquise de Maintenon, in the Palace of Fontainbleu, France

A fine early sixteenth century Italian chest, complemented with roses

The ordinary flower arranger too needs to know about period designs, and how best to go about making them correctly and to a good standard. After all, most homes possess one or two pieces of good antique furniture that will be greatly enhanced by flowers and containers that are authentic in feeling to the time the item of furniture was made. It should be said that the arrangement need not be in a genuine period container in order to give this sense of unity with the chest or side-table or other furniture that the bouquet is placed on when completed. Indeed it would be virtually impossible to own or find an antique vase, bowl or container of the exact period that was suitable for the flowers. It is, however, vital that the flowers, containers, colours and type of design should give the impression of bouquets contemporary with the furniture and its period setting. This knowledge can only be acquired by a study of what influences worked upon the arrangers of that time.

The Saloon of Saltram House, Plymouth, England, which was decorated by Robert Adam. Stylized foliage and flowers are to be found in many of the eighteenth century embellishments

Another reason why the ordinary flower arranger should be conversant with period work, is that these kinds of designs are often called for in exhibition or competitive show work. However delightful the finished exhibit may be, or however skilled the arranger, the work will not be considered by the Judge if all the components – that is, the flowers and foliage chosen, the container they are in, the colours, the kind of design, and the background and bases and accessories (if used) – do not conform to the requirements of the particular period portrayed. For instance, an early Flemish style would exclude hybrid flowers, for they did not exist at that time. It is, however, in order to use flowers that were known to be grown at that time and were suitable for the 'Flemish picture' type of design. It would also be acceptable to use a glass goldfish bowl of the globe-shaped variety, that is similar in shape and texture to some of the pots used by the decorators and artists of the Flemish Period. The base and holders of Victorian oil lamps sometimes provide suitable substitutes in feeling to the old bronze or brass urn-type containers used at that time. It is useful to refer to the NAFAS Definition (1974) Show Schedule (still in force) of a Period Exhibition: 'This must be in keeping with the furnishings and decor of a past era. Present day flowers and containers are permitted but they should convey the atmosphere of the period.' The arranger cannot hope to carry out such a design with any success unless she is very familiar with the characteristics of the particular period in question. Challenging as the task is, the average arranger gets immense satisfaction and happiness from carrying out such designs. The necessary research reveals many aspects of life in earlier times: preference in colour, medicinal uses of plants, social patterns and interiors of homes and buildings.

The reassuring thing about Period design is that, generally speaking (providing you are aware of the essentials required) the actual practical making of the arrangement is relatively simple. It is still necessary to follow the four basic rules of good **scale**, **harmony**, **balance** and **design**. Most period designs used in Europe more or less conform to a semi-ovoid shape and a mass use of flowers and foliage. There are variations of course – such as the medieval upright design used in churches, and the Victorian épergne – but given the basic shape, it is the containers, settings, and kinds of flowers available that provided the differences. This is very different from the designs used by ancient people like the Egyptians, Greeks and Romans, where there is no design shape in common. They vary considerably in construction and materials used. But these are described later individually as are the European styles. The American Colonial follow the latter in outline shape for they were derived from the European styles. The Chinese and Japanese early Periods have had a great influence on the design forms and shapes latterly, and chapters are devoted to this subject elsewhere in the book. The Japanese style (Ikebana) demands many years of dedicated study and although it has thousands of students, many others reject the discipline which the art of ikebana demands. The contrast between the extrovert west and restrained east is reflected in the marked difference between the comfortable furnishings of the European and the severity of décor in a Japanese home. The distinctive evolution of the Japanese style is dealt with separately in Chapter 17.

Carpets, upholstery and wood fires are comforting in the cold winters of the Westerner. A copper bowl filled with a quantity of rich coloured autumn leaves, berries and chrysanthemums with their warm pungent scent can bring an aesthetic comfort and happiness on a grey day just as no doubt a Japanese has his spirits raised by contemplating the beauty of a bough, blossom and leaves arranged with maximum simplicity.

Because of the totally different evolvement of the Western and Eastern styles, the latter are dealt with in another chapter in detail by Stella Coe the acknowledged master and leader in the Western and Oriental world of this specialist art form in Europe. Leaving the description and

detail of the Japanese art form and development, let us turn to the part flower decoration has played from the early days of history, and see how the development of styles set a pattern of loveliness through the ages.

Primitive beginnings

The first look back over our shoulders to the dim past will be to a time when – to use the words of Genesis – 'The earth was without form, and void, and darkness was upon the face of the deep.' So we learn from Genesis; but on the third day of creation, we are told, 'the earth brought forth grass, the herb yielding seed, and the fruit tree yielding fruit after its kind, whose seed is in itself, upon the earth' and 'God saw that it was good.' We know, then, that even before Man, there were the grasses, herbs and fruits. The earliest reliable evidence of how, when and where man first used flowers, fruits and leaves, comes from the Chinese and early Egyptians. Although paintings and manuscripts of earlier times do not exist or have not survived, surely we can believe that man, with his special gifts, will have given grasses, herbs and fruits a special place in his world, however primitive? We cannot know for sure, but can surmise that early man not only offered flowers and fruits to his god, but also to his chosen mate, to put in her hair or to breathe its fragrance and see its beauty.

For more recent times, there is much information about what in fact took place in the daily lives of men and women and how they used the flowers around them. It is helpful for a student new to the study of the development of flower arrangement to be aware from the beginning that, (in common with many other artistic interests) during times of political or economic tension or war the standard of work and the interest in it diminish sharply, or even disappear completely, as they did in the Dark Ages. It is during periods of peace, and the prosperity associated with such eras, that we find the greatest creativity, standard of skills and their development. Only in such times was there leisure for the cultivation and enjoyment of flowers and foliage. The continent of Africa and India do not show us any ethnic style of flower arrangement developing and peculiar to themselves. Indeed, to this day, the garlands given to honoured guests in India are similar to those beloved and used by the Greeks 600–146 B.C. and the Romans A.D. 28–325.

China

As early as the Han era, 207 B.C.–A.D. 220 the Chinese had classified and described medicinal herbs. A love of Nature, and a tradition of philosophical thought and religious teaching (Taoist, Buddhist and Confucian) has meant that the Chinese not only placed cut flowers in water on the altars of their temples since the beginning of the T'ang dynasty, A.D. 618–906, but that they have left a legacy beyond price in folk-lore and artefacts of all kinds: exquisite paintings of blossoms and boughs on silk, scrolls, porcelain vases, bowls and plates; embroidery, and carving in wood, ivory and bronze. All these express the

Previous page: 'The Immaculate Conception' by Carlo Crivelli (c.1495–1500). *Lilium candidum* or the Madonna lily is emblematic of the Virgin Mary, and appears, denoting or accompanying her, in religious paintings throughout the ages. Here, Crivelli shows the Madonna flanked on one side by a stem of three lily blooms and on the other by roses and pinks (*Dianthus caryophyllus*). These flowers are traditionally associated with the Virgin and with humility.
The painting shows rich Renaissance beauty in the Virgin's robe and the elaborate hanging tapestry. There is, however, a deliberate simplicity in the jug and glass carafe and the natural way in which the flowers are placed; this yet accords perfectly with the ornate setting. A student of design would gain much knowledge by examining the way Crivelli has achieved unity and symmetrical balance in the overall design.
The symbolic qualities of almost everything included in a Renaissance religious painting have long been accepted. We can gauge from this fact the real and metaphorical significance of flowers; they are beautiful, and they are also emblems of more beauty

Above: Chinese painting on silk, seventeenth century. The Chinese often used such baskets for informal flower arrangements. The decorative handle is a feature, providing a frame for a bouquet of mixed flowers

Left: Chinoiserie. Using dried plant material on a black fabric base and background, the designer has skilfully reproduced a Chinese ivory carving on black hardwood. The slender weeping willow tree with flowers at its base and the small pagoda in the background are subjects often represented in Chinese painting and carving. All is achieved with a spare use of line and colour, in all things avoiding overstatement

Chinese love and appreciation of flowers, fruit branches and leaves. Because the Buddhist teaching forbids taking life, they were sparing in their cutting of plant material. The only time when we see reasonably full groups of flowers and leaves are in the highly esteemed basket arrangements.

Although restraint is always present in the Chinese use of flowers and branches, they are always arranged naturally. With each portrayal comes a feeling of the personal expression of the artist and his response to the ephemeral beauty of nature. In some way it conveys to the viewer the feeling that behind the finished work lies the inspiration provided by first viewing the growing flower and branch, the joy of bearing it in to the house and placing it in the chosen vessel and the care and devotion given to the cutting and to the final positioning. For all the care and thought given to it, paradoxically it has a sweet spontaneity.

There is a wealth of examples of Chinese works of art available in literature, paintings and artefacts, in galleries and museums. The vases originally all had their own stands, but few have survived with the original pot. Many of the designs are set on tables, and have with them scrolls, lamps and other vases or pots. Such designs suggest that the flowers belonged to a home or courtyard personal to the designer, and emphasizes the uniqueness of what we see. The influence of the Chinese upon the art of flower arranging has been profound. Most of the flowers and leaves that were used had a symbolic meaning. The pear, the peach tree, and the bamboo express the importance to the Chinese of long life. Very often they use a certain fungus known as 'the plant of long life'. The New Year, which begins in February, bears the emblem of the paper white tazetta narcissus which was often forced into early bloom. The four seasons are denoted by white plum blossom for winter, cherry and peach blossom for spring, lotus for summer, and the chrysanthemum for winter. A combination of pine, bamboo and plum is known as 'The Three Friends of the Cold Season'. Orchids, tiger lily and pomegranate are emblems of fertility. The flower honoured above all others was the peony (*Paeonia suffruticosa*, syn *P. moutan*) known as 'The King of Flowers'. Not only was it an emblem of good fortune, but also of wealth and high position.

From the seventeenth century plant collectors have brought to the west large numbers of plants and shrubs, that now are universally grown and easily available to most flower arrangers for their use and enjoyment. More details of flowers can be found in *Gardens of China* by Oswald Siren (Ronald Press Co., New York, 1949).

From China, Buddhist missionary priests carried their flower skills to Japan, where the art of Ikebana subsequently developed.

Ancient Egypt

The ancient Egyptians were using plant material for decorative purposes as far back as 2,500 B.C., as carved stone reliefs and painted wall decorations bear witness. Rules were laid down and strictly followed, so that there was little variation in style for over 3,000 years. Flowers were cut and

Left: a seventeenth century Chinese flower painting

Above: a replica of an ancient Egyptian design, taken from the representations in the tomb of the Pharaoh Tutankhamun (c.1361–1352 BC). Typical plant material was used. Bamboo stems are grouped together to make a central pillar and the bronze reverse side of rhododendron leaves are used to form the clusters at the base, centre and top. Glycerined ficus leaves create the brown fan-shaped placement at the apex. The three triangular sections are made from shaped pampas grass seedheads, and their small decorative points from hare's foot grass. Grapes are used at the points where the column is intersected by the curving vine-stem. There is something very akin, in result, if not in conception, to modern abstract plant design in these Egyptian examples

placed in vases. The latter were sometimes glazed and decorated faience, often with spouts for holding flowers. Glass was much used, and the cup-shaped pieces were placed into terracotta cups (which would be porous) and mounted on stands. The spouted pots are strikingly similar to those used thousands of years later in Persia, and also to seventeenth-century Delft tulip pots in Holland. All Egyptian foliage or flower arrangement designs - whether for the decoration of banquet tables, for burial in tombs, or for processions - were highly stylized, and the containers dictated by convention. Religious beliefs influenced the choice of flowers and foliage. The lotus flower (*Nymphaea lotus*, the Egyptian lotus, a water-lily) was considered sacred to the goddess Isis, and during the long reigns of the Pharoahs this flower and the herbs, the palm tree and the papyrus plant were the most used. Other flowers found in tomb garlands such as mallow and corn poppy were not of the same significance. Not until considerably later did the rose appear to be used and it is probable that when it was so it was due to the spread of Graeco-Roman culture. Other identifiable flowers which are available to present-day arrangers include the blue scilla, *Iris sibirica*, poppy-flowered anemone, tazetta narcissus and *Delphinium orientale*.

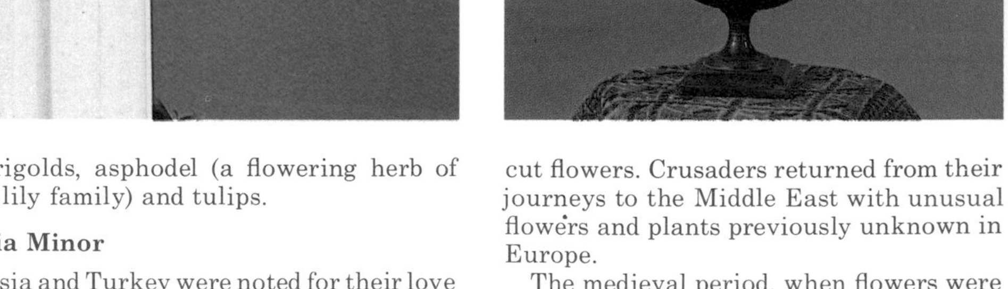

Greek and Roman

The decorative uses of flowers in the Greek (600–146 B.C.) and the Roman (A.D. 27–325) periods can be looked at together by the student, for they follow a similar pattern. The surprising thing is that although flowers and foliage were lavishly used, they were not set in water or pots, but used principally as wreaths, garlands and chaplets as a mark of distinction, whether worn, wound round pillars, or carried on staves. Flowers and petals were freely strewn upon floors, beds, and even the guests at banquets!

The garlands, wreaths and chaplets were made from oak leaves and acorns, ivy, laurel and box, parsley, bay and yew, and other foliage. Fruits such as apples, grapes, pomegranates, and figs abounded. Sweetly scented flowers such as hyacinth, rose and violets, honeysuckle, and lilies were favoured but many were chosen simply for their colour, form and shape, like larkspur, marigolds, asphodel (a flowering herb of the lily family) and tulips.

Asia Minor

Persia and Turkey were noted for their love and interest in flowers. In the fifth century B.C., for example, the Persian king Darius I had no less than fifty flower growers and florists attached to his household.

The Byzantine Empire (A.D. 500–1453) continued to enjoy much of the Greek and Roman culture while Western Europe was in chaos. The cone-shaped design was their particular contribution to floral decoration. Long slim tapering cones of foliage were constructed and placed in urns or chalices and were decorated with fruits and flowers of jewel colours. Lilies, daisies, carnations, and cypress and pine were all used. The Byzantines loved to use ribbons, winding them into the manes of their horses, and spiralling round their foliage and flower cones. Sometimes a low container had a central stem from which symmetrical flowers or fruit were placed at intervals up the stem. Arrangements were highly stylized and formal.

The Renaissance

After the fall of the Roman Empire, the so-called 'dark ages' enveloped Europe. It was not until A.D. 1000 that a revival of interest in the use of flowers and plants for decoration can be found. As the chief centres of learning, monasteries and churches cultivated plants, flowers and herbs for medicinal purposes as well as for food and decoration. Illuminated manuscripts of the time carry exquisite flower paintings, and the altars of churches were embellished with cut flowers. Crusaders returned from their journeys to the Middle East with unusual flowers and plants previously unknown in Europe.

The medieval period, when flowers were confined mostly to use in churches and cathedrals, was the preliminary to the fourteenth-century Italian Renaissance during which the art of flower arrangement was reborn. During this period different styles evolved all over Europe. From medieval darkness, there emerged great richness of colour, from shapelessness, came graceful form. New expression of art blossomed. In the renowned Italian gardens flowers were grown for their beauty alone, without consideration for their usefulness. The Renaissance reached its climax in the fifteenth and sixteenth centuries. The student can gain an immediate visual understanding of the period by looking at the paintings of Botticelli, Titian and Tintoretto, Raphael, Carlo Maratta, and many others.

Georgian Design

Lilian Martin

Arrangement 1: George III

Perhaps the easiest approach when beginning a historically-based arrangement is to select one span of time and consolidate one's knowledge of its more *domestic* details. (Do not forget, however, that despite historical periodization, the saying 'The King is dead – long live the King' does not apply to the customs and culture of a people. Changes in architecture, art, fashion and interior decoration slowly filter through the various reigns.) The whole period from George I to George IV is relatively vast, extending as it does from 1714–1830, so for Arrangement 1 I have chosen to create the atmosphere of the time of George III, roughly about 1770.

This was a great period and there were still strong links with the East and the Colonies to introduce many new and exotic plants. It may be remembered that Phillip Millar was still at the Chelsea Physic Garden and Sir Joseph Banks at Kew; it is said that 7,000 new species were introduced during his time there. The influence of Capability Brown, the famous landscape gardener, was pervasive, with the idea that Nature is best appreciated when discreetly translated into Art. This attitude is seen in the poetry of the time, and the portraits of the mid-eighteenth century British artists; the ordered and subdued conversation pieces, with Milord, his family and pets stiffly posed against the formal background of his parkland, or by the side of a Georgian garden ornament. It is this atmosphere of quiet restraint and ordered elegance which prevails in the architecture of Robert Adam, the furniture of Chippendale, the heavy rich fabrics of the curtains and hangings and the classical urn-shaped vases.

These vases, either of lead or stone, are far too heavy and large for demonstrations or home use today, but fortunately now there are many good plastic containers of classical design which may be 'mocked up' to give an authentic effect. The one used in the George III design was white plastic, painted all gold. A wash of dull Adam Green emulsion was superimposed, and before this dried was wiped off the raised areas. Thus the dull green remained in the recessed areas, while the gold shone through the highlights of the mouldings. In this way one may recreate the patina of years! This was placed on a base treated similarly.

The atmosphere was created with flowers and foliage more easily and locally obtainable than a Great House could have found. Unfortunately more exotic material was not available, including the pineapple so beloved by Robert Adam for his finials. The required points, therefore, were obtained with grasses. The parrot was incorporated as a reminder of the aviaries which the fashionable world of the eighteenth century introduced into its hothouses along with its plants from foreign climes

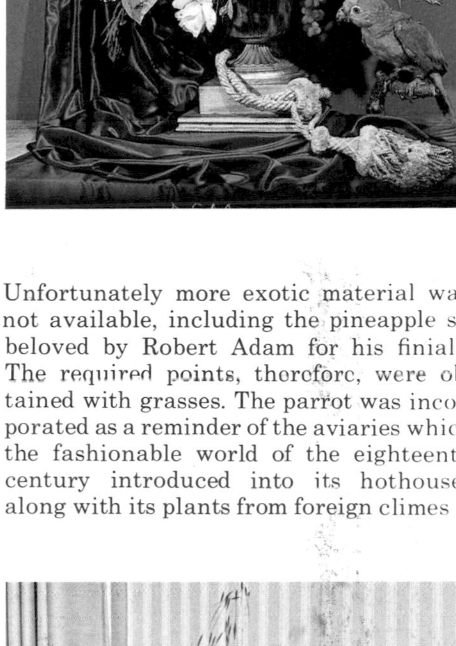

Arrangement 2: 1810–1837

This period, from the beginning of the Regency to 1830, is in many respects particularly attractive; and though not officially Georgian, one feels that William IV should also be included, ending the period with Victoria's accession. During this period there was gradual change from the previous more formal solidity, to a preference for classical simplicity in home furnishings and in personal fashion. It is to these domestic changes that one may turn for inspiration on which to base an arrangement of the times.

There was great stress on the elegance of simplicity as a result of the contemporary revival of 'Imperial' forms and styles. One may see this in the 'Empire' style of the gowns of Empress Josephine, and those probably worn by the young ladies of Miss Jane Austen, with their flowing, elegant lines. These young ladies sat hopefully in Bath or Brighton next to their chaperones on chairs made by such cabinet makers as Sheraton and Hepplewhite; smaller 'occasional' pieces of furniture were being introduced into homes. Chinoiserie was becoming very popular. Gentlemen joined the Horticultural Society which was formed in 1804. Joseph Paxton had just started at Chatsworth House in the capacity of landscape gardener.

All these details are present in the mind when setting up this arrangement on a Sheraton tea urn stand, using an old alabaster vase. The arrangement keeps a slender line from the *Stipa gigantea* grass to the mauve floribunda and 'Gloire de Dijon' roses lower down, which give weight yet do not spoil its slenderness. The tints and tones here are more muted, in deference to the late Georgian preference for heavier colouring.

Lilian Martin

Left: a Flemish fresh flower arrangement, distinguished for its sensitive authenticity, its celebration of colour, form and texture in a style worthy of the seventeenth and eighteenth century masters

Left: an ornate arrangement in the style of the Late Regency, embellished with fruit, embroidered satin, bullion tassel and figured container

Left: a beautiful period design of peonies, carnations, roses, honeysuckle and lilies in warm pastel colours. The elaborate elegance of the setting is typical of the French Rococo style

Right: portrait of Queen Charlotte, by John Zoffany (1771). Queen Charlotte (the wife of George III of England, m1761, d1818) is depicted against magnificent silk hangings, her arm resting on a velvet cushion. In her elaborate blue dress with its deep edgings of exquisite lace she presents a very regal figure, surrounded by all the material trappings of majesty. A less formal note is struck by the bouquet of garden flowers, the kind often seen in present-day English homes. The arrangement of the flowers is fresh and naturalistic, and it seems they are included to indicate, in the midst of pomp, something of the Queen's true preferences. One might imagine her turning her head during the tedious portrait sitting to relax and enjoy the flowers

Seventeenth-century Holland

The Dutch and Flemish schools of the seventeenth and early eighteenth centuries present us with a marked change from the elegant French Baroque to a simpler presentation. Gay bold colours and varieties of flowers are mixed with abandon. This contrast of styles in choice and use of flowers at approximately the same time in history, provides a most useful example to the student of how important features in flower decoration were influenced by the interiors of the houses in which they were placed, and by the characteristics and tastes of the people who used them. While the French are renowned for refinement in décor the Flemish and Dutch - great seamen, travellers, and horticulturists - had a forthright enjoyment of life which is clearly reflected in the paintings of the interiors of their homes. The lives they led required reasonably practical - rather than elegant - clothes, yet the beauty of their flower bouquets is breathtaking. Their fascination has indeed grown rather than diminished through the centuries. It was paintings, curiously enough, that brought colour and interest to their homes. Such magnificence of real and living flowers was not placed for everyday enjoyment. Indeed, this would have proved impossible for many combinations consisted of flowers of all seasons. They were composed from studies of flowers made at different times, and then very skilfully brought together. The textural qualities, not only of the flowers and leaves, but also draperies, fruits, birds, and other objects included in the paintings, were exceptional. The fragility of a butterfly's wing or the sheen of a petal were portrayed by the Flemish and Dutch painters with perfect fidelity. Posterity must always be grateful for their skills, but flower arrangers must feel an even deeper gratitude for what was the foundation and inspiration of the groupings of mixed flowers. The student has literally hundreds of inspiring and instructive paintings to observe in this particular period from which she can gain detailed knowledge and understanding of the Dutch and Flemish styles. The great painters are too numerous to list but the names of Jan Brueghel (1568-1625), Peter Paul Rubens (1577-1640) and Jan Vermeer van Delft (1632-75) must be mentioned.

The containers used are very varied in shapes and textures. They included jugs and ewers, beautiful glass shapes from Venice and Germany, often green in colour and with glass prunts or knobs, Chinese blue and white porcelain, and of course the cheaper blue and white Delft ware may all be used. The classic urn - often in terracotta - was an excellent shape for the quantity of flowers used. The design was mostly based on an oval with flowers, leaves and stems gracefully flowing within the ovoid shape. There is a free rhythmic line, with colours highlighted. The rim of the container is always visually 'broken' by flower placements to avoid a hard horizontal line at the base of the flowers. A rhythmic assymetric 'flow' can be perceived in the design, starting from the top of the arrangement, where an important flower would be placed, and continuing to the base of the design in such a way that the eye is led easily by plant forms and shapes, or by colour, to the lower placements.

Surprisingly large flowers - even sunflowers - are used, but when the scale of such flowers is too challenging, then they are turned in profile rather than full-faced to reduce the visual impact. The effect is not only to reduce 'scale', but provides a lesson in the beauty of the profile - sometimes even the reverse side - of a leaf or flower. Garden flowers, especially tulips, poppies, marigolds, morning glories, auriculas and countless other flowers, leaves, grasses and fruits were all used to provide a constant delight to the eye.

The later period of Dutch and Flemish designs demonstrates a particularly magnificent use of colour. Orange, terracotta and deep reds are mingled with pale pink, white and pale yellow, always with a pure shade of blue - almost sky-blue. Of course many shades of green combine with these colours. The handling of colour combinations in these paintings is masterly.

The English tradition

Although the British are an island race, through history they have happily absorbed people and ideas from many sources. Famed for a passionate love of gardening and nature, they have been responsible for filling their own gardens and those of the rest of the world with plants, trees and shrubs from all continents. Many of these were provided by plant hunters, and many by their seamen merchants and explorers. Invaders and refugees alike, from the Romans, Anglo-Saxons and Danes to the Normans and Huguenots brought new flowers, fruits, and plants to their shores. All these flowers, notably the carnation, auricula, tulip and narcissus have found their place in the English garden both small and stately.

The ancient Druids used mistletoe (the golden bough) in their religious ceremonies. In modern times it is hung up at Christmas to kiss beneath - a relic from an age when it was not allowed to touch the ground, nor strife permitted near it. The Romans introduced their own flower festivals. The one dedicated to Flora, goddess of spring, still survives in May day festivals all over England, celebrated with floral dances and the crowning of a May queen. In Derbyshire, village wells are beautifully

Above: a very fine seventeenth century multi-spouted tulip pot in Dutch Delft ware

Left: an illustration by Sir George Naylor (1837) of a part of the Coronation service for George IV in 1820. A royal Herb-woman and her six attendant maidens are strewing herbs and flowers in the path of the procession. The illustration is of great interest for two reasons: one is that it shows the last occasion on which this ceremony was performed at the coronation of a king or queen of England. The other reason is that it indicates the continuation of the Roman custom of wearing floral wreaths and chaplets on the head and garlands over the shoulder and breast. The handle-less baskets (called 'canistra') in the illustration are made in the same pattern as the Roman ones

decorated with thousands of flowers and religious texts. This is a survival of the worship of water spirits known as 'well-dressing'. (See right)

From very early times, before reliable medical treatment was available, people have used flowers in the belief that they would keep noxious odours at bay and make the air sweeter. Herbs and petals were strewn about the floor, posies carried and chaplets worn on the head. The unsophisticated arrangements could be described as 'folk' bunches. The choice of flowers and leaves was informal and random, although the Church had certain ritual uses for flowers. In the thirteenth century the priests of St Paul's, London, wore flower crowns (*coronae sacerdotales*). To this day the judges carry posies at the opening of the Law Sessions.

The Dutchman Leivius Lemnius wrote after visiting England in 1560: 'Their chambers and parlours strewed over with sweet herbs refreshed me, their nosegays finely intermingled with sundry sorts of fragraunte flowers, in their bed-chambers and privy rooms, with comfortable smell cheered me up and entirely delyted all my senses,' and continued, 'Altho' we do trimme up our parlours with greene boughes, freshe herbs or vine leaves, no nation does it more decently, more trimmely nor more sightly than they doe in Englande.'

Contemporary paintings are an equally useful source of information about the use of flowers in sixteenth-century England. Hans Holbein, for example, painted a delightful picture of the family of Sir Thomas More (see p. 152-3) which shows three groups of arranged flowers from his Tudor garden. They contain lilies, carnations, iris, columbine and peonies, and they are put fairly loosely and vertically in pewter pots, and a china jug. Two very important books were published at about this time. John Parkinson's *Paradise* (*In Sole Paradisus Terrestris*, 1629) throws light on what flowers were used to 'deck up houses'. He writes of the German iris: 'It well doth serve to deck up both a garden and House with Natures beauties.' John Gerard's *Herball* has two flower arrangements depicted in the frontispiece in interesting containers which are 'footed' and of the urn variety, one of them with two handles. The flowers are clearly seen and the overall shape is a tall oval with an outline that is loose and flowing.

Georgian and Regency

This period saw some of the greatest social and political changes of our times, and the beginning, for both Europe and America, of the modern world. In England the stiff *ancien régime* and the new 'Romantic' love of the unconventional, the mysterious and the informal began to co-exist uneasily. They were finally brought together in the sentimental formality of the Victorian age. In this 'Romantic' period then, there arose a love of Nature for its own sake, which partly showed itself in the new naturalism in landscape design. After 'Capability' Brown, 'natural' trees and lakes, and 'rustic' paths and dwellings stood in artfully-planned curving vistas, flowers being relegated to the kitchen garden. At the same time, 'classical' formality was generally observed in the large, dignified set-piece flower arrangements (still often undertaken by head-gardeners) and in their imposing containers. More latitude was allowed as the period advanced into the Regency.

Two such arrangements, one Georgian, one Regency, are described and illustrated by Lilian Martin, an expert in this area, on page 161.

The Victorian period

The early Victorian period is characterized by a breaking away from the pseudo-classicism of the Regency. Certainly from the 1850s to the end of her reign, Victoria's personal taste was universally adopted by her subjects. This meant a preponderance of dark colours, such as mulberry, mustard, purple, magenta, royal blue, brown and dark crimson for curtains and furnishings as well as for personal dress. Since mahogany and rosewood were much used for furniture, a somewhat sombre interior prevailed. Perhaps as a reaction there was a tremendous upsurge of interest in horticulture and flower arrangements in popular ladies' magazines as well as scholarly journals. In her famous book on household management, Mrs Beeton commented on flower arrangement:

> The decoration of tables at the present time is almost universal, and so does the taste for it grow and develop, that what was formerly left in the hands of the head servants in large establishments, who had no difficulty in packing the épergnes with fruit or flowers, now forms a wide field of labour for artistic taste and skill. Hostesses in the season vie with each other as to whose table shall be the most elegant, and often spend almost as much upon the flowers as upon the dinner itself, employing for the floral arrangement people who make a profession of this pleasant occupation. Home decoration is practised by those who have the time, and we can imagine no household duty more attractive to the ladies of the house than that of making their tables beautiful with the exquisite floral produce of the different seasons, exercising their taste in devising new ways of employing the materials at their command. Young people should have their taste for arranging flowers encouraged, and be allowed to assist in decorating the table. Care should be taken not to overload the table with flowers.

Mrs Beeton's warning about not overloading the table is as timely today as it ever was. This extract from a book written during the Victorian period paints a very clear picture of the great houses with many staff and the wealth to employ professional florists. It also shows that the more ordinary Victorian hostess was concerned with the tasteful arrangement of her flowers.

Thousands of petals on a china clay base assembled in the manner of the Derbyshire well-dressings. The original design was carved in a small Devon church in AD1220

An enduring example of Victorian floral arrangement is the posy. It was carried on many and varied occasions, with a frill of lace (real or paper) or some kind of foliage encircling it. Around the raised centre, usually formed by a rose-bud at the top, several other kinds of flowers were placed in perfect concentric circles of differing colours. Wire was used to assist in the construction and hold the stems rigidly. When the neat circular posy or bouquet was finished, the wire-supported stems could be tapered off so that the 'tuzzy-muzzy' would have a slim handle easily held in the hand. An additional embellishment – many of which have great charm (and are now collectors pieces) – was a 'posy holder' made of porcelain, precious metal, or enamel. Some had a tripod stand on a spring mechanism so that the posy could be placed on a side table when tea was to be taken during an afternoon visit. (See p. 166.) Modern bridesmaid bouquets are a reminder of this custom of carrying posies. Ladies wore flowers in their hair and bosom, while gentlemen wore button holes which were virtually small bouquets in themselves.

Church decoration which, previously, had been confined to restrained and traditional work, became a new field of invention for Victorian ladies. Their activities ranged all round the church building and were not confined to the altar. Wooden laths, bent into curves and arches, were decorated with greenery. Whether at home or in church, the Victorian style of flower decoration reflected in its unforgiving symmetry the conventional formality of contemporary life.

Flowers had to be suited to the containers used, of which there were many types. Glass, in all its forms, coloured, cut, moulded and pressed, was very popular, as was porcelain and pottery, usually decorated with pattern or painting. The trumpet and cornucopia shapes were much favoured. Larger containers like urns and chalices owed a great deal to the classical shapes of the Italian Renaissance and were made in marble, alabaster and other stone materials. Jardinières fitted with practical metal liners were much used. Foliage plants were placed within them and cut flowers in water were added, in the manner of modern *pot-et-fleur* designs. Bamboo, wicker and wood stands abounded and held flowers or potted plants.

Despite the cluttered rooms in which they sat, Victorian flower designs have a certain precision and clarity and are not without grace, especially when used in épergnes for table decoration. The outline shapes were round or semi-ovoid or triangular. Height was not a feature, but the horizontal and low shape was used. We must be grateful to the Victorians for making known the decorative value of ornamental grasses, ferns, and even bulrushes. They 'grouped' colours, and combined maroon, scarlet and white with green leaves and added (according to a widely-read periodical of the time), a single gold calceolaria – a brave combination and one peculiar to this period.

The Victorians developed 'the language of flowers', as if to introduce some sentiment into the orderly pattern of their designs. Certain combinations of flowers conveyed a message of love or condolence.

Inevitably, there was a reaction to all this visual impact of colour and mass in the environment. In the latter part of the nineteenth century a group of painters set up the 'Pre-Raphaelite Brotherhood' in an attempt to return to the ideals of a more primitive age. They were championed by John Ruskin, who, with the writer, painter and designer William Morris looked forward to a 'new art' or *art nouveau* which would take its expression from natural forms. William Morris's designs enjoyed much success in his day, and have a well-established place in modern design. *Art nouveau* shows the influence of oriental sparseness of line. No doubt the elongated shapes and graceful curves of tendrils and stems with one or two flowers seen in isolation, provided the perfect contrast to the tight-packed bouquets, precise patterning and bold use of colour that had surfeited the artistic sense for so long.

The traditional period, extending from the Edwardians to the end of the Second World War is described in Chapter 4.

American Colonial eighteenth century

Early Puritan settlers in North America had too tough a time of it to grow flowers and herbs other than for medicinal and culinary use. In New Amsterdam, however, the situation was rather easier. The Dutch colonists, known for their skill in horticulture, set about making orchards and

Far left: a colourful Victorian arrangement in a china cornucopia

Left: a Victorian posy-holder, the base tripod open for free-standing while its owner has her hands occupied. (See p. 165)

Below left: 'The Cousins: Queen Victoria and Princess Victoire, Duchesse de Nemours' by Franz Winterhalter (1852)

Right: Flowers as a corsage, on the hat and worn as a button hole, from a Victorian painting by Edwin Roberts

Far right: Mr T C March, a nineteenth century head gardener, was the author of *Fruit and Flower Decoration*, which has immortalised his skills as a table decorator. One illustration from this book (below, right) shows three elegant épergnes or table centrepieces (sometimes called March stands) using fruit, flowers and ferns. The other picture (above, right) illustrates circular arrangements of different coloured blossoms

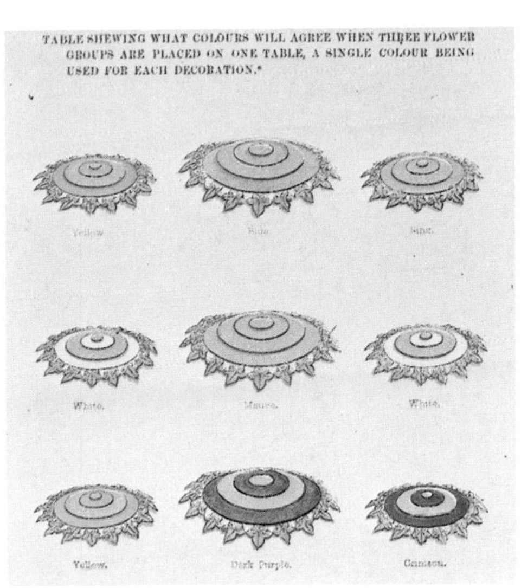

flower gardens from 1626 until 1664 when the settlement was taken over by the English. The Dutch picked tulips, guelder roses, violets, marigolds and gilly flowers that they had brought with them from Holland and then placed them in simple vessels that they had in their possession.

In 1698 Williamsburg was founded by the English as the capital city of Virginia. Very rapidly the colony prospered. There was a close link with England, and soon fine English furniture, rich fabrics, porcelain and the trappings of fine mansions were shipped across the Atlantic to furnish large wooden houses built in the neo-classical style. Naturally, the gardens that were created for settings for these homes were in keeping with this style. In this relaxed and prosperous society a real interest in bringing cut flowers into the houses became important to the community. From the beginning, the native flowers and grasses which flourished in the mild climate as well as the flowers and foliages that came from other countries were used and appreciated. Flowers were dried for household use during the winter months, when lavender and straw flowers, cat-tails and corncobs and other suitable materials were made into mixed groups. This interest and skill in drying and pressing plant forms reached the very high standard still to be observed in American work.

There are a few glimpses of the kind of arrangement of cut flowers that was made in the eighteenth century in some early paintings, where they figure in the backgrounds. Vases were imported from England, China, Holland, and elsewhere. In the absence of written records it would seem reasonable to suppose that the style of the arrangements was similar to that being used in France, Holland and England at the time, although they were probably less elaborate. Carnations and pinks, ranunculus, foxgloves, roses, bulb flowers and lilies, irises and alliums, tulips and crown imperials were imported, given love and care in gardens and then brought in to houses to give pleasure. It is interesting to find that 'spouted' vases and pots were used about this time, as they had been long before in Egypt and later in Holland and England.

Enthusiasm for flower arrangement developed very rapidly in nineteenth-century America where interest in cut flowers and pot plants grew apace. New colours and shapes in flowers were available with the importation from Mexico of brilliant dahlias and nasturtiums. Azaleas and camellias were planted. South Africa provided gladioli, roses and chrysanthemums; tree peonies came from China. Dahlias and fuchsias were especially prized. Women's magazines, which were widely read both in Victorian England and in America at a time when women had few leisure occupations outside the home and garden, contained good advice on what was described as 'the proper management' of cut flowers. In the American 'Flower Garden Companion' magazine of 1838 Edward Sayers stated that it was 'now an almost universal practice to have cut flowers in rooms as natural ornaments'

Over the years America has developed the art of flower arrangement to a standard and diversity that has absorbed all that is best of the European designs, and in addition has taken from the Far East the principle of using line and space within the design fusing both elements into a new and distinctive style. With brilliance the American arranger has widened the possibilities of new forms and stimulating shapes and has created a form of expression that is unique. The garden clubs of America have made a supreme contribution in this field. The National Council of State Garden Clubs, an international organization, continues to bring new life to an art with centuries of history. Arrangers of all countries are increasingly enjoying gaining knowledge and experience in period designs prompted by a desire to interpret the feeling and spirit of a great era.

12. Church Flowers and Church Festivals

Glorious the song, when God's the theme.
CHRISTOPHER SMART 1722–1771

The beautiful frontal of Salisbury Cathedral's High Altar is framed by two 'trees' of red flowers which not only repeat the colours of the embroidery, but also provide a contrast in both texture and colour to the magnificent stone pillars. The silver cross stands alone in space and rightly becomes the most important feature. Design interest is provided by the contrast between the horizontal line of the altar top and the strong vertical lines of the candles, pillars and flowers. The occasion was a 'Flowers in Glory' festival. (See p. 128)

·TE·GLOSVS·APTOM·CHORVS
·SCS·SANCTVS·SCS·
·TV·PATRIS·SEMPITERNVS·ES·FILIVS
VENAND·TVV·VERV·ET·VNICV·FILIV

Every week thousands of cathedrals, abbeys and other churches and chapels of many denominations are decorated with flowers and foliage. There are, of course, certain exceptions, such as the period of Lent, and a few religious sects who do not allow flowers to be used in their places of worship. A great number of people carry out this work – usually on a rotating basis – and there is no duty which is performed with greater pleasure. It could be that the quiet surroundings and the spiritual atmosphere of the buildings help the arranger to be relaxed and absolved from daily worries and cares. Whatever the reason, there can be no doubt that there is a particular and very special happiness felt while church flowers are being arranged.

Left: in an ancient Dorset church a mellow stone seat provides a serene setting for a simple but beautiful design which includes stripped lime, *Stephanandra, Hosta* foliage and lilies

The church rota

The performance of a flower arranger's duties will, of course, vary from church to church but there will always be someone who organizes the committees and who will give the necessary details. The important things to be sure about are:

1. The days on which the work is to be done and what time.
2. Whether the arranger supplies the flowers or whether there is a fund from which a sum is allocated.
3. Where the arrangements are to be placed.

Generally speaking, in smaller churches the flowers are donated by the arranger, but this is not always the case. The essentials are:

(a) To pick or buy really fresh flowers.

(b) Condition them well in whatever way is appropriate and give them a deep drink for several hours.

(c) Having arranged the flowers, see that they remain in perfect condition for the period you have agreed to undertake.

Unfortunately, this last point is overlooked by arrangers who seem to consider that their responsibility ends with the completed work. This is not so, for each arrangement must be taken care of until the next arranger's date comes round. It is most distressing to see wilted and dead plant material in a church. It is better to have no flowers than those that are withered. Make it a point of honour that your flowers are perfect from start to finish. If some flowers let you down and expense is a problem, perhaps because you have no garden, then use well-conditioned fresh foliage as a substitute. Dried or preserved foliage with a few flowers will also make the task easier.

Sadly, many churches are now kept locked, except for services, for security reasons. Make sure that you know where the key can be obtained when the church is closed, as you may be expected to remove the previous week's flowers. If lilies or other long-lasting flowers have been used they may still have some days of life left in them. Even so, it is wise not to use them at

Below: visitors to this church are welcomed by a colourful arrangement conveniently placed between pillar and bench-end in the porch entrance

Left: a red carpet and cords of the kind often seen in churches provide the arranger with an opportunity to outline the font corner with summer garden flowers, repeating the warm colour of carpet and cords in soft tints and tones. In the background a flower border can be seen at the base of the pews

Below: these two 'kneelers' or hassocks were made entirely of flowers for a wedding. Queen Anne's lace provides the background for a pattern of white flowers. In order to make an accurate design for such decorations the shapes and colours are usually first worked out on graph paper, in much the same way as embroiderers plan their tapestries. The design is then made up using one of the following methods: 1) prepared fresh flowers and foliage are pressed into a base of damp plastic foam; 2) prepared fresh flowers and foliage are pressed into a base of damp sphagnum moss, which keeps the plant material in good condition and provides a pleasant green background to the design; or 3) prepared dried flower heads and foliage are pressed into a base of dry plastic foam

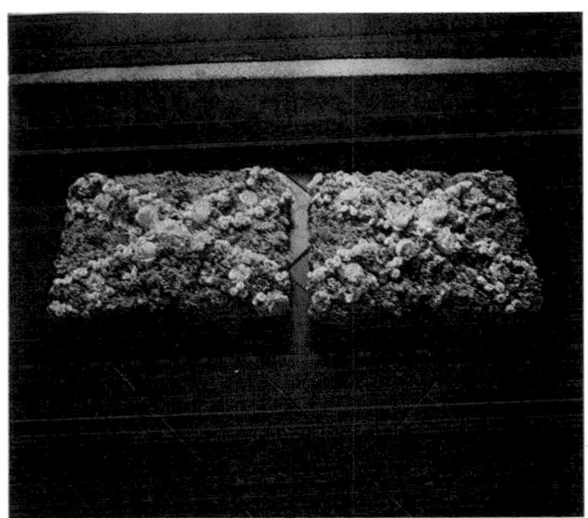

Above: this all-foliage design using green peppers as a centre point is an excellent example of the way in which easily-obtainable leaves can look both imposing and beautiful in a cathedral setting

the altar or principal position. A few tired flowers amongst fresh ones will be very noticeable as the week progresses. Some nonconformist and other churches have the flowers taken to the sick or bereaved, after the conclusion of the Sunday evening service. Should this be your local custom, find out whether it is your task to deliver them. The majority of churches leave the flowers for the whole week.

It is usual to make the arrangements on a Friday or Saturday so that they are ready for the Sunday services. Narrow vases, carefully filled with water on the first day, may be a quarter empty two or three days afterwards. So remember, whatever containers you use, to fill them up and replenish them with water as required. If plastic foam is used, see that it is well-saturated at the beginning and then kept thoroughly moist all the time. Nip, or cut out any dead or tired flowers or foliage. Do not try to pull out the whole stem. You will almost certainly make a muddle and have to start all over again. Bought flowers must have their stems re-cut, as the stem ends seal up to form a kind of callous that prevents the water being drawn up. Cut off about 1 cm ($\frac{1}{2}$ in.) of stem and see that the stems of a bought bunch of flowers are of uneven length.

Transport

If you take flowers and foliage to the church by car, long cardboard boxes of the kind used to transport flowers to florists are excellent, placed in the boot or on the back seat of the car. A florist will probably give or sell you one of these boxes. Lay the flowers so that their heads are supported by tissue, and stretch a piece of polythene across the box top as a lid to keep the plant material in good shape. If you walk to the church, or travel by bus or public transport, then place well-conditioned foliage in a plastic bag and seal the top. A flat flower basket is good to hold your plant material. Pack the basket as carefully as you would the box and again use a polythene cover. Flower baskets are a little expensive but can also be used in the garden when picking. Even if you have no garden you can arrange flowers in them for the church or house if you put a container as a lining inside them.

Equipment

Remember to take along all the equipment for your work. Flower scissors or secateurs are essential for tough woody stems, so invest in purpose-made scissors as they last for ever. Include a square of polythene to work on to prevent any mess from water or stem-ends, and an old polythene bag to hold rubbish when work is over. If there is no facility for rubbish to be disposed of at the church, take the bag home.

In most church flower cupboards you should find wire-netting, plastic foam and pinholders – but make sure this is so in your church, and if not, take your own requirements.

Above: when there is little space available, a vertical design can be placed between the pews. Such a design shows up well against a bare wall

Left: rich autumn colours are enhanced by boldly-used brown foliage in Piddlehinton Church, Dorset

Containers

It would be very unusual if flower vases and containers were not available in a church. The variety of containers is admittedly not very great and some are not the best shapes for inexperienced arrangers to cope with. One of the most useful is the loaf-shaped oblong baking tin, painted a plain grey or soft green. The tin rarely shows when the arrangement is finished, and if it does, blends inoffensively with the architecture. These tins are deep enough to hold a reasonable amount of water or a plastic foam brick. They stand securely on a long wide base, wherever they are needed.

If upright rather than horizontal designs are required, then pottery urn containers are to be recommended. Their classical shape fits in well with the formal church background. Urns can be bought in medium or large sizes, and the latter look very well standing on the floor against a pillar. Fibre-glass or plastic garden urns are very suitable and light in weight.

Many churches have bought boat-shaped containers. These are difficult to arrange well, for the horizontal line of the container should be followed and the curved base cavity does not make this easy. The large looped handles at each end of the container are rather intrusive. Earthenware jars are pleasing in feeling, and many utilitarian bowls and pots make good standbys. Candlecups, plastic saucers and other holders are all of use at different times and in different positions. The main considerations for all containers will be their suitability to the place and occasion and most of all, to the scale of the building.

Colours

Since the colour of vases and containers used in a church is very important, careful thought should be given to this point when the containers are first purchased. Best are stone, dull greens and earthy colours – in other words colours that are the least eye-catching and will not conflict with those of the flowers. Although there are occasions in summer when the all-white containers that one often sees in churches can look cool and lovely, dead-white can be difficult. Because it is so dominant, it 'separates' visually from the flower design, which should appear as one with its container. If permission is obtained, much can be done by painting on two coats of matt emulsion paint to make an unpromising pot into a useful one. Plastic pots which do not take paint well should be rubbed over with sandpaper to help give them a surface that paint will cling on to more easily. The texture can also be changed by adding some sand to the paint or using special cement paint: this effectively takes away the over-smooth look of plastic. The high shine of

Above: the carved wooden organ screen in St Saviour's Church, Dartmouth, has its centre decorated with a slim swag of dried and preserved plant material mounted on a linen panel. The central design contains a small bronze cherub and two crossed recorders

Above: a green and white swag of fresh flowers decorates a stone pillar

Right: superb colour used in swags of fresh flowers in St Paul's Cathedral, London

gloss paint is not at all pleasing with flowers.

Sometimes a church cupboard is packed solid with a miscellaneous collection of jam-jars and pots that have accumulated over the years and generations of church workers. Call the church rota together and decide just which of these items are really liked and used. Retaining these, sell or dispose of the rest. Any funds raised by this can be put towards more suitable and useful equipment which can then have space to be properly stored.

Baskets

Baskets, though seldom found in church equipment, look lovely on the window sills of country churches, filled with spring or summer flowers or with greenery at Christmas. They are excellent for wedding arrangements. The inexperienced arranger who may find a formal trough daunting will enjoy working with baskets. Certainly troughs require far more leaves and long-stemmed flowers. A more unified effect will be achieved if all the baskets are the same size and design, although this is not essential. If eight, ten or twelve baskets are being bought it is sometimes possible to get them at wholesale prices. Each basket must of course have a liner, and it is wise to buy a set that is identical for all the baskets. Find plastics or other liners that are long and not too high at the sides (but sufficient to provide a good depth of water), so that the flowers and leaves flow over the basket edge. The basket length should be extended by trails of ivy or other vines or greenery. One basket will usually be sufficient in each church window, and will be more attractive than a bank of flowers that is not easy to construct well and requires much more material.

Troughs

For very long window sills in larger churches, trough-shaped containers are very suitable. Stable and capacious, they can be bought in various materials, amongst which stoneware accords especially well with church interiors. For permanency – stoneware and pottery tend to crack if banged around with constant use – choose galvanized iron chicken or pig feeding troughs. They are oblong in shape, usefully deep and come in various sizes. Paint the outside matt grey or soft green – or whatever is suitable for your church. These are practical containers, and the metal keeps flowers and leaves cool. In very long windows the trough can be placed centrally and two upright arrangements positioned at each end to elongate the flower designs. Be sure to get the scale correct for a large window and use extra long stems to gain height. Seedheads, either from the garden or roadside, are

A pedestal of red flowers brings warmth to the grey stone of Cookham Church

The grey stone of the font and walls provides a perfect background for a fine arrangement of scarlet gladioli

useful for this. Flowers can be elevated by funnels on false stems. Plastic foam can, of course, be used in either baskets or troughs but by using the cheaper wire-netting you will have more money to spend on flowers and can use the wire-netting repeatedly. All flowers last well in water, but not all flowers take kindly to plastic foam.

Pedestals

Because of their scale, pedestals (described in detail in Chapter 4) are ideal in churches. They will hold a large group of flowers, elevated in a graceful way so that they may be seen from a distance. Many churches have had memorial pedestals given by one of the members of their congregation. Since few churches have flowers arranged on the altar, a pair of well-executed pedestal designs flanking the altar look very beautiful and equally appropriate in large or small churches, as long as the design is in scale.

Wrought iron pedestals should be adjustable in height to suit different places and occasions. Iron pedestals generally have their own container, many of which are far too small for the large quantity of plant material you will need to use. Make sure you buy one with a deep container. Wooden pedestals usually have a flat top on which a separate container stands. Heavy containers such as an old metal preserving pan are useful here. They have great stability and, most important, hold a lot of water: it is surprising how much water is 'taken up' by a large group of stems. If plastic foam is used, the container must offer room for more than one brick.

Pedestals of traditional design are not always suitable in modern churches. In this situation, arrangements can be raised on earthenware or plain grey drain-pipes. These plain functional pipes also look well in older churches. Wooden stands can be made fairly cheaply by a handyman with a framework of wood, over which can be stretched hessian or furnishing felt of a suitable colour. Place the bowl or containers on top of the drain-pipe or constructed stand. Wooden stools are also useful for raising a bowl to stand against a pillar or elsewhere.

Brass altar vases

It is not possible to write of church flowers without making special mention of these traditional Victorian vases, which very many churches still retain. Their design is probably based on medieval church vessels intended for a single stem of lilies or a few stems of flowers. The present-day arranger can very rarely use lilies (though few flowers are more perfect or long-lasting for church work) and will also be aware that in the average church as few as four or five flowers will be invisible from 6 m (20 ft) or more away, particularly if they are not white, cream, or pink. There are three ways in which these narrow vases can be adapted for more generous arrangements:

This arrangement for the commemoration of the Battle of Britain in Westminster Abbey uses flowers in the soft blue colours of the Royal Air Force

A choir pew end decorated with white and cream flowers for a wedding

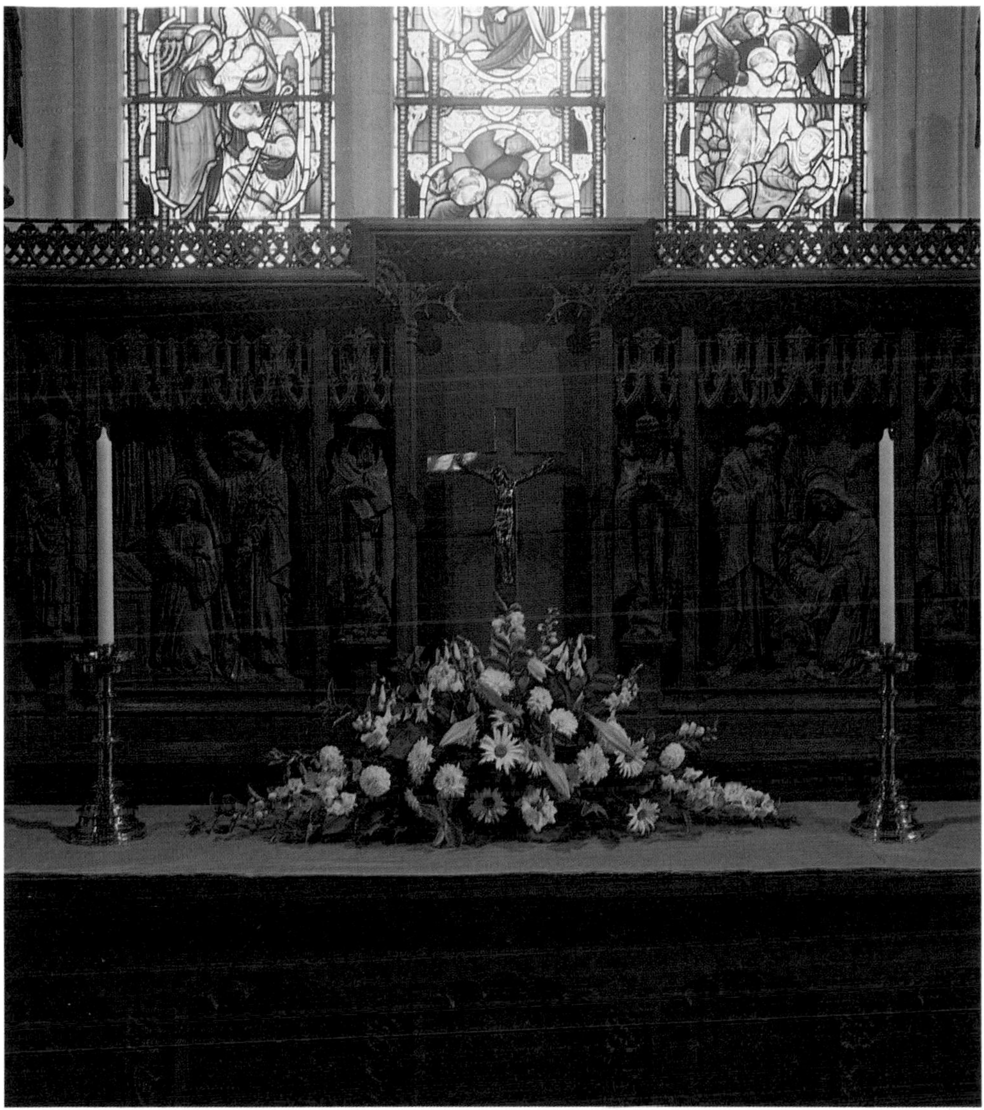

Left: simple flowers massed at the foot of the crucifix at the centre of the altar in Ideford Church are not overwhelmed by the heavily-carved wood or the colour of the stained glass window above them

Below: the classical urn-shaped container has the solidity required for the heavy stone alcove in which this lovely mixture of summer flowers is placed

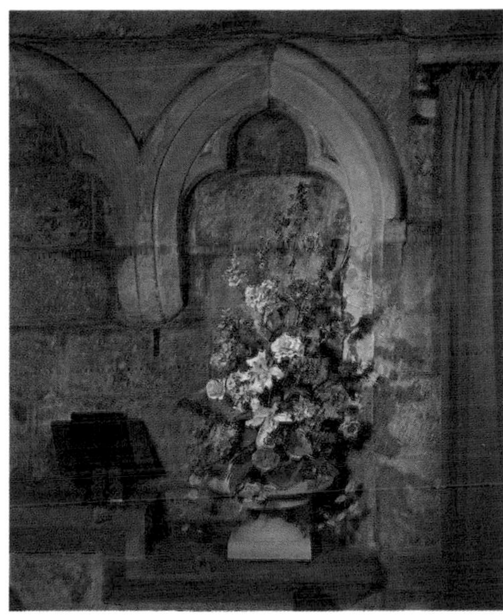

1. With plasticine or modelling clay, fix a candlecup in the mouth of the vase; or use plastic foam; or insert a pinholder and wire-netting as mechanics.

2. Put a piece of wire-netting cut like a snake inside, extending from the vase top to the base with a piece reaching above the vase edge. Make a cross of two slim plant rods. One should be upright with its lower end in a blob of clay fixed to the base of the empty *dry* vase. Thread this rod through the wire. Fix the second rod crosswise with wire, above the vase rim. This wooden construction helps to give a rigid support to a quantity of flowers and foliage.

3. Perhaps the easiest and best solution is to arrange the plant material in the vase and add to it a funnel fixed on a stick to raise the top placements. The funnel and stick must be painted matt green and placed at the back of the vase. The funnel must be well-concealed by the foliage and flowers used lower down.

The positioning of flowers varies with the practice and customs of each particular church, chapel and occasion. Generally speaking, however, there is a pattern that applies to them all, or there is so little difference that it is of no importance.

Church features

The altar is the most important place in the church. If flowers are placed on the altar they must always be subservient to the cross and in no way impinge upon it. Two matching asymmetrical designs sweeping each side in to the foot of the cross look very beautiful. More often the cross is flanked on each side by formal symmetrical arrangements of a vertical design. Sufficient foliage to provide a good background for the flowers should be used, and the flowers that are chosen should have a clear form and shape and in order to be clearly visible, should be of white, cream or pastel colours. Blue, however, is unsuitable as it is a receding colour, and disappears at quite a short distance away. Few flowers excel the lily for this work; although they are expensive they will last a long time if cut or bought in the early stage of development. Very few need be used and if the 'pips' or single blooms are taken from the main cluster and placed in tubes, they can be positioned in the design where they will show best. If flowers are not used on the altar then two large arrangements placed each side of the altar usually look best. In chapels with communion tables then either a matching pair each end, or a central arrangement will look best, paying due regard to the functional needs of the church service. Altar frontals are changed in colour for various festivals and dates. The main feasts of the Christian church are Christmas, Easter, Whitsuntide, and Harvest Festival. There are no hard and fast rules about the colours of flowers and leaves to be used on these occasions, but tradition, the spirit of the festival and the availability of plant material have made familiar the use of particular plants.

Christmas decoration relies on the use of evergreen leaves of holly, bay, laurel and ivy, fir branches with cones, and as many holly and other berries as can be found. Flowers are scarce and expensive at this time but single white and gold chrysanthemums or the bolder large blooms in rich colours are available and are long-lasting. Evergreens can look rather heavy, so the gold of variegated golden holly, privet or elaeagnus will help to give a lighter and more festive feeling. Red carnations and gladioli should be available. In large groups, two or three poinsettia plants will introduce a note of cheerful long-lasting colour. Many churches bring in Christmas trees which when decorated with candles, a few baubles or some fruit and cones, will give pleasure to the children of the congregation and be evocative to the adults.

Easter provides the first flowers of the year and this happy festival sees the church filled with the gold and white of Arum and Longiflorum lilies together with narcissus of all kinds. Primroses, pussy willow, catkins and all the fresh flowers of spring make this celebration one of the loveliest of the whole year.

Whitsun is perhaps the most difficult festival for the arranger to conform to, with its traditional colours of red, often combined with white. As there seem to be few red flowers available in gardens at this time bought flowers often have to be relied on. Remember that some help can be given by red-tinted foliage if you have any in your garden, but generally speaking the arranger has difficulty unless gladioli, red carnations or other red flowers are available. A great standby are large heads of hydrangeas which have been dried at the end of the previous summer.

Harvest Festival presents no problems. At this time leaves, flowers and fruits are abundant. Hedgerows are loaded with sprays of lustrous blackberries and their leaves, hawthorn berries, and golden bronze bracken. Gardens are generous with dahlias and chrysanthemums in all their rich colours, and the fruit and vegetable garden offers apples and pears and every other kind of form and shape – a wide choice at last for the decorator, which allows the spirit of thankfulness to be expressed as it should be. The priest in any particular church should always be consulted when more extensive decorations are to be carried out. The patterns of decoration described are the ones usually followed.

Other festivals are as follows:

Advent The Sunday nearest Christmas; colour, blue.

Epiphany 6th January and the following Sunday; white and gold. For the remaining five Sundays of Epiphany, green is used.

Septuagesima, Sexagesima, and Quinquagesima These are the Sundays falling closest to the seventieth, the sixtieth, and the fiftieth day before Easter. Colours are purple or blue. Occasionally green is used from Septuagesima to Shrove Tuesday.

Lent It is unusual for any flowers to be placed in a church during this period of penitence. Lent includes six Sundays and lasts for forty days before Easter (not including Sundays). Church colours are purple or blue.

Good Friday No flowers; church colour black.

Easter Day and five following Sundays; gold and white.

Whit Sunday until Trinity Sunday; red.

Trinity Sunday Gold.

The Sunday after Trinity Sunday Green. Green continues to be used for the following twenty-two Sundays.

All Saints Day Colours used are white and red or a mixture of all colours.

The colours described will be followed in some churches in the altar frontals, vestments of the clergy, the chalice veil, burse, pulpit fall and bible markers. Smaller churches may not have sufficient changes of these articles but in large churches the pattern described is followed. The colours do not have to be necessarily followed in the flowers used on the particular church year days, but the arrangement should be in harmony with the church accoutrements and the spiritual meaning of these special days. It is necessary to be familiar with the fixed celebrations of the liturgical year.

Altar frontals White and gold is used for all special occasions such as weddings, ordinations, confirmations, and dedication of a church, Harvest Festival, the feast of saints (excepting those of the martyrs, when red frontals are used).

In general these particulars will not apply to the nonconformist churches. Many diaries print the dates of the various festivals for those who need them and the details appear in parish magazines.

Larger designs and construction

Special occasions such as Easter and Christmas and Church Festivals provide opportunities to use arrangements and designs on a very large scale. Details of such designs and their mechanics, and of swags, garlands and plaques can be found in Chapter 9.

Fonts come in all shapes and sizes, ancient and modern, but whether in a cathedral or simple little chapel there will almost certainly be a circular ledge around the rim of the font. This is the perfect place for flower decoration to be placed. Choose simple flowers and small ferns or foliage. Place a ring of fresh sphagnum moss on a plastic base to hold the small flowers. Small patty pans filled with flowers could be used and linked with ivy or periwinkle trails. Scallop shells look delightful filled with primroses or forget-me-nots, pinks or any other small and unsophisticated flowers. Simplicity is the keynote. Remember to leave a small break on the font rim so that the priest can carry out the ceremony of baptism without disturbing the flowers. If more decoration is wanted tiny garlands can be linked around the font, but careful detailed work on the rim should suffice.

Pulpits are often highly decorated wood or stone structures that need little embellishment. Sometimes there are small niches that can carry delicate work, but generally speaking the pulpit is best left without floral arrangement.

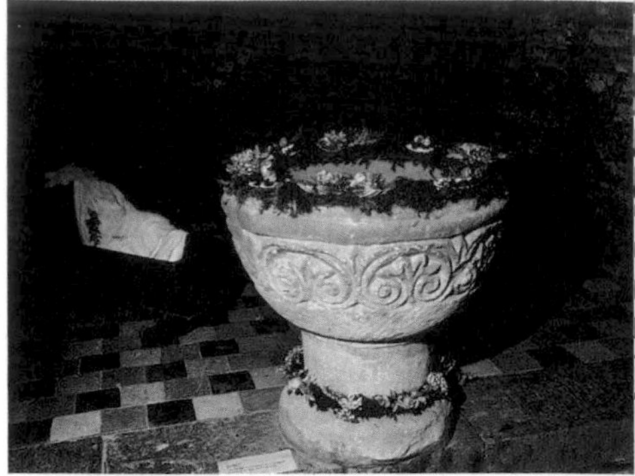

The Saxon font in the Church of St Petrox, Dartmouth, has been garlanded around its rim with shells and flowers, which also encircle its base

In contrast, the font in St Paul's Cathedral has an inspired design in keeping with its larger size. The boat-shaped arrangements at the base are a special feature

Below: decorated pulpit in Ideford Church, Devon

Lecterns do offer scope if flowers and foliage are used from the base and following the column of the lectern. Lecterns are usually made of brass or wood, both of which accord well with plant material.

Monuments often have small flat ledges on which flowers can be placed. This would only be suitable at a church festival of flowers - but on such an occasion much local history can be rediscovered by people admiring the flowers and reading the words on the monument.

Choir stalls Care must be taken in all the places decorated in a church that the flowers will in no way interfere with the services and the functional use of the church. Choir stalls are meant for the use of the choristers who may be wearing surplices, and therefore any decorations must be well out of the way of choristers entering and leaving. The best way to decorate choir stalls is to range a line of flowers and foliage on the floor running each side of the aisle to lead the eye to the altar. This is very easily done by using loaf-shaped tins placed end to end. The centre of the line can be made taller, or remain low and the two ends of the line be raised. The same system can be used along a church gallery that has a ledge sufficiently wide.

Church pillars Garlands and swags look splendid wound around pillars or plaques hung on them. This was the way they were first used and they have a splendid decorative value (see Chapter 9).

Side chapels Decoration should be restrained to be effective, especially in a confined space. Most chapels are dedicated to a specific saint. Some research into their emblems and colours can usually give a lead to what can be done to enhance the chapel.

Aisles Progress of clergy and congregation must not be impeded by flower arrangements in the aisles. Topiary trees for weddings (Chapter 8) and for Christmas if space allows, are effective. Pew ends can be decorated by using special holders for a plastic foam brick, or with arrangements at floor level against the pew end (Chapter 9).

Window sills can hold baskets and troughs as described above. If the window-ledge slopes, then it is wise to have a wood or hardboard ledge made so that the surface can be used to stand the flowers on. Failing

Top left: an example of the decorative value of well designed garlands of fresh flowers in a country church

Left: a garland made by the church flower helpers at Ideford Parish Church is placed around a pillar

St Edmund's Chapel, Salisbury Cathedral, contains so much beauty in the decorative work of its reredos, altar frontal and banner that unless the task of planning the flower decoration is undertaken by an experienced designer the result can be overpowering. Here the choice of muted golden colours and great restraint on the part of the arranger have succeeded in creating both unity and beauty

Below left: the stone window reveal provides a background for an arrangement that will be viewed from the body of the church. This position rather than a central placement allows the light from the window to fall upon the flowers

that, a foam brick wrapped in polythene can be hung or rested on a ledge made from adhesive clay. The latter will hold only a lightweight design. It is best to keep flowers against the 'reveals' or sloped sides of the window where a background is provided. Strong light coming from *behind* the flowers if placed in front of the glass makes them difficult to see clearly.

Radiators are best left alone unless space is very restricted elsewhere. In summer, however, the tops of radiators can be used for a special occasion if a piece of hardboard is cut to size and either painted or covered in suitable fabric.

Unsightly areas exist in many churches. It is better to draw attention away from them with a very outstanding design close by, than to attempt a 'cover-up' job that probably will not succeed.

Winter flowers

Winter is a special and recurrent problem for church arrangers. Garden flowers are practically non-existent and shop flowers are very expensive. Here are a few suggestions that may help to improve the situation:

1. Prepare during the summer a quantity of glycerined beech and other foliage leaves in different lengths and sizes. With a few fresh flowers, or some dried hydrangea, achillea and other flowers quite large arrangements can be made. Use berries and fruits in place of flowers, or with them, as an alternative.
2. Use a suitable small table and place on it a *pot-et-fleur* (see Chapter 9). In a group of growing plants, conceal a funnel or other container, in which to place a few fresh flowers.

Frequently, incidents in the history of a parish church provide subjects for interpretation in flowers and foliage. This gives the arranger an opportunity for research and evokes interest in those visiting the festival. The imprisonment of Mary, Queen of Scots, was the inspiration for this window decoration in a country church

Below right: neglected stone carvings or other disused embellishments discovered in the church environs can be utilized. Here a pair of discarded rood screen doors become a focal point. Flowers are placed behind them and they are lit from below. Slim vertical designs on each side serve as a frame

3. In late autumn plant some large bowls of hyacinths, daffodils or other bulbs. When the bulbs are sufficiently grown place them in the church and for many weeks the developing plants, and subsequently the flowers will give much pleasure and colour.

Church flower festivals

These occasions have become a frequent and regular part of church activities everywhere, giving happiness to all who are involved in them, whether in great cathedrals or abbeys or in little parish churches and chapels. They have also performed a practical purpose by raising substantial funds to preserve church fabric. To be successful, Flower Festivals must be carefully planned for some months or even a year beforehand. Under the guidance of their priest, the church officers should be responsible for all the administrative arrangements such as publicity, stewarding of the public, car parking, refreshments, and a brochure if there is to be one. The flower and foliage decoration should be the responsibility of a team led by an experienced artistic planner backed up by a committee to carry out the scheme envisaged. This scheme – and a theme, if one is chosen – must be outlined and approved by the clergy of the church. The period for a Festival is usually a day for staging, three days for the Festival, and a day for dismantling the arrangements. The church must always be left immaculately tidy. Keep any lettering required to a very high standard, otherwise the effect is undignified.

Artistic planning of church festivals

Practical planning, and knowing how to make best use of the architectural features in a church can be a very demanding task.

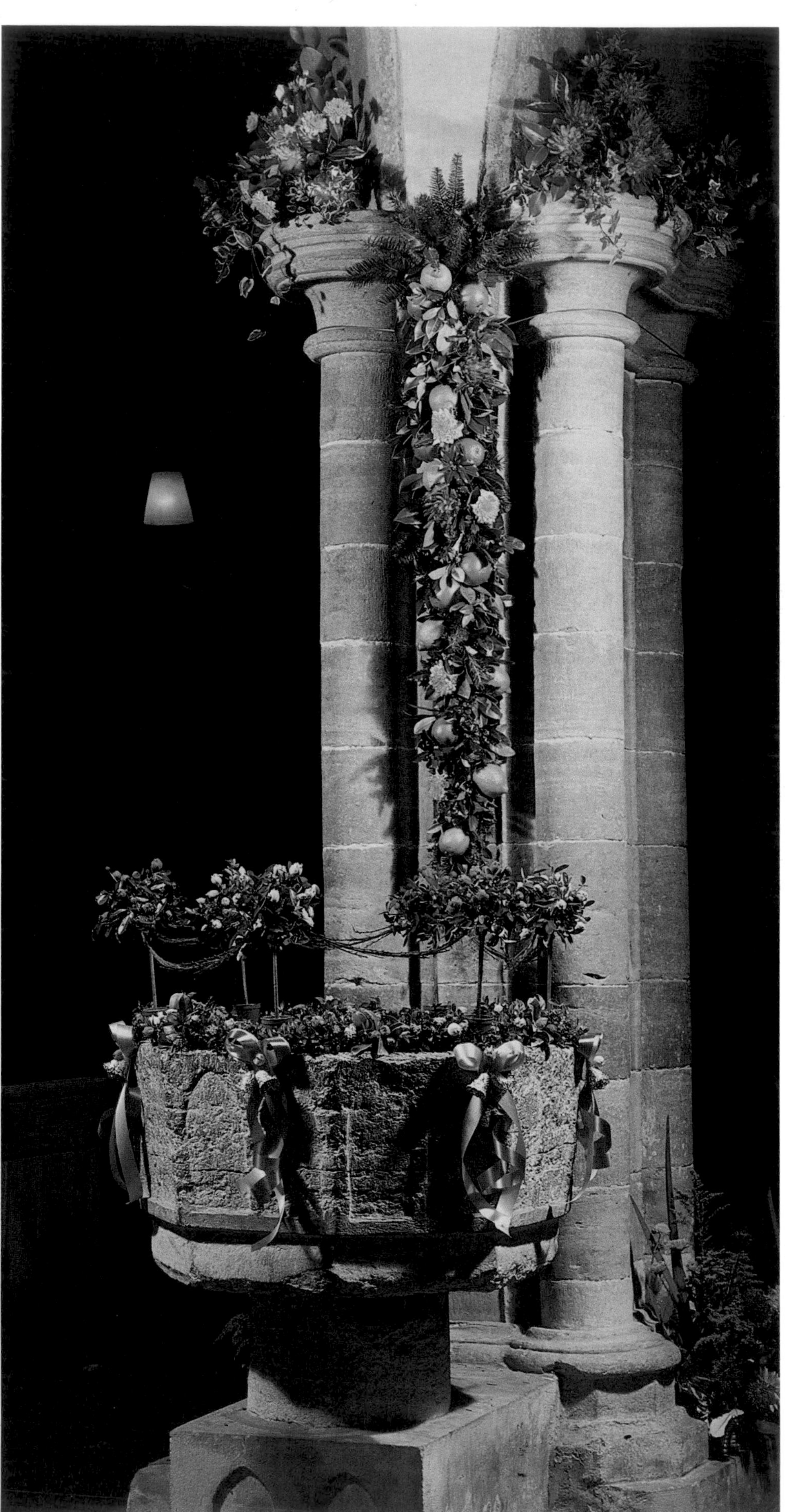

An even more daunting feature of flower festivals, however, is the artistic planning. Although ideas may be forthcoming from many of the people involved in the festival, the final plan and allocation of work and positions should be in the hands of one person who is responsible for the artistic direction. Any other course leads to confusion and an uncoordinated result. The person given this task should be sensitive to the church architecture and the character of the church. She must be able to exercise great restraint even when there is opportunity for a more dramatic approach and planning. Churches and occasions will vary. The artistic planner should visit the building frequently before finalizing her plan. She should mark down where, on a sunny day, certain windows on the south side will become like small heated conservatories. On cold dark days she must consider where the heating system will make fresh flowers flag. These are the places for dried and preserved material. It is necessary to view the church in artificial light as well as in daylight, for the aspect will be entirely changed. If there are very dark corners, she should find out if there are plug points for lights, or if there are possibilities for floodlighting. One of the most important things is to discover if there will be any services during the festival period. If so, it is essential to attend the church when the congregation is there to observe the effect of their sitting and standing. It is a waste of effort to plan for features that will be out of sight when the service takes place.

Themes

A church may be decorated for a festival with no aim in mind other than to enhance the architectural features. All schemes of decoration should reflect a quiet simplicity; not a vestige of a 'flower show' should be apparent. If a specific theme is asked for, there are many possibilities. For instance, the history of the church or village or the life of the saint to whom the church is dedicated may be drawn upon. Biblical texts or verses from hymns can be illustrated. Very often, flower festivals are held to raise funds for church repair. Many imaginative ideas can be drawn from the theme of church builders, such as 'wood carvers', 'stone workers', and 'glass makers'. Inspiration is not difficult if you think along these lines. Allocating the positions will be governed by the kind of work and the skills available from the helpers you have. There is scope for everyone on such an occasion. The shy and anxious arranger can be encouraged in her work by being given a quiet position. On another occasion she will be more confident about taking a more active part.

Planning a festival requires hours of dedicated thought and work. When the planning is completed, each participant should be given written details setting out (a) the place, (b) the kind of design, (c) the

Left: a font decorated to interpret the name of the church, St Clements, by utilizing its association with the nursery rhyme 'Oranges and Lemons'. Miniature orange and lemon trees are placed around the rim of the font with knots of ribbons. The orange and lemon theme is carried through to the decorations of the capitals and the panel decoration on the pillars

Top right: a favourite theme is that of church builders. Here greater impact was achieved by using a background on which the tools of the trades concerned in church building were depicted in natural materials. Examples of the work of stone-carvers, glaziers and wood-workers were placed with the flowers at the base

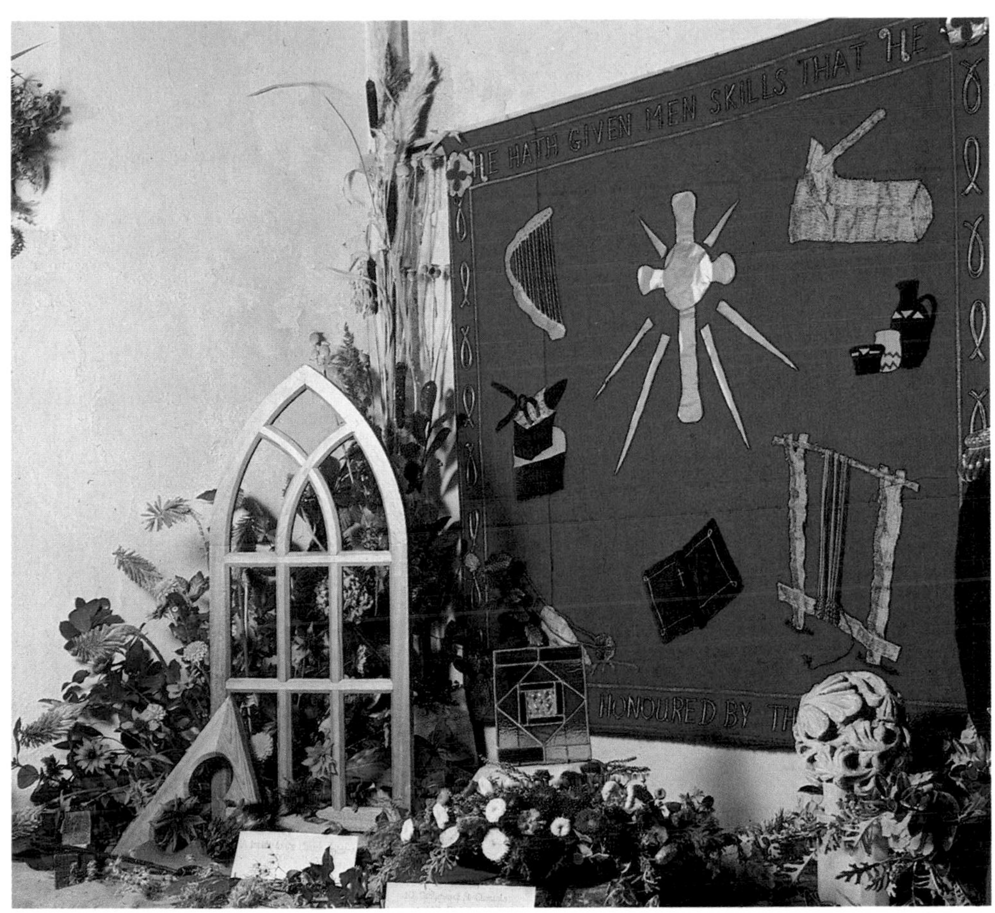

Bottom right: memorials on church walls sometimes provide inspiration. Here a wine importer, who died in Portugal and whose body was returned by sailing ship for burial in England, is remembered by his descendant who, in this arrangement, depicted his occupation in flowers

measurements of where she is to work and (d) the colours. The place and measurements must be specific but the others can often be left to the individual, unless, of course, it is for an area of special planning. After the festival is over, it is courteous to send a note of thanks to each person who has given her time and skills to make the occasion a success.

When festival work is done with skill, combined with the beauty of flowers and foliage, it can be hoped that the following words of the Reverend Christopher Hildyard, M.V.O., M.A. will apply. After the Festival of Flowers arranged by NAFAS and held in Westminster Abbey to celebrate its 900th anniversary, he wrote: 'Never could the Abbey have looked more glorious . . . The flowers declared the Glory of God, we could only add our thanks.' Beneath the cloisters of Westminster Abbey has been laid a fitting tribute by the National Association of Flower Arrangements Societies of Great Britain. To commemorate the Silver Jubilee of Queen Elizabeth II and, it is to be hoped, for the eyes of posterity, a freeze-dried arrangement of flowers and leaves was made. A simple Tudor rose in pink marble marks the flagstone underneath which the arrangement lies.

13. Colour

Jean Taylor

All sorts of flowers the which on earth do spring
In goodly colours gloriously array'd . . .
EDMUND SPENSER 1552–99

Brilliant, scarlet poppies (*Papaver atrosanguinea maxima*)

It is usually the colour of a flower which first attracts our eyes. If all flowers were grey it is doubtful if we would ever cut them to place in our homes. Their colours give life and gaiety to our surroundings, both inside and out. Because this is so important to us it is well worthwhile making a study of how to use colour in flower arrangements to achieve the effect we want.

An artist mixes colours with paints, but someone who arranges flowers works with colours that are already provided by nature. You may think that these colours are enough in themselves and that therefore they need not be a subject of study. However, a grouping of flowers and leaves usually looks more attractive when the arranger has thought about the colours combined together. Do you think, for instance, that brown leaves would be a better choice to blend with peach-coloured roses than green ones? Or that perhaps yellow flowers would look more dramatic against a blue wall than a beige one? Could a grouping of orange and red flowers be more attractive on a cold day than blue flowers? Which colours show up better in candle-light?

It is rewarding to make a study of colour not only as a guide when arranging flowers, but because it will help you to appreciate colour in all your surroundings. There will be many colours that you have not really noticed before, and as you grow more and more colour conscious, your new awareness will bring you increasing enjoyment.

Beginning with colour

Most people have favourite colours and when you begin to arrange flowers it is important to arrange flowers you enjoy. It is off-putting to begin by studying colour theory and terminology which can so easily make a fascinating subject tedious. Theories can be highly scientific and academic. It is more important at first to improve one's own natural eye for colour and later to learn helpful terms and explanations.

The way to extend one's colour consciousness is first of all to mix different colours together. Take a bunch of garden roses, for example, and arrange them simply in a household jug. Try several reds together, then pinks and reds and then oranges and reds. Decide which grouping you prefer. Then try grouping all pale colours together, followed by only dark colours and finally see if you can combine both pale and dark. Notice the different effects you achieve each time.

Study a flower or a leaf

Try looking at the colours in one flower. You will notice that it has a characteristic colour scheme and that the colours seem harmonious. This is probably because in any one plant there is a limited amount of colour-producing matter and therefore the colours are related.

Colour combinations in flowers are a great source of inspiration to both artists and designers, not only because of the actual colours present in the blooms but because of the various tints and shades in close proximity. For example, a 'Peace' rose has many tints of creamy yellow with a touch of yellow-pink. This colour scheme could be repeated in an arrangement of yellow and pink flowers.

Look especially at the colours in the centre of a flower, in the stems and in the leaves. Turn over a flower to see if the reverse side is a different colour. Look to see if opening buds are slightly different in colour to the full-blown flower.

Flower and leaf colours can be rich as in a velvety pansy, dramatic as in a scarlet poppy with a blue-black centre, and gentle as in an 'Iceberg' rose which is white with the palest pink flush. Leaves turning colour in autumn can look like a resplendent sunset. Sunshine dappling the pale-green leaves of spring can be ethereal in effect. There are so many moments of colour beauty in nature to be studied and to store in the mind for inspiration when arranging flowers.

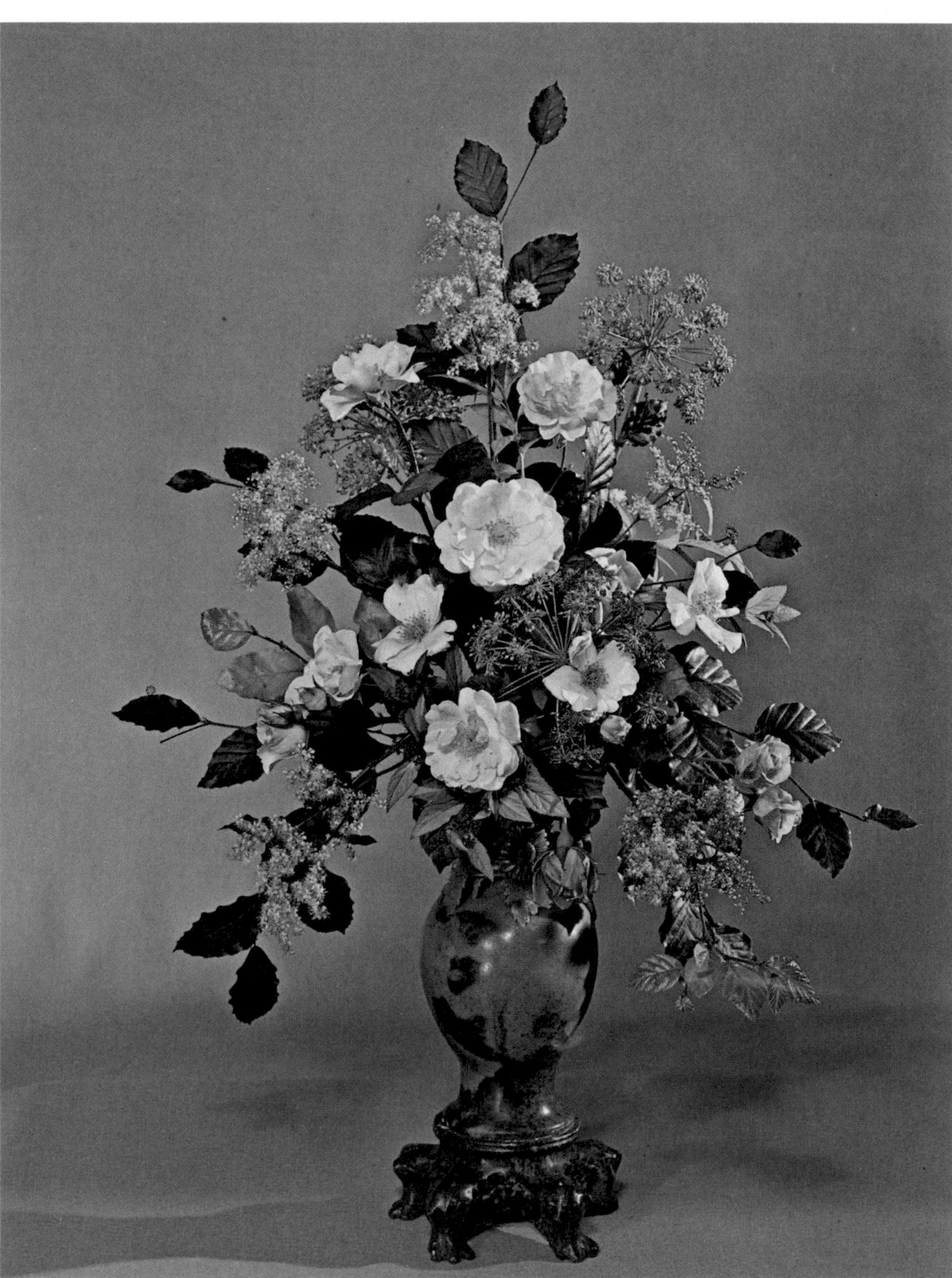

Left: dark and light colours combine together to create a design of great harmony

Right: there are many greens in Nature; this highly varied foliage pedestal arrangement makes clear the extensive range of this colour family

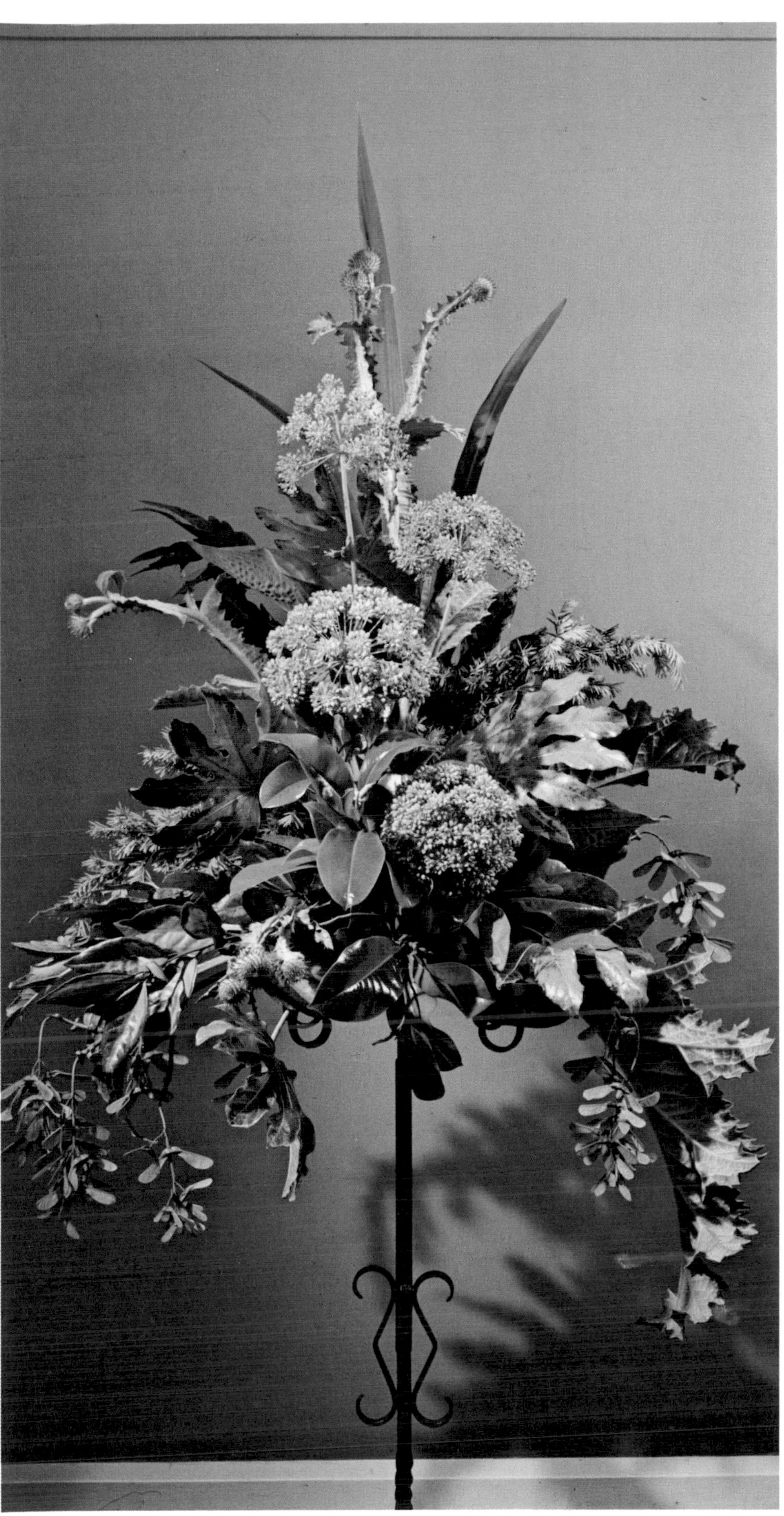

Colour families

Try picking as many greens as you can in a garden or the countryside. Notice that there are yellow-greens, blue-greens, light and dark greens, brilliant and dull greens, greens splashed with brown, red, yellow or white. There are indeed many variations of the sensation we call 'green'. We learn colour groupings in childhood and this helps us to catalogue colours. We need to do this so that we reserve some order from the thousands of colour sensations we receive from our surroundings. We call the colour families red, orange, yellow, green, blue and violet. But there are many other names within the families, usually derived from colour associations.

Within the red family, for instance, there is ruby, claret, burgundy, shrimp, raspberry, cherry, tomato, pillar-box, rose, coral, brick, lobster, strawberry, salmon, cyclamen, poppy, geranium, peony, plum, damson, garnet, flame and Indian red – to name but a few.

Colour variations

If you are lucky enough to see a rainbow, the six colour families can be seen easily, starting with red at the top. The colours are brilliant and clear. They are usually called *hues*. But colours are not always brilliant and clear as in a rainbow, or in jewels, feathers of tropical birds, butterflies' wings and certain flowers. Most colours we see are complex mixtures, often modified to a colour that looks dark, light or greyed with a strong or a weak sense of the family hue. Blue, for example, can be the strong clear blue of the rainbow, dark 'navy' blue, pale 'baby' blue or a watery sky blue. Many of these modified colours are very beautiful. Think of the soft greys in a pigeon's feathers, the delicate touches of pink and cream in a sky at dawn, the whites when snow falls, the gentle colours of a misty evening, the dark, dramatic clouds of a storm, and the delicate sheen of a pearl.

Colour qualities

To help classify colours and relate them to each other it is necessary to define the qualities that can modify a hue.

Hue is the quality of a colour that decides its family name; brilliant, unmodified colour.

Value means the lightness or darkness of a colour in relation to white and black. This is easy to understand if you try mixing water-colour paints together. Make a pool of blue paint and add a little black. This causes the blue to become dark. If instead of black you add white to blue it becomes a light blue. Add both white and black (grey), and a greyed blue is the result. A dark colour is called a *shade*. A light colour is called a *tint*. A greyed colour is a *tone*.

Colour wheel

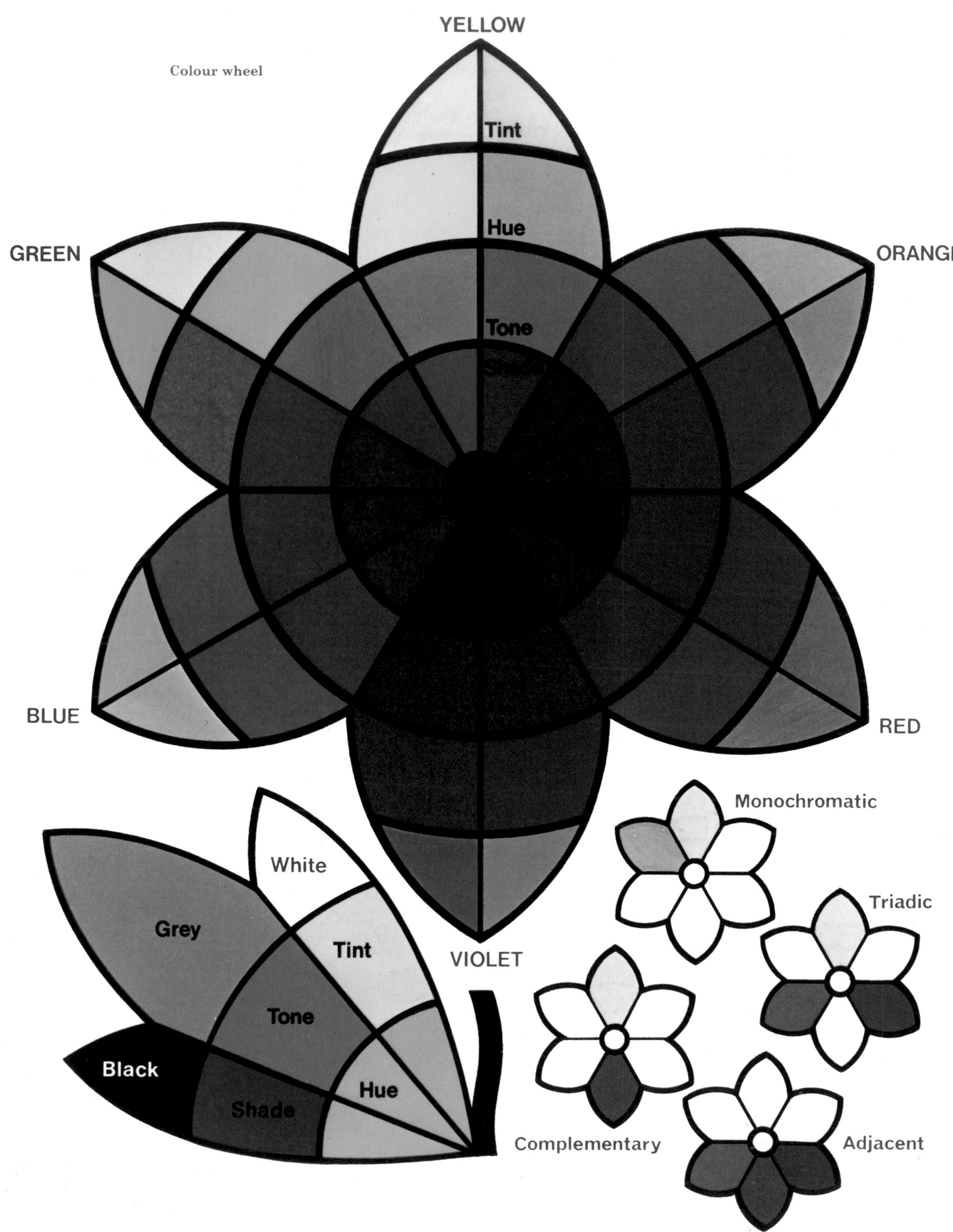

Intensity is a quality sometimes called *chrome* or *saturation*. It refers to the strength or weakness of a colour. A blue may have so much white in it that, as in ice-blue, there is only a faint sense of blueness. However, in the flower of a gentian, the colour is strong and seems fully saturated with blue.

Colours then belong to a family; may be light or dark or greyed; may be strong or weak. These three qualities, also referred to as properties or dimensions of colour, combined in innumerable ways, give us the many thousands of colour sensations that we are aware of in the world around us every day.

Colour qualities are the dimensions used to describe every form of colour just as height, width and depth may be used to describe an object. Colour also has additional characteristics that add to its complexity but at the same time make it all the more fascinating.

Luminosity Some colours show up better in poor lighting than others. Yellow and white flowers can be seen in the garden at twilight or in the dim lighting of a church far better than others of different colours. Tints, colours with white in them, have higher luminosity than shades and tones which contain black. Violet, even at full saturation, shows up poorly and is not a good colour to use if the lighting is dim. Knowledge of the luminosity of colours is invaluable when arranging flowers in churches and in big halls, and when flowers are to be used in candle-light.

Weight quality The amount of white, black and grey in a colour, the tonal value, gives a sense of lightness or heaviness. White appears the lightest, black the heaviest. Pure yellow is light and lifting, but pure violet appears heavy. Colours of equal weight, whether a hue or a value of a hue, do not usually enhance each other. For example, dark-green leaves with deep bronze chrysanthemums appear heavy and dull, whereas yellow-green leaves, or brighter orange dahlias in place of the chrysanthemums, could give a more pleasing effect.

Temperature Colours give impressions of warmth and of coolness. Warm colours are cheerful when arranged for a cold day, and cool colours are pleasing in hot weather. Red and orange are warm colours, blue and green are cool. Violet and yellow can appear warm or cool according to the colours with which they are grouped. Violet with reds appears warm, but with blues it looks cold. Yellow looks warm with oranges, but cooler with greens.

The sensation of warmth or coolness is brought about largely through our associations – blue with the cold sea, orange with the sun, and so on. Experiments have demonstrated a difference of 2.5°C (5–7°F)

Left: a striking fruit and foliage arrangement. The figurine's suggested strength and power are reinforced by the 'heaviness' in the dark, matt colouring of most of the selected material. Included are *Monstera deliciosa*, gourds, green peppers, artichokes and *Cucurbita pepo ovifera* 'Zucchini' (courgettes)

Right: the dramatic qualities of a concentrated area of colour. The neutral quality of the container and foliage serves only to emphasize the impact

Advancing and receding colours

in the subjective feeling of heat or cold between a workroom painted in blue-green and one painted in red-orange. Johannes Itten reports that in a blue-green room occupants felt that 15°C. (59°F.) was cold, whereas in a red-orange room they did not feel cold until the temperature fell to 11-12°C. (52-54°F.). Objectively, he says, this means that blue-green slows down the circulation and red-orange stimulates it.

In cold climates people tend to use oranges and reds for interiors, but in hot climates blue and green are normal. The properties of cold and warm colours are essential to colour therapeutics in hospitals.

Movement Colours give a sense of movement upwards, downwards, forwards and backwards. Orange and red give the illusion of being nearer to the viewer than violet and blue, which give the illusion of receding. Yellow, especially a light yellow, gives a feeling of lifting; but violet is a sinking colour. Green is neutral in movement. Much depends on the make-up of the colour – how much black or white it has in it whether it is a blue-red or an orange-red. Orange-reds advance, but blue-reds tend to move downwards. Much depends also on the surrounding or background colours. When yellow appears on a black background it advances sharply, but when against a white background yellow stands out only slightly.

There are so many colours and possible backgrounds with different effects that guaranteed rules are not advisable, other than the general ones indicated earlier. Experience and observation must govern the use of colours for the quality of movement in different situations.

Neutrals

Black, white and grey are regarded as neutrals or achromatic colours. All other colours are called chromatic colours. Their use in a grouping of colours is not supposed to affect the colours in any way. This is the reason why there are so many black-and-white containers for flowers. They neither clash with nor contribute to the colour impression of an arrangement, and although they can be useful they do not enhance the flowers. However, colours seen against a mid-grey background will appear at their truest. It is normal to call grey, white and black *neutrals* and not neutral colours.

In nature it is impossible to find any true black, white or grey. The trace of a hue can be seen in seemingly grey rocks, white flowers, and in the black centres of flowers. The centre of a tulip is not black, but purple or blue-black. White flowers are usually either pink-white, as a daisy, green-white, as a lily, or cream-white, as a magnolia bloom. There are many so-called 'whites', as can be recognized when white flowers are placed next to white fabric, which is much whiter. Brides' bouquets usually harmonize better with a white wedding dress when made in definite tints of a colour.

Neutralized colours

These are colours weak in hue. Beige driftwood is an example. Although weak in hue such colours are invaluable to the flower arranger. They enhance other brighter colours and can be used in greater quantities. They are excellent for backgrounds, containers, bases, accessories and drapes because they do not detract from the brilliant colours of flowers by competing with them.

Neutralized colours can be dark or light. They are usually the tones that John Freeman described

Than these November skies is no sky
lovelier
The clouds are deep
Into their grey the subtle spies of
colour creep

They are seen in the feathers of many British birds and in landscapes. They have more character than neutrals and seem to contribute more to a grouping of colours.

Container colours

Invaluable colours for containers include the earthy browns and beiges of stoneware, the bronze and pewter of metal, and the dull cream of basketry, all of which have a natural affinity with flowers. They are also adaptable and can be used with any flower colours without obtruding.

Containers in bright colours can sometimes help achieve a very dramatic or beautiful effect, but care must be taken to blend the flowers and the container together otherwise the design separates in the middle, dividing the flowers and the container into two separate parts. This can be avoided if the container colour is repeated somewhere in the plant material.

Choosing colours to combine

Flower arrangement is essentially a matter of colour grouping, of both flowers and leaves within the container, taking into account the background. There are no rules. Any colours can be combined together to give a variety of effects. Some of the truisms about them, such as 'clashing reds' (which can achieve a dramatic effect), should be discarded. Try to look at each colour and each combination of colours with a fresh eye.

It is helpful, in finding an agreeable companion for one or more colours, to see related colours at a glance with a colour circle. There is a definite relationship between colours and once observed it is rarely forgotten. The value of making a colour circle cannot be overestimated and even a simple one is helpful to the understanding of colour. You will find a ready-made one in this book (see p. 184) and another in the NAFAS *Guide to Colour Theory*. Colour circles are for explanation and have no scientific basis.

Colour grouping

The shades, tints and tones are just as important, if not more so, than the hues, and the most interesting colour groupings are often made with the modified hues rather than with the hues themselves, which need not be included in a colour grouping. It is the shade, tone or tint of a hue that needs more consideration than the selection of a hue. This applies to all aspects of colour as well as flower arrangement, and it is not the fact that green is used for the leaves in an arrangement but which green – blue-green, yellow-green, dark or light green and so on.

Practice in colour grouping

In addition to experimenting with flowers and leaves in different colours, it is helpful to collect 'shade' cards of artists' colours, house paints, embroidery threads, knitting wools, cut-up squares of fabrics in many

monochromatic

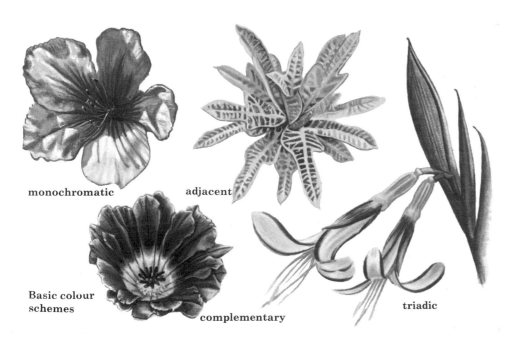

adjacent

Basic colour schemes

complementary

triadic

colours, and small chippings of solid colour from magazines. Try the different colours in various combinations: colours that seem related; all dark shades; a grouping of tones; a mixture of tints; brilliant colours together; colours that appear to have no relationship. Discover interesting, dramatic, pretty, subtle, sombre and rich effects and find which colours produce them. Try achieving the same effects with flowers.

Colour schemes

This is the term given to recognized groupings of colours. These are basic groups which have evolved because viewers can see easily the relationship between the colours used and give the grouping a name.

Although it is better to assemble colours intuitively than by attempting to follow a set scheme, knowledge of the basic colour schemes is useful because it increases your awareness of colour relationships. However, it should be stressed that there are no inflexible rules and you can combine any colours for the effect you want to achieve. In the words of Johannes Itten, 'the flow of intuition should not be damned by rigid prescription'.

Related colour schemes

Monochromatic This term means 'one-coloured'. But it does not mean only one variation of a colour, referring rather to the whole segment of a hue on the colour circle, including the tints, tones and shades. There is in fact far more interest in a monochromatic colour scheme when several variations or modifications of a hue are present. The pure hue itself need not necessarily be used. The colour is constant but the values can be varied.

In flower arrangement it is a difficult colour scheme to achieve because plant material is rarely one-coloured. Flowers normally have green stems and leaves, although there are a few with brown ones. Many flowers have dark or yellow centres, and often there are colour variations in petals and leaves. These can be lovely and should not be ignored in order to follow an academic exercise in a monochromatic scheme. Green is the easiest colour in which to achieve it in flower arrangement because there are green flowers and many variations of green leaves.

Instead of trying to reach a strict monochromatic colour scheme in a flower arrangement, it is better to give an all over impression of a predominating colour by using greater amounts of it. By attempting to exclude all but one colour we deny the beauty of nature's endless colour variations such as a green leaf shot with yellow in autumn, the red backing of blue-grey begonia leaves, the many red, blue and mauve tones in a mature hydrangea flower, even the colours sometimes produced by disease on a leaf. These variations give life to a flower arrangement. When you do wish as a challenge to make a monochromatic flower arrangement, you can avoid dullness by using strong contrasts of value such as pale pink with dark maroon and by using strong textural contrasts such as shiny red with dull red. Strictly speaking, the container, base, accessory and background in the design should also conform to the chosen monochrome.

Adjacent In an adjacent colour scheme, you use colours with the common bond of one primary such as the group – red, orange, red-orange and yellow-orange. In fact the common primary is also present in red-violet and violet and theoretically these are also part of the family. However, the relationship is rather similar to second cousins and too remote for people to recognize the common bond. As a guide-line use one-third of the colour circle whether it is a six-, twelve- or eighteen-hue circle. This gives a limitation which strengthens the feeling of relationship because the colours are similar to each other. They are called adjacent colours because they lie near to each other on a colour circle. Red is not used in the make-up of blue or yellow, so when these colours are used with red the colour scheme is not adjacent, or analogous as it is sometimes called.

Really lovely adjacent colour schemes can be achieved with plant material and it is the easiest scheme for flower arrangers to follow. There are the autumnal colours of browns (shades of orange) with gold, yellow and yellow-green which can be placed in a copper container. The common primary of yellow is in all these colours. Or a summer grouping of violet-blue delphiniums, blue-pink peonies and roses can be arranged in a blue-grey container, and there are many other attractive adjacent groupings. When such similar hues with their many variations are woven together they seem to reinforce each other, giving greater richness and importance. It is not essential to use the pure hue, and subtle effects can be achieved with tones, shades or tints either alone or combined.

Contrasting schemes

Complementary In a complementary colour scheme, you use colours lying opposite or approximately opposite on the colour circle. They have none of each other in their make-up and so are not related through any common bond, but it is an interesting fact that one of the hues is made from the other two primary colours. Red is opposite green, and green is mixed from yellow and blue. Many people find all the primaries together, although two are mixed, satisfying to the eyes. Red and

An adjacent colour scheme. The transition from the almost pure yellow of the narcissi to the green within the scheme is achieved with variegated foliage: *Aucuba japonica* 'Maculata' (spotted laurel) and *Hedera helix* 'Aureovariegata' (variegated ivy)

green, blue and orange, yellow and violet are the simple complementaries, but the green could be a blue-green and the red a red-orange.

There are also colour schemes called split-complementaries and double complementaries, but it is not necessary for a flower arranger to be so technical nor is it easy to follow these schemes with plant material. The availability of plant material limits the choice of colour. A use of approximately opposite colours is enough.

Red and green are the easiest of the complementary colours to combine in a flower arrangement and they are readily obtainable. Yellow and violet are a challenge because they are at the opposite end of the luminosity scale, an extreme light-dark contrast, and they tend to separate because of this. More violet is necessary than yellow and the yellow needs careful placement. Blue and orange separate because of the extreme cool-warm contrast, but a pleasing balance can be achieved when more blue is used than orange, but this depends on the value of the colour. For example, brown is a shade of orange and can be used with brown beech leaves and blue hydrangeas for a pleasing grouping. In this case the value of orange alters the effect and more brown can be used with less blue. Achieving pleasing proportions is an interesting exercise, especially when it involves the use of different values of the hues. An approximate guide to harmonious relative areas of pure hues in a complementary colour scheme is:

yellow and violet	$\frac{1}{4}$–$\frac{3}{4}$
blue and orange	$\frac{2}{3}$–$\frac{1}{3}$
red and green	$\frac{1}{2}$–$\frac{1}{2}$

When opposite colours are used together in their purest forms they incite each other to maximum vividness. This is especially true of red and green, and the oscillation becomes dazzling and too much for the eyes. There is also a physiological and unexplained fact about our eyes which has a bearing on complementary colour schemes. The eyes require any given colour to be balanced by its complementary and will spontaneously generate the complement if it is not present. Try looking at a red spot for a minute or two and then close your eyes. The unalleviated power of red will make you see a green spot as relief. The same happens, though to a lesser extent, with orange and blue and with violet and yellow. This is called successive contrast. It therefore follows that a scheme using complements should be pleasing to the eyes.

Polychromatic This term has been adopted by flower arrangers for an arrangement that uses all the hues together. The Flemish and Dutch flower painters were skilled at combining many colours and they have been an inspiration. But brilliant, pure hues are difficult to combine because they are tiring to the eye and success is more easily achieved when values and not pure hues are used.

Triadic The use of three colours equidistantly apart on the colour circle is termed triadic. This may not sound attractive if the colours are pure blue, red and yellow, but if these colours are modified to gold, maroon and palest blue the scheme becomes more subtle. Many old masters thought that a triad was an ideal colour scheme, and red, yellow and blue in varying values and proportions can often be seen in old paintings.

Delacroix kept a colour circle on a wall

Orange and blue are complementary colours but the green foliage and the yellow achillea prevent it from being a direct complementary

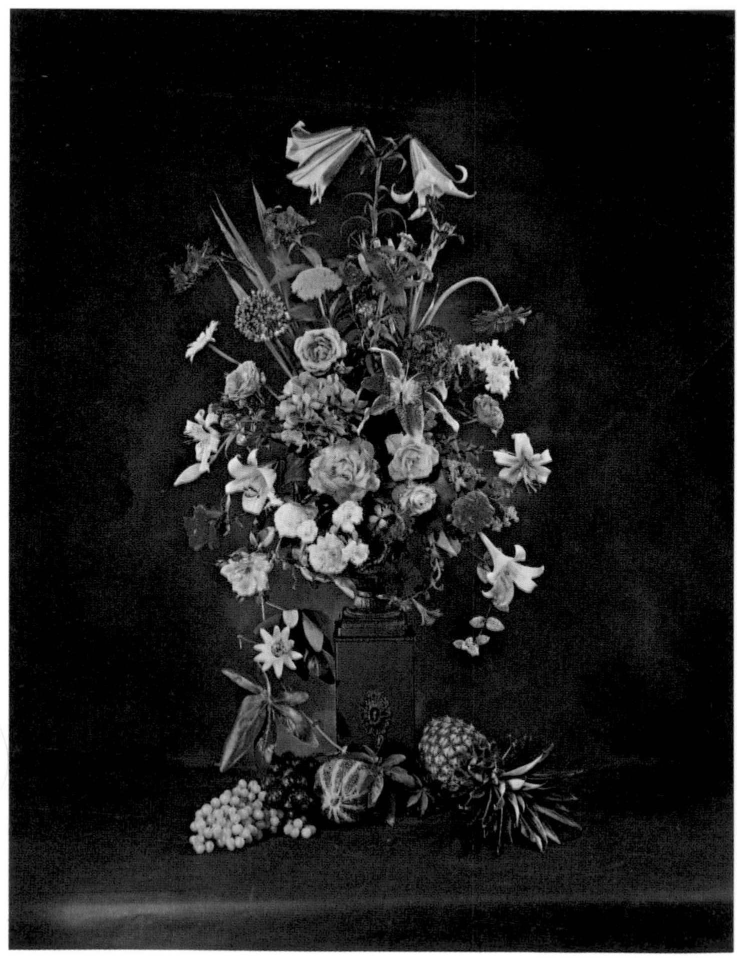
A very fine polychromatic arrangement in the manner of a Flemish flower painting

of his studio, each colour labelled with possible combinations. The Impressionists esteemed him as a colourist.

Nature's colour schemes

Nature combines colours in the most remarkable way and many flowers, leaves, skies, weathers, shells, stones, landscapes, birds, animals, minerals and seasons provide ideas. Although set schemes based on the colour circle are a most useful exercise, there is more inspiration to be found in the natural things about us. Try arrangements inspired by the colours of:

richness	fantasy	anger
frugality	subtlety	tranquillity
gaiety	sadness	jealousy
drama	delicacy	depression

The expressiveness of colour

This is one of its most fascinating assets. Colour can be used to give a dramatic or gentle effect. It can be harsh, pretty, rich, gay. Colours seem to have personality in the same way as people, and this varies with the tonal value. For example, a light yellow is youthful, while a deeper yellow is mature like ageing fruit. It is possible to evoke certain atmospheres through the use of colour in flower arrangement, especially for competitive work in flower shows, such as:

jewels	dawn	sea-shore	storm
shells	high noon	moorland	rainbow
rock	sunset	woodland	mist
stone	dusk	jungle	snow
butterflies	sunlight	flowers	china
fish	moonlight	leaves	paintings
birds	candle-light	fruit	textiles
animals	shadow	bark	wallpaper

For this it is also helpful to have a knowledge of colour associations, and although associations can differ from people to people there are many that are common. There are pleasant and unpleasant associations, often dependent on the value used.

yellow	sunshine, springtime, cheerfulness, youth, wealth, sickness, luminosity, deceit
red	danger, aggression, passion, excitement, hatred, joy, fire, heat, richness, courage, torture, friction, the devil
blue	space, peace, transparency, cold, cleanliness, sea, sky, nothingness, loneliness, boundlessness, fidelity
orange	warmth, autumn, vitality, strength, decay, activity, earthiness, dullness, action, cordiality, energy
green	youth, woodlands, jealousy, hope, neutrality, faith, immortality, contemplation, immaturity, nature, rest
violet	melancholy, primness, humility, retirement, solemnity, luxury, richness, aestheticism, splendour, fantasy, dignity
black	depression, drama, darkness, sophistication, severity, piracy, neutrality, contrast, evil, witches, magic, solemnity
grey	passivity, old age, humility, melancholy, serenity, dignity, resignation, restraint, frugality, twilight
white	innocence, chastity, truth, serenity, cleanliness, delicacy, coldness, purity, crispness, honesty, lightness, airiness

The subtle merging and mixing of Nature's colour scheme as it is seen in a rock pool

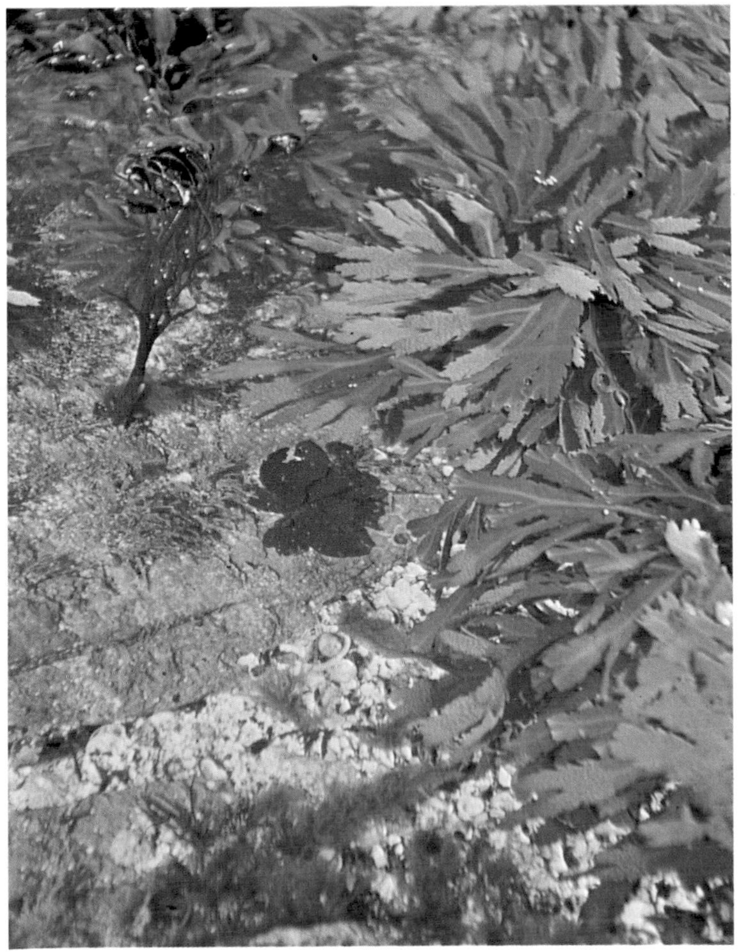

The vibrant orange of these *Lilium* 'Enchantment', emphasized in the base and reinforced by the springing willow wands, perfectly expresses vitality

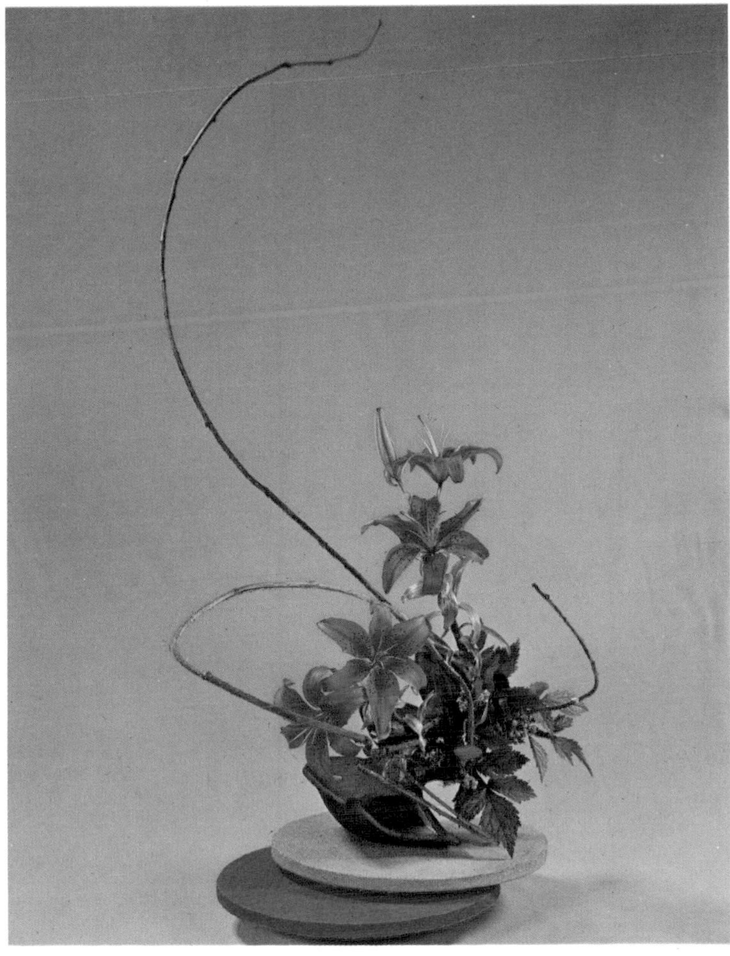

Colour terminology

Colour is a complex subject and many of its mysteries remain unsolved despite constant research. There are few precise laws for guidance particularly in selection for colour grouping, but artists should anyway be concerned with effects not rights or wrongs. Different specialists use colour theories according to their needs and a physicist, a physiologist, a psychologist, an artist, a chemist and a flower arranger all study it in different ways depending on their needs. A number of systems have been devised, but because the field is so diverse it is sensible at first to limit your field to the aspects of colour that most concern you, especially the selection and grouping of colours and the effect of surrounding colours and lighting. Books use different terminology, which can be confusing. Some people argue that no terminology is necessary, but a little does help communication and understanding. The terms given so far are those commonly used by knowledgeable flower arrangers.

Colour harmony

When people speak of colour harmony they are evaluating the joint effect of two or more colours on themselves or a viewer. However, experience and experiments with subjective colour combinations show that individuals differ in their evaluation of harmony and of discord. Some people enjoy one grouping of colours to live with in their homes, others a quite different grouping of hues or values of hues. Combinations of colours, like most things, do not meet with universal acclamation or approval. Objectively, harmony implies a pleasing balance of colours. Wilhelm Ostwald wrote:

> These colours are pleasing among which some regular, i.e. orderly relationship obtains. Lacking this the effect will be displeasing or indifferent. Groups of colour whose effect is pleasing we call harmonious.

Although there are no rules, there are guide-lines to help us achieve colour harmony in arrangements, but these should only be regarded as signposts:

1 Smaller areas of brilliant colour are more acceptable to most people than larger areas because pure colour is more exciting to the eye and so more tiring. One guide-line in any scheme is to use much less of the more brilliant colours than of the duller and paler ones. Witness a garden where we see brightly coloured flowers against a background of earth, sky and green foliage, in other words a natural balance. The same guide-line applies to the flower arrangement itself, and also to the arrangement within its setting – for instance, a design of brilliant hue will achieve the right harmony in a room of paler or duller colours.

2 It is almost impossible to isolate colours from their surroundings. Thought must always be given to the lighting. The more luminous colours show up better in dim lighting; reds turn muddy in appearance and lose all vitality in fluorescent lighting; blues and violets are at their best in daylight, poor in tungsten lighting but better in fluorescent lighting. Sunlight bleaches colours and gives a feeling of lightness.

Surrounding colours also change the effect and colours alter against different coloured backgrounds. A colour changes as another is placed beside it. There is a reaction between the colours. Experiments with large sheets of coloured paper behind a design are quite fascinating. Colour has an ever-changing quality which is both a challenge and a frustration.

3 A colour has more life and depth when variations are used even though only one dramatic colour is featured. For example, many reds together enhance each other, making the design appear redder and more vibrant.

4 Colours of equal weight do not usually enhance each other.

5 Repetition of a colour used in an arrangement gives unity. When a colour is used by itself, perhaps in one flower, it achieves the focal effect of a 'bull's-eye'. The eyes tend to put like colours together and to link them into a pattern which causes the eye to move from one flower to another of the same colour. When there are many colours, several patterns intertwine, which is why a multicoloured arrangement can look confusing. The pattern of a colour should be considered when arranging and this is especially necessary when arranging white flowers with dark green foliage in a church. From a distance the spots of white stand out, and unless the pattern appears ordered, white blobs seem to be placed indiscriminately around the arrangement.

The patterns of colours can be lines of one colour through an arrangement or groupings of colours such as warm and cool, dark and light. To avoid loss of continuity, the groupings can be combined with plant material that has both colours such as a hydrangea flower with blue and red petals or a begonia leaf with red colouring on the green.

6 Unless a dramatic effect is wanted, a more gentle harmony is achieved by small gradations in colour, such as yellow-orange, orange, orange-red, red instead of yellow directly to red. White is very far from most colours, and for instance, dark red and white rarely look well together because of their extreme contrast. Add other values of red – that is, many pinks – and the effect can be better. White is normally more pleasing when used with tints modified by white.

7 A colour 'theme' can be helpful. Many artists limit their palettes to a certain number of colours. In a design of all-brilliant colouring, a small amount of subtle colour may look overshadowed and out of place; one brilliant hue, unless a specially dramatic effect is desired, may jar the eye in a grouping of all-soft colours. The chosen theme may be subtle, brilliant, delicate, strong, dark and so on. It is helpful to think of the probable 'theme' when collecting plant material.

8 The weight of colours should be considered. A dark red flower at the top may give a feeling of impending weight but used for a container it can give stability. A brilliant yellow hue at the top can be weightless but at the bottom of a design may give an impression of buoyancy imprisoned.

9 Colours usually appear at their best when they are kept in the same value relationship as that shown on the value scale (the natural order of values). If the reverse order of values is used the areas of each colour will need varying.

10 A colour grouping is usually more pleasing when there is a dominant colour, light or dark effect, warm or cool effect and/or a combination of these.

Backgrounds

A flower arrangement is almost always seen against a background. It may be the wall of a room, the fabric of a church, a niche in a show, or a background devised by the arranger. It is an integral part of the arrangement because the colours selected for the arrangement depend for maximum effect on the colour of the background.

An exhibitor making a background can choose flower colours first and then plan a background colour to enhance the arrangement, but normally the background is unchangeable and must be considered first when planning the arrangement. There are certain guide-lines which help, but there are innumerable types of background of many colours and textures ranging from plain to highly decorative and each must be considered individually.

It is the *contrast* between the colours of the arrangement and those of the background that must be decided. Our eyes function in this instance only by means of comparison and therefore we compare the colours, which are weakened or intensified in contrast to the background colour. Distinct differences must be perceived if an arrangement is to show up, but the

Right: the influence of background colour on an arrangement. The same polychromatic design is set against four differently-coloured backgrounds. This shows the changes made in our perception of the colours and therefore in our response to their qualities of warmth, depth and weight

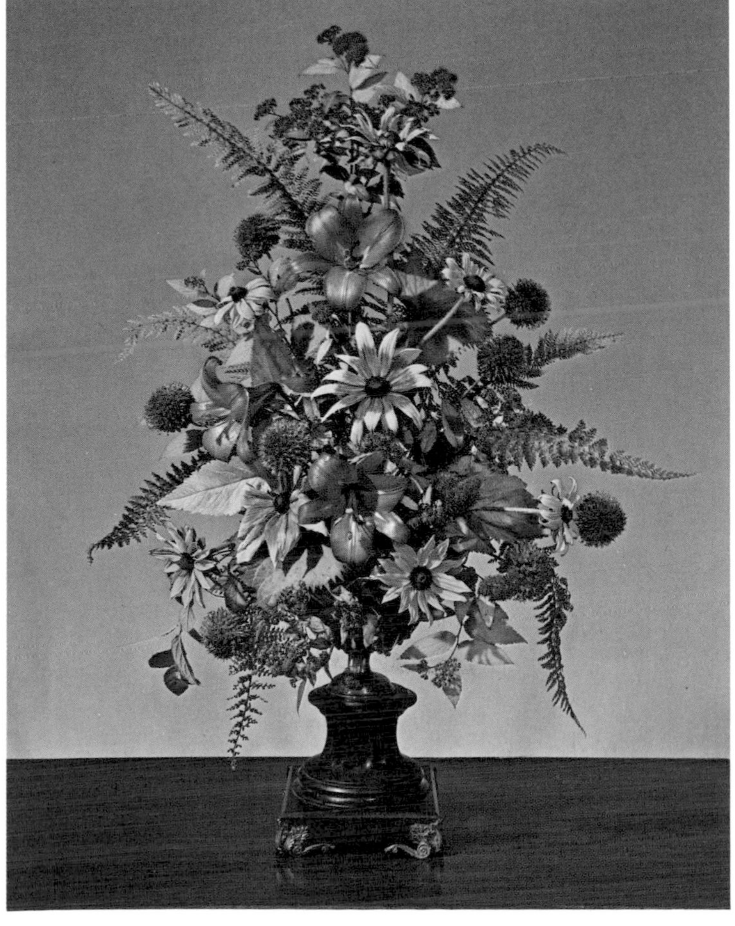

degree of contrast depends on the effect you wish to achieve.

1 Larger areas

The background is the larger area and one of the guide-lines to harmony is that larger areas should be in a more subdued colour. When choosing flower colours, select those brighter than the background. If devising your own background, paint or cover it in a colour less brilliant than the flowers.

2 Hues

The aim of a flower arranger is to enhance the flowers. Pure hues behind a design will normally subtract the potency unless the hue is not a brilliant one, such as violet. A brilliant background or a highly patterned one will usually attract attention to itself first and predominate, which is not the object of the exercise. If strongly patterned wallpaper cannot be avoided, then the arrangement must be exceptionally dramatic if it is to have any effect. It could be a mass of flowers of the most brilliant hue seen in the background. When an arranger provides a background, brilliant colours may be chosen for special effect in a free-form or abstract design, but normally pure hues should be avoided.

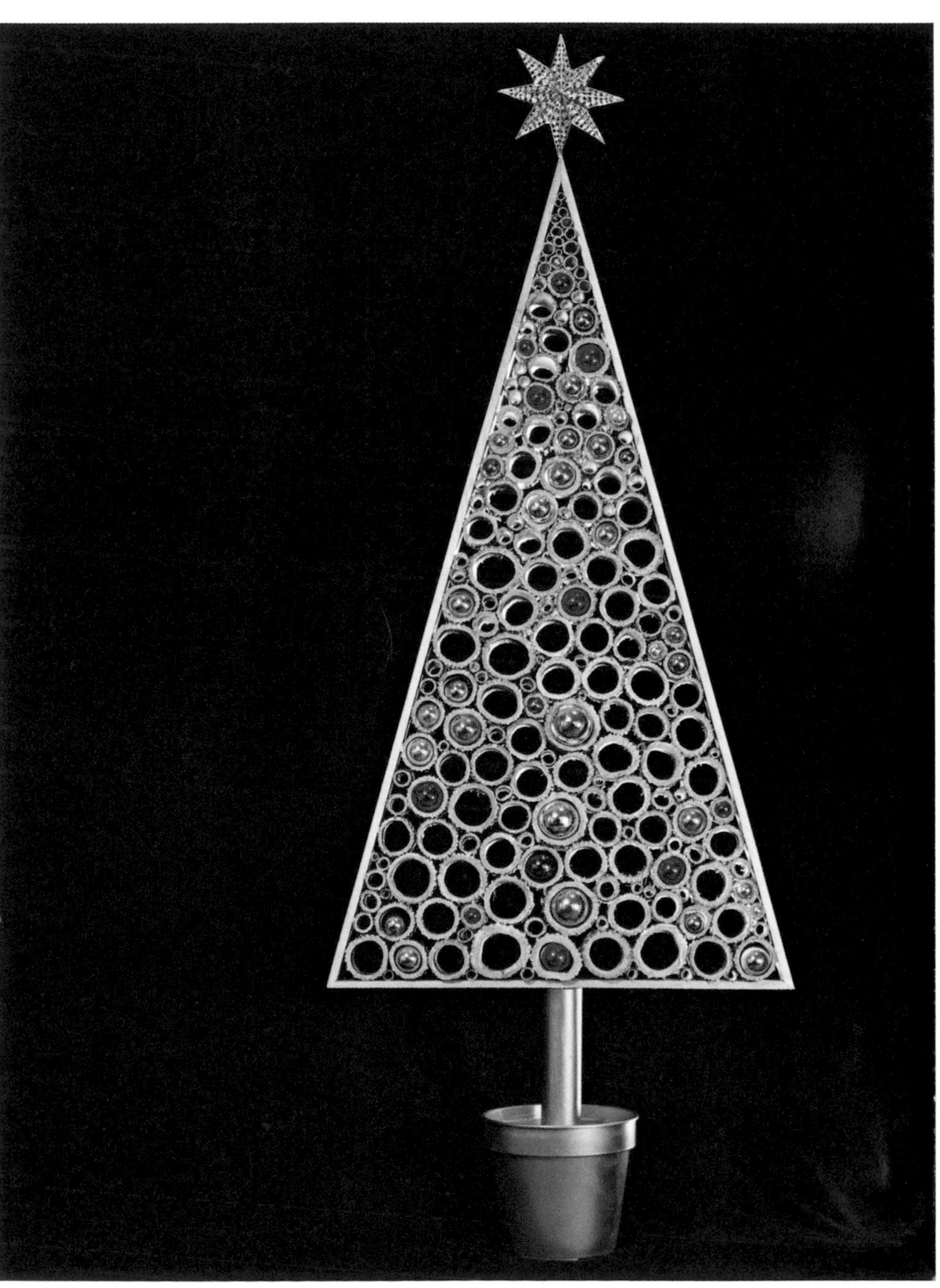

A modern Christmas tree: hogweed stem slices painted gold, inset with glass baubles. Gold and other metallic colours look best contrasting with a dark dull background

Right: the coolness of this all-green arrangement, of blue cedar, *Hosta* and Solomon's seal foliage and poppy seedheads, is emphasized by the almost virginal quality of the young greenish hydrangea and the comparatively warm apricot background

3 Light-dark contrast

If an arrangement is made of darker flowers it normally shows up better against a lighter background, and lighter flowers appear at their best in front of darker backgrounds. Too great a contrast is usually to be avoided if possible because strong contrasts of value give a sense of space and may separate the background and the flowers.

4 Warm-cool contrast

Warm pinks and oranges against a cool blue-green background are especially appealing. Itten wrote that this combination of warm and cool colours is the most sonorous. Cool coloured flowers are also attractive against a warm background. Each makes the other appear warmer or cooler. The important guide-line, that of making the background more subdued and less dominant, should still be followed. Generally speaking, warm backgrounds are better than cool ones because they unify colours placed against them, whereas cool backgrounds tend to separate colours.

5 Neutrals

Black strongly defines the outline of an arrangement placed against it and tends to make it look smaller. But it has a dramatic quality and gives great depth.

Grey is rather characterless and indifferent, although it is said that colours are the truest against mid-grey. It does not add much to the colour scheme.

White can provide too strong a contrast, especially with dark flowers, which look even darker against white. Tints are a better choice against white.

Usually the subtle colours, or neutralized ones, make a more interesting background for flowers than neutrals.

6 Complementary contrast

This is a clever form of contrast, especially as complementary colours enhance each other. An all-green design is pleasing against a light background; dulled red, yellow flowers are effective in front of violet, and blue in front of a shade or tone of orange. Red also looks excellent in front of green, and orange does in front of blue; but violet in front of yellow has to be used with care because the yellow is normally much more luminous and eye-catching.

7 Texture

The surface texture of a background should not be shiny. A shiny surface reflects light and attracts the eye away from the arrangement.

Colour Appreciation

All nature manifests itself by means of colour to the sense of sight.

Goethe.

A study of colour increases awareness and, through this, appreciation. There are so many lovely colours and colour groupings in the world about us to enjoy, store in our minds and reproduce in our own creative activities.

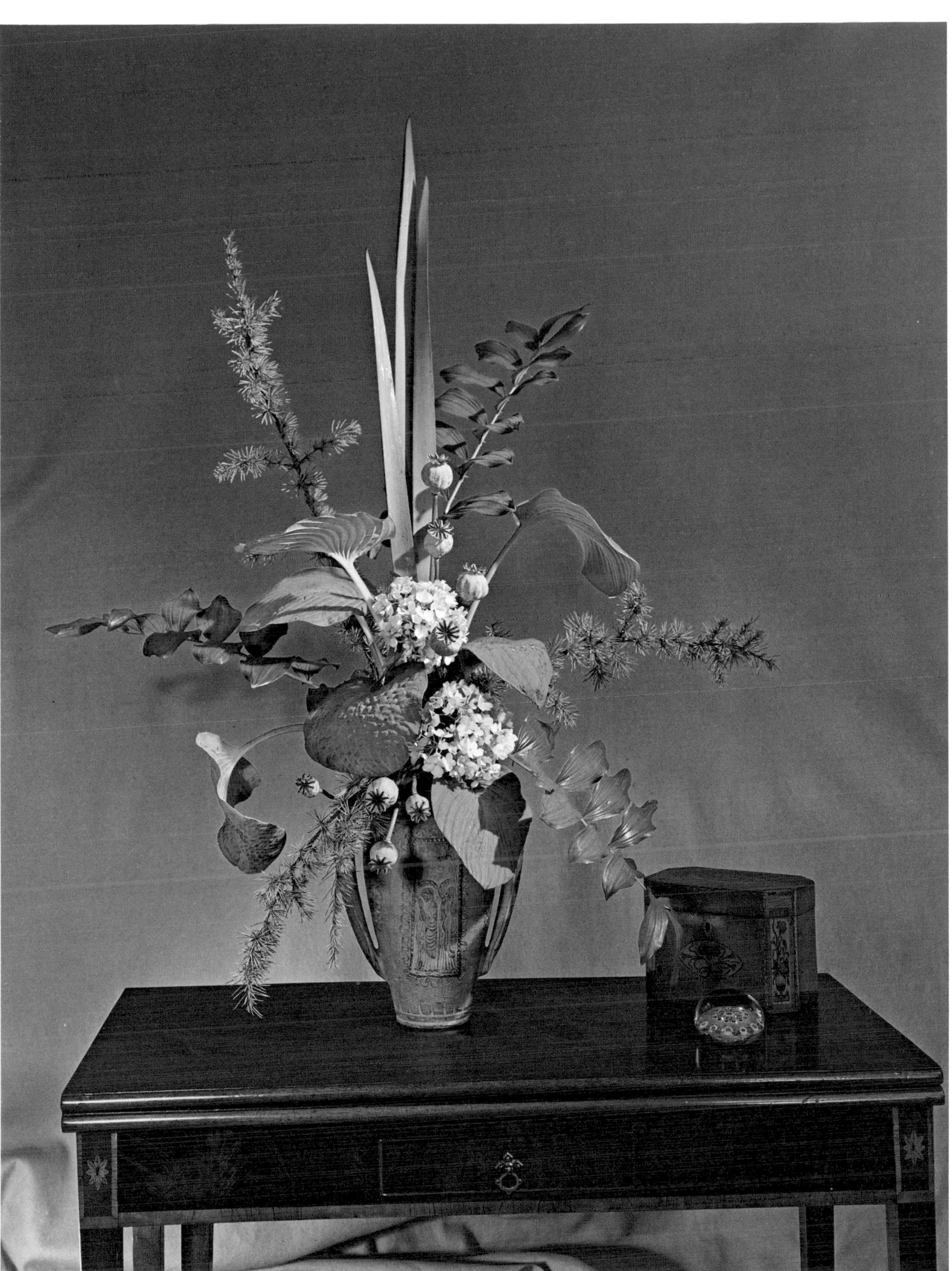

14. Additional Design Elements

Joan Weatherlake

. . . Creative art . . . demands the service of a mind and heart.

WILLIAM WORDSWORTH 1770–1850

An arrangement in Westminster Abbey, where the author of this chapter, Joan Weatherlake frequently provides the floral decorations

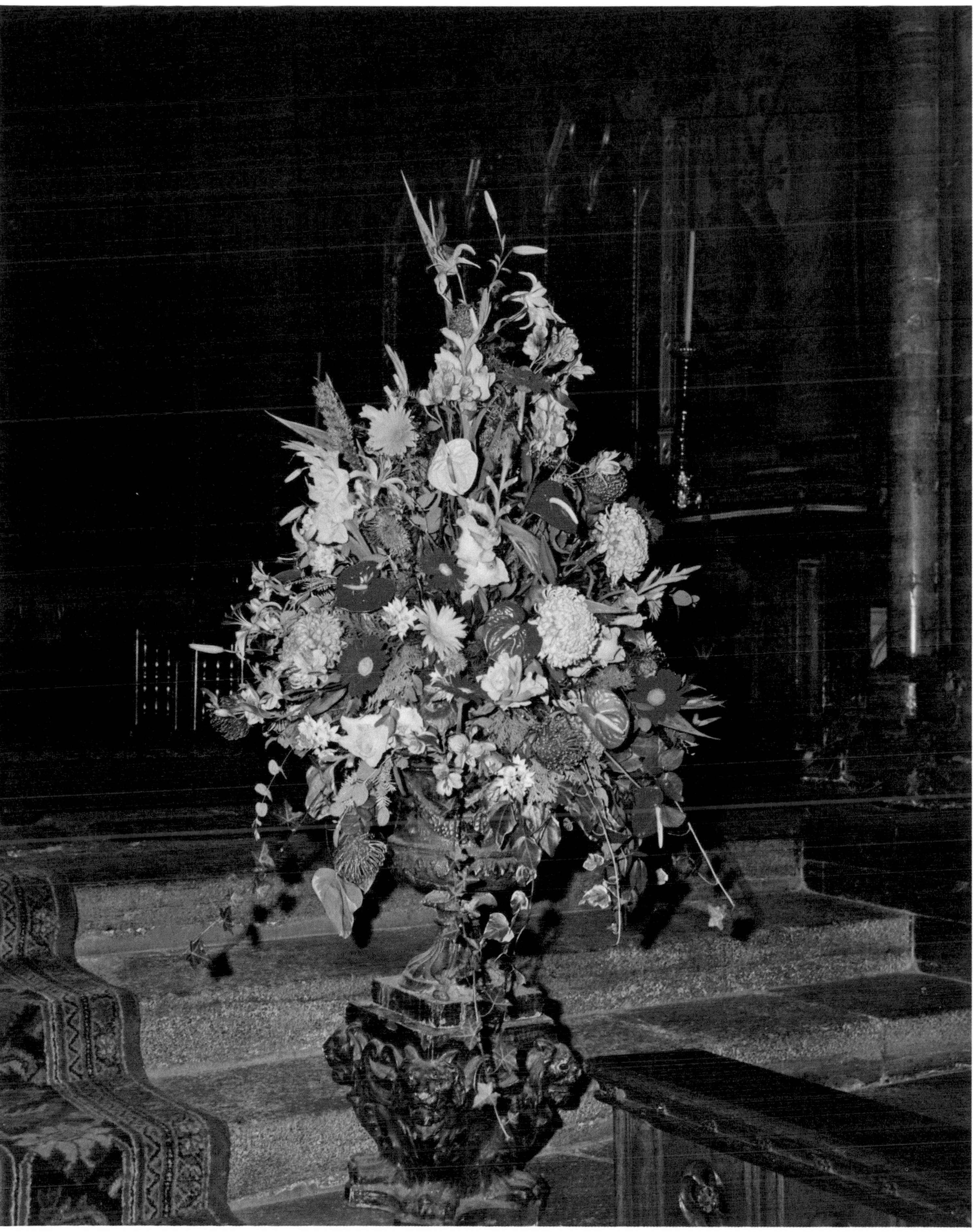

The first aim of this chapter is to consider some important design elements which are vital to artist, sculptor and flower arranger alike, and then to look at natural materials and lighting. A knowledge of design elements helps one to select materials, to envisage a design and to carry it out successfully. If a completed arrangement seems unsatisfactory, then probably one of these basic principles has been abused or ignored. Some elements are already present in all things, while others are introduced from outside when an arrangement is being made. For instance an apple has **colour**, a waxy **texture**, a rounded **form**, and **space** in the dimpled ends where the flower and stem grew. These four elements are present in every object included in an arrangement, from a bare branch to the flowers, foliage and container. They must be used with understanding if the design is to have maximum effect.

The factors imposed on a design by the craftsman are sometimes called *design principles*. They include **rhythm, repetition, contrast, dominance, depth** and **proportion**. All need to be observed with skill and sensitivity when making an arrangement and when checking it after completion.

Proportion

This is probably one of the first elements to consider when making a design, because the size of the space in which the arrangement is to be placed determines the size of the flower arrangement and the container, and the quantity of plant material. Usually a visually satisfying proportion of plant material to container is at least one and a half times to twice, so that if the container is 25 cm (10in.) high, the tallest stem would be 37.5-50 cm (15-20 in.) tall. Table arrangements, for instance, often need quite small containers to start with, if there is to be room left for the place settings. Many women consider proportion when they buy clothes – a short woman will look wrong in a gathered, tiered skirt and wide brimmed hat because the proportions are wrong in relation to her own and the clothes overwhelm the person. In flower arrangement the plant material should usually be the most important element and the container and accessories subsidiary.

If the arrangement is to stand in a contained space such as a niche, then the arrangement should be framed in space to enhance it rather than completely filling the niche – a useful average proportion would be for the arrangement to be two-thirds the height of the niche. A common fault in exhibition work is to make arrangements proportionately too small, so that the top two-thirds of the niche is empty. These small arrangements need taller plant material, but could also be helped by a raised base which would bring the proportions nearer to the ideal (Figure 1).

Space

We are surrounded by space. Flower arrangements are three-dimensional objects, like pieces of sculpture, placed in their own area of space; they could be in the contained space of a niche or free-standing in open space on a table. The arrangement in the niche is surrounded by an area of space, like a mount round a watercolour, and this can be thought of as having a definite shape and identity of its own almost as important as the shape of the arrangement itself.

A further important way of thinking about space is to consider how it can be brought into the design itself, so that it links the surrounding space with the arrangement and gives it a lighter look. Think of a solid Victorian arrangement with full-blown flowers closely packed together, and no space within the design. (Gertrude Jekyll, who pioneered the idea of looser arrangements at the turn of the century, allowing space to show between the flowers, called them 'the old pudding-like masses'.)

Then picture an *ikebana* arrangement, with three branches of blossom spaced out like a one-sided fan with lots of space between each stem. The eye travels into the centre of the arrangement and out again before returning to rest at the centre where the branches meet. Ideas for modern and free-form designs stemmed from these traditional *ikebana* arrangements, in which, because the plant material is limited, space becomes an integral part of the design. Try placing three curved branches of different lengths on to a pinholder, each spaced apart from the other, and then stand back and look at them. Within the design spaces have been outlined and defined by the branches – could they be made more interesting by a change of angle? Alternatively, try sticking dried curving stems on to a background to make interesting two-dimensional shapes. Use the stems as outlines for the shapes between them. Collage often makes a good starting point for experiments because work on a flat surface leaves out the third dimension of depth. The shapes between the stems on the pinholder are, however, likely to be more interesting than the collage because it can be viewed from the side and from different angles as well as from the front.

Further experiments employ materials that will loop and twist. Popular as cane is, irregular stems of honeysuckle, old man's beard or tree ivy are more satisfying to work with. When the two ends of a long piece are held together, an oval slightly asymmetrical shape is formed, the basis for an interesting arrangement (Figure 2). Impale these stem ends on to a pinholder. Add one or two flowers like dahlias or roses, low down on short stems so that the space within the looped stem is not obscured. Bold rather than fussy flowers which are difficult to handle in a sparse design. Then mask the pinholder with a few stones, a leaf or two, or a piece of driftwood. Many a simple design like this is spoilt by the

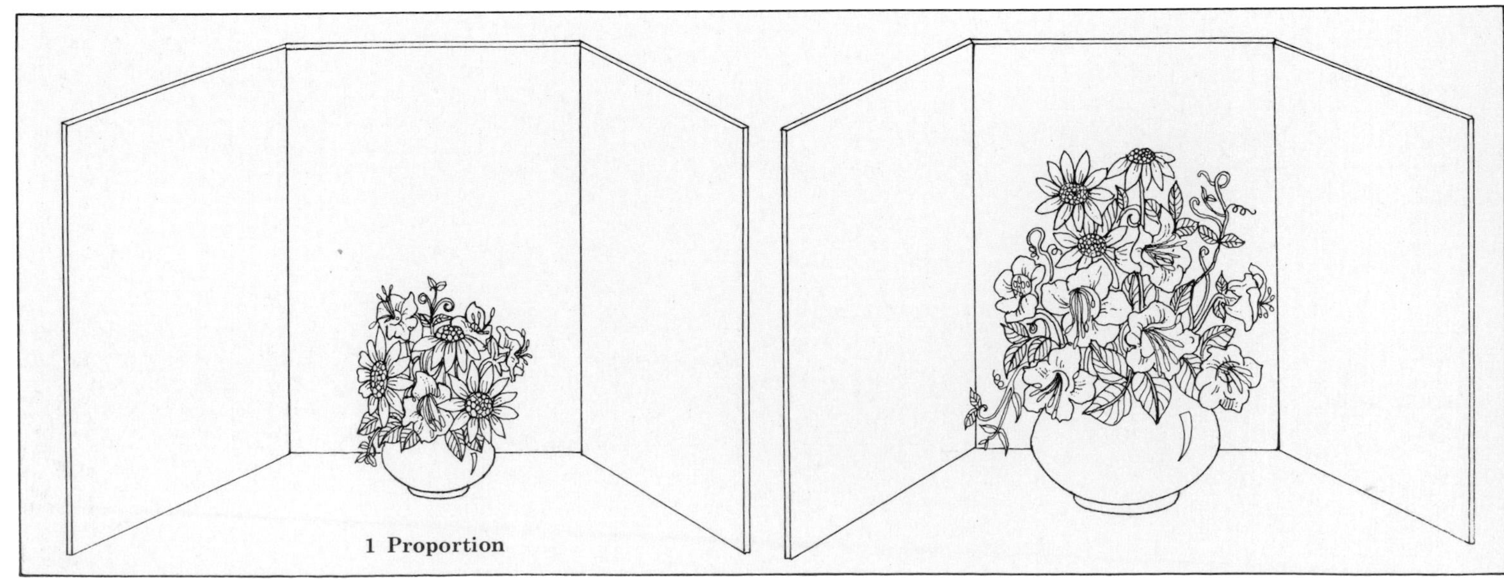

1 Proportion

2 Space
Enclosed space used in a design

3 Space
Space beneath a design used to impart lightness

addition of too much material intended to cover the mechanics; a frill of leaves at the base detracts from the feeling of space and simplicity. Small curved pieces of driftwood about the size of a clenched fist can be placed over the pinholder or plastic foam; sometimes two pieces are needed, one at the front and one at the back. Often a single leaf, for example a rose leaf, can be pressed flat on to the pinholder, or a single senecio leaf on a couple of centimetres of stem could be pushed into the foam to conceal that last distracting glimpse of the mechanics.

Much has been written about the use of space in modern arrangements, but space can make all the difference in traditional designs also, changing an old-fashioned close-packed look to a freer more up-to-date one. To start with, the outline stems can be well separated so that the space surrounding the design is brought in and integrated. When putting in the outline, one or two stems placed to come forward near the centre and above the rim of the container, help as a reminder that the arrangement should not be flat in the front. The area of space at the back of the arrangement should also be used: use stems slanting slightly backwards each side of the tallest stem and also lower down behind the side stems at a diagonal. This helps to give a feeling of depth which is so important. Depth and space are closely related; both would be lacking from the front and back of a flat two-dimensional arrangement, for example.

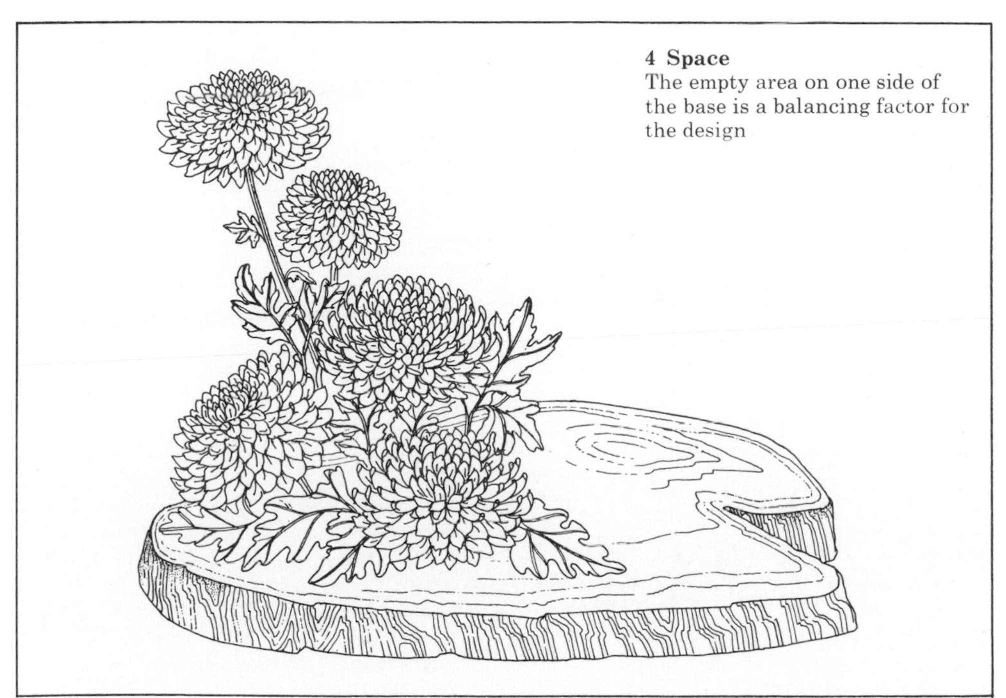

4 Space
The empty area on one side of the base is a balancing factor for the design

Depth and space are also created when short stemmed flowers are tucked into the centre of the arrangement with other longer stemmed flowers placed in front of them. A pedestal design incorporating this principle might have a line of mauve rhododendron flowers on short stems masking the plastic foam and, coming from these, a line of pink roses on longer stems. The space between the two different flowers gives a light airy look while the deep-set receding-coloured rhododendrons give depth. Look at any good pedestal arrangement and see how space has been used on the outer edges between the outline stems. The lowest side stems do not stop at a horizontal angle but flow downwards, making the space below important too (Figure 3). View the front of the arrangement from one side and see that the flowers have space between them. There is a soft in-and-out look rather than a solid bow front.

An arrangement raised on to a base or pedestal is given lightness by the space beneath. Space can create balance in water arrangements or arrangements on a base, when the placements are at one end; though free of plant and other materials, the clear area of the container or base is not 'empty', but is a positive design element, 'full' of space, which is the crucial balancing factor (Figure 4). In asymmetric, L-shape, upturned crescents or Hogarth curve designs this use of space comes into play. In modern arrangements, space is often used in order to counteract solid areas; a heavy pot, for instance, could be balanced by the space enclosed by a tall curved stem.

Rhythm

An important element to foster in flower arrangement is the suggestion of music and movement often found in the natural growth patterns of plants. Natural growth can, however, be confusing and the flower arranger may have to improve on nature by cutting out confusion for, as Whistler said, 'an artist is born to pick and choose'.

The heart-beat has a regular rhythm. Seen from a moving train, evenly spaced telegraph poles or sleepers on the track provide an example of rhythm sensed visually. Although this type of rhythm could be useful in free form designs, generally uneven rhythm patterns are used in flower arrangements. Many organic patterns found in nature have a hidden order and system governing them. The spiral curve of a snail shell is based on the same system as the arrangement of segments in sunflower centres; a river system and the branching of trees are based on a similar order.

In flower arrangement, a straight stem of bamboo would not in itself suggest rhythm, but two stems placed an inch apart on a pinholder, with a curved stem of tree ivy twisting round them, could do so (Figure 5). Curved stems and diagonal ones suggest movement, straight stems are static like columns and suggest alertness, repose or calmness. Think of a human figure standing still, dancing and running and see how these actions are interpreted

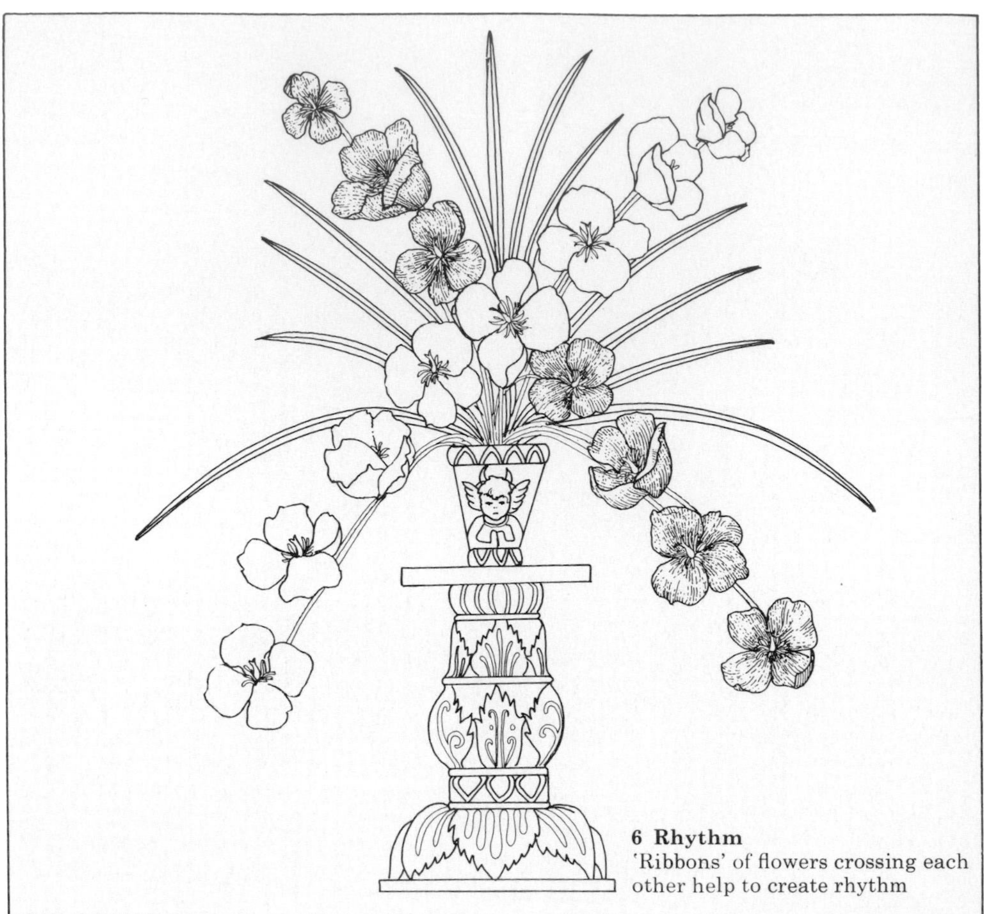

6 Rhythm
'Ribbons' of flowers crossing each other help to create rhythm

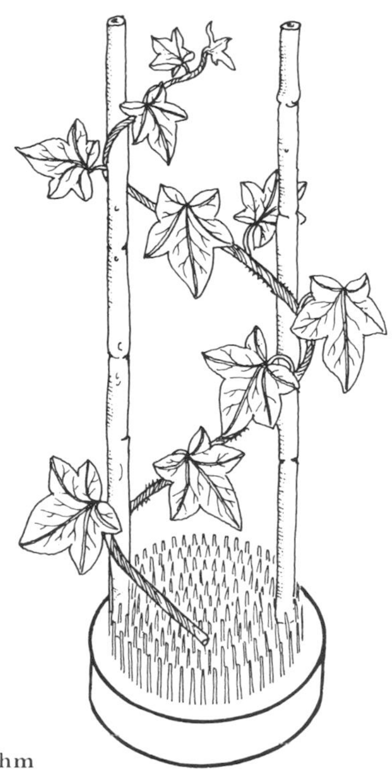

5 Rhythm

by the straight, curved and diagonal stems.

Curved branches and symmetrical shapes will give a rhythmic feeling also. Usually the tallest stem should be placed so that its tip is over the mechanics, otherwise it will have an uncomfortable look of tipping over. It can, however, curve and bend between tip and stem end, as much as you like. Like most 'rules' this is only a general guide. You might, for example, want to plan a design to suggest a windy day and use curved branches at a diagonal.

Rhythm is important even in a traditional symmetrical triangle design because too static an arrangement could look boring. Curved stems can be used at the sides and also by running down 'ribbons' or lines of flowers in an uneven line from one side of the tallest stem to low down on the opposite side, with a reversed line of a different flower or colour crossing it (Figure 6). Drapes can help with rhythm by following the sweep of the arrangement to accentuate the curve. Other placements in the front of an arrangement such as fruit can also be placed to follow the curve.

Repetition

A recurring feature is found in art and music as well as in nature. It can be used to great advantage in arrangements to help unify a design and bring harmony out of a miscellaneous collection. An interior designer uses repetition when, for example, he chooses lampshades and cushions to repeat the colour of a flower motif in the curtains; nature provides the model with, say, an unplanned drift of cow parsley by the roadside, which looks more restful than a gaudy border planted with single specimens of many different kinds of plants. A flower arranger might use repetition by matching the pink of some roses with a pink velvet base; she could plan a set of bases in favourite colours to mix and match with flowers, like co-ordinated clothes.

Colour is only one way to explore the effect of repetition. Texture can be repeated in different materials to help with harmony; for instance a rough knubbly fabric, a hand-thrown pot, and the back of a sea shell might all have a similar coarse texture, while a silky drape could repeat the texture of peony petals. Shape or form could be repeated too; an organic shaped container might have its curve echoed in a branch, or the round form of an apple could repeat the shape of a carnation.

Contrast

Too much repetition could make a design boring. This can happen when one of the elements is restricted as in a monochrome or one-colour arrangement, in a foliage arrangement or a dried design. The element of contrast can come to the rescue in these situations. Repetition and contrast should be used hand in hand like the yin and the yang, the one enhancing the other in a positive-negative way. (See p. 241.)

A monochrome arrangement which, as we have seen, might be monotonous if only one shade of say, red was used, could have a contrast of light to dark reds, from pale pink to darkest maroon; or it could keep the one shade of red but use a contrast of textures, such as aubergines, black grapes and glycerined eucalyptus foliage with black parrot tulips and a velvet base. A foliage arrangement could have a colour

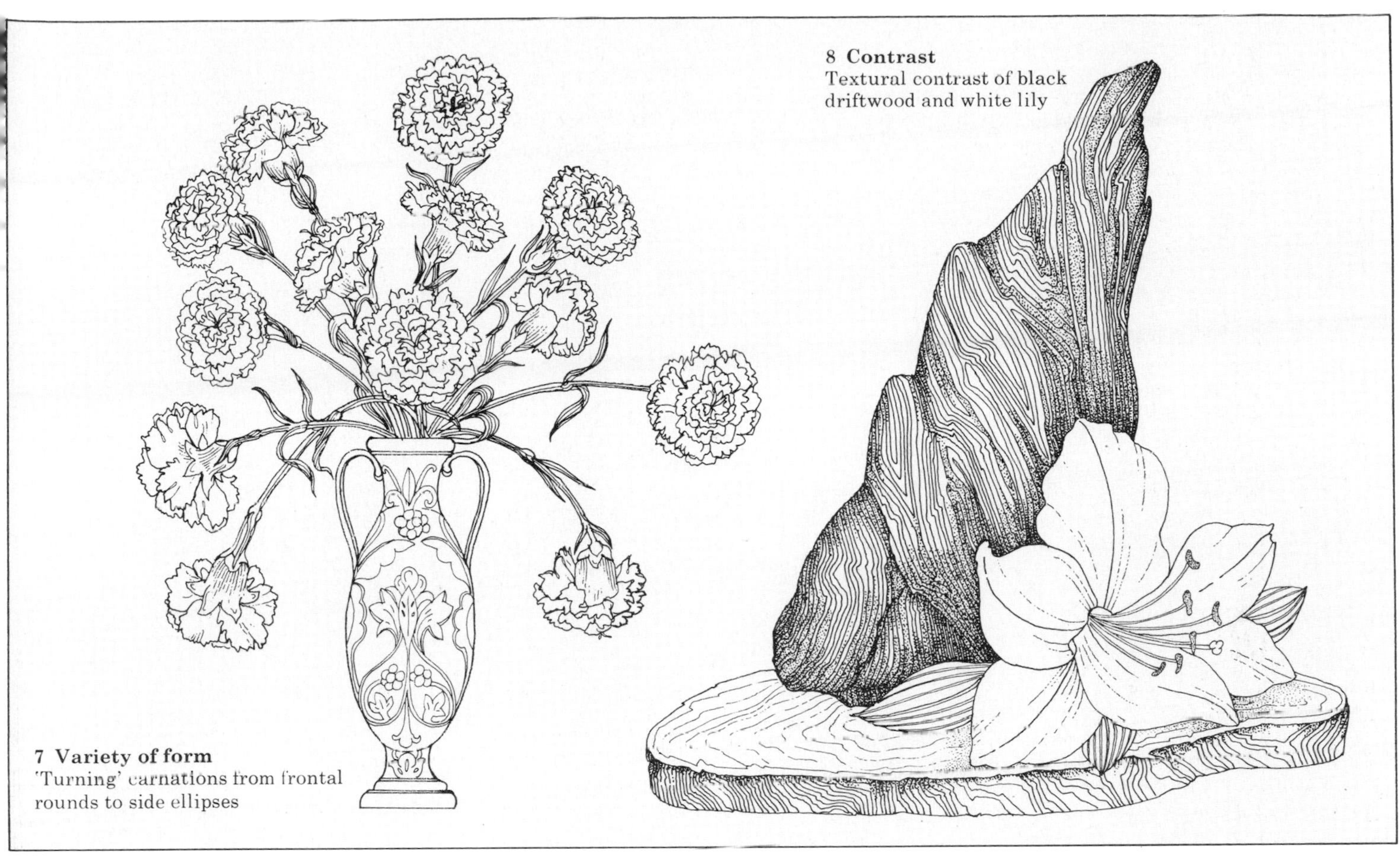

8 Contrast
Textural contrast of black driftwood and white lily

7 Variety of form
'Turning' carnations from frontal rounds to side ellipses

contrast of grey, gold and red foliage, or if it was to be all green then texture could be varied and ribbed *Hosta* leaves could contrast with shiny *Fatsia* and soft *Tellima*. The shapes of the leaves could also give both repetition and contrast in a foliage design. One only has to look at a well-planned border where interesting herbaceous plants grow to see how many different shapes there are and how they can enhance one another when placed side by side: the lacy leaves of *Dicentra* against matt, scalloped-edged *Tiarella*, and upturned Solomon's-seal leaves with the bloom of a grape on them. Contrast and variety of shape can be thought about every time the materials are selected for a design. It is usually more interesting if some spiky flowers and some rounded flowers are used together, rather than making a whole design depend on chrysanthemums, for instance. Gladioli, larkspur or slender-flowering branches of forsythia are examples of the first, and rounded flowers include roses, dahlias and carnations. Some rounded flowers with centres, such as single spray chrysanthemums, give variety. It is always possible to make variety in an arrangement with carnations only (or other rounded flowers), by turning some flowers sideways, some looking upwards and some downwards at the base of the arrangement. The form of the flower will then change to elliptic instead of round (Figure 7). Leaf shapes can also give variety and again spiky shapes like winter jasmine stems give interest when used with intermediate shapes like privet and larger simple shapes like ivy or *Hosta* leaves.

Contrast of shape and texture are also vital to dried designs, especially when predominantly beige and brown materials are involved. Slender velvety bulrushes might have their texture repeated in a brown velvet base, while contrast could be found in a piece of rough bark, the polished mahogany of a horse chestnut and the powder puff texture of a cardoon centre. Contrast gives vitality and prevents monotony, but like repetition it needs to be used with discretion if a harmonious effect is wanted. In modern designs a more aggressive type of contrast could be achieved using opposing directions, or strong colour contrast, or surprising combinations of contrasting textures, for instance a blackened piece of driftwood, charred in a fire and the pure shimmering white of a lily (Figure 8).

Dominance

In many types of design it is held that some part of the finished work must be more important or eye-catching than the rest. The idea is seen at work in the use of a centre of interest or focal point to which the eye should travel and rest. Unfortunately this sometimes suggests a bull's-eye, with one extra large flower used in the middle near the rim of the container, in a colour stronger than the rest of the flowers. It has an eye-riveting effect which should be avoided. It would be more satisfying, in a traditional design, to use several of the more important flowers to make a line running through the centre of the design – not dead straight but slightly on the diagonal, to add rhythm. Perhaps in a pedestal these could be five stems of lilies; in a smaller arrangement roses or dahlias could be used because they have an important look which smaller fussier flowers lack. 'Face' flowers – those with centres like *Rudbeckia*, single spray chrysanthemums or water-lily dahlias – are eye-catching and more dominant than round flowers like carnations or pom-pom dahlias. Flowers with a strong form like lilies or cardoons and seedheads like lotus are examples of dominant forms. They can be used to advantage towards the centre of the arrangement because they attract the eye which should, in a satisfying balanced design, be invited towards the centre.

Smaller fussy flowers like sprays of rambling roses, *Tellima* spikes, or sweet peas are the types of flowers one would not normally use to create dominance. There are, however, many surprising possibilities. In a petite design, single little roses nipped off the spray of rambler roses could create a centre of interest. The spikes of *Tellima* could create a dominant line of lime green in an all-green arrangement, and the sweet peas could be the most eye-catching colour in a table arrangement of small flowers. It is also possible to group smaller flowers together to create dominance.

Colour can easily create dominance especially when bright, light colours or white are introduced. When two different colours are used together it is usually more pleasing to have unequal parts of each with the dominant colour in the lesser quantity. Equal parts of, say, red and green would give a restless effect – which might, of course, be what one wanted in interpretative work.

Shiny textures with the quality of reflecting light are more dominant than those that are restrained and matt: compare a green pepper and the shell of an egg. It is worth remembering this when buying containers, because however beautiful a glazed pottery container is, it should not overpower the plant material which it is to hold. Very coarse textures also can be dominant because of the contrast of light and shade on the surface.

With sparse arrangements the line material could be the dominant feature. A slender curved piece of driftwood used with three flowers would predominate. In a design using a loop of honeysuckle stem the enclosed space could be the most important part.

Plant material should always be more important than accessories or containers, but man-made materials used in designs can all too easily dominate. A patterned or shiny container can easily be too eye-catching. To avoid this happening it is possible to use repetition, and choose the same flowers or colours as are used in the pattern, say roses with rose sprigged china, or plum and mauve coloured dahlias in a container with a similar coloured pattern. If the container has a repeating pattern of circular shapes then round flowers like carnations could be used. This has the effect of unifying the pattern with the plant material. Usually it is best to use neutral coloured containers such as earth colours, grey or black. If using a brightly coloured container then use dominating flowers. It is very difficult to use patterned or shiny bases or drapes, as they too should blend without dominating.

Accessories also need using with care and usually should not be taller than the arrangement, as they should be subordinate partners to the plant material. Often last minute additions to an exhibit in a show can be too dominant, for example a white card with a quotation, an open book or a bright label on a bottle. These may need to be partly masked by some plant material, while titles or quotations are better if written on tinted paper. Pale grey or cream are less dominant than white.

Accessories such as a ginger jar with the open space turned towards the viewer, or an empty bird's nest, can also be too dominating. It may be better to turn the jar sideways and place eggs in the nest to hide the eye-catching space.

Depth

As well as recessing flowers on short stems into the centre of a design, and taking some stems to the back of the arrangement, there are other ways to create depth. For instance, when making an exhibit with more than one placement, depth is created if one is placed back and one forward. This applies to a simple water arrangement with two pinholders in a long low dish. If one pinholder holding the taller plant material is placed towards the back and at one end of the container, and the smaller pinholder with shorter material towards the front at the other end, then depth and perspective are created (Figure 9). One can follow the same idea in more complex exhibits with several placements and accessories. It is far more interesting if these are placed at different depths in the niche to give an effect of going back in space. Stones or moss or driftwood could link the different placements and create a unified whole. Accessories such as figurines can be placed slightly behind an arrangement in a niche to give depth and interest.

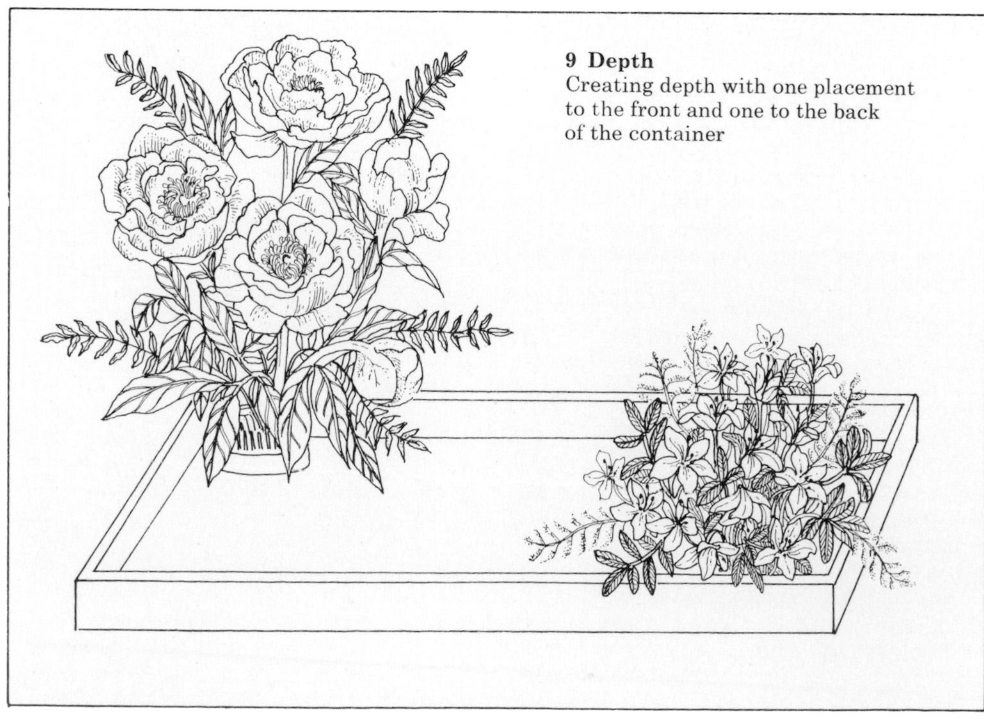

9 Depth
Creating depth with one placement to the front and one to the back of the container

Natural materials

Natural materials like water, stone and wood are ideal companions for flowers and foliage. They can be introduced in many ways. **Water** arrangements suggest repose when low containers are used with an expanse of water showing and the plant material on mechanics at one end. A little scene can be constructed with suitable materials like bulrushes and iris; branches of blossom would introduce an oriental air.

Stone can enhance the character of an arrangement. Thin slabs of sandstone or slate could be used as bases in landscape designs. A sawn slab of marble would look right with a Dutch period arrangement. Chunky off-cuts of stone or marble are sold more cheaply and can simulate pillars or be used to make a raised base, or to add textural interest beside an arrangement.

Small stones are invaluable for covering up the mechanics; it is worthwhile collecting sets of these in different colours and sizes. Small smooth white stones are found on beaches, or black stones could be picked out of a gravel path. Shops selling Japanese goods have boxes of beautiful smoothly polished black and dark grey pebbles, which are traditionally used for covering the pinholder in *ikebana* arrangements.

Wood is an even more versatile material. It is equally suitable as a base, to cover the mechanics, or as an important part of the design itself. There are countless types of wood to be found. 'Found' is an important word where driftwood is concerned, as it is most exciting to find a beautiful piece on the beach or in the woods.

Useful bases are simple slices of wood cut through a tree trunk or branch, but oval shapes are more versatile than round ones. Wood slices are available from some wood yards but, as the wood may not be seasoned properly, it is necessary to leave them flat in a cool place for several months to dry out without warping. These bases could be left in their natural state with the bark on, and a slightly rough texture to the wood; or they could have the bark removed and be sanded and polished. The natural base would be useful for landscape arrangements and the polished one for more sophisticated designs.

Small pieces of driftwood or bark are very useful for masking mechanics or for placing in front of a tin or other small container that needs to be hidden. Larger beautifully shaped pieces can also be used in front and slightly to one side of an

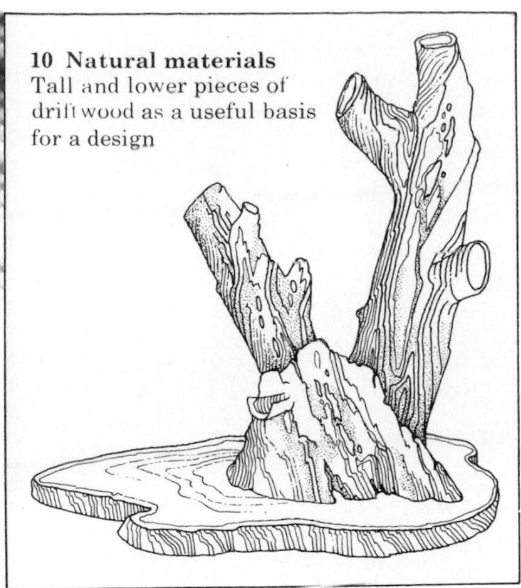
10 Natural materials Tall and lower pieces of driftwood as a useful basis for a design

arrangement, with the plant material flowing round, and thus incorporating the wood into the design. Tall pieces of wood used to give height, and low pieces to give weight at the base can sometimes be used in combination with one another. It is useful to have pairs of tall and low driftwood in similar colours, for instance some greyish, and some a golden brown, which when used together make the basis of an arrangement and may need only a few flowers to complete it (Figure 10). Bleached tree ivy or fire-blackened gorse stems are also very useful and give variety to a driftwood collection. Pine bark is worth searching for. After pine trees have been felled the bark is sometimes sliced off on the spot where it dries out very hard in beautiful shapes. Tree ivy, gorse stems, pine bark and other slender pieces of wood can be used in many different types of arrangement to give height. They may be pushed into the mechanics or may need the extra support of a special driftwood holder.

Lighting

Consider the effects which different types of lighting have on colour, as this will help when selecting flowers for different occasions. Daylight does not alter colours in the way that artificial lighting does, but it can vary a lot from dim winter light to strong sunlight. Subtle soft colours would be hard to distinguish in the dim interior of a church, but could be appreciated in a well-lit room. The church might need clear advancing colours like yellow, pink, or orange rather than blues and mauves.

Artificial lighting actually alters colours as it picks up and accentuates its own hue. Since household lighting is yellow/orange, orange and red flowers will look pure and strong while blues may look muddy. White strip lighting is bluish and so it enhances blue and mauve flowers; they stand out even more than if seen in daylight; but reds do not appear pure. Candlelight is soft, and so receding colours like blue and mauve will not show up well and may look like holes in the arrangement. White, yellow and cream will look lovely by candlelight as they are luminous colours, and any pastel colour will be preferable to a darker hue. Coloured lights which might be used at exhibitions with dramatic effect will exaggerate flowers of their own colour and alter other colours. For instance red light would dramatize a red arrangement, but would turn yellow flowers orange.

Lighting can also have an effect on texture. Any shiny texture will be accentuated by direct lighting because it has a reflective surface. This applies to tomatoes for instance; the plastic-like texture of an anthurium would appear more shiny. Side lighting will emphasize rough texture because it strengthens the shadows made by the surface structure of the object.

At first the separate design elements will have to be consciously considered but with practice their use will become almost instinctive. It will, however, be useful to check through the design elements one by one after the arrangement is completed.

Practice makes it possible to visualize the sort of plant material to pick to achieve a particular effect, thinking about texture, form and colour, contrast and repetition. Choose a container which will give an arrangement good proportions for the space it will occupy.

When making the design it will become easy to use space to give a light airy look and to create rhythm and movement by the use of curved stems, to use dominance in a subtle way and unobtrusively to suggest depth and perspective. It will be useful to be able to find beautiful natural materials to complement the plant material, and to understand the different types of lighting and their effect on colour and texture.

Joan Weatherlake

The seven main comparative components

Students who are beginners or at the intermediate stage may find some difficulty in discerning the design principles underlying traditional, free form (modern) and abstract arrangements. This simple chart has been drawn up to illustrate what the differences are and to show how they can be put into practice. Iris Webb

	Traditional	**Free form (Modern)**	**Abstract**
Shape and use of space	*Massed plant material*	*Often linear, using space*	*Use of enclosed space*
Quantity	*A* lot *of plant material*	Less *plant material*	*Often (though not always) restricted to one type of plant material made into patterns*
Movement from central area	*Radiates from a* centre	*Radiates from a central* point	*There is usually no central radiation point. Radiating lines rarely used.*
Focal point	*Central area of greater interest*	*No central area of interest, but there is a point of interest introduced to provide balance*	*More than one area of interest. Places to which the eye is drawn.*
Harmony and contrast	*Harmonious use of colours and shapes. Shapes graded to link materials ('transition')*	*Sense of contrast greater than feeling of harmony*	*Extremely strong contrasts e.g. between round forms and straight lines*
Degree of realism	*Element of naturalism present*	*Though subsidiary, a sense of naturalism remains*	*No naturalistic appearance*
Container	*Traditional or concealed*	*A modern design, usually in stonework or pottery*	*An integrated part of the design. Often more than one opening*

15. Modern and Abstract Design

Marion Aaronson

Speak of the moderns without contempt,
and the ancients without idolatry.
THE EARL OF CHESTERFIELD 1694–1773

The evocative line of this lovely driftwood, in harmony with that of the Easter lilies (Lilium longiflorum), suggests a title such as 'Winged Victory'

In modern design, once the basic traditional methods are mastered, and the eye is more trained in artistic judgement, many enthusiastic flower arrangers wish to explore more imaginative channels, and to experiment with more progressive areas of design. All the while nature, with its kaleidoscope of strange, beautiful and bewitching objects, is still the most constant source of inspiration, and the extravagant range of form, colour and textures of the natural world are the greatest spur to artistic development.

Fine, traditional arranging can still remain a pleasure, and will always be practised when the occasion, setting and availability of material lend themselves to the more conventional style. Indeed, there is no reason why all types of arranging cannot be practised and enjoyed for their different aims and qualities. Yet, while there is a natural temptation to repeat a pattern one is well versed in, there is no challenge in constant repetition, which dulls the creative impulse. Therefore a change of attitude or technique is often a necessary stimulus. Most creative artists feel the need from time to time to find new ways of using their particular medium, and different means of expression, and these help keep their art forms fresh.

In modern design, the arranger can use plant material more adventurously, and through experiment discover new and interesting ways of communicating ideas in an individual way. A sparse design, for instance, needing just one or two flowers, is not only economical, but practical for town dwellers or those with small gardens. Flower arrangers with traditional homes may feel modern design is out of place in settings such as theirs, but these need not restrict their ventures, as there are always shows, exhibitions and demonstrations providing good opportunities for experimentation.

Defining the terms

In the context of flower arranging, **modern design** – which includes free form, abstract, and all the various extensions – implies a swing from the familiar basic shapes to the more original styles with no set pattern or formula.

Free form is generally taken to mean a style with no precise geometric shape. It developed as a breakaway from stiff, rigid, conventional patterns to arrangements with a more fluid and flexible outline dictated by the nature of the material used.

Abstract design uses plant material in a non-naturalistic way – it is a departure from the 'natural'.

Mobile, stabile, sta-mobile, collage and *free-standing constructions* are further extensions of modern design. However, they are terms for methods of assembling rather than distinct styles, in which artistry and skill can be further exercised to result in more permanent constructions.

Above: dramatic effects with amazing, textured wood, arresting container and orange lilies

Below: Two dried agave leaves combine with strips of dried seaweed to make an arresting setting for two *L. auratum* (golden-rayed lilies)

Mobile is a light construction of delicately balanced plant material, planned on the principles of movement as an art form.

Stabile is a construction which has the appearance of movement, without actually being suspended in space, i.e. implied not actual movement.

Sta-mobile is a combination of a mobile and a stabile. Some parts may actually move in space, whilst other items have implied motion only. (See p. 75.)

Collage is a collection of different objects, plant material and non-plant material, mounted and fixed to a background for colour and texture effects.

Construction means plant material fitted together to form a decorative structure in a three-dimensional effect that resembles a piece of sculpture.

The boundaries between different modern styles are quite flexible, and one type can overlap another with a similarity of characteristics, so there is no rigid, clear-cut dividing line between the varieties. But they all have one thing in common, and that is the strong accent on **design** – the motivating factor in modern work with plant material considered in terms of design elements.

Characteristics of modern design

Even though the basic laws of design are always, and without exception, observed, the final appearance of the modern arrangement is a dramatic change from the conventional mass, basically because the designer uses far less material, and concentrates chiefly on design impact. A study of these characteristics will be helpful for appreciating modern design generally and be a guide to the choice of plant material and everything relevant to the plan of the design. They are:

1. A clear and well-defined outline. One is conscious of the beauty and force of line – lack of superfluous items keeps it pure – and there is obvious restraint in the amount of material used. This approach will have the effect of keeping the design crisp and uncluttered.

2. Space is a far more dominant feature than in a traditional arrangement, where voids are filled to present a massed effect. The modern designer organizes space to be part of the rhythm, depth and beauty of the arrangement, so the individual items are seen in greater isolation, with their special characteristics more sharply defined than in the mass. An interesting and dynamic balance of spaces and solids is part of the design impact.

3. Because there is a sparseness of

Above: dramatic line made with branches of burnt gorse, in a Clive Brooker container of harmonizing texture. Sharp colour contrast is provided by flowers and background

Below: an abstract design, stressing space, shape and rhythm. The round emphasis points are made of beech nuts impaled in dry foam united rhythmically with cane

material, a modern arrangement relies for effect on sharp contrasts. This may be of any of the elements of line, form, colour or texture. Colour contrasts are often bold and exciting, powerful rhythms are created with line contrasts, daring form and texture combinations are used for stunning effects. The overall effect is kept dramatic by the minimum of transition from one element to another – from hue to hue, shape to shape, and so on.

4. Proportion and scale are not always of a conventional nature, and often appear exaggerated to suit the effect required, and to give more emphasis. A tall, vertical arrangement of more than the customary height soaring upwards into space is typically modern. Balance is also not usually achieved in a conventional way, though in the overall effect every good design is finely balanced.

5. Plant material is handled more adventurously in a modern arrangement, and placed in more original and imaginative ways. One heavy focal area with everything radiating from it is avoided, and the design is kept lively and rhythmical with several points of interest. The result is that the eye is pleasantly stimulated to appreciate every possible facet of the design.

6. Because designing is along less repetitive lines, the character of the modern construction is altogether more individual and unique than the stereotyped pattern, and though everything is put together in an unconventional way, the visually pleasing design has overall harmony and unity with all the separate parts working for the whole.

Abstract is generally considered a distinct style in flower arranging. It is a facet of 'modern', and could be described as an exaggerated version of its basic form. The design approach is along similar lines, but plant material is used in a less natural way to give non-naturalistic effects. The more extreme examples of this style have more empathy with another art form such as modern sculpture than true flower arranging, and become extensions beyond the limits of the conventional arrangement. Plant material is regarded merely as objects with special qualities of line, colour, shape and texture, juxtaposed in such a way as to create interesting patterns. The aim is not to emulate nature faithfully as in traditional flower arranging, for in taking the plant material out of its natural context the values are changed. This may suggest a clinical or prosaic approach, with the beauty and charm of the plants disregarded. It is true that the attitude is analytical, but it can also be lyrical, and at times poetic, with the essential character of the plants presented in a fresh light.

Above: an expressive abstract with seedheads of giant hogweed, gold wire and a metal sculpture against a black background, entitled 'Escapism'

What is abstract?

Abstracting is a simplifying process, the taking away of non-essentials. An abstract arrangement is the simple basic form without the details. The more that is eliminated, the more abstract the design, which can be to a degree where there is nothing but pure form. Think of a mass arrangement, based on a triangular or pyramid framework. This basic, underlying structure is filled in with the detail of graduated form, colour and texture to become a mass. By eliminating some of the detail, to leave a stronger line and structure visible, a simpler form emerges. By eliminating even further, the simple, basic structure without the detail is all that remains. (See fig A, overleaf).

In its simplest form an abstract design is rather stark and of a dramatic simplicity. A strong pattern is evident; often the composition is nothing other than a pattern of solids and spaces. The organization of line and shape and space is really the subject; there is no theme or subject other than the design itself. This type of abstract is classified as **non-objective** or **decorative**. It is somewhat austere, but can also be serene and restful. An expressive or interpretative abstract on the other hand is based on a theme or subject, and is a little more lyrical, romantic, compositional.

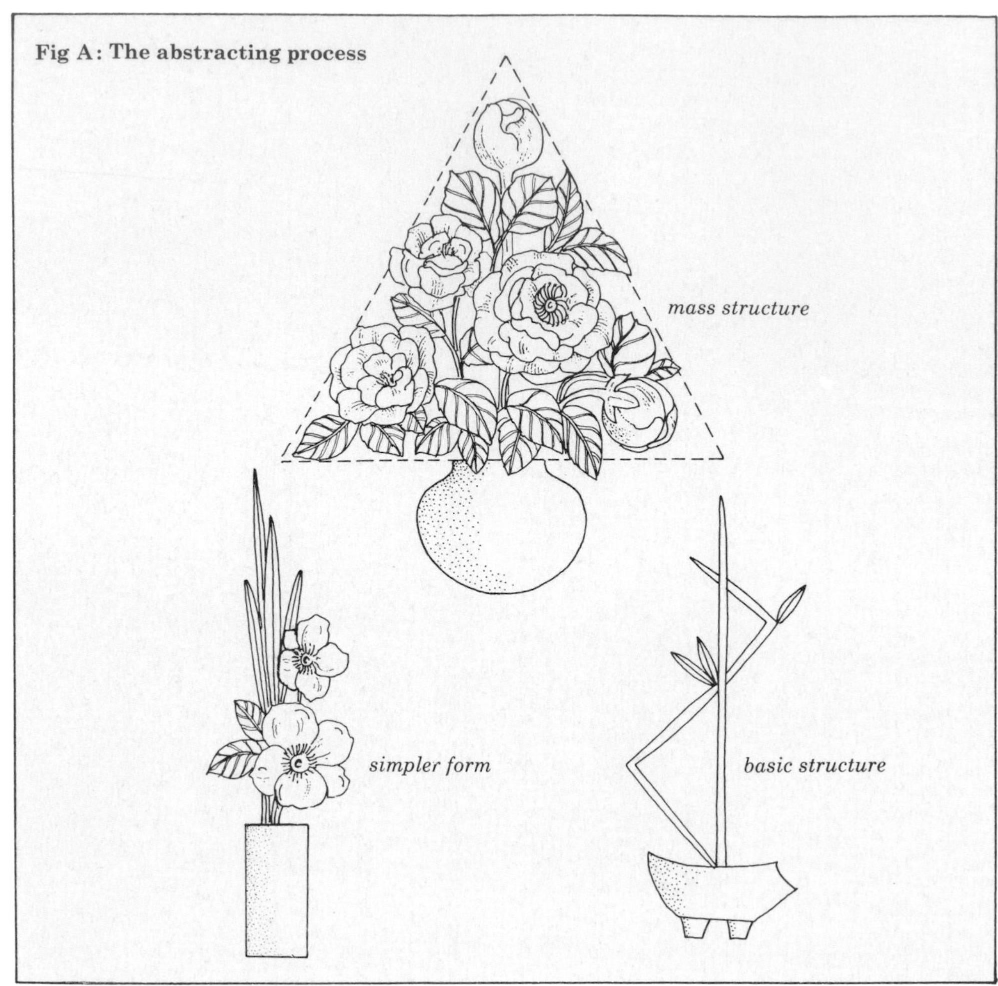

Fig A: The abstracting process

Fig B: a mobile
Actual rather than implied movement

Here the arranger is expressing her feelings, using plant material as symbolism. The statement is simple, with nothing superfluous included, so that the interpretation is the essence of the subject rather than the realistic image – an impression of an object rather than the object itself. In other words, the aim is not to be literal, but to abstract from the subject.

Since abstract is a comparatively new phase in flower arranging, looking at other abstract art forms can be helpful, and a source of inspiration. One can study examples of the two categories discussed. Looking at modern painting and sculpture can teach us how other artists have used their media to communicate ideas and impressions. How, for example, in a non-objective painting the painter has organized colour to advance and recede, how line and space can create a flow of movement. Abstract paintings are often based on very simple elements, with perhaps just a variation on a single shape, like a circle or square. It is the thoughtful putting together that creates a rhythmical and unified composition.

Again, in an expressive abstract, much can be learnt about the principle of symbolism: how the painter or sculptor has managed to convey a world of expression and emotion with a few simple strokes, or a shape, or a gesture. The sculptor Brancusi said, 'When you see a fish, you think of its speed, its flashing, floating body seen through water – I've tried to express just that.' He simplified and abstracted to get the essence, the inherent traits of his subject. His inspiring fish and bird sculptures, full of grace and movement, express a personal impression in a simple but powerful way. Distortion and exaggeration can be seen in the strange, emaciated and elongated figures of the sculptor Giacometti. These characteristics emphasize a particular quality – loneliness, or human isolation perhaps, or suffering. The distortion is for a purpose, that of interpretation and emphasis.

The media for flower arranging are less easy to alter and manipulate than clay or paint and set certain limitations on abstractness, for one works with recognizable objects associated with the natural world. Yet, by seeing each item of plant material as a design symbol, the flower arranger abstracts a quality from it. For instance a thin, curving branch becomes a piece of delicate calligraphy; a heavier piece of driftwood suggests strength, a flower, delicacy; an allium head has a spherical shape; a chrysanthemum is rounded with a distinctive texture; a reedmace presents a strong vertical line. The arranger sees the abstract qualities rather than the familiar role of the plant in nature.

Design characteristics – abstract

Since the intrinsic quality of an abstract design is the non-natural, placements are unconventional. Plants can be put anywhere, placed where they most benefit the pattern required. The item of greatest visual weight is not necessarily at the heart of the design – it is often high in the arrangement. A non-realistic effect is also quite often created with items that appear suspended in space without too obvious a means of support.

Plant material is handled unconventionally too, its natural appearance often being altered to suit the particular concept. Painting, bleaching and other techniques can dramatize the special qualities, making them more noticeable. Plants of an insignificant nature often look more interesting in an altered form, becoming as they do less 'natural'. With abstract techniques, it is the essence, or significant character of plants, rather than the mere surface prettiness, that is featured. The line and shape of certain items are also seen in an altered form, bent, twisted or manipulated into exciting patterns quite unlike their original growing appearance. Greater colour and texture emphasis are achieved with flowers grouped closely together. In this way they lose their identity as growing plants, and become merely colour and texture emphasis points.

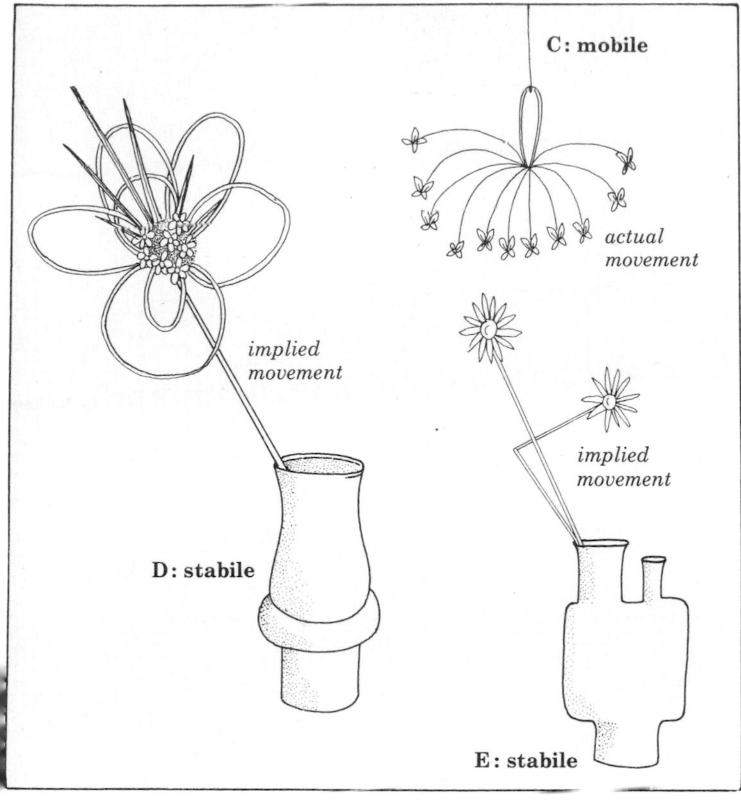

Right: an abstract composition which is merely an interesting pattern made with palm fronds (trimmed), incorporated into a metal structure

Below: a black and white collage emphasizing form and texture. The heavier strips are skeletonized ponga bark strips (from New Zealand), and sea-fern

These techniques are for the purpose of emphasis on interpretation – the greater the move away from natural presentation, the more abstract the design.

Mobile, stabile and other extensions

The methods of construction for these innovations differ somewhat from general flower arranging. In a **mobile**, for instance, there is actual, physical movement, as opposed to implied rhythm within an arrangement. The charm of a mobile is the ever-changing pattern created by the motion of its various parts. It should have a quality of lightness and buoyancy; a mobile is more than just a 'hanging' arrangement. It hangs in space, but is at its most effective and 'mobile' when each unit revolves in continuous motion, without touching or getting entangled.

Plant material should promote the qualities mentioned. Small, delicate objects are buoyant, and visually light; the idea is to give an impression of the parts floating in space. The designer has to work for both physical and visual balance – very thin, transparent material, like a fishing line, is strong and almost invisible, so is suitable for suspending each item. Where the aim is to create an *illusion* of movement, as in a **stabile**, the line of the design should have a soaring quality and the structure not appear too firmly held to the ground. If a container is used, space left between material and point of anchorage will strengthen the illusion. The illusion of movement is of course present to a certain degree in design generally, but the quality is more pronounced, and more deliberately cultivated, in constructions like the stabile. (See figs B, C, D, E above.)

In a **collage**, the design is made on a flat surface, but a three-dimensional effect is possible with proper organization of the elements used. Objects are generally glued to the background to make an attractive pattern of form, colour and texture. The result can provide a more lasting record of an arranger's efforts than more conventional flower arrangements.

Classes for these sort of constructions are being included more and more in flower shows. They extend the range of interest and presentation of the exhibition, and though not as widely practised as other forms of arranging, they afford a good exercise in designing. For, even if the assembling technique differs, the basic laws of design apply in the same way. It is essential to have balance and rhythm for a pleasing construction, the contrast of advancing and receding colour and texture, variety of form and all the other requirements that make up a good composition. Briefly then, the modern designer aims for:

1. Clarity of line
2. Positive use of space
3. Strong contrasts
4. Interesting balance
5. Originality of execution
6. Overall harmony and unity

with, additionally, in abstract, a conscious aim for:

(a) A non-naturalistic design
(b) A simplified statement

Selection of material

Once acquainted with the basic aims, the arranger can select items to suit these. A sensible choice at the start saves discouragement even if the original idea needs to be modified as the design evolves. Items involved are plant material, container, accessories, background, and anything relevant to the design and particular effect required.

Containers

These can enhance the beauty of any type of arrangement. In a modern design where, generally, there is but little plant material, the quality of the container used is even more noticeable. It must therefore be wholly compatible with the nature of the arrangement and harmonize with the plant material in every feasible way. Vase and plants should work together for the benefit of the design – the line, form, colour or texture of the one promoting the effectiveness of the other. Since the emphasis is strongly on design and the aim is to be unconventional, the vase should not of course be too traditional in character. Certain modern pots lend the right sort of feeling, and can provide the initial inspiration for a design as well as guide the line and layout of the arrangement. There are now many pleasing modern containers of pottery, glass, metal, etc., available. Quite humble ordinary objects can also function as attractive vases and add a touch of originality. Containers with more than one opening offer scope for original patterns, an unconventional effect, or an extra dimension. Vases of a particularly *avant-garde* design are perhaps a little restrictive, and can be difficult to use, but at the same time they can be a challenge to the imaginative.

As well as making an aesthetic contribution, the vase should meet the practical demands of a design. Mechanics can be a problem in modern work, where there is a

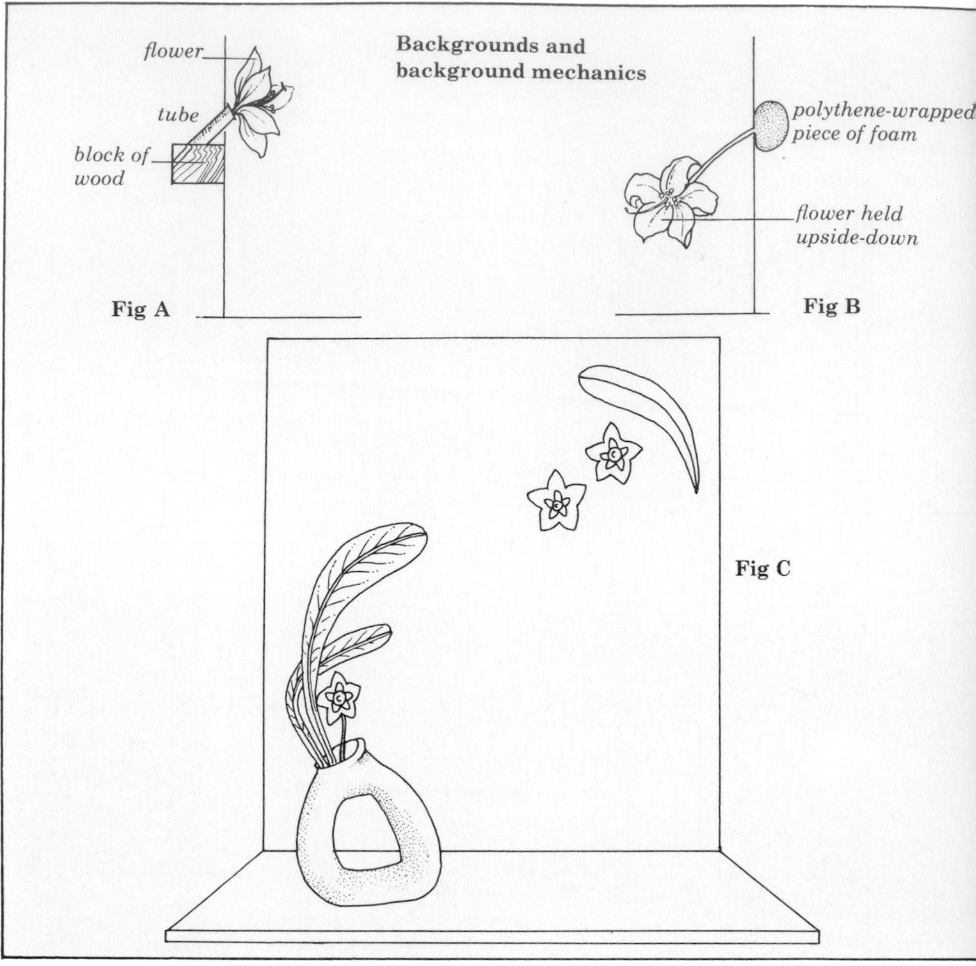

Below: wood, weathered to a rusty hue, is arranged on two levels with the aid of a vase harmonious to its character

need to keep everything immaculate. The less obvious the holding devices the better. Therefore containers where these devices are hidden from sight are the answer. Space can then be left above the rim of the case instead of camouflaging material; when flat dishes needing a pinholder are used, the covering leaves, bark, stone, and so forth, should look part of the arrangement. Mechanics of this nature are not totally suited to an abstract design, as such natural items would create too realistic an effect. Sometimes the use of two containers is a satisfactory solution, where the mechanics, placed in one, can be subtly hidden by the other. This can also add extra depth and rhythm: two flat containers, stacked on top of each other, with one left empty or with water, can create a feeling of space and tranquillity.

Bases, underneath a vase, which give balance and stability to a mass arrangement, are not always appropriate in modern design. This does not mean a base is *never* necessary, and there are numerous instances where it can enhance the line or rhythm of the design through continuity. But the space areas of the vase affording visual weight in ratio to the plant material more often than not supply the necessary balance. An oversized base can spoil the force of the dominant line of the design. For instance, a strong, ascending movement can be reduced with a horizontal line

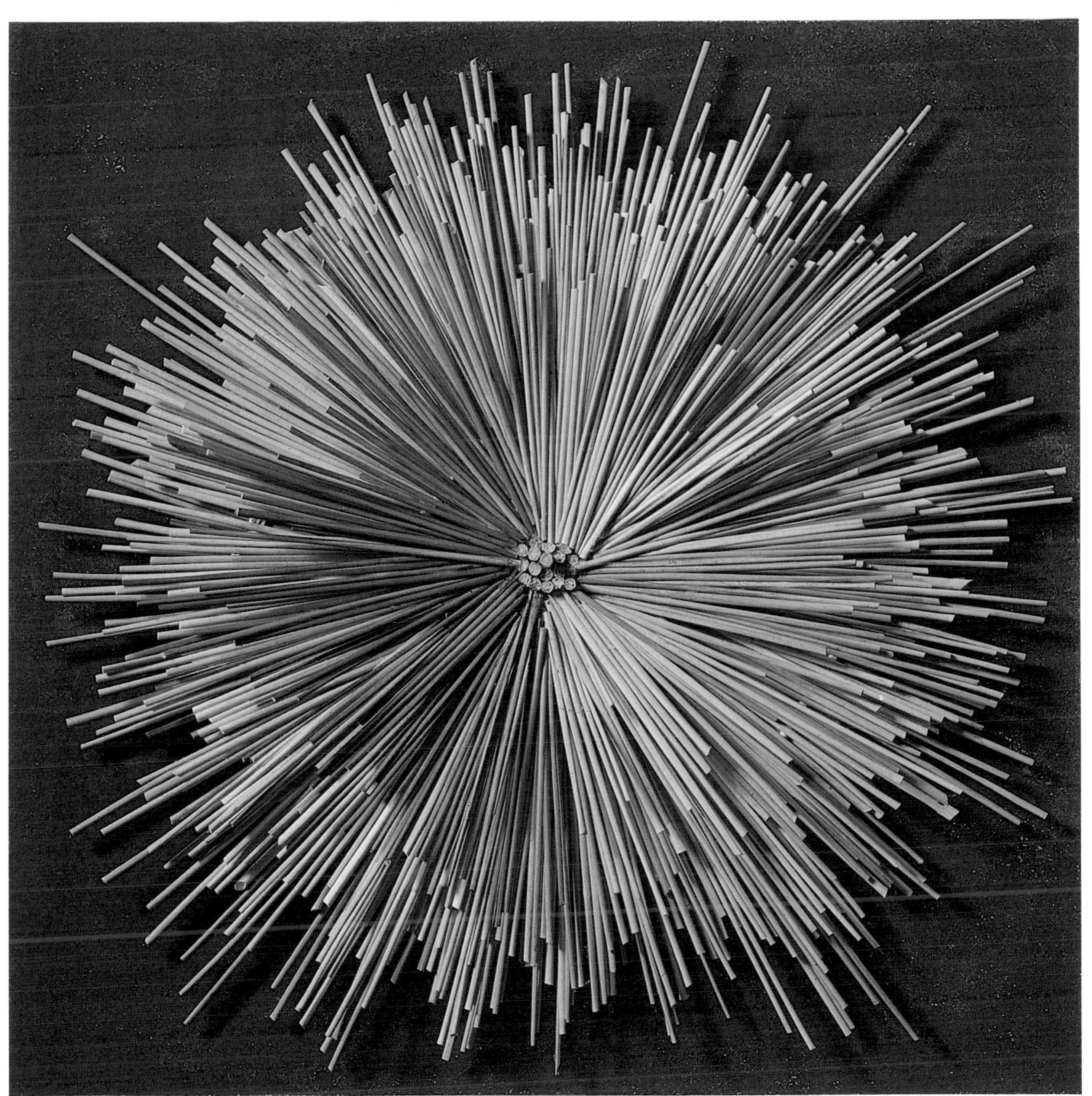

Above: a 'sunburst' of dried and preserved reeds

supplied by a base. In Fig. A the eye movement upward is uninterrupted, the arrangement having a strong vertical thrust. In Fig. B the horizontal line of the base brings the eye down, where it is held by the opposing movement. If a base is necessary it should (1) add to the design effect, and (2) be in character with the arrangement. A traditional type base detracts from the modern effect. (See figs A, B below.)

The designer today often makes use of a free-standing background to promote a scheme or idea, and to add an extra dimension to the design. The background can be in strong contrast, or blend with the main elements of the arrangement. A textured background can introduce extra light-and-shade effects. Again, an aspect or item in the design can be repeated in the background, to increase its three-dimensional aspect and unite background with arrangement. In abstract work, backgrounds can provide the means for unusual placements to promote an unrealistic presentation. A fresh flower, for example, can be placed in the background by pushing the holding device unobtrusively through a small hole behind the stem. A small tube with water or a tiny block of wet foam wrapped in polythene will keep the flower fresh. Some kind of support, like a small block of wood for the tube to rest on, allows a more flexible positioning of the flower. (See figs A, B, C on page 210.)

Many other novel ideas for abstract and modern work can become effective through the aid of a background, more especially when it becomes an integrated part of the overall design. When a scene or impression is painted on the background, care is necessary to avoid the background becoming too dominant. We see many beautifully executed backgrounds at shows and exhibitions that are far too powerful for the subject in front of them, so that the eye is magnetized by the painting rather than the arrangement. Often the merest suggestion of landscape, sea or sky, with subtle blendings of colour and texture, is enough. It is so easy to get carried away and overdo the background effect.

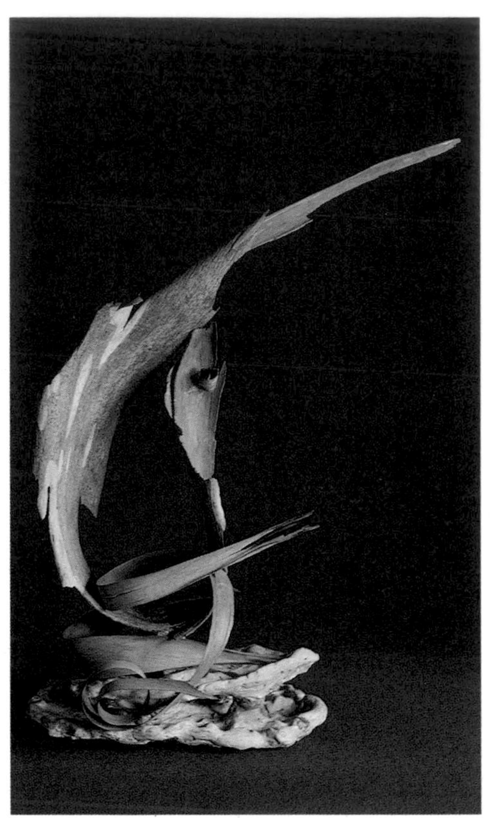

Above: strips of eucalyptus bark integrated with a home-made container for an interesting structure

Plant material

This is the basic ingredient in any type of flower arrangement, and though many modern designs are flowerless, they are generally not plantless, with all types of flora in all stages of development being used. Modern design gives the arranger ample opportunity to collect and use all the strange and wonderful trivia he or she fancies, their qualities being seen with a new eye, so that many specimens once destined for the bonfire gain a new status. Twisted and misshapen stems or seedheads may be abhorrent to the keen horticulturist, but to a design-conscious flower arranger they have a strange allure. For it is plants with good design potential that the modern arranger seeks. Broadly speak-

Below: Rings of clear perspex on a glass base gain an added sparkle with *Lilium rubrum*

Opposite: an abstract construction emphasizing the dramatic use of space with beech nuts and cane incorporated into a background

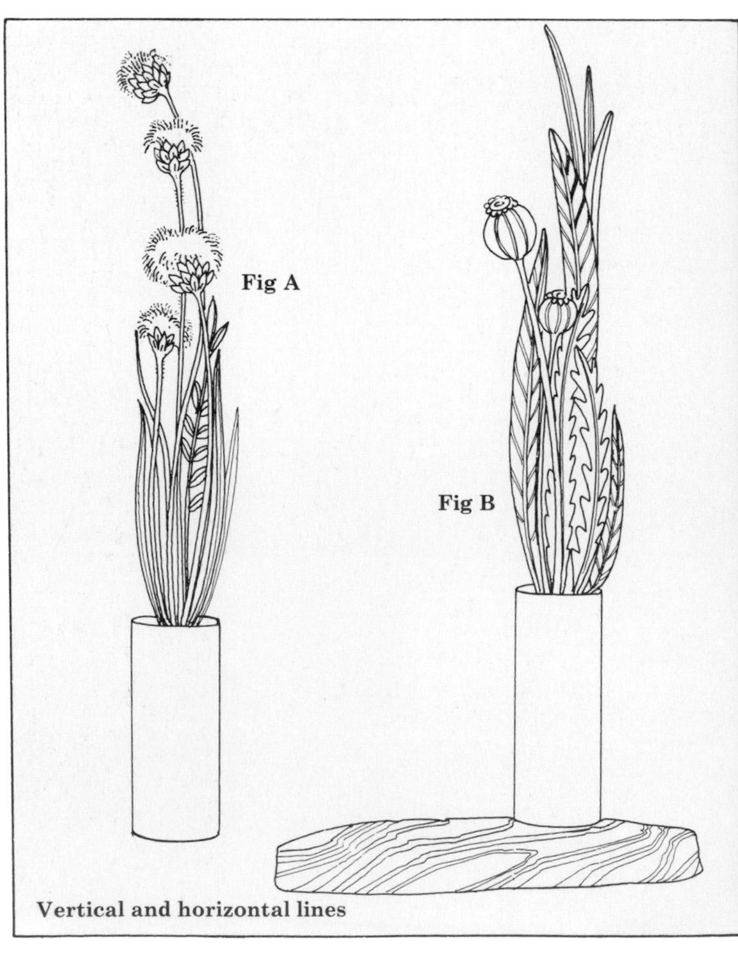

Vertical and horizontal lines

ing, they are items with a strong, clear line or shape, rather than those of a weak, fussy or indeterminate form. Colour and texture selection will be motivated by similar design needs.

There are many suitable types of plant material to choose from, and in addition the imaginative designer can adapt whatever is available to suit a particular scheme. Plants with a good line and form are leaves like *Phormium tenax* of several varieties, yucca, iris spears, dracaena, cordyline, reedmace, and flowers like kniphofia, delphinium, foxglove, gladioli and verbascum, to name a few. These pointed forms are excellent for tall designs with a forceful line. Other flowers with bold, interesting forms are: allium, oriental poppy, cardoon, achillea, echinops, centaurea and agapanthus. Lilies of all kinds (and there are many lovely varieties) are wonderful for modern work, with their purity of line and sculptural structure.

Exotic blooms like anthurium, strelitzia and heliconia seem tailor-made for dramatic effects. They have an arresting line, form and colour, and the anthurium a very distinctive texture. Gerbera too are bold and colourful. Flowers like roses, carnations and spray chrysanthemums, which lack the impact of larger, bolder blooms, can be grouped solidly together to form a concentrated array of colour and texture; while spectacular leaves like those of monstera, palm and aspidistra can be used on their own for their highly sculptural look. *Fatsia, Hosta, Bergenia* and arum leaves are also bold and attractive. Pliable leaves like reeds, and various iris spears, dracaena, willow, etc., are very useful for making patterns in abstract design.

Dried and preserved plant material has certain obvious advantages for the less conventional construction. It need not be in water, and so can be placed in all sorts of positions not possible with fresh flowers and leaves. Its natural appearance can also be easily altered with painting or bleaching to extend the design and interpretative possibilities. It is less fragile than fresh plants and lasts indefinitely, so more time can be taken in experimenting, perfecting and refining the design. The sculptural beauty of dried leaves and seedheads is another facet to commend their use. The altered textures are also interesting, often dramatic, which more than compensates for the absence of strong colour. The idea of shape and form being inherently satisfying is one which can be profitably fostered and followed.

Driftwood, which includes roots, bark and dried branches of all types, is ideal for a bold framework or powerful line. Weathered wood has a wonderful texture which, when combined with an interesting form, can stand alone as a superb piece of natural sculpture, quite unequalled by any man-made effort. Natural wood has a

Above, left: tall stems of dried *verbascum* seedheads and two sun-bleached sunflower husks

Above, right: driftwood makes a sculptural framework for one cardoon plant and onopordum leaves

most satisfying visual quality. It can also serve as a practical solution in abstract work, for unusual and daring placements can be fixed in its structure.

Suggestions for the designing procedure

1. Aim from the start for a good framework based on general art principles, remembering that line and clarity are of prime importance in a modern design.

2. Choose material, container and any additional props that are most likely to promote the idea or pattern envisaged; but be prepared to chop and change a little if necessary as the design evolves.

3. Concentrate on the characteristics of the material, the best guide to the pattern that will most readily emerge. Doing this will also prevent preconceived ideas taking over. Let the material 'speak' to you.

4. Having developed the 'feeling' for the design, stick to the concept of 'modern', without reverting to traditional methods; especially in organizing the space pattern of the design.

5. Avoid monotony in the space areas. Balance a large void with two or more smaller areas to avoid an uninspired, static look. Make your space shapes as beautiful as the plant material.

6. Keep an eye all the time on the way the balance of the design is progressing, making this as interesting as possible. Here and there put something deliberately out of balance, then adjust it with another placement. This is a stimulating way of working which keeps the eye and mind alert, and away from repetitive methods.

7. Experiment with a background to see whether it can add interest and atmosphere, or help the design in any way. It might compensate for what is lacking by bringing the right contrast or added depth. But be discriminating and do not let the background detract from the arrangement in any way.

8. Assess the finished arrangement for overall unity and visual harmony. Readjust balance where necessary. Carefully examine the colour and texture distribution. Check that there is sufficient contrast. Is the design rhythmical, does it 'live'?

9. Eliminate anything which reduces design impact. Be ruthless. If something has been added because it is irresistibly attractive rather than for its design contribution, take it out. Stick to simplicity

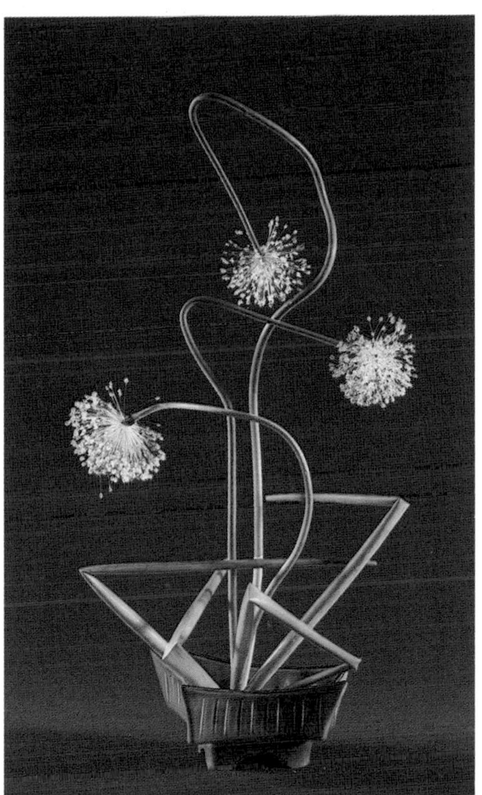

Left: the bold forms of strelitzia flowers and monstera leaves give great impact
Above: a pottery container which lends aesthetically to the design of twisted allium seedheads

of purpose; overstatement is less powerful and confuses the issue.

10. In an abstract design, remember it is a non-naturalistic effect you are striving for. But this means more than just putting plants in exaggerated positions, the techniques being for a *purpose*. In a non-objective abstract, try for attractive patterns that are sympathetic to the line of the material. Eliminate all unnecessary detail in order to leave a simplified form. In an expressive abstract, use plant material in a symbolic way to express your feelings. Do not be too literal and remove anything too realistic in the way of props and accessories. Paint, dye or reshape plants only when it increases the interpretation or adds to the design quality. Use containers where the holding devices are hidden or unobtrusive, and remember all the time that you are aiming for balance and beauty in the finished design.

11. Let your work evolve in a way that suits your particular talent. The design should reflect the way you see things, and the freedom of modern arranging gives ample opportunity to do just this. Experiment with as many design techniques as possible, and try to be more than just a competent designer – work from the heart as well, so that your arrangements have that little bit of magic which transforms the prosaic into the poetic.

16. Exhibition and Show Work

Mary Napper

Good order is the foundation of all good things
EDMUND BURKE 1729–1797

'The Romans Came'. An example of a competitive exhibit which is immaculately staged and is a perfect interpretation of the class title. The figurine and ship's prow are well incorporated in the design. Blue-green sedums and brown cones blend with the muted colours at the base; the red roses and the gold ficus and other leaves near the figure give a satisfying richness of colour in such a bold design

Shows and exhibitions are an important part of the flower arranger's way of life. The competitor in club and area shows is taking the first step on the road to competing at national level; new members will be attracted to their local flower club by publicity for the show, which will also raise money for club, area and other worthwhile charities, and above all generate a wonderful feeling of fellowship and friendship for those who are involved.

The show hall

Whether you are staging a small club show in a village hall or a large National Festival or state garden show you must start by making a plan of the hall on graph paper. Make the outline as large as possible. Measure the hall accurately. The plan must show doors, fire exits, windows, radiators, pillars, fixtures, recesses, position of overhead lights and electrical points for additional lighting. At the same time, mark in any extra space in corridors or lobbies which could be used for a publications table, sales counter or raffle. Check the length of available tabling, and whether they have laminated tops (which will not take drawing pins) or are wooden. Find out whether they are all the same size, especially in width and height so that any necessary adjustments can be made. Check water points, cloakrooms and refreshment facilities. To determine the position of the tables, cut out to scale in card or graph paper the length of tabling and other staging required and juggle the cards about on the plan of the hall to achieve a satisfactory layout which allows gangways of at least 1.8 m (6 ft) for the general public to walk around the show in comfort.

There are some important 'dont's' to be observed at the advance planning stage. (a) Avoid positioning any classes with their backgrounds against windows, as this reduces light. If the hall relies on artificial light, ascertain the type of lighting as some types of fluorescent tubes affect colours. (b) Do not place classes in front of radiators or tabling over underfloor heating grids if you are staging a winter show, when the heating is likely to be on. This would be a suitable spot for the dried/glycerined class, publications desk or sales table. (c) None of the classes should be situated just inside the entrance to the hall in such a way that it cuts off the visitor's view of the exhibition as a whole. As they walk in, people should see a complete view which gives the most impact. Because of this, open staging or low bases are best in the centre. An alternative would be to place an exhibition piece as a central focal point. (d) Do not place a competitive class on a stage that only has one set of steps; it is better to have an exhibition which can be viewed from the floor, otherwise there will be a bottleneck as people go up and down the same steps to read the comment cards or take a closer look. If you need the stage for prize-giving, but would like an exhibition staged

A typical hall available for smaller club exhibitions showing trestle tables and conduit pipe backing in preparation

as well, have ready in the wings an easily moveable covered table with the cups and trophies laid out upon it. The table can be moved into position just before the presentation of prizes, and taken away directly the prize-giving is over.

Decide on various types of staging the show will embrace: open; backed with straight fabric backing; niches; in single rows or back-to-back; low bases for club classes or exhibition arrangements; round tables for petites or miniatures; and space for pedestals. If you are planning for a small club and members are reluctant to enter you must be prepared to be flexible with your plan. Encourage your members to enter by accepting their entries even if it does mean rearranging the position of classes; this can be managed if the height and width in several classes are the same. Perhaps some classes will be better supported than expected and others less, so be prepared to lengthen or shorten the tabling without spoiling the overall plan. This is rarely the case at most area and National Festivals, where each class is oversubscribed and has a waiting list. Do not, however, be tempted to include an extra class or too many extra entries, if by so doing the public would be crowded; it is far better to have one less class with ample space for viewing. Visualize the hall at the busiest time to decide whether you have allowed sufficient space between staging. This is of great importance, so if in doubt work out a one-way viewing route, especially for larger area and National Shows. Perhaps your show will be smaller and more intimate, where it does not matter if neighbours stop for a chat in the middle of viewing. They have come to see the show, meet their friends, have a cup of tea and buy their cakes from the home-produce stall. This is what flower arranging clubs are all about – friendship through flowers, and to this end all sizes of shows are appropriate, from the smallest with 30 to 40 entries to national exhibitions with 300 to 400. But large or small, they must be carefully planned and immaculately staged.

Tables

If you are using wooden tables, wooden battens for uprights may be nailed to them, one at each end and one in the centre. A 1.8 m (6 ft) table needs three uprights. Fix another batten along the top from which to hang backing material. A second row of tables may be placed the other side and material hung over the top to cover both sides, the upright extending from the floor to the required height of staging. If the show is taking place in a marquee, wood battens are the best method to employ. The ground is not always sufficiently level to use the following alternative idea which is less time-consuming on staging day, most of the preliminary preparation having been done beforehand. Many modern halls have tables with laminated surfaces, which means that the uprights must be free-standing. For this situation use electric conduit, not wood. This can be obtained from your local electrical suppliers in 3 m (10 ft) lengths. The uprights are made by setting a 1.8 m (6 ft) length of conduit into a 20 cm (8 in.) deep tin filled with cement, the bar for the top being joined by means of T-junctions with elbows at either end (see diagram I). The tins at each end of the tabling should either be painted, or covered with the same material as the table skirting.

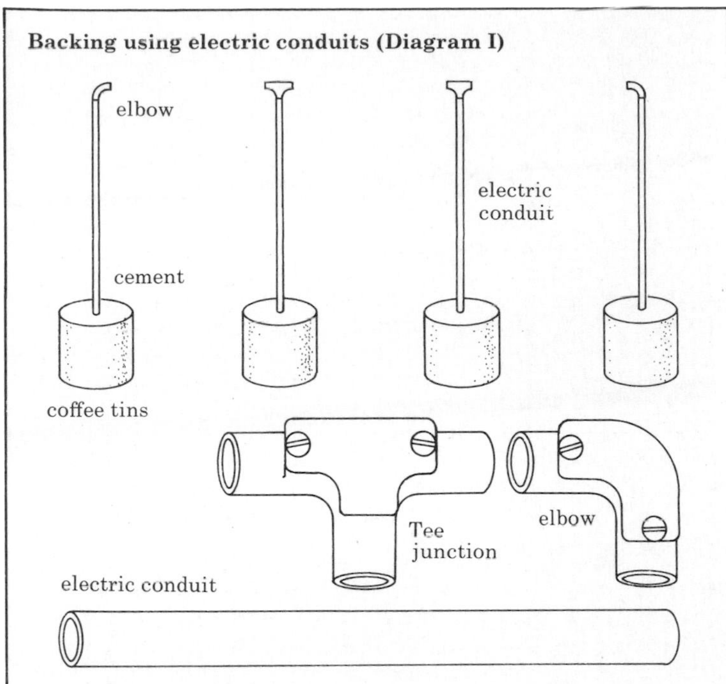

If tabling is in short supply a long run can be improvised by mounting planks on plastic bottle crates

If you are using low bases for staging club or individual exhibition arrangements and need something which will take up the minimum of storage room between shows, the following method is suggested. For a 1 m (3 ft) diameter circular base have two pieces of 13 mm ($\frac{1}{2}$ in.) chipboard cut measuring 60 cm (2 ft) by the desired height of base, say 20 cm (8 in.). In the centre of each of these cut a slit 10 cm (4 in.) long by 1.5 cm ($\frac{5}{8}$ in.). Slot one into the other and place the 1 m (3 ft) circle of chipboard on top (see diagram II).

The fabric which is to be used for covering the tables must be immaculately clean and without a crease. To press the fabric successfully you will of course need iron(s), blankets to work on, extension leads and, not least, willing workers. Anything less than a first-class finish is demoralizing for competitors, bad for photography (as creases are accentuated in photographs), an eyesore to the public, and disaster to the overall look of the show.

Whatever the staging, and whatever the material used, no thumbtacks, tacks, staples or adhesive should show. If you are buying new material, order it well before the show as orders can take up to eight weeks to arrive. In Britain material may be available after a National Festival at a slightly reduced price. Before purchasing fabric, give some thought to its maintenance. If your club is likely to use the material annually, easy laundering is essential, especially for table-top covering which can easily become stained by spilt water. Spun rayon or polyester/cotton sheeting is worth considering. All fabric should be stored on cardboard rolls and covered with plastic.

Skirting Suitable materials for skirting are: spun rayon, sheeting, hessian, felt, window or display drape. When using wooden tables, fix the cut edge to the table top with thumbtacks; staples may also be used but are more difficult to extract when dismantling. If the tops are laminated, use adhesive cellophane tape all the way along. If the tables are against a wall, start 30 cm (1 ft) in at the back, pulling the fabric taut round the sides and front. With a double row of tabling, start the material at the side where the tables join, allowing 30 cm (1 ft) overlap at the end, which may be neatened with double-sided adhesive tape. Should you be staging in a marquee, try to avoid the material touching the grass, because, whatever the time of year the air is very damp at night and the material will draw moisture from the ground.

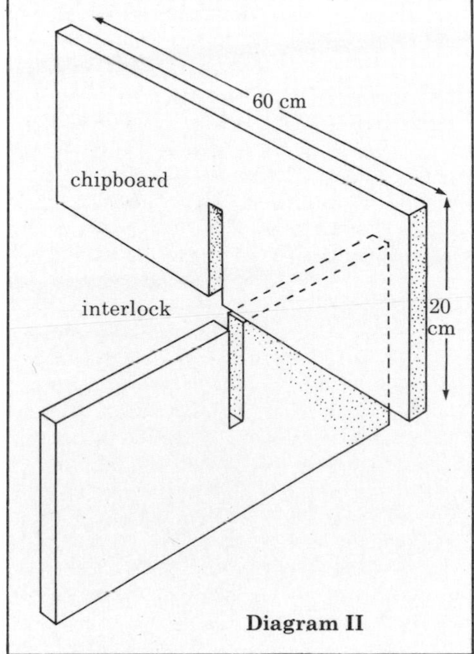

Diagram II

Background Suitable materials are: sparva spun rayon, casement, window or display drape and polyester/cotton sheeting. This last one is particularly suitable if the backing is to serve two classes back-to-back, as it is 2.3 m (90 in.) wide and if hung with the centre of the width at the top, would allow for a class height of 1 m (39 in.), plus 15 cm (6 in.) to hang below the table or be taped to the table top either side, and then cut to the required length of the class. It should be pulled taut and the edges at the ends turned in and stuck with double-sided adhesive. Thin casement or muslin should be slightly gathered. If employing this method, take care which classes are staged against a gathered background: some arrangements need a more tailored look. Material backgrounds should be put on before covering the tops of tables. Cardboard niches, if used as an alternative, should be put up after the top is covered.

Table tops Suitable materials are: spun rayon, window or display drape, casement and sheeting. This may be laid on the top coming just to the front edge. No frayed edges should be visible. If the material is non-fraying, it may overlap the edge by about 18 cm (7 in.) and the edge be scalloped. In the event of lack of funds, tops may be covered with unprinted newspaper obtainable from the offices of your local paper, which it is to be hoped will be sending a reporter and photographer to your show. After covering the tables and perhaps putting a layer of thin plastic sheeting over the top to prevent marks from spilt

The legs of the trestle tables are now concealed by fabric but preparations are still in progress

water, the space allowed for competitors should be marked with cord or ribbon, ensuring that the measurement is the same at the back as at the front. A 1 m (3 ft) length of dowel with 60 cm (2 ft) and 75 cm (2 ft 6 in.) also marked on it is easier to use than a tape measure.

Round tables Affix the skirting by the method explained above, taking care not to pull the material too tight, otherwise it 'bellies in' at the top. Neaten the join with double-sided clear adhesive tape. If using non-fraying material for the top, cut it 30 cm (1 ft) wider than the table giving a 15 cm (6 in.) pelmet which may be scalloped. For this cut a template of strong cardboard 12.5 cm (5 in.) wide by 6.25 cm ($2\frac{1}{2}$ in.) deep; this will give 30 scallops on a 1.2 m (4 ft) cloth to cover a 1 m (3 ft) table (see diagram III). If using material which frays such as rayon or sheeting, turn up a narrow hem and neaten with either braid or fringe. Another alternative is casement or muslin draped and caught up with ribbon bows.

Low bases Suitable materials are: hessian, felt, window or display drape. Cover the tops first in exactly the same manner as you cover cake-board bases to stand under the containers. Pull the material taut and fix underneath with staples or fabric adhesive. The material used for the sides needs backing with a medium weight cardboard obtainable in a roll from any good art shop. This should be cut 12.5 mm ($\frac{1}{2}$ in.) narrower than the depth of the base and covered with material, allowing a 2.5 cm (1 in.) hem top and bottom to be turned over and glued to the cardboard. This is then attached to the top with double-sided adhesive tape. For safety put in a tack where the edges meet.

Fixtures

Niches If niches are used as an alternative to fabric backgrounds, they should be spotless: a coat of plain emulsion works wonders in cleaning up any which may have become grubby in storage. These may be fastened together with the kind of plastic stripping used to hang wall-posters, which comes complete with a feed-in device for easy insertion. It is cheaper, however, to use tiny dog-clips painted the same colour as the niches. One near the top and one at the bottom will hardly show, and will look much neater and less conspicuous than paper clips. If using niches back-to-back, ensure they are the same height. There is something to be said against using niches in a marquee, as they tend to absorb moisture from the atmosphere and become flimsy; on a windy day they may be blown over.

Miniatures or petites Individual frames for miniature arrangements are very simple to make (see diagram IV). For a petite size you will need a sheet of stiff card 40.5 × 33 cm (16 × 13 in.). Cut out of it an aperture 30 × 22.5 cm (12 × 9 in.) leaving a 5 cm (2 in.) edge all round. Cover the card with adhesive backed hessian or felt or similar material. For the backing you need a length of corrugated paper 40.5 × 39 cm (16 × $15\frac{1}{2}$ in.) with the ribs running parallel to the shorter edge. This may be painted with emulsion or covered with wood grain wallpaper. Attach the corrugated paper to the back of the frame at the sides of the aperture, using either adhesive tape or liquid glue. The ribs should run vertically, level with the top edge of the frame and 12.5 mm ($\frac{1}{2}$ in.) from the bottom. Cut for the base a semi-circle of very stiff card (use two stuck together if one is not thick enough) 22.5 cm (9 in.) across the front and to a depth of 12.5 cm (5 in.), which, to give support and to raise it slightly may be stuck to a shallow tin of suitable diameter. Push the base into the bottom of the frame, thus pushing out the back to give a taut semi-circle. The front of the frame may be trimmed with braid. These frames may be ranged along the front of a stage, or round a circular table; nine will fit round the top of a 1 m (3 ft) table, and twelve round a 1.2 m (4 ft) one. With the base removed, the frames will store flat.

Cards Cards bearing class titles should be clearly visible above the top of the backgrounds and attractively handwritten or printed. They may be attached to the wall with adhesive or to a dowel rod set in cement in a painted plastic flower pot.

Competitors' entry cards are best placed alphabetically to avoid disagreements over sequence. Just before judging commences the stewards should check to ensure the cards are turned name downwards. They should be consistently placed in the niches or spaces – all in the same corner or all central, *not* some in the middle, some in one corner and some in another. If possible, work tables should be provided in the aisles enabling the competitors to have a little more working space, to work away from their niche, at the same time helping to keep the material in the niche clean. Have the work tables removed before judging commences.

Decide whether you will need ropes to indicate a viewing route, or to rope off the 'best-in-show' or the centre-piece. Wrought iron stands and chains are ideal for this purpose but expensive. A substitute can be made using 75 cm (2 ft 6 in.) dowel rods painted and set into cement in painted plastic flower pots; attach cup hooks near

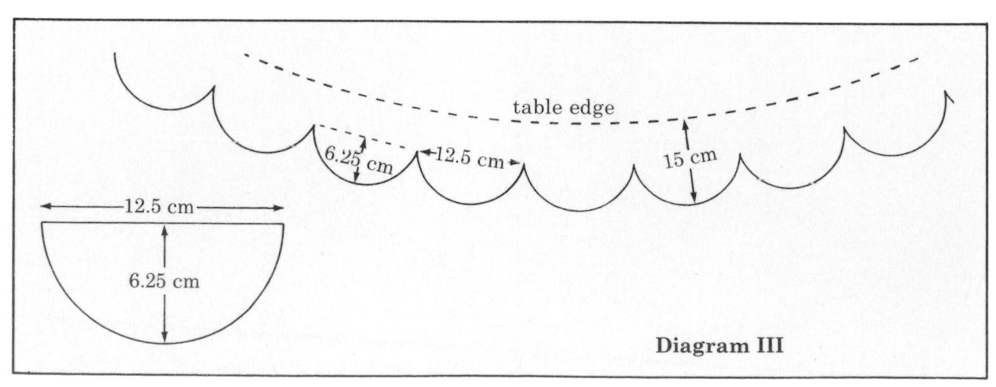

Diagram III

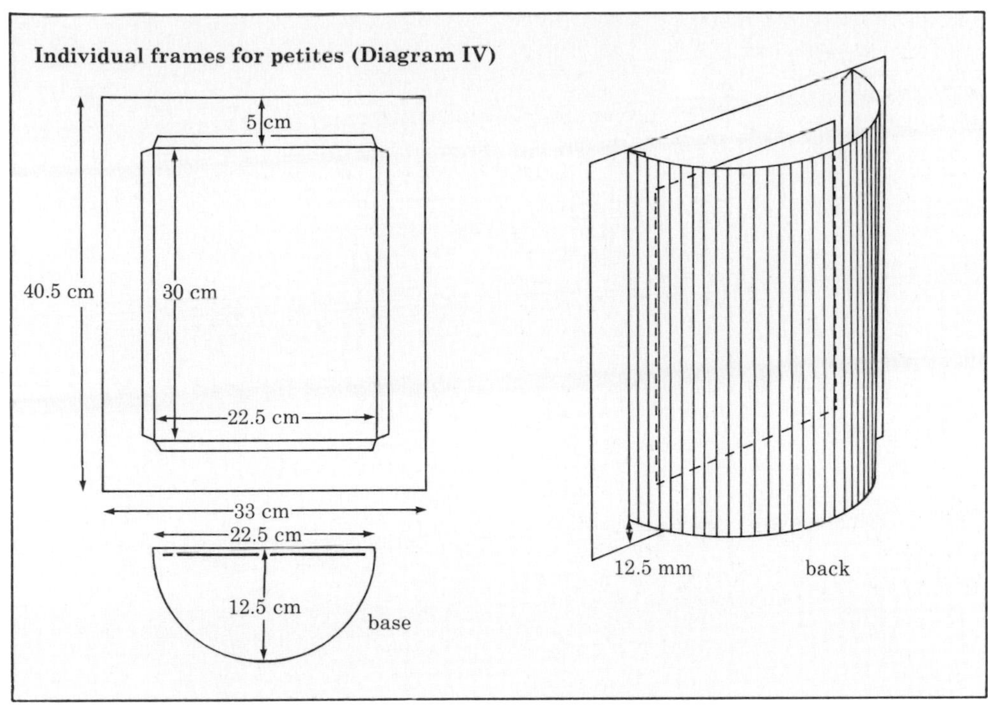

the top of the rods and join them with plastic chain link, obtainable by the metre from any good garden centre.

The schedule

Since the schedule sets the standard for the show, it must be carefully planned by a small sub-committee made up of the Competition Secretary, Staging Chairman and one or two experienced competitors, who all have a complete understanding of the relevant NAFAS or NCSGC handbooks. The committee should choose an inspiring title, bearing in mind that all the class titles must link with the overall theme, and one that is different from any used in the past. The wording of the classes should fulfil three demands: it should be clear, leaving no doubt in the minds of either the competitors or judges exactly what is required; concise, expressing what is called for in as few words as possible. The more open the classes are left, the more variety will be produced and the creative ability of the competitors seen to the full; and its presentation should be consistent, specifying plant material (if this needs to be named), dimensions, conditions of eligibility of entry, and whether or not accessories are allowed. Always state if painted plant material is forbidden. If your schedule is for a Christmas show, state clearly which classes may have artificial plant material.

The class titles should not be restrictive, Aim for themes which will require the Advanced members to do a little research, give the Intermediate members a variety of choice, and create confidence for the Novices. There should be a variety of type of classes bearing in mind the season of the year, space available for staging, the standard of the exhibitors, and last but certainly not least the overall appearance of the show. To visualize the overall appearance a simple analysis of your classes should be undertaken. List your classes and by the side indicate the type of exhibit in each, noting whether plant material and accessories are allowed, and the possible colouring. In this way you can easily ascertain whether or not you have been too restrictive in each category. Remember that accessories may always be used (unless otherwise stated) when the word 'exhibit' is used. Consider whether too many classes are likely to be staged on flat bases.

The following classes might be included in a typical schedule:

Period	Landscape
Traditional	Pedestal
Abstract	Miniature or Petite
Contemporary	Dinner or Buffet Table
Pot-et-fleur	Swags, plaques, collage or flower pictures.

Avoid colour classes and classes stating number of flowers.

Picture your schedule staged as the judges see it when they walk into the hall: does it have impact, colour, variety of designs and staging? If you think it has all of these, present it to the main committee for comment, preferably well before a committee meeting so each member has had time to consider it. Then, when any amendments have been made, the schedule should be sent to the judges for approval *before* it is printed. The cover of the schedule should be eye-catching and in an attractive colour. Perhaps there is an artist in your club, who will design your own unique cover, or you may be able to buy attractive ready-made folders into which the schedule can be stapled.

On the front cover the following information must appear: the title, date, times of opening, venue and price of admission. On the back cover give details of available refreshments, parking facilities, attractions such as a demonstration or exhibition, plant stall, raffle or tombola, sales table, and any other features. For the competitors you will also need to include the Rules and Regulations which should be as clear and concise as possible and should include:

(a) Whether the competitions are open to all or only to members.

(b) Closing date for entries, entry fee and to whom cheques and postal orders are to be made payable.

(c) Name, address and telephone number of Competition Secretary.

(d) Cancellation procedure, stating whether fees (if any), will be refunded.

(e) Times of staging and dismantling; number of members allowed to stage an inter-club or inter-area exhibit.

(f) Height and width, if not included under class heading.

(g) Colour backgrounds and height of tables.

(h) Whether backgrounds are allowed in all classes.

(i) Whether drapes may be attached to the staging.

(j) Whether competitors' property is displayed at owner's risk.

(k) Whether all exhibits must be arranged in the hall, and if not, which classes are exempt.

(l) That all exhibits will be judged in accordance with the current NAFAS or NCSGC handbooks.

(m) Whether the judges' decision is final and if a protest procedure is to be adopted.

(n) Restrictions on photography (if any).

After the description of classes, list what awards and other prizes are to be presented, stating at what time they will be given and by whom. Give the names of the judges and state at what time judging will take place.

Include a separate entry form listing the classes and entry fee, leaving ample space for the entrant's signature, name, address and telephone number, as well as club or area (according to eligibility of entry) and repeating to whom cheque or postal order is made payable, and to whom it should be sent together with the closing date for entries.

Entering a show

The competitor's prime motive in entering an exhibit should be enjoyment rather than simply the idea of winning, and she should be prepared to accept constructive criticism. There is great value in showing: competitions are a stimulus, and an incentive to do one's best; they help the individual to acquire knowledge, gain experience, and at the same time to support her club. You will achieve a higher standard of flower arranging by complying with the show schedule and competing with others than by only having your own domestic standard to satisfy. Show exhibits are different types of arrangements from those arranged in your home, and should be tackled in a different way. Before entering a show for the first time, visit other shows, obtain their schedule and study it, see how the classes have been interpreted, and then read the judges' comment cards. Buy a copy of the NAFAS or NCSGC handbook, familiarize yourself with the contents and if there is anything you do not understand – ask. Help a friend to stage her exhibit by acting as her 'odd-job' man and then take the plunge yourself – you will never regret it.

Competing for the first time

Obtain the schedule and read carefully both the class wording and the Rules and Regulations. Decide on the class or classes for which you will enter. It is better not to try for too many at first, although two classes are better than one. This is because the beginner is likely to become too tense over a single entry and it shows in her work. Make sure that you are eligible to enter your chosen class or classes. If there is anything in the schedule you do not understand contact the Competition Secretary whose name, address and telephone number should be on the entry form.

The first stage in preparing your entry is to devote quiet time and thought to its composition. Sit and think about your class title, and either mentally or, better still, on a piece of paper, list everything which springs to mind about it. Which container could you use? What plant material do you have available without spending too much on flowers? It is not always the arrangement with the most expensive flowers that gains an award. Garden plant material gives more variation in form and colour, and if your garden cannot meet all your requirements, friends are always willing to help. Gather your plant material either early in the morning or in the evening when transpiration is lowest. Is the use of accessories permitted? If so, do you have accessories that are suitable in size, colour and texture? Do you need a base, background or drape? Have a practice run.

Never be tempted to copy from a photograph in a book, however much you admire it. Since points are awarded for originality, you would be downpointed at once. The value of exhibits in photographs is that they may show you unusual combinations of plant material, or good outline and shape, but you will win no prizes for copying them to the last detail.

The chief difference between arranging flowers at home and for a competition is that in the latter you are obliged to conform to the restrictions of the rules. When decorating your home, you have used what plant material you wanted in the container of your choice and made your arrangement as small or large as you wished, but now you must use certain plant material and conform to the size stated. For every practice run, mark out the space allowed remembering your exhibit should fill the available space but not overcrowd or appear too small. If you are staging in a niche, allow 5 cm (2 in.) either side and at the top and do not allow plant material to touch the sides. If straight backgrounds are used, never go above the top or over the dividing tape or ribbon. Plan the shape and size of flowers similar to the ones you anticipate using. If you will be using florist's flowers such as gladioli or roses, remember that you will need them in different stages of development, although they may be all at the same stage when buying them. Leave some in a very cold, frost-free place, bring some into a warm room and even stand some near the boiler or radiator.

If you plan to use a base, drape or background, ensure that they are clean and crease-free, that no frayed edges show, and that they are of the correct colour and texture. A light drape or background is suitable behind a dark-coloured arrangement, while a darker shape or background can accompany a light-coloured arrangement. The texture of bases, drapes and backgrounds is just as important as the colour. If using sophisticated flowers such as carnations, gladioli or Arum lilies then choose velvet, satin, crêpe or taffeta; for dried arrangements or ones containing berries, fruit or vegetables, then hessian, linen or tweed would be better. Bases can help to integrate the separate components of an exhibit, especially when accessories are used. Drapes or backgrounds should not be too distracting so avoid patterns, which, like painted scenes, confuse the flowers in front. Do not introduce into the arrangement any dominant feature which will immediately draw the eye to the back. Excellent free-standing backgrounds can be made by painting chipboard or the reverse side of hardboard, or covering them in hessian, cork tiles or textured wallpaper.

Accessories must be chosen and used with great discretion, producing a well-balanced and pleasing exhibit, and together with your flowers and style of arrangement should help depict the title of your class. Since they must look part of the design it is well to put them in place before the plant material, remembering that your plant material must predominate over all else. Do not be tempted to use all the accessories you have; the careful use of one or perhaps two is far more eloquent than too many. If in doubt, remove one at a time and see whether they will be missed. If they are not vital, leave them out. Make sure you are using the correct plant material: for example, berries and fruit may or may not be permitted. If you seem to be short of ideas, perhaps you need more research into the title.

It is very important to ask yourself whether the judges will understand your interpretation. Points which the judges look for are:

Interpretation: has your exhibit depicted the title? Read every word of the title and wording to ensure that it has.

Condition: use plant material that is interesting and fresh, not limp, dirty, damaged or blemished.

Design: the arrangement must be the correct size for the container. The exhibit must be in scale with the space allowed. Contrast of form and textures must be considered.

Plant material must be in scale. This is very important, especially with miniatures, petites and landscapes, and applies not only to the arrangement itself, but also to the container, plant material, base or background, accessories and title card (if any) which all contribute to the overall design.

Staging: Press drapes well. Cover bases neatly. Choose containers suitable to plant material, e.g. marigolds or dahlias would look better in pottery or wood, while more sophisticated flowers such as freesia, carnations or roses would suit silver or alabaster.

Distinction: be original without being gimmicky. Exercise restraint in the use of plant material and accessories. Aim for beautiful colouring and atmosphere.

Transport and staging

To transport your paraphernalia to the show, pack pinholders, chicken wire, scissors, watering can and spray into a basket or large strong cardboard box, together with container and accessories carefully wrapped in a newspaper or an old towel. Be sure to include the schedule, background and base (if used), and drapes carefully pressed and rolled on a cardboard tube and covered with plastic. After careful conditioning of plant material (see Chapter 2), pack it carefully, putting the foliage in plastic bags. Flowers should be packed in flower boxes lined at the bottom with plastic and covered with very damp tissue or kitchen paper before closing the lid. This may be transported in a bucket with a brick or large pinholder at the bottom to give weight and prevent falling over, filled one-third full of water. Include a small sheet of plastic to put on the floor where you are staging; this helps to confine the mess and facilitates preparing the hall for judging.

When you arrive at the hall or marquee, leave everything in your car until you have found your space or niche, and when unloading do not spread out too far as space is always limited. It is a cardinal rule that competitors never put any of their belongings in a neighbour's space. When you have finished staging your exhibit recheck the following points with your schedule: that you have only used what is allowed; your mechanics are not showing; all your plant material is in water or water-retaining material, and there are no frayed edges on the drapes. If all is well, spray, avoiding drapes. Stage your next arrangement, come back to look at the first with a fresh eye (but not to make fiddling last-minute touches) and go home, knowing that, having finally taken the plunge, you have done your best.

Staging larger exhibits

There are several occasions upon which the arranger with some experience may be invited to stage a large exhibit: for a club in the inter-club class at an area show, for an area exhibit at a National Festival or at the Royal Horticultural Society's show at Chelsea, a county show, a church festival or a large exhibition tableau. A useful background to such work may be gained by acting as steward at one of the large shows, affording an opportunity to see how the larger exhibits have been staged and studying the cards with the judges' comments. It is always a most rewarding experience to help in this manner, and invaluable if you think you might ever be involved with staging an exhibit at Chelsea or a National Festival. It gives a wonderful chance to note the pitfalls and make mental notes on how exhibits could be improved, as well as helping the show committee. Whether as a steward or spectator, visit as many large shows and festivals as you can: you will always see something fresh and learn something new.

Larger exhibits are staged by three or four members, according to the space allocated or the number stipulated in the schedule. They must all work together as a team rather than as individual arrangers, and should be selected simply for their proven ability and skill and not because 'it is such a long time since they were invited to stage an entry'. A great deal of time, effort and money is involved staging an exhibit of any great size, and the most talented members should be invited, not just for the reputation of the club or area, but also for the sake of the show committee who will probably have worked very hard with planning and organization and deserve to be rewarded with a good overall standard. The member of the team who is appointed captain must be a perfectionist, because this exhibit must be impeccably staged. She should be a gifted flower arranger with plenty of imagination and foresight, who will work hard if not harder than the rest, and above all should have a sense of humour. If possible include in the team a less experienced member who is keen to learn and willing to perform the more menial tasks while gaining invaluable experience for the future. In the early stages of planning involve the members of your club or area and keep them informed of your progress. They will all be proud that their club/area is participating in an important event and will be encouraged to visit the show or festival to see what their members have achieved.

When planning an exhibit of 3.6 m (12 ft) or more, it is advisable to plan the floor space to scale on graph paper, making sure you have allowed sufficient but not too much space, with additional sketches giving base size, height and outline of the main arrangements. Discuss this before the team meet with their containers, bases, accessories, drapes and backgrounds for the first trial-run meeting. This could take place in a garage or shed, with the width and height marked on the walls and the base space marked on the floor. If the exhibit is to be raised, then the practice stage needs to be raised to the required height. This is very important: arrangements can look quite different if raised up even knee-high. The background should be the same colour as will be used on the day. Dye some old sheets, and obtain colour samples of the possible material to be used on the floor or table top. Decide on containers and any bases (immaculately covered) needed for additional height, taking the eye nearly up to the top with your main arrangement, and staging the others at different levels, staggered at different depths. Use the space well: visualize it as a cube that has height and depth as well as width, and needs calculated space but not voids. Many exhibits are spoilt when the height is unvaried and not used to the full in a way that gives more scope for different types and a less crammed look to the exhibit. Bring in your accessories, eliminating all that are not strictly necessary.

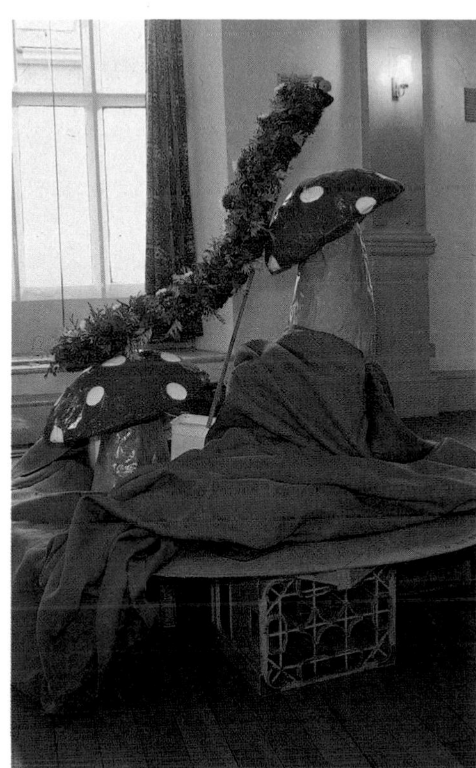

'Alice in Flowerland', a centrepiece for a small show, consists of a floral caterpillar on toadstools Bottle crates support a circular fabric-covered hardboard top

Substitute flowers and foliage of the same shape and colour may need to be used in the second trial-run as the season of the year may not make plant material available for both the trial-run and the day of exhibition. When planning plant material, remember that it is not always the most expensive and exotic flowers which gain the awards, but often simple blooms, well-chosen and artistically arranged. Have at least two, but preferably three, of these trial-runs: the first will determine the containers and colour, the style of arrangements which you thought you could use but now find are too big or too small, and what plant material is too fussy. At the second meeting substitute plant material should be used; the correct containers, beautifully covered bases and necessary accessories will be in place. Material linking one arrangement with another will be added, ensuring that the exhibit appears as a whole and not just a series of unrelated arrangements. By this time the title, beautifully printed on suitable card, should be ready. A third meeting may be necessary if the arrangement still leaves room for improvement, and to this or even to the second meeting could be invited a member of the club or area who has had experience in staging exhibits of this size and who will be seeing it with fresh eyes. At the final meeting, mark the position of all the placements on the graph paper plan: this saves a tremendous amount of time on the actual day. Driftwood which fitted like a jig-saw at the practice run never goes together in quite the same way unless marked. Make a list of everything required on the day, including exhibitors' entrance cards and car pass and correspondence regarding overnight accommodation (if any). It is surprising how much can be packed into a car with a little careful thought, especially if the front passenger seat is removed to take flower boxes.

On arrival at the site, find the space allocated to you, the water tap, your plan and your refreshments. Put plant material into water, re-cutting the stems; put the background, bases and containers into place and lay down plastic sheets on which to work. Check on the plan that all is in the correct place and stand back to take a critical look before setting to work to arrange the flowers. Leave sufficient time at the end for any final adjustments; clean the floor; make sure the title card is well-placed for easy reading, and that the drapes have no frayed edges showing. Administer a final watering and last, but most important, a spray, taking care of course not to stain the drapes or background. If the exhibit is to remain in place for two or three days it will need maintaining by you unless the schedule states otherwise. This includes watering, spraying, removing any faded flowers or foliage and giving the floor a gentle brush. The exhibit should look as fresh on dismantling day as the day it was staged, and it will if your plant material was well-conditioned, carefully handled, and, it cannot be said too often, sprayed.

17. Ikebana / the Japanese Art of Flower Arrangement

Stella Coe

. . . and cherry blossoms, and white cups,
whose wine
Was the bright dew, yet drained not
by the day . . .
PERCY BYSSHE SHELLEY 1792–1822

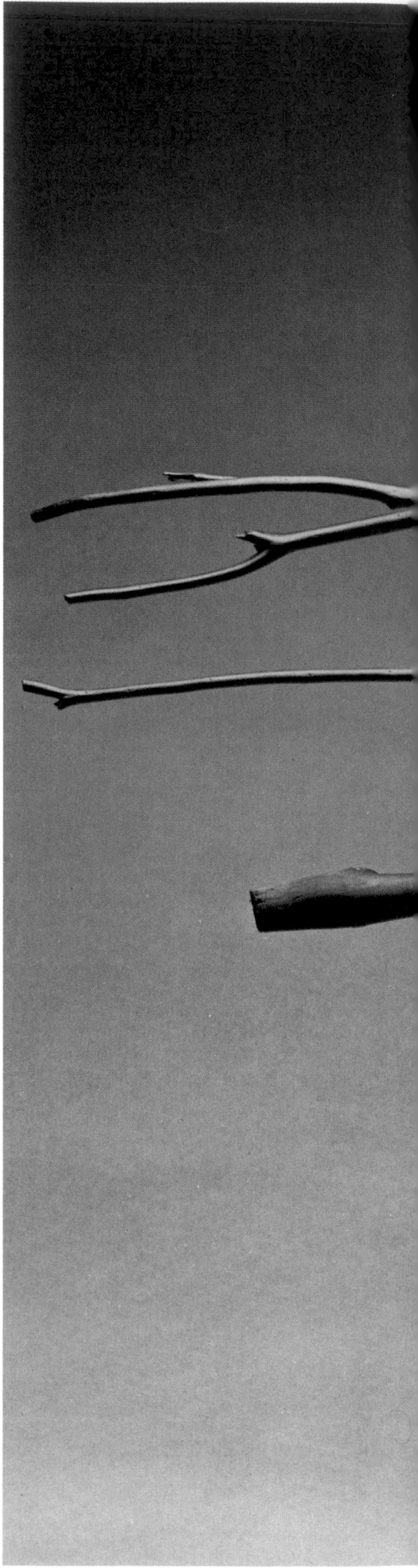

A dramatic Ikebana arrangement. To the ideals of Japanese culture, exaggeration or overstatement are inimical to beauty. Thus the maximum effect is achieved through skilful and dedicated use of sparse, carefully-chosen material

Ikebana, the Japanese art of flower arrangement, is one of Japan's most influential artistic contributions to the world. This art form dates from the sixth century when Buddhism was introduced into Japan. Originally, arrangements were done by priests for the temples. Then the noblemen became interested, and gradually the art form became available to all classes. While on the one hand the Buddhist priests cultivated the art for centuries, on the other it reflects the Japanese people's deep love and reverence for nature. This goes back to the primitive belief that spirits, or gods (*kami*) lived in mountains, streams and trees, indeed in all natural living things. Small wonder then that love and reverence for the Buddha would be shown in a floral offering.

During the sixth century Ono-no-Imoko went to China as an emissary of the Emperor and returned to Japan with examples of painting, literature, sculpture, drama and gardening. It is believed that it was his idea to place cut flowers before the Buddha image. He conceived the notion that flowers should not be placed carelessly before the Buddha but that care and thought should be given to the way they were presented. When he retired he lived in a priest's house near a pond in the grounds of the Rokkado-do, the hexagonal temple, in Kyoto. Tradition has it that the first flower arrangements were made here. His priest's name was *sen-mu*. From this time dates the Ike-no-bo (temple by the river) school of *ikebana*, and his successors have always carried 'sen' in their names.

This print showing a woman and a flower arrangement is taken from a woodblock by Utagawa Kuniyoshi (1798–1861)

Historically, all forms of Japanese art have been associated with Buddhism, and the particular forms of *ikebana, cha-no-yu* (tea ceremony) *sumi-e* (ink painting) and *haiku* (seventeen-syllable poems) with Zen Buddhism. It should be understood that in any art performed in the spirit of Zen there is no division between art and life, or art and spirituality. Thus for the study of *ikebana*, discipline and intuition, art, life and spiritual experience are all fused together. One begins the study of *ikebana* by adhering strictly to the rules, and, by becoming thoroughly conversant with them, one's intuitive, creative powers are developed to the full. Needless to say, it is a lifelong study, no matter which school of *ikebana* one takes up. While one begins with technique, in time there comes the realization that there is much more to it than mere technique.

While Western students may be interested only in arranging flowers in a different style, those students who have made *ikebana* a way of life have found much personal enrichment, and that they have put themselves on a path of self-discovery. *Ikebana* in Buddhist terms is known as the 'way' or path of flowers (just as *cha-no-yu* is the 'way' of the tea cere-ceremony), the taking of which results in the development of the 'seeing eye' for the wonders of all nature. What first appears to be inanimate material simply to be manoeuvred into a visually attractive formation, soon takes on a life and personality of its own. Not only is this true of types of trees and shrubs and flowers, but of each flower and each branch. Each has individuality, and is as different as people are different from each other in characteristics and in their way of life. Working with branches and flowers day after day brings this home to the serious student.

When one starts *ikebana*, one feels separated from the arrangement, it seems a thing apart. With perseverance, however, comes the feeling that the arranger and the arrangement are one, so that the minute the student takes a branch or flower in his or her hand, he or she instinctively knows exactly how to work with it – just how far it can be bent or curved into a special pattern if need be. To achieve this sense of unity one first studies the basic principles of *ikebana* and then practises them over and over again. One must know the precise angle at which a piece of material should be placed, and the relationships between materials. All of this demands conscious thought and effort at the beginning, but through constant practice the day comes when the action is entirely instinctive and the distinction between separate parts disappears.

The teacher of *ikebana* cannot force this feeling, or the philosophy behind it, on a student. These must evolve from the student's growing awareness of the 'way' being taken, and the desire for greater understanding must come from within. Then it is possible to proceed towards the meaning of *ikebana*.

Exercise of the six perfections

The essence of *ikebana* is what the Buddhists call the exercise of the six perfections.

These are:

1. *Giving* One gives in the right way; that is, one gives to all without reservation, just as trees and flowers give their beauty to all without reservation. One gives kindly, humbly, fearlessly, immediately, quietly, following the example of nature.

2–3. *Morality and Patience* Purity of thought is always necessary in planning an arrangement, and how patient one must be with branches and flowers when putting them into place! It is no good trying to make an arrangement in a hurry. The result will show that this just doesn't work.

4. *Energy* This, too, is needed not only in the gathering of the material but also in its arrangement, especially in the twisting and the bending of a stubborn or recalcitrant branch in order to give it the desired line.

5. *Concentration* One must really 'lose' oneself in the process of arranging the materials to achieve a satisfactory result. Utter concentration leads to complete serenity.

6. *Wisdom* Wisdom comes through years and years of practice. This can be expressed in the active submission of one's ego to the work at hand, a state in which no thoughts arise, and there is no separation between the doer and the deed. This training leads naturally into meditation, the complete stilling and emptying of the mind. The 'way', regularly followed, leads to inner balance and harmony, which one can only fully express when one has acquired it.

A facet of life exemplified in all flower arrangements is impermanence. While one knows that everything is always changing, one clings to the idea of things being everlasting. Through the study of *ikebana* one comes to realize that there can be beauty in impermanence. Nowadays, of course, by using artificial flowers, one can almost achieve an 'everlasting' arrangement. After all, many artificial flowers look very real. Yet somehow they are unsatisfactory, the reason for which is simply that in the permanence of the artificial one is losing the fragile appeal of the real. With living material one starts with the buds and experiences the joy and wonder of watching them open into beautiful flowers. It is the same with each new arrangement. Also, in *ikebana* simplicity and restraint are emphasized so that the student is stimulated to create living beauty with as little material as possible.

Shibui and furyu

Let us now turn to two subjects of great importance to all Japanese art, the words for which have no direct translation in English. They are *shibui* and *furyu*. *Shibui* refers to the ultimate goal in Japanese art forms, the attainment of supreme beauty with the minimum amount of material – the fewest words as in a *haiku*, the fewest strokes as in *sumi-e*, the fewest flowers as in *ikebana* – and the exercise of the greatest restraint. The Japanese attitude is that when feelings are expressed too fully, there is no room for the unknown, which is where art begins. Another way of looking at *shibui* is as subdued elegance. *Furyu*, on the other hand, is not so easy to describe in Western terms as it is a state of being few Westerners would have reached through cultivation of Western arts. *Furyu* refers to that which is beyond the ultimate in sophistication and refinement, a sense of the imperfection of perfection. This is expressed in the schools of *ikebana* by the tearing of a leaf at the point of finishing an arrangement as if to remind one that what is perfect in nature is sometimes painful, or missing, lonely, transitory or unique. The instance of catching this 'truth' gives rise to what are known as the moods of *furyu*, which are themselves expressed in flowers, poetry, painting, the taking of a cup of tea. The first is *sabi*, a sense of loneliness which comes from being completely detached, and seeing things as if they are happening by themselves. Then comes *wabi*, a recognition of ordinary things but seen in a very clear, almost transparent light. *Aware* is to be able to see in a split second a moment of life which seems timeless. In other words a moment of time in a timeless moment. And *yugen*, the mystery of there being constant change while at the same time eternal sameness. It has been stated that without some understanding of *furyu* a student cannot grasp the spirit of *ikebana*.

Furyu can be stated through *ikebana*, which is a very real and meaningful way to work through and overcome the troubles and sorrows of life, to heal wounds, and to give up all worldly desires. The appeal in a twisted branch or a moss-covered tree, things seemingly of no use or value, exemplifies *furyu* because it is useless, valueless, fragile, old or tender. One comes to understand in one's heart more about *furyu* as one's study of *ikebana* progresses. *Furyu* exemplifies peace and serenity, the turning away from worldly things. As a concept and as a working reality, it is hard to attain in our materialistic culture; but it is one which carries its own rewards.

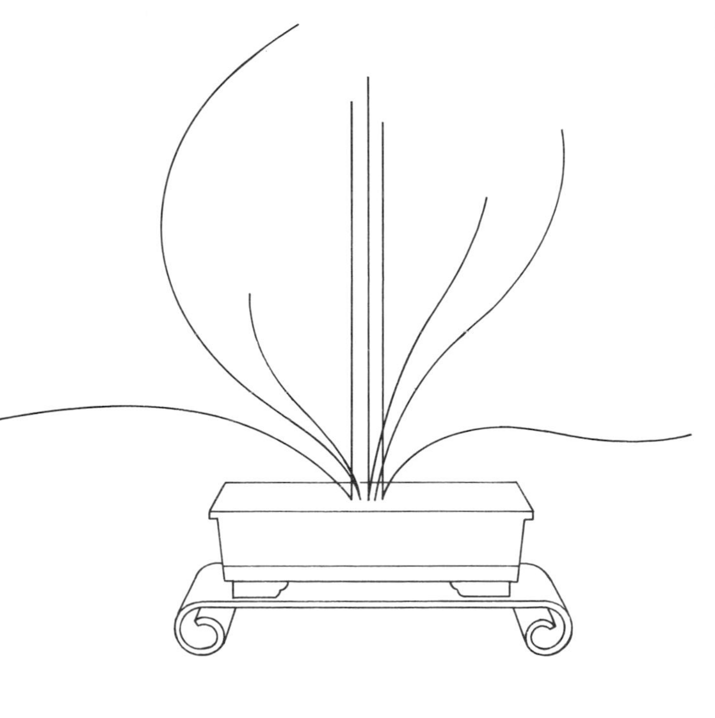

A bronze *suiban* holds a *rikka* arrangement using a large root, evergreens, bare branches and flowers. (See p. 226)

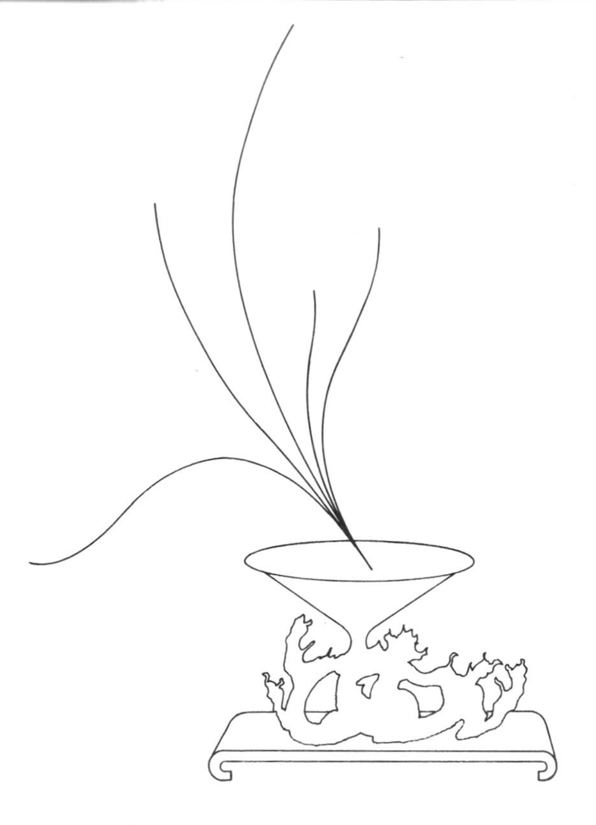

A strictly classical arrangement of five evergreen stems in the *seika* or *shoka* style, in a fine old bronze container

Styles

The oldest styles of *ikebana*, the classical as opposed to the modern, are *rikka* and *shoka* or *tenchijin* (heaven–earth–man). The *rikka*, or standing style, is a towering, almost overwhelming style in which the flowers and branch tips point towards heaven. It accorded well with the spaciousness of the temples and palaces, and the time and trouble entailed were in keeping with its spiritual significance. For any other purpose it would have been quite impractical, though at the time in question no other use for it was envisaged. The vases used for *rikka* were huge, deep bronzes that came from China. They were filled with bundles of straw into which the stalks of the branches and flowers were inserted. They were intended to represent landscapes showing mountains, hills, forests, waterfalls and the like.

Rikka arrangements are still to be seen today in exhibitions in Japan, and as they are so massive and stylized and difficult to make, students prefer the simpler styles. The *shoka* (also called *seika*) is modified *rikka* intended for use in the home. In Japan a *shoka* arrangement is usually placed in the *tokonoma*, an alcove cut into the wall of the principal room of the house in which a sacred scroll or painting is placed. *Shoka* exemplifies the idea of heaven, man and earth – heaven being the tallest line, man the next tallest and earth the shortest.

Today the classical styles are taught by the Ikenobo school, which has been mentioned as the first school of *ikebana*. Mr Senei Ikenobo, the present master, is the forty-fifth in succession. He has visited the West many times, demonstrating Ikenobo styles. As *ikebana* moved from the temples and palaces into the home, a simpler and freer way of arranging evolved, known as *nageire*, or 'thrown in'. A *nageire* is done in a tall vase and gives the impression of great casualness, although it is not something that can be accomplished in a casual manner. Knowledge of several basic techniques is necessary to gain a firm balance of the materials. A tall branch, cut in a fork to an extent of about 7.5 cm (3 in.), is stood in the container with the split uppermost and touching the wall of the vase. The next step is to split the end of the branch to be secured and insert it so that the forked end of the branches interlock. The effect is a vertical arrangement delicately but firmly balanced.

The easiest style to arrange is known as the *moribana*, which is also known as 'natural style' because it so often depicts a little scene. It is an arrangement in a flat dish, 6.5–7.5 cm (2½–3 in.) deep. The dish can be round, oblong or irregular in shape. Branches and flowers are secured in a *kenzan*, or pinholder, placed at the side or at the back of the container. A *kenzan* is seldom placed in the middle, as the Japanese point out that nothing in nature is quite symmetrical, and they do not want symmetry in their arrangements. Anything perfectly balanced, they believe, has no movement and thus appears dead. All arrangements must have the appearance of living and growing.

The angles that most *ikebana* arrangements take are 10, 45 and 75 degrees from the vertical zero. For a basic upright arrangement, the *shin* (heaven) line is 10 degrees, *soe* (man) 45 degrees and *hikae* (earth) 75 degrees. When the flowers are added they are placed in the centre of the branches at varying lengths, the longest being roughly half the measurement of the *shin* branch.

When the student has thoroughly mastered the basic rules of *ikebana* he or she can express themselves in their own way. as students of the Sogetsu school do.

As there is no method of teaching 'free style' it would be inviting confusion to attempt one, short of a full study of traditional methods. Free style replaced the naturalistic and scenic qualities of the traditional styles with a more contrived look and a basis of design which must be interpreted as a sign of the times – a sign, perhaps, that the world is becoming more materialistic. It maintains the basic balance of opposites in the use of lightweight and heavyweight material and contrasting colours. True free style can be acquired only after the basic principles have been studied and mastered.

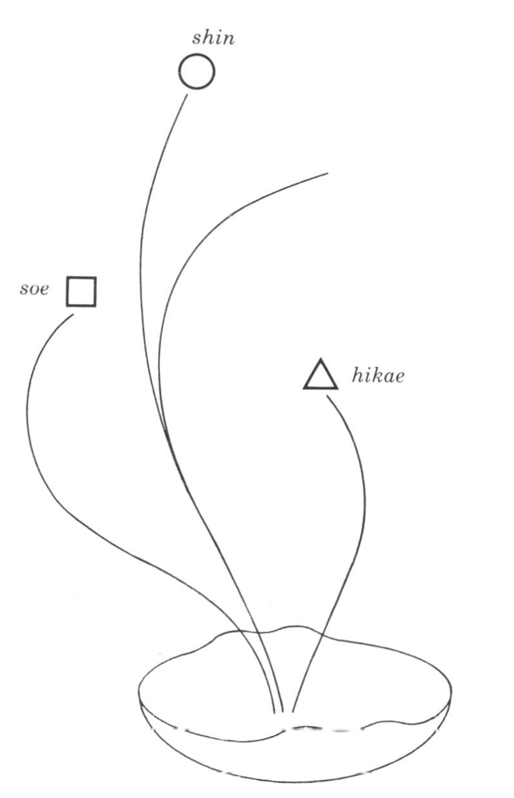

The low, flat container characteristic of *moribana* supports willow branches which stand for 'heaven' and 'man'. The 'earth' line is represented by the tallest flower

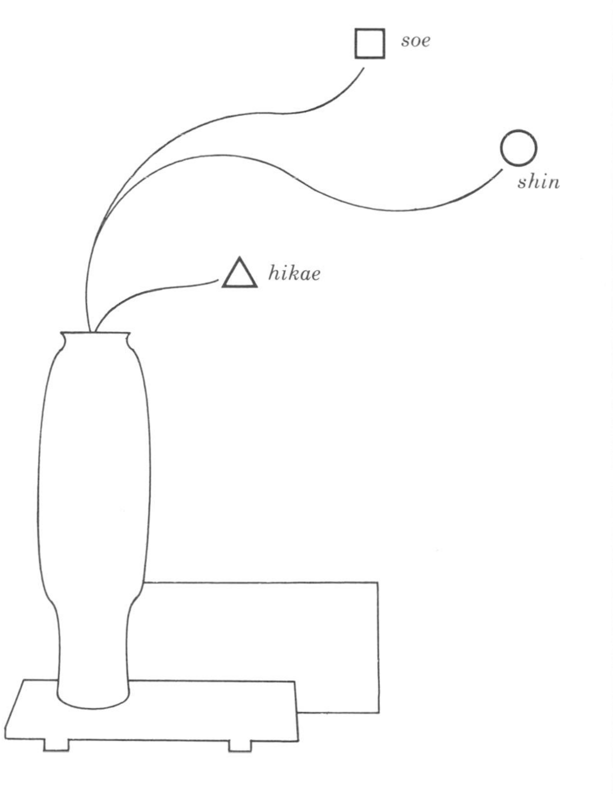

With three strong lines for 'heaven', 'earth' and 'man', *nageire* is made in a tall vase, here holding a windswept arrangement of foliage and flowers

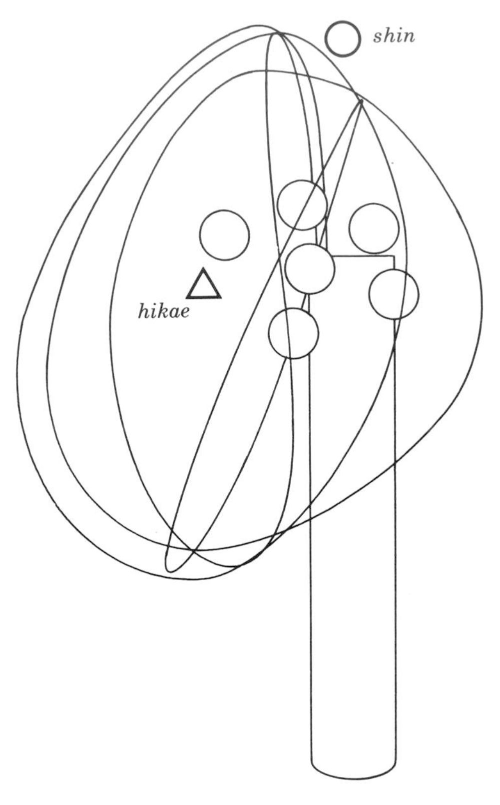

A modern free-style in a straight, dark container which uses curved cane, carnations and feathers

Schools

The oldest and the best known of the *ikebana* schools, as already mentioned, is the Ikenobo school. Another of the older schools is the Saga school. Its headquarters are in the Daitokuji in Kyoto, where annually a memorial service is held to perpetuate the memory of the Emperor Saga. Although he reigned only fourteen years, from 809 to 823, when he abdicated in favour of his younger brother, his influence continued, as he was one of the foremost scholars of his time. In the thirteenth century Daitokuji was authorized to issue degrees of rank to the priests for flower arranging; and in the sixteenth century the imperial household recognized the awarding of these degrees to the Flower Masters. Although the Chief Abbot is the titular head of the Saga school, *ikebana* is just one of his responsibilities. Daitokuji is also a centre for calligraphy and the tea ceremony (*cha-no-yu*). The 1976 annual exhibition was particularly festive as it was the 1,155th anniversary, and Mr Hakushu Tsujii, who has often come to the West, demonstrated modern as well as classical arrangements in the Saga tradition.

The Soami school was founded in the Muromachi period (1330–1568). Nineteen consecutive headmasters of the school have kept to the school precept, 'not to arrange flowers as (his) main occupation'. This means that the head cannot become commercially involved in the school. The seventeenth head was a Buddhist priest, the eighteenth (the father of the present head) a medical doctor, and the present head, Socheon Yokochi, is a painter and university professor. Soami school students have been invited many times to arrange flowers for ceremonial occasions by the imperial household.

The Soami school has a distinctive *rikka* style arrangement called *sotenka*, composed of 'light' forms and 'shade' forms – the *In* and the *Yo* (*Yin* and *Yang* in Chinese) – which symbolize men as the central axis of the arrangement, the light and the shade on either side in asymmetrical lines. The school is not influenced by present trends, handing down the classical spirit and traditional techniques it has inherited. Mr Yokochi has written that he feels great responsibility in that while *ikebana* has a long history behind it, the original spirit may gradually be lost. He says: 'In the course of development, and to my regret, most of the *ikebana* schools in Japan are deeply involved in profit-seeking competition and are losing the very essence of flower arrangement.'

The Ohara school is a modern school of *ikebana*. The founder and first headmaster, Ushin Ohara, first studied with his father, who was a master of the Ikenobo school. At the beginning of this century, Ushin Ohara devoted his life to *ikebana*, though his first love was ceramics. This was the time when Japan was opening up to the West and beginning to import brightly coloured flowers from the Western countries. He was fascinated by these flowers and began to use them in his arrangements. Finding that they were unsuitable for the classical styles, he began to use low, flat containers. So the *moribana* style came into being – *moribana* meaning piled-up flowers in a flat dish. While the old masters flatly rejected this style it appealed greatly to most people, so Ushin opened his own school.

Houn Ohara, the present head, succeeded his father in 1961. He outlined basic measurements, gave exhibitions using step-by-step instructions and started training women as teachers. The *moribana* style is now accepted by all schools in Japan and is one of the styles most favoured by Western students. In his book, *The Best of Ikebana*, Mr Ohara states: 'The spirit of its foundation, inherent in the Ohara school today, constitutes its objective as determination to strive always to improve. The aim of the Ohara school study is not to adhere strictly to tradition, but to keep pace, creatively, with life's progress, while retaining the integrity of traditional principles. In the attainment of this aim, the Ohara school has developed in every form of *ikebana* from natural to abstract.'

Undoubtedly the most outstanding modern school is the Sogetsu. Mr Sofu Teshigahara, headmaster and founder of

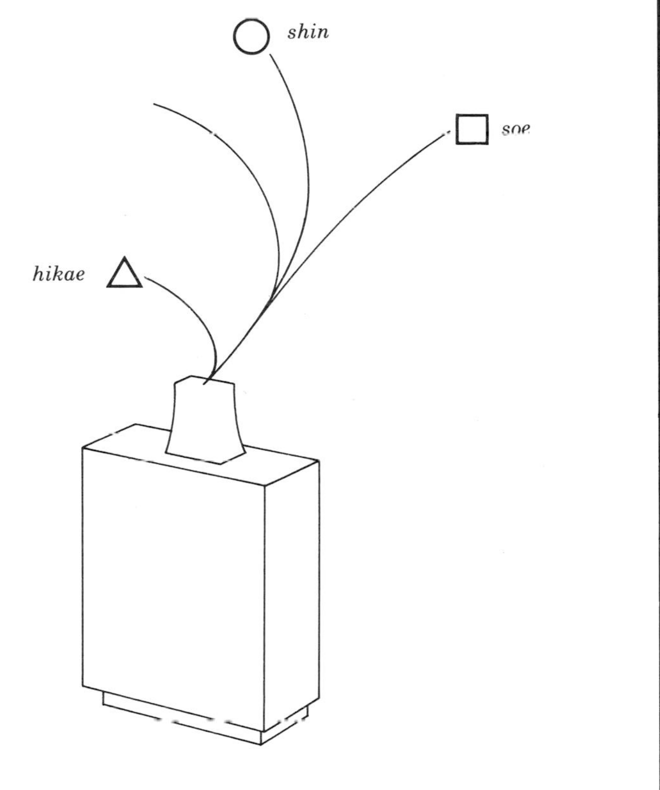

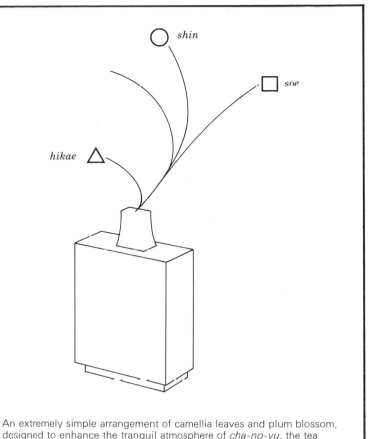

An extremely simple arrangement of camellia leaves and plum blossom, designed to enhance the tranquil atmosphere of *cha-no-yu*, the tea ceremony

the school, studied with his father, who was a teacher of the classical style. He thought a freer way of arranging flowers should develop, in keeping with the times, so in 1926 he broke with the classical and developed the Sogetsu school. In this school, the students learn thoroughly the basic arrangements in the *moribana* and *nageire* styles and then they are encouraged to put their own personality into their arrangements. The main feature of the Sogetsu is the beauty of line. Every piece of material is arranged in such a way as to bring out the beauty of each. Mr Teshigahara gave a new life to *ikebana* by his imaginative and inventive genius. He has made many trips to the West, and in 1978 he celebrated the fiftieth anniversary of the Sogetsu school by holding exhibitions and demonstrations in Tokyo, when the new building of the school was opened. Mr Teshigahara is fortunate in having his talented daughter, Kasumi Teshigahara to carry on the tradition of the Sogetsu school. She was invited to represent the Japanese people by making an arrangement in Westminster Cathedral for Queen Elizabeth's Silver Jubilee in 1977.

Cha-no-yu

Ikebana is an important part of the tea ceremony, *cha-no-yu*, which is becoming increasingly popular in the West. A school to teach it has recently been opened in London. *Cha-no-yu* is also one of the 'ways' of Zen Buddhism.

The art of *cha-no-yu* is the creation of a gentle tranquillity. The room in which it is situated is quite small, about 3×3 m (10×10 ft), or four and a half *tatami* mats, and is in a tea-house built in the garden of a house rather than being a part of the house itself. As one walks along the *roji*, the winding path to the tea-house, through the pine trees, one can break free of the outside world. At the entrance to the tea-house there is a stone basin into which spring water runs. One pours the cool, clean water from a bamboo dipper over one's hands as a symbol of purification. To enter the tea-room it is necessary to bend almost double through the small door. This is a sign of humility. The atmosphere of the tea-room is quiet and subdued. Light filters through the paper *shojii* (windows and doors), the tea-kettle sizzles over a charcoal stove. There is a faint smell of incense, and the pine trees rustle outside. One feels quiet and close to nature, a simple and restrained *ikebana* arrangement completing the scene. It is always utterly simple, sometimes consisting of a single flower. Everything unnecessary has been eliminated.

Haiku

Just as *ikebana* is an integral part of the tea ceremony, it is also an integral part of the writing of a poem – and poetry is an integral part of *ikebana*. The Japanese excel at the seventeen-syllable verse known as the *haiku*, in which few words are used to capture a timeless moment. *Haiku* have been written on the occasion of viewing a flower arrangement just as they have inspired many arrangements – as 'one flower expresses Spring, a falling leaf can express Autumn'. *Haiku* and *ikebana* share that spirit, exemplifying the significance of a single moment.

Here are a few examples of Japan's most famous *haiku* poets, Basho being perhaps the first and foremost.

Autumn evening
A crow perched
On a withered branch.

The mood of autumn evening catches the loneliness of winter soon to come.

Another famous *haiku* is:

The old pond
A frog jumps in –
The sound of water.

And another by Basho:

The sea darkens;
The voices of the wild ducks
Are faintly white.

Haiku and *ikebana* have come to be such a combination that many of the exhibitions

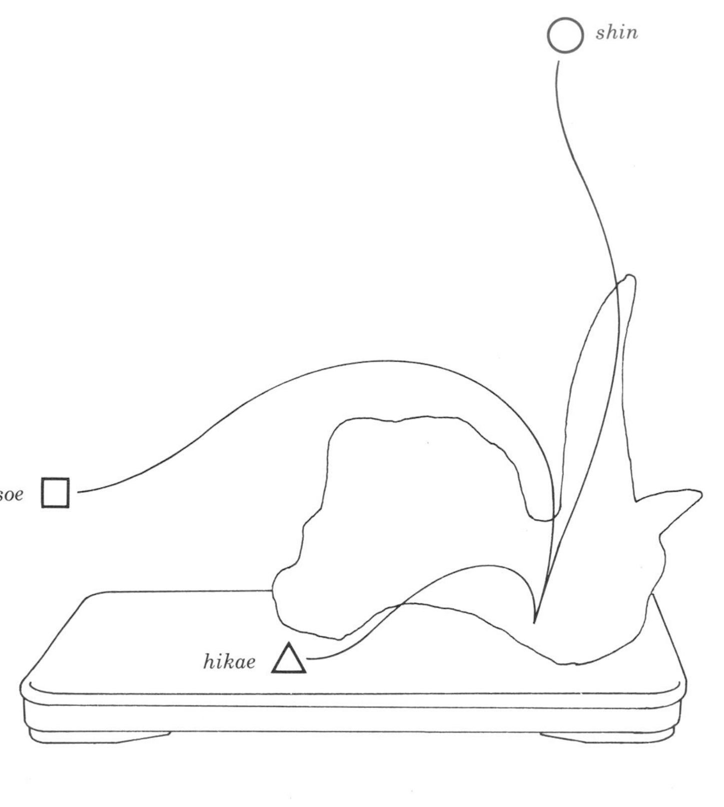

A *haiku* poem provided the inspiration for this contemplative waterside composition in subdued tones

in the West will have one or two *haiku* as the themes to be interpreted in an arrangement. A *haiku* must be read and absorbed, as each one has a deeper meaning than appears at a superficial glance.

Festivals

Ikebana and the festivals of Japan are also closely connected. These are usually very colourful and enjoyed by everyone. The most important is the Festival of the New Year, at which time an arrangement of pine, bamboo and plum blossom is made. The pine, as an evergreen, represents everlasting life; the bamboo, as it bends and sways in the storms but returns to an upright position when the storm has passed, represents resilience; and the plum blossom, as it is the first to bloom even when snow is still on the ground, stands for courage.

The Japanese always greet January dressed in their best kimonos, and everywhere there are decorations. Even the first trucks to be taken out in the new year will have bamboo or evergreens at each corner.

The Girls' Festival, *O'hina Sama*, is held on 3 March. For this, young girls put their ceremonial dolls on display. These may be heirlooms handed down in one family for generations. They consist of the Emperor and Empress, court musicians, ladies in waiting, and the like. For this festival the *ikebana* arrangement is done with pink and yellow flowers, originally with peach blossom and mustard flower, but now any combination of yellow and pink flowers may be used.

The Boys' Festival, *tango-no-sekku*, held on 5 May, is dedicated to young boys. The arrangement for this festival is of iris flowers and leaves. The leaf symbolizes the *samurai*, or warrior spirit, since it resembles the blade of the sword. Outside the home, on a long bamboo pole, paper or cloth carp are flown – one carp for each son. The carp has great strength and courage, as it can swim against the stream and leap up waterfalls. Thus it is the emblem of perseverance and courage.

The Chrysanthemum Festival, held in November, is very colourful. The Japanese value this flower very highly. The sixteen-petal chrysanthemum is the imperial crest, so that no one but the Emperor can show a design of sixteen petals. There are large displays of these flowers of hundreds of blossoms trained in a bamboo frame to create different designs such as a waterfall or large circles, the flowers all coming from the one stem. One sees also large lifelike dolls clothed in fresh flowers, as well as horses, birds and castles made from chrysanthemums.

Ikebana International

On 17 August 1956, Ellen Gordon Allen, the wife of an American army general, spoke to a group of women at the Washington Heights Club in Tokyo about an idea she had had for some time. What she proposed was the formation of an international association devoted to the art of *ikebana*. She recommended a framework for an association which would aim to stimulate and cultivate the continuous study and spread of *ikebana*, thereby engendering a better understanding of the Japanese people – indeed a better understanding of all people of all nationalities. The aim would also be to strengthen the friendship between masters, teachers and students, keeping the *ikebana* family together; but above all, to stimulate international friendship and spread goodwill around the world.

Chapters were opened all over the world. In Great Britain there are now nine, and in the rest of the world about 200. Chapters exist in practically every state in America, in South America, South Africa, Australia, Hawaii, Okinawa and Taipei, as well as in many European countries. The activities of individual chapters are rewarding socially as well as artistically. Chapter meetings bring together people with an absorbing common interest – peoples of all colours, races, nationalities and creeds, who find in *ikebana* the creative outlet they seek. Ikebana International is certainly spreading the art of *ikebana* with a warmth of friendship and understanding that recognizes no barriers.

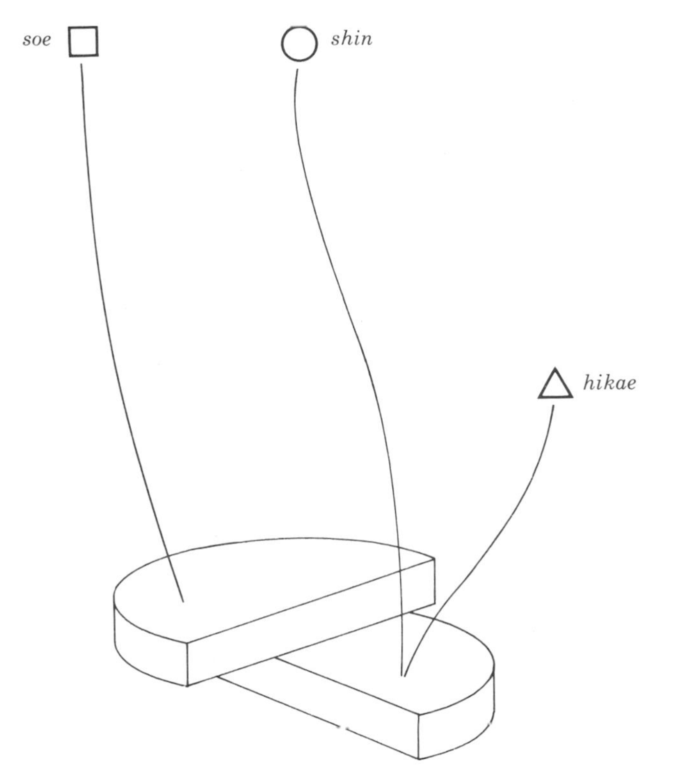

Arrangements celebrating the Boys' Festival always include iris because of its sword-shaped leaves, an attribute which is emphasized in this modern design

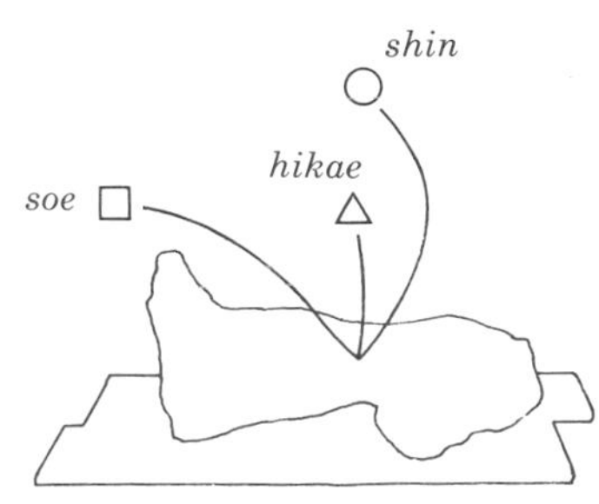

Flowers for the Girls' Festival traditionally include light, dainty blooms of yellow and pink like the mimosa and plum blossom in this free-style arrangement

18. East and West
Differences and Influences

Pamela South

By different methods different men excel;
But where is he that can do all things well?
CHARLES CHURCHILL 1731–1764

Two Japanese girls picking blossom. This Ukiyo-e woodcut clearly shows the universal urge to satisfy a personal love of beauty by finding and using a very particular flower or branch

Appreciation of the beauties of nature and especially the love of flowers, together with a delight in fragrance, has been recorded since the beginnings of civilization. Traces of flowers have recently been discovered in a Neanderthal grave, thought to date back 46,000 years and situated in a cave at Shanidar, south of Baghdad. The grave contained very large quantities of flower pollens; among which, eight different species have been positively identified. So it would seem that when Western Europe was still in the grip of its last Ice Age, or before any written or known spoken language existed, primitive man was already expressing his emotions with flowers.

Much fascination can be derived from studying the motivation behind flower arrangement: why flowers were placed in a certain way and how these forms were adapted to changing ideas and different styles of décor, and why certain plants and species were especially selected and favoured when there were no preconditioning factors.

Over a long period of time man had changed from a hunter to a tiller of the soil and plants were grown for culinary, medicinal and eventually for purely decorative reasons.

There arose two separate and entirely different mainstreams of flower arranging, geographically placed in areas of the East and the West. The Eastern one began in China and spread to Japan, where it developed its own highly distinctive styles. Buddhism, though originating in India, was a strong influence. The Western mainstream lay within the boundaries of the Roman Empire and the sphere of influence of the early Christian Church. Even today, with evolution continuing, the main influences upon flower arranging throughout the world can still be divided into occidental and oriental, each stemming from their separate cultural backgrounds with their different religious beliefs, some of which have a connecting symbolism of materials. The present exchange of ideas between the two has been greatly accelerated by the post-war American presence in Japan, and later by relatively cheap air travel, the mass media, and improved colour printing techniques. Especially in the last thirty years, the flood of floral art literature with its high quality photographic illustrations has proved a great stimulus. Then, as the numbers of floral enthusiasts increased, the ease of air travel enabled previously island-bound Flower Masters from Japan, together with top British and some European and American demonstrators, to traverse the world displaying their talents.

It is possible to trace how, latterly, the East and West have influenced and altered each other's styles. The interaction of influences has been profound, but no one form or style has been adopted in its entirety by the other. There has been a

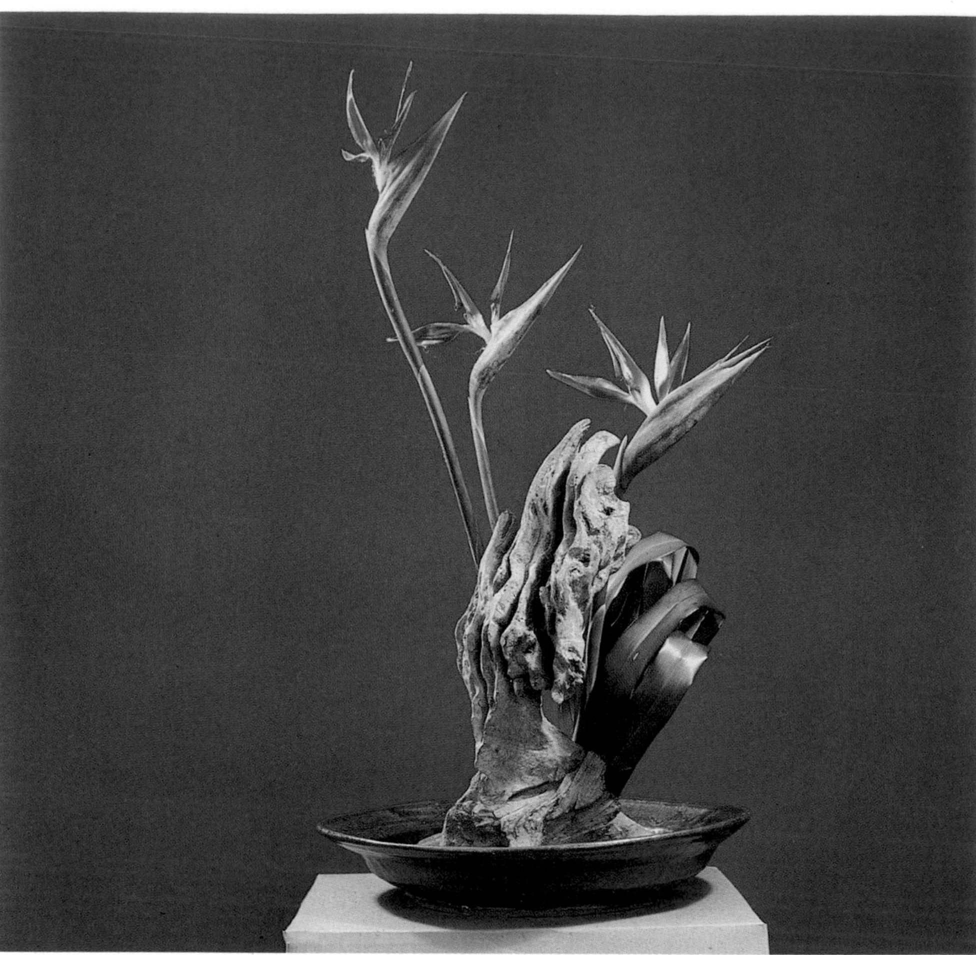

Above: a Free Form expressive design entitled 'Flight to Paradise'. Three strelitzias and petrified wood recovered from a Scottish bog. The three *tenax* leaves provide textural interest

Opposite top: a Colin Kellam multiple pot in which a bleached mulberry branch is used with pink belladonna lilies and eucalyptus bark

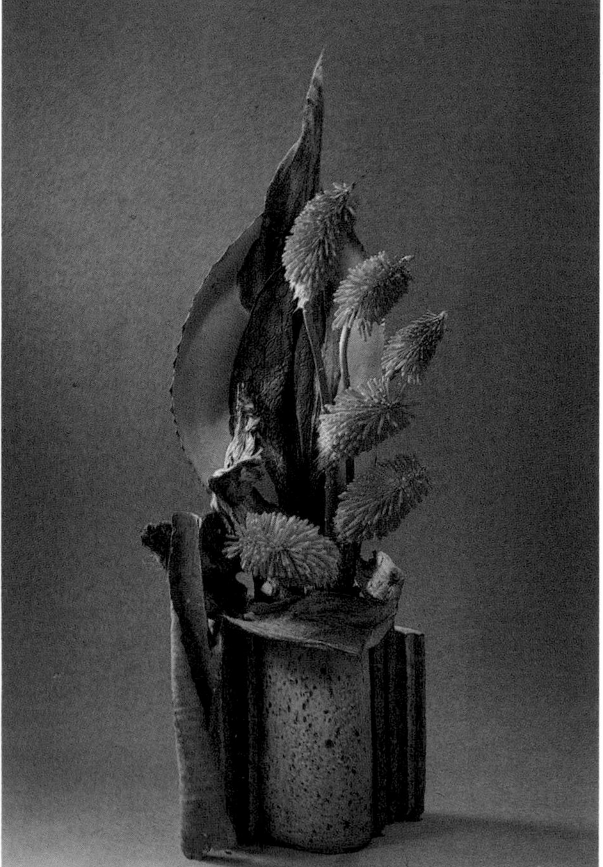

Left: Western Modern. Orange and red *kniphofia* used with giant agave leaves, fresh and dried, and eucalyptus bark. The Colin Kellam pot of 'slat' design provides repetition of colour and form

continual process of absorption and assimilation of the different national characteristics, which has altered the original concepts and ideas. To the trained observer of modern or abstract styles it is still possible to say about an arrangement, with a high degree of accuracy, whether its primary influences originated in the East or in the West. The accompanying illustrations seek to demonstrate this.

To understand how floral art evolved in the East it is necessary to know something of the underlying philosophy. In China, man was considered to be but one of the manifestations of nature. Ultimately, it was believed, he returned to the cosmic element. In the East man was always more aware of his relationship to nature and did not seek to dominate or subdue it. Harmony with nature has always been the key to understanding the arts of the East.

The first country in the East to evolve a distinct and recognizable form of flower arrangement was China. This was *linear*, following the style of her paintings and calligraphy, mass being subordinated to line. The flowers themselves were selected for the arrangements on the basis of their felicitous associations and the auspiciousness of their ascribed meanings; odd numbers of branches and flowers were chosen. The form was asymmetrical, the use of space in and around the composition being of great importance. Space was considered to be an integral part of the design. The basic principles of composition and painting were stated in the fifth century A.D. in the famous Six Canons of Hsieh Ho, the most important being *Ch'i Yun Sheng Tung*, which translates as 'the life of the spirit in the rhythm of things'. This spiritual-orientation means that the artist, whatever the medium in which he works, must grasp the essence of life which flows through all the universe by developing a total oneness with his subject, a principle at the basis of all Chinese and Japanese art. The asymmetry of line gives the arrangement rhythm and movement, as though the branches and stems were springing out of the ground. Compositions which lack the inward depth promoted by *Ch'i Yun*, however good technically and mechanically, are considered sterile and dead. In the West we might describe them more prosaically as being competent but uninspired.

When Buddhism slowly infiltrated into China from India in the early centuries A.D., it brought with it the tradition of making religious floral offerings, especially of the Lotus flower, which was considered sacred to Buddha.

In China itself a recorded history of flower arrangement existed from very early times. Strict formalization of styles and rigid rules did not develop as they did in Japan. In 1595 *A Treatise of Vase Flowers* was written by Chang Ch'ien-tê, giving details of techniques, choice of

A mid-eighteenth century Chinese wall-hanging, on which the design is both woven and painted

containers and classification of plants. Another well-known book, *The Painting Patterns of the Mustard Seed Garden*, compiled by Wang Kai in 1682, expounded principles of painting equally relevant to flower arrangement.

In China domestic floral decoration was considered in relation to other furnishings. Flower vases were placed on wooden stands and were often grouped with other table decorations, which would be placed at different levels, but with a unity of balance and composition. The table decorations could include any of the following: incense burners, peacock feathers, wooden figurines, carved jade or rock. The most prized rocks were often fantastic shapes of convoluted stone eroded and hollowed out by wind and water, showing the Tao web of time and change. In the East stones have never been thought of as alien to floral arrangements or as accessories, quite unlike Western conventions. This derives from a different attitude to nature, which in the East is viewed in its entirety.

The principle of three parts, the triangle, was used symbolically in China. The entire universe was said to be contained in it. Later, it was taken from the teachings of the great teacher Confucius that one line is symbolic, two lines are harmonious, but three lines represent fulfilment. Subsequently, in Japan the three main lines of the asymmetrical triangle in a flower arrangement were called heaven, earth and man, the combination of the three making for complete harmony. This asymmetrical triangle form has been adopted for informal and modern work by Western flower arrangers.

In the sixth century Buddhism, together with the art of flower arranging, was brought from China to Japan. The existing form of religion of the Japanese was animistic, and called Shinto. From the start Shinto and Buddhism have managed to coexist successfully, the majority of Japanese adhering to both. To this day the Japanese have retained their Shinto beliefs and regard for complete harmony with nature, whether it be plants, rocks or water. In Shinto the duality of male and female, plus the universe, make up the whole. To symbolize this, three sprigs of sacred evergreen laurel are placed on Shinto altars. The reverence felt for sacred trees by the followers of Shinto provided inspiration to arrange flowers as a way to bring the individual closer to his God. The *Sendensho* is the oldest Japanese work on flower arranging. Dating from 1445, it gives details of techniques and arrangements for special festivals.

In Japan, with its paternalistic employment traditions, many factories and offices regularly organize flower lessons for the employees as a leisure aid to relaxation. It is usual for pupils to remain faithful to one chosen school and there is a special quality of respect and depth of relationship between pupil and teacher, fostered by many, many years of disciplined study. In the West courses of study are mainly of shorter duration and the student seeks further instructions and inspiration from many different sources. It is a less disciplined and freer approach after the initial absorption of traditional styles and techniques. In Japan the initial male orientation made the creation of arrangements up to 4.5 m or 6 m (15 or 20 ft) high, and often in complementary pairs, physically possible. The ultra large exhibition piece remains today because of the still high proportion of male teachers in Japan.

The austere refined simplicity of Zen Buddhism had a very profound effect on cultural life, acting as a catalyst on all branches of Japanese art, and maintaining a considerable influence today. In Japan the completed arrangement was not necessarily a prime objective of the exercise, merely a felicitous outcome, whereas in the West the finished arrangement was an end in itself. The particular internal disciplines of the Eastern approach led to strong forms emphasized by line and space. Restrictions on the number of colours and the variety of materials selected avoided distractions from the perfection of line, which was of prime importance. In the West, in total contrast, because flower arranging had a mainly decorative purpose, it was used to enhance and embellish décor and furnishings, and to reflect the tastes and customs of each age. The variety of materials, and of the colours used, derive from the Western love of growing a wide range of plants and a generally inquisitive botanical disposition. In other words, because the underlying philosophical attitudes were different, the techniques and styles which evolved from these philosophies were different, as were the end results. Flower developments in the West can be traced as far back as 2800 B.C. The history of the many periods from Ancient Egyptian times to more recent ones has been described already in Chapter 11. It therefore suffices to note here that, during these long periods of history, flower decoration moved from purely religious contexts into the house and home environment.

The great thirst for knowledge, exploration, adventure and commercial gain led the rising merchant classes to use some of their new wealth in the decoration of their homes and gardens. As the commercial frontiers expanded beyond the confines of Europe, new varieties of plants and new species were brought back by the merchant fleets and overland caravans. Highly prized porcelain was introduced from China via Venice, the shapes ultimately having considerable influence on European ceramic design.

The dominant floral style in Europe has remained that of the large massed multi-

Driftwood is used in place of a ceramic container; a well pinholder sustains the auratum lilies

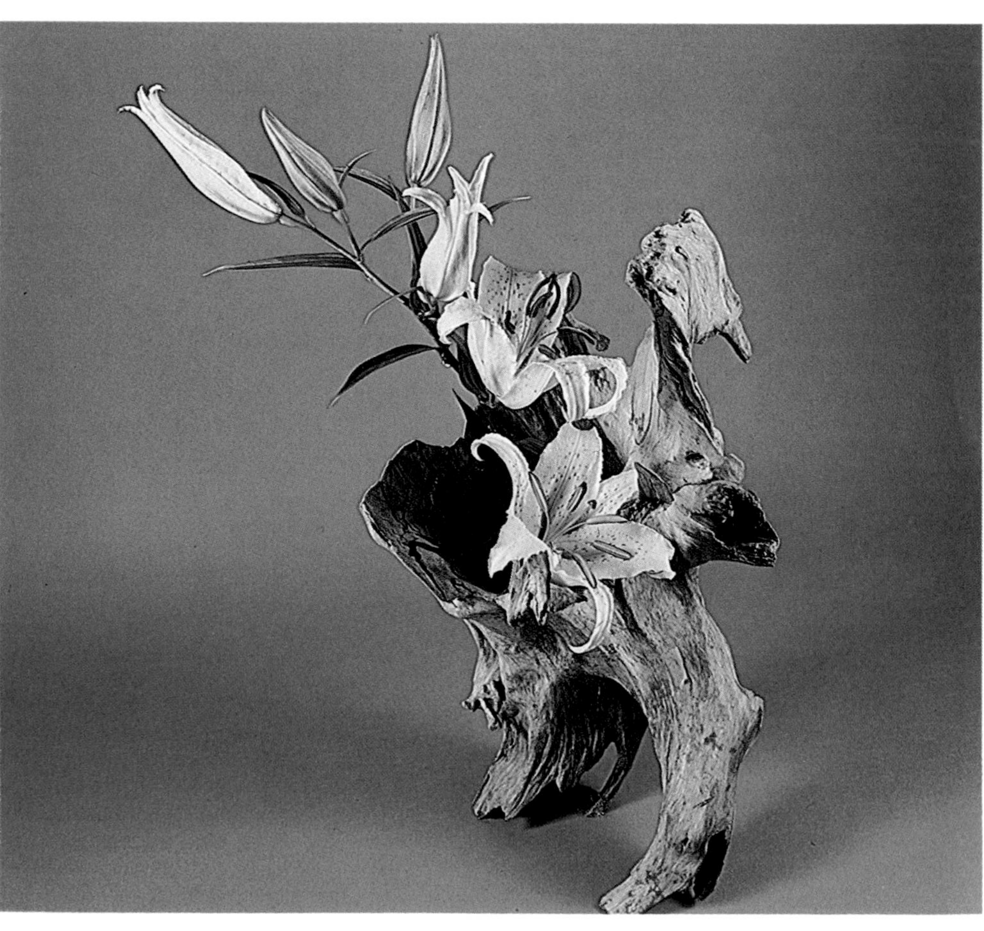

coloured bouquet of mixed flowers with a lavish variety of material. Space within the arrangements was often non-existent, flowers being tightly packed together, even overflowing their containers. The richness of colours advancing and receding was the defining factor, making their own dimensions and appeal to the senses.

In the nineteenth century, books purely on flower arranging began to appear. Miss Mallings was one of the earliest writers on the subject and in 1862 her work *Flowers for Ornament and Decoration and How to Arrange Them* was published. The books of Gertrude Jekyll at the turn of this century, and in the twenties and thirties those of Constance Spry, have been strong influences on the development of the art in Britain.

In the last twenty years NAFAS in Britain has worked tirelessly to raise the standard of knowledge and skills across the country, providing demonstrations, lectures, exhibitions and teaching. Flower arranging in Britain has now achieved recognition as an educational creative study by the City and Guilds Institute. Similarly the National Council of State Garden Clubs have made their Flower Show Schools available throughout the United States.

The traditional Western style of a massed pyramid with triangular form and symmetry of balance, solid weight at the base and, latterly, a central focal point, stemmed from an intellectual construction akin to Greek architecture and sculpture, based on a mathematical ratio. The basis of scientific thought of the early Greeks was the origin of the Western process of logic and rational thinking, which, in turn, influenced Western art forms and what is commonly called the classical tradition. The early Greek philosophers sought to find a geometric law in art. Art and beauty, they considered, were harmony – and harmony came from due proportions. If this was the case, then these proportions must be fixed. The golden section was formulated by Euclid in mathematical propositions. The usual formula is to cut a finite line so that the shorter part is to the longer part what the longer part is to the whole. The resulting proportion is roughly the ratio of five to eight, eight to thirteen, twenty-one to thirty-four, or about 1:1.6 (see above right). The golden section at times was accorded mystical and religious connotations, some writers relating its parts to the Trinity. Plato called relative beauty that which is inherent in living things. It has been shown by scientific measurements comparatively recently that many different plants do in fact use this constructional principle of proportion. It provides for an economical use of space, for example, in the single blooms and seeds of the giant sunflower. Artists had recognized this proportional beauty in nature long before its existence could be proved scientifically.

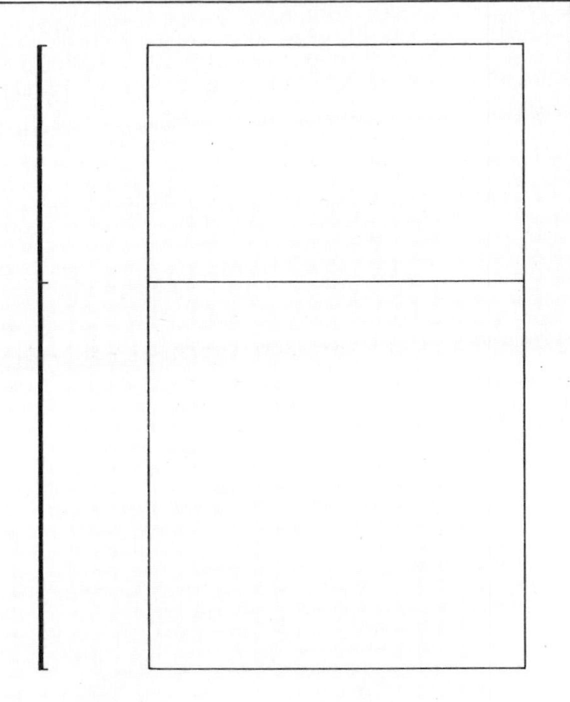

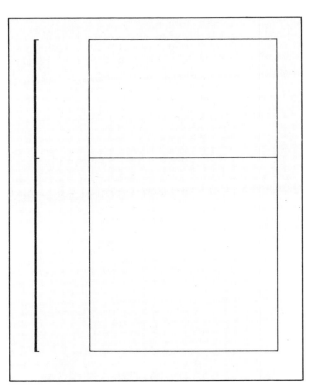

A diagrammatic representation of the golden section

Western Abstract. A right-angled geometrical construction using four vertical and two horizontal bean pods, and four rounded spheres of seed pods asymmetrically placed. The smaller red bean, vertically placed at the centre, provides depth

Ikebana Abstract. Another geometrical construction created by the use of vertically-placed palm spathes with defined spaces between them. At the base the smaller forms of the *lysichiton americanus* flowers give colour impact and formal repetition of the palm spathe tips

An *art nouveau* arrangement whose beauty evinces the influences of both West and East

Plato called absolute form those constructions or abstractions which consisted of straight lines and curves. The surfaces of three-dimensional assemblages produced out of living things, where instruments of measurement were used in the construction process to arrive at precision of placement, could also achieve absolute form. Absolute form was beauty. It is this pure form that is the basis of non-representational art whether it be cubist, constructional, or abstract, and which is brought into play by a flower arranger when she selects a distinctively shaped leaf or seedhead and uses it in a non-naturalistic manner purely as a design element. Abstract work cannot be undertaken seriously, whether in painting or flower arranging, without some appreciation or thought being given to the underlying structure of all nature and natural forms, whether it be of the planetary system or of the bank of information stored in a grain of wheat which controls its growth and development.

Major historical events initiated the two main periods of impact between art ideas from East and West. The Tokugawa Shogunate system of government lasted from 1600 to 1867, during which time development in Japan was frozen in a medieval system of government and outlook, her ports and country being closed to foreigners. Commodore Perry with his black-painted American warships sailed into the harbour of Uraga in the year 1854 and within a short time trade treaties had been signed with the United States and the United Kingdom. At last Japan was open to commerce, and a flood of Western ideas entered the country, at the same time exposing the West to Japanese art. When displayed at the London International Exhibition of 1862, its linear lines and asymmetry, especially in the *Ukiyo-e* woodblock prints, influenced profoundly the emerging style of *art nouveau* which was sweeping Europe. Even in flower arranging it had some impact among the intellectuals as they started placing a few flowers simply in upright vases with their new simplified furniture, part of a reaction to the prevailing mass style of flowing épergnes. An interpretative illustration of this new era, showing an elongated lily and an extended whiplash line of poppy-heads can be seen on the left.

For its part in the two-way flow of ideas the West helped to free Japanese flower arranging from the rigid rules and petrification of style which had predominated. When the Shogunate fell and power was restored to the young Emperor Meiji, a new era of Westernization and modernization began. Among the European items pouring into Japan were new plants and flowers. In Britain and America this was a time of wealth and prosperity. There were many large gardens with teams of gardeners, and wealthy owners vied with each other in the acquisition of plants from all over the world. Plant-hunting expeditions were financed in the search for new varieties and rarities. Rooms were filled with hothouse plants and dinner-tables groaned under lavish displays of flowers. The impact of colour and abundance of material made a strong impression on Japanese Flower Masters.

In 1910 a young man, Ushin Ohara (mentioned in the previous chapter) founded his own school, having seized the opportunity of using Western flowers in low, flat containers. He called his new style *moribana*, meaning literally 'piled-up flowers'. He also initiated realistic representations with flowers, rocks and moss. These scenic arrangements had three forms showing distant, middle and near landscape views, and the plants used for them accorded with the season and their natural habitat. The early Buddhist style of piling up or floating flowers in low dishes is still practised in India and South-East Asia, but without the use of a pinholder to raise the stems.

The placing of branches and flowers impaled on *kenzans*, or pinholders, in low dishes, was a technical breakthrough. It was this mechanical device of holding a branch or stem at any desired angle that made possible some of the later and exciting free-style forms. The pinholder was adopted by the West from the thirties onwards. In the twenties flower stems were still being placed in small glass domes, called roses, which incorporated many tapering holes to hold the stems rigidly in a contrived manner.

The landscape style became very popular in the West, accessories of figurines or animals sometimes being added, in competitive show work for instance. The whole modern art movement in painting and sculpture began in Europe, and these developments were closely followed in Japan, starting with the influence of colour from the impressionist movement. Colour had hitherto been of minor importance in Japanese arrangements. In contrast, Chinese arrangements had always shown a more exuberant display of colour, although the number of colours used at any one time had always been limited, basket arrangements being the exception.

In the West branches and leaves, if used at all, were subordinate to flowers. Their main function in period arrangements was to achieve height, the leaves acting as a quiet background to a colourful mass of blooms. The present use in Western free-style arrangements of branches and stems as strong line material, dominating and creating the shape with the added use of space as a positive design element, springs directly from Eastern influence.

The exception to limited variety of material in Japan occurs in the ancient formal upright *rikka* arrangements which date from the fifteenth century. In these, between seven and nine primary branches were utilized in order to create a globular

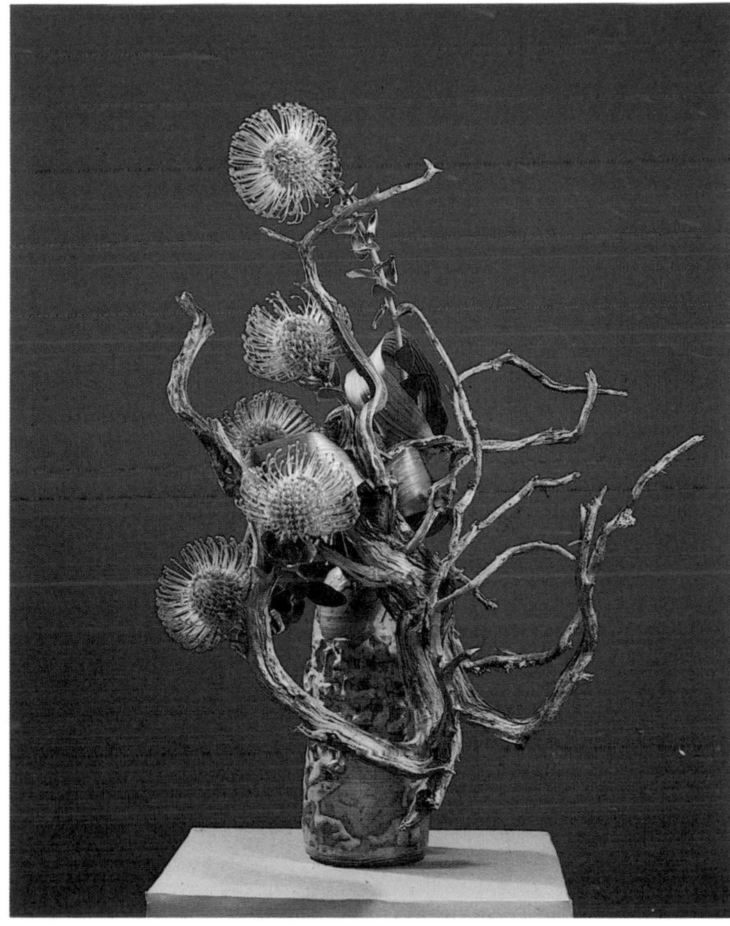

three-dimensional effect, the organized elements symbolizing the universe. This was symbolically expressed in the form of a mythical mountain, while the main lines represented different aspects of nature. The names of the branches themselves have changed over the years, and have been variously called 'mountain peak', 'hill', 'waterfall', 'valley', 'village', 'Buddha welcoming', 'dew receiving', 'smoke restricting' and 'strength-giving'. The object was to show, with the branches coming from a central core, the harmony of nature. Space was carried outwards with the branches from this core. The whole arrangement had a *Yō*, or light positive male side, and an *In*, a shade or negative female side. In China these were termed *Yang* and *Yin*. The principle of *Yō-In* is also applied in classical arrangements to the surface or front, *Yō*, of a leaf, and the underneath or back, the *In*, perfect balance between the two dualities always being aimed for. These often very large arrangements were placed in huge bronze vases on lacquered or polished wooden bases or stands.

In traditional, formal Western mass triangular arrangements, a base is sometimes used in order to lend visual balance and stability, or to achieve contrast of colour or texture. The base or bases may be of wood or stone but are often covered with fabric material, very formally in velvet and less formally in a coarser material such

Above left: freedom of placement, made possible by the use of pinholders. The three pink gerberas and *phormium tenax* leaves (cut and shredded) are held in three separate containers but result in one unified design

Above right: Western Free Style. Contrasting line and texture; rhythmical driftwood defines space. Pink proteas provide radiation and curved aspidistra leaves give texture contrast with rugged pot

Below: the traditional depiction of the Yo-In principle, with light positive male and dark negative female aspects

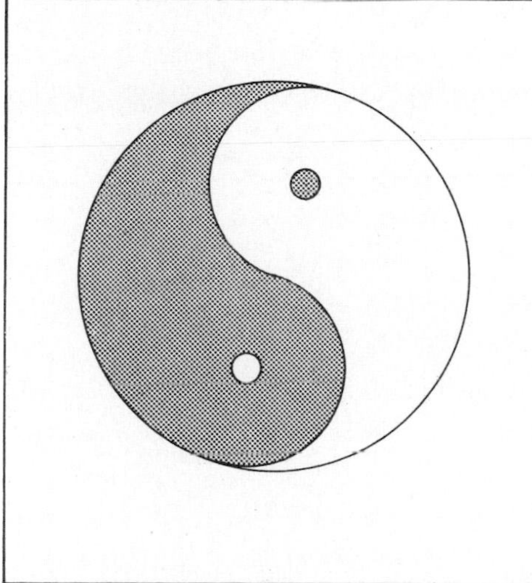

as hessian. In the East, however, fabric material bases have never been used, but tatami mats have been. The Western custom of raising large massed arrangements on columns of wood or marble, and latterly the use of wrought-iron pedestals to obtain height, may have influenced modern Japanese arrangements which are sometimes elevated on geometrically shaped metal stands and are often placed in groups. The difference being that the Japanese metal stands are frequently painted in bright primary colours that have an affinity with other similarly painted modern metal sculptures.

The whole of this century has seen a rebellion in all art forms and a breaking away from traditional forms and styles, whether Eastern or Western. An assertion of the freedom of the individual artist to express himself has been a keynote. In 1930 a manifesto was issued by some of the young Japanese Flower Masters, saying:

> We regret the botanical restrictions of flowers. We embrace a free use of containers. We are revolutionary to an extreme and, therefore, without fixed form. We are, however, concerned with the styles of modern living and we have strong artistic consciences. Our task is entirely different from that of earlier flower arrangers. We must express a new image in a new spirit.

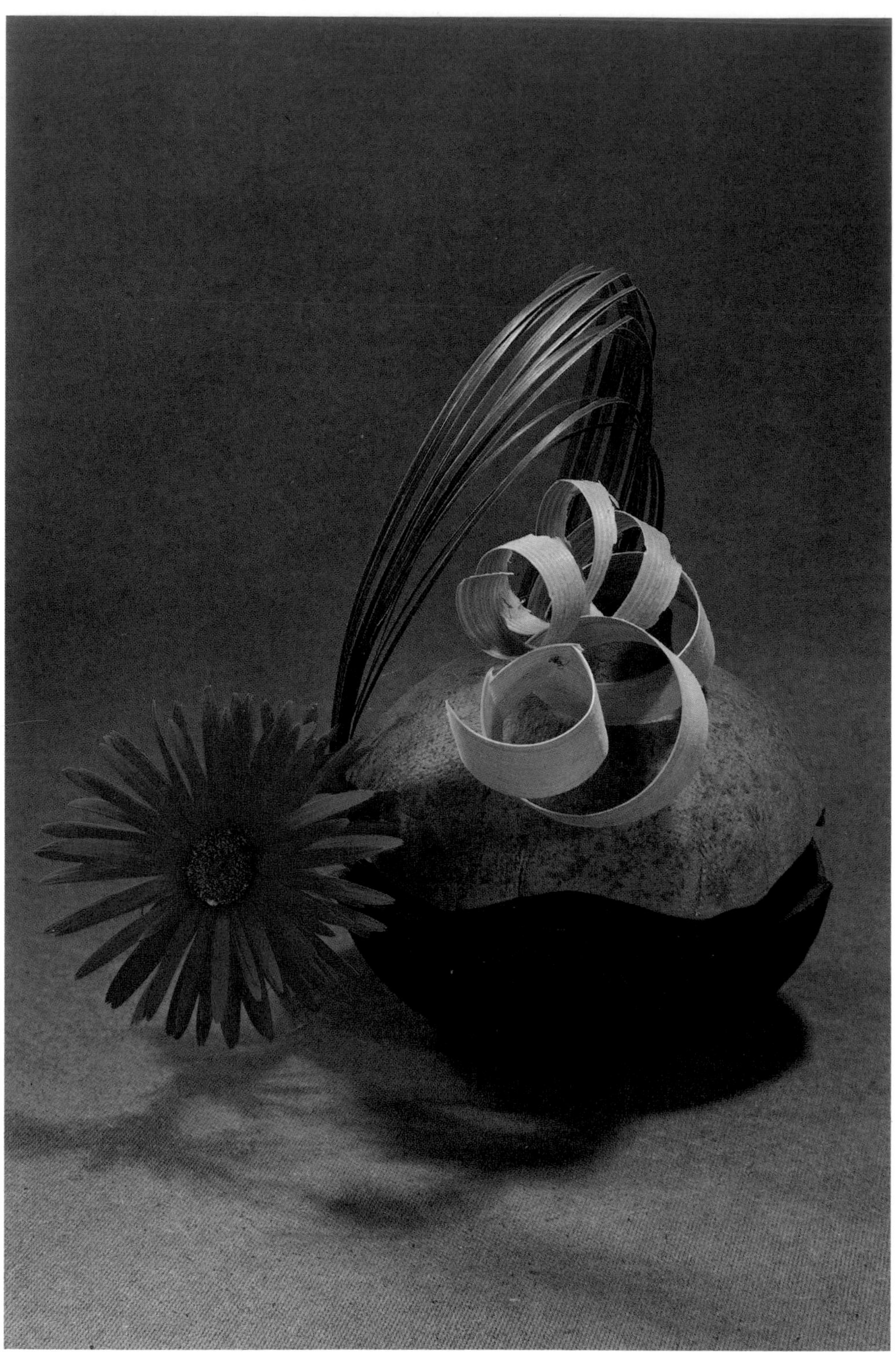

Free Style Ikebana. Exciting contrasts of three main groupings. Bubbling spirals of wood shavings, gentle arcs of shredded *phormium tenax* leaves and the dramatic colour emphasis of a gerbera flower

Among this group was Sofu Teshigahara, often called the Japanese Picasso, who founded the Sogetsu school. He has always pointed out that the affinity between sculpture and Japanese flower arrangement lies in their both being of three-dimensional form, and has stated that he moulds living things as a sculptor moulds clay or plaster. Following the manifesto quoted above, experimental work was done using huge tree trunks, rocks, items of steel, feathers and other *avant-garde* materials. Dried material, consisting of driftwood, grasses and plants, also started to be used, as well as bleached and dyed material.

The second major historical event to affect East-West influences was Japan's widespread adoption of American ideas after the outcome of the Second World War. The American military presence after 1945, and especially during the period of the Korean War, allowed the wives of American servicemen with leisure at their disposal, to embrace Japanese arts, and this they did with a great enthusiasm, especially the art of flower arrangement. They rapidly became proficient in their chosen flower schools, and on their return to America started demonstrating and writing about their new skills. This helped spread the new ideas of form and style. Gradually, through experimentation and keen competitive work, talented arrangers evolved a distinctive American modern style which initially gave the lead to Europe in the new free form and abstract styles. The dominant position taken by American art in the forties and fifties with abstract expressionism influenced and helped the American arrangers. In their turn, the Japanese Flower Masters were seeking new forms themselves and were profoundly influenced by all modern Western art, especially the three-dimensional art of sculpture.

Eastern and Western arrangers have for many years used large pieces of tree root, or driftwood of interesting forms with devices attached for placing plant material. The Japanese also partially cover the wood with hammered-on panels of metal or even completely cover the wood, using it as the structural basis for abstract forms, moulding the metal to the wood's shape, and dispensing entirely with any visible plant material. This is alien to Western practice, but in the oriental view is only an extension of the concept of unity of the whole cosmos, whether of plant material or minerals. Some abstract work is done with no plant material at all, being of glass, stone or metal, but it always follows the same design principles as would have been applied with plant material. The pace of modern life and the ever-increasing popularity of flower demonstrations has led to a consistent demand for change, experimentation and novelty. New forms such as mobiles have been introduced, and those inspired by surrealistic and pop art; there have even been exploding or disintegrating arrangements. These experiments encourage very different reactions, and some may even be found amusing, humour being a new ingredient in flower arranging.

The widely differing styles of architecture and interior décor of Eastern and Western homes have played their part in the past in determining the forms of domestic flower arrangement. The traditional Japanese home was of lighter construction, being built mainly of wood, with at one time a height restriction imposed by the frequency of earthquakes

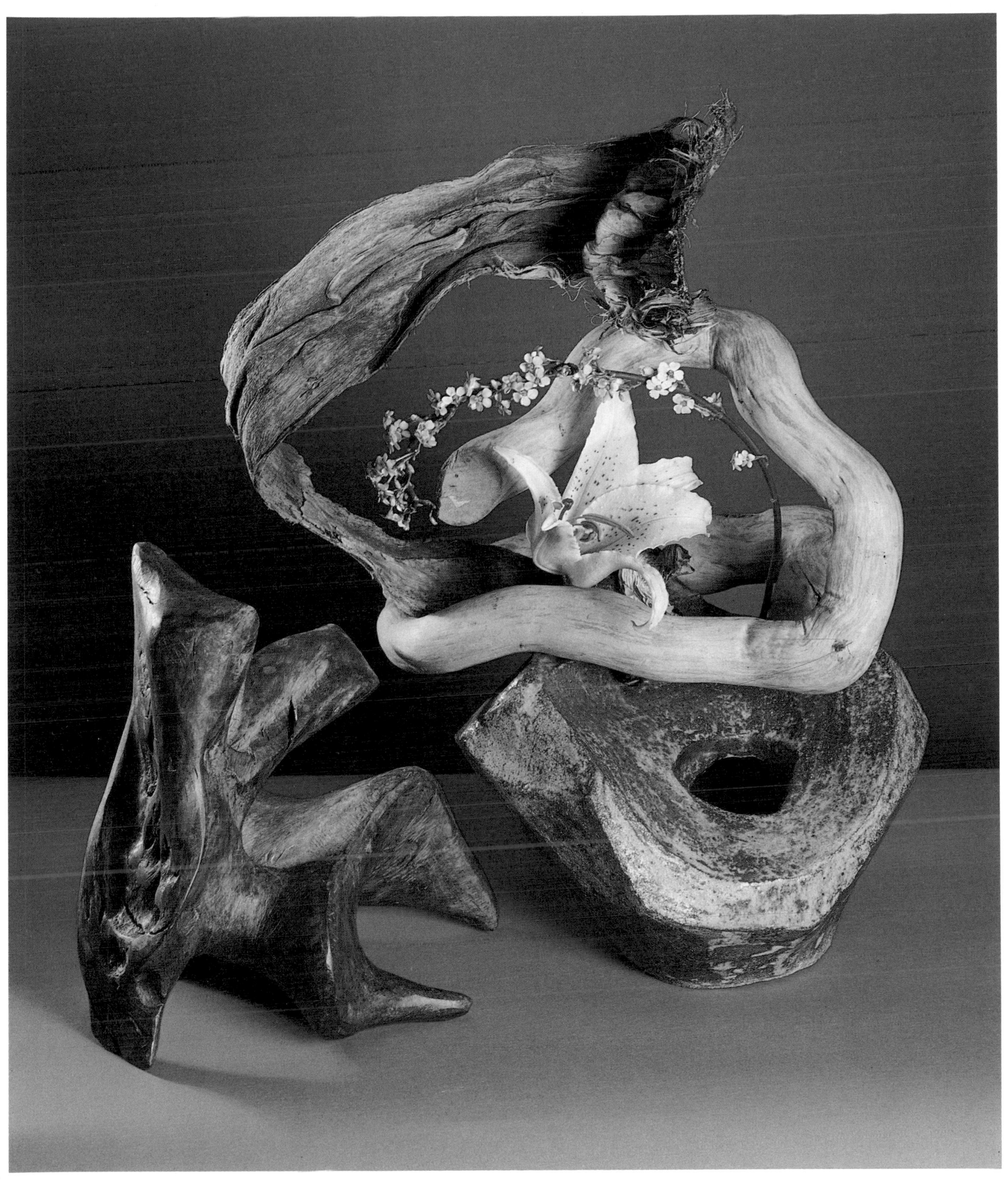

Western Free Style. A lily and *euphorbia* emerge majestically from the sculptured wood, which provides the feeling of imminent movement. The design was inspired by the work of Henry Moore

and fires as well as the limitation of materials. Often two of the outer walls were sliding and opened on to verandas or gardens. The interior divisions again consisted of sliding walls and screens, and the wooden floors were covered with tatami rush matting, thereby providing a neutral background. Furniture was sparse in the extreme and the overall effect was one of simplicity and space. The focal point of the room was a large built-in alcove, called a *tokonoma*, in which the flower arrangements were displayed, forming a perfect setting for a sparse line arrangement of branches with few flowers.

The more solidly built Western home, mainly of stone or brick construction, had patterned carpets, furnishings and wall hangings, a fireplace forming a focal point, and often a profusion of furniture and ornaments. This busy background called for a mass arrangement of flowers to compete in colour and solidity of form. The world-wide movement from the countryside to towns and cities, with flats in monolithic concrete blocks, has meant that the urban dweller cannot readily pick a handful of branches and wild flowers and so has to rely in part on dried, preserved and bleached materials for the framework of a design, adding florists' flowers.

Not all Japanese homes now have a *tokonoma*, where flowers were placed for frontal viewing only, and so flowers are increasingly placed on low tables for all-round viewing. Similarly, most Western houses now have simplified furnishing and less ornamentation, and thus line arrangements can be shown to advantage against the plainer backgrounds.

Some people think that there has been a complete about-face from traditional styles in modern work of both East and West. This, of course, is far too sweeping a generalization. The orientals are, however, taking to mass form and vigorous colour. It is also true that the Japanese are making very large exhibition structures of wood with groups of massed flowers, the whole encompassed in writhing, stripped vines, pattern placed on pattern. These arrangements can be likened loosely to a very modern adaptation of the old *rikka* form. In some ways they resemble the works of the American artists who obtained their images from biomorphic forms related to plant and animal structures. On the other hand, modern Western work does now consist mainly of strong line and limited material. Perhaps both sides, in breaking away from their traditional styles, go to the extreme opposites to obtain the maximum contrast with their own country's former conventions.

The Japanese Flower Masters have been quicker to absorb ideas from Western modern art and translate them into usable forms with flowers, coming as they do from a tradition which has always viewed arrangement as an art form. Many Westerners, who are primarily gardeners, think that some of the more extreme adaptations of modern Western art cannot be considered beautiful, only interesting or stimulating.

In summary, the East has taught the use of line and space, while the West has demonstrated the glories of colour and abundant plant material. Each has influenced the other, and together they have created the whole that is the art of flower arranging – an ephemeral art, but yet a significant expression of man's spiritual vision.

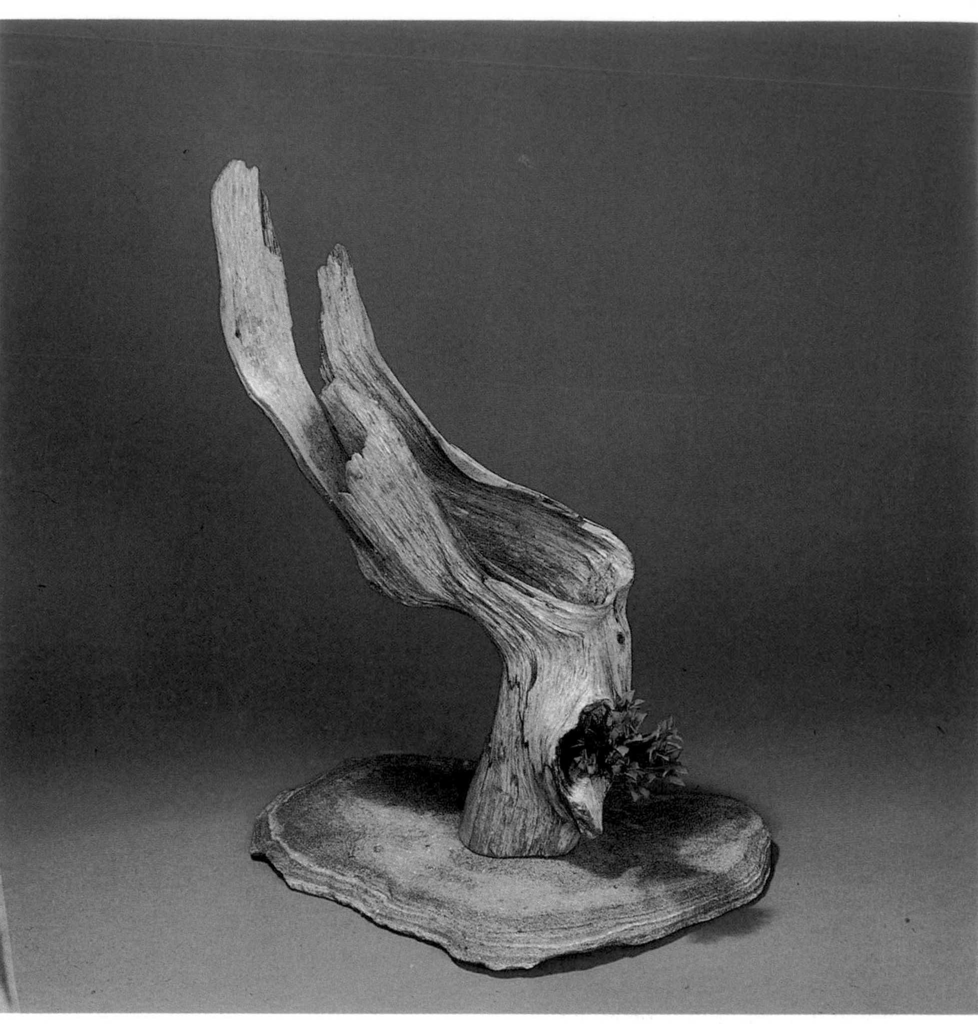

Above: a sculptural piece of silver driftwood on a natural stone base. The highlight is a small placement of blue gentians

Right: a geometrical construction of silver birch with radiating whorls of two *rhodostachys pitcairnifolia* and stripped wisteria leaves

Far right: an expressive semi-abstract, with pink hydrangeas massed and used purely as form; echoing the contours of the pot, and becoming a unified whole with it. A radiating palm leaf echoes the sun's rays. Inspired by Henry Moore's series of heads

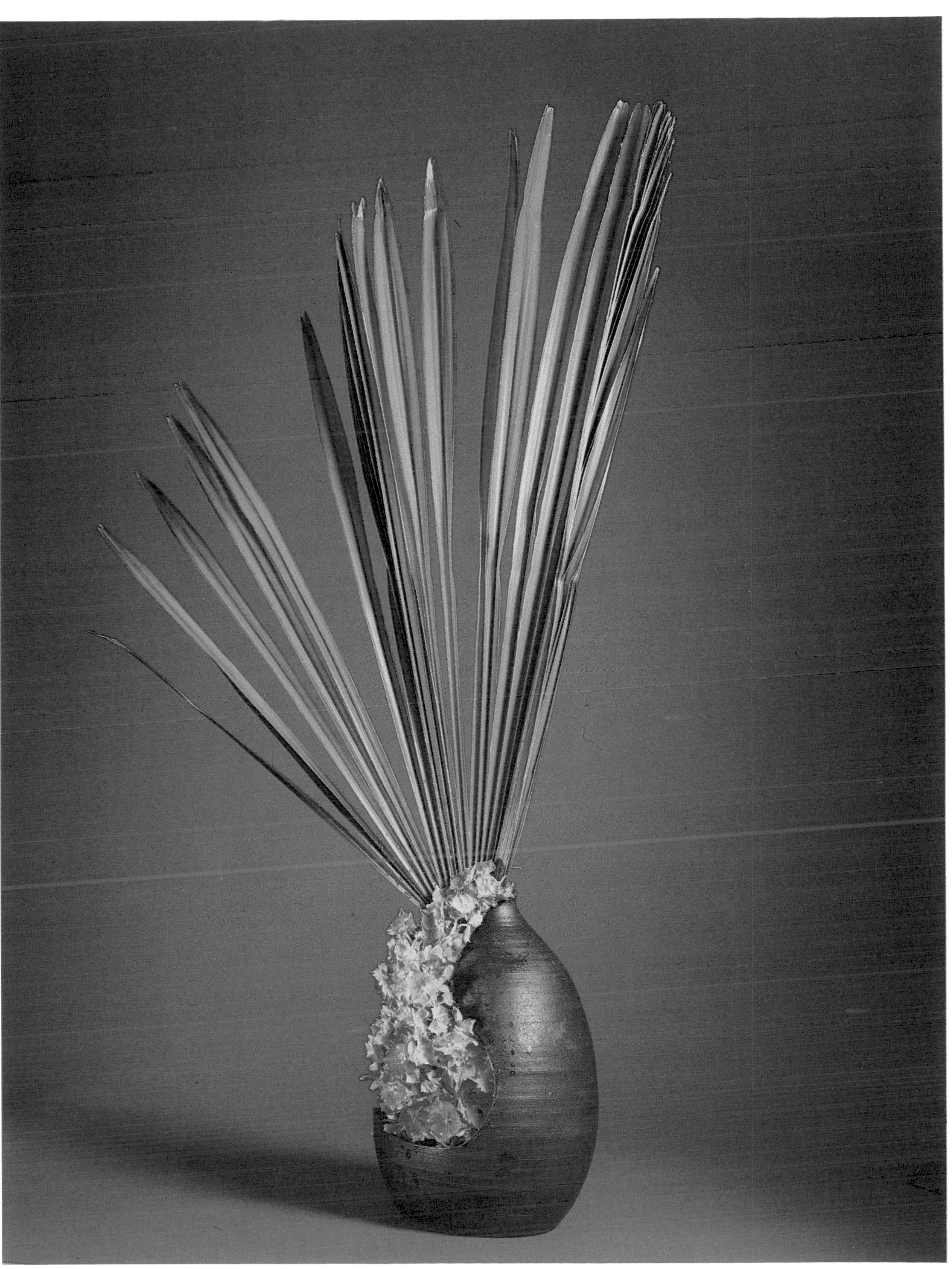

Glossary

Abstract A design where plant material is used in a non-naturalistic way with a strong pattern and dramatic simplicity. A *Decorative Abstract* is based on design qualities and has no special theme. An *Expressive Abstract* interprets the essence of a subject or theme.

Accessory Anything other than plant material used as part of an exhibit, such as a figurine. Carved wood or other plant material made into a recognizable shape, such as corn dollies, is considered to be an accessory. In NAFAS shows bases, containers, drapes and backgrounds are not classed as accessories.

Background A self-supporting fixture placed behind an arrangement to enhance it in some way. For a competitive class in a show details should be stated in the schedule, such as type, colour and height.

Base A placement under an arrangement which should enhance or add to its balance and colour harmony. In NAFAS shows it is not considered to be an accessory.

Bracts Modified leaves often brightly coloured, just below the small flower or flower cluster. In NAFAS shows they may be considered as flowers or foliage.

Candlecup A small cup-shaped container which has a centre made to fit into the top of a candlestick.

Collage A collection of materials assembled to form a picture, in which plant material should predominate. It can be made either to hang or to stand.

Conditioning The treatment of plant material before arranging to encourage longer life.

Container The receptacle of any shape into which plant material is placed, usually containing water or water-retaining foam.

Contrived or Made-up Flowers Pieces of dried plant material assembled into a flower shape. In NAFAS shows no wire or other aids should be visible.

Desiccants Material used for removing moisture from flowers and foliage to preserve them as dried plant material. Silica gel, borax and sand are desiccants.

Drape Material, usually fabric, placed behind or in association with an arrangement to enhance it or to contrast with it, by colour, form or texture.

Driftwood Any type of dried wood, roots or bark, which may have had some cleaning treatment. In addition to wood weathered by water the term driftwood describes wood from forest or hedgerow.

Exhibit In NAFAS shows this term denotes an arrangement of plant material with or without accessories.

Focal Point or Centre of Interest The part of an arrangement with the strongest visual weight, usually at the centre of the design and at the base of the main stem.

Freeze-drying The removal of moisture at a very low temperature in a vacuum or in an atmosphere containing an inert gas.

Fruit This term can include edible and inedible fruit, berries, seedheads, nuts, cones, fungi and vegetables. In NAFAS shows grasses, sedges, rushes, reeds, bulrushes, catkins and cereals are allowed as flowers or fruit according to the stage of their development.

Glycerine Solution A mixture of one-third glycerine to two-thirds hot water. The water must be hot or the two liquids will not blend.

Garlands Plant material assembled to hang in rope form.

Hogarth Curve or Lazy S An arrangement which follows the line of an S, called by Hogarth 'the line of beauty'.

Mechanics The means by which the plant material is held in position in an arrangement.

Miniature In NAFAS shows these are limited to 4 in (10 cm) in width, depth and height.

Mobile Plant material assembled to hang and move in space.

Modern Design In contrast to the traditional mass arrangement modern design uses an economical approach to plant material in keeping with the modern style of furnishing and decor, yet necessarily observing the principles of good design.

Niche A recess in which an exhibit is staged. In a show schedule the type, size and height are described.

NAFAS The National Association of Flower Arrangement Societies of Great Britain.

NCSGC The National Council of State Garden Clubs, Inc.

Outline Plant material chosen for its design qualities to establish the overall shape of an arrangement, usually of delicate or tapering character.

Period Design This should be in keeping with the furnishings and decor of a past era. Present day flowers, foliage and containers are acceptable but they should convey the atmosphere of the period.

Petite In NAFAS shows an arrangement more than 4 in (10 cm) and less than 9 in (22.5 cm) in width, depth and height.

Plaque A collection of materials assembled together on a visible background, made to hang or stand, with plant material predominating.

Plastic Foam A man-made substance which retains water and is used for positioning flowers and foliage. It should be well soaked before use and should not entirely fill the container so that more water can be easily added.

Pot-et-fleur A collection of growing plants and some cut flowers assembled in one container. Plants may be in or out of pots. Flowers must be in water or water-retaining material and should not include additional foliage.

Seaweed This is accepted as plant material, but sea fern, sea fan and coral are of animal origin and are considered to be accessories.

Stabile, Sta-mobile A mobile suspended from a stand.

Silica Gel Crystals used as a desiccant.

Swags A collection of materials assembled without a visible background, to hang or stand, with plant material predominating.

Transition Plant material chosen for its design qualities to bridge the visible gap between tapering outline and the focal point or centre of the arrangement.

Useful Addresses

Information and enquiries

The National Association of Flower Arrangement Societies of Great Britain (NAFAS), 21a Denbigh Street, London SW1V 2HF.

The National Council of State Garden Clubs, Inc. (NCSGC), 4401 Magnolia Avenue, St. Louis, Missouri 63110.

Bulbs:

P. DeJager & Sons, Inc., 188 Asbury Street, South Hamilton, MA 01982.

Van Bourgondien Bros., Box A, Babylon, NY 11702.

John Scheepers, Inc., 63 Wall Street, New York, NY 10005.

Clematis:

F. & R. Farrell Co., 6810 Biggert Rd., London, OH 43140.

The D.S. George Nurseries, 2491 Penfield Rd., Fairport, NY 14450.

Roses:

Armstrong Nurseries, Inc., 1265 S. Palmetto, Ontario, CA 91761.

The Conrad-Pyle Co. (Star Roses), West Grove, PA 19390.

Jackson & Perkins Co., Box 1028, Medford, OR 97501.

Thomasville Nurseries, Inc., 1842 Smith Ave., Box 7, Thomasville, GA 31792.

Seeds:

W. Atlee Burpee Co. Headquarters: 300 Park Ave., Warminster, PA 18974.

Joseph Harris Co., Inc., Moreton Farm, Rochester, NY 14624.

Geo. W. Park Seed Co., Inc., Box 31, Greenwood, SC 29647.

Stokes Seeds, Inc. Box 548, Buffalo, NY 14240.

Thompson & Morgan, 401 Kennedy Blvd., Somerdale, NJ 08083.

Trees, shrubs and nursery stock:

Kelly Bros. Nurseries, Inc., Maple St., Dansville, NY 14437.

Sheridan Nurseries, 700 Evans Ave., Etobicoke, Ont. M9C 1A1.

The Wayside Gardens Co., Hodges, SC 29695.

White Flower Farm, Esther Ln., Litchfield, CT 06759.

Flower-arranging supplies:

Dorothy Biddle Service, Hawthorne, NY 10532

Junior's Plant Shop, Glen St., Rowley MA 01969.

Bibliography

The Editor has found the following books invaluable for reference purposes and enjoyment over many years. Some may be out of print, but they can sometimes be procured through libraries or second-hand book shops.

Flower Arrangement

Aaronson, Marion, *The Art of Flower Arranging*, Grower Books, 1970

Aaronson, Marion, *Design with Plant Material*, Grower Books, 1972

Berrall, Julia, *A History of Flower Arranging*, Thames & Hudson, 1969

Bode, F., *New Structures in Flower Arrangement*, Hearthside, 1968

Brack, Edith, *Flower Arrangement Free Style*, Whitethorn Press, 1977

Coe, Stella, *The Art of Japanese Flower Arrangement*, Barrie & Jenkins, 1965

Cyphers, Emma, *Modern Abstract Flower Arrangement*, Hearthside, 1964

Cyphers, Emma, *Nature, Art and Flower Arrangement*, Hearthside, nd

Foster, Maureen, *Preserved Flowers*, Pelham Books, 1973

Hawkes, Frances Ann, *The Pulbrook and Gould Book of Flower Arrangement*, Barrie & Jenkins, 1968

Knight, Mary, *Abstract Not So Abstract*, Van Nostrand, nd

Li, H. L., *Chinese Flower Arrangement*, Van Nostrand, nd

McDowell, Pamela, *Pressed Flower Pictures*, Lutterworth Press, 1971

MacQueen, Sheila, *Encyclopaedia of Flower Arrangement*, Faber & Faber, 1969

MacQueen, Sheila, *Flower Arrangement from Your Garden*, Ward Lock, 1977

NAFAS, *The Flower Arranger* (magazine)

NAFAS, *Guide to Church Flowers*

NAFAS *Instruction leaflets*

NAFAS, *Teachers' Association Guides to Period Arranging*

Nichols, Beverley, *The Art of Flower Arrangement*, Collins, 1967

Reister, Dorothy, *Design for Flower Arrangers*, Van Nostrand, nd

Rockwell, F. F. & Grayson, Esther, *The Rockwells' New Complete Book of Flower Arrangement*, Doubleday, 1960

Smith, George, *Flower Arrangements and Their Settings*, Studio Vista, 1967

Smith, George, *Flower Arranging in House and Garden*, Pelham Books, 1977

Spry, Constance, *Favourite Flowers*, J. M. Dent, 1959

Taylor, Jean, *Creative Flower Arrangement*, Stanley Paul, 1973

Wilson, Helen van Pelt, *Flowers, Space and Motion*, Simon & Schuster, 1971

Gardening and Growing

Collingridge, *Collingridge Guide to Garden Plants in Colour*, Hamlyn, 1976

Emberton, Sybil, *Garden Foliage for Flower Arrangement*, Faber & Faber, 1968

Emberton, Sybil, *Growing Plants for Flower Arrangement* (RHS Wisley Handbook 20), 1975

Emberton, Sybil, *Shrub Gardening for Flower Arrangement*, Faber & Faber, 1965

Fish, Margery, *Gardening in the Shade*, David & Charles, 1972

Hay, Roy & Synge, Patrick M., *The Dictionary of Garden Plants in Colour*, Michael Joseph, 1976

Ingwersen, Will, *Classic Garden Plants*, Hamlyn, 1975

Kaye, Reginald, *Hardy Ferns*, Faber & Faber, 1968

Keble Martin, W., *The Concise British Flora in Colour*, Ebury Press & Michael Joseph, 1969

Mansfield, T. C., *The Border in Colour*, Collins, 1948

Perry, Frances, *Water Gardens*, Penguin Handbooks, 1962

Reader's Digest, *Encyclopaedia of Garden Plants and Flowers*, Reader's Digest, 1971

Royal Horticultural Society, *Dictionary of Gardening*, Oxford University Press, 1956

Stearn, W. M., *A Gardener's Dictionary of Plant Names*, Cassell, 1972

Synge, Patrick M., *Collins' Guide to Bulbs*, Collins, 1971

Taylor, Jean & Davidson, William, *The Garden Indoors*, Stanley Paul, 1971

Thomas, Graham Stuart, *Colour in the Winter Garden*, J. M. Dent, 1967

Thomas, Graham Stuart, *Perennial Garden Plants*, J. M. Dent, 1966

Thomas, Graham Stuart, *Plants for Ground Cover*, J. M. Dent, 1970

Thomas, Graham Stuart, *Old Shrub Roses*, J. M. Dent, 1976

Thomas, Graham Stuart, *Shrub Roses of Today*, J. M. Dent, 1963

Underwood, Mrs Desmond, *Grey and Silver Plants*, Collins, 1971

Related Subjects

Bell, F. Carlton & Lovoos, J., *Making Pottery Without a Wheel*, Van Nostrand, 1976

Coats, Alice, *Flowers and Their Histories*, Adam & Charles Black, 1968

Coats, Peter, *Flowers in History*, Weidenfeld & Nicolson, nd

Fry, Roger, *Vision and Design*, Pelican, nd

Gordon, Lesley, *Green Magic*, Ebury Press, 1977

Meilach, Done & Ten Hoor, Elvie, *Collage and Found Art*, Studio Vista, 1973

Mitchell, Peter, *European Flower Paintings*, Adam & Charles Black, 1973

NAFAS, *Guide to Colour Theory*

Tampion, John & Reynolds, Joan, *Botany for Flower Arrangers*, Pelham Books, 1971

Tritten, Gottfried, *Colour and Form*, Van Nostrand, 1975

Photographic Credits

Photographs were supplied or are reproduced by kind permission of the following:

Reproduced by gracious permission of Her Majesty The Queen, 163, 164 bottom left, 166 bottom right.

Michael Alexander: 13, 14 right, 15 top, 24, 25, 26, 49 top, bottom, 50 top, bottom, 52 bottom left, 56, 57 top left, centre and right, bottom left, 61, 66 top, 67 left, 69 top right, bottom left, 71 top right, bottom right, 78 top, bottom, 85 top left, bottom, 86 top, centre left and right, bottom left and right, 87 top left and right, bottom left and right, 88 right, 93 top right, 94 top right, bottom right, 95 bottom right, 98 top left, top right, bottom left, 108 bottom left, 116, 122 top, 125 top, bottom, 126 left, right, 127 right, 129 top right, bottom right, 157 right, 158 right, left, 159 bottom right, top left, 164 left centre, 165, 166 top left and right, 167 top right, right, 170 top, bottom, 171 top left, top right, 172 left, top right, 174 bottom right, 175 left, 176 bottom, 177 top, bottom, 178 bottom, 179 top, bottom, 180, 181 top, bottom, 218, 219, 220, 223, 236 top, bottom, 237 top, 238, 239, 240 top, bottom, 241 right, left, 242, 243, 244 top, bottom, 245; Harry Angel: 7, 48 top, bottom, 70 bottom; Denis Barnard/*The Flower Arranger*: 77; David Barwick: 19 bottom left; John Bethell: 18 bottom left, bottom right; Pat Brindley: 20; Martin Chambers: 29; Peter Clayton: 34; Cooper-Bridgeman Library: 120–1; Keith Ferguson: 51 bottom left and right, 53; Charles Harding/*The Flower Arranger:* 57; Iris Hardwick: 18 top right, 144 left, 148 left, 149 right; Michael Holford Library: 154 top right, 156 right, 157 left; India Office Library: 15 bottom; Leslie Johns: 38; Edna Johnson: 66 bottom, 95 top left, 173 left, 174 top left; Peter Keverne: 112, 113, 114, 115; Vagn-Ebbe Kier, Copenhagen: 62–3; Scott Lauder: 10, 47 top, 58 right, 60, 64 bottom, 80 left, 81 right, 82 right, 92, 95 top right, 102, 103, 104, 105, 106, 107, 108 top left, top right, bottom right, 109, 110, 111, 132–3, 135 top, 137, 143, 148 right, 159 top, 182–3, 187 right, 204–5, 206 top, bottom, 207 top and bottom left, top right, 209 top, bottom, 210, 211, 212 centre top, bottom left, 213, 214 right, left, 215 right, left, 224–5, 227, 228, 229, 230, 231, 232, 233; Ken Loveday: 91; Contessa Camilla Cagli Malvasia: 74 centre left, 75 bottom right; The Mansell Collection: 33; Joëlle Caroline Mayer: 75 bottom left; J. McGuffie, 74 top right; Tim Megson, New Dimension Photography, Leeds: 65; NAFAS Education Committee: 58 left; NAFAS Photographic Committee: 44–5, 46, 55, 67 right, 68 top left, bottom, 69 top left, 70 top right, top left, 71 top left, 72 top right, top left, 79, 80 right, 83, 84, 88 left, 89 right, 97 bottom left, 122 bottom, 123, 124 left, right, 127 left, 129 top left, 131, 156 left, 160, 172 top right, 178 top, 179 bottom, 191 left, 217; NAFAS/St Paul's Cathedral: 173 right, 176 centre; NAFAS/Salisbury Cathedral: 168–9, 171 bottom right, 178 top; NAFAS Teachers' Association: 82 left; The National Gallery, London: 9, 155, 159 bottom left; The National Portrait Gallery, London: 152–3; The National Trust: 16 top, bottom left, 17, 154 bottom; The Floral Art Society of New Zealand: 74 bottom right, 75 top right; Keith Petersen: 39; The Floral Art Society of Queensland: 74 bottom left, bottom centre, 75 centre left; Douglas Rendell/*The Flower Arranger*: 52 top, bottom right, 81 left, 85 top right, 89 left; Douglas Rendell/Jean Taylor: 162 bottom, 174 bottom left, 175 right, 184, 185, 187 left, 189, 190 left, right, 193, 194, 195; Sotheby's, Belgravia: 14 left, 21 bottom right, 101, 167 top left; Pamela South: 235; Jean Taylor: 191 right, 197; Thames Television Ltd: 94 bottom left; Victoria and Albert Museum, London. Crown Copyright: 16 bottom right, 226, 237 bottom; Joan Weatherlake: 174 top right, 197; Virginia Weaver: 74 centre right, 75 top left; Iris Webb: 21 top left, 47, 95 top right, 135 bottom right, 136 bottom, 139, 144 centre, 146 bottom, 147 bottom left, 151, 154 top left, 172 bottom right, 176 top; Don Wildridge: 134, 135 bottom left, 136 top, 138 top, bottom, 140, 142 bottom, 144 right, 145, 146 top, 147 bottom right, 149 centre, left, 150 top, bottom; Col W. B. Wright: 141, 142 top left, top right; Yerbury Galleries, Edinburgh: 161, 162 top; ZEFA: 19 top left, right.

Index

Page numbers in italic type refer to illustrations.